lonely

Nova Sc
Brunswick & Prince Edward Island

Newfoundland & Labrador
p181

Prince Edward Island
p153

New Brunswick
p113

Nova Scotia
p52

Oliver Berry, Adam Karlin, Korina Miller

PLAN YOUR TRIP

LASZLO PODOR/GETTY IMAGES ©
BALD EAGLE, SHUBENACADIE P93

JULIE DESHAIES/SHUTTERSTOCK ©
FIDDLEHEADS P44

ON THE ROAD

Contents

COVID-19

We have re-checked every business in this book before publication to ensure that it is still open after the COVID-19 outbreak. However, the economic and social impacts of COVID-19 will continue to be felt long after the outbreak has been contained, and many businesses, services and events referenced in this guide may experience ongoing restrictions. Some businesses may be temporarily closed, have changed their opening hours and services, or require bookings; some unfortunately could have closed permanently. We suggest you check with venues before visiting for the latest information.

UNDERSTAND

SURVIVAL GUIDE

SPECIAL FEATURES

Right: View from Gros Morne Mountain Trail (p217)

WELCOME TO

Nova Scotia, New Brunswick & Prince Edward Island

I first visited Atlantic Canada as a backpacker in my early twenties, and there's one image from that trip that's imprinted onto my brain: riding a Zodiac boat off the coast of Cape Breton, and watching a humpback whale breach out of the water before slamming back down into the Atlantic. I've since traveled pretty much the whole way round the Maritimes, but that image still encapsulates the place for me: wild, surprising and elemental.

By Oliver Berry, Writer
@olivertomberry olivertomberry
For more about our writers, see p288

Nova Scotia, New Brunswick & PEI

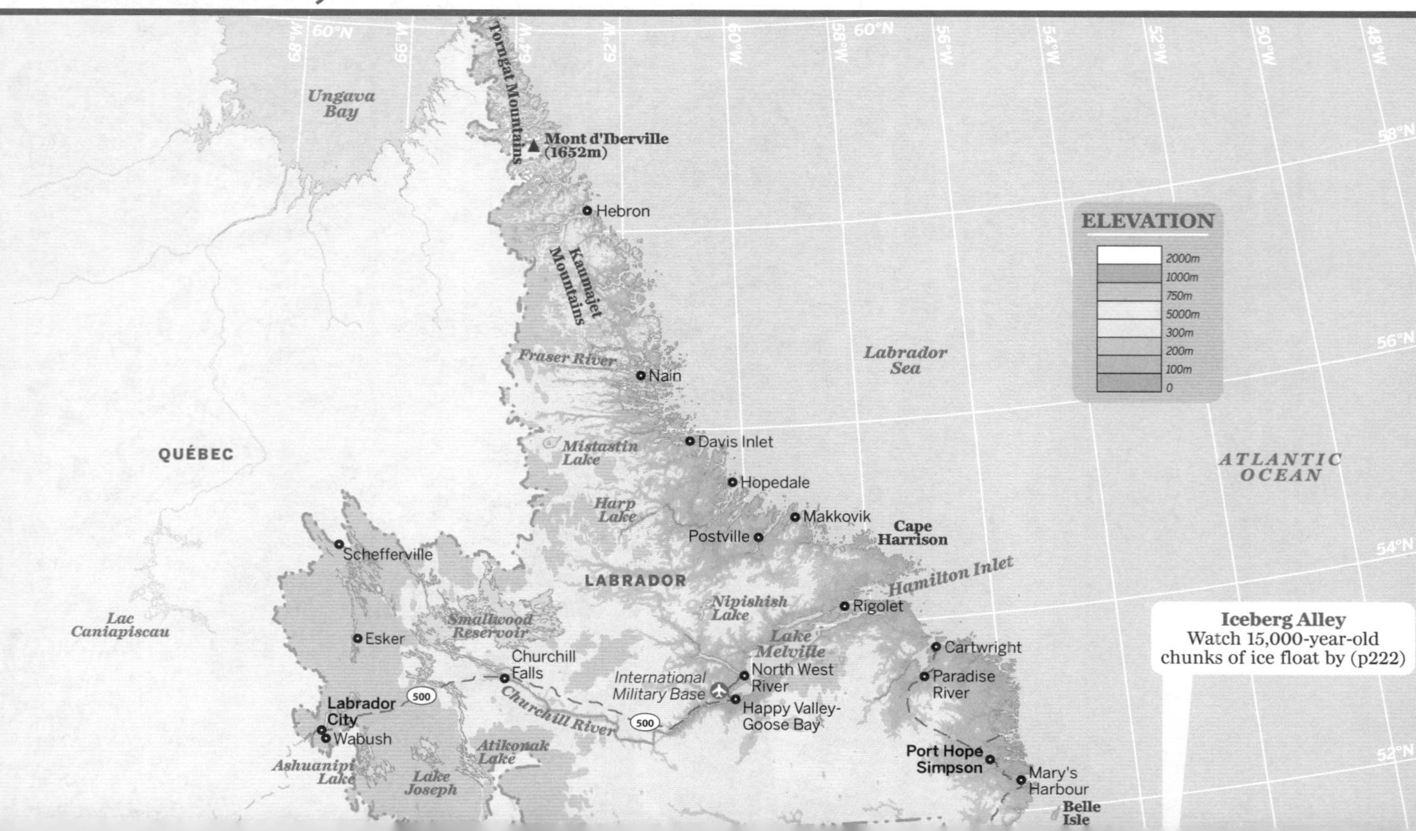

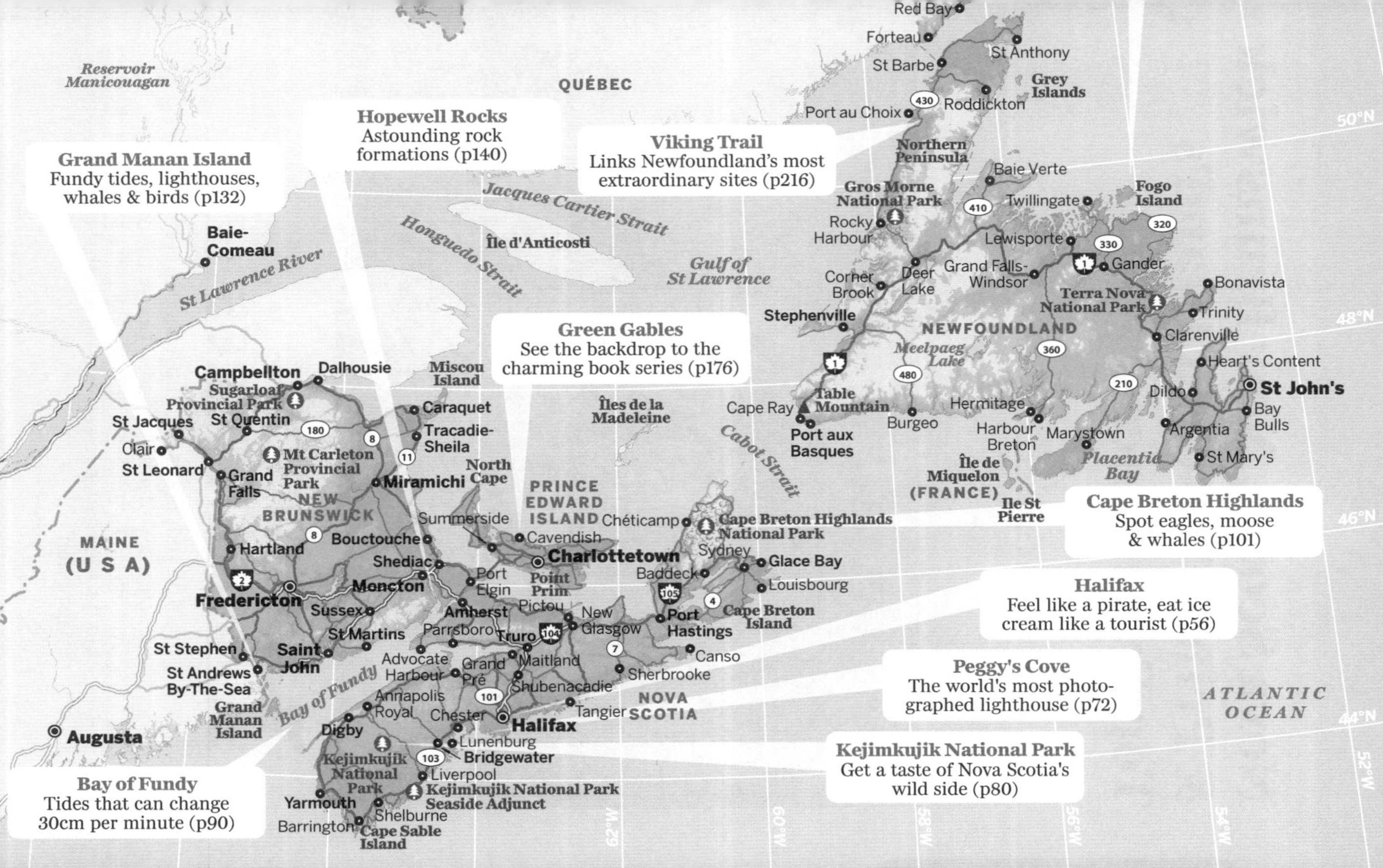
Grand Manan Island
Fundy tides, lighthouses, whales & birds (p132)
Hopewell Rocks
Astounding rock formations (p140)
Viking Trail
Links Newfoundland's most extraordinary sites (p216)
Green Gables
See the backdrop to the charming book series (p176)
Cape Breton Highlands
Spot eagles, moose & whales (p101)
Halifax
Feel like a pirate, eat ice cream like a tourist (p56)
Peggy's Cove
The world's most photographed lighthouse (p72)
Kejimkujik National Park
Get a taste of Nova Scotia's wild side (p80)
Bay of Fundy
Tides that can change 30cm per minute (p90)
Reservoir Manicouagan
QUÉBEC
Baie-Comeau
St Lawrence River
Jacques Cartier Strait
Honguedo Strait
Île d'Anticosti
Gulf of St Lawrence
Îles de la Madeleine
Cabot Strait
Red Bay
Forteau
St Anthony
St Barbe
Grey Islands
Port au Choix
Roddickton
Northern Peninsula
Baie Verte
Gros Morne National Park
Rocky Harbour
Twillingate
Fogo Island
Lewisporte
Gander
Corner Brook
Deer Lake
Grand Falls-Windsor
Terra Nova National Park
Bonavista
Trinity
Stephenville
NEWFOUNDLAND
Clarenville
Meelpaeg Lake
Heart's Content
Dildo
St John's
Table Mountain
Cape Ray
Port aux Basques
Burgeo
Hermitage
Harbour Breton
Marystown
Argentia
Bay Bulls
St Mary's
Placentia Bay
Île de Miquelon (FRANCE)
Ile St Pierre
Campbellton
Dalhousie
Sugarloaf Provincial Park
Miscou Island
Caraquet
Tracadie-Sheila
St Jacques
St Quentin
Clair
St Leonard
Grand Falls
Mt Carleton Provincial Park
Miramichi
North Cape
NEW BRUNSWICK
MAINE (U S A)
Hartland
Fredericton
Summerside
Bouctouche
Shediac
Moncton
Sussex
PRINCE EDWARD ISLAND
Cavendish
Charlottetown
Port Elgin
Point Prim
Pictou
Chéticamp
Cape Breton Highlands National Park
Sydney
Glace Bay
Baddeck
Louisbourg
Cape Breton Island
Port Hastings
Canso
Amherst
New Glasgow
St Martins
Parrsboro
Truro
St Stephen
Saint John
St Andrews By-The-Sea
Advocate Harbour
Grand Pré
Maitland
Sherbrooke
Shubenacadie
Bay of Fundy
Grand Manan Island
Annapolis Royal
Chester
Tangier
NOVA SCOTIA
Halifax
Augusta
Digby
Lunenburg
Bridgewater
Kejimkujik National Park
Liverpool
Kejimkujik National Park Seaside Adjunct
Yarmouth
Shelburne
Barrington
Cape Sable Island
ATLANTIC OCEAN
50°N
48°N
46°N
44°N
62°W
60°W
58°W
56°W
54°W
52°W

Nova Scotia, New Brunswick & Prince Edward Island's Top Experiences

1 OUTDOOR ADVENTURES

Strap on your boots, pick up a paddle, break out the binoculars – Atlantic Canada lives for the outdoors. Cycling, walking, sailing and kayaking are all popular here, but it's the chance to see wild whales that really fires the imagination.

Above: Hiking in Cape Breton Highlands National Park (p101)

SURINAWILD/SHUTTERSTOCK ©

Whale-Watching

Few places on the planet are better for cetacean spotting than Atlantic Canada. From June to October these deep-sea leviathans cruise the region's waters: humpbacks, minke, North Atlantic right whales, pilot whales, orcas and mighty blue whales can be seen depending on the season. Remote Brier Island is one of many whale-watching locations (pictured right). p33

CURTIS WATSON/SHUTTERSTOCK ©

LUCIE KUSOVA/SHUTTERSTOCK ©

DAMIAN LUGOWSKI/SHUTTERSTOCK ©

Hiking

Coast hikes, beach walks, mountain jaunts, forested trails: there's a host of hikes to be had, with many charismatic animals to see along the way (moose, bear, sea eagles, beavers and more). Fundy National Park makes a great start, with trails winding along the wooded coastline. p33

Above: Hopewell Rocks, Bay of Fundy (p140)

Canoeing & Kayaking

Piloting your own canoe or kayak allows you to reach parts of the Maritime provinces most people never see. From mellow lake paddles to multiday ocean expeditions, there's a wealth of watery adventures – including along Nova Scotia's under-explored Eastern Shore. p32

2 HIT THE HIGHWAY

Foggy coast roads, hillside loops, backcountry backroads – there's a whole atlas of Maritime road trips to discover. Some, like the famous Cabot Trail and Viking Trail, span days, but there are many shorter routes if time is tight.

Below: Skyline Trail, Cape Breton Highlands National Park (p101)

The Cabot Trail

Sea-fringed Cape Breton Highlands National Park offers the classic Nova Scotian road-trip, the Cabot Trail: rugged mountains, dense forests, remote beaches and sleepy villages. The circuitous road snakes its way around the peninsula, with numerous hiking, kayaking and cycling possibilities. Look out for moose on the highway and whale spouts on the skyline.

p101

GNAGEL/GETTY IMAGES ©

CWORTHY/SHUTTERSTOCK ©

ROB CRANDALL/SHUTTERSTOCK ©

The Viking Trail

The Viking Trail, aka Rte 430, connects Newfoundland's two World Heritage sites on the northern peninsula. Gros Morne National Park rests at its base, while the sublime, 1000-year-old Viking settlement at L'Anse aux Meadows (pictured above left) stares out from the peninsula's tip. p216

Fundy Trail Parkway

Every day, earth's highest tides swirl around the Bay of Fundy (pictured above right): a billion tons of water with a range of up to 50ft, the height of three double-decker buses. It's a surreal sight: when the tides recede, boats are beached, huge sand-flats are revealed and you can walk out onto the sea floor which hours earlier was submerged underwater. p139

3 SPIRIT OF THE SEA

Wherever you go in this part of Canada, the Atlantic is never far away: you can taste it on the air, hear it on the breeze and, if you're feeling really brave, feel it on your skin too.

Islands

Islands pepper the coastline, some near at hand, some fabulously remote, but each with their own distinctive island character. Grand Manan (pictured below) is a popular day-trip, but there are countless others for island hoppers to explore. p132

LAZYLLAMA/SHUTTERSTOCK ©

Seaside Towns

Coastal cities such as Halifax and Saint John are full of life, but it's the quieter seaside towns that have the most character. You'll find the prettiest of all, Unesco-listed Lunenburg (pictured above), along Nova Scotia's lovely South Shore. p75

Lighthouses

When most people envision the Maritimes, there's probably a lighthouse in the image somewhere. There are scores to see: Cape Forchu (pictured right) is the most unusual, with a distinctive 'apple core' profile. p83

4 GEOLOGICAL WONDERS

Sculpted by the wind and the waves, Atlantic Canada has some wonderfully weird landscapes – from fossil-studded cliffs and otherworldly rock formations to wild icebergs.

Joggins Fossil Cliffs

Some of Canada's oldest fossils can be found studding the cliffs around Joggins – including ancient trees and shrimp-like creatures that lived 300 million years ago. p94

Hopewell Rocks

Arches, giant mushrooms, flowerpots and animals can all be discerned in the extraordinary rock formations at Hopewell Rocks, best seen at low tide. p140

Iceberg Alley

Off the Newfoundland coast, this ocean sound (pictured above) offers a glimpse of the Arctic: great shards of ice that have sailed down from Greenland. Steer a kayak through them, take a boat-trip or cool your drink with ancient ice cubes. p222

5 INTO THE WILD

They might not have the big mountains of BC or Alberta, but the Maritimes still offer some fantastically wild locations to escape the madding crowd. For the ultimate experience, pack a tent and camp out for a few nights in the backcountry: the stars are out of this world.

THOMAS FAULL/GETTY IMAGES ©

SHARP/SHUTTERSTOCK ©

Kejimkujik National Park

Mi'kmaw people have been tramping, paddling, exploring and tending this vast wilderness of lakes and forest (pictured top) for thousands of years. A national park since 1967, it's the optimal place to experience Nova Scotia's wild side – especially in the Tobeatic Wilderness Area. p80

Witless Bay Ecological Reserve

Birdspotters make a beeline to these four faraway islands: they're home to North America's largest puffin colony, along with kittiwakes, gulls, storm petrels and many other species. p198

Above left: Atlantic puffins

Gros Morne National Park

Perhaps the wildest of Newfoundland's national parks, this 1800 sq km reserve encompasses mountains, fjords, bogs and deserted beaches where you won't see another soul. p216

Above right: Tablelands, Gros Morne National Park

6 TASTES OF THE ATLANTIC

MARK MAHABIR/SHUTTERSTOCK ©

MAURITIUS IMAGES GMBH/ALAMY STOCK PHOTO ©

EYESTRAVELLING/SHUTTERSTOCK ©

Whether it's a simple bowl of chowder or a perfectly-brewed beer, tasting your way around the Maritimes is a great way to immerse yourself in local life.

Lobster Suppers

A lobster supper is a rite of passage: armed with claw-crackers and paper bib, you'll tackle mountains of just-caught crustacean until you can consume no more. New Glasgow on PEI offers the full feast experience. p173

Craft Beer

Canada's craft beer boom is alive and well: big name breweries like Alexander Keith's, Propeller and Garrison can be found in Halifax, but for something truly local, try Tatamagouche Brewing Co. p97

Wine Tasting

Vineyards carpet the Annapolis Valley, where renowned winemakers like Lightfoot & Wolfville (pictured left), Luckett and Domaine de Grand Pré open their cellars to visitors. p92

7 LIVING HISTORY

From Viking sites to hilltop fortresses, the Maritimes are awash with history – including several places where the past comes to life before your eyes.

Fortress of Louisbourg

Razed to the ground and painstakingly rebuilt, this coastal fortress (pictured below) is populated by costumed guides – including soldiers, orderlies and artisans – who'll transport you back to the 18th century. p110

GINA SMITH/SHUTTERSTOCK ©

Sherbrooke Village

An early 1900s town is the model for this living museum (pictured above), where you can watch potters and printers at work, try your hand at weaving or woodwork, get a tintype photo taken or just sit down for a hearty homecooked lunch. p111

Kings Landing

Capturing the spirit of New Brunswick c 1800, this fascinating village has a collection of period buildings and people role-playing 19th-century characters: bakers, blacksmiths, publicans, farmers, carpenters and more (pictured right). p116

8 TRADITIONAL CULTURE

ROB CRANDALL/ALAMY STOCK PHOTO ©

REGINE POIRIER/SHUTTERSTOCK ©

HEMIS/ALAMY STOCK PHOTO ©

Waves of settlers from many different parts of the globe have settled in the Maritimes, but no-one knows this land better than the First Nations, who have called this region home for thousands of years.

First Nations

The Mi'kmaq and Maliseet people are the oldest inhabitants of Atlantic Canada, and visiting one of their reserves offers a fascinating insight into their way of life, legends and mythology. The informative First Nations guides of Lennox Island offer fascinating walking tours and craft workshops. p180

Celtic & Acadian Music

Scottish, Irish and French immigrants have left an indelible mark on the region's culture, notably in the toe-tapping music that can be heard in many a bar, pub or concert hall. Don't miss a traditional *ceilidh* (gathering) at the Red Shoe Pub (pictured above) near Mabou. p100

Need to Know

For more information, see Survival Guide (p259).

Currency
Canadian dollar ($)

Language
English, French

Visas
With the exception of US nationals, all visitors to Canada require either an electronic travel authorization (eTA; visa-waiver) or a formal visa.

Money
ATMs are widely available and credit and debit cards are accepted almost everywhere.

Cell Phones
Local SIM cards can be used in unlocked GSM 850/1900 compatible phones.

Time
Atlantic (GMT minus four hours)

When to Go

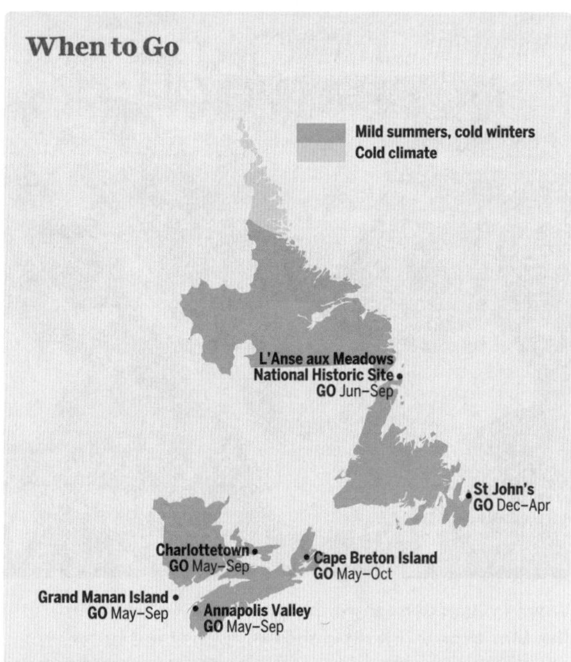

High Season (Jul & Aug)

➡ Warm weather and long, sunny days mean busy highways and slower travel times.

➡ Summer means festival mode, with theater, music and food extravaganzas.

➡ Attractions and visitor centers keep longer hours.

Shoulder (May–Jun & Sep–Oct)

➡ Wildflowers in spring and crimson leaves in the fall.

➡ Cool but comfortable. You may have things all to yourself.

➡ Some lodgings close and restaurants may open under reduced hours.

Low Season (Nov–Apr)

➡ Few lodgings and attractions outside the big cities and ski resorts remain open.

➡ Darkness and cold take over. Driving can be fraught with challenges.

➡ Christmas festivals liven up December and January.

Useful Websites

Lonely Planet (www.lonelyplanet.com/canada) Destination information, hotel reviews and more.

Newfoundland & Labrador Tourism (www.newfoundlandlabrador.com)

Nova Scotia Tourism (www.novascotia.com)

Parks Canada (www.pc.gc.ca) Official website of the National Parks Service.

Tourism New Brunswick (www.tourismnewbrunswick.ca)

Tourism Prince Edward Island (www.tourismpei.com)

Important Numbers

Nova Scotia and Prince Edward Island's area code is 902, New Brunswick is 506, and Newfoundland and Labrador is 709. Many accommodations have toll-free numbers that are free to dial from Canada and the US. For local calls, you need to use the area code but not the country code.

Country Code	☎1
International Access Code	☎011
Emergency	☎911
Directory Assistance	☎411

Exchange Rates

Australia	A$1	C$0.90
Europe	€1	C$1.48
Japan	¥100	C$1.26
New Zealand	NZ$1	C$0.86
UK	UK£1	C$1.60
US	US$1	C$1.33

For current exchange rates, see www.xe.com.

Daily Costs

Budget: Less than $100

- Dorm bed: $25–40
- Campsite: $20–35
- Markets and supermarkets for self-catering

Midrange: $100–250

- B&B or room in a midrange hotel: $90–200
- Restaurant meal: $15–25 plus drinks
- Rental car: $25–60 per day
- Attractions: $5–25

Top End: More than $250

- Four-star hotel room or luxury B&B: from $180
- Three-course meal in a top restaurant: from $45 plus drinks
- Sea kayaking or canoe day tour: $65–175

Opening Hours

The following list provides standard opening hours for high-season operating times.

Banks 10am to 5pm Monday to Friday; some open 9am to noon Saturday.

Bars 5pm to 2am.

Clubs 9pm to 2am Wednesday to Saturday.

Museums 10am to 5pm; may close on Monday.

Restaurants 8am to 11am and 11:30am to 2:30pm Monday to Friday, 5pm to 9:30pm daily; some open 8am to 1pm weekends.

Shops 10am to 6pm Monday to Saturday, noon to 5pm Sunday.

Supermarkets 9am to 8pm; some open 24 hours.

Arriving in the Region

Halifax Stanfield International Airport MetroX bus 320 runs every 30 to 60 minutes (5am to midnight). Maritime Bus (www.maritimebus.com) operates an hourly airport shuttle ($22, 30 to 45 minutes) between May and October. Taxis cost $56 to downtown (30 minutes).

Moncton Airport Bus 20 travels from the airport to Champlain Pl nine times a day on weekdays. A taxi to the center costs about $20.

St John's International Airport Taxis cost $25 plus $3 for each additional passenger to downtown (10 minutes).

Land Border Crossings The Canadian Border Services Agency (www.cbsa-asfc.gc.ca/bwt-taf) posts updated wait times hourly; it's usually less than 30 minutes.

Getting Around

Public transportation is available in cities and between larger towns, but most visitors rent a car for flexibility.

Car Good-value rentals are available in Nova Scotia and New Brunswick. There are fewer vehicles and higher prices in Prince Edward Island. In Newfoundland, this is even more the case.

Train Clean, economical and reliable VIA Rail connects Halifax to Montréal via various stops in New Brunswick.

Bus Buses cover more ground than trains; places not serviced by buses usually have private shuttle services for similar fares, more cramped seating and door-to-door service.

For much more on **getting around**, see p270.

What's New

Like the rest of the world, the Maritimes have been weathering some seriously stormy waters recently. Hopefully brighter times are on the horizon, with intriguing developments from a new pan-island trail on PEI to a stunning tree-top gondola at Cape Smokey.

The Island Walk

Launched in fall 2021, this epic 700km trail (www.theislandwalk.ca) loops pretty much the whole way around PEI, encompassing blustery bluffs, dirt tracks, beaches and quiet backcountry roads along the way - along with stops in the island's main towns of Charlottetown and Summerside. It takes around 32 days to complete, or more like 35 if you take things at a more leisurely pace.

Ingonish Gondola & Treewalk

The first gondola in Atlantic Canada, this new cable car near Ingonish (https://capesmokey.ca/gondola-ticketing) carries visitors from the bottom of Cape Smokey to a viewpoint at 285m, from where there's a grandstand view of the Cape Breton coastline. Construction is also underway on the Ingonish Treewalk, a 30m-high treetop walkway, which is due to open in late 2022.

Georges Island National Historic Site

The newest of the designated national historic sites around Halifax, this island fortress (www.pc.gc.ca/en/lhn-nhs/ns/georges) can be reached by boat from the city's waterfront. Notorious as a prison and internment camp, it once formed part of the defensive system that protected the city from seaborne attack.

LOCAL KNOWLEDGE

WHAT'S HAPPENING IN NOVA SCOTIA

By Oliver Berry, Lonely Planet Writer

Like the rest of Canada, the Maritimes have been hit hard by COVID-19 – even though they've fared far better compared to Canada's more populous provinces, with some of the lowest case and death rates in the country. The effect of repeated lockdowns and huge disruption to the tourism industry has caused major damage to the Atlantic economy, and with a tentative reopening scheduled for 2022, it remains to be seen what the long-term fallout will be. Pandemics haven't been the only problem, however. Severe winter storms rocked the Atlantic coast in late 2021, causing storm surges and knocking out power to some areas for days – an early warning sign, many fear, of the tempestuous future that lies ahead for the Maritimes as a result of climate change. Still, there's hope in the region's move towards renewable energy: several provinces have put themselves on track towards carbon neutrality, and Canada's first tidal stream energy project is slated to open in 2022, designed to harness the massive tides that sweep through the Bay of Fundy every day. It's a potentially unlimited energy source that could utterly transform the region's prospects – but just how fast, and how far, remains to be seen.

Waterfront Trailer Village, St John

The port city's waterfront has a new look thanks to the addition of 60 shipping containers housing a mixed-use space of shops, food trucks, bars, pop-ups, a performance space and a beer garden (www.area506.ca/village).

Fossil hunting on PEI

PEI is the only place in Canada where fossils from the Permian period can be found in abundance – including big dinosaurs. The discovery of fossilized footprints in 2018 belonging to the sail-backed Dimetrodon has really put the island on the paleontological map: the fossils' discoverer, Laura MacNeil, now offers guided fossil-hunting tours (www.prehistoricislandtours.ca) around the island's cliffs and beaches.

Lighthouse tours at Cape Forchu

Nova Scotia's most distinctively shaped lighthouse (p83) has recently opened up for guided tours, offering the chance to climb the 77 spiral steps up into the lantern room for incredible views over the coastline around Yarmouth.

Véloroute Bike Trail

This 610km-long cycle trail (www.veloroutepa.ca) loops New Brunswick's Acadian Peninsula, and is split into 22 sections offering views of Chaleur Bay and the Gulf of St. Lawrence.

Queen's Marque, Halifax

Several years in development, this huge complex on the Halifax waterfront has finally opened with the five-star Muir Hotel, along with restaurant, art gallery, speakeasy and even a private yacht.

Founders' Food Hall, Charlottetown

Charlottetown now has its own trendy food hall (www.foundersfoodhall.com), with twenty vendors offering some of the best eats and drinks on PEI – from French-Caribbean *bokit* sandwiches to donuts, sushi burritos, vegan wraps and tacos.

LISTEN, WATCH & FOLLOW

For inspiration and up-to-date news, visit www.lonely planet.com/canada/articles.

CBC (www.cbc.ca) Latest news courtesy of Canada's national broadcaster.

Saltwire (www.saltwire.com) News, features and views from across the four Atlantic provinces.

Curated (curatedmagazine.ca) Insights into Nova Scotia's food and drink scene, published online along with a quarterly magazine and annual guide.

FAST FACTS

Food trend Craft beer

Length of coastline 43,000km

Number of whale species 22

Pop 2.3 million

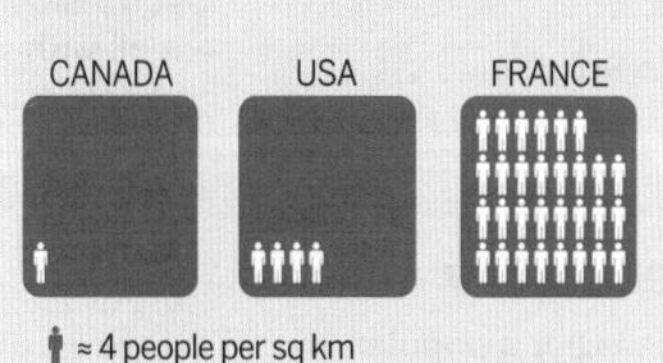

Dining on the Ocean Floor

For Nova Scotia's most unusual eating experience, how about a slap-up meal on the sea-bed? Several times a summer at low tide, dinners are hosted out on the mud flats around Burntcoat Head. Tickets sell out lightning quick: book at www.foodfantastique.ca/dining-on-the-ocean-floor.

Developments at Beaverbrook Art Gallery

Fredericton's top art gallery (p116) has added a new pavilion, allowing extra exhibition space, along with the new Harriet Irving Gallery.

Hearst Lodge on the Fundy Trail

Formerly a private salmon-fishing lodge, this backcountry cabin complex is reached via a 2.6km hike and a suspension bridge off the beautiful Fundy Trail Parkway.

Month by Month

TOP EVENTS

Lobster suppers June–September

Whale-watching June-October

Stan Rogers Folk Festival August

Celtic Colours October

Ceilidhs July

February

This is not a popular month to visit this part of Canada unless you're looking for deep snow and hard ice.

World Pond Hockey Tournament

Hockey purists shouldn't miss this event at Plaster Rock in New Brunswick. Around 120 teams come to shoot pucks around the ice, with the event helping to support the ongoing cost of a new recreation centre for the people of the Tobique Valley. (p122)

South Shore Lobster Crawl

Lobster-themed events spring up all along the South Shore in February, from a challenge to find the finest lobster roll to a grand chowder showdown (www.lobstercrawl.ca).

April

The land is usually thawing by April and trees are sprouting new leaves, but if you visit you'll be enjoying it all with very few other people around.

Mi-Carême

Mid-Lent, usually in March or April, is marked in the Acadian town of Chéticamp by going in disguise and visiting neighborhood homes to see if anyone can guess who you are.

PEI Burger Love

Carnivores go crazy at this month-long celebration of the humble burger. Restaurants around the province devise mouthwatering creations that compete for the title of Most Loved Burger: all are crafted with love and imagination using homegrown ingredients. (p159)

June

June weather can be sunny but brisk. In some areas many tourist-oriented attractions may still be shut or keep low-season hours, but in general you'll find the Maritime provinces ramping up for the summer season.

Whale-watching

Whales begin to be seen in the Bay of Fundy and off the coast of Newfoundland this month, then hang around to feed until around October or November. On Nova Scotia's South Shore the season runs from July to October.

Iceberg Festival

Spring and early summer are the best times to see some of the tens of thousands of icebergs that break off in Greenland to sail down the coast of Newfoundland's 'Iceberg Alley.' In honor of these giant white monsters, Northern Newfoundland even hosts its own weeklong iceberg festival in early June.

Acadian Concerts

In late June you'll start to find summer Acadian concerts and kitchen parties along the Nova Scotia coast between Yarmouth and Digby. More are scheduled through July, and by August you can find a performance most nights of the week.

July

Summer starts to heat up, days are long and festivals bring music and food to the streets. All outdoor activities are go! If you're lucky, things can still be relatively uncrowded early in the month.

Lobster Suppers

During the summer lobster season (which varies depending on the region), tasty crustaceans get boiled up en masse and served to hungry crowds with all-you-can-eat fixings and pie for dessert. Try New Glasgow Lobster Supper (p173) on PEI or Halls Harbour Lobster Pound in Nova Scotia. (p87)

Ceilidhs

Cape Breton is the capital of these foot-tapping Scottish music performances, where most people in the small communities show up as audience and get up and dance. While found year-round, they occur almost every night in July and August.

Canada Day

Canada's national holiday is celebrated throughout the region with parades, fireworks, music and picnics. Many businesses close their doors in observance of the holidays, so be sure to have plans and a picnic packed before the big day, July 1.

Cavendish Beach Music Festival

Some of the biggest names in country music head to Cavendish, PEI, to play one of the largest outdoor music festivals in North America. (p248)

Indian River Festival

As an antidote to Cavendish partying, this Kensington festival from the end of June into October showcases classical, jazz and world music in an acoustically sublime St Mary's Church. The French Gothic architecture complements the beautiful music in a wonderful summer experience. (p176)

Peak of Lupine Season

Lupine usually begin blooming in June but by July they cover hillsides, colorfully border the highways and decorate home fronts. Purple is the dominant color but you'll also see scatterings of pink lupine, especially in PEI.

Halifax Pride Week

Halifax booms with events for Pride Week, the largest this side of Montréal. Don't miss the annual, highly entertaining Dykes vs Divas softball game, the Queer Acts Theater Festival, nightly parties and one hell of a parade.

Bastille Day

Celebrate the July 14 French national holiday with bona-fide French nationals in St-Pierre. The town comes alive with music, food stalls and family-oriented games for nonstop fun. Stop in for a few éclairs while you're there as well.

Antigonish Highland Games

Always wanted to see a caber being tossed? Harbor secret dreams of doing a Highland dance? You'll get your chance at this long-running event held in Antigonish, Nova Scotia, since 1861 – making this the longest-running Highland Games outside Scotland. (p98)

August

High season is in full swing by August. The weather is at its sunniest, everything is open extended hours and festivals are going on everywhere.

Stan Rogers Folk Festival

The tiny remote seaside town of Canso swells with visitors once a year for what many claim is one of the best music festivals in the Maritimes. It's a mellow scene with camping, easy-going people and amazing live performances. (p112)

Halifax International Busker Festival

Comics, mimics, daredevils and more from Canada and around the world perform on several outdoor stages over 11 days. This is the oldest festival of its kind in Canada and the audience usually exceeds 500,000 people. (p63)

Festival Acadien

The largest Acadian cultural festival kicks off in Caraquet during the first two weeks of August. Along with 100,000 other visitors, you'll be entertained by top Acadian singers, musicians and performers from all across the Maritimes, and from further afield too. (p150)

GGW/SHUTTERSTOCK ©

Top: Fall foliage, Cape Breton Island

Bottom: Royal St John's Regatta

Halifax Seaport Cider & Beerfest

The Maritimes sure do love a good brew, and this three-day event at the Cunard Centre in Halifax is a must for beer and cider lovers, with new brews from many of the region's leading brewers, plus guest ales from around the world. (p63)

Panmure Island Powwow

Learn the art of tribal drumming, hear First Nations stories and even brave a sweat lodge at this important powwow, which brings more than 5000 people to little Panmure Island, off the PEI's coastline. (p164)

Digby Scallop Days

Celebrating Digby's massive scallop fleet, this five-day festival in early August lets you try out different styles of preparation. Alongside it are parades, dances, car shows and even a kids' pie-eating contest.

Miramichi Folksong Festival

This is North America's oldest folk-fest set along its winding, namesake river in New Brunswick. Expect a low-key family vibe set to the tune of fiddlers and singers with all the old folks getting up to boogie.

Royal St John's Regatta

Newfoundland keeps up the action with this rowing regatta, claimed to be the oldest sporting event in North America, on Quidi Vidi Lake. St John's becomes a ghost town as thousands head to watch and enjoy the sunshine. (p188)

September

Summer gets extended for a slew of music festivals, while the harvest of food and wine is enjoyed to the fullest. Temperatures become more brisk but the sun still makes regular appearances.

PEI Fall Flavours

Called 'the biggest kitchen party in Canada,' here you get your hands juicy with interactive culinary demos, gorge on the best seafood in the world and enjoy two chowder championships. Meanwhile there's live music, a widely regarded oyster-shucking contest and chef challenges.

Atlantic International Film Festival

Atlantic Canada and Canada's best films plus some gems from around the world get screened at this intimate yet internationally recognized film festival in Halifax. Of course, this is Nova Scotia so there are plenty of music performances scheduled alongside. (p63)

Canadian Deep Roots Festival

Enjoy live folk music and move to the beats of Mi'kmaw, Acadian and other unique musical genres, all with Canadian roots, in the fun university town of Wolfville. Workshops are available with some of the artists. (p91)

October

Ah, the colors of fall. As the world turns from green to red and the temperatures start to drop, there's still plenty to enjoy in the Maritimes. Canadian Thanksgiving is the perfect time to experience the warmth and hospitality of the locals.

Fall Foliage

One of nature's most spectacular shows of color begins late September and peaks in October. Panoramas are filled with brick reds, rust, gold and copper that eventually turn brown before dropping to the ground. The forests of Cape Breton put on a particularly fine show.

Halifax Pop Explosion

Up-and-coming bands play a series of intimate gigs at various venues across Halifax during this lively music festival. The lineup is skewed towards Canadian names, but there's usually a pretty broad spectrum to the schedule. (p63)

Celtic Colours

The who's who of the Maritimes' music world make it to this Cape Breton music festival, which is highly regarded among lovers of Celtic music. (p99)

Itineraries

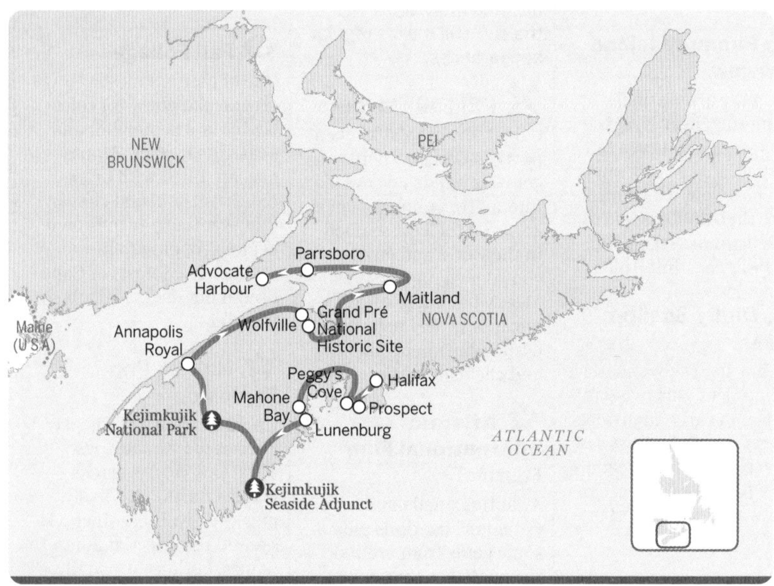

Nova Scotia Loop

This compact itinerary showcases the historic and natural diversity within easy reach of Halifax.

Soak up some music and culture in **Halifax**, then travel to nearby **Peggy's Cove** and jostle for position to snap the most photographed lighthouse in the world. Don't forget your sunscreen in **Mahone Bay**, where the sun shines on great craft shopping and sea kayaking. Move on slightly south to **Lunenburg**, a World Heritage site known for its colorful boxy buildings and *Bluenose* schooner. The **Kejimkujik National Park** offers a range of terrain from its coastal beaches (in the section of park known as the Keji Seaside Adjunct) to inland rivers, which are the perfect spot to float a canoe and drift through the woods. Cross the province to **Annapolis Royal** to stay at a heritage B&B; explore its fort by day and graveyard by night. The next day visit the wineries around the fabulous college town of **Wolfville** and the **Grand Pré National Historic site**, before stopping to down a meal at a fine vineyard restaurant. Lastly, explore the Fundy coast around **Parrsboro** and **Advocate Harbour**, or go to **Maitland** to get right in and raft the tidal bore. From here you can easily continue on to PEI, or return to Halifax.

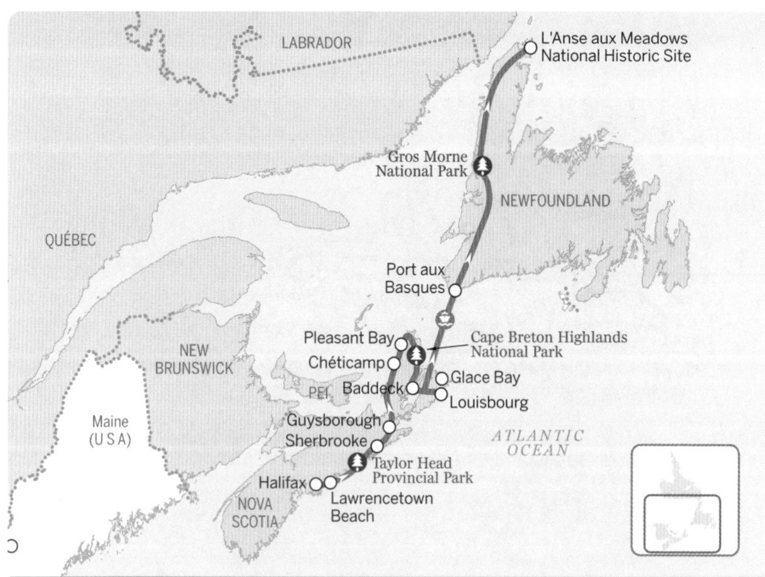

Cabot & Viking Trails

Experience the living world at its most magnificent and explore the juxtaposing cultures that have shaped eastern Canada in this grand northerly tour, best suited to those who love hiking, wildlife and photography.

Spend a couple days in **Halifax** enjoying lively bars and a nonstop music scene, then hit the road up the Atlantic Coast. Stop for a chilly surf at **Lawrencetown Beach** or a hike through pine forest to a spectacular white-sand beach at **Taylor Head Provincial Park**. Visit the historical village at **Sherbrooke** then cut up Hwy 7 for a shortcut to Cape Breton Island. Just after arriving on Cape Breton from the causeway, veer left toward Hwy 30 and stop in at one of the many ceilidh music gatherings along this route. Hook up with the **Cabot Trail** at **Chéticamp**, a deeply Acadian town. Next you can watch whales or chant with monks at the Tibetan monastery in **Pleasant Bay** and look for moose and nesting bald eagles in **Cape Breton Highlands National Park**. Get your art fix at the studios dotted along the last section of the trail before heading over to **Baddeck** to learn everything you ever wanted to know about Alexander Graham Bell at the town's fabulous museum. From here take a jaunt east to **Louisbourg** to visit the massive, windy restored French Fort, complete with costumed thespians and activities to take you back to the 18th century. Stop at the **Cape Breton Miners' Museum** in Glace Bay before arriving in industrial North Sydney for the ferry to Newfoundland.

It's a six-hour sail over the sometimes rough swell of the Cabot Strait to Port aux Basques. Alight and drive north to **Gros Morne National Park**, rich with mountain hikes, sea-kayaking tours, fjords and weird rock formations. Take the Viking Trail from here to its awe-inspiring endpoint: **L'Anse aux Meadows National Historic Site**, North America's first settlement. Leif Erikson and his Viking pals homesteaded the place 1000 years ago, and it probably looked much the same then as it does now. After coming all this way, you too will feel like an Atlantic explorer.

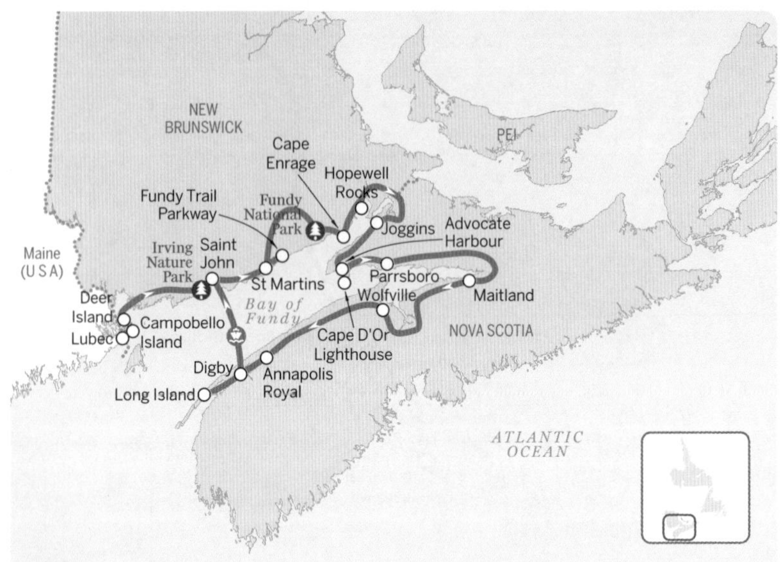

Bay of Fundy Tidal Tour

Experience the dramatic Fundy tides and wildlife on this loop that can be tackled from Maine, USA.

Cross the bridge to **Campobello Island**, the childhood home of 32nd US president Franklin D Roosevelt, from **Lubec**, Maine, then visit Roosevelt's home, which is now a fascinating museum. The next day take the car ferry to fisher-funky **Deer Island** to check out Old Sow, the world's second-largest natural tidal whirlpool, before boarding another ferry that shuttles you to the mainland. Drive north to gritty yet cosmopolitan **Saint John** to fill up on fine dining, and warm up your hiking boots at **Irving Nature Park** the following day to see hundreds of birds and possibly seals.

Follow the coast as far as **St Martins** – with an optional detour to the **Fundy Trail Parkway** if you wish to break in your hiking boots – then head north towards Sussex, gateway to the wilds of **Fundy National Park** and its extensive coastal trails. Continue north to **Cape Enrage** to take a tour of the lighthouse, and sea kayak or rappel down the rock cliffs that meet the rise and fall of the powerful tides. Move on to a day trip to the bizarre **Hopewell Rocks** formations, a must-see –but expect hundreds of visitors.

Now it's time to change provinces. Drive across the border to Nova Scotia and down to **Joggins** to see the Unesco World Heritage fossil cliffs. Continue along driftwood-strewn Chignecto Bay to stop for lunch in **Advocate Harbour**, then move onto **Parrsboro** via the **Cape D'Or Lighthouse**, to look for semiprecious stones on the beach and stay the night. Enjoy the views of the Cobequid Bay tides, which can change up to a foot per minute, until you reach **Maitland** where you can get into inflatable dinghies for an exhilarating rafting adventure on the tidal bore. Scoot southwest to fabulous **Wolfville** for a night or two to explore the surrounding countryside, before heading deeper into the Annapolis Valley to delightful **Annapolis Royal**, and onwards to **Digby** where you can dine on succulent scallops before resting your weary head. In the morning, head over to **Long Island**, home to the region's most spectacular whale-watching, before turning back to Digby for the car ferry to Saint John, New Brunswick, where the adventure began.

Top: Charlottetown (p157)

Bottom: Cabot Trail, Cape Breton Highlands National Park (p101)

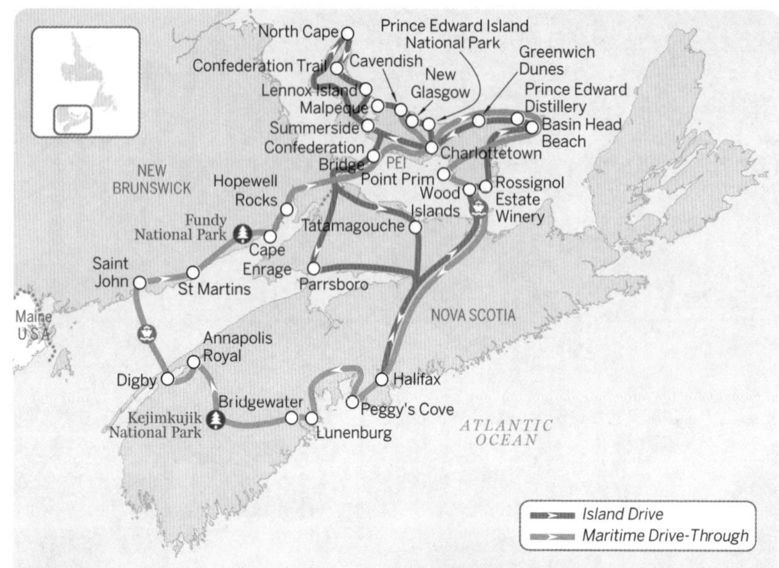

Island Drive

Start with a day in **Halifax**, walking the waterfront, visiting the museums and soaking up the city's dining and drinking scene. Take the Prince Edward Island (PEI) ferry from Pictou. Spend your first day exploring the east; stop at **Rossignol Estate Winery**, stroll on **Basin Head Beach**, swig some potato vodka at **Prince Edward Distillery** and walk among the **Greenwich Dunes**. Head south to **Charlottetown**, a perfect base for exploring the island's centre. Devote a day to the beaches of **Prince Edward Island National Park** and the home of Anne of Green Gables in **Cavendish**, stopping in **Malpeque Oyster Barn** for an oyster lunch and **New Glasgow** for a lobster supper.

Overnight in **Summerside**, then drive up the west coast through Acadian villages to lighthouse vistas. If time allows, spend a day or two cycling along the **Confederation Trail**, driving up to **North Cape**, and learning about Mi'kmaw culture on **Lennox Island**.

Take the **Confederation Bridge** to drive back to Halifax via the wine region around **Tatamagouche**, or head down the Fundy Coast to **Parrsboro** for geological explorations.

10 DAYS

Maritime Drive-Through

This whistle-stop, three-province tour takes in the essential sights. Enjoy **Halifax** for a day before swinging down to snap a few photos at **Peggy's Cove**, then stop for the night in World Heritage–listed **Lunenburg** with your camera at the ready at every turn. The next day cross via Bridgewater up Hwy 8, stopping for a day hike or a paddle in **Kejimkujik National Park**, then stay in **Annapolis Royal** and take the town's famous nighttime graveyard tour, if you're not easily spooked! Take a short drive to **Digby** for a lunch of fried scallops, then take the ferry to **Saint John**, New Brunswick. If you're a nature lover, press on to camp in **Fundy National Park**; otherwise, stay in adorable **St Martins**. Spend the next day hiking and continuing up the Fundy Coast to view the tides at **Cape Enrage** and **Hopewell Rocks**. The next day, drive across the **Confederation Bridge** into Prince Edward Island (PEI) and **Charlottetown**. Meet Anne of Green Gables in **Cavendish**, have a lobster supper, then tour PEI's east coast the following day, with a stop at **Point Prim**, before taking the car ferry back to Nova Scotia and Halifax.

Hiking on Brier Island (p87)

Plan Your Trip

Outdoor Activities

There are numerous ways to get out and explore the glorious environments of Atlantic Canada, whether it's kayaking the seashore, hiking in the forests or braving whitewater rapids. Keep in mind, though, that the season is short for most activities, running May to October.

Best for...

Kayaking & Canoeing

Eastern Shore (p110) and South Shore (p78), Nova Scotia

Cape Breton (p99), Nova Scotia

Fundy Isles (p127), New Brunswick

Eastern Fundy Shore (p138), New Brunswick

Witless Bay Ecological Reserve (p198), Newfoundland

North Rustico (p169), PEI

Whale-Watching

Twillingate Island (p210), Newfoundland

Digby Neck (p86), Nova Scotia

Grand Manan Island (p132), New Brunswick

Pleasant Bay (p104), Nova Scotia

Witless Bay Ecological Reserve (p198), Newfoundland

Kayaking & Canoeing

Atlantic Canada is chock-full of possibilities to get out on the water, be it a lazy canoe trip or a battle with rolling rapids. Sea kayaking has exploded here, with myriad places to paddle. Top spots include Nova Scotia's South Shore, the under-appreciated Eastern Shore between Halifax and Canso, and the Bay of Fundy, especially the area around Advocate Harbour.

Canoeing and kayaking is also a great way to explore the interior, as practised by First Nations people for thousands of years. Kejimkujik National Park ranks high on the list thanks to its wealth of lakes and rivers. In New Brunswick, the place for canoeing is pristine though moose- and bear-trodden Mt Carleton Provincial Park, while those who wish to remain closer to city life can push off from Fredericton and paddle the Saint John River. Canoeing in Newfoundland centers on the region's Terra Nova National Park. Maps and equipment rentals are usually available from the park information centers, where staff can also give route recommendations and point you in the direction of local kayaking companies.

Many operators now also offer SUP (stand up paddleboards), giving you another way to explore the region's waterways.

Sea Kayaking

If there's any one activity that is Atlantic Canada's specialty, it's sea kayaking. It's everywhere and is absolutely the best way to see the remarkable coastlines. You'll often be kayaking alongside whales, seals and a huge amount of birdlife.

Most companies cater to beginners, so no need to feel unworthy if you've never kayaked before. Conversely, advanced paddlers can rent crafts and head out on their own. It can be very rough out there due to volatile weather, high winds and strong currents, so know your limits. The Canadian government publishes an excellent resource titled *Sea Kayaking Safety Guide* available via download from Transport Canada (www.tc.gc.ca). The guide details each province's weather and kayaking terrain, and also provides trip-planning tips.

Trips range from paddling around icebergs in Newfoundland to navigating protected inlets ringed by forest on uninhabited isles along the Eastern Shore of Nova Scotia. If you're a beginner, the best place to start are calm waters where your boat won't get jostled around by waves or currents. Some companies make multiday trips, including camping in places you couldn't get to otherwise.

Tidal Bore Rafting

One activity that's unique to this part of Canada is the opportunity to brave a tidal bore: a churning maelstrom of whitewater, created when a strong incoming sea tide meets a river's outgoing flow. The region's best-known (and most powerful) tidal bore is on the Shubenacadie River, where the river's flow smashes into the great Fundy tides, creating some of the roughest and most exhilarating whitewater anywhere in Atlantic Canada. Local rafting companies lead expeditions into the chaos, although the power of the whitewater depends both on the season and the moon's phase.

Whale-watching

More than 22 species of whale and porpoise lurk offshore throughout Atlantic Canada, drawn to the rich fishy feeding waters. The standout species include the leaping and diving humpback whale, the highly endangered North Atlantic right whale and the largest leviathan of all, the mighty blue whale.

Whale-watching boat operators are ubiquitous and will bring you close to the creatures. Popular tour areas include Cape Breton and Nova Scotia's Cabot Trail coastline, especially around Pleasant Bay. The most common sightings here are humpback, minke and pilot whales. In New Brunswick, right whales and blue whales are frequently observed along the eastern Fundy Shore and around the Fundy Isles. Newfoundland is generally surrounded by whales, with humpback and minke commonly seen; tour operators cluster around Witless Bay Ecological Reserve and Twillingate.

Some tours get you closer to the action in Zodiacs while others are on big, relatively comfortable ferry-like motorboats. Look for smaller tours such as Ocean Explorations Whale Cruises (p88) on Digby Neck, which are led by marine biologists. Many tours take in more than just whales and will take you to see seals, puffins or other seabirds as well.

Standard trips last about two hours and cost around $60 to $90 per adult. The sighting success rate is often posted and you should ask if there's any sort of money-back guarantee if you do not see whales. Remember, you're heading out on open sea for most of these tours, so be prepared for a wavy ride. If you're at all prone to seasickness, medicate beforehand. It's also cold out there, so take a jacket or sweater. The season varies by location but usually is in July and August.

And while whale-watching tours are great, never underestimate what you can see from shore, especially from places such as Cape Breton's Cabot Trail and throughout Newfoundland's Avalon Peninsula. Seeing the far-away spout of a whale from a clifftop while a bald eagle soars overhead is a true Maritime experience.

Gray seal

Hiking

Trails – from gentle jaunts around an interpretive path to breath-sapping slogs up a mountain – crisscross the area's national and provincial parks. Hiking them can be the most enjoyable and inexpensive way to absorb the region.

The hiking season runs from May to October, with optimal conditions from June onwards, when the trails are fully thawed. Early in the season, you'll frequently find yourself blissfully (depending on your inclination) alone. During the height of the season (July and August), especially on popular sections of the Cabot Trail and other well-publicized walks, you'll be sharing your isolated paradise with scores of other hikers. Having realistic expectations

MARINE CONDITIONS

Kayakers, fisherfolk and anyone else sailing out to sea can check www.buoyweather.com for marine conditions all around Atlantic Canada.

Cape Breton Highlands National Park (p101)

will help you choose when to set out. Maps are available at park information centers, although for extended hikes you may need topographic maps.

Canada is notably home to one of the most ambitious paths ever conceived, the **Trans Canada Trail** (www.thegreattrail.ca). Finally completed in 2017, the trail spans approximately 24,000km from Cape Spear in Newfoundland to Victoria, British Columbia, but work is ongoing to improve access, signage and trail conditions.

Nova Scotia

Nova Scotia holds such a variety of terrain and well-tended backcountry that you'll be spoiled with options.

Cape Breton Highlands National Park (p101) Exquisite hiking over dramatic coastline. The Skyline Trail is the most popular path, but it's hard to go wrong with any of them.

Cape Split (p87) Probably the best hike to view the scale and might of the Fundy tides.

Taylor Head Provincial Park (p111) A slender sprig of land on the eastern shore, with trails traversing forest and beach.

New Brunswick

Rugged, forested New Brunswick holds a huge number of hiking options ranging from mountains and river valleys to the dramatic Fundy coastline.

Fundy National Park (p138) and Fundy Trail Parkway (p139) A variety of paths along the wooded coastline.

Mt Carleton Provincial Park (p121) Adventurous hikes over mountain peaks to river valleys and lakes. Expect to see wildlife but few humans.

Grand Manan Island (p132) Great for seaside-themed mellow hikes, taking in cliffs, marshes and lighthouses.

Newfoundland

Remnants of old walking paths that used to connect local communities and provided escape routes inland from pirates now make for fantastic hiking. Most clutch the shoreline and often provide whale views.

East Coast Trail (p198) An epic 265km trail along the Avalon Peninsula; the 9.3km path between Cape Spear and Maddox Cove is a great taster.

Razorbills off the coast of New Brunswick

Skerwink Trail (p204) On the Bonavista Peninsula, a fabulous 5km loop reveals picture-perfect coastal vistas.

Gros Morne National Park (p216) Renowned for its spectacular landscapes.

Prince Edward Island

PEI is very flat, so there are far fewer hiking opportunities than the other provinces. That said, there are plenty of beaches to stroll.

Prince Edward Island National Park (p168) Follow the shoreline for big views of beaches and bluffs.

Bird-watching

No need to be a binocular-toting ornithologist to get into the scene here. Birds swarm the region, and whether you're a birder or not, you'll find it tough to resist the charm of a funny-looking puffin or common murre.

Seabirds are the top draw. Many whale-watching tours also take visitors to seabird colonies as whales and birds share a taste for the same fish. You'll be able to feast your eyes upon razorbills, kittiwakes, arctic terns, and yes, puffins and murres. The colonies can be up to one million strong, their shrieks deafening and their smell, well, not so fresh. Still, it's an amazing sight to behold.

Also impressive to watch are the Arctic-nesting shorebirds that migrate south through the Bay of Fundy. Each year millions of tiny sandpipers refuel in the rich mudflats exposed by the world's highest tides. The prime time is mid-August, and the best places are around Windsor and Grand Pré in Nova Scotia's Annapolis Valley.

The *Sibley Field Guide to Birds of Eastern North America* (2003) by David Sibley makes an excellent, illustrated and portable companion for bird-watchers.

Cycling & Mountain Biking

Most people explore the Maritimes on four wheels, but there's no reason you can't do it on two – as long as you're prepared for changeable weather and plenty of up-and-down terrain. The best idea is to explore one of the region's dedicated bike trails: there's at least one in each province, although PEI has the real jewel in the crown.

Nova Scotia

Long distances and rugged terrain make Nova Scotia a tough proposition for cyclists, so it's probably best left for experienced pedalers. Having said that, there are a number of short trails dotted around the province that make for great day trips: among the best is the Rum Runners Trail (p74), a 119km route between Halifax and Lunenburg which is split into seven easy-to-manage sections (the Mahone Bay to Lunenburg jaunt makes a fabulous day trip). And if all you want is a quick pedal, hiring a bike for a spin along Halifax's lovely waterfront is hard to beat.

Hardcore cyclists head for Cape Breton Highlands National Park (p101): completing the Cabot Trail is a huge achievement, but not to be underestimated. The scenery is wonderful, but peak-season traffic and

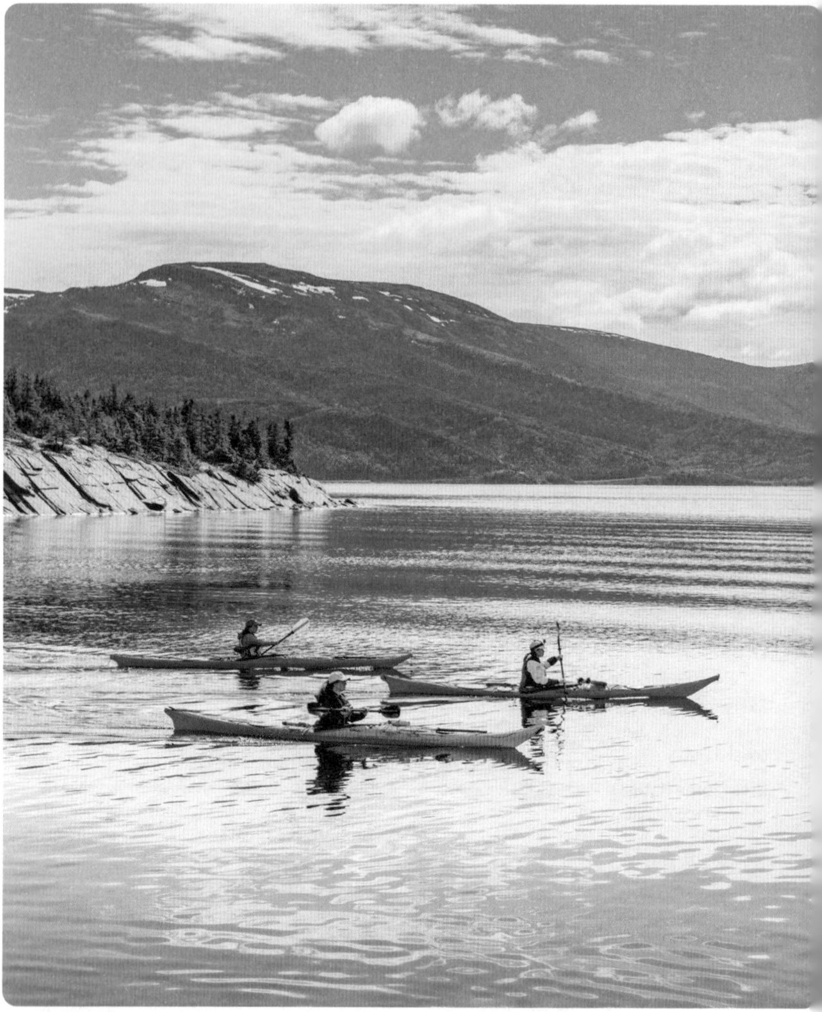

WILDNERDPIX/SHUTTERSTOCK ©

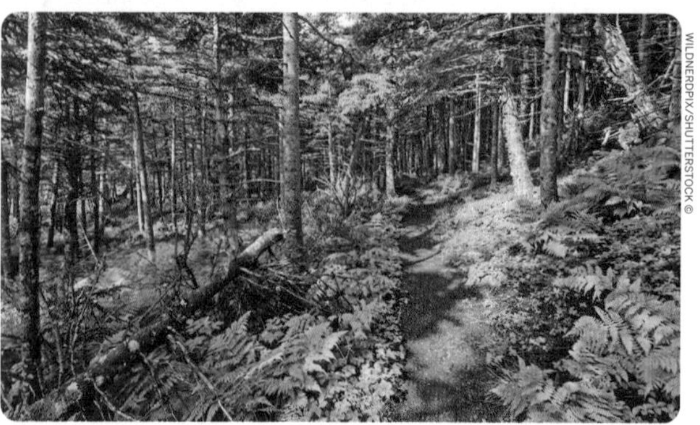

Top: Kayaking in Gros Morne National Park (p216)

Bottom: Hiking trail, Gros Morne National Park (p216)

sections of punishing elevation make it very hard going indeed.

Prince Edward Island

PEI's most celebrated bike route is the Confederation Trail (p161), a long-distance bike route that follows the course of the island's railway, which ceased operations in 1989. It's established PEI as an international cycling destination, and cycling the trail remains one of the most popular ways to experience the province today. Traversing the length of the island, with feeder paths connecting most towns, the trail is lined with top-notch services and facilities, many provided in quaint, reconditioned train stations. This access to services, combined with manageable distances between sections and predominantly flat, scenic terrain, make cycling here an attractive prospect even for those with limited experience.

The main east–west route covers 273km from Tignish in the northwest to Elmira in the northeast, but branch trails bring the total cyclable distance to an impressive 435km. The seaside stretch from St Peters to Mt Stewart is a lovely day trip.

New Brunswick

Rewarding rides include the Fundy Trail Parkway (p139) along coastal wilderness, and paths through the backcountry in Kouchibouguac National Park (p148). Although not yet a cohesive entity, the **New Brunswick Trail** (www.nbtrail.com) offers unconnected sections of trail around the province.

Newfoundland

Rugged terrain, high winds, poor road conditions and long stretches of road between towns make Newfoundland a difficult cycling destination. If you really want to give it a try, Gros Morne National Park (p216) and CA Pippy Park (p186) in St John's are potential options.

Fishing

Fly-fishing in this region is downright legendary – particularly for Atlantic salmon and trout (speckled and brown, among the many).

TYING KNOTS

Unleash your inner sailor (or fisher or rock climber) by learning to tie a half hitch, bowline and others with *Knots and Splices* (2006) by Cyrus Day and Colin Jarman. Also helpful for budding escape artists.

On the tranquil Miramichi River in New Brunswick, everyone from Prince Charles to Dick Cheney to Marilyn Monroe has reeled one in. The Margaree River on Cape Breton is another fabled fishing run. The Humber River in Newfoundland and Pinware River in Labrador Straits are known for salmon fishing. If the latter isn't remote enough, Labrador offers several fly-in lodges that have hosted the likes of George Bush Sr. Some rivers are stocked, others wild – but either way, fishing on a catch-and-release basis is the more environmentally friendly option.

Depending on where you fish, a fishing license may be required, and make sure you're aware of proper catch and release techniques, and that you adopt careful handling to ensure fish health and survival. It's well worth consulting the relevant anglers' handbooks, which are all available for download from the relevant governmental websites.

Deep-sea fishing is huge around North Rustico in PEI, where you can sign on with any of a fleet of fishing boats, often captained by bearded seamen who come from long generations of plying the waters. There are plenty of other opportunities to cast a line for the big one – try boats around Lunenberg and along the Cabot Trail in Nova Scotia. Obviously issues around fish stocks and sustainability should be considered before you head out on a trip – make sure you discuss the boat's specific fishing policy with the captain before you sign up.

And finally, lobster fishing provides a unique experience, one that kids will love. Haul up crustacean-filled pots in Lunenburg in Nova Scotia. Then grab a bucket and a shovel to go clamming in PEI.

Fishing Rules & Licenses

Staff at any tourist office will have the most current information about fishing

Fishing in Cape Breton Island (p99)

regulations and outfitters. Each province also produces its own 'angler's guide' booklet that includes licensing rules. License prices vary by province and by species fished; a seven-day license costs anywhere from $35 to $95. Check with each province's environmental or natural resources department for further information.

Fishing Hot Spots

Miramichi River Valley (p147) New Brunswick's most fabled salmon run.

Pinware River Provincial Park (☎709-927-5516; www.nlcamping.ca; Rte 510; campsites $18; ⊙Jun-Sep) The Pinware is well-known for its salmon fishing.

Fishing for Success (p197) Learn cod-jigging, net-knitting and rope work the Newfoundland way.

Cape Breton (p99) Fly-fish for trout and salmon in the Margaree River.

ICE-SKATING

Windsor, Nova Scotia, claims to be the birthplace of ice hockey, so as you'd expect, there are plenty of ice-skating areas around the region, although not many cater to visitors. Your best bet for gliding across the ice is the world-class Emera Oval (p62) in downtown Halifax where you can even borrow skates for free.

Surfing & Kitesurfing

Surfing seems an unusual sport for Atlantic Canada – too damn cold, right? Think again. People do surf here and not only is it cold, it's bloody freezing, since the best waves break in winter. Luckily, the best time for beginners is summer when the waves are smaller and the water is at least a little bit warmer.

The place to partake of the madness is Lawrencetown Beach on Nova Scotia's eastern shore. L-town, as it's called, faces due south and picks up stormy weather from hundreds of kilometers away; this results in exceptional wrapping waves, especially plentiful in the colder months.

Kitesurfing at Lawrencetown Beach (p111)

So bundle up in your 7mm wetsuit, try not to freeze your ass off in the almost freezing water and join the lineup. People do surf at warmer times of the year, too. Board rentals cost about $40 per day, lessons about $90.

The Seaside Adjunct in Kejimkujik National Park provides additional waves and the prices are similar.

If kitesurfing is more your thing, Shippagan in northeastern New Brunswick is a good place to try it. Lawrencetown Beach in Nova Scotia is also a great place to watch a spectacular show of kitesurfers flying along and over the waves.

Skiing & Snowboarding

Atlantic Canada's best skiing and snowboarding take place at Newfoundland's Marble Mountain (p223) outside Corner Brook. It may not have the height of Whistler or other top resorts, but it's lower cost with shorter lift lines, so you get more time on the slopes.

Marble has 39 trails, four lifts, a 519m vertical drop and annual snowfall of 5m. There are snowboarding and tubing parks, as well as night skiing on Friday. The region caters to cross-country skiers at **Blow-Me-Down Cross-Country Ski Park** (☎709-639-2754; www.blowmedown.ca; Lundigran Dr; day pass $20; ⊙sunrise-9pm Dec-Apr), about 10 minutes from the mountain.

Serious cross-country skiers will want to head far north to where the Canadian national team trains in Labrador West. The Wapusakatto Mountains let loose with good, cold, dry snow from late October to late April, a much longer season than elsewhere in the region – or anywhere in Canada.

Wentworth (www.skiwentworth.ca) is the favorite spot in Nova Scotia, although it's small with 815 vertical feet and 20 runs. The park also offers cross-country skiing and snowshoeing.

New Brunswick has three ski parks, the biggest being Poley Mountain (www.poleymountain.com) near Sussex, with more than 40 hectares of skiable terrain and 10 night skiing trails.

Plan Your Trip

Travel with Children

These Canadian provinces were made for kids. As if seeing moose, eagles and whales or running around in the snow or on the beach all day wasn't fun enough, everywhere you turn those crafty Canadians have cooked up some hands-on learning experience, living history lesson or child-oriented theater.

Best Regions for Kids

Halifax, Nova Scotia

Cartoonlike tug-boat rides, cycling, kayaking, a free year-round skating area, parks and family-friendly festivals galore through summer.

Prince Edward Island's Beaches

Sandy stretches of white or pink sand with lightly lapping, bearably cool waves.

Fundy National Park, New Brunswick

Low-tide flats to putter around, trails leading to waterfalls, lakes to swim in.

St John's, Newfoundland

Nearby whale-watching tours.

Nova Scotia, New Brunswick & Prince Edward Island For Kids

Between learning about pirate history on antique sailing vessels, playing on low-key beaches and climbing to the top of lighthouses, it's impossible to make a bad decision about where to take your kids in these provinces. Canada caters to families better than nearly anywhere else in the world and the mix of coast and forest, easy-to-manage cities and lakes galore make this region a top choice in the country. The food isn't daunting, people are exceptionally friendly and there's a prevalent sense of peace and welcome.

Museums, Monuments & Lighthouses

Halifax, Saint John and St John's all have science museums that specialize in hands-on activities to get all ages involved, while at historic sites strewn across the region costumed thespians get you right into the period and often have demonstrations of everything from blacksmithing to cooking. At some of these places there are also puppet or theatrical performances for children and other events such as hayrides. Teens often enjoy these sites as well, since they are large, diverse and great for exploration.

Lighthouses seem to be perched on every headland and you can climb up to the top of many of them, usually for a small fee. If you're lucky there will be a hand pump horn to set off.

Outdoor Activities

Endless coastlines, fresh air, wildlife, snow, sand, rivers, lakes and mountains make almost any outdoor activity you may be yearning for entirely possible. Prince Edward Island's mostly flat Confederation Trail traverses the island and can be picked up from almost any point; the coastline of the Prince Edward Island National Park has dedicated cycling lanes that run scenically along the beaches. The Halifax waterfront is also a great place for family bike rentals. Canoeing is a Canadian activity par excellence, available in lakes in Nova Scotia and New Brunswick, and most sea-kayaking outfits throughout the region cater to families. Skiing and snowboarding are available at small family-friendly slopes in winter.

But perhaps the most exciting thing to do with all the surrounding seas is to set sail, either to explore and feel the wind in your hair or to look for the many species of whale thriving in the Bay of Fundy, Cabot Straight and the mighty Atlantic Ocean.

Children's Highlights

Historic Locations

Fortress of Louisbourg (p110) Step back to the 18th century at this historic fort.

Citadel Hill (p57) Look out from the battlements of Halifax's hilltop stronghold.

Joggins Fossil Cliffs (p94) Spot 300-million-year-old fossils in the cliffs.

L'Anse aux Meadows (p220) Visit Leif Eriksson's viking village.

Kings Landing (p116) Wander through a Loyalist village from the 1800s.

The Great Outdoors

Whale-watching (p33) Spy whales on Brier Island, Cape Breton or Grand Manan Island.

Kejimkujik National Park (p81) Explore Nova Scotia's largest wilderness area.

Greenwich Dunes (p168) Spot birds amongst PEI's dunes and wetlands.

Kouchibouguac National Park (p148) Stroll, bird-watch, camp and clam-dig in this New Brunswick park.

Witless Bay Ecological Reserve (p198) Watch out for Newfoundland wildlife, including whales and puffins.

Family-Friendly Attractions

Shubenacadie Provincial Wildlife Park (p93) Get up close to Nova Scotian wildlife.

Green Gables Heritage Place (p176) See the real-life location where *Anne of Green Gables* was set.

Memory Lane Heritage Village (p110) Walk through a Nova Scotian town c 1940.

Maritime Museum of the Atlantic (p60) View a flotilla of boats from Nova Scotia's past.

Fundy National Park Swimming Pool (p139) Splash around in a solar-heated saltwater swimming pool.

Activities Galore

Sea Kayaking on the Eastern Shore (p111) Paddle a kayak to the 100 Wild Islands.

Cycling the Confederation Trail (p161) Pedal your way along PEI's premier bike trail.

Anchors Above Zipline Adventure (p99) Conquer your vertigo on two huge zip lines.

Rafting the Fundy tidal bore (p90) Get very wet indeed on a whitewater adventure.

Canoeing in Kejimkujik National Park (p80) Bring out your inner paddler on Kejimkujik Lake.

Hopewell Rocks (p140) Explore weird rock formations on the Bay of Fundy.

Planning

When to Go

➡ Summer is the best season for travelling with kids: everywhere will be open and all activities will be available, and there are often seasonal visitor programs at national parks and historic sites.

DON'T FORGET!

- Waterproof jacket
- Insulating layers
- Sunscreen
- Bug spray
- Wildlife field guides

- Fall is the next best time to visit: most attractions stay open until October, the weather is usually quite settled and mild, and the fall colors are fabulous.
- Spring can be a tricky time: many places won't open up until late May or early June, and the changeable weather makes for guaranteed tantrums.
- Few visitors come to Atlantic Canada in winter, unless they're coming specifically for winter sports.

Travel Documents

Children under 18 are considered minors and will need to apply for their own eTA and travel on their own passport.

Single parents, grandparents or guardians traveling with anyone under the age of 18 should carry proof of legal custody, or a notarized letter from the nonaccompanying parent authorizing the trip. Unaccompanied children will also need a notarized letter of consent from both parents or legal guardians. This is in addition to their passport and/or proof of citizenship.

Accommodations

- Kids often stay for free in hotels and motels.
- B&Bs are not so gracious, and may even refuse to accept pint-sized patrons. Ask when booking.
- Camping can be a really good way to keep costs down – many campgrounds offer pre-pitched tents, chalets or cabins.

Food

- Fast food is ubiquitous in Canada so healthy eaters may find that the biggest hurdle is finding food that's not processed or fried.
- Cabins and family suites often have kitchens so you can self-cater; in cities you'll find options for any type of diet.
- Most restaurants offer kids' menus or half-sized portions of main meals.

Admissions & Discounts

- Once in Canada, kids receive a wide range of discounts on attraction admissions and transportation fares.
- Usually kids aged six to 17 are half-price; younger children are free.
- Kids receive free admission to National Historic Sites.
- Ask about family admissions if your posse consists of two adults and two or more kids.

Practicalities

- Baby food, infant formula, milk, disposable diapers (nappies) and the like are widely available in drugstores and supermarkets.
- Breastfeeding in public is legal.
- Most supermarkets and larger visitor attractions offer baby-changing facilities.
- In all vehicles, children under 18kg must be restrained in safety seats.

Lobster chowder

Plan Your Trip

Eat & Drink Like a Local

Long celebrated for its seafood, Atlantic Canada is becoming a serious culinary destination, thanks to PEI's meteoric rise on the foodie circuit and Nova Scotia's emergence as one of the top wine-producing regions in Canada. That said, dining in the Maritimes remains a simple affair. Main meals usually feature fish or shellfish with a veggie thrown in, and perhaps a hearty bowl of seafood chowder.

The Year in Food

Spring (April & May)

Warming waters open up previously icebound fishing grounds for scallop, crab, lobster and oysters.

Summer (June–September)

Summer brings food and wine festivals and outdoor dining, plus the best time for salmon and trout fishing.

Autumn (October & November)

End-of-summer harvests bring a bounty of produce, from new potatoes to bakeapples.

Winter (December–March)

Despite the winter weather, lobster fishing continues in some areas such as southwestern Nova Scotia.

Food Experiences

Local Treats

Lobster Supper (p173) The original Maritime feast, traditionally served in churches and village halls.

Digby Scallops (p86) The Bay of Fundy is famous for its huge, succulent scallops.

Malpeque Bay Oysters (p176) The best place on PEI to try the prized bivalves.

Kitchen Parties (p246) These Acadian celebrations are a feast of food, drink and music.

Wolfville Wineries (p92) Tour the vineyards of the Annapolis Valley.

Cheap Eats

Lobster Roll (p161) The cheapest way to enjoy the costly crustacean: sold all over Nova Scotia and PEI. Water Prince Corner Shop & Lobster Pound in Charlottetown is particularly good.

Rappie Pie (p85) An Acadian meat-and-potato pie that you can find along Nova Scotia's French Shore. Stop in at La Cuisine Robicheau.

Seafood Chowder (p162) A Maritimes classic, rich, filling and full of fishy flavor; try it at Point Prim Chowder House in Charlottetown.

Ice cream (p157) PEI is the home of Cows ice cream, but there are lots of other excellent makers across the region.

Dare to Try

Solomon Gundy (p78) Pickled herring *and* chopped meat? Yum.

Lunenburg pudding (p78) More sausage than pudding: pork and spices cooked in pig intestines.

Dulse (p133) Never tried seaweed? New Brunswick's Grand Manan Island is the place.

Fiddleheads Edible fern shoots eaten like vegetables.

Cod Tongues (☎709-639-1895; 13 West St; mains $13-30; ⊙noon-9pm Mon-Fri, from 4pm Sat) A dubious Newfoundland delicacy.

Local Specialties

Nova Scotia

Seafood in all its forms dominates Nova Scotian menus. You'll find a huge variety of sea-based specialties to try here, most of it served fresh off the boats.

The region's most famous treat is, of course, lobster. The richest lobster grounds anywhere in Canada are dotted around the shores of Nova Scotia, Prince Edward Island and New Brunswick, so it's no surprise that Maritimers have developed a taste for it. The signature way to enjoy it is at a lobster supper, where the crustacean is served alongside a smorgasbord of other seafood, but a simple lobster roll tastes just as good and doesn't have the associated price-tag. Scallops (especially from the Digby area) and snow crab are also highly prized, and Atlantic cod and salmon are also fairly ubiquitous. The province also has its own variety of lightly smoked salmon called Nova: it's fairly similar to lox.

Seafood chowder is another common dish you'll be guaranteed to try: it's a rich, creamy soup usually made with lobsters and clams, generally eaten as an appetizer but sometimes as a main dish too.

The province's Acadian past has left it with a rich legacy of Acadian dishes: rappie pie (also known as la rapure), a potato and salted-pork dish; *tourtière* (meat pie); poutine *râpée* (a mixture of grated raw and mashed potatoes wrapped around fresh pork) and *fricot* (a hearty soup or stew). Similarly, Celtic settlers brought over many old dishes that are still served in some areas, such as oat-cakes in Cape Breton.

The Annapolis Valley is also a major fruit-producing area, particularly for apples: there's a huge Apple Blossom Festival in early June every year, followed by a superb strawberry crop from July through August.

New Brunswick

Acadian lobster and Atlantic salmon are the best-known seafood specialties in New Brunswick. Seasonal produce abounds, and there's a strong penchant for foraged ingredients – fiddleheads (the coiled heads of young ferns) are one of the more unusual delicacies you'll be able to try. Look out, too, for Acadian-style mussels, steamed with onions, celery and garlic.

Berries are also a big crop: blueberries, partridgeberries (similar to cranberries) and bakeapples (cloudberries) get shoveled into muffins, pies and jams. The best time of year for the harvest is mid-August.

Prince Edward Island

Like Nova Scotia, PEI is absolutely mad about seafood. In summer many towns host lobster suppers, and you'll find a huge variety of other fish and seafood on island menus. A particular PEI specialty to look out for is oysters: the area around Malpeque Bay catches the best oysters in Atlantic Canada, and you'll be able to try them at seafood shacks and fine-dining restaurants across the island.

PEI is also celebrated for its potatoes, so the humble spud features in many dishes, from lobster poutine to potato soup.

Newfoundland

Fishing has provided the backbone of Newfoundland's economy for generations, and no fish is more important than Atlantic cod. It's most likely to arrive battered and fried, but sometimes you'll see it baked or pan-fried and served with a sauce. Atlantic salmon, cousin of the better-known Pacific salmon, usually arrives broiled and sauced, perhaps with dill or hollandaise.

Poached cod fillet

EDIBLE SEAWEED

Maritime provinces harvest seaweeds that are eaten or used for their medicinal properties. Stop by Roland's Sea Vegetables (p133) on Grand Manan Island, New Brunswick, for a bag of dulse to eat as-is or to sprinkle on fish, or to Point Prim, PEI, for Seaweed Secrets, where you collect, learn about and eat the region's vegetables from the sea.

Other Newfoundland specialties to look out for include figgy duff (a sweet pudding with raisins and molasses) and jig's dinner (meat and vegetables boiled together and eaten with pickles, gravy and figgy duff).

Local Tipples

Beer

The craft-beer revolution has taken the Maritimes just as much by storm as the rest of Canada. There's now a huge number

Oysters with lemon and cocktail sauce

LOBSTER SUPPERS

The classic Nova Scotia, New Brunswick and Prince Edward Island (PEI) dining experience is a no-frills lobster supper, held in dining halls, churches and community centers. The lobster is generally unadorned with sauces and fanfare; the suppers are a place to enjoy these critters as simply as possible (or perhaps with a little melted butter), often accompanied by other types of seafood, like seafood chowder, clams, snow-crab, oysters and mussels. It's a hands-on, get-stuck-in kind of experience: you'll be supplied with an arsenal of tools, from pickers to crackers, to help you extract all the meat you can. Expect to get messy: juices will fly.

Held daily for dinner from roughly mid-June to mid-October, the most suppers per capita are found on PEI. The cost of dinner depends on the market price of lobster but generally hovers around $35 for an all-inclusive meal with a 1lb crustacean.

of craft breweries dotted across the region, not just in the major cities but in many smaller towns too. In Nova Scotia, among the best-known are Garrison Brewing Company, Alexander Keith's Brewery and Propeller, all based in Halifax, but there are plenty of up-and-coming breweries hot on their heels, often making exciting experimental brews: Tatamagouche Brewing Co produces a chocolate porter and plum beer, Rare Bird in Guysborough makes ales infused with spruce and maple, while Cape Breton's Big Spruce Brewing makes an organic (and aptly named) Kitchen Party Pale Ale. New Brunswick's best-known is Moosehead, brewed in Saint John. In Newfoundland, Quidi Vidi microbrews flow through the provincial taps; try Eric the Red.

Wine

The winemaking tradition in Nova Scotia goes back to the early 1600s – this may have been the first place in North America where wine grapes were grown. Today

Glenora Inn & Distillery (p100)

wineries are springing up everywhere. There are six distinct wine-growing regions in the province, although most wineries are found in the Annapolis Valley and on the Malagash Peninsula. Domaine de Grand Pré, Blomidon Estate Winery and Jost Vineyards are among the biggest; you'll often see their wines on restaurant menus. Newer wineries to try include Lightfoot & Wolfville and Luckett Vineyards, which make excellent reds, whites and fruit wines.

L'Acadie Blanc, a French hybrid, grows particularly well in Nova Scotia and has become the province's signature grape. It makes a medium-bodied, citrusy white wine that pairs well with scallops or smoked salmon. New York Muscat also grows well and is often used for dry white and ice wines. The area also has its own appellation, Tidal Bay, a crisp blended white.

There are just a few wineries on PEI: Rossignol Estate specializes in fruit wines, while Newman Estate produces renowned fruity reds.

Spirits

For something a little boozier, you'll find plenty of distilleries to take a tipple. The Glenora Distillery on Cape Breton Island produces a very sip-worthy single-malt whiskey. Lunenburg's Ironworks Distillery produces Bluenose Dark Rum which is smooth as silk poured over a cube of ice. Prince Edward Distillery makes award-winning spirits from, you guessed it, potatoes, as well as a few grain-based beverages. Just around the corner, Myriad View cooks up a tonsil-searing 'Strait Lightning' that's 75% alcohol and the only legal moonshine in Canada. Newfoundland is famous for its Screech, a brand of rum that's actually made in Jamaica.

A signature Canadian drink worth trying is the Caesar, a Bloody Mary-ish cocktail made with Clamato (a tomato- and clam-juice-based beverage), vodka, hot sauce and Worcestershire sauce. It's a good Sunday morning hair-of-the-dog drink, imbibed on ice in a salt-rimmed glass and garnished with lime and a stalk of celery.

FOOD FESTIVALS

Lobster Carnival (p97) Pictou, Nova Scotia

Tyne Valley Oyster Festival (p180) Tyne Valley, PEI

Digby Scallop Days (p86) Digby, Nova Scotia

Fall Flavours (p159) Charlottetown, PEI

PEI Burger Love (p159) Charlottetown, PEI

Roots, Rants & Roars Festival (p206) Elliston, Newfoundland

How to Eat & Drink

When to Eat

Most restaurants open for lunch (usually between 11:30am and 2:30pm) and dinner (from around 5:30pm), although more upscale establishments sometimes only open for dinner. Dinner tends to be the main meal of the day, but it's worth noting that in rural areas (especially out of season), many restaurants close early – last orders are often around 7:30pm or 8pm.

Sunday brunch is a popular weekly treat for many Maritimers: it's generally served from around 11am to 2pm.

Where to Eat

In the larger towns and cities there's usually a fairly good selection of restaurants, from simple cafes to pubs, diners and fine-dining bistros. In rural areas, the choice tends to be more limited: in most places you'll be able to find at least one restaurant or diner for dinner, although you might well find they're closed outside the main tourist season.

Some establishments specialise in one type of food (eg seafood), but generally you'll find a selection of dishes, including meat, fish, pasta and vegetarian.

Vegetarians & Vegans

Vegetarians will be well catered for in the region's principal cities, such as Halifax, Fredericton and St John's, but as you move away from urban areas your options become extremely limited. Vegans can expect an even rougher ride. Strict adherents should stick to any vegetarian-only eateries they come across, since 'vegetarian' items in mainstream restaurants may well have been prepared with meat stock or lard.

Specialty health-food shops are found almost exclusively in the larger cities or hip college towns, so you'll want to stock up on supplies before going to more remote regions. Chinese eateries occasionally pop up in remote areas and may be another option. Many fine restaurants (some that have unexpected rural locations) will nearly always cater to dietary restrictions, as will many B&Bs.

Menu Decoder

Appetizer Starter.

Entrée Main course.

Locavore Ingredients sourced from local producers and farmers.

Growler Pitcher or bottle used to contain draft beer.

Regions at a Glance

Yaar! This is the Canada for enjoying steel-colored seascapes and salt air with a big bowl of chowder and a pint of ale to wash it down. Everything here revolves around the cold Atlantic Ocean, from today's whale-watching adventures and lobster feasts to the history of Vikings and pirates. While tied together by geography and history, each province has its own personality, from the iceberg-clad desolation of Newfoundland to the forested inland rivers and lakes of New Brunswick, the storybook farmlands of Prince Edward Island (PEI) and the never-ending coastal variations of Nova Scotia. Wherever you choose to go, you'll never be far from the sound of waves crashing on a beach or a simple supper of fresh fish.

Nova Scotia

Coastline
Activities
Culture

Coves, Cliffs & Tides

The sea has shaped and sculpted this corner of Canada, carving out its complicated coastline, wrecking countless ships and providing a diverse habitat for all manner of marine creatures. Most majestic of all is the Bay of Fundy, home to the highest tides on earth.

Outdoor Pursuits

Nova Scotians need no excuse to get out and explore the great outdoors, whether it's kayaking to a remote island on the Eastern Shore, cycling the Rum Runners Trail, camping out in Kejimkujik National Park or braving the Shubie tidal bore.

Culture Trip

As you travel round Nova Scotia, you'll experience a surprising array of cultures, including Acadian, Celtic and Mi'kmaw. Dance along at a kitchen party, listen to fiddle and pipes at a traditional ceilidh, or sweat it out at a pow-wow.

p52

New Brunswick

Activities
Beaches
Wildlife

Canoe Like a Canadian

From tranquil lakes to the quicksilver Tobique River, New Brunswick is fantastic for canoeing, the most Canadian of activities. For the ultimate authentic experience, join a Voyageur tour, hearing tales of old as you paddle just like the first settlers.

Beach Time

You might not think it, but New Brunswick is home to a surprising number of superb sandy beaches – many of them empty for much of the year. Parlee Beach has the warmest ocean water in Canada.

Puffin Lovin'

Whether you're a hard-core bird-watcher or just want to be able to tell your friends you saw a moose, New Brunswick's got plenty of animal action to go around. Your best bet: observing rare Atlantic puffins on desolate Machias Seal Island.

p113

Prince Edward Island

Food
Culture
Scenery

Lobster Suppers, Oysters & Potatoes

PEI might be famous as Canada's potato capital (it even has its own potato museum), but it's seafood that dominates most menus. Delving into a table-sized lobster supper is a longstanding PEI tradition, but leave room for Malpeque oysters if you can.

It's All About Anne

Personified by Anne Shirley, LM Montgomery's red-headed star of the *Anne of Green Gables* series, Prince Edward Island is as pretty as it's portrayed in the books. Red dirt and sands mimic Anne's hair, while white-picket fences and fields of wildflowers paint the real-life backdrop.

Island Landscapes

PEI is only small, but it packs in a real diversity of scenery: pan-flat fields, grass-backed dunes, lonely lighthouses and sienna-colored cliffs, not to mention a wealth of white beaches and some of the warmest waters in the Gulf of St Lawrence.

p153

Newfoundland & Labrador

Seascapes
Culture
History

Great Big Sea

'There's one,' someone shouts, and sure enough a barnacled humpback steams through the water. Or maybe they're referring to the icebergs. Whether you're along-shore, out in a boat or by your window, Newfoundland's sea delivers.

Strange Brew

The peculiar brogue is vaguely Irish, the slang indecipherable enough to merit its own dictionary, plates arrive with cod tongues, bakeapple jam and figgy duff (sweet pudding made with raisins and molasses), while towns have names such as Dildo and Jerry's Nose. This region is so offbeat it even has its own time zone: a *half*-hour ahead of the mainland.

Viking Vestiges

They've taken a low-key approach at L'Anse aux Meadows, Leif Erikson's 1000-year-old settlement, but the forlorn sweep of land is more powerful that way. You can feel the Vikings' isolation.

p181

On the Road

Nova Scotia

902 / POP 923,598

Includes ➡

Best Places to Eat

- ➡ Edna (p65)
- ➡ Canteen (p71)
- ➡ Lincoln Street Food (p79)
- ➡ Le Caveau (p92)

Best Places to Stay

- ➡ Prince George Hotel (p64)
- ➡ Alicion B&B (p78)
- ➡ Quarterdeck (p80)
- ➡ Oceanstone Seaside Resort (p72)

Why Go?

Facing the restless swells of the Atlantic, Nova Scotia is a place that's steeped in the sea. With its candy-striped lighthouses, salty fishing towns and towering red cliffs, this Maritime province feels thrillingly rugged and wild, especially in winter, when storms thrash the coastline and the ocean freezes. But come summer it's a different picture: Nova Scotians emerge to hike the trails, lounge on the beaches, tuck into gigantic lobster suppers and celebrate their Celtic roots with lively ceilidhs (parties with music and dancing). Life here has always been tough, but the locals' warm-hearted humor can't fail to make you feel welcome.

Most adventures begin in seaside Halifax, followed by postcard-perfect Peggy's Cove and Unesco-listed Lunenburg. Further afield, the vineyards of the Annapolis Valley beckon, along with the wild coastline of Cape Breton, the lakes and forests of Kejimkujik National Park and the incredible tides of the Bay of Fundy.

When to Go

Halifax

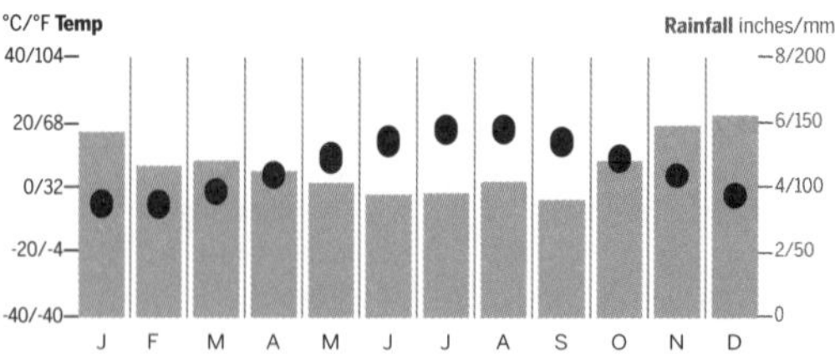

May & Jun You'll beat the summer crowds and prices – but some things may be closed.

Jul & Aug Peak summer season means long, warm days and events galore.

Sep & Oct Locals make the most of stunning fall foliage before the long winter comes.

History

From time immemorial the Mi'kmaq First Nation has lived throughout present-day Nova Scotia. When the French established the first European settlement at Port Royal (today's Annapolis Royal) in 1605, Grand Chief Membertou offered them hospitality and became a frequent guest of Samuel de Champlain.

That close relationship with the French led to considerable suspicion by the British after they gained control of Nova Scotia, and rewards were offered for Mi'kmaw scalps. Starting in 1755, most French-speaking Acadians were deported to Louisiana (where they became known as Cajuns) and elsewhere for refusing to swear allegiance to the British Crown.

Nova Scotia was repopulated by some 35,000 United Empire Loyalists retreating from the American Revolution, including a small number of African slaves owned by Loyalists as well as freed Black Loyalists. New England planters settled other communities, and from 1773 waves of Highland Scots arrived in northern Nova Scotia and Cape Breton Island.

Most Nova Scotians trace their ancestry to the British Isles, as a look at the lengthy 'Mac' and 'Mc' sections of the phone book easily confirms. Acadians who managed to return from Louisiana after 1764 found their lands in the Annapolis Valley occupied. They settled instead along the French Shore between Yarmouth and Digby, on Cape Breton Island around Chéticamp, and on Isle Madame. Today Acadians make up some 12% of the population, although not as many still identify French as their first language. African Nova Scotians make up about 5% of the population. Nova Scotia has close to 34,000 people of Indigenous identity, of which around 22,000 are First Nations people, predominantly from 18 Mi'kmaq communities.

Information

Tourism Nova Scotia (☎902-425-5781, 800-565-0000; www.novascotia.com) operates visitor centers in Halifax and other locations within Nova Scotia province, plus a free accommodation-booking service, which is useful when rooms are scarce in midsummer. It publishes the *Doers & Dreamers Guide*, which lists places to stay, attractions and tour operators.

Getting There & Away

AIR

The province's main air hub is Halifax Stanfield International Airport (p70), which has year-round daily flights to Canadian cities including Toronto, Montréal, Ottawa, Calgary, Fredericton, Saint John, Charlottetown and Moncton, as well as US cities including New York, Boston, Chicago, Philadelphia and Orlando.

In summer and fall there are also regular flights (some direct, some via a Canadian hub) to London, Paris and Frankfurt. Air Canada and Westjet cover nearly all the Canadian flights, with United and Delta handling most US flights.

In addition to the main airport at Halifax, Nova Scotia has two smaller airports: **JA Douglas McCurdy Sydney Airport** (www.sydneyairport.ca), which has regular flights to Halifax, Toronto and Montréal, and Yarmouth International Airport (www.yarmouthairport.ca/), which generally only handles charter and private flights.

PAL Airlines (PB; ☎800-563-2800; www.palairlines.ca) can be useful for getting to Nova Scotia from regional locations in Québec, New Brunswick and Newfoundland.

Air St-Pierre (☎877-277-7765; www.airsaintpierre.com) offers flights between Sydney and the French territory of St Pierre and Miquelon.

BOAT

As of July 2019, the **Bay Ferries** (☎877-762-7245; www.ferries.ca) service from Yarmouth to Portland, Maine, has been suspended; check the website for updates.

Prince Edward Island

Bay Ferries (www.ferries.ca; adult/car $20/79; ⏲May-Dec) operates the ferry between Caribou, near Pictou, and Wood Islands on Prince Edward Island (PEI) up to nine times daily. No reservations are required, but it's wise to show up half an hour before departure. Vehicle fees include all passengers for the 1¼-hour trip.

The ferry is free if you're traveling from Nova Scotia to PEI, but it's worth making a reservation anyway to guarantee a space. Note that there is no ferry service from January through April.

New Brunswick

Bay Ferries operates boats from Digby to Saint John, NB (adult/child from $39/23, 2¼ to 2¾

NOVA SCOTIA FAST FACTS

- Population: 923,598
- Area: 55,284 sq km
- Capital: Halifax
- Quirky fact: Has the only tidal power plant in the western hemisphere

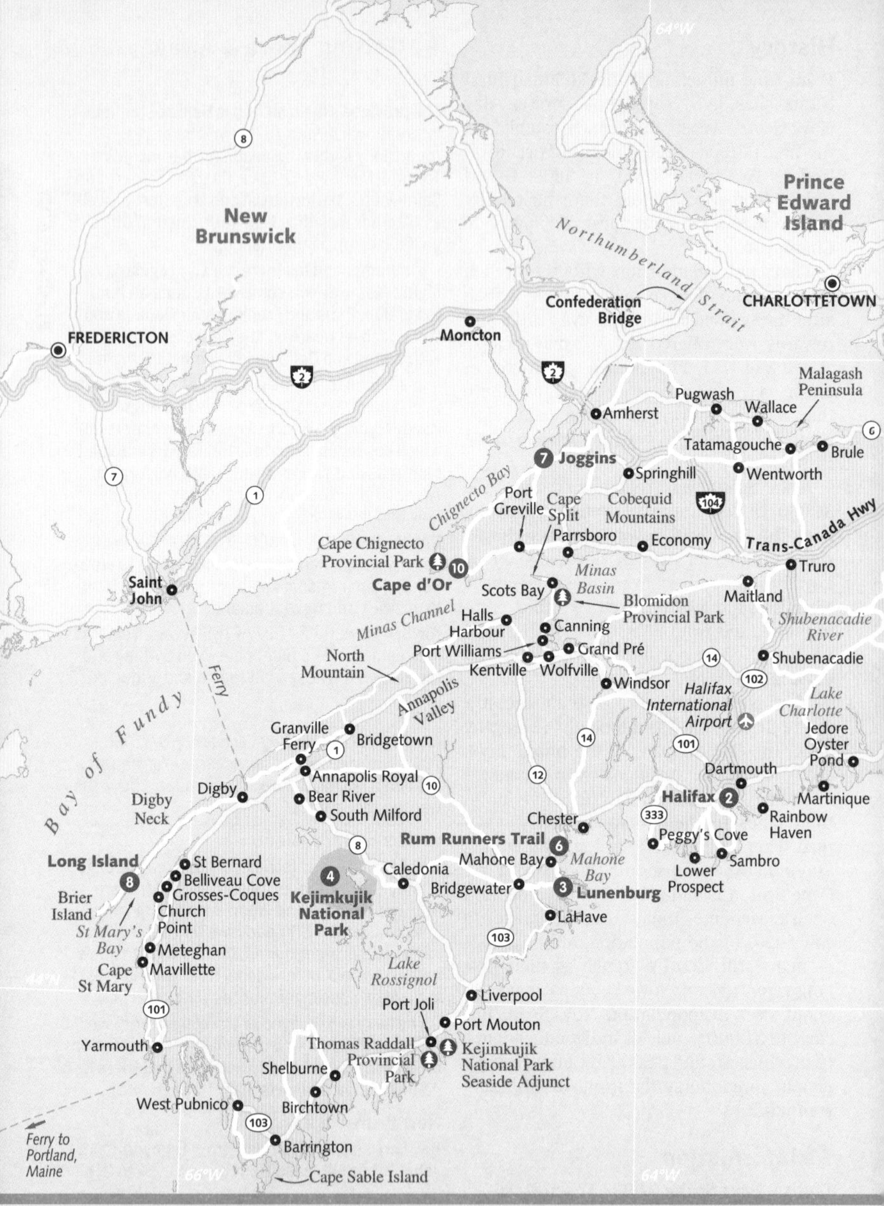

Nova Scotia Highlights

1 Cabot Trail (p101) Driving Cape Breton's snaking coastal road.

2 Canadian Museum of Immigration at Pier 21 (p57) Learning about the immigrant experience.

3 Lunenburg (p75) Wandering the orderly streets of this model colonial town.

4 Kejimkujik National Park (p80) Hiking this wonderfully preserved wilderness.

5 Louisbourg National Historic Site (p110) Exploring Nova Scotia's colonial past at this fascinating fortress.

6 Rum Runners Trail (p71) Cycling along the beautiful South Shore.

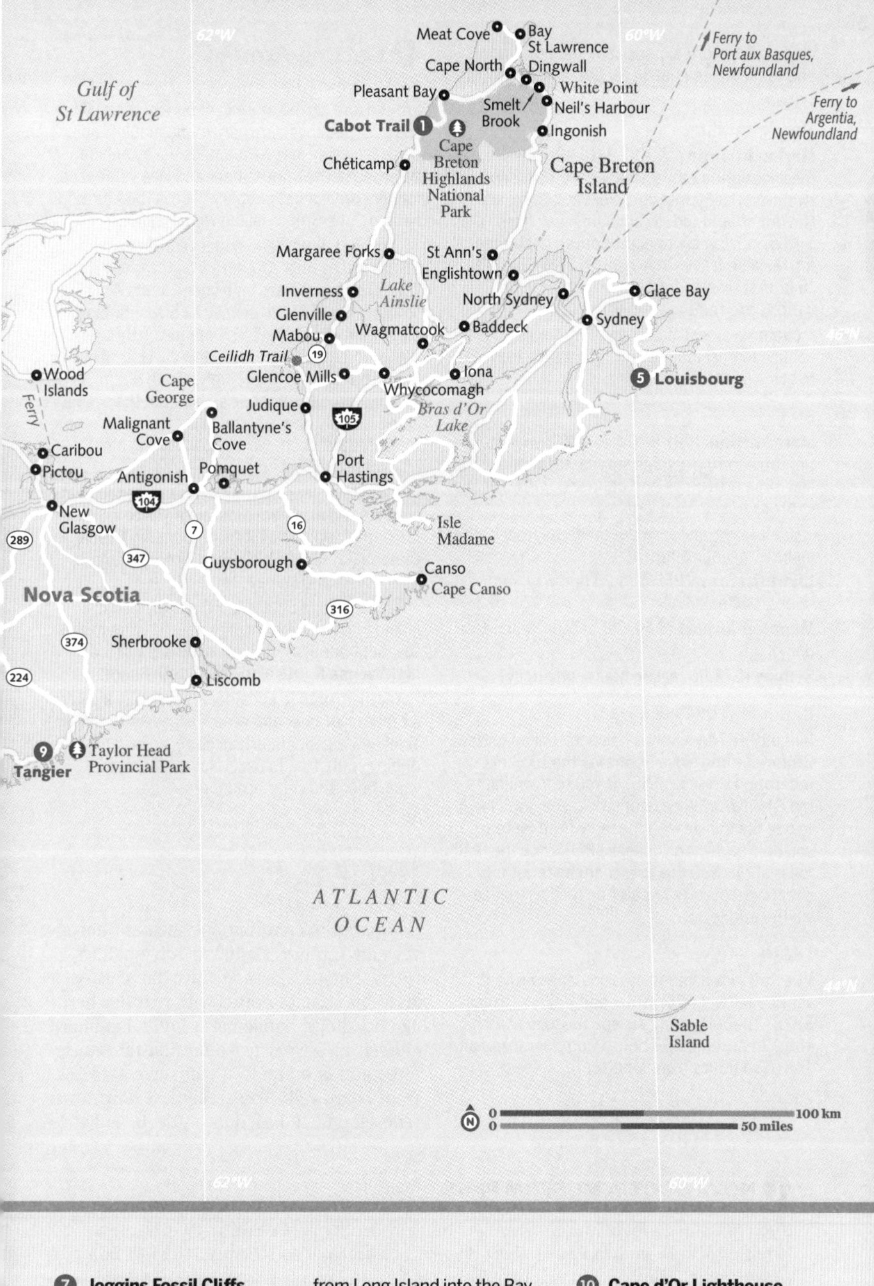

7 Joggins Fossil Cliffs (p94) Viewing 300-million-year-old fossils.

8 Whale watching (p88) Getting up astonishingly close to cetaceans on an expedition from Long Island into the Bay of Fundy.

9 Sea kayaking (p111) Paddling into the spectacular 100 Wild Islands.

10 Cape d'Or Lighthouse (p95) Gawking at the view from this lighthouse near Advocate Harbour.

hours); it's more expensive if you don't book ahead. Vehicles cost $113/119 in low/peak season.

Newfoundland

Marine Atlantic (☎800-341-7981; www.marineatlantic.ca) ferries ply the route between North Sydney and Port aux Basques, Newfoundland (adult/child one way from $45.57/21.24, six to eight hours). In summer, ferries also travel to Argentia ($121.26/58.88, 16 hours) on Newfoundland's east coast. Reservations are required for either trip.

Factor in an extra $114 to bring a standard-size vehicle to Port aux Basques, and an extra $203 to bring one to Argentia.

BUS

Maritime Bus (☎1-800-575-1807; www.maritimebus.com) provides service throughout the Maritime provinces and connects with Orléans Express buses from Québec.

Useful long-distance destinations from Halifax include the following:

Charlottetown (PEI; $58.25 one way, 4½ hours, twice daily)

Moncton Airport ($49, 3½ to four hours, five daily)

Sydney ($72.50, seven hours, one daily)

CAR & MOTORCYCLE

Since 1997, Nova Scotia has been linked to New Brunswick and Nova Scotia via the 12.9km Confederation Bridge (p156). If you're traveling to the island from New Brunswick, you don't have to pay the toll; as with the ferry from Pictou, you only pay when you leave PEI. Since the road toll is about $30 cheaper than the ferry, the cheapest option is to enter on the ferry and exit via the bridge.

TRAIN

VIA Rail (www.viarail.ca) runs an overnight service between Montréal and Halifax (from $223, 21 hours, daily except Tuesday), with stops in Amherst (17 hours from Montréal) and Truro (18 hours from Montréal).

Getting Around

Renting a car is by far the easiest way to get around and can be more economical than taking the bus. Distances are very manageable; you can easily stay in the Annapolis Valley and do day trips to the South Shore and vice versa. The longest drive most people will do is the four-hour haul to Cape Breton Island from Halifax.

The most direct (and fastest) route to most places will be on a 100-series highway (eg 101, 102, 103); these have high speed limits and limited exits. There's usually a corresponding older highway (eg 1, 2, 3) that passes through communities; these roads have varying speed limits, but they're rarely higher than 80km/h. The older roads might be slower, but the scenery along the way is much, much better, so take these routes whenever you can for the most enjoyable experience.

Ubiquitous car-rental agencies can be found at airports and in larger cities, but if you're looking for something with a bit more room, try **Cruise Canada** (☎800-671-8042; www.cruisecanada.com) for RV and camper rentals.

Tourism Nova Scotia (p53) has divided the island into a number of organised driving routes, the most popular of which is the signposted **Lighthouse Route** along the South Shore.

Another route to consider – especially if you're a fan of craft beer and wine – is the **Good Cheer Trail** (www.goodcheertrail.com), an organised driving route that takes in Nova Scotia's top wine, beer and cider producers.

HALIFAX

☎902 / POP 403,390

Compared to conurbations such as Vancouver and Toronto, Halifax barely qualifies as a city, but this seaside town punches well above its size: it's dotted with redbrick heritage buildings, public parks and a landmark citadel; blessed with some first-rate museums; and is home to a truly epic 4km seafront boardwalk. True, relentless downtown redevelopment has done little to enhance

NOVA SCOTIA MUSEUM PASS

If you're visiting a lot of museums around the province, it might be worth investing in a **Nova Scotia Museum Pass** (https://museum.novascotia.ca; adult/family $46.85/92.65), which grants unlimited admission to 28 museums for 12 months.

Museums covered by the pass include the Museum of Natural History (p61) and Maritime Museum of the Atlantic (p60) in Halifax, the Fisheries Museum (p77) in Lunenburg, the Dory Shop (p82) in Shelburne, the Acadian Village (p83) in Yarmouth, the Fundy Geological Museum (p93) in Parrsboro and loads more.

You can buy the pass online or at the first participating museum you visit.

the city's charm: boxy office blocks and uninspiring concrete carbuncles are rising where handsome ironstones and Victorian town houses once stood, although some exceptions (notably the new Central Library) show what can be achieved when planners exercise a little more quality control.

Above all, Halifax is a livable city: its small size, fresh air and easygoing lifestyle mean it scores high in quality-of-life tables. The nightlife and dining scene has come on in leaps and bounds in recent years: there are craft breweries and locavore bistros galore, especially around the trendy North End.

History

Pirates, warring colonialists and exploding ships make the history of Halifax read like an adventure story. From 1749, when Edward Cornwallis founded Halifax along what is today Barrington St, the British settlement expanded and flourished. The destruction of the French fortress at Louisbourg in 1760 increased British dominance and sealed Halifax's place as Nova Scotia's most important city.

Despite being home to two universities from the early 1800s, Halifax remained a rough-and-ready sailors' nest that, during the War of 1812, became a center for privateer black-market trade. As piracy lost its government endorsement, Halifax sailed smoothly into a mercantile era, and the city streets, particularly Market and Brunswick Sts, became home to countless taverns and brothels.

On April 14, 1912, three Halifax ships were sent in response to a distress call: the 'unsinkable' RMS *Titanic* had hit an iceberg. Over 1500 people were killed in the tragedy and many were buried at Fairview Cemetery, next to the Fairview Overpass on the Bedford Hwy.

A lesser-known piece of tragic local history occurred in 1917, during WWI, when the SS *Mont-Blanc,* a French munitions ship carrying TNT and highly flammable benzol, collided in the Halifax Narrows with a Norwegian vessel, the *SS Imo,* causing a fire. The French ship burned for 20 minutes before the fire reached its toxic cargo. The subsequent blast that ripped through the city became known as the Halifax Explosion and was the world's most powerful detonation prior to the testing of the atomic bomb. More than 1900 people were killed, and 9000 were injured. The entire suburb of Richmond was leveled by the blast and First Nations Mi'kmaq communities along the shoreline were inundated by the resultant tsunami. The event remains the most significant disaster in Haligonian history.

Sights

The downtown area, three universities and the older residential neighborhoods are contained on a compact peninsula cut off from mainland Halifax by an inlet called the North West Arm. Almost all sights of interest to visitors are concentrated in this area, making walking the best way to get around.

Point Pleasant Park is at the extreme South End of the peninsula, and the lively and multicultural North End neighborhood – home to African Nova Scotians, art-school students and plenty of hipsters – stretches from the midpoint to the northern extreme.

Two bridges span the harbor, connecting Halifax to Dartmouth and leading to highways north (for the airport) and east. The MacDonald Bridge at the eastern end of North St is closest to downtown.

The North End has been a distinct neighborhood for almost as long as Halifax has existed. In the early 1750s the 'North Suburbs' area became popular and subsequently grew thanks to its larger building lots. It's now the city's hippest district.

★Canadian Museum of Immigration at Pier 21 MUSEUM

(☎902-425-7770; www.pier21.ca; 1055 Marginal Rd; adult/child $12/8; ⏰9:30am-5:30pm May-Nov, reduced hours Dec-Apr) There's an argument that this dockside museum is Canada's most important institution. Between 1928 and 1971, Pier 21 was the Canadian version of the USA's Ellis Island, where all prospective immigrants arrived. More than a million people passed through these redbrick halls, and it's an emotional experience to walk through the very same doorways where refugees from across the globe began new lives. A mix of audiovisual exhibits, poignant artifacts and personal testimonies make for a powerful and moving museum.

★Citadel Hill National Historic Site HISTORIC SITE

(☎902-426-5080; www.pc.gc.ca/en/lhn-nhs/ns/halifax; 5425 Sackville St; adult/child Jun–mid-Sep $11.70/free, May & mid-Sep–Oct $7.80/free, other times free; ⏰9am-6pm Jul & Aug, to 5pm rest of year) Perched atop the grassy hillock looming over town, this star-shaped fort played

Halifax

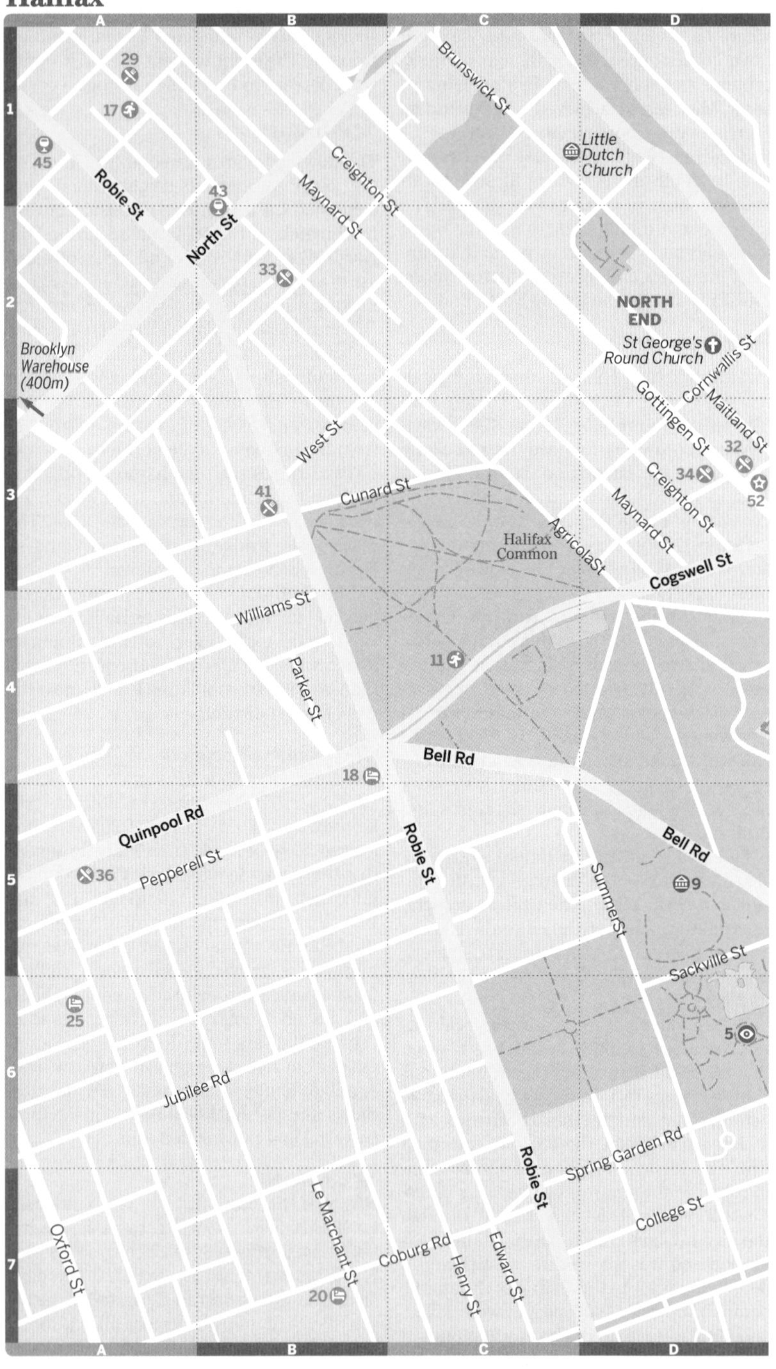
A
B
C
D
1
2
3
4
5
6
7
Brunswick St
Little Dutch Church
Robie St
North St
Creighton St
Maynard St
NORTH END
St George's Round Church
Cornwallis St
Gottingen St
Maitland St
Brooklyn Warehouse (400m)
West St
Cunard St
Creighton St
Maynard St
Halifax Common
Agricola St
Cogswell St
Williams St
Parker St
Bell Rd
Quinpool Rd
Robie St
Pepperell St
Bell Rd
Summer St
Sackville St
Jubilee Rd
Spring Garden Rd
Robie St
College St
Oxford St
Le Marchant St
Coburg Rd
Henry St
Edward St
29
17
45
43
33
41
32
34
52
11
18
36
9
25
5
20

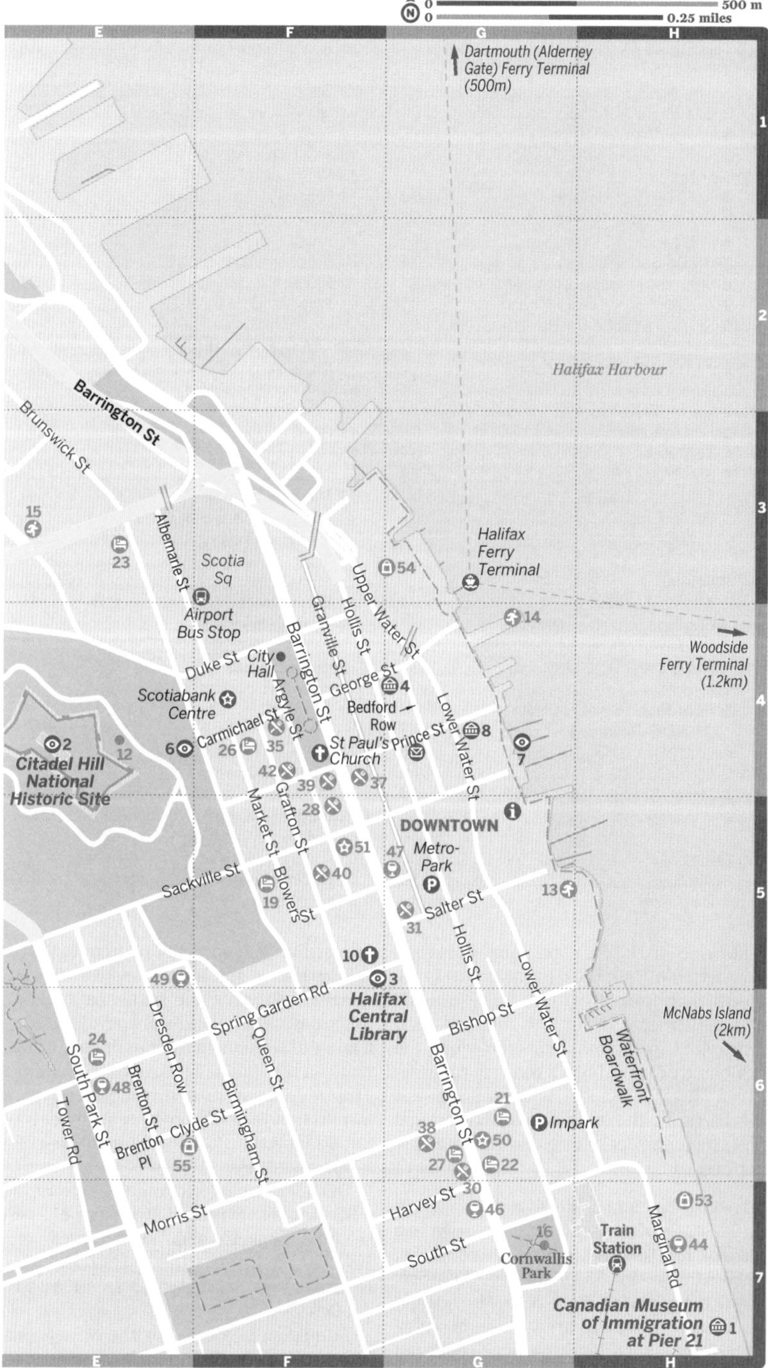

0 500 m
0 0.25 miles
Dartmouth (Alderney Gate) Ferry Terminal (500m)
Halifax Harbour
Barrington St
Brunswick St
Albemarle St
Scotia Sq
Airport Bus Stop
Halifax Ferry Terminal
Upper Water St
Hollis St
Granville St
Barrington St
Duke St
City Hall
George St
Woodside Ferry Terminal (1.2km)
Scotiabank Centre
Carmichael St
Argyle St
Bedford Row
Prince St
Lower Water St
Citadel Hill National Historic Site
St Paul's Church
Market St
Grafton St
DOWNTOWN
Metro-Park
Sackville St
Blowers St
Salter St
Hollis St
Lower Water St
Halifax Central Library
Spring Garden Rd
Queen St
Dresden Row
Bishop St
McNabs Island (2km)
Waterfront Boardwalk
South Park St
Tower Rd
Brenton St
Brenton Pl
Clyde St
Birmingham St
Barrington St
Impark
Morris St
Harvey St
South St
Cornwallis Park
Train Station
Marginal Rd
Canadian Museum of Immigration at Pier 21

Halifax

Top Sights
1 Canadian Museum of Immigration at Pier 21 ... H7
2 Citadel Hill National Historic Site ... E4
3 Halifax Central Library ... F5

Sights
4 Art Gallery of Nova Scotia ... G4
5 Halifax Public Gardens ... D6
6 Halifax Town Clock ... E4
7 HMCS Sackville ... G4
8 Maritime Museum of the Atlantic ... G4
9 Museum of Natural History ... D5
10 St Mary's Cathedral Basilica ... F5

Activities, Courses & Tours
11 Emera Oval ... C4
12 Halifax Free Tours ... E4
13 I Heart Bikes ... G5
14 J Farwell ... G4
15 Seven Bays Bouldering ... E3
Tall Ship Silva ... (see 14)
16 Tattle Tours ... G7
17 Timber Lounge ... A1

Sleeping
18 Atlantica Hotel ... B4
19 Cambridge Suites Halifax ... F5
20 Dalhousie University ... B7
21 Halliburton ... G6
22 HI Halifax ... G6
23 Homewood Suites by Hilton Halifax-Downtown ... E3
24 Lord Nelson Hotel & Suites ... E6
25 Marigold B&B ... A6
26 Prince George Hotel ... F4
27 Waverley Inn ... G6

Eating
28 Antojo Tacos ... F5
29 Bar Kismet ... A1
30 Board Room Game Cafe ... G6
31 Chives Canadian Bistro ... G5
32 Edna ... D3
33 enVie: A Vegan Kitchen ... B2
34 Field Guide ... D3
35 Five Fishermen ... F4
36 Heartwood Bakery ... A5
37 Highwayman ... F4
38 Morris East ... G6
39 Press Gang ... F4
40 Stubborn Goat ... F5
41 Studio East ... B3
42 Wooden Monkey ... F4

Drinking & Nightlife
43 Chain Yard Urban Cidery ... B2
44 Garrison Brewing Company ... H7
45 Good Robot ... A1
46 Henry House ... G7
Lot Six ... (see 28)
47 Middle Spoon Desserterie & Bar ... G5
Propeller Brewing Company ... (see 15)
Stilwell ... (see 39)
48 Stilwell Beer Garden ... E6
49 Tom's Little Havana ... E5

Entertainment
50 Bearly's House of Blues & Ribs ... G6
Carleton ... (see 28)
51 Neptune Theatre ... F5
52 Seahorse Tavern ... D3

Shopping
53 Halifax Seaport Farmers Market ... H7
54 Historic Properties ... G3
55 NSLC Clyde St ... E6

a key role in Halifax's founding. Construction began in 1749; the current citadel is the fourth, built from 1818 to 1861. The grounds and battlements inside the fort are open year-round, with free admission when the exhibits are closed, but it's better to come between May and October, when you can visit the barracks, the guards' room, the signal post, the engineer's store and the gunpowder magazines.

Maritime Museum of the Atlantic MUSEUM
(☎902-424-7490; http://maritimemuseum.novascotia.ca; 1675 Lower Water St; adult/child May-Oct $9.55/5.15, Nov-Apr $5.15/3.10; ⌚9:30am-5pm May-Oct, closed to 1pm Sun & all day Mon Nov-Apr) Sea dogs will love this briny museum on the waterfront, which houses a huge collection of maritime memorabilia relating to Atlantic Canada's many nautical activities, from merchant shipping and small-boat building to the days of the world-war convoys. There's a range of permanent exhibits, including displays on the Halifax Explosion (p57) and the *Titanic* (you can sit in a replica deckchair), a collection of small boats, scale models of important steamships, and a recreation of a 1900s chandlery.

Outside at the dock you can explore the **CSS Acadia**, a retired hydrographic vessel from England, and WWII corvette the **HMCS Sackville** (☎902-429-2132; www.hmcssackville.ca; adult/child $3/2; ⌚10am-5pm Jun-Oct).

Admission is covered by the Nova Scotia Museum Pass (p56).

Art Gallery of Nova Scotia GALLERY

(☎902-424-5280; www.artgalleryofnovascotia.ca; 1723 Hollis St; adult/child $12/5, 5-9pm Thu free; ⏲10am-5pm Sat-Wed, to 9pm Thu & Fri) The province's premier art institution is a must-see. It has a strong collection of local art, particularly the work of folk artist Maud Lewis, including the original tiny house (measuring 3m by 4m) where she lived most of her life, and which she turned into a living canvas. The main exhibit in the lower hall changes regularly and features anything from ancient art to the avant-garde.

Halifax Public Gardens GARDENS

(www.halifaxpublicgardens.ca; 5665 Spring Garden Rd; ⏲sunrise-sunset) FREE Established in 1867 to mark Confederation, but formally opened to the public in 1875, Halifax's delightful 6.5-hectare public gardens are a fine example of Victorian horticultural planning. Stocked with lakes, statues, fountains, bridges, ponds and a huge variety of trees and formal flower beds, the gardens also have a bandstand where old-time tunes parp away on Sunday afternoons.

★ **Halifax Central Library** LIBRARY

(☎902-490-5700; www.halifaxpubliclibraries.ca; 5440 Spring Garden Rd; ⏲9am-9pm Mon-Thu, to 6pm Fri & Sat, noon-6pm Sun) FREE Built on a former parking lot, this stunning modern library, composed of glass boxes stacked artfully on top of each other, was opened in 2014 and has become a much-loved meeting spot for Haligonians. Inside, concrete staircases ascend Escher-like through the central atrium, leading toward a rooftop where there's an excellent cafe and viewing garden.

Halifax Town Clock NOTABLE BUILDING

(Old Town Clock; Brunswick St) Atop Citadel Hill, Halifax's Palladian-style town clock looks as though it would be more at home in a Venetian lane, but it has been faithfully keeping time here for over 200 years. The inner workings arrived in Halifax from London in 1803, after being ordered by Prince Edward, the Duke of Kent.

Museum of Natural History MUSEUM

(☎902-424-7353; http://naturalhistory.novascotia.ca; 1747 Summer St; adult/child $6.30/4.05; ⏲9am-5pm; 👪) Natural history with a Nova Scotian bent is the modus operandi of this interesting museum, where informative exhibits cover everything from the gold rush to Mi'kmaw culture, whaling and Nova Scotian woodlands. A perennial favorite is Gus the Gopher Tortoise, who's been a resident here for more than 70 years.

St Mary's Cathedral Basilica CHURCH

(☎902-429-9800; www.halifaxyarmouth.org/cathedral; 1508 Barrington St) You can't miss Halifax's most ornate cathedral, which has the largest freestanding granite spire in North America.

Fairview Lawn Cemetery HISTORIC SITE

(☎902-490-4883; 3720 Windsor St) When the RMS *Titanic* sank, the bodies of those not lost at sea were brought to Halifax. Among other sites, there are 19 graves at **Mt Olivet Catholic Cemetery** (7076 Mumford Rd) and 121 here at the Fairview Lawn Cemetery. Frequently visited graves include the touching Celtic Cross and Unknown Child monuments, and one belonging to J Dawson, a possible namesake of Leonardo DiCaprio's character in the film *Titanic* – although according to director James Cameron, the name echo is simply an eerie coincidence.

Activities

I Heart Bikes CYCLING

(☎902-406-7774; www.iheartbikeshfx.com; 1507 Lower Water St; rentals per hour from $12; ⏲10am-6pm May, 9am-8pm Jun-Aug) If you prefer two wheels to two legs, you'll heart these folks, too. Centrally located near the Halifax waterfront, it's a great spot to pick up a chariot and start pedaling. It offers a range of city bikes and e-bikes, and also runs city tours.

Timber Lounge ADVENTURE SPORTS

(☎902-453-8627; www.timberlounge.ca; 2712 Agricola St; per person $30; ⏲4:30-10:30pm Tue-Thu & Sun, noon-10:30pm Fri & Sat) Always harbored lumberjack fantasies? Head here and learn

AFRICAN HALIFAX

The **Africville Heritage Trust Museum** (www.africvillemuseum.org; 5795 Africville Rd; adult/child $5.75/free; ⏲10am-4pm Tue-Sat) tells the story of Halifax's predominantly African suburb, the residents of which were evicted and their homes razed in what became the local scandal of the 1960s. In 2010 Halifax's mayor issued a formal apology to the community. Poignantly, the museum is housed in a replica of the Seaview United Baptist Church that was once the center of the neighborhood.

how to chuck an ax like a pro. The aim is to hit a target using a double-headed ax; staff are on hand to show you the ropes. For a confirmed booking, you'll need a minimum of six, although walk-in spots are often available on the day.

If not, you can always just turn up, have a beer and enjoy the ax-tion.

Seven Bays Bouldering CLIMBING
(☎902-407-9656; www.sevenbaysbouldering.com; 2019 Gottingen St; bouldering day passes $16; ⊙8am-11pm Mon-Sat, to 9pm Sun, boulder wall closed 8am-1pm Tue) Now this is something you'd only see in Canada: a coffee shop with its own bouldering wall and gym next door. Kick yourself into gear with a cortado and buckle up, or just sit back and watch the show. There's an early-bird discount of $3 before 2pm.

McNabs Island HIKING
(https://mcnabsisland.ca) Fine sand and cobblestone shorelines, salt marshes, forests and abandoned military fortifications paint the landscape of this 400-hectare island in Halifax Harbour. The website has a list of local boat operators who can shuttle you over (from $20 per person). It's a popular hiking and bird-spotting location, and in summer there are guided tours once a week.

Point Pleasant Park HIKING
(☎902-490-4700; 5718 Point Pleasant Dr; ⊙sunrise-sunset; 🚌9) Some 39km of nature trails, picnic spots and the beautiful 18th-century **Martello Tower** are all found within this 75-hectare sanctuary, just 1.5km south of the city center. Trails around the perimeter of the park offer views of McNabs Island, the open ocean and the North West Arm.

Emera Oval SKATING
(☎902-490-2347; www.halifax.ca/skatehrm; 5775 Cogswell St; ⊙7am-7pm) FREE This fabulous municipal facility features in-line skating in summer and ice-skating in winter, including free winter skate rentals. Photo ID is required.

Tours

Halifax Free Tours WALKING
(www.halifaxfreetours.wixsite.com/halifaxfreetours; ⊙10am & 3pm Jun-Sep) FREE You can't beat the price of these free 1½-hour walking tours of downtown Halifax, led by friendly local guides. Send an email to reserve a spot, and please remember to tip! All tours leave from the viewing platform next to Halifax Citadel.

Ambassatours CRUISE
(☎1-800-565-9662; www.ambassatours.com; 6575 Bayne St) This operator runs Halifax Harbour tours, including popular family-oriented trips on the Harbour Hopper amphibious bus (adult/child $37/21, 55 minutes) and the Theodore Tugboat ($21/16, 30 minutes).

It also runs cruises on the **Tall Ship Silva** (www.tallshipsilva.com; 1751 Lower Water St; 1½hr cruises adult/child $33/21.50) and the yacht **J Farwell** (adult/child $80/70), as well as hop-on, hop-off bus tours.

All trips run from one of the piers along the waterfront, but head office is way out of town in the Hydrostone district.

Tattle Tours WALKING
(☎902-494-0525; www.tattletours.ca; $25; ⊙10am & 2pm mid-Jul–mid-Oct) Lively two-hour tours filled with local gossip, pirate tales and ghost stories depart from Cornwallis Park, opposite the Westin Nova Scotian Hotel.

Festivals & Events

TD Halifax Jazz Festival MUSIC
(www.halifaxjazzfestival.ca; tickets from $28; ⊙Jul) Now in its fourth decade, Halifax's beloved jazz festival boasts free outdoor jazz concerts and evening performances ranging from world music to classic jazz trios.

Nova Scotia Tattoo CULTURAL
(www.nstattoo.ca; ⊙Jul) Honoring Nova Scotia's Celtic heritage, this military-style musical tattoo features an array of marching bands.

Halifax Pride Week LGBTIQ+
(www.halifaxpride.com; ⊙Jul) The largest LGBTIQ+ Pride festival east of Montréal paints the town pink and every other shade of the rainbow.

Halifax International Busker Festival PERFORMING ARTS
(www.buskers.ca; ⊙Aug) The oldest and largest festival of its kind in Canada draws comics, mimes, daredevils and musicians from around the world to the Halifax waterfront.

Halifax Seaport Cider & Beerfest FOOD & DRINK
(www.seaportbeerfest.com; ⏲Aug) Brewers from across the Maritimes and other beer-loving areas around the world congregate on Halifax for this summertime celebration of craft beer and cider.

Atlantic International Film Festival FILM
(www.finfestival.ca; ⏲Sep) Halifax's week-long film fest showcases quality flicks from the Atlantic region, Canada and beyond.

Atlantic Fringe Festival THEATER
(www.atlanticfringe.ca; ⏲Sep) The theater comes to town for 10 days in September, showcasing offbeat and experimental works by emerging and established artists.

Halifax Pop Explosion MUSIC
(www.halifaxpopexplosion.com; passes from $80; ⏲Oct) Venues across the city host established and emerging acts over four heady days in October.

Sleeping

Halifax has plenty of hotels, from heritage properties through to modern aparthotels and the usual chain suspects. Unlike in the rest of the province, there isn't a huge selection of B&Bs, nor are there any luxury hotels that could be considered truly world-class. Be sure to book ahead during the peak months of June to September, when beds fill fast and prices are at their highest.

HI Halifax HOSTEL $
(☎902-422-3863; www.hihostels.ca; 1253 Barrington St; dm members/nonmembers $26/30; Wi-Fi) In a rambling, wood-clad Victorian house, this hostel is a cheery place to stay, even if the building does look as though it's about to fall down. Rooms are shabby: basic steel bunk beds, minimal frills. The common areas, including a good kitchen and a small back garden, are the best part. Several pubs and venues are a walk away.

Marigold B&B B&B $
(☎902-423-4798; www.marigoldbedandbreakfast.com; 6318 Norwood St; s/d $75/85; P, non-smoking, Wi-Fi) Feel at home in this welcoming artist's nest full of bright floral paintings and fluffy cats. Marigold is located in a tree-lined residential area in the North End, with easy public-transport access.

LOCAL KNOWLEDGE

CRYSTAL CRESCENT BEACH

Eighteen kilometers south of Halifax, near the village of Sambro, this gorgeous **provincial park** (http://parks.novascotia.ca/content/crystal-crescent-beach; 223 Sambro Creek Rd) boasts three distinct beaches in separate coves; the third one out, toward the southwest, is clothing optional and gay friendly. An 8.5km hiking trail begins just inland and heads through barrens, bogs and boulders to Pennant Point.

Dalhousie University HOSTEL $
(☎902-494-8840; www.dal.ca/dept/summer-accommodations.html; 6230 Coburg Rd; s/d from $45/69; ⏲May-Aug; P, Wi-Fi, pool) The single and twin dorm rooms with shared bathrooms here are clean but bland. Most are adjacent to all the included university amenities, a short walk from the Spring Garden Rd area.

★ **Cambridge Suites Halifax** HOTEL $$
(☎902-420-0555; www.cambridgesuiteshalifax.com; 1583 Brunswick St; d $159-209, ste $169-299; P, non-smoking, air-con, Wi-Fi) It's not the prettiest from the outside, but this large, well-run hotel offers perhaps the most practical rooms in the city, with modern studio-style spaces that include kitchenettes, sofas and desks. Best value are the one-bedroom suites. Free continental breakfast is served in the dining room downstairs.

Halliburton INN $$
(☎902-420-0658; www.thehalliburton.com; 5184 Morris St; d $169-229, ste $299-350; P, air-con, @, Wi-Fi) Smart, refined and with a dash of Haligonian history that's getting increasingly hard to find, the Halliburton occupies a classic redbrick Victorian edifice in the middle of downtown. It offers 29 traditionally decorated rooms with varying layouts, and a very pleasant hidden garden out the back.

Lord Nelson Hotel & Suites HOTEL $$
(☎902-423-5130; www.lordnelsonhotel.ca; 1515 S Park St; d $169-239, ste $289-399; P, non-smoking, air-con, @, Wi-Fi) Opened in 1928 opposite Halifax's Public Gardens (p61), this heritage beauty is the choice for those who like their hotels with a touch of class (the chandelier-lit,

wood-paneled, painting-lined lobby alone makes a stay here worthwhile). After the grand entrance, the rooms feel a tad generic, but spoils like Nespresso machines and Aveda spa products don't go amiss.

Homewood Suites by Hilton Halifax-Downtown HOTEL **$$**
(902-855-605-0320; www.hilton.com; 1960 Brunswick St; r $226-473;) Tapping into the Airbnb trend, these multiroom studios and suites are ideal for families or long stays, with fully kitted-out kitchens and space to spare. Admittedly, they're fairly bland, but rates include daily breakfast, use of the pool and occasional guest socials. The location on the corner of a busy intersection isn't ideal.

Atlantica Hotel HOTEL **$$**
(902-423-1161; www.atlanticahotelhalifax.com; 1980 Robie St; d $129-214;) This North End hotel feels old school, mostly in a good way. The office-block facade is downright ugly, but inside it's spruced up and modern, with big pluses such as a restaurant and an attic-style indoor pool. Rooms fall into three tiers (silver, gold and platinum), plus there are suites and family studios; go gold or higher for any kind of view.

Waverley Inn INN **$$**
(902-423-9346; www.waverleyinn.com; 1266 Barrington St; d $135-245;) In business since 1876, this lemon-yellow inn has rooms with their own little quirks, from bold antiques to luxurious linens, swagged curtains and Turkish rugs. It feels rather theatrical, and fittingly the guest book includes both Oscar Wilde and PT Barnum. The period building means that, apart from the suites, rooms are small, and some are only accessible by stairs.

★**Prince George Hotel** HOTEL **$$$**
(902-425-1986; www.princegeorgehotel.com; 1725 Market St; d $229-367;) This suave city hotel is as slick as Halifax gets: every inch looks as though it's been designed for an Instagram post, from the arch-windowed interior pool to the landscaped patio and the **LevelBar** cocktail corner. Rooms are equally stylish (Crown-floor rooms have their own private lounge), and the **Gio** restaurant is really good.

Pebble Bed & Breakfast B&B **$$$**
(902-423-3369; www.thepebble.ca; 1839 Armview Tce; r $245-345;) The two suites of this luxurious B&B, in a posh, waterfront residential area, feature plush, high beds, gorgeous bathrooms and modern-meets-antique decor. Irish owner Elizabeth grew up in a pub-owning family and brings lively, joyous energy from the Emerald Isle to her delightful home. It's a stone's throw from downtown. There's a two-night minimum stay from June to October.

Eating

If you're going to splurge on eating out anywhere in Nova Scotia, Halifax is the place to do it. The city has some fantastic restaurants, with a particular concentration in the trendy North End. Bars and pubs nearly always serve food, too.

The free quarterly *Curated* (www.curatedmagazine.ca) keeps track of the city's hot dining tips and publishes a popular annual guide. It's available at restaurants and bars around the city.

Board Room Game Cafe CAFE **$**
(902-423-7545; www.boardroomgames.ca; 1256 Barrington St; wraps $8.50-9.50, pizzas $6-8; 11am-midnight Mon-Thu & Sun, to 2am Fri & Sat) There's a choice of 500 board games, from classic to contemporary, at this fun hangout, with wraps, pizzas, good coffee and craft beers to guzzle as you play. Don't worry if you're a beginner: the staff's encyclopaedic knowledge will match you up with something fun.

It seems a *lot* busier since Nova Scotia relaxed its pot laws...

Heartwood Bakery VEGETARIAN **$**
(902-425-2808; www.iloveheartwood.ca; 6250 Quinpool Rd; mains $11-16; 11am-8pm;) Everything feels as though it's doing you good at this fantastic veggie-vegan restaurant, which became so popular it now has a second location (at 3061 Gottingen St), plus a seasonal spot on the harbor. Delicious salads, kamut-crust pizzas, buddha bowls, veggie burgers – Heartwood really nails it. In fact, for non-carnivores there's nowhere better to eat in Halifax.

★**Bar Kismet** BISTRO **$$**
(902-487-4319; www.barkismet.com; 2733 Agricola St; small plates $12-15, large plates $25-

27; 5pm-midnight Tue-Sun) Impeccable small plates of seafood have made this tiny bar-bistro a favorite among foodie North Enders, and deservedly so: dishes zing with surprising combinations and flavors, such as bass with morel mushrooms and artichokes, or raw scallop with lemongrass and turnip. The decor's stripped right back – bare wood, mirrors, pendant lights – putting the focus firmly on the food.

★**Edna** CANADIAN **$$**
(902-431-5683; www.ednarestaurant.com; 2053 Gottingen St; brunch $12-20, mains $24-36; 5-11pm Fri & Sat, 5-10pm Tue-Thu & Sun) At the edge of the North End, this hipster diner has strong competition but is still many people's first choice. It's bare bones as far as decor goes: a long wooden table for communal dining, a tiled bar, metal stools and tables for two. Food is modern bistro: risotto, seared scallops, classic steaks, all lovingly prepared. Edna equals excellence.

★**Field Guide** BISTRO **$$**
(902-405-4506; www.fieldguidehfx.com; 2076 Gottingen St; mains $12-24; 5pm-midnight Tue-Sat, 10am-2pm & 5pm-midnight Sun) At this hipster diner you order according to hunger level (from 'Sorta Hungry' starters to 'Still Hungry' desserts). It's a gimmick, but the food is first rate: fresh, surprising and modern, from cured salmon on seed bread with ricotta to fried chicken on a biscuit. The decor is minimal: brushed-concrete floors, a long bar, and big windows onto the street.

★**Brooklyn Warehouse** CANADIAN **$$**
(902-446-8181; www.brooklynwarehouse.ca; 2795 Windsor St; mains lunch $12-18, dinner $23-30; 11:30am-10pm Mon-Sat;) It's aptly named: there's definitely a New York flavor to this neighborhood eatery, with its worn wood, tobacco-yellow walls and chalkboard menus. The food selection changes fast, but it's strong on rich, hearty bistro fare.

Hopefully the Dragon's Breath (a take on the classic Caesar salad) will be on when you visit.

Antojo Tacos MEXICAN **$$**
(902-405-2790; www.antojo.ca; 1667 Argyle St; tacos $4.50-6, mains $12-22; 4-10pm Sun & Mon, 11:30am-10pm Tue-Thu, 11:30am-midnight Fri & Sat) This downtown taco joint is equally popular for a midday lunch or a late-night mescal-fueled feria. Tacos are the star, of course: zingy chipotle chicken, spicy battered Baja fish, spit-roasted pork or crispy cauliflower, accompanied by barbecued corn and a bewildering tequila selection. Day of the Dead decor adds to the Mex-themed fun. It's popular: reserve or queue – your call.

Highwayman SPANISH **$$**
(902-407-5260; www.highwaymanhfx.com; 1673 Barrington St; small plates $5-12; 4pm-midnight Sun & Tue-Fri, 2pm-midnight Sat) You could be in a backstreet of Barcelona at this moody tapas joint, which specializes in Spanish-inspired small plates and Basque-style *pintxos:* manchego and jamon, quail egg and chorizo, Arctic char. There's a great cheese and charcuterie selection, and a fantastic cocktail bar. It looks lovely, too, with its tall windows, dark tones and intimate nooks. No reservations.

Studio East ASIAN **$$**
(902-422-8096; www.studioeastfood.ca; 6021 Cunard St; mains $13-22; 5-10pm or 11pm Tue-Sat) Asian fusion of the first order: sticky hoisin-braised ribs, pork- and fish-curry ramen, Thai salads and Japanese 'Karaage' chicken dinners, with pickles, fried rice and spicy gochujang mayo. It's good for non meat-eaters, too: most dishes can be made with tofu. Order a tiki cocktail, an event in itself.

enVie: A Vegan Kitchen VEGETARIAN **$$**
(902-492-4077; www.enviehalifax.com; 5775 Charles St; mains $11-18; 11am-9pm Tue-Thu, to 10pm Fri, 10am-10pm Sat, to 9pm Sun;) Halifax's roster of vegan restaurants is growing fast, but enVie is one of the first and best. It serves exactly the kind of food you'd want: delicious homemade soups, crunchy pear and arugula salads, loaded flatbreads, and imaginative non-meat versions of cheeseburgers, wings, tacos and pad thai (thanks to the miracles of tofu, seitan and oyster mushrooms).

Stubborn Goat PUB FOOD **$$**
(902-405-4554; www.stubborngoat.ca; 1579 Grafton St; small plates $9-19, mains $14-28; 11:30am-2am) Belly-filling pub grub, from generous burgers to fish-and-chips, is what's on offer at the Goat. The beer selection is good, and it also has a seasonal beer garden down on the waterfront.

(Continued on page 68)

PCHOUI/GETTY IMAGES ©

BRIGITTE SMITH/GETTY IMAGES ©

BENEDEK/GETTY IMAGES ©

MOLLIEGPHOTO/SHUTTERSTOCK ©

1. Cape Breton Highlands National Park (p101)
The best known of Nova Scotia's two national parks.

2. Lunenburg (p75)
A perfect example of a Nova Scotian fishing town, Lunenberg's architecture has earned it Unesco World Heritage status.

3. Joggins Fossil Cliffs (p94)
One of the most complete fossil records anywhere in Canada.

4. Fortress of Louisbourg (p110)
Built by the French but battled over countless times before being burned to the ground in 1760, the current site recreates the 1744 fortress.

(Continued from page 65)

Morris East ITALIAN **$$**
(☎902-444-7663; www.morriseast.com; 5212 Morris St; pizzas $15-20; ⌚11:30am-9pm, to 10pm Fri & Sat) Halifax has some good pizza joints, but this is the pick. Pies are available in your choice of white, whole-wheat or gluten-free dough, and there are some really left-field options: try the peach, rosemary aioli, goat's cheese and prosciutto.

It's proved so popular that there are three other outlets dotted around the city.

Wooden Monkey CANADIAN **$$**
(☎902-444-3844; www.thewoodenmonkey.ca; 1707 Grafton St; mains $15-30; ⌚11am-10pm;) A cross between a neighborhood diner and a city pub, the Monkey is a good stop if you're just looking for a simple supper and pint of something local and cold. It looks convincingly worn in, with a Victorian facade and lots of dark wood. Pasta, seafood, burgers, steaks – the menu covers it all.

Chives Canadian Bistro CANADIAN **$$$**
(☎902-420-9626; www.chives.ca; 1537 Barrington St; mains $25-35; ⌚5-9:30pm) Proper, formal Canadian fine dining in the heart of downtown is on offer at Chives, one of the city's longest-running restaurants. Seasonally driven, artfully presented dishes are the stock-in-trade of chef Craig Flinn, and the food tastes as lovely as it looks. Freshened up by a 2018 refit, it features dark wood, blue-velour benches and antique-mirrored walls.

Press Gang SEAFOOD **$$$**
(☎902-423-8816; www.thepressgang.ca; 5218 Prince St; single oysters $3.25, mains $35-46; ⌚5-10pm) This is one of the city's old-school supper spots, in more ways than one. The building (erected in 1759) is one of the oldest stone structures in downtown Halifax, and the walls give it a cellar-like atmosphere very different from that of most of the city's restaurants. Oysters are the specialty, plus indulgent 'from the sea' and 'from the land' mains.

Five Fishermen SEAFOOD **$$$**
(☎902-422-4421; www.fivefishermen.com; 1740 Argyle St; mains $29-49; ⌚5-9pm Sun-Thu, to 10pm Fri & Sat) As the name suggests, this upscale place focuses on the fruits of the fisher's art: oysters, lobsters, halibut, Arctic char, swordfish and plenty more, alongside premium steaks and classic lobster dinners. There are booth seats and tasteful lighting in the formal main restaurant, plus a more relaxed oyster bar next door.

Drinking & Nightlife

Halifax rivals St John's, NL, for the most drinking holes per capita. The biggest concentration of bars is on Argyle St, where temporary street-side patios expand the sidewalk each summer (it can get a little boisterous on weekends). Pubs and bars close at 2am (a few hours earlier on Sunday).

★ **Stilwell** CRAFT BEER
(☎902-421-1672; www.barstillwell.com; 1672 Barrington St; ⌚noon-2am Thu-Sat, 4pm-2am Sun-Wed) A massive, wall-size chalkboard of brews from across Canada and beyond (all with a handwritten description and each delivered through a brass tap) gives this downtown bar probably the best beer selection in the city. Staff are incredibly knowledgeable and will help guide your choice. There's a menu of delicious small plates for late-night snacking.

It also runs a summer **beer garden** (5688 Spring Garden Rd; ⌚noon-late in fine weather).

★ **Good Robot** CRAFT BEER
(☎902-446-1692; www.goodrobotbrewing.ca; 2736 Robie St; ⌚noon-2am Mon-Fri, 10am-2am Sat & Sun) This new North End microbrewery has become known for its wild beers: you might taste a watermelon-and-kiwi fruit Pink Flamingo, a coffee-and-cherry-pie pale ale or a jalapeño-spiked lager (the names are equally wild). It's in a warehouse-style space with a pleasant beer garden; the pub snacks are delicious, too.

★ **Lot Six** COCKTAIL BAR
(☎902-428-7428; www.lotsix.ca; 1685 Argyle St; cocktails $12-15; ⌚4pm-2am, plus brunch 11am-2pm Sat & Sun) The soaring glass atrium that floods the room with light adds an extra touch of class to this slinky cocktail joint, which mostly crafts its own mixes but also offers a few shaken-up classics. Try the Springtime Smash, with tequila, Aperol, lemon, grapefruit and mint. It also serves fantastic food (mains $14 to $24).

Chain Yard Urban Cidery PUB
(☎902-407-2244; www.chainyardcider.com; 2606 Agricola St; ⌚11:30am-11pm or 11:30pm) Craving a change from the craft-beer tsunami in Halifax? No sweat: head for the city's only craft cidery, with wares made from 100% Nova Scotia apples. Try a dry Pippin Russet,

a super-tart Farmhouse Sour or a Polar Perry (made with pears), or really offbeat brews laced with kombucha, grape skins and rose petals. There's a patio for outdoor drinking.

Propeller Brewing Company MICROBREWERY
(☎902-468-1026; www.drinkpropeller.ca; 2015 Gottingen St; ⊙10am-8pm Mon & Tue, to 10pm Wed & Thu, to midnight Fri & Sat, noon-10pm Sun) In the first wave of Halifax microbreweries, Propeller is still leading the way with its consistently good beers: the core range includes a pilsner, a lager, a porter and several pale ales, with seasonals based on pumpkin, coffee, dark berries and stone fruit.

Even better, there's a vintage arcade in the basement: let the Asteroids tournament commence!

Tom's Little Havana BAR
(☎902-423-8667; www.tomslittlehavana.wix.com/cafe; 1540 Birmingham St; ⊙11:30am-2am) Craft beers, game nights, Scotch nights and a daily happy hour (5pm to 8pm) make Tom's feel like an extension of the living room at your best mate's place.

Garrison Brewing Company BREWERY
(☎902-453-5343; www.garrisonbrewing.com; 1149 Marginal Rd; ⊙10am-8pm Sun-Thu, to 9pm Fri, 8am-9pm Sat) A grandaddy of the Halifax brewing scene, Garrison is down by the waterfront in an impressive warehouse space full of upturned beer barrels and scuffed wood. There's a huge range of brews: if you're not sure which to pick, order a tasting flight of five (or 16, if you're really indecisive). There's a small patio out the front.

Henry House PUB
(☎902-423-5660; www.henryhouse.ca; 1222 Barrington St; ⊙11:30am-12:45am) Solid as a brick, this National Historic Site is one of the city's best surviving examples of the Halifax House, a 19th-century stone style developed by Scottish masons. These days it's a cozy pub downstairs and a stylish drawing-room bar upstairs. There are plenty of wines, beers and classic pub dishes to choose from.

Middle Spoon Desserterie & Bar COCKTAIL BAR
(☎902-407-4002; www.themiddlespoon.ca; 1559 Barrington St; ⊙4-11pm Mon-Wed, to midnight Thu, to 1pm Fri & Sat) One for those late-night sweet cravings: a cocktail bar that also serves ice-cream sundaes and sinful desserts such as lemon pavlova, peanut-butter pie and chocolate lava cake.

☆ Entertainment

Check out the *Coast* (www.thecoast.ca) to see what's on. This free weekly publication, available around town, is the essential guide for music, theater, film and events.

Halifax loves its music, with folk, hip-hop, alternative, country and rock gigs around town every weekend. Cover charges depend on the band.

Seahorse Tavern LIVE MUSIC
(☎902-423-7200; www.theseahorsetavern.ca; 2037 Gottingen St) Indie acts and local bands are the mainstay at the rough-and-ready Seahorse. It also hosts a monthly dance party, plus retro nights devoted to the '80s and '90s. It's worth a visit just to see the giant seahorses on the bar.

Carleton LIVE MUSIC
(☎902-422-6335; www.thecarleton.ca; 1685 Argyle St; ⊙noon-2am) The Carleton's lineup is famously eclectic: folk, indie, jazz, rock and Celtic all regularly feature. There's a good dinner menu, too, served till late if you want a post-gig supper.

Neptune Theatre THEATER
(☎902-429-7070; www.neptunetheatre.com; 1593 Argyle St) This downtown theater presents musicals and well-known plays on its main stage and edgier stuff in the studio.

Bearly's House of Blues & Ribs LIVE MUSIC
(☎902-423-2526; www.bearlys.ca; 1269 Barrington St; ⊙5pm-midnight) Some of the best blues musicians in Atlantic Canada play here, often at very low cover charges.

Shopping

★Halifax Seaport Farmers Market MARKET
(☎902-492-4043; www.halifaxfarmersmarket.com; 1209 Marginal Rd; ⊙10am-5pm Mon-Fri, 7am-3pm Sat, 9am-3pm Sun) Although it has operated in several locations since its inception in 1750, what's now known as the Halifax Seaport Farmers Market (in its present location since 2010) is North America's longest continuously operating market. With more than 250 local vendors from a province that prides itself on strong farm-to-table and maritime traditions, it's well worth a visit.

NSLC Clyde St DISPENSARY
(☎902-423-6716; www.mynslc.com; 5540 Clyde St; ⊙10am-10pm Mon-Sat, noon-5pm Sun) This is the flagship NSLC cannabis store in Halifax;

the staff are well informed, so head here if you're after advice, equipment or supplies.

Historic Properties SHOPPING CENTRE (www.historicproperties.ca; 1869 Upper Water St; ⏲store hours vary) The Historic Properties are a group of restored warehouse buildings on Upper Water St, built between 1800 and 1905, that have been converted into boutiques, restaurants and bars connected by waterfront boardwalks. The 1814 Privateers Warehouse was the former storehouse of government-sanctioned pirates and is the area's oldest stone building.

Information

Useful websites include Discover Halifax (https://discoverhalifaxns.com) and the Halifax Regional Municipality (www.halifax.ca).

Family Focus (☎902-420-2038; www.thefamilyfocus.ca; 5991 Spring Garden Rd; ⏲8:30am-9pm Mon-Fri, 11am-5pm Sat & Sun) Walk-in or same-day medical appointments.

Halifax Airport Visitor Information Centre (VIC; ☎902-873-1223; www.novascotia.com; Halifax International Airport; ⏲10am-9pm Jun-Oct, 9am-4:30pm Mon-Fri Nov-May) The official province-run welcome center at Halifax airport.

Halifax Infirmary (Charles V Keating Emergency and Trauma Centre; ☎902-473-3383, 902-473-7605; www.cdha.nshealth.ca; 1796 Summer St; ⏲24hr) For emergencies.

Halifax Waterfront Visitor Information Centre (VIC; ☎902-424-4248; www.novascotia.com; 1655 Lower Water St; ⏲9am-7pm Jul & Aug, to 5pm mid-May–Jun, Sep & Oct) On the Halifax waterfront, this official province-run center will load you up with maps and friendly advice.

Main Post Office (☎902-494-4670; www.canadapost.ca; 1660 Bedford Row; ⏲9am-5pm Mon-Fri)

Getting There & Away

AIR

Halifax Stanfield International Airport (YHZ; ☎902-873-4422; www.hiaa.ca; 1 Bell Blvd) is 32km northeast of town on Hwy 102, toward Truro.

BOAT

Catch the Alderney (to downtown Dartmouth) and Woodside ferries from Halifax's central **terminal** (www.halifax.ca/transit/ferries.php).

BUS

Maritime Bus (p56) runs services from Halifax to various points around Nova Scotia, as well as Prince Edward Island (PEI) and New Brunswick. Some services require you to book at least three hours ahead.

A few useful destinations from Halifax:

Charlottetown (PEI; $58.25 one way, 4½ hours, two daily)

Lunenburg ($25.50, 1¾ hours, two daily)

Mahone Bay ($20.25, 70 minutes, one daily) Three-hour advance booking required.

Moncton Airport ($49, 3½ to four hours, five daily)

Truro ($25.50, 1¾ hours, five daily)

Wolfville ($20.25, 1½ hours, two daily)

For journeys along the South Shore, **Cloud Nine Shuttle** (☎902-742-3992; www.thecloudnineshuttle.com) can drop you at any point as far as Yarmouth for a flat $75 fare. It also offers airport transfers for $80.

TRAIN

One of the few examples of monumental Canadian train-station architecture left in the Maritimes is found at 1161 Hollis St. VIA Rail (www.viarail.ca) operates an overnight service to Montréal (from $223, 21 hours, daily except Tuesday).

Getting Around

TO/FROM THE AIRPORT

By far the cheapest way to get to/from the airport is by public bus 320 ($3.50), which runs half-hourly to hourly between 5am and midnight to/from the **bus stop** on Albemarle St between Duke and Cogswell Sts.

If you arrive in the middle of the night, as many flights do, your only choice is a taxi, which costs $56 to downtown Halifax. There are often not enough taxis, so it's prudent to reserve one in advance. Try **Halifax Airport Taxi** (☎902-999-2434; www.halifaxairportlimotaxi.com), which has 24-hour airport service. The journey shouldn't take much longer than 30 minutes.

Maritime Bus (www.maritimebus.com) operates an hourly airport shuttle ($22, 30 to 45 minutes) between May and October. You'll need the exact fare; buy tickets in advance online or at the airport's Ground Transportation Booth. The shuttle picks up and drops off at most city-center hotels, as well as the main bus station. From the airport, buses run from 8am to 7pm; from downtown they run from 7am to 6pm.

CAR

Pedestrians almost always have the right of way in Halifax, so watch out for cars stopping suddenly.

Outside the downtown core you can usually find free on-street parking for up to two hours. Halifax's parking meters are enforced from 8am to 6pm Monday to Friday.

All the major national car-rental chains are represented at the airport and in downtown Halifax. Most will let you pick up in town and drop off at the airport free of charge.

PUBLIC TRANSPORTATION

Halifax Transit (902-480-8000; www.halifax.ca/transit; single ride $2.50-3.50) runs the city bus system and the ferries to Dartmouth. Maps and schedules are available at the ferry terminals and at the information booth in Scotia Sq mall.

Bus 7 cuts through downtown Halifax and the North End via Robie and Gottingen Sts, passing both of Halifax's hostels. Bus 1 travels along Spring Garden Rd, Barrington St and the southern part of Gottingen St before crossing the bridge to Dartmouth.

AROUND HALIFAX

Dartmouth

902 / POP 92,301

Founded in 1750, just a year after its counterpart across the harbor, working-class Dartmouth was long regarded as Halifax's grubby little brother – but as the cost of living spirals in the capital, many young people and commuters are finding more space to breathe on the other side of the water, turning formerly down-at-heel Dartmouth into a rather trendy little town in its own right.

Dartmouth's compact, historic downtown is a pleasant place for a stroll and a pint: getting here on the ferry from Halifax – the oldest saltwater ferry system in North America – is half the fun, especially at sunset. Before you return, head west on Alderney Dr to climb the bluffs of **Dartmouth Commons** for excellent views across the harbor. Exercise the usual caution in the park after dark.

Eating & Drinking

Cafe Good Luck CAFE $
(902-469-9658; www.manualfoodanddrinkco.com/goodluck; 145 Portland St; mains $6-14; 8am-3pm Tue & Wed, 8am-9pm Thu & Fri, 10am-9pm Sat, 10am-3pm Sun) Dartmouth's latest brunch-spot love affair, the Good Luck is the place for a comforting croque monsieur, a freshly baked muffin or a hangover-fixing breakfast sandwich. It's a fresh, friendly place, with the requisite retro-meets-modern decor, reclaimed furniture and, of course, plenty of potted plants.

Portland Street Creperie CRÊPES $
(902-466-7686; www.portlandstreetcreperie.com; 55 Portland St; crepes $6-9; 8:30am-5pm Mon-Thu & Sat, to 7pm Fri, 10am-2:30pm Sun) A beloved snack stop for locals, this hip creperie corners the market in all things pancakey: go savory with a mushroom melt or ham and Swiss, or indulge that sweet tooth with an Oreo-cheesecake, honeycomb or chocolate-covered-berry crepe.

Two If By Sea BAKERY $
(902-469-0721; www.twoifbyseacafe.ca; 66 Ochterloney St; pastries $3-5; 7am-6pm Mon-Fri, 8am-5pm Sat & Sun) Be warned: if you want to gorge on the massive, buttery chocolate croissants that TIBS is famous for, get in quick as they're often sold out by 1pm.

★ **Canteen** BISTRO $$
(902-425-9272; www.thecanteen.ca; mains lunch $10-18, dinner $18-24; 11am-2:30am & 5-11pm Tue-Fri, 10am-2pm & 5-11pm Sat) This pared-back bistro has become Dartmouth's dining hot spot for its fresh, flavoursome dishes: big bowls of mussels, panzanella salad, lobster tagliatelle and scallop risotto, all driven by the seasons and served in a light, minimal space. It's very popular, so bookings are advised. If you miss out, its sandwich takeout, **Little C**, is next door.

★ **Battery Park Beerbar & Eatery** MICROBREWERY
(902-446-2337; www.batterypark.ca; 62 Ochterloney St; 11:30am-midnight Sun-Thu, to 1am Fri & Sat) The best place for a brew in Dartmouth, this industrially styled beer bar has 20 taps, plus a super menu of snacky food such as burgers, chicken skewers, tacos and calamari. Drinkers make the pilgrimage from Halifax just to come here – it's that good.

DON'T MISS

RUM RUNNERS TRAIL

This 119km bike route runs from Halifax to Lunenburg via most of the main South Shore towns, including St Margaret's Bay, Chester and Mahone Bay. The website and route maps handily split the route into seven subsections that can each easily be done in a day. The 10km Mahone Bay to Lunenburg section is particularly popular.

Train Station Bike & Bean (902-820-3400; www.bikeandbean.ca; 5401 St Margaret's Bay Rd; cafe 8am-5pm, bike shop 10am-5pm) in Tantallon, about 25km west of Halifax, is a handy place to hire a bike for a quick day trip.

Getting There & Away

BOAT

Halifax Transit (www.halifax.ca/transit) operates an extensive, easy-to-use network of buses and ferries. You can catch the ferry to Halifax ($2.50, 12 minutes) from the **Dartmouth Ferry Terminal** (complete with public-use piano) at Alderney Gate.

CAR

The Macdonald Bridge (built 1955) and the Mackay Bridge (built 1970) provide 24-hour links between Halifax and Dartmouth. The toll for each is $1.

A sidewalk on the Macdonald Bridge allows cyclists and pedestrians to cross (for free); the Mackay Bridge is for cars only.

Peggy's Cove

☎902 / POP 640

With its red-and-white-striped lighthouse, colorful clapboard cottages and boulder-strewn shoreline, this tiny fishing cove presents the classic Nova Scotia picture that every visitor wants to snap. And it is undeniably pretty – especially on a calm summer's day when the sea shines china blue, seagulls wheel overhead and you can watch the lobster boats chugging out to sea. Unfortunately, the hordes of tourist buses that descend on the cove somewhat shatter the illusion, so visit early or late in the day (before 10am or after 6pm) if you don't want to be caught in the crush, or save your visit for any time but summer.

If you're looking for the same vibe without the mass of visitors, albeit without the iconic lighthouse as well, cute-as-a-button **Lower Prospect** is 30km east via Terence Bay.

Sights & Activities

Peggy's Point Lighthouse LIGHTHOUSE
(185 Peggys Point Rd; ⏲9:30am-5:30pm May-Oct) The highlight of the cove is this picture-perfect lighthouse, built in 1914. It's supposedly the most photographed lighthouse in Canada, and for many years served as a post office.

You can wander freely around the granite landscape that undulates much like the icy sea beyond, but take care: several people have been swept away by freak swells here.

William E deGarthe Gallery & Monument GALLERY
(☎902-823-2256; 109 Peggy's Point Rd; $2; ⏲gallery 10am-4pm May-Oct) Finnish-born local artist William deGarthe (1907–83) carved the magnificent *Lasting Monument to Nova Scotian Fishermen* into a 30m granite outcrop behind his home. The sculpture depicts 32 fishermen, their wives and children, St Elmo with wings spread, and the legendary Peggy of her eponymous cove. The homestead is now a gallery showcasing 65 of deGarthe's other works.

Swissair 111 Memorial MEMORIAL
(8250 Hwy 333) This moving memorial commemorates the 229 people who lost their lives on September 2, 1998, when Swissair Flight 111, bound for Geneva, Switzerland, plunged into the ocean 8km off the coast of Peggy's Cove not long after taking off from New York's JFK airport.

Peggy's Cove Boat Tours BOATING
(☎902-541-9177; www.peggyscoveboattours.com; Government Wharf; tours adult/child from $35/21.50) Get a different perspective on the cove and the lighthouse with this experienced local guide. The standard sightseeing tour runs several times daily in summer; there are also seal- and puffin-watching trips, lobster dinner cruises, and special sunset trips on Tuesday, Thursday and Friday.

Sleeping & Eating

Wayside Camping Park CAMPGROUND $
(☎902-823-2271; www.waysidecampground.com; 10295 Hwy 333, Glen Margaret; tent/RV sites $30/40; ⏲May-Oct; 📶🐾) About 10km north of Peggy's Cove and 36km from Halifax, this camping park has lots of shady, wooded sites but gets crowded in midsummer. Firewood is available by the armload ($5).

★**Oceanstone Seaside Resort** RESORT $$
(☎902-823-2160; www.oceanstoneresort.com; 8650 Peggy's Cove Rd, Indian Harbour; r $170-235, ste $270-315, cottages $410-570; P🚭❄@📶🐾) Smart rooms and lovely sea-view cottages are on offer at this large complex just a short drive from Peggy's Cove. The decor is very stylish, with lots of distressed wood, maritime detailing and big windows that make the most of the briny scenery.

Rhubarb (mains $15 to $17), the inn's dining room, is considered one of the region's best seafood restaurants.

Peggy's Cove Bed & Breakfast B&B $$
(☎902-823-2265; www.peggyscovebb.com; 17 Church Rd; d $159; ⏲Apr-Oct; 📶) If you want

to stay in Peggy's Cove proper, this B&B has an enviable position with one of the best views in Nova Scotia, overlooking the fishing docks and the lighthouse; it was once owned by artist William deGarthe.

You'll definitely need advance reservations.

Information

Visitor Information Centre (VIC; ☎902-823-2253; 109 Peggy's Point Rd; ⏱9am-7pm Jul & Aug, to 5pm mid-May–Jun & Sep–mid-Oct) There's a free parking area with washrooms and a tourist office as you enter the village. Free 45-minute walking tours leave from the tourist office daily from mid-June through August.

Getting There & Away

Peggy's Cove is 43km southwest of Halifax on Hwy 333.

SOUTH SHORE

This is Nova Scotia's most visited coastline (for good reason) and it's here you'll find all those quintessential lighthouses, protected forested coves with white beaches, and quaint fishing villages turned tourist towns. The area from Halifax to Lunenburg is cottage country for the capital's elite and ever-popular with day-tripping tourists and locals.

A great way to explore the area on two wheels is along the excellent Rum Runners Trail (p71), which runs for 119km from Halifax to Lunenburg.

Getting There & Away

Hwy 3 from Halifax – labeled the 'Lighthouse Route' by tourism officials – can be busy and slow. Take this scenic route if you're not pressed for time and want to check out antique shops or artisans' wares along the way. Travel times can be halved by taking Hwy 103 directly to the closest exit for your destination. You'll need your own vehicle to get down here.

Chester

☎902 / POP 1200

The clapboard seaside village of Chester is one of the prettiest stops along the South Shore. Established in 1759, it's had a colorful history as the haunt of pirates and Prohibition-era bathtub-gin smugglers, and it keeps its color today via the many artists' studios about town. It's also a popular place for well-to-do Haligonians to buy a summer home.

Many visitors to Chester also take a day trip out to Big Tancook Island, the largest of the islets in Mahone Bay. It offers some great walking and interesting settlement history. The one-way trip takes about 50 minutes.

Sights & Activities

Big Tancook Island ISLAND

(www.tancookcommunitynews.com; adult/child round-trip $7/free) Big Tancook Island (population 120) is a 50-minute ferry ride from Chester's government wharf. Settled by Germans and French Huguenots in the early 19th century, the island is famous for its sauerkraut, and is crisscrossed with **walking trails**. It also has some pleasant beaches at Southeast Cove and Gravel Cove. The best way to get around is by bike; rentals are available as you step off the ferry. Ferries sail at least twice daily.

The **Tancook Ferry** (☎902-275-7885) runs four times daily Monday to Friday (first sailing from Chester at 6am, last sailing from Tancook at 5pm), with two extra sailings on Friday evening, at 6:30pm and 9:30pm (returning at 8:30pm and 11pm). The ferry runs twice daily on weekends (first sailing from Chester at 9am; last sailing from Tancook at 6pm on Saturday and 5pm on Sunday). The ferry stops en route at Little Tancook.

Kayak Shack KAYAKING

(☎902-221-2298; www.kayakshack.ca; 89 Water St; kayaks & SUPs per 2hr $30; ⏱8am-7pm mid-May–mid-Oct) Single and double kayaks and stand-up paddleboards are available here for you to explore the bay under your own paddle power.

Sleeping & Eating

Graves Island Provincial Park CAMPGROUND $

(☎902-275-4425; https://parks.novascotia.ca/content/graves-island; campsites $26.70-35.60; ⏱mid-May–mid-Oct) An island in Mahone Bay connected by a causeway to the mainland has 95 wooded campsites, 33 of which are serviced. RVs usually park in the middle of the area, but some shady, isolated tent sites are tucked away on the flanks of the central plateau. It's 3km northeast of Chester, off Hwy 3.

Mecklenburgh Inn B&B B&B $$
(902-275-4638; www.mecklenburghinn.ca; 78 Queen St; r $149-169; May-Dec;) Known as 'The Meck', this 1902 house is the only B&B in central Chester, with four heritage-style rooms featuring upscale touches such as clawfoot tubs, wooden floors, Frette linens and Lindt-chocolate pillow treats. Owner Suzi is a Cordon Bleu–trained chef, so expect a breakfast treat.

Kiwi Café CAFE $
(902-275-1492; www.kiwicafechester.com; 19 Pleasant St; mains $9-16; 8am-4pm Sun-Wed, to 8pm Thu-Sat;) Friendly as anything and serving comforting food cooked with love by an NZ-born chef, this is exactly the kind of community cafe you'd hope to find in a place like Chester. Choose from lobster rolls, fish cakes, burgers, superfood salads and an entire page of all-day breakfasts. Leave room for dessert: the cookies and cakes are divine.

★ **White Gate inn** CANADIAN $$$
(902-275-4400; www.whitegate.ca; 28 Pleasant St; mains $26-38; 5-8pm, 8:30pm or 9pm Wed-Sun) This beautiful heritage inn is by far Chester's swishest place to eat. The sophisticated menu features the likes of rack of lamb, lobster pie and chicken ballotine, served in the elegant surroundings of a gabled, white-weatherboard building right in the town center. Upstairs there are delightful rooms, decked out in pale blues and tasteful creams.

Drinking & Entertainment

Fo'c'sle PUB
(902-275-1408; www.focslechester.com; 42 Queen St; 11am-11pm) Dubbing itself 'Chester's Living Room', this ramshackle pub is a lively place to rub shoulders with the locals. There's been a pub of some sort on this site since 1764.

Chester Playhouse THEATER
(902-275-3933; www.chesterplayhouse.ca; 22 Pleasant St; tickets around $25) This quaint theater space has great acoustics for live performances. Plays or dinner theater are presented most nights in July and August, with occasional concerts during spring and fall.

Information

Since the closure of the visitor center, Tourism Chester (www.tourismchester.ca) is the best resource for things to see and do around town.

Getting There & Away

Chester is 67km southwest of Halifax via Hwy 103.

Mahone Bay

902 / POP 950

The sun shines more often in Mahone Bay than anywhere else along the coast, apparently. With more than 100 islands in its bay, and a location less than 100km from Halifax, it's a great base for exploring this section of the South Shore. Take out a kayak or a bike or simply stroll down Main St, which skirts the harbor and is scattered with shops selling antiques, quilts, pottery and works by local painters.

Sights & Activities

Mahone Bay Settlers' Museum MUSEUM
(902-624-6263; www.mahonebaymuseum.com; 578 Main St; 10am-4pm late May–mid-Oct) FREE This modest little local-history museum is worth a visit to understand the development of Mahone Bay, particularly the 1754 settlement, the building of the three churches and the long tradition of shipbuilding.

Sweet Ride Cycling CYCLING
(902-531-3026; www.sweetridecycling.com; 523 Main St; half-/full-day rentals $25/35; 10am-5pm Mon-Sat, noon-5pm Sun) This friendly bike shop rents out a good range of bikes, including fat-wheeled cruisers. It's devised some good local routes, and can also help you out with the Rum Runners Trail (p71).

Sleeping

Heart's Desire B&B B&B $$
(902-624-8470; www.heartsdesirebb.com; 686 Main St; cottages $116, r $126-130;) John and Denise Perry's house, originally built for a local schoolteacher, is a quintessential example of a Victorian 'Foursquare', and it retains lots of its original fixtures. The three rooms have hardwood floors and are prettily decorated with cheery quilts, and there's a separate cottage in the lovingly tended garden.

Eating & Drinking

LaHave Bakery DELI $

(☎902-624-1420; www.lahavebakery.com; 3 Edgewater St; sandwiches $5-9.50; ⏰8:30am-5:30pm; ✎) This bakery is famous for its hearty bread. Sandwiches are made on thick slabs of it.

★**Biscuit Eater** CAFE $$

(☎902-624-2665; https://thebiscuiteater.com; 16 Orchard St; mains $14-21; ⏰9am-4pm Mon-Fri, to 7pm Sat, 10am-3pm Sun; ☎) This is many people's dream come true: a vintage bookstore that doubles as a cafe, serving homemade soups, burgers and all-day breakfasts, not to mention absolutely knockout cakes. The house special is the 'biscuit bowl': roast chicken, barbecue brisket, lobster or veggies served on a bed of greens and a homemade biscuit.

Oh My Cod! SEAFOOD $$

(☎902-531-2600; www.oh-my-cod.ca; 567 Main St; mains $14-18.50; ⏰11am-8pm) For quick and easy eating, this friendly seafood diner is hard to beat: enjoy clams, scallops, battered haddock and fish tacos, along with hand-cut chips, a cold beer and a great view over Mahone Bay. What's not to like?

★**Mateus Bistro** CANADIAN $$$

(☎902-531-3711; www.mateusbistro.ca; 533 Main St; mains $23-35; ⏰5-9pm Tue-Thu, 11:30am-9pm Fri-Mon) The Bratislavan-born chef has made this little restaurant into a real destination address: people drive to Mahone Bay just to eat here. The food is really fresh and tasty, with lots of herbs and garnishes, running the gamut from Moroccan lamb shank to panko-crusted haddock.

Saltbox Brewing Company MICROBREWERY

(☎902-624-0653; www.saltboxbrewingcompany.ca; 363 Main St; ⏰11am-9pm Mon & Tue, 10am-10pm Wed-Sat, 11am-7pm Sun) Mahone Bay's very own small-batch craft brewery has a taproom where you can try all the latest brews.

Information

Mahone Bay Visitor Information Centre (☎902-624-6151; www.mahonebay.com; 165 Edgewater St; ⏰9am-6pm May-Oct) Lots of info on the town, plus self-guided walking-tour brochures.

Getting There & Away

Mahone Bay is 86km southwest of Halifax on Hwy 103 and 11km northwest of Lunenburg.

Maritime Bus (p56) has services to Halifax ($20.25, 70 minutes, one daily). Three-hour advance booking required.

Lunenburg

☎902 / POP 2263

After Peggy's Cove, lovely Lunenburg is the place that everyone stops off to see on their trip along the South Shore. And no wonder:

THE TREASURE OF OAK ISLAND

Oak Island, near Mahone Bay, is home to a so-called 'money pit' that has cost over $2 million in excavation expenses – and six lives. Few facts are known about what the pit is or what might be buried there, but if you're keen to find out more, *The Curse of Oak Island*, an ongoing reality-TV series, documents the efforts of a team of treasure hunters.

The mystery began in 1795, when three inhabitants of the island came across a depression in the ground. Knowing that pirates (including the legendary Captain Kidd) had once frequented the area, they decided to dig and see what they could find. Just over half a meter down, they hit a layer of neatly placed flagstone; another 2.5m turned up one oak platform, then another. After digging to 9m, the men temporarily gave up, but they returned eight years later with the Onslow Company, a professional crew.

The Onslow excavation made it 27.5m down; when the crew returned the next morning, the shaft had flooded and they were forced to halt the digging. A year later, the company returned to dig 33.5m down in a parallel shaft, which also flooded. It was confirmed in 1850 that the pit was booby trapped via five box drains at Smith Cove, 150m from the pit. The beach was found to be artificial.

Ever since, people have come from far and wide to seek their fortune at the 'money pit', including Rick and Marty Lagina, stars of *The Curse of Oak Island*. They've made progress – recent finds include coins, a lead cross and a garnet brooch – but so far they're yet to strike it really rich.

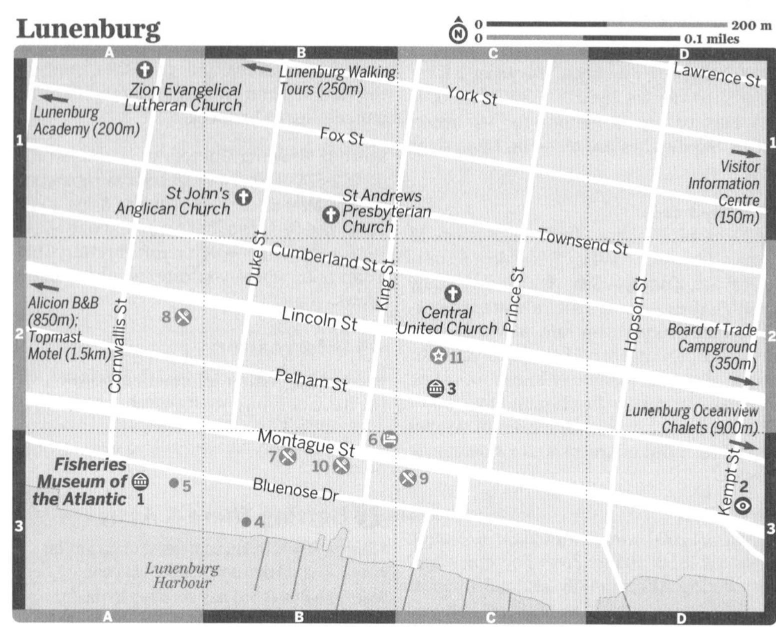

Lunenburg

Top Sights
1 Fisheries Museum of the Atlantic A3

Sights
2 Ironworks Distillery D3
3 Knaut-Rhuland House C2

Activities, Courses & Tours
4 Bluenose II B3
5 Trot in Time A3

Sleeping
6 Sail Inn B&B B3

Eating
7 Half Shell Oyster Bar B3
8 Lincoln Street Food A2
9 Salt Shaker Deli C3
10 South Shore Fish Shack B3

Entertainment
11 Lunenburg Opera House C2

with its brightly painted weatherboard houses, lawned squares and slate-topped churches, it's such a perfect example of a Nova Scotian fishing town that it almost looks like a model. And in some ways that's exactly what it is: it was designed according to the standard British blueprint for colonial settlements in the 18th century, and it seems barely to have changed since it was built. The old town's beautifully preserved architecture has earned it Unesco World Heritage status, and deservedly so, but it gets very busy in summer – visit in May or September to see it at its pastel-tinted best.

History

The Mi'kmaq lived for many centuries along this area of the South Shore prior to the first European arrivals, the Acadians, who founded the small farming community of Mirliguèche in the mid-1600s.

A century later the area was claimed by the British, who established one of their earliest Nova Scotian settlements here, naming it in honor of the Duke of Braunschweig-Lüneburg (later George II). The town was populated by 'Foreign Protestants' (mostly Germans, Swiss and Protestant French), who gradually switched from farming to fishing for their livelihood.

Lunenburg subsequently established itself as an important fishing and shipbuilding port, and during Prohibition in the 1920s it became a major rum-running center. The town remains a working fishing town, although dwindling stocks have made many fishers give up the trade in search of a more secure income. The town was listed as a World Heritage site by Unesco in 1995.

Sights & Activities

Look out around town for the distinctive 'Lunenburg Bump', a distinctive architectural feature of older buildings whereby a five-sided dormer window on the 2nd floor overhangs the 1st floor.

There are four handsome 18th- and 19th-century churches in the old town (each of the different religious denominations – Anglican, Presbyterian, Lutheran and Methodist – built its own, in an astonishing show of ecclesiastical one-upmanship). Look out for the weathervane atop **St Andrews Presbyterian Church** on Townsend St; it's cod shaped. Only in Lunenburg!

★Fisheries Museum of the Atlantic — MUSEUM

(☎902-634-4794; http://fisheriesmuseum.novascotia.ca; 68 Bluenose Dr; adult/child $13/3.50; ⌚9:30am-5pm or 5:30pm mid-May–Oct) You simply can't understand Lunenburg unless you've visited this maritime museum, which traces the history of fishing from the days of the Mi'kmaq through to the present time. Fascinating exhibits explore fishing grounds, vessels and techniques, and film screenings and talks are scheduled throughout the day. The museum also has two vintage vessels: the *Theresa E Connor*, the oldest saltbank dory schooner in Canada, built in 1938; and the *Cape Sable*, a steel-hulled side trawler built in 1962.

There's a large parking lot opposite the museum. Admission is covered by the Nova Scotia Museum Pass (p56).

Ironworks Distillery — DISTILLERY

(☎902-640-2424; www.ironworksdistillery.com; 2 Kempt St; ⌚4 tours daily mid-Jun–mid-Sep, contact for other times) Lunenburg's renowned brewery crafts a selection of fruity liqueurs, a strong apple brandy, a pear eau-de-vie, an apple vodka and – fittingly for a maritime town – several rums. You can follow the distilling process on a guided tour.

The name comes from the distillery's location in Lunenburg's former blacksmith's shop, which produced ironworks for the shipbuilding industry.

Knaut-Rhuland House — MUSEUM

(☎902-634-3498; www.lunenburgheritagesociety.ca/museum; 125 Pelham St; ⌚11am-5pm Mon-Sat, noon-4pm Sun Jun-Sep) FREE This 2½-story house – named after its first owners, merchants Benjamin Knaut and Conrad Rhuland – is considered the finest example of Georgian architecture in the province. It's an intriguing insight into how a wealthy Lunenburg home would have looked to early settlers, although some of the rooms are quite spartan.

Pleasant Paddling — KAYAKING

(☎902-541-9233; www.pleasantpaddling.com; 245 The Point Rd, Blue Rocks; kayak rentals from $38, tours from $60; ⌚May-Oct) The knowledgeable folks at this beautiful place to paddle offer rentals and tours in single or double kayaks. They're based at Blue Rocks, about 9km east of Lunenburg.

Tours

Lunenburg Walking Tours — WALKING

(☎902-521-6867; www.lunenburgwalkingtours.com; tours adult/child from $25/15) The enthusiastic and very experienced Sheila Allen and her team lead informative history tours during the day and spooky lantern-lit ones at night. Tours begin outside the impressive edifice of the Lunenburg Academy, built in 1895 and currently undergoing restoration.

Trot in Time — TOURS

(☎902-634-8917; www.trotintime.ca; adult/child $30/15; ⌚Jun–mid-Oct) For that old-timey photo op, take a half-hour tour of town in a

THE BLUENOSE

Designed by renowned boat maker William J Roué, the original *Bluenose* was built right here in Lunenburg in 1921. She was the largest schooner ever built: 25 tonnes. She served as a fishing vessel and an award-winning racing yacht under local captain Angus Walters before being wrecked in a storm near Haiti in 1946. You might well have seen her without ever being aware of it: the boat features on one side of the Canadian dime.

The **Bluenose II** (☎902-634-1963; https://bluenose.novascotia.ca; 2hr cruises adult/child $65/36), a replica of the original vessel launched in 1963, runs unforgettable trips along the South Shore during summer; depending on the day, it might be moored in Lunenburg or Halifax. Check the website to see when it's next in town.

If you're just after a souvenir, there's a Bluenose Company Store at 121 Bluenose Dr.

LUNENBURG, THE MODEL TOWN

Lunenburg was laid out as a colonial 'planned settlement' along a geometric grid pattern drawn up by British planners: eight blocks, each divided into 14 lots measuring from 12m to 18m, with a four-block area in the center (including a parade ground) designated as public space. Each settler family received a 'town lot', and a 'garden lot' where they could grow vegetables and keep animals; most of the town's houses have small or no gardens as a result. Unfortunately, the off-the-shelf design made no allowance for topography, which explains why some of Lunenburg's streets are so ludicrously steep. Originally the town would have been protected by forts, blockhouses and palisades, but these are now mostly gone (although one still houses the town's visitor center).

horse-drawn cart. It leaves from outside the Fisheries Museum of the Atlantic (p77).

Festivals & Events

Nova Scotia Folk Art Festival ART
(www.nsfolkartfestival.com; Aug) Buffet dinner, artist talks and then a big art show and sale on the first Sunday in August.

Boxwood Festival MUSIC
(www.boxwood.org; festival pass $50; Jul) Flautists and pipers from around the world put on stellar public concerts.

Lunenburg Folk Harbour Festival MUSIC
(902-634-3180; www.folkharbour.com; Aug) Singer-songwriters from Canada and beyond, plus traditional music and gospel.

Sleeping

Board of Trade Campground CAMPGROUND $
(902-634-8100; www.lunenburgns.com/campground; 11 Blockhouse Hill Rd; sites from $36.80; late May-early Oct;) Perched on Blockhouse Hill, high above Lunenburg (the site of the old fort), this campground guarantees you a pitch with a view, although the sites are pretty packed together and there's not much shade.

★ **Alicion B&B** B&B $$
(902-634-9358; www.alicionbb.com; 66 McDonald St; r $159-179; P) Wow, what a beauty: a 1911 former senator's home, built on a hilltop, with a wraparound veranda that radiates Revival elegance. There are four beautiful nature-themed rooms: tranquil Kingfisher, garden-view Periwinkle, south-facing Tamarack and double-aspect Dragonfly, all stuffed with antiques and thoughtful touches. Owners Christopher and Joe do everything with class (there's even a sweet treat in the afternoon).

★ **Sail Inn B&B** B&B $$
(902-634-3537; www.sailinn.ca; 99 Montague St; r $120-180; P) If you want to be down by the harbor, this smart B&B is a really lovely choice. It's housed in a heritage building, but the rooms are bright, airy and modern, and all have harbor views. Look out for the old well on the ground floor that's been turned into a fishpond!

Lunenburg Oceanview Chalets COTTAGE $$
(902-640-3344; www.lunenburgoceanview.com; 78 Old Blue Rocks Rd; cottages $149-179; P) For something a little different, these rustic log cabins with private decks atop a hill on Lunenburg's outskirts might be just what the doctor ordered. They're fully self-contained, and have wi-fi, log fires, ocean views (at a distance) and the refreshing sound of horses neighing in the meadows. Basic, but rather romantic and reasonably priced. Two-night minimum stay June to September.

Topmast Motel MOTEL $$
(902-634-4661; www.topmastmotel.ca; 76 Masons Beach Rd; d $139-154) Arguably the best prospect in Lunenburg is the main selling point at this simple, friendly and spotlessly clean motel. Yes, the rooms are no-frills – but the views more than make up for any shortcomings.

Eating

There are plenty of great restaurants here. Lunenburg's offbeat dining specialties include Solomon Gundy (pickled herring with onions) and Lunenburg pudding (pork and spices cooked in the intestines of a pig), which goes well with whiskey and water.

★ **South Shore Fish Shack** SEAFOOD $$
(902-634-3232; www.southshorefishshack.com; 108 Montague St; mains $12-20; 11am-8pm

Sun-Wed, to 9pm Thu-Sat) There are two main reasons to swing by this place: to eat the best fish-and-chips in Lunenburg and to enjoy the view from the deck. Chuck in great lobster buns, panko-crusted scallops and a fun sea-shack vibe, and you really can't go wrong.

Salt Shaker Deli DELI $$
(902-640-3434; www.saltshakerdeli.com; 124 Montague St; mains $12-20; 11am-9pm) This friendly downtown diner is where everyone, local or tourist, heads for a meal in Lunenburg: crispy-crust pizzas, piles of mussels, salmon cakes and fisherman's stew keep the punters packed in, and there's a great selection of craft beers and Nova Scotian wines. Try for a spot on the deck on summer nights.

It's recently added upstairs **rooms** (from $130), several of which have water views, but inevitably there's spillover noise from the restaurant.

Half Shell Oyster Bar SEAFOOD $$
(902-634-8503; www.halfshelloysterbar.com; 108 Montague St; oysters from $3.25, mains $12-22; noon-midnight Jul & Aug, to 9pm Jun & Sep) A long ice bar loaded with such seafood goodies as snow-crab claws, chilled lobsters, littleneck clams and, of course, freshly shucked oysters is the main feature at this newly opened restaurant, run by the team behind the Salt Shaker Deli and the South Shore Fish Shack. The idea is hands-on seafood – yes, you'll get messy, but what fun!

★**Lincoln Street Food** CANADIAN $$$
(902-640-3002; www.lincolnstreetfood.ca; 200 Lincoln St; mains $26, 3-course prix fixe $47; 5-9pm Tue-Sat;) This smart, contemporary bistro is a sign of the town's changing times: stripped back in style, with exciting dishes such as halibut with charred-cucumber salsa verde and summer panzanella salad that feel unusually urban for olde-worlde Lunenburg. Unsurprisingly, it's popular: bookings are essential.

Entertainment

Lunenburg Opera House THEATER
(902-634-4010; www.lunenburgoperahouse.com; 290 Lincoln St; tickets $5-25) This recently refurbished 400-seat theater is rumored to have a resident ghost. Built as an Odd Fellows Hall in 1907, it's now a favorite venue for rock and folk musicians. Check the posters in the window for what's coming up.

Information

Visitor Information Centre (VIC; 902-634-8100; www.lunenburgns.com; 11 Blockhouse Hill Rd; 7:30am-7pm Jul & Aug, 9am-5pm May, Jun, Sep & Oct) Perched high above town, this helpful center has loads of information on old Lunenburg, and can help find the last available rooms around town if you're stuck in summer.

Getting There & Away

Lunenburg is just shy of 100km from Halifax on Hwy 103.

Maritime Bus (p56) runs a regular bus along the South Shore to Halifax ($25.50, 1¾ hours, two daily).

Liverpool

902 / POP 2549

Like that of other South Shore settlements, Liverpool's history takes in fishing, privateering, shipbuilding, rum running and pretty much every other maritime trade you could mention. Despite this, Liverpool has never managed to reinvent itself as a tourist center as many of the other towns have. As such, it looks a little run-down, but it's worth a stop for its attractive beaches and the distinctive lighthouse at Fort Point.

It makes a particularly handy base for exploring Kejimkujik National Park's Seaside Adjunct.

Every June, the town celebrates its piratical history during the **Privateer Days** (www.privateerdays.ca).

Sights

★**Rossignol Cultural Centre** MUSEUM
(902-354-3067; www.rossignolculturalcentre.com; 205 Church St; adult/child $5/3; 10am-5pm Tue-Sat) This brilliantly oddball museum explores the eclectic fascinations of local photographer Sherman Hines, born in Liverpool in 1941. There are halls of taxidermy animals, cases of gorgeous indigenous beadwork, walls of Hines' beautiful photography (including some from his Mongolian adventures), the interior of a Halifax apothecary and – most bizarre of all – a room dedicated to outhouses around the world.

Hank Snow Home Town Museum MUSEUM
(902-354-4675; www.hanksnow.com; 148 Bristol Ave; $5; 9am-5pm Mon-Sat, 1-5pm Sun) Country-music star Clarence Eugene 'Hank' Snow was born on May 9, 1914, in the village of

Brooklyn, not far from Liverpool. Housed in the old train station, this little museum explores his life, along with that of Wilf Carter and fellow crooners and yodelers.

Fort Point Lighthouse LIGHTHOUSE
(☎902-354-5260; 21 Fort Lane; ⏰cafe 10am-6pm May-Oct) FREE Built in 1885, this lighthouse at the end of the spit of land overlooking Liverpool harbor stands on the place where Frenchmen Pierre Dugua and Samuel de Champlain landed in 1604. Before the lighthouse was built, a privateer fort stood on the site to guard the harbor, hence the name.

There's now a pleasant seasonal cafe here, operated by the owners of Lane's Privateer Inn, and some small displays on the lighthouse's history.

Sleeping & Eating

Lane's Privateer Inn INN $$
(☎902-354-3456; www.lanesprivateerinn.com; 27 Bristol Ave; d $125-175; P) Liverpool's main place to stay, this rambling, old-school inn on the main road through town was once the residence of a Liverpudlian privateer. Rooms are large; the best have wooden floors and attractive artwork, but the budget ones look very dated. Downstairs are a **coffee shop and restaurant** (mains $18 to $25). There's lots of parking next to the inn.

★ **Quarterdeck** BOUTIQUE HOTEL $$$
(☎1-800-565-1119; www.quarterdeck.ca; 7499 Hwy 3, Summerville; villas $299-429) Like a contemporary take on a family-friendly resort, Quarterdeck has modern, luxurious weatherboard villas on Summerville Beach and offers digs ranging from one-roomers to swanky multiroom lofts. There's an on-site **grill** (mains $24 to $30) and a rec center with its own movie screen. Style galore on the South Shore.

Five Girls Baking CAFE $
(☎902-354-5551; 181 Main St; sandwiches $4-8; ⏰8am-5pm Tue-Fri, 9:30am-4pm Sat, 10am-4pm Sun) Sandwiches, muffins, cookies and freshly baked buns, plus lots of local foodie treats, are reason enough to check out this attractive little cafe on Main St.

Getting There & Away

Liverpool is 67km southwest of Mahone Bay on Hwy 103, and 64km northeast of Shelburne.

Kejimkujik National Park

Some of Nova Scotia's most unique, magnificent and unspoiled terrain is found within the boundaries of Kejimkujik National Park (shortened to 'Keji' by locals). Generations of Mi'kmaw people paddled, camped and hunted here, and the area is dotted with ancient camping sites, many marked by rock engravings known as petroglyphs. In summer you can join a fascinating guided hike led by Mi'kmaw guides.

These days Keji remains popular for hiking, backcountry camping, bird-watching and kayaking. The main park occupies 381 sq km in the center of the mainland, while its smaller **Seaside Adjunct**, protecting an important coastal habitat of dunes, beaches and creeks between Port Joli and Port Mouton, is 107km south.

Incredibly, even today less than 20% of Keji's wilderness is accessible by car; the rest can only be reached on foot or by canoe.

Activities

Petroglyph Tour HIKING
(⏰10:30am daily Jul & Aug, 10:30am Sat & Sun Sep) FREE Hike into restricted areas of the park to see some of the 500 ancient petroglyphs left behind by Mi'kmaw people. Located mainly around Kejimkujik's lakes, the carvings depict figures, symbols, animals, sailing ships and clothing. There are only 20 places, so bookings should be made well ahead through the visitor center. Tours leave from the Merrymakedge parking lot.

Whynot Adventure OUTDOORS
(Keji Outfitters; ☎902-682-2282; www.whynotadventure.ca; 1507 Main Pkwy; canoe rental per hour/day/week from $15/40/165; ⏰8am-8pm Jun-Sep) This company rents out kayaks, canoes, bikes and paddleboards for adventures around Keji. It offers 'Quickie Adventure' guided trips (from $50/80 for a two-/four-hour expedition), plus multiday trips including overnight camping. Its shuttle service is useful, and it also rents out camping gear.

Mi'kmaw Encampment CULTURAL
(Wejisqalia'ti'k; ⏰2pm Tue-Sat Jul & Aug) FREE Hear local tales and legends from Mi'kmaw guides while sipping a cup of bush tea at these fascinating storytelling sessions (in Mi'kmaw, *wejisqulia'ti'k* roughly translates as 'tell us that we grew from the earth'). They also offer stories around a campfire at

10pm on Saturdays in July and 9:30pm in August.

Birch Bark Canoe Carving Demonstration CULTURAL

(⌚2-4pm Thu-Sun Jul-early Sep) Seventh-generation Mi'kmaw and master craftsman Todd Labrador demonstrates the art of birch-bark-canoe carving. If you'd like to have a go yourself, he also holds workshops from 10am to 12:30pm on Sunday morning ($65).

Demonstrations take place at the Merrymakedge car park on the shore of Kejimkujik Lake.

Sleeping

★ Jeremy's Bay Campground CAMPGROUND $

(☎877-737-3783; www.pc.gc.cax; campsites $25.50-29.40, cabins & yurts $70, oTENTiks $100; ⌚May-Oct) This excellent campground is one of the best places in the park to sleep under the stars. There's a wide choice of campsites (both serviced and unserviced), plus rustic wooden cabins, yurts and pre-pitched tents (called oTENTiks) that come with mattresses, furniture, a private deck, a firebox and a picnic area. It's in a great lakeside location near Jake's Landing.

Thomas Raddall Provincial Park CAMPGROUND $

(☎902-683-2664; http://parks.novascotia.ca/content/thomas-raddall; campsites $25.60-35.70; ⌚May-Oct) Thomas Raddall Provincial Park, across Port Joli Harbour from Kejimkujik's Seaside Adjunct, has large, private campsites, eight of which are walk-in. The forested campground extends onto awesome beaches.

★ Mersey River Chalets CABIN $$

(☎902-682-2447; www.merseyriverchalets.ns.ca; 315 Mersey River Chalets Rd E, Caledonia; tipis $90-120, cabins $185-208; 🚭📶) Get back to nature at this cabin complex, deep in the woods beside Harry's Lake. There's a choice of pine chalets, a spacious log house, a four-room lodge and (best of all) tipis. Cabins have wood-burning stoves and private porches with barbecues; rooms in the lodge have private decks with lake views; and the cozy tipis have fully equipped kitchens.

Canoes and kayaks are available for guests.

Information

There are black bears in the park: campers should take the usual precautions when hiking and backcountry camping.

Biting insects, including some seriously large mosquitoes, are rampant in summer. Also watch out for eel-like leeches in the lakes.

Kejimkujik National Park Visitor Centre (☎902-682-2772; www.parkscanada.gc.ca/keji; 3005 Main Pkwy, Maitland Bridge; park entry adult/child $6/3; ⌚8:30am-7pm or 8pm mid-Jun–Aug, to 4:30pm mid-May–mid-Jun & Oct) Get an entry permit and park maps and reserve backcountry campsites here. It also reserves places on various activities and tours around the park. It's off the main road through the park, Hwy 8.

Getting There & Away

Entry to Kejimkujik National Park is through the visitor center (on Hwy 8), which can be approached from Annapolis Royal, 49km northwest. From the east, the park is 68km from Liverpool, from where it's another 19km to Lunenburg.

The only access into Kejimkujik National Park's Seaside Adjunct is via Hwy 103 and then along a 6.5km gravel road. The adjunct is 47km east of Shelburne and 32km west of Liverpool. For GPS navigation systems, search for 1188 St Catherine's River Rd, Port Joli.

Shelburne

☎902 / POP 1690

Shelburne's historic waterfront area bobs with sailboats and has 17 homes that were built before 1800 – it feels like a historical recreation, but it's real. The wonderfully maintained, low-in-the-earth buildings once housed Loyalists who retreated here from the American Revolution. In 1783 Shelburne was the largest community in British North America, with 16,000 residents, many from the New York aristocracy, who exploited the labor of Black Loyalists living in nearby Birchtown. Shelburne's history is celebrated with **Founders' Days** over the last weekend of July.

Sights

Black Loyalist Heritage Centre MUSEUM

(☎902-875-1310; https://blackloyalist.novascotia.ca; 119 Old Birchtown Rd; adult/child $9.20/5.75; ⌚10am-5pm) In 2015 Birchtown's Black Loyalist Heritage Centre and museum was moved to its shiny new facility 7km outside town, on the site of what was Canada's

WORTH A TRIP

TROUT POINT LODGE

Situated at the edge of the Tobeatic Wilderness Area, this fabulously luxurious **forest lodge** (☎902-761-2142; www.troutpoint.com; 189 Trout Point Rd, East Kemptville; r from $358; P) offers a taste of the wild blended with old-fashioned country comfort. Built from giant eastern-spruce logs, the three-story lodge is the epitome of rustic chic, with beamed ceilings, stone fireplaces, handmade log furniture, a mezzanine library and an excellent Atlantic Acadian restaurant.

Guides offer a range of backcountry experiences, including stargazing, forest bathing and geological excursions. You're way, way off the map here – cell-phone coverage is nonexistent – so switch off for a few days and feel the call of the wild.

largest free African settlement in the 1780s. The museum offers an insight into this largely untold Canadian story.

Dory Shop Museum MUSEUM
(☎902-875-3219; https://doryshop.novascotia.ca; 11 Dock St; adult/child $4/free; ⏲9:30am-5:30pm Jun–mid-Oct) Shelburne dories (small wooden open boats used for fishing from a mother schooner) were the staple craft for Nova Scotian fishermen on the Grand Banks fishery, thanks to their lightweight construction, shallow draft, durability and maneuverability. This fascinating workshop is one of the only places in the world that still makes them to order, and it has a collection of vintage craft.

Ross-Thomson House MUSEUM
(☎902-875-3141; https://rossthomson.novascotia.ca; 9 Charlotte Lane; adult/child $4/free; ⏲9:30am-5:30pm Jun–mid-Oct) Go shopping, 1780s style, at this merchant's house, once owned by traders George and Robert Ross, who supplied Shelburne's residents with staple goods and luxury items. There's a replica of the original store counter, and you can also see around the sparsely furnished house and the pleasant gardens.

Sleeping & Eating

Cooper's Inn B&B B&B $$
(☎902-875-4656; www.thecoopersinn.com; 36 Dock St; r $140-230;) Part of this waterfront building dates from 1784 and was brought here from Boston. Now it's a relatively modern but still charmingly heritage-style inn with eight rooms. There's also a flower-filled garden.

Bean Dock CAFE $
(☎902-875-1302; Dock St; sandwiches $3.50-7; ⏲8:30am-4pm Mon-Fri, 9am-3pm Sat & Sun) A chilled coffee shop overlooking the waterfront, serving grilled cheese sandwiches, muffins and paninis. There's also a gift shop selling souvenir tees, candles and kitchen items – although the giant Adirondack chair isn't up for sale, so don't ask.

★ **Charlotte Lane Cafe** CANADIAN $$$
(☎902-875-3314; www.charlottelane.ca; 13 Charlotte Lane; mains lunch $11.50-22, dinner $20-42; ⏲11:30am-2:30pm & 5-8pm Tue-Sat) This colorful cafe is everyone's top tip; evening reservations are highly recommended. Swiss chef Roland Glauser serves a varied menu of seafood, meat and pasta dishes, featuring dashes of spice and exotic ingredients picked up on his travels.

Information

Visitor Information Centre (VIC; ☎902-875-4547; www.shelburneandlockeport.com; 43 Dock St; ⏲9am-4pm May-Sep) In a dinky little building at the end of the harbor, the town's tourist office has a few historical walking trails to try.

Getting There & Away

Shelburne is 64km southwest of Liverpool on Hwy 103, and 97km east of Yarmouth.

ACADIAN SHORES

Acadian culture has left a strong influence on the history of this part of Nova Scotia: you'll often spy the Stella Maris, the single-starred, tricolored Acadian flag, and you'll still hear the Acadian dialect spoken in many areas. The area's main town is Yarmouth, an important lobster port and – theoretically – the transit point for ferries to Portland, Maine.

The Acadian Shores cover roughly 120km of coast between Digby to the north and the city of Yarmouth and the communities of the Pubnicos to the south. This area is a lot less prettified than the coastal communities of the South Shore and the Annapolis Valley: this is hardworking country, and proud of it.

Yarmouth

902 / POP 7217

Founded in 1761 by New Englanders from Massachusetts, Yarmouth reached the peak of its prosperity in the 1870s. It's still the biggest town in southern Nova Scotia, and one of the province's largest centers for lobster fishing.

It's very much a working town, but there are a few compelling reasons to stop on your way through, including an outpost of the Art Gallery of Nova Scotia and a landmark lighthouse at Cape Fourchu.

Sights

★ Cape Forchu Lightstation LIGHTHOUSE

(Yarmouth Light; 902-742-4522; www.capeforchu.com; Hwy 304; 9am-5pm Jun-Sep) FREE Instantly recognisable thanks to its strange 'apple core' shape (designed to deflect winds around the structure), the present-day lighthouse on the lonely headland of Cape Forchu was built in 1962, but there's been a beacon here since 1839. It's a wild location with epic views: even on clear days, rogue waves have been known to crash over the parking lot. There's a small seasonal cafe, the **Keeper's Kitchen**, and a couple of walking trails to explore.

Art Gallery of Nova Scotia GALLERY

(902-749-2248; www.artgalleryofnovascotia.ca/visit-yarmouth; 341 Main St; adult/child $6/2.50, from 5pm Thu free; 10am-5pm, to 8pm Thu) The work of Maritime artists provides the backbone of the collection at this impressive outpost of the main Halifax gallery (p61), spread over three floors. If you save your ticket you'll get 50% off admission to the gallery in Halifax.

Yarmouth County Museum MUSEUM

(902-742-5539; www.yarmouthcountymuseum.ca; 22 Collins St; adult/student $5/3; 9am-5pm Mon-Sat Jun-Sep, 2-5pm Tue-Sat Oct-May) This museum in a former church has a typically eclectic collection of artifacts: look out for a Victorian funeral hearse and stagecoach, an original Fresnel lamp from the Cape Forchu Lightstation, and a mysterious 'runic stone' that some people claim was left by Viking explorers.

Your ticket includes admission to **Pelton-Fuller House** (20 Collins St) next door, which is filled with period artwork, glassware and furniture.

Le Village historique acadien de la Nouvelle-Écosse HISTORIC SITE

(Historical Acadian Village of Nova Scotia; 902-762-2530; http://levillage.novascotia.ca; 91 Old Church Rd, Lower West Pubnico; adult/child $8/3; 9am-5pm Jun-Oct) This 17-acre site overlooking Pubnico Harbour recreates an Acadian village, with vintage Acadian buildings and a cemetery. The village is located in West Pubnico, one of Nova Scotia's original Acadian communities (and not to be confused with all the other nearby Pubnicos), about a 40-minute drive southeast of Yarmouth.

Sleeping

★ Ye Olde Argyler Lodge HOTEL $$

(902-643-2500; www.argyler.com; 52 Ye Old Argyle Rd; r $140-260) Situated 34km from central Yarmouth, the Argyler has nothing olde worlde about it: it's a modern, veranda-encircled lodge built in a truly glorious spot overlooking a creek. Set along a central corridor, the smart rooms have comfy beds, feather-down pillows and lovely bathrooms (ask if you want a water view). There's great food, too, including lobster parties and Acadian dishes.

DUMPING DAY

If you happen to be in Yarmouth around the end of November, you might be lucky enough to see one of the area's most exciting events: Dumping Day. This long-standing tradition is held to mark the beginning of the main lobster-fishing season: scores of boats head out from the harbors at the crack of dawn, watched by hundreds of locals cheering them on from the dockside. It's a lucrative business: after months of not being fished, the best lobster grounds can yield huge hauls, with experienced boats pulling in thousands of pounds of lobsters on each trip. The first week of the season is the richest of all, and many skippers will stay out as long as possible, only heading back to shore to land their catch. But it's a dangerous business, too: sinkings are not unknown, and the first day of the fishery is usually watched over by search-and-rescue teams from the Canadian Coast Guard.

Lakelawn B&B Motel MOTEL $$
(☎902-742-3588; www.lakelawnmotel.com; 641 Main St; r $129-179;) This place is as cute and service-oriented as motels come. Rooms are clean and basic, and some of the better meals in town are available in the country-style dining area. Go even classier in the four B&B-style rooms in the central Victorian house.

MacKinnon-Cann House Historic Inn INN $$
(☎866-698-3142; www.mackinnoncanninn.com; 27 Willow St; r $149-289;) Each of the six rooms here represents a decade, from the Victorian 1900s to the groovy 1960s, and depicts the era at its most stylish while managing to stay calming and comfortable. Two rooms can be joined to create a family suite.

Eating & Drinking

Shanty Cafe CAFE $
(☎902-742-5918; www.shantycafe.ca; 6b Central St; items $4-9; 7am-7pm Mon-Sat;) Fishers and shoppers alike head for the all-day breakfast at this simple town cafe, which dabbles in Indian and Mexican flavors alongside burgers, salads and steaks.

★**Gaia Global Kitchen** FUSION $$
(☎902-881-2627; www.gaiaglobalkitchen.com; 222 Main St; mains $14-19; 11am-8pm Tue-Sun, to 9pm Fri & Sat) This little restaurant takes a surprisingly pan-global trip on its menu, which includes everything from Jamaican jerk chicken to dhaba curry, Lebanese meze, drunken noodles and even Korean barbecue-pork poutine. It has a whole-food, eco-conscious ethos. They mix a pretty mean cocktail, too, and the desserts are divine.

Rudder's Brew Pub PUB FOOD $$
(☎902-742-7311; www.ruddersbrewpub.com; 96 Water St; mains $13-30; 11am-late) Join a local crowd tucking into no-nonsense Maritime classics such as bar clams and fries and Acadian *rappie* pie (meat pie topped with grated potato) at this waterfront pub, which also brews its own ales, including an English-style brown, a raspberry-red wheat beer and a malty Scottish-style 'wee heavy.'

Heritage Brewing Co MICROBREWERY
(☎902-881-2777; www.heritagebrewing.beer; 250 Main St; noon-11pm Sun-Wed, 11am-11pm Thu-Sat) Founded in 2017, this brewery has fast become Yarmouth's drinking venue of choice, with a range of core ales supplemented by guest ales from around Nova Scotia. The taproom is a cool warehouse-style space; you can see the vats at work through little windows off the bar.

Perky Owl Coffee CAFE
(☎902-881-2140; www.perkyowlcoffee.com; 255 Main St; 7:30am-5:30pm Mon-Fri, 8:30am-4:30pm Sat, 10am-3pm Sun) Pop into the Perky Owl for a caffeine pick-me-up or something sweet and sticky for the road.

Information

Visitors Information Centre (VIC; ☎902-742-5033; 228 Main St; 9am-5pm Jun & Sep–mid-Oct, to 7pm Jul & Aug) Has maps and a couple of walking tours.

Getting There & Away

Yarmouth is 300km southwest of Halifax on Hwy 103 and 104km south of Digby on Hwy 101.

There are no scheduled bus services from Yarmouth to Halifax and beyond, but if you're unable to rent your own wheels, Cloud Nine Shuttle (p70) can get you to the capital or to Halifax International Airport for a flat $75 fare.

Since 2016 Yarmouth has been served by a regular catamaran to Portland, Maine, but at the time of writing the service had been suspended due to construction work. See www.ferries.ca/thecat for the latest updates.

French Shore

The villages of Church Point, Grosses-Coques, Belliveau Cove and St Bernard, on the mainland directly across St Mary's Bay from Digby Neck, make up the heart of the French Shore. This is where Acadians settled when, after trekking back to Nova Scotia following deportation, they found their homesteads in the Annapolis Valley already occupied. Now linked by Hwy 1 – pretty much the only road in each town – these are small fishing communities.

The best way to explore this fading but unique part of the province is to follow Hwy 1 as it hugs the shoreline from Belliveau Cove as far south as Mavillette Beach. It can also be approached in the reverse direction.

Sights & Activities

★**Gilbert's Cove Lighthouse** LIGHTHOUSE
(☎902-837-5584; www.gilbertscovelighthouse.com; 244 Lighthouse Rd, Gilbert's Cove; 10am-4pm Mon-Sat, noon-4pm Sun mid-Jun–Sep) FREE Built in 1904, this gorgeous little lighthouse had only two light keepers throughout its

OFF THE BEATEN TRACK

BEAR RIVER

Bear River is a delightful riverside enclave popular with artists and those who moved here from larger centers for a tree change. There's a strong Mi'kmaq presence here: the **Bear River First Nation Reservation** (☎902-467-0301; www.bearriverfirstnation.ca; 194 Reservation Rd) FREE is spread out on the hills above town. Some buildings near the river are on stilts, while other historic homes nestle on the steep hills of the valley.

A few wineries are starting to pop up just out of town, including the excellent **Bear River Winery** (☎902-467-4156; www.wine.travel; 133 Chute Rd; ⊙11am-6pm May-Thanksgiving), which makes award-winning using solar energy, biodiesel, wind power and the natural slope of the property. Stop by for a free tour and tasting (July to September) or stay at the one-room B&B (from $90 per night) to enjoy wine-making workshops and retreats.

Bear River is 16km from Digby, off Hwy 101. There's no public transport.

years of service: William Melanson and his daughter Louise. It was rescued in 1982 from vandalism and decay by the local historical society, who have turned it into a charming museum. There's a scenic picnic area and a great spot for beachcombing and swimming.

Mavillette Beach Provincial Park BEACH

This huge, dune-backed beach sprawls for 1.5km overlooking Cape St Mary, and can be accessed by boardwalks from the parking lots. The receding tide reveals huge areas of sand flats, and in summer the shallow water heats up fast, making for great paddling. The beach is only supervised on Saturday and Sunday in July and August.

Smuggler's Cove Provincial Park STATE PARK

(http://parks.novascotia.ca; 7651 Hwy 1, Meteghan; ⊙mid-May–mid-Oct) Named for its popularity with 19th-century pirates, this park is today frequented by picnickers. A hundred wooden stairs take you down to a rocky beach and a good cave for hiding treasure. There are picnic sites containing barbecue pits at the top of the stairs, with a view across St Mary's Bay to Brier Island.

Rendez-Vous de la Baie CULTURAL CENTER

(www.rendezvousdelabaie.com; 23 Lighthouse Rd, Church Point; ⊙8am-6pm Mon-Fri, 9am-5pm Sat & Sun) FREE This interpretive center on the grounds of Université Sainte-Anne in Church Point is a really useful stop as you drive along the coastal road. You can acquire background about Acadian culture at the small museum, then get tourist tips at the information center. There is also a theater and a few walking trails to explore.

Église Ste-Marie CHURCH

(St Mary's Church; ☎902-769-2808; 1713 Hwy 1, Church Point; incl guide $2; ⊙9am-5pm May-Oct) The town of Church Point, also commonly known as Pointe de l'Église, takes its name from Église Ste-Marie, which towers over the town. Built between 1903 and 1905, the church is said to be the tallest wooden church in North America. An informative guide will show you around. Adjacent is the **Université Ste-Anne**, the only French university in the province and a center for Acadian culture.

Eating

Roadside Grill ACADIAN $

(☎902-837-5047; 3334 Hwy 1, Belliveau Cove; mains $9-18; ⊙8am-9pm) Try the steamed clams or the *rappie* pie at this pleasantly old-fashioned and long-running local restaurant. There's live Acadian music Tuesday night from 5:30pm to 7:30pm June through August.

La Cuisine Robicheau ACADIAN $$

(☎902-769-2121; www.lacuisinerobicheau.ca; 9651 Hwy 1, Saulnierville; mains $12-25; ⊙8am-7pm Tue-Sun Apr-Oct) This is the most elevated Acadian cuisine on the French Shore. The *rappie* pie, seafood lasagna and chocolate pie are so good and affordable they may make you exclaim *'sacre bleu!'* It's family-run and always busy, and there's often live music at suppertime during summer.

Getting There & Away

The French Shore begins in Belliveau Cove, 43km south of Digby, and hugs Hwy 1 south as far as Mavillette Beach, 35km from Yarmouth.

ANNAPOLIS VALLEY

Historically, the fertile and sparsely populated Annapolis Valley was known as the breadbasket of colonial Canada. Today the region still produces much of Nova Scotia's fresh produce, especially apples, but the real excitement surrounds the growth of the valley's wine industry. The valley's vineyards, which boast a similar latitude to that of Bordeaux, France, have taken advantage of the sandy soil and reconnected with the area's French roots.

Regional highlights include the **Annapolis Valley Apple Blossom Festival** (www.appleblossom.com; late May), the Fundy coast at Annapolis Royal for tidal vistas over patchwork farmland, the vibrant and spirited town of Wolfville, and taking a moment to contemplate the past while gazing upon the World Heritage landscape of Grand Pré.

Getting There & Away

Hwy 101, which begins on the outskirts of Halifax, continues for 74km to Wolfville at the northern edge of the Annapolis Valley, then runs straight down to Digby in the south. Because of the distance between towns and the many side trips to discover, self-driving is the most practical and enjoyable way to explore the region.

Maritime Bus (www.maritimebus.com) runs a direct service from Halifax to Wolfville.

Bay Ferries (www.ferries.ca) links Digby to Saint John, New Brunswick, via car ferry. The journey takes approximately 2¼ hours in peak season and 2¾ hours in low season.

Getting Around

Kings Transit (www.kingstransit.ns.ca) runs a bus every other hour from 6am to around 7pm from Weymouth (just north of Church Point) to Bridgetown (just north of Annapolis Royal) and then as far as Wolfville, stopping in every little town along the way. The fare is $3.50.

Kentville-based **Valley Stove & Cycle** (902-542-7280; www.valleystoveandcycle.com; 353 Main St; bike rental half/full day from $25/35; 9am-5:30pm Mon-Thu, to 7pm Fri, to 5pm Sat) rents out trail bikes, fat bikes, tandems and e-bikes.

Digby

902 / POP 2060

Nestled in a protected inlet off the Bay of Fundy, Digby is known across Nova Scotia for one thing: scallops. These sought-after shellfish grow in great numbers on scallop beds just offshore and command a premium price – you'll find them at most of the town's restaurants. Digby is now home to the largest fleet of scallop boats in the world, and hosts its own scallop-themed festival, **Digby Scallop Days** (www.digbyscallopdays.com; Aug), in honor of its most prized export.

The town may lack the quaint charm of the other Annapolis Valley settlements, but it's an honest, down-to-earth base for exploring the valley and nearby Digby Neck.

If you're here only briefly, the best things to do are to stroll the waterfront, watch the scallop draggers come and go, eat as much of their catch as you can, and then squeeze in a sunset at **Point Prim**.

Sleeping & Eating

Digby Backpackers Inn HOSTEL $

(902-245-4573; www.digbyhostel.com; 168 Queen St; dm/r $30/65;) Saskia and Claude keep their solid four-bed dorms spotless and often spontaneously host barbecues or take the whole hostel out to see the sunset. The heritage house has plenty of communal areas, including a deck, and there's a lively, welcoming vibe. Internet access, a light breakfast and towels are included in the price. Cash only.

Hillside Landing B&B $$

(902-247-5781; www.hillsidelanding.com; 152 Queen St; d $150-180) Originally from Ontario, owners Henry and Linda have renovated this wonderful mansion with real love and care. The three rooms are spankingly stylish: one looks over the street, while Vye and Rutherford both have panoramic aspects over the harbor. Throw in posh jet showers, a magnificent veranda and a copious breakfast, and you have Digby's top B&B.

Shoreline Restaurant SEAFOOD $$

(902-245-6667; 88 Water St; mains $12-30; 11am-9pm) This is *the* spot in Digby for top-notch scallops – and clams, crab, lobster, haddock and pretty much every other fish you care to mention – along with salads and steaks. Grab a booth or head out to the waterfront deck and dig in. It's easy to miss, located at the back of a gift shop.

Sydney St PUB $$

(902-245-1066; www.sydneystreetpub.ca; 14 Sydney St; mains $14-26; noon-9pm Sun-Thu, to 11pm Fri & Sat) In a turreted, decked building just off the main drag, this lively pub is where everyone heads for a pint of some-

WORTH A TRIP

CAPE BLOMIDON

The **North Mountain**, which ends at dramatic Cape Blomidon, defines one edge of the Annapolis Valley. On the other side of the mountain are the fishing communities of the Bay of Fundy. The valley floor is crisscrossed with small highways lined with farms and orchards. It's a great place to get out your road map – or throw it away – and explore.

Around 3km from the village of **Port Williams**, the 1814 **Prescott House Museum** (902-542-3984; http://prescotthouse.novascotia.ca; 1633 Starr's Point Rd; adult/student $3.90/2.80; 10am-5pm Mon-Sat, 1-5pm Sun Jun-Sep) – considered one of the finest examples of Georgian architecture in Nova Scotia – is the former home of the horticulturalist who introduced many of the apple varieties grown in the Annapolis Valley.

In the quaint, historic town of **Canning**, stop for a fair-trade coffee (or an art class) at **ArtCan Gallery & Café** (902-582-7071; https://artcan.com; 9850 Main St; mains $10-14; 9am-5pm;) or head just out of town to sample wines at **Blomidon Estate Winery** (902-582-7565; www.blomidonwine.ca; 10318 Hwy 221; 10am-6pm Mon-Fri, to 7pm Sat, 11am-6pm Sun Jun-Sep).

North of Canning, along Hwy 358, stop at the well-signposted **Look-Off**. About 200m above the Annapolis Valley, it's the perfect spot to view the farmlands below and, if you're lucky, bald eagles above: from November to March they number in the hundreds, attracted by local chicken farms.

Hwy 358 ends in **Scots Bay**, where the dramatic 13km **Cape Split hiking trail** (https://parks.novascotia.ca/content/cape-split) leads to views of the Minas Basin and the Bay of Fundy. If you're not up for the hike, nearby **Blomidon Provincial Park** (902-582-7319; https://parks.novascotia.ca/content/blomidon; 3138 Pereau Rd; campsites $26.70-35.60; mid-May–mid-Oct) has a picnic area and plenty of easier walks.

If you need some lunch after all that fresh air, head to **Halls Harbour Lobster Pound** (902-679-5299; www.hallsharbourlobster.com; 1157 W Halls Harbour Rd, Centreville; mains $15-24; noon-7pm mid-May–Jun, Sep & Oct, 11:30am-9pm Jul & Aug) and gorge yourself on ocean delicacies straight from the source.

Round out your afternoon with a visit to **Kentville**, the county seat for the area, where you can rent a bike at Valley Stove & Cycle to admire the town's stately old homes, or check out the region's apple-farming history at **Blair House Museum** (Kentville Agricultural Centre; 902-678-1093; www.nsapples.com/museumb.htm; 32 Main St; 8:30am-4:30pm Mon-Fri Jun-Sep) FREE or other local history and art at **Kings County Museum** (902-678-6237; www.kingscountymuseum.ca; 37 Cornwallis Ave; 9am-4pm Mon-Sat Jun–mid-Aug, 9am-4pm Mon-Fri Apr, May & mid-Aug–mid-Dec) FREE.

thing cold and local. It also does decent grub, including (of course) pan-fried Digby scallops.

Getting There & Away

Digby is 32km southwest of Annapolis Royal, just off Hwy 1. From Yarmouth, it's 104km along Hwy 101 heading northeast.

Kings Transit (902-628-7310; www.kbus.ca; 1 way adult/child $4/2.25) operates a local bus service that runs as far north as Wolfville, via Annapolis Royal.

Bay Ferries (www.ferries.ca) operates a daily car-ferry service to Saint John, NB, on the *Fundy Rose* (adult/child from $39/23, 2¼ to 2¾ hours). Rates are about $10 more expensive in peak season, and much pricier if you don't pre-book. Vehicles cost $113 in low season and $119 in peak season.

Long Island & Brier Island

The long, narrow strip of land that resembles a giraffe's neck craning out to take a peek into the Bay of Fundy is known as **Digby Neck**. At the far western end of this appendage are two islands: Long Island and Brier Island, connected by ferry with the rest of the peninsula. The entire area is a haven for whale and seabird watchers.

Long Island is easier to get to and has a few more residents. The main towns are **Tiverton** at the northeastern end and **Freeport** at the southwestern end, connected via Hwy 217.

Brier Island is best known as the onetime home of sailor Joshua Slocum who, in 1895, became the first man to sail solo around the world. These days it's also famous as a whale-watching spot. The only town is **Westport**, a quaint fishing village and a good base for exploring the island's numerous excellent, if rugged and windy, hiking trails.

Sights & Activities

★Ocean Explorations Whale Cruises WHALE WATCHING
(☎902-839-2417; www.oceanexplorations.ca; Tiverton; adult/child $85/60; ⊙Jun-Oct) One of the best whale-watching tours in the province is led by biologist Tom Goodwin and has the adventurous approach of getting you down to whale-breaching level in a Zodiac. Shimmy into a coastguard-approved orange flotation suit and hold on tight! Times depend on weather, whale sightings and demand. It's based in a white-gabled building 100m from the ferry wharf.

Brier Island Whale & Seabird Cruises WHALE WATCHING
(☎902-839-2995; www.brierislandwhalewatch.com; 223 Water St, Westport; adult/child from $50/28; ⊙mid-May–Oct) You can book excellent whale-watching tours (2½ to five hours, depending on where the whales are) with this eco-conscious company. Tours are very popular, so it's worth booking as far ahead as possible.

Brier Island Lighthouse LIGHTHOUSE
(Western Light; 720 Lighthouse Rd) Originally built in 1809, this rugged outpost has seen many incarnations over the years. Its present form, a striking red-and-white-striped concrete tower standing 18.3m tall, was built in 1944 and has been automated since 1987.

Islands Historical Society Museum MUSEUM
(☎902-839-2034; www.islandshistoricalsociety.com; 243 Hwy 217, Freeport; by donation; ⊙9:30am-4:30pm Jun-Sep) Island life is explored at this little museum, which has lots of boat models, vintage fishing gear, sepia-tinted photos and a small exhibit on one-time Brier Island resident Joshua Slocum.

Sleeping

Brier Island Lodge LODGE $$
(☎902-839-2300; www.brierisland.com; 557 Water St, Westport; r $109-169; ⊙May-Oct;) Atop cliffs 1km east of Westport, Brier Island Lodge has 37 rooms, many with ocean views. Its pine-paneled **restaurant** (mains $10 to $30) has views on two sides, friendly service and fabulously fresh seafood. Boxed lunches are available.

Hooking by the Sea B&B $$
(☎902-308-2107; www.hookingbythesea.com; Church St, Westport; r $80-125;) Centered on Westport's first schoolhouse, this working farm also has cozy B&B rooms inside the traditional tin-roofed farmhouse. There's a barbecue and fire pit for guests' use, and you can try your hand at the old craft of rug hooking with the owners, should you so desire.

Getting There & Away

Long island is connected to Digby Neck by ferry from East Ferry to Tiverton, departing on the half-hour and returning on the hour. From Tiverton, it's another 18km along Hwy 217 to Freeport, where you can catch a second ferry over to Westport on Brier Island.

Both ferries run hourly (after midnight they're on an 'on-call' basis); each costs $7, payable only for travel toward Brier Island (the trip back to Digby is free). There's more information in the 'Important Details – Getting Here' section of www.brierisland.org.

Annapolis Royal

☎902 / POP 491

The epitome of a homey Nova Scotian town, with a lovely main street lined by cafes and B&Bs, Annapolis Royal also has historical significance: the area was the location of Canada's first permanent European settlement and was the capital of Nova Scotia until the founding of Halifax in 1749.

Named in honor of the English Queen Anne, the town's main sight is its dramatic 17th-century fort. Its ramparts are now covered in grass, but the fort once commanded control of the nearby Annapolis River.

Sights & Activities

★Fort Anne National Historic Site HISTORIC SITE
(☎902-532-2397; www.parkscanada.gc.ca/fortanne; Upper St George St; adult/child $3.90/free; ⊙9am-5:30pm daily mid-Jun–Aug, Tue-Sat only mid-May–mid-Jun & Sep–mid-Oct) The strategic importance of Annapolis Royal, particularly its access to the Annapolis River, led to decades of conflict, mostly centered on this impressive fort. The first redoubt was built by the French in the 1630s; the current structure was designed by French military architect Vauban in 1702. You can wander

the bulwarks and battlements (now mostly grassed over), and there's an interesting **museum** in the old officers' quarters with exhibits including a four-panel tapestry depicting 400 years of the fort's history.

Port Royal National Historic Site HISTORIC SITE
(☎902-532-2898; www.pc.gc.ca/en/lhn-nhs/ns/portroyal; 53 Historic Lane; adult/child $3.90/free; ⏲9am-5:30pm daily mid-Jun–Aug, Tue-Sat mid-May–mid-Jun & Sep–mid-Oct) Some 14km northwest of Annapolis Royal, Port Royal National Historic Site is the location of one of the earliest permanent European settlements in North America, established by French colonist and explorer Samuel de Champlain as a fur-trading outpost. A replica of the settlement, complete with wooden stockades and timber buildings, has been created here. Brought to life by guides in period costume, it gives a surprisingly convincing insight into early colonial times.

Annapolis Royal Historic Gardens GARDENS
(☎902-532-7018; www.historicgardens.com; 441 St George St; adult/child 12-18yr/child 6-11yr $14.50/6/3; ⏲9am-8pm Jul & Aug, to 5pm May, Jun, Sep & Oct) These gorgeous gardens cover a rambling 6.5 hectares and have various themed areas, such as an Acadian kitchen garden one might have seen in the late 1600s and an innovative modern one. Munch blueberries, ogle the vegetables and look for frogs. The **Secret Garden Café** offers lunches and German-style baked goods.

Delap's Cove Wilderness Trail HIKING
Over the North Mountain from Annapolis Royal, the Delap's Cove Wilderness Trail lets you get out on the Bay of Fundy shore. It consists of two loop trails connected by an old inland road that used to serve a Black Loyalist community. Today only foundation relics and apple trees remain in the woods. Each loop trail is a 9km round-trip.

★**Tour Annapolis Royal Graveyard Tour** WALKING
(☎902-532-3034; www.tourannapolisroyal.com; adult/child 13-18yr/under 12yr $10/5/3; ⏲Jun–mid-Oct) This company runs several local history walks. The best is where a guide in undertaker's garb leads a creepy tour of the Fort Anne graveyard. Everyone carries a lantern and winds through the headstones to discover the town's history through stories of those who've passed. Hour-long tours run nightly at 9:30pm.

There's also a regular historical tour of Annapolis Royal at 2pm every Monday and Wednesday, departing from the lighthouse. Proceeds go to the Annapolis Royal Historical Society.

Sleeping

Annapolis Royal has some glorious Victorian architecture, including several fine Queen Anne–style mansions that have been turned into heritage B&Bs.

Dunromin Campground CAMPGROUND $
(☎902-532-2808; www.dunromincampground.ca; 4618 Hwy 1, Granville Ferry; sites $33-47, cabins from $65; ⏲May-Oct; P📶🐾) This popular, offbeat campground has some secluded riverside sites as well as nifty options such as waterfront 'camping cabins' and a rustic caravan.

★**Queen Anne Inn** INN $$
(☎902-532-7850; www.queenanneinn.ns.ca; 494 Upper St George St; r $129-209; ⏲May-Oct; P❄📶) The most elegant property in Annapolis Royal, this eye-popping B&B looks as though it's blown straight off the *Gone with the Wind* set. Built in 1865 as a private home for local notables William Ritchie and Fanny Foster, it's a real museum piece: sweeping staircases, carriage clocks, four-poster beds, Tiffany-lamp replicas and a glorious central turret.

Bailey House B&B B&B $$
(☎902-532-1285; www.baileyhouse.ca; 150 Lower St George St; r $145-175; P📶) The only B&B on the waterfront, Bailey House is also the oldest inn (built around 1770) and one of the best in town. The friendly owners have managed to keep the vintage charm (anyone over 6ft might hit their head on the doorways!), while adding all the necessary modern comforts.

Eating & Drinking

★**Restaurant Compose** EUROPEAN $$
(☎902-532-1251; www.restaurantcompose.com; 235 St George St; mains lunch $11-18, dinner $16-34; ⏲11:30am-2pm & 5-8:30pm; 📶) This waterfront bistro is the place for dining with a view: there's a wonderful outlook over the Bay of Fundy. It majors in classy seafood, steaks and schnitzels, and there's a greenhouse-covered patio for sunny days.

Bistro East BISTRO $$
(☎902-532-7992; www.bistroeast.com; 274 St George St; mains $16-28; ⏲11am-10pm) Annapolis Royal's down-home downtown diner serves pretty much every kind of food you could fancy: quesadillas, chicken Alfredo, Cajun haddock and great pizza. It's in an attractive redbrick corner building on the main street.

German Bakery Sachsen Cafe GERMAN $$
(☎902-532-1990; www.germanbakery.ca; 358 St George St; sandwiches $9.25-10.95, mains $19.45-23.95; ⏲9am-7pm) The owners of this Teutonic-themed cafe hail from Saxony in Germany, and specialize in goodies such as schnitzel, sausages and *belegte brötchen* (sandwiches on Kaiser bread). Baking has been in the family for three generations.

Annapolis Brewing MICROBREWERY
(☎902-286-2080; www.annapolisbrewing.com; 302 St George St; ⏲noon-8pm Sun-Tue, to 10pm Wed & Thu, to 11pm Fri, 10am-11pm Sat) With a cannon-themed logo commemorating the historic 40th Regiment of Foot, this great new brewery and taproom has become a firm town favorite: all its beers have names relating to the town's history, from King George to Acadian Honey.

Sissiboo Coffee Roaster CAFE
(☎902-286-3010; www.sissiboocoffee.com; 262 St George St; ⏲7:30am-4pm Mon-Fri, 9am-4pm Sat & Sun) Great home-roasted coffee and delicious homemade biscotti keep this cafe busy throughout the day.

Shopping

Farmers & Traders Market MARKET
(www.annapolisroyalfarmersmarket.com; cnr St George & Church Sts; ⏲8am-1pm Sat May-Oct, plus 10am-2pm Wed Jul & Aug) Annapolis Royal's thriving community of artists and artisans offer their wares alongside local farm produce at this popular market. There's live entertainment most Saturday mornings.

Information

Tourist Information Centre (☎902-532-5769; www.annapolisroyal.com; 236 Prince Albert Rd; ⏲10am-5pm Jun–mid-Oct) Located at the tidal-power station in summer and at the town hall in winter.

Getting There & Away

Annapolis Royal is 108km southwest of Wolfville on Hwy 101. Continuing a further 32km on Hwy 101, you'll come to Digby, from where you can catch the ferry to Saint John, NB.

Kings Transit (www.kbus.ca) shuttles along the valley between Wolfville and Digby for a flat $3.50 fare.

Wolfville & Grand Pré

☎902 / POP 4195

Wolfville has a perfect blend of old-college-town culture, small-town homeyness and a culinary scene that has developed in concert with the surrounding wine industry. When added to the town's permanent residents, the students and faculty of the local Acadia University bump the population to more than 7000, injecting youthful vigor into this otherwise quiet district and making Wolfville one of the most livable and ethnically diverse towns in the province.

Essentially just down the road is the small bilingual community of Grand Pré, Wolfville's bucolic neighbor. In the 1750s, however, it was the site of one of the most tragic but compelling stories in eastern Can-

DON'T MISS

BRAVE THE BORE

Tiny Maitland is the place to brave the Shubenacadie River's legendary **tidal bore**, a mass of churning white water caused by the river's outflow meeting the blasting force of the incoming Fundy tide. Depending on the phase of the moon, the tidal bore can create wave heights of up to 3m, a wild washing machine of water that has to be experienced to be believed.

There are plenty of rafting companies in the area, including **Shubenacadie River Runners** (☎902-261-2770, 800-856-5061; http://riverrunnersns.com; 8681 Hwy 215; 2/3hr tour $65/85; ⏲Jun-Sep) and **Shubenacadie River Adventures** (☎902-261-2222; www.shubie.com; 10061 Hwy 215; tours from $85; ⏲Jun-Sep); check their websites for tour times and bore conditions. Outboard-powered Zodiacs plunge right through the white water for the two to three hours that the rapids exist. Prepare to get very, very wet indeed.

ada's history: the Acadian deportation. In 2012 the marshland and polder farmland of Grand Pré were given Unesco World Heritage status.

Beyond the two towns you'll find Acadian dikes, scenic drives and some of the best hiking along the Bay of Fundy.

Sights

★Grand Pré National Historic Site HISTORIC SITE
(☎902-542-3631; www.pc.gc.ca/en/lhn-nhs/ns/grandpre; 2205 Grand Pré Rd, Grand Pré; adult/child $7.80/free; ⏱9am-5pm May-Oct) This interpretive center explains the historical context for the deportation of the French-Acadian people from Acadian, Mi'kmaw and British perspectives, and traces the many routes Acadians took from, and back to, the Maritimes. Beside the center, a serene park contains gardens, an Acadian-style stone church, and a bust of American poet Henry Wadsworth Longfellow, who chronicled the Acadian saga in *Evangeline: A Tale of Acadie,* and a statue of his fictional Evangeline, now a romantic symbol of her people.

★Tangled Garden GARDENS
(☎902-542-9811; www.tangledgarden.ca; 11827 Hwy 1, Grand Pré; $8; ⏱10am-6pm May-Oct) A one-woman passion project, these glorious terraced gardens are a must-see for horticulturalists. Split into a series of 'rooms' by hedges of beech, box and yew, and stocked with a wonderful array of flowers, trees and herbs, this is a lovely place to wander. At the delightful **tearoom** (open 11am to 4:30pm Wednesday to Sunday) all the jams and chutneys are made with garden goodies.

The gift shop is probably the best-smelling shopping experience in Nova Scotia; there's a huge selection of herb jellies, vinaigrettes, cordials, liqueurs and chutneys to try and buy.

The gardens are 5.5km from Wolfville along Hwy 1.

Festivals & Events

Canadian Deep Roots Festival MUSIC
(www.deeprootsmusic.ca; ⏱late Sep) If you're in Wolfville in early fall, rock out to modern roots music at this annual festival.

Sleeping

★Olde Lantern Inn & Vineyard INN $$
(☎902-542-1389; www.oldlanterninn.com; 11575 Hwy 1, Grand Pré; r $137-157; 📶) Among the world-famous Grand Pré vines, this little vineyard has a pleasant guesthouse with four attractive, clutter-free rooms, all with whirlpool bath. Two are in the timber-framed main house, while another two are in a modern wing. There are wonderful views over the Bay of Fundy and the Grand Pré landscape.

★Roselawn Lodging MOTEL $$
(☎902-542-3420; www.roselawnlodging.ca; 32 Main St, Wolfville; d $95-185; P🚭@🏊) This fun 1960s-style complex features a variety of motel-like rooms and freshly updated, cute-as-a-button cottages with full kitchens. It makes a welcome alternative to Wolfville's sedate B&Bs. With a pool, a tennis court and spacious grounds, it's easy to make this place your home away from home.

Victoria's Historic Inn INN $$
(☎902-542-5744; www.victoriashistoricinn.com; 600 Main St, Wolfville; r $149-229) This elegant inn is directly opposite Acadia University. The luxuriously appointed rooms vary in style, but all are decorated with sumptuous taste: four-poster beds, period furnishings, antiques, fine linens. The Chase suite is hard to top for old-world grandeur. Ask for the main inn; the carriage-house rooms are underwhelming.

Blomidon Inn INN $$
(☎800-565-2291; www.blomidon.ns.ca; 195 Main St, Wolfville; d $149-169, ste $189-219; ❄@📶) Old-fashioned elegance is on offer in this imposing house set amid 2.5 hectares of lawned grounds. This isn't one for minimalists: expect dark wooden furniture, four-poster beds and ornate Victoriana. There's no elevator.

Eating

★Noodle Guy PASTA $
(☎902-697-3906; https://thenoodleguy.wordpress.com; 964 NS 358, Port Williams; small/large plates $7/11; ⏱10am-7pm Mon-Thu, to 8pm Fri & Sat, 11am-7pm Sun) Owner Ross Patterson perfected his art running a noodle stall, and diners now travel from far and wide to his laid-back pasta place in the village of Port Williams, 4km from Wolfville. Every day there's a ravioli, tagliatelle, spaghetti and conchiglie dish, plus a Japanese-style soba-noodle bowl. The pasta's 100% handmade and tastes like it.

LOCAL KNOWLEDGE

WOLFVILLE WINERIES

Most of Nova Scotia's best wineries and vineyards are found in the rolling hills and valleys around Wolfville and Grand Pré. If you want to dodge the problem of deciding on a designated driver, hop on the vintage double-decker **Magic Winery Bus** (902-542-4093; www.magicwinerybus.ca; hop-on/hop-off pass $50; Thu-Sun Jun-Oct).

Lightfoot & Wolfville (902-542-7774; www.lightfootandwolfville.com; 11143 Evangeline Trail; 10am-6pm Mon-Wed, to 9pm Thu-Sun mid-Jun–mid-Oct, shorter hours rest of year) This organic, biodynamic winery produces vintages from a bubbly rosé and blanc de blancs to a crisp chardonnay and an ice wine. It has a great bistro.

Domaine de Grand Pré (902-542-1753; www.grandprewines.com; 11611 Hwy 1, Grand Pré; tours $9; 10am-6pm Mon-Wed, to 7pm Thu-Sat, 11am-6pm Sun Jul & Aug, shorter hours rest of year) A great destination winery and one of the best known in the province, Grand Pré features a delicious spicy muscat and a nice sparkling Champlain Brut.

Luckett Vineyards (902-542-2600; www.luckettvineyards.com; 1293 Grand Pré Rd, Wolfville; tastings from $5; 10am-5pm May-Oct, tours 11am & 3pm) Palatial views over the vines and hillsides down to the Bay of Fundy cliffs are on offer here. Sample the red, white, fruit and dessert wines, and the particularly good ice wine, then stay for lunch on the patio.

Gaspereau Vineyards (902-542-1455; www.gaspereauwine.com; 2239 White Rock Rd, Gaspereau; 10am-6pm Jun-Sep, to 5pm rest of year) One of the province's best-known wineries, Gaspereau has award-winning ice wine and an elegant estate Riesling.

L'Acadie Vineyards (902-542-8463; www.lacadievineyards.ca; 310 Slayter Rd, Wolfville; 11am-5pm May–mid-Oct, by appointment other times) Overlooking the Gaspereau Valley, this geothermally powered winery grows certified-organic grapes to make traditional-method sparkling and dried-grape wines.

Naked Crepe CRÊPES **$**
(902-542-0653; www.thenakedcrepebistro.ca; 402 Main St, Wolfville; crepes $3-12; 9am-11pm) Who doesn't enjoy a flaky, wafer-thin crepe filled with delicious sweet or savory goodness? Hardly anyone, it seems, judging by this newcomer's rise to become one of Wolfville's best-loved eateries. Catering to the breakfast crowd *and* the late-nighters, Naked Crepe boasts a huge range of inventive fillings.

★**Troy** MEDITERRANEAN **$$**
(902-542-4425; www.troyrestaurant.ca; 12 Elm Ave, Wolfville; mains $18-32; 11am-9pm Mon-Sat, noon-9pm Sun;) Zingy meze dishes, kebabs, falafel and stuffed vine leaves bring the flavours of the Mediterranean and the Middle East to well-to-do Wolfville. Order a selection of items and eat tapas style. There are loads of veggie options.

★**Le Caveau** EUROPEAN **$$$**
(902-542-1753; https://grandprewines.com/pages/le-caveau; 11611 Hwy 1, Grand Pré; mains lunch $14-21, dinner $28-38; 11:30am-2pm & 5-9pm May-Oct) Overseen by head chef Jason Lynch, this upscale bistro at the Domaine de Grand Pré winery has become a destination in its own right. The ethos is rich, indulgent dining with a taste for game and seafood; as much produce as possible comes from surrounding farms. The beautiful patio is paved with fieldstones and shaded with grapevines.

Drinking & Nightlife

Annapolis Cider Company BAR
(902-697-2707; www.drinkannapolis.ca; 388 Main St, Wolfville; 10am-7pm) Red-and-white-striped awnings and a swanky tasting room provide an impressive introduction to this craft cidery, which makes all its brews from local apples, with a particular penchant for heirloom and heritage varieties. Occasionally it produces a 'Something Different' brew: a cherry-and-cilantro cider has featured in the past.

Library Pub & Wine Tavern PUB
(902-542-4315; www.thelibrarypub.ca; 472 Main St, Wolfville; 11am-midnight Mon-Sat, 11:30am-8pm Sun) This friendly pub, with a wood-lined interior and plenty of wines by the glass, makes a great place to sink a pint or three. Downstairs has more of a wine-bar feel; upstairs it's more like a pub.

Entertainment

Acadia Cinema's Al Whittle Theatre THEATER
(☎902-542-3344; www.acadiacinema.coop; 450 Main St, Wolfville) Operated by the volunteer-run Acadia Cinema Co-op, this fabulous historic building, a Wolfville cultural icon, functions as a multipurpose cinema, theater and performance space. Check the website for regular event listings and screening times and to learn a little about the theater's history.

Information

Wolfville Visitor Information Centre (☎902-542-7000; www.wolfville.ca; 11 Willow Ave, Wolfville; ⊙10am-6pm May-Oct) A well-run center with lots of info on local vineyards and the wider valley.

Getting There & Away

Wolfville is linked to Halifax by Hwy 101; the journey takes an hour in good traffic.

Maritime Bus (www.maritimebus.com) services from Halifax stop at Acadia University in front of Wheelock Hall off Highland Ave (Wolfville; $20.25, 1½ hours, two daily).

Kings Transit (www.kingstransit.ns.ca) buses run between Cornwallis (southwest of Annapolis Royal) and Wolfville, stopping at 209 Main St. The fare is a flat $3.50.

CENTRAL NOVA SCOTIA

Hiking, rafting and rock-hounding are the activities of choice around this pleasant and often overlooked region. For those traveling overland from the rest of Canada, the town of Amherst, geographic center of the Maritimes and a crossroads between New Brunswick, Prince Edward Island and Nova Scotia, will be your first taste of the province if you swing off the Trans-Canada Hwy (Hwy 104 at this point).

From Amherst you can follow the 'Glooscap Trail' – named for the figure in Mi'kmaw legend who created the unique geography of the Bay of Fundy – as far as Wolfville in the Annapolis Valley, or take the road less traveled and hug the shoreline, visiting the World Heritage–listed Joggins Fossil Cliffs, the delightful hamlet of Advocate Harbour and the village of Parrsboro.

This is the part of Nova Scotia famed for the legendary Fundy tides and tidal-bore rafting.

Information

Amherst Visitor Information Centre (VIC; ☎902-667-8429; ⊙9am-7pm Jul & Aug, to 5pm mid-May–Jun, Sep & Oct, to 4:30pm Nov-May) This massive visitor center is at exit 1 off Hwy 104, just as you cross the border from New Brunswick.

Getting There & Away

Amherst is the gateway to Nova Scotia for visitors arriving overland, although the town is largely bypassed by the Trans-Canada Hwy (Hwy 104).

Maritime Bus (www.maritimebus.com) connects Amherst with Moncton, NB ($14, one hour, three daily) and Halifax ($41.75, three hours, three daily), and Truro with Halifax ($25.50, 1¾ hours, five daily).

Parrsboro

☎902 / POP 1205

Rock hounds come from far and wide to forage on the shores of Parrsboro, the largest of the settlements along the Minas Basin. The town's Fundy Geological Museum has wonderful exhibits and good programs that take you to the beach areas known as Nova Scotia's 'Jurassic Park.'

Sights

★**Fundy Geological Museum** MUSEUM
(☎902-254-3814; http://fundygeological.novascotia.ca; 162 Two Islands Rd; adult/child $6/4; ⊙10am-5pm mid-May–mid-Oct) If you want to understand the geological history of the Bay

WORTH A TRIP

SHUBENACADIE PROVINCIAL WILDLIFE PARK

Shubenacadie, or simply 'Shube', 35km south of Truro off Hwy 2, is best known for this wildlife park (☎902-758-2040; https://wildlifepark.novascotia.ca; 149 Creighton Rd; adult/child $4.75/2; ⊙9am-6:30pm mid-May–mid-Oct, to 3pm Sat & Sun mid-Oct–mid-May). It's the place to commune with Nova Scotia's native fauna: moose, porcupines, timber wolves, lynx, bobcats, cougars, black bears and bald eagles. Contained within large enclosures, the animals were mostly born in captivity, but a few have been rescued from private ownership as 'pets' and thus cannot be released into the wild.

of Fundy this excellent museum should be your first port of call. It has a wide range of interactive exhibits, but inevitably the highlights are the fossils and dinosaur skeletons unearthed around the Fundy coastline – perhaps the most famous are the tiny dinosaur footprints found in 1984 by Eldon George. You can also peer into a working lab where new specimens are being processed.

Fun beach tours ($15 to $25) allow you to try out your newly acquired knowledge in the wild.

Age of Sail Museum MUSEUM
(☎902-348-2030; www.ageofsailmuseum.ca; 8334 Hwy 209, Port Greville; $4; ⏰9:30am-5pm daily Jul & Aug, Thu-Mon Apr-Jun, Sep & Oct) This museum on the banks of the tidal Greville River, about 20km west of Parrsboro, memorializes the age of sail and the area's shipbuilding past. A restored church and a working blacksmith shop are also on-site.

Sleeping

★**Gillespie House Inn** B&B $$
(☎902-254-3196; www.gillespiehouseinn.com; 358 Main St; d $129-149; Ⓟ📶) The pick of Parrsboro's B&Bs, this lovingly restored sea captain's mansion has heritage-themed rooms stocked with burnished sleigh beds, clawfoot tubs, antique settees and wingback chairs. There's a fabulous staircase and veranda, a yoga studio and a blueberry field where you can pick your own berries in summer. A real stunner.

Maple Inn B&B $$
(☎902-254-3735; www.mapleinn.ca; 2358 Western Ave; d $99-169; ⏰May-Oct; Ⓟ🚭❄📶) There's a room to suit every taste and budget at this huge heritage house, from a basic buttercup-colored twin to two grand bay-windowed suites (there's also a Freemasons-themed room and one that served as a delivery ward when the house was still a hospital). Standards are very high throughout, and there's a daily special for breakfast.

Sunshine Inn MOTEL $$
(☎877-706-6835; www.thesunshineinn.net; 4487 Hwy 2; r $117-122, cottages $139-149; ⏰May-Nov; Ⓟ🚭📶) Practical, no-frills motel rooms are what to expect from the Sunshine, out on the Glooscap Trail 3km north of Parrsboro. In addition to the motel units there are self-contained cottages on the grassy grounds (some have views of the motel's own lake).

Eating & Drinking

Black Rock Bistro BISTRO $$
(☎902-728-3006; www.blackrockbistro.ca; 151 Main St; mains $14-20; ⏰7am-8pm; Ⓟ) New owners have brought fresh flavors to this downtown bistro, pretty much the pick of Parrsboro's eating places. Steak-frites, handmade burgers, slow-roasted ribs, and the odd pasta and risotto dish will make sure you don't leave hungry, and there are on-tap brews from Two Islands Brewing down the road.

DON'T MISS

JOGGINS FOSSIL CLIFFS

Buried deep in the cliffs along the edge of the Bay of Fundy is one of the most complete fossil records anywhere in Canada. Laid down during the Carboniferous period – sometimes known as the 'Coal Age', when much of the surrounding landscape was covered in swampy forest – the life-forms preserved in these ancient cliffs predate the dinosaurs by about 100 million years.

Start at the impressive **Joggins Fossil Cliffs Visitor Centre** (www.jogginsfossilcliffs.net; 100 Main St, Joggins; tours from $10.50; ⏰9:30am-5:30pm Jun-Aug, 10am-4pm late Apr–May, Sep & Oct), which explains the geological context through audiovisual displays and exhibits before you take a guided tour down to the cliffs. Hidden in the rocks here lies an entire ecosystem, including fossilized lycopsid trees, root systems known as stigmaria and ancient shrimp-like creatures called pygocephalus. Tours range in duration and difficulty from an easy half-hour trip to two- and four-hour expeditions that visit more remote sections of the cliffs.

The best time to visit is at low tide, when all of the beaches can be accessed; at other times you'll be cut off from some of the more interesting sites by high water. Note that tours leave on an irregular schedule that depends on the tides. It's a good idea to reserve ahead.

Harbour View Restaurant CANADIAN $$
(☎902-254-3507; 476 Pier Rd; mains $12-24; ⏱7am-8pm) If it's fish-and-chips, homemade chowder, delicious pies and supersize club sandwiches you want, this homey diner down by the water will definitely fit the bill. Zero pretension, checked tablecloths, bottomless coffee and a warm welcome.

Two Islands Brewing MICROBREWERY
(☎902-728-2221; www.twoislandsbeer.ca; 169 Main St; ⏱10am-8pm Sun-Wed, to 11pm Thu-Sat) This newly opened microbrewery has four core ales: a blonde, an Irish red, a porter and an American pale ale. It also runs a small cafe next door.

Entertainment & Shopping

Ship's Company Theatre THEATER
(☎902-254-3000; www.shipscompanytheatre.com; 18 Lower Main St; tickets from $15; ⏱Jul-Sep) Surely the most unusual theater space in Nova Scotia, this place is built around the MV *Kipawo,* the last of the Minas Basin ferries. There's a summer season of plays, plus kids' shows, comedy, readings and music gigs.

Tysons' Fine Minerals GIFTS & SOUVENIRS
(☎902-728-8364; www.tysonsfineminerals.com; 114 Lamb's Hill Rd; ⏱10am-4pm) This place is more like a museum than a shop, displaying some of the most sparkling, massive and colorful minerals you're likely to see anywhere.

Getting There & Away

Parrsboro is closer to New Brunswick's largest city (Moncton, 120km away) than it is to Nova Scotia's (Halifax, 180km). There are no scheduled bus services to the area.

Advocate Harbour

Advocate Harbour is a breathtaking little cove with a 5km-long beach, piled high with driftwood, that changes dramatically with the tides. Behind the beach, salt marshes – reclaimed with dikes by the Acadians – are now replete with birds. The town's best-known sight is the dramatic Cape d'Or lighthouse, and nearby is the hikers' paradise of Cape Chignecto.

Otherwise, most visitors pass through here on the scenic route to Amherst or on the way to the famous Unesco World Heritage–listed fossil cliffs in Joggins, 32km south of Amherst.

Sights & Activities

★**Cape d'Or Lighthouse** LIGHTHOUSE
(☎902-670-0534; www.capedor.ca; 1 Cape d'Or Rd, Diligent River) This spectacular cape of sheer cliffs was misnamed Cape d'Or (Cape of Gold) by Samuel de Champlain in 1604 – the glittering veins he saw were actually copper. Mining from 1897 to 1905 removed the sparkle. The present lighthouse was added in 1922. Access is via a partly unsealed road off Hwy 209 to Cape d'Or; you must then hike down a dirt trail. If you can't bear to leave, the former keeper's residence is now a seasonal **guesthouse and restaurant** (r $135, houses $490; ⏱May-Oct; 📶🐾).

★**Cape Chignecto Provincial Park** STATE PARK
(☎902-392-2085; http://parks.novascotia.ca/content/cape-chignecto; Red Rocks Entrance, W Advocate Rd; campsites $26.70-35.60; ⏱mid-May–mid-Oct) This isolated wilderness on the Bay of Fundy offers some of the best coastal hiking in Nova Scotia. The 55km **coastal loop** usually takes three days to complete, encompassing dramatic coastline, isolated bays and lofty sea cliffs, but there are plenty of options for easier hikes. The tides are dangerous, so stick to the trail. All hikers must register at the visitor center, where you can discuss itineraries and make backcountry-campground reservations.

NovaShores Sea Kayaking KAYAKING
(☎866-638-4118; www.novashores.com; 3838 Hwy 209, Advocate Harbour; day tours $129) See the Bay of Fundy from a different perspective – on a sea-kayaking trip with this excellent outfit. There are regular day trips to see the Three Sisters sea stacks and the lovely beach at Horseshoe Cove, plus two- and three-day camping tours. You're pretty much guaranteed to see seals and seabirds; if you're really fortunate you'll see bears and whales.

Sleeping & Eating

★**Wild Caraway Restaurant & Cafe** CANADIAN $$
(☎902-392-2889; www.wildcaraway.com; 3721 Hwy 209; mains lunch $8-16, dinner $22-38; ⏱11am-3:30pm & 5-7:30pm Thu-Mon mid-May–Oct; 📶) Local products and seasonal cooking underpin the menu at this superb coastal cafe, in a little house with a view of the driftwood-strewn beach of Advocate Harbour. The food is as good as you'll find in this part of Nova Scotia: crumbed fishcakes, mackerel

bento bowls, pan-seared scallops, and cheeses from That Dutchman's Cheese Farm.

There are also two upstairs **rooms** ($100), with wi-fi, breakfast and shared bathrooms.

Getting There & Away

Advocate Harbour is 46km west of Parrsboro on Hwy 209 and 90km south of Amherst.

SUNRISE TRAIL

It's claimed that the Northumberland Strait between Nova Scotia's north shore and Prince Edward Island has some of the warmest waters north of the US Carolinas, with sea temperatures averaging slightly over 20°C in summer. The Sunrise Trail is a prime area for beach-hopping, cycling and exploring friendly countryside towns.

The Sunrise Trail runs 227km from Amherst in the west to Antigonish in the east. You'll need your own wheels to get around.

Tatamagouche

☎902 / POP 2037

The Malagash Peninsula, which juts into protected Tatamagouche Bay, is a low-key, bucolic loop for a drive or bike ride. Taste local wines, go beachcombing or visit some interesting museums found just inland. Tatamagouche is the largest town on the Northumberland Shore coast west of Pictou and makes a great base for exploring the region.

Sights

Jost Winery WINERY

(☎902-257-2636; www.jostwine.ca; 48 Vintage Lane, Malagash; tours $5; ⏲wine store 10am-5pm Mar-Dec, tours noon & 3pm Mon-Fri, 11am Sat Jun-Sep) Among Nova Scotia's best-known wineries, Jost offers informative guided tours including two tastings, and you can pick up vintages in the shop. It produces well-regarded whites, rosés and reds (including the rather brilliantly named Great Big Friggin' Red), as well as unusual skin-fermented wines, ice wines and maple wines.

Signs direct you about 5km off Hwy 6; it's about 17km from Tatamagouche.

Balmoral Grist Mill HISTORIC SITE

(☎902-657-3016; http://balmoralgristmill.novascotia.ca; 660 Matheson Brook Rd, Balmoral Mills; adult/child $3.90/2.80; ⏲10am-5pm Jun-Oct) In a gorgeous setting on the stream that once provided it with power, the Balmoral Grist Mill still grinds wheat in summer. From Tatamagouche, turn south on Hwy 311 (at the eastern edge of town) and then east on Hwy 256. It's about a 14km drive south of Tatamagouche.

Sutherland Steam Mill HISTORIC SITE

(☎902-657-3365; http://sutherlandsteammill.novascotia.ca; 3169 Denmark Station Rd, Denmark; adult/child $3.90/2.80; ⏲10am-5pm Wed-Sat Jun-Oct) During the 19th century wood was the wonder material that underpinned nearly every aspect of construction. Built in 1894, this steam-powered sawmill produced an incredible range of products, including furniture, windows, shingles, decorations known as 'Gingerbread Trim', and even bathtubs. It's 15km east of Tatamagouche.

To get here from Tatamagouche, follow Hwy 6 for about 10km until the junction with Hwy 326, then drive south for 5km.

Wallace Bay National Wildlife Area BIRD SANCTUARY

(☎800-668-6767; www.ec.gc.ca) About 30km northwest of Tatamagouche, this vast sanctuary protects 585 hectares, including tidal and freshwater wetlands. A 4km loop trail winds through the reserve; it's great for bird-watching, especially for waterfowl and, if you're lucky, bald eagles.

Sleeping

★ **Train Station Inn** INN $$

(☎902-657-3222; www.tatatrainstation.com; 21 Station Rd; carriages $129.50-189.50; ⏲May-Nov; 📶🐾) Top prize for Nova Scotia's quirkiest accommodations has to go to this train-spotters' paradise, where several railway cabooses have been converted into cozy accommodations, decorated with period posters, toy trains and locomotive books. There's also a railway dining car for dinner.

The dreamer behind the inn, James LeFresne, grew up across the tracks and saved the train station from demolition when he was just 18.

Eating & Drinking

Sugar Moon Farm CANADIAN $$

(☎902-657-3348; www.sugarmoon.ca; 221 Alex MacDonald Rd, Earltown; mains $12-30; ⏲9am-4pm Jul & Aug, reduced hours Sep-Jun) The food – simple, delicious pancakes and locally made sausages served with maple syrup – is the highlight of this working maple farm and woodlot. To reach the farm from Tatamagouche, take Hwy 311 south for 25km, then follow the signs on Alex MacDonald Rd.

★**Tatamagouche Brewing Co** MICROBREWERY
(☎902-657-4000; www.tatabrew.com; 235 Main St; ⏲10am-6pm Sun-Thu, to 9pm Fri, to 8pm Sat) Tata's beloved brewery now has a Nova Scotia–wide reputation, and for good reason: its beers are world-class. The lagers and session ales in particular are worth trying, and look out for 'weird' beers such as a chocolatey breakfast porter and a wild-yeast plum beer.

Pictou

☎902 / POP 3186

Many people stop in Pictou for a side trip or as a stopover via the ferry from Prince Edward Island, but it's also an enjoyable base for exploring Northumberland Strait. Water St, the main street, is lined with interesting shops and beautiful old stone buildings. Unfortunately, the views are blighted by a giant, smoking pulp mill on the opposite side of the estuary; the mill has long been slated for closure due to environmental concerns.

The town is sometimes known as the Birthplace of New Scotland because the first Scottish immigrants to Nova Scotia landed here in 1773.

Sights

Hector SHIP
(☎902-485-4371; www.shiphector.ca; 33 Caladh Ave; adult/child $8/3; ⏲10am-4pm Jun-Oct) A replica of the ship *Hector,* which carried the first 200 Highland Scots to Nova Scotia, is tied up for viewing on Pictou's waterfront. You can descend into the bunk-crammed hull to get a sense of how challenging the crossing would have been. The historical context is explored in the heritage center nearby.

Northumberland Fisheries Museum MUSEUM
(☎902-485-8925; www.northumberlandfisheriesmuseum.ca; 21 Caladh Ave; adult/child $8/3; ⏲10am-6pm Mon-Sat) In the old train station, this museum explores the area's fishing heritage. Exhibits include a replica of a fishermen's bunkhouse and the spiffy *Silver Bullet,* an early-1930s lobster boat. You can also visit the nearby lobster hatchery, where baby lobsters are reared before being released into the wild, and a small lighthouse research center just along the front.

Festivals & Events

Pictou Landing First Nation Powwow CULTURAL
(☎902-752-4912; www.plfn.ca; ⏲Jun) Across Pictou Harbour (a 25-minute drive through New Glasgow), this annual powwow on the first weekend in June features sunrise ceremonies, drumming and craft demonstrations. Camping and food are available on-site; it's strictly alcohol and drug free.

Lobster Carnival FOOD & DRINK
(☎902-485-5150; www.pictoulobstercarnival.ca; ⏲Jul) Started in 1934 as the Carnival of the Fisherfolk, this four-day event now offers free entertainment, boat races and lots of chances to feast on lobster.

Sleeping & Eating

Caribou-Munroes Island Provincial Park CAMPGROUND $
(☎902-485-6134; https://parks.novascotia.ca/content/caribou-munroes-island; 2119 Three Brooks Rd; campsites $26.70-35.60) Less than 10km from Pictou, this park is set on a gorgeous beach. Sites 1 to 22 abut the day-use area and are less private; sites 78 to 95 are gravel and suited for RVs. The rest are wooded and private.

★**Pictou Lodge** RESORT $$
(☎902-485-4322; www.pictoulodge.com; 172 Lodge Rd; r $199-239, cottages $215-445;) In business since the 1920s, this complex feels rather quaint, with cedar-log cabins, paddleboats and family-friendly 60-hectare grounds (including a private beach). Cabins range in size from one to three bedrooms, or you can book lodge-style rooms; most have been attractively renovated. The restaurant (mains $25 to $30) is the best place for dinner in town.

Customs House Inn INN $$
(☎902-485-4546; www.customshouseinn.ca; 38 Depot St; d $95-125;) Probably the grandest building in Pictou, this imposing brick building looms over the waterfront and offers eight spacious, rather old-fashioned rooms with hardwood floors and antique furniture. Rarely full, it can feel a little spooky if you're the only guest.

Willow House Inn B&B $$
(☎902-485-5740; www.willowhouseinn.com; 11 Willow St; r $105-140; P) A blue-slatted house dating from around 1840, Willow

House has pleasant rooms, all named after trees and accessed via an unusual double flight of staircases. Owners Brenda and George are really friendly, and serve an extremely good breakfast.

Information

Eastern and Northumberland Shores Visitor Information Centre (902-485-8540; Pictou Rotary; 9am-6:30pm Jun-Thanksgiving) is a large info center situated northwest of town to meet travelers arriving on the Prince Edward Island ferry.

Town of Pictou (www.townofpictou.ca) has links to sights and festivals.

Getting There & Away

Pictou is familiar to most Nova Scotians as the departure point for ferries to Prince Edward Island. Bay Ferries (p53) operates the service from May to December, with around five sailings a day in spring and autumn, up to nine per day in summer.

The terminal is a few kilometers north of Pictou.

Antigonish

902 / POP 4364

The pleasant student town of Antigonish is best known for its well-regarded seat of learning, St Francis Xavier University, and for its Celtic roots: since 1861 the town has hosted its own Highland Games (www.antigonishhighlandgames.ca; Jul), and the event continues to attract thousands of visitors.

A 4km hiking and cycling trail to the nature reserve at Antigonish Landing begins just across the train tracks from the Antigonish Heritage Museum, then 400m down Adam St. The landing's estuary is a good bird-watching area where you might see eagles, ducks and ospreys.

Another popular destination for beach walks and swimming is Crystal Cliffs Beach, about 15km northeast of Antigonish.

Sleeping & Eating

Antigonish Victorian Inn B&B $$
(902-863-1103; www.antigonishvictorianinn.ca; 149 Main St; d $140-210;) As its name suggests, this turreted B&B is solidly Victorian throughout, in terms of both architecture and decor. The rooms are all different in style; it's worth bumping up to a Queen for space. There are also apartments on the ground floor. Breakfast is very generous.

Antigonish Evergreen Inn MOTEL $$
(902-863-0830; www.antigonishevergreeninn.ca; 295 Hawthorne St; d $159-179;) A really homey motel about five minutes' drive from Main St, with side-by-side rooms offering big beds, work desks, armchairs, and views over the lawned grounds. Rates include breakfast in the little dining room in the office, and there are often fresh muffins and cakes.

Gabrieau's Bistro CANADIAN $$
(902-863-1925; www.gabrieaus.com; 350 Main St; mains lunch $8-16, dinner $18-30; 10am-9pm Tue-Fri, 4-9pm Sat & Mon;) Fine dining inspired by classic French and Italian cuisine is chef Mark Garibeau's stock-in-trade, and his restaurant is far and away Antigonish's top table.

Brownstone Restaurant CAFE $$
(902-735-3225; www.brownstonecafe.ca; 244 Main St; mains $8-20; 11am-9pm Mon-Sat) This attractive little cafe on Main St has some surprises inside, including Italianate murals, brick-effect wallpaper and a bizarre copper-effect stucco ceiling. It's the town's any-time-of-day choice for something to eat, with generous breakfasts; big salads and flatbread pizzas for lunch; and stir-fries, steaks and pasta for dinner.

Antigonish Townhouse PUB FOOD $$
(902-863-2248; www.antigonishtownhouse.com; 76 College St; mains $15-25; 4pm-midnight Tue-Sat, 10am-11pm Sun, 4-11pm Mon) Swing by this popular town pub for a pint of something local or a plate of chicken-confit poutine or moules frites. It's a favorite hangout for students and locals, especially at Sunday brunch.

Information

Antigonish Visitor Information Centre (902-863-4921; www.visitantigonish.ca; 145 Church St; 8am-8pm Mon-Sat, 1-6pm Sun Jun-Sep;) Brochures, free local calls and free internet access. Located in the Antigonish Mall parking lot at the junction of Hwys 104 and 7.

Getting There & Away

Antigonish is at the northern end of Hwy 7, 62km from Sherbrooke. New Glasgow is 57km to the west on the Trans-Canada Hwy (Hwy 104).

WORTH A TRIP

CAPE GEORGE

The eastern arm of the Sunrise Trail, from New Glasgow to Antigonish, has some gorgeous diversions – it's perfect for a half-day excursion when the weather's fine. Be sure to pack some snacks and remember your beach towel.

Perhaps start your day with a hands-on visit to the **Museum of Industry** (902-755-5425; http://museumofindustry.novascotia.ca; 147 N Foord St, Stellarton; adult/child $8.90/3.90; 9am-5pm Mon-Sat, 10am-5pm Sun Jul-Oct, shorter hours rest of year;), which has lots to interest the kids, including a working water tower, a machine shop and assembly line, loads of vintage machinery and vehicles, a model railway, and Samson, one of the oldest locomotives in Canada, then head along the coast to pretty **Arisaig Provincial Park** (902-863-4513; https://parks.novascotia.ca/content/arisaig; 5704 Hwy 245), where you can take a dip or search for fossils.

Continue to **Malignant Cove**; from here the 55km coastal stretch of Hwy 245 has been compared in beauty to parts of the Cabot Trail, although it's less mountainous and more accessible.

After a short drive east you'll reach **Cape George Point Lighthouse** (www.parl.ns.ca/lighthouse), the handsome jewel in the day's crown, where you can look out over the calm waters of St Georges Bay. The present light (the third) was built in 1961, but there's been a beacon of some sort here since 1861. If it's nearing lunchtime, head just around the cape to the fish-and-chip truck near the **Ballantyne's Cove Tuna Interpretive Centre** (902-863-8162; 57 Ballantyne's Cove Wharf Rd; 10am-5:30pm Jul-Sep) FREE, then enjoy a dip or a stroll at **Crystal Cliffs Beach** (Crystal Cliffs Farm Rd).

Just 15 minutes south, there's plenty to see and do in Antigonish, or keep to the outdoorsy theme and round out the day with a roar, high above the trees at **Anchors Above Zipline Adventure** (902-922-3265; www.anchorsabovezipline.ca; 464 McGrath Mountain Rd, French River; 1 ride $30; 10am-5pm), where you can lose your stomach on two hair-raising zip lines, one 335m long, the other 275m long. The first line is slower thanks to its shallower pitch, but the second drops about 10 stories and reaches pretty hairy speeds. It's about 40km from Antigonish – watch for the signs on the Trans-Canada Hwy (Hwy 104).

Maritime Bus (www.maritimebus.com) has various services from Antigonish. Most stop at the Bloomfield Centre at St Francis Xavier University. Useful destinations include the following:

- Halifax ($41.75, 3½ hours, two daily)
- Sydney ($46, 3¼ hours, one daily)
- Truro ($25.50, 1½ hours, two daily)

CAPE BRETON ISLAND

Rugged, wooded and genuinely wild, the northwestern region of Nova Scotia almost feels like a province apart. Famous for its circuitous coastal road, the 297km-long Cabot Trail, which dips and dives round the edge of Cape Breton Highlands National Park, it's a dream destination for road-trippers, and figures pretty high on everyone's must-see list – so expect traffic jams aplenty in summer. The best time to visit is in fall, when the area's roads are quieter and the forests light up with color.

Beyond the borders of the national park, Cape Breton has a rich Celtic and Acadian heritage, so you'll almost certainly hear live music wafting out from many pubs and bars, especially during the **Celtic Colours** (www.celtic-colours.com; Oct) festival. Also well worth visiting is the historic fort at Louisbourg, arguably the most evocative fort in all of Nova Scotia.

Getting There & Away

Cape Breton Island is linked to mainland Nova Scotia by the Canso Causeway. The Trans-Canada Hwy (Hwy 105) runs straight up the middle of the island to Sydney, which has air and ferry links to other Canadian centers.

The Cabot Trail forms a massive loop around the island's northwestern corner.

Maritime Bus (p56) operates limited services from Halifax into the region, but by far the best way to explore the dramatic scenery at your own pace is by renting a car. From Halifax, Hwy 102 meets the Trans-Canada Hwy heading north through the middle of Nova Scotia to the Canso Causeway. For a more scenic route, consider taking some smaller roads up the Eastern Shore (p110).

Ceilidh Trail

The snaking road along the western coast of Cape Breton Island from Port Hastings (Hwy 19) has been dubbed the Ceilidh Trail thanks to its history of Scottish settlement and a regular program of ceilidhs (parties with music and dancing), Celtic gigs and square dances in summer – not to mention a renowned whisky distillery.

The small town of **Mabou** makes the most logical base. From here, the trail continues to the former coal-mining town of **Inverness**, with its sandy beach and 1km-long boardwalk, and then twists north to **Margaree Forks**, where you can pick up the Cabot Trail.

Sights & Activities

★Glenora Inn & Distillery DISTILLERY

(902-258-2662; www.glenoradistillery.com; 13727 Hwy 19, Glenville; guided tours incl tasting $7; tours hourly 9am-5pm Jun-Oct) The first distillery in North America (and the only one in Canada) to make single-malt whisky, this renowned producer claims to take its secrets straight from the old country. Guided tours explore the process and include an all-important tasting.

The distillery also has its own **pub** (mains $12 to $17) and a fine-dining warehouse **restaurant** (mains $32 to $47). From June to October you can catch a ceilidh at lunch or dinner. There are also attractive **rooms** ($189 to $319), either in the original inn or in a separate lodge, as well as a selection of self-contained timber **chalets** (from $359).

Celtic Music Interpretive Centre MUSEUM

(902-787-2708; www.celticmusiccentre.com; 5473 Hwy 19, Judique; exhibit room from $8; 10am-5pm Mon-Fri Jun-Aug) This well-run center is one of the region's best places to experience Celtic music. The main exhibit room explores the origins and styles of the local musical culture, and there are often fiddling sessions and step-dancing workshops during summer, as well as 1½-hour walking tours with one of the center's instrument-playing guides. The restaurant hosts regular lunchtime ceilidhs (parties with music and dancing).

Cape Mabou Highlands HIKING

(www.capemabouhiking.com) Within the Cape Mabou Highlands an extensive network of hiking trails extends between Mabou and Inverness toward the coast west of Hwy 19. The trails are sometimes closed when the fire danger is high; otherwise, hikes ranging from 4km to 12km start from three trailheads.

The most-used trailhead is at Mabou Mines, about 12km from Mabou; the other two are at Cape Mabou and Sight Point Rd, near Inverness.

When the trails are open an excellent trail guide ($5) is available at the grocery store across the road on Hwy 19. Maps are also posted at the trailheads.

Sleeping & Eating

Duncreigan Country Inn INN $$

(902-945-2207; www.duncreigan.ca; 11411 Hwy 19, Mabou; r $165-210;) A pleasant inn set among oak trees, the Duncreigan feels rather dated, but its rooms offer plenty of space, and some have terraces and water views. There's a licensed **dining room** (mains $12 to $25) that serves breakfast to guests or dinner by reservation.

★Red Shoe Pub PUB FOOD $$

(902-945-2996; www.redshoepub.com; 11533 Hwy 19, Mabou; mains $13-25; noon-11pm Sun-Wed, to 2am Thu-Sat) The Red Shoe is *the* place to catch a bit of Celtic music as you mosey down the Ceilidh Trail. The homey, ramshackle pub hosts at least one gig seven nights a week, from country crooners to folky fiddlers, and you can tuck into a menu of hot wings, fish-and-chips and homemade gingerbread as you listen.

The pub is run by the renowned Rankin Sisters, who hail from Mabou and whose Celtic-tinged music has scooped them numerous national awards; they often join in with the show.

Getting There & Away

The Ceilidh Trail begins near the Port Hastings visitor center and runs north through the towns of Mabou and Inverness for 107km until it links up with the Cabot Trail in Margaree Forks.

Cabot Trail

This is the big one: the incomparable Cabot Trail is a looping, diving, dipping roller coaster of a road that snakes for 297km around the northern tip of Cape Breton, with epic views of rolling seas, mountain passes and thick forests, and – if you're lucky – perhaps the sight of a moose, an eagle or even a whale along the way.

From Englishtown to St Ann's Bay, artists' workshops dot the southeastern flank of the trail like Easter eggs: there are pottery, leather, glass and pewter workers, plus painters and sculptors, and you can also discover living remnants of Mi'kmaw and Acadian culture.

This is not a road to rush. Many people race through in a day, but the real pleasure of the trail is taking your time, stopping at the roadside lookouts, hiking the hidden trails and really getting the most out of the scenery.

Cape Breton Highlands National Park

The better known of Nova Scotia's two national parks, **Cape Breton Highlands** (☎902-224-2306; www.pc.gc.ca/en/pn-np/ns/cbreton; adult/child day pass $7.80/free, summer season pass adult/family $39.20/78.50) offers visitors some of Maritime Canada's most dramatic scenery. Most people visit it as they follow the Cabot Trail, a third of which runs along the park edge. Established in 1936 and encompassing 20% of Cape Breton's landmass, it's the fancy feather in Nova Scotia's island cap, with mountain scenery that early visitors thought was powerfully reminiscent of the Scottish highlands: deep glens, high heaths, dark forests and snowy mountains aplenty.

Entry is free if you already hold a **Parks Canada Discovery Pass** (adult/family $67.70/136.40). If you're visiting outside the July–October summer season, you can purchase an 'early bird' park pass for $19.60/49 per adult/family.

There are two entrances, one at Chéticamp and one at Ingonish Beach; park permits can be purchased at either one. A one-day pass remains valid until noon the next day. It's a drive of about 104km between the two entrances, but due to the winding, twisting road and seasonal traffic, you should allow a minimum of 2½ hours to cover the distance, plus extra for stops.

Activities

Hiking

Aside from the stunning scenery, the other reason many people come to Cape Breton Highlands is for the hiking. Plenty of trails crisscross the park, the most famous of which is the **Skyline Trail**, an 8.2km loop that runs along a ridge to an impressive cliff with amazing views of the Cape Breton coast. The trailhead is near the top of French Mountain, about 22km north of Chéticamp and 20km south of Pleasant Bay; it's very well known, so don't expect to be alone in summer.

Two other notable routes are the **Coastal Trail**, an 11km round-trip along the eastern coast of the park, just south of Neil's Harbour. On the west coast, **Fishing Cove Trail** descends 330m over 8km to the mouth of rugged Fishing Cove River; a steeper, shorter hike of 2.8km runs from a second trailhead about 5km north of the first. Round-trip distances are double; the park's only backcountry campsite is located at the bottom if you feel like overnighting.

A good alternative to the popular Skyline Trail is **Broad Cove Mountain**, a 1.6km hike with 168m of ascent to the top of the eponymous mountain: the view of the coast, Middle Head and Cape Smokey is superb, and you may see eagles soaring over the summit.

The Cabot Trail website (www.cabottrail.com) has loads more suggestions for hikes. Parks Canada runs a program of guided hikes and interpretive events during summer; contact the park offices for details.

Wheelchair-accessible trails are indicated on the free park map available at either entrance.

Cycling

Don't make this your inaugural trip: the riding is tough, there are no shoulders in many sections and you must be comfortable sharing the incredible scenery with RVs. Alternatively, you can mountain bike on four inland trails in the park; only **Branch Pond Lookoff Trail** offers ocean views.

DRIVING THE CABOT TRAIL

The best way to enjoy the trail, with the freedom of starting and stopping as you choose, is by self-driving. Most folks rent a car in Sydney or Halifax and drive across, although it's worth noting that car-rental agencies charge high one-way fees for returning the vehicle in a different town, so it's a good idea to plot your route in a loop.

The next decision is which way round you're going to follow the trail. The majority of drivers drive from west to east, starting in Chéticamp and ending in Ingonish, but there's a good case for doing it in the opposite direction: there's less traffic and you get to drive coast-side the whole way, making for better views and easier stops. It also means that, if you do the trail in a day, you'll hit the west coast for sunset: cue photo ops aplenty.

Note that there are very few gas stations along the way: make sure you fill up in Chéticamp or Ingonish before you set out.

Accommodations along the way are limited. If you intend to drive the trail in one or two days, base yourself at Baddeck or Ingonish on its eastern flank, or Chéticamp or Pleasant Bay in the west. In the peak times of July and August, book well ahead.

The official Cabot Trail website (www.cabottrail.travel) has loads of information on accommodations, activities and stops along the way, as well as useful planning tools.

Sleeping

Cape Breton Highlands National Park Campgrounds CAMPGROUND
(☎1-877-737-3783; https://reservation.pc.gc.ca; unserviced tent sites $17.60-27.40, serviced RV sites $29.40-38.30, oTENTiks $100; ⊙mid-May–late Oct) The park operates six campgrounds; from west to east, they are: Chéticamp, Corney Brook, MacIntosh Brook, Big Intervale, Broad Cove and Ingonish Beach. You can reserve online or at park visitor centers (essential in summer). The largest campgrounds are at Chéticamp and Broad Cove, with 122 and 202 sites, respectively; smaller campgrounds away from the main entrances are usually quieter.

Chéticamp, Ingonish and Broad Cove all have ready-pitched cabin-tents called oTENTiks, which are very handy if you don't have gear. Discounts are available for stays of seven nights or more.

There's also one backcountry campground at Fishing Cove; with just eight sites, booking is mandatory here.

Information

Chéticamp Information Centre (☎902-224-2306; 16646 Cabot Trail; ⊙8:30am-7pm Jun-Sep, 9am-5pm Oct-May) Has displays and a relief map of the park, plus a bookstore, Le Nique. Plans are afoot to redevelop the center.

Ingonish Beach Information Centre (☎902-285-2535; 37677 Cabot Trail; ⊙8am-8pm May-Oct) At the park's eastern edge, with displays, maps and friendly bilingual staff. A short trail nearby leads to a lookout over Freshwater Lake.

Chéticamp

☎902 / POP 3039

Chéticamp is not only the western gateway to Cape Breton Highlands National Park; more importantly, it's Nova Scotia's most vibrant and thriving Acadian community, owing much of its cultural preservation to its geographical isolation – the road didn't make it this far until 1949. Strung out along the coastal road, it's a busy little summer town with a working fishing fleet, a couple of interesting museums and a few craft shops (Chéticamp is famed for its hooked rugs), but outside the warmer months it's extremely quiet.

Sights & Activities

Les Trois Pignons MUSEUM
(☎902-224-2642; www.lestroispignons.com; 15584 Cabot Trail; adult/child $5/4; ⊙8:30am-6pm Jul & Aug, to 5pm mid-May–Jun & Sep–mid-Oct) This excellent museum explains how rug hooking went from home-based activity to international business. Artifacts illustrate early life and artisanship in Chéticamp. Almost everything – from bottles to rugs – was collected by one eccentric local resident, Marguerite Gallant. Among the amazing array of hooked

rugs, look out for portraits of Jacqueline Kennedy Onassis, the Queen, and Christ attended by angels.

Le Centre de la Mi-Carême MUSEUM
(902-224-1016; www.micareme.ca; 51 Old Cabot Trail Rd, Grand Étang; adult/child $5/free; 10am-5pm Jun-Aug, to 4pm Mon-Fri Sep & Oct) Mi-Carême, celebrated in the middle of Lent, is Chéticamp's answer to Mardi Gras. Locals wear masks and disguises, and visit houses in a bid to get people to guess who they are. This museum covers the history of the celebration and displays traditional masks.

Sleeping

Albert's Motel MOTEL $
(902-224-2077; www.albertsmotelcheticamp.com; 15086 Cabot Trail; d $75-120; May-Oct; P) Colorful patchwork quilts really liven up the decor at this simple but homey motel, where the rooms also have mini-fridges, microwaves and large flat-screen TVs, plus there's a communal deck overlooking the harbor.

★ **Maison Fiset House** B&B $$
(902-224-1794; www.maisonfisethouse.com; 15050 Cabot Trail; d $159-179, ste $169-229; P) A little luxury in Chéticamp is found in this grand old 1895 home, once owned by the town's first doctor. All the rooms are nicely appointed in a heritage style; if you're in a suite, lounge in your hot tub and enjoy the ocean views.

Unusually for Chéticamp, it's open year-round.

Chéticamp Outback Inn MOTEL $$
(902-224-8025; cheticampoutbackinn@bellaliant.com; 909 Chéticamp Back Rd; r $155-225; P) Inland from Chéticamp, this back-road country motel looks standard, but the rooms are a bit of a surprise: they have wood-effect walls, enormous TVs, comfy beds with scatter cushions, and a work desk with coffee machine. Each room has a small deck area for mountain contemplation.

There's no breakfast, but sometimes the owner supplies pastries from La Boulangerie Aucoin.

Cornerstone Motel MOTEL $$
(902-224-3232; www.cornerstonemotel.com; 16537 Cabot Trail; d $99-169; May-Oct; P) Last stop before the national-park gates, this endearingly retro motel is about 7km from town. It offers pretty much what you'd expect in terms of accommodations; the rural location, communal fire pit and gray-clapboard exterior are nice touches.

Eating & Drinking

La Boulangerie Aucoin BAKERY $
(902-224-3220; www.aucoinbakery.com; 14 Lapointe Rd; items $3.50-9; 7am-5pm Mon-Sat;) If you've never tried an Acadian meat pie, this fine little bakery, founded in 1959, will happily oblige. It also has fresh home-style breads (including baguettes), cinnamon rolls, molasses cookies, scones and sandwiches for the trail.

Harbour Restaurant SEAFOOD $$
(902-224-1144; www.baywindsuites.com; 15299 Cabot Trail; mains $13-39; 11am-9pm) A reliable stalwart in central Chéticamp, with windows looking onto the strait and a slightly alarming slope in the floors at low tide. Seafood's the specialty: chow down on a snow-crab or lobster dinner, or go for the 'best of both' if you can't decide.

Le Gabriel DINER $$
(902-224-3685; www.legabriel.com; 15424 Cabot Trail; mains $15-24; 11am-10pm) This big pub-diner is buzzing on the weekend: locals come for the generous plates of fish, steak and seafood (all served with potato or rice, vegetables and a baguette), and to play free billiards. It's not fancy, but it'll definitely fill your belly.

Go for the gargantuan Captain's Platter if you're absurdly hungry.

Information

Tourist Information Centre (902-224-2642; www.lestroispignons.com/visitor-information; 15584 Cabot Trail; 8:30am-6pm Jul & Aug, to 5pm mid-May–Jun & Sep–mid-Oct) In the same building as Les Trois Pignons museum (p102).

Getting There & Away

Chéticamp is 104km from Ingonish, 56km northeast of Inverness on Hwy 219, and 88km from Baddeck via the Cabot Trail. There's no public transport.

Pleasant Bay

Situated 43km north of Chéticamp, aptly named Pleasant Bay is cradled in a sheltered cove framed by brooding, forested mountains. It makes a useful break as you drive the Cabot Trail, especially at sunset, and it's also a good place for whale-watching.

Somewhat unexpectedly, there's a **Tibetan monastery** (☎902-224-2752; www.gampoabbey.org; 1533 Pleasant Bay Rd; ⊙tours 1:30-3:30pm Mon-Fri Jun-Sep) 8km north of town.

Sights & Activities

Whale Interpretive Centre MUSEUM
(☎902-224-1411; 104 Harbour Rd; adult/child $5/4; ⊙9am-5pm Jun-Oct) Get some background on cetaceans at this modest visitor center, which has illustrations of 16 whale species, and a life-size model of a pilot whale suspended from the ceiling.

Captain Mark's Whale & Seal Cruise WHALE WATCHING
(☎902-224-1316; www.whaleandsealcruise.com; adult/child $60/40; ⊙May-Sep) The best of the whale-watching operators in Pleasant Bay, Captain Mark and his team pilot fast Zodiacs into the bay in search of cetacean visitors; as always, sightings aren't guaranteed, so it's worth asking about recent activity before you book.

Tours leave from the wharf next to the Whale Interpretive Centre.

Sleeping & Eating

Pleasant Bay has a few motels strung along the main street, but Chéticamp and Ingonish have better options.

Rusty Anchor DINER $$
(☎902-224-1313; 23197 Cabot Trail; mains $10-28; ⊙11am-9pm) Pit stops are few and far between on the Cabot Trail, which makes this waterfront diner a boon if you've run out of picnic snacks. The food's mostly good; pan-fried fish, scallops and lobster rolls are all on offer.

You can't miss it – look out for the fiberglass fisherman in the yellow sou'wester brandishing a lobster.

Getting There & Away

Pleasant Bay is 43km north of Chéticamp and 61km west of Ingonish.

Ingonish

☎902 / POP 1250

At the eastern entrance to Cape Breton Highlands National Park are **Ingonish** and **Ingonish Beach**, small settlements sheltering in a large bay under the headland of **Cape Smokey**, where there's a community-run ski area in winter. The region is a sensible base for beginning or ending a jaunt along the Cabot Trail, but there's not a huge amount to see or do, so one night is likely to be as much as you'll want to spend here.

As you drive north over Cape Smokey you'll first come to Ingonish Beach, set above a large inland lagoon. Ingonish itself is 10km further north; you'll pass into the national park as you drive there.

Sleeping

Driftwood Lodge INN $
(☎902-285-2558; www.driftwoodlodge.ca; 36139 Cabot Trail, Ingonish; d/ste from $55/100; ⊙May-Nov; P) It's hard to find wallet-friendly accommodations along the Cabot Trail, but this rustic beside-the-beach inn definitely fits the bill; it's been going since 1973, and is still run by the same family. The main building has pine-paneled rooms and apartments, and there's an old housekeeper's cottage in the grounds: a little dated, maybe, but quite comfortable.

Seascape Coastal Retreat CABIN $$
(☎902-285-3003; www.seascapecoastalretreat.com; 36086 Cabot Trail, Ingonish; cottages $139-279; P) Seascape's pleasant cottages are set in pretty landscaped gardens only a five-minute drive from central Ingonish. Each cottage has a separate sitting room and bedroom, a private bathroom with whirlpool tub, a deck with barbecue and a cracking ocean view. Free kayaks and mountain bikes are available for guests' use.

Lantern Hill & Hollow COTTAGE $$$
(☎902-285-2010; www.lanternhillandhollow.ca; 36845 Cabot Trail, Ingonish; r $250-260, cottages $225-335; ⊙May–mid-Oct; P) For a proper spoil, head to this fancy cottage complex that sits in a dreamy beachfront location and offers extremely stylish rooms, decorated in soothing grays and blues, with mod-

ern furniture and top-notch fixtures. There's a choice of one- or two-bed cottages, plus enormous suites in the main house. If you fancy a twilight cookout on the beach, they'll supply you with firewood.

Eating

Dancing Moose Cafe CAFE $
(☎902-929-2523; www.thedancingmoosecafe.com; 42691 Cabot Trail, Birch Plain; pancakes $5-10; ⏰7:30am-4pm Jun-Oct) Stop in here for Dutch *pannenkoeken* (pancakes), either savory (loaded with green onions and Gouda cheese) or sweet (whipped cream, honey, fruit, nuts – the works). There are some fun souvenirs to browse, and it also has a cottage and a few camping cabins for rent.

Clucking Hen Deli & Bakery CAFE $
(☎902-929-2501; 45073 Cabot Trail; mains $7-18; ⏰7am-7pm May-Oct) This fun cafe and bakery makes an ideal stop at the start or end of your Cabot Trail drive. The decor centers on chickens and hen-based puns, while the menu serves a solid choice of sandwiches, soups and salads, along with made-on-the-day cakes.

★**Main Street Restaurant & Bakery** CANADIAN $$
(☎902-285-2225; 37764 Cabot Trail, Ingonish Beach; mains $10-24; ⏰8am-8pm) Come breakfast, brunch, lunch or dinner, Ingonish's friendly diner is the place most people head for when they're feeling hungry. Chunky BLT sandwiches, homemade waffles, big plates of chicken, pasta and seafood, and yummy cakes – what's not to like?

Getting There & Away

Ingonish and Ingonish Beach are at the eastern entrance to Cape Breton Highlands National Park. From here it's 93km to Baddeck via the Cabot Trail and 134km to Sydney via the Cabot Trail and the Trans-Canada Hwy (Hwy 105).

The Far North

Heading north of Ingonish, the Cabot Trail (p99) skirts the coastline as far as the little fishing settlement of **Neil's Harbour**, where you can take a scenic detour away from the main trail and travel through small coves, including picturesque **White Point**, where fishing boats outnumber houses. From here you can follow winding White Point Rd before rejoining the main trail near South Harbour. Shortly afterward, another turnoff leads to the village of **Dingwall**.

If you're determined to reach the top of Nova Scotia you'll need to turn off at **Cape North** and follow Bay St Lawrence Rd along a beautiful valley; you'll eventually reach the eponymous fishing village after about 18km. From here the road gets rougher and the scenery wilder as you head toward unedifyingly named **Meat Cove**; the last 7km of road is bone-jarring gravel.

Sights & Activities

★**Captain Cox's Whale Watch** WHALE WATCHING
(☎902-383-2981; www.whalewatching-novascotia.com; 578 Meat Cove Rd, St Margaret Village; adult/child $45/25; ⏰mid-Jun–Oct) One of the first three whale-watching operations in Nova Scotia, Captain Cox's tours leave from the fishing harbor at Bay St Lawrence and have a very good rate of whale sightings (around 96%). Trips run at 10:30am, 1:30pm and 4:30pm in July and August, with afternoon-only sailings in late June and late September.

Pilot whales, minke whales and dolphins are all regularly seen; fin whales are much rarer, but if anyone can find them, Captain Cox can.

★**White Point** HIKING
This little-known 2km trail follows a single-track path along the coast out to a headland with fine views of several offshore islands. The area was once a notorious ships' graveyard, and locals claim that many sailors were buried here in unmarked graves. On a sunny evening it's one of the best short walks anywhere along the Cabot Trail.

Cabots Landing Provincial Park STATE PARK
(☎902-662-3030; https://parks.novascotia.ca/content/cabots-landing) Stop in this wonderful provincial park, 10km north of the Cabot Trail en route to Bay St Lawrence, to enjoy Aspy Bay and its spectacular beach.

The area is supposedly the site of the historic 1497 landing of John Cabot, the first European to set foot in North America; a cairn marks the spot, although some historians still dispute the claim that Cabot actually landed here.

Grassy Point HIKING

You can't beat the views over the coast from Grassy Point, accessible via a small trail (about 40 minutes round-trip) that starts just past the Meat Cove Campground. Sit for a while at the point to look for whales and nesting bald eagles.

Dixon's Zodiac Safari WHALE WATCHING

(☎1-855-259-4122; www.dixonszodiacseafari.com; 36 Lighthouse Rd, Neil's Harbour; adult/child $49/25; ⊙May-Sep) Four daily whale-watching tours leave from little Neil's Harbour; your vessel is the 25ft *Highland Hurricane,* a fast Zodiac designed for maximum maneuverability.

Cabot Trail Adventures CYCLING

(☎902-383-2552; www.cabottrailoutdooradventures.com; 299 Shore Rd, Dingwall; bike rental per day/week $45/225, kayak tours $65; ⊙9am-5pm Jun-Oct) Sea-kayaking tours, guided hikes and bike rental are all offered by this outdoors company near the Cape North turnoff.

Sleeping & Eating

Meat Cove Campground CAMPGROUND $

(☎902-383-2379; www.meatcovecampground.ca; 2475 Meat Cove Rd, Capstick; tent sites/cabins from $35/80; ⊙Jun-Nov; P 📶) This is the place if you enjoy camping in the middle of nowhere. The campground sits on a grassy bluff with incredible ocean views: gorgeous on a sunny day, spooky as anything when the fog rolls in. There are basic cabins, plus ample space for camping, with a shared toilet and shower block. You'll need your own gear and bedding.

The **Chowder Hut** (mains $8 to $15) serves simple meals, and there's also a small store.

Blue Bayou Resort TENTED CAMP $$

(☎647-995-1633; www.bluebayouresort.com; 25 Old Road Loop, South Harbour; domes $180-200, tipis $120; P) Sleep under the stars in a geodesic dome or traditional tipi at this wooded campground. Domes are set on a wooden base, feature proper beds and private bathrooms, and have a skylight to see the stars; tipis are set around a central fire pit, but you'll be in sleeping bags and will have to use the communal toilet block.

Chowder House SEAFOOD $$

(☎902-336-2463; 90 Lighthouse Rd, Neil's Harbour; chowder $7-12, mains $14-24; ⊙noon-6:45pm Tue-Sun May-Oct) This establishment, out beyond the lighthouse at Neil's Harbour, is famous for its chowder, but it also serves great-value suppers of snow crab, lobster, mussels and more. There are plenty of dining locals, who like to chat with folks from far away while they splatter themselves with seafood juice.

Getting There & Away

Neil's Harbour and White Point are 16km and 23km from Ingonish, respectively, via the Cabot Trail, New Haven Rd and White Point Rd.

Meat Cove is at the northernmost tip of Nova Scotia, 60km from Ingonish. The road is steep, winding, and in poor condition in parts, with the last 7km rough gravel. It's not advised to come here in a compact rental car; a 4WD or SUV is highly recommended.

Baddeck

☎902 / POP 769

The small resort town of Baddeck sits beside mighty Bras d'Or Lake, the largest lake in Nova Scotia – at 1099 sq km, it's more like an inland sea. The town makes a useful staging post before you head up to the highlands. Its main claim to fame is its link with inventor Alexander Graham Bell: he built himself a grand country estate across the water from Baddeck in the late 19th century, and the town now has an interesting museum (and National Historic Site) dedicated to the great man.

Sights & Activities

★**Alexander Graham Bell National Historic Site** MUSEUM

(☎902-295-2069; www.pc.gc.ca/en/lhn-nhs/ns/grahambell; 559 Chebucto St; adult/child $7.80/free; ⊙9am-5pm May-Oct) Telecommunications pioneer and inventor Alexander Graham Bell fell in love with Bras d'Or during a family holiday – apparently the hilly scenery reminded him of his Scottish homeland. In the late 1880s he built a lavish summer estate, **Beinn Bhreagh** (Gaelic for beautiful mountain), on a peninsula across the bay from Baddeck. This fascinating museum at the edge of town houses full-scale replicas of Bell's groundbreaking Silver Dart aircraft, along with electrical devices, telegraphs, telephones, kites and medical inventions.

Though he's understandably best known as the inventor of the telephone, Bell explored many areas, particularly the idea of human flight. He conducted his first experiments at Beinn Bhreagh, culminating in the development of the Silver Dart airplane, which took off from the ice of Baddeck Bay on 23 February, 1909, just over five years after the Wright Brothers' first flights.

Amoeba CRUISE
(☎902-295-7780; www.amoebasailingtours.com; 2hr tour adult/child $30/15; ⏲Jun-Oct) Climb aboard this handsome schooner for tours around Bras d'Or Lake. Trips include fine views of Alexander Graham Bell's estate Beinn Bhreagh, the site of the first flight of the Silver Dart, and the chance to spot local wildlife, including bald eagles and seals.

Donelda's Puffin Boat Tours BIRD-WATCHING
(☎902-929-2563; www.puffinboattours.com; 1099 Hwy 312, Englishtown; adult/child $52/22) Boats head to a bird sanctuary off Cape Dauphin where puffin sightings are guaranteed. You may well see gray seals lounging on the rocks, too. There's a discount of $4/3 per adult/child if you pay in cash.

Highland Village Museum MUSEUM
(☎902-725-2272; http://highlandvillage.novascotia.ca; 4119 Hwy 223, Iona; adult/child $11/5; ⏲10am-5pm Jun-Oct) Perched on a hilltop overlooking the Bras d'Or Lake, this living-history museum explores the region's Gaelic heritage. Costumed Scots demonstrate the day-to-day activities of early settlers' lives, from storytelling to weaving, cooking, music and daily chores. There are Celtic-inspired workshops from spring through fall.

Sleeping

★**Silver Dart Lodge** LODGE $$
(☎902-295-2340; www.silverdartlodge.com; 257 Shore Rd; r/chalets from $165/195; P ⊜ ❄ ☜ ☒) Cracking views over Bras d'Or Lake are the main selling point here. There's a wide choice of accommodations, with rooms divided between the original main house, three motel-style lodges and several cute clapboard chalets, and you can eat with a lake view in **McCurdy's Dining Room** (mains $15 to $26).

★**Broadwater Inn & Cottages** INN $$
(☎902-295-1101; www.broadwaterinn.com; 975 Bay Rd; r & cottages $129-169; ⏲May-Nov; P ☜ 🐾) Situated 2km northeast of Baddeck, this 1830s home belonged to JD McCurdy, who worked with Alexander Graham Bell on early aircraft designs. The rooms in the main house are full of character; the best is the A-frame library room, but they're all spacious and most have a lake view. For even more space, ask for one of the self-contained cottages.

Telegraph House HOTEL $$
(☎902-295-1100; www.baddeckhotel.com; 479 Chebucto St; r $110-155; P ☜) This hotel-motel has Alexander Graham Bell connections: opened in 1861, it served as the town's telegraph office for many years, and the inventor himself stayed in room 1. There are 18 rooms in the main lodge – some old-fashioned and frilly, others modern – supplemented by 13 bland rooms in the motel alongside.

Dunlop Inn B&B $$
(☎902-295-1100; www.dunlopinn.com; 552 Chebucto St; d $175-270; P ❄ ☜) A great B&B choice in downtown Baddeck, this modern gabled house has fabulous lake frontage – most of the tasteful rooms have a water outlook. There's a self-serve breakfast in the swish modern kitchen.

Eating & Drinking

Highwheeler Cafe CAFE $
(☎902-295-3006; www.visitbaddeck.com/highwheeler-cafe; 486 Chebucto St; sandwiches $9; ⏲7am-6pm Tue-Sun May-Oct; ☜) Everyone's choice for lunch, this Baddeck cafe ticks all the boxes: grilled sandwiches, delicious quesadillas, homemade soups, and delicious muffins and blueberry-raspberry scones, plus a pleasant deck. You can phone ahead and ask for a packed lunch if you're hiking or hitting the Cabot Trail.

Herring Choker Deli DELI $
(☎902-295-2275; www.herringchokerdeli.com; 1958 Hwy 105; items $6-17; ⏲9am-5pm Tue-Sun May-Oct; ☜) Swing by this roadside diner-deli, 12km southwest of Baddeck, for a pit stop. It serves up soups, sandwiches, wraps and salads, plus breads, pastries and cakes cooked on-site.

★**Baddeck Lobster Suppers** SEAFOOD $$$
(☎902-925-3307; www.baddecklobstersuppers.ca; 17 Ross St; mains $24-36; ⏲4-9pm Jun-Oct) In Baddeck's former legion hall, this local institution offers your choice of lobster, salmon, snow crab or strip loin with all-you-can-eat mussels, chowder and dessert for an all-in $50. It's no-frills dining: you're encouraged to just get stuck in.

Big Spruce Brewing MICROBREWERY
(☎902-295-2537; www.bigspruce.ca; 64 Yankee Line Rd, Nyanza; ⊙noon-7pm) Pop into this farmyard brewery, about 14km southwest of Baddeck, to grab a growler of unfiltered, unpasteurized, 'unbelievably good', locally brewed beer.

Baddeck Gathering Ceilidhs LIVE MUSIC
(☎902-295-0971; www.baddeckgathering.com; St Michael's Parish Hall, 8 Old Margaree Rd; adult/child from $10/5; ⊙7:30pm Jul & Aug) Proper community ceilidhs (parties with music and dancing) with plenty of fiddling, twirling and Celtic atmosphere are held in Baddeck's parish hall, opposite the tourist-information center. Tickets are only available on the night, and it's cash only.

Information

Baddeck Tourist Information Centre (☎902-295-1911; www.visitbaddeck.com; 454 Chebucto St; ⊙10am-5pm Jun-Oct) A small visitor center offering useful info on the Bras d'Or area and the Cabot Trail.

Getting There & Away

Baddeck is located on the Trans-Canada Hwy (Hwy 105), 78km southwest of Sydney.

Maritime Bus (www.maritimebus.com) services from Sydney to Halifax stop in town once or sometimes twice a day.

Sydney & North Sydney

☎902

The second-biggest settlement in Nova Scotia and the only real city on Cape Breton Island, Sydney is the embattled core of the island's collapsed industrial belt. The steel mill and coal mines – once the region's largest employers – have all closed down, and as a result the city feels a bit empty, but there are some lovely older houses, especially in the North End residential areas where most of the B&Bs are found. Overall, the city is well serviced and you get more bang for your buck making this your base for exploring Louisbourg and the Cabot Trail than you would in more scenic areas.

Industrial North Sydney is a small and friendly town, although there's not much to see or do. The main reason you'll be passing through is if you're heading to the Cabot Trail from Sydney, or traveling to or from Newfoundland on the ferry.

Sights

★**Cape Breton Miners' Museum** MUSEUM
(☎902-849-4522; www.minersmuseum.com; 42 Birkley St, Glace Bay; museum adult/child $6.95/5.65, tour & mine visit $16/8; ⊙10am-6pm mid-May–Oct) Coal mining played a central role in the development of this part of Nova Scotia, so you shouldn't pass up the chance to venture into a disused mine in the company of a former miner. It's fascinating, a little spooky, and not for the claustrophobic. The museum has interesting exhibits on this aspect of Cape Breton's past. It's at Glace Bay, 22km east of Sydney.

Membertou Heritage Park CULTURAL CENTER
(☎902-567-5333; www.membertouheritagepark.com; 35 Su'n Awti, Membertou; adult/child $8/5; ⊙9am-4:30pm) This First Nations reserve has an interesting visitor center where you can learn about Mi'kmaw culture, and workshops (from $25) where you can try your hand at making a traditional tribal basket, drum or dream catcher. There's also a good restaurant, Kiju's, where you can sample Mi'kmaw dishes, and a shop selling indigenous crafts and petroglyph engravings.

Old Sydney Society Ghost Tour TOURS
(☎902-539-1572; www.oldsydneysociety.org; 173 Charlotte St; $13; ⊙7pm Thu Jul & Aug) In the town's old Bank of Montreal building, this local-history society offers a weekly ghost tour in July and August, leaving from **St Patrick's Church Museum** (☎902-562-8237; 87 Esplanade; $2; ⊙9am-5pm Mon-Sat Jun-Oct).

It maintains a few heritage museums around town, including **Cossit House** (☎902-539-7973; http://cossithouse.novascotia.ca; 75 Charlotte St; adult/concession $2/free; ⊙9am-4pm Tue-Sat), **Jost Heritage House** (☎902-539-0366; 54 Charlotte St; $3; ⊙9am-5pm Mon-Sat Jun-Aug, 10am-4pm Sep-Oct) and St Patrick's.

Sleeping

★**Colby House** B&B **$$**
(☎902-539-4095; www.colbyhousebb.com; 10 Park St; r $100-130; 📶) This 1904 house makes a grand spot to stay in Sydney, with three handsome rooms tricked out in turn-of-the-century style. It's been beautifully maintained, from the central staircase to the elegant veranda, and the tree-lined location is surprisingly peaceful. A real delight.

WORTH A TRIP

GOAT ISLAND

Lying 40km southwest of Sydney, in Bras d'Or Lake, Goat Island is home to one of Nova Scotia's largest Mi'kmaq communities. **Eskasoni Cultural Journeys** (902-322-2279; www.eskasoniculturaljourneys.ca; 1 Goat Island Trail; adult/child $40/20; 9am-5pm Mon-Fri May-Oct) offer enthralling tours that provide an introduction to Mi'kmaw culture and allow you to participate in a smudging ceremony (a smoke bath used for purification). This is one of the best cultural experiences in Nova Scotia; book ahead.

You'll also have the opportunity to weave baskets, try traditional dances, learn about hunting and cooking techniques, and hear tribal stories. Along the way you'll get to sample some bush tea and luskinigan: a bannock-style bread (sometimes known as 'four-cent bread' because it's so cheap to make) cooked over an open fire. The 2.4km trail winds along the lake and offers lovely views.

Cambridge Suites Sydney HOTEL $$
(902-562-6500; www.cambridgesuitessydney.com; 380 Esplanade; d $160-200; P ❄ wi-fi) This smart hotel in a hard-to-beat downtown location has comfortable, nicely renovated rooms in a variety of configurations, many with water views (although some still smell a bit from pre-nonsmoking days). Rates include a decent serve-yourself breakfast spread and free wi-fi. The **Trio Restaurant** (mains $22 to $35) is high quality, if a little overpriced. Parking costs $7 a night.

A Boat to Sea B&B $$
(902-794-8326; www.aboattosea.com; 61 Queen St, North Sydney; r $120-140; P nonsmoking wi-fi pets) Right on the water and surrounded by beautiful gardens, this grand home is accented by stained glass and has a quirky antique collection. Relax on the waterfront patio and enjoy hearty breakfasts. There are only three rooms, so book ahead in high season, when there's a two-night minimum stay. There's a dock if you're arriving by yacht.

Eating

Governors Pub & Eatery PUB FOOD $$
(902-562-7646; www.governorseatery.com; 233 Esplanade; mains $9-22; 11am-11pm) Governors is easily the most popular place in Sydney. Stop by to mingle with the after-work crowd for drinks, dine on gourmet pub grub or just sink a beer on the 1st-floor deck. There are regular live-music jams.

Flavor on the Water BISTRO $$
(902-567-1043; www.cbflavor.com/flavor; 60 Esplanade; mains $11-28; 11am-9pm; family-friendly) Sydney's swankiest restaurant, this high-ceilinged bistro in a large waterfront complex serves upscale plates of salmon, blackened cod, strip loin and halibut. Go for the monster sharing platters ($99), loaded with East Coast goodies, if you're feeling flush. There's a second branch downtown.

Flavor Downtown BISTRO $$
(902-562-6611; www.cbflavor.com; 16 Pitt St; mains lunch $8-12, dinner $15-20; 8am-8pm Mon-Sat, 10am-3pm Sun) If you can't make it to the main Flavor on the waterfront, this downtown diner is the next best thing: an urban-style cafe serving sandwiches, soups and salads, along with more substantial mains like Thai curries and panko-crusted haddock after 4pm.

★ **Black Spoon** CANADIAN $$
(902-241-3300; www.blackspoon.ca; 320 Commercial St; mains $12-19; 11am-9pm Mon-Thu, to 10pm Fri & Sat) If you ask a local where to eat in North Sydney, they'll point you straight to the Spoon. It's a small space that goes big on flavours – hazelnut-crusted salmon, scallop carbonara, bacon-bourbon ribs – washed down with a good selection of Nova Scotian wines. Sometimes there'll be a band playing while you dine.

Kiju's NATIVE AMERICAN $$$
(902-562-6220; www.kijus.com; 50 Maillard St, Membertou; mains $22-46, 3-course menu $40; 11am-9pm Sun-Thu, to 10pm Fri & Sat) Based at Membertou Heritage Park, this restaurant provides the rare opportunity to try Mi'kmaw-inspired dishes, such as four-cent bread, cedar-plank salmon, barbecued duck and a foraged-fruit-and-berry salad.

Drinking & Entertainment

★ **Breton Brewing** MICROBREWERY
(902-270-4677; www.bretonbrewing.ca; 364 Keltic Dr; 10am-8pm Mon-Wed, to 11pm Thu-Sat, noon-5pm Sun) The top place around Sydney

DON'T MISS

LOUISBOURG

The fortunes of the province that became Nova Scotia are inextricably bound up with the mighty **Fortress of Louisbourg** (☎902-733-3552; www.fortressoflouisbourg.ca; 58 Wolfe St; adult/child $17.60/free; ⌚9:30am-5pm mid-May–mid-Oct, to 4pm Mon-Fri mid-Oct–mid-May), built by the French but battled over countless times before finally being burned to the ground in 1760. The current site recreates the fortress as it was in 1744, right down to the people – costumed soldiers, cooks, orderlies, musicians, gardeners and artisans create a real sense of time travel, and bring the place to life with stories and free guided tours.

Built to protect French interests in the region, Louisbourg was the area's administrative capital. It developed from around 1713 to 1745, when the British captured it after a gruelling 46-day siege. The fortress then changed hands twice more until 1760: that year, when British troops under the command of General James Wolfe took Québec City, the walls of Louisbourg were destroyed and the city was put to the torch.

In 1961 the federal government funded the largest historical reconstruction in Canadian history. Fifty buildings are now open to visitors, although three-quarters of Louisbourg remains in ruins. The 2.5km **Ruins Walk** guides you through the untouched terrain and out to the Atlantic coast.

Louisbourg is 35km from Sydney on Hwy 22.

for a beer is the taproom of this up-and-coming brewery, jointly run by Welsh and BC beer masters. You can watch the brewing process while you drink, and maybe have a food-truck snack on weekend nights. Look out for seasonal beers, such as the rhubarb kettle sour and the maple lager.

Highland Arts Theatre ARTS CENTER
(☎902-565-3637; www.highlandartstheatre.com; 40 Bentinck St) Housed in the old St Andrew's Church, the HAT has become the town's top venue for live performance, music and dance. There are often Celtic music nights in summer.

Getting There & Away

AIR

Air Canada and Westjet offer direct services to Halifax, Toronto and Montréal from Sydney's compact JA Douglas McCurdy Airport (p53), 13km from downtown.

BUS

Maritime Bus (p56) travels from Sydney to Halifax ($72.50, seven hours) and Truro ($63.50, five hours), from where you can connect to services bound for New Brunswick and Prince Edward Island.

It's faster and slightly cheaper to book the **Cape Shuttle Service** (☎855-673-8083; www.capeshuttleservice.com), which runs a private shuttle direct to Halifax (one way $70). The pickup in Sydney starts around 7am; you should be in Halifax sometime between noon and 1pm, when the shuttle runs in the opposite direction. It also runs shuttles to Truro and Baddeck ($65 one way), New Glasgow ($60), Antigonish ($55) and a few other local destinations.

CAR & MOTORCYCLE

Sydney is 403km by road from Halifax via Hwy 104, a journey of four to 4½ hours depending on traffic.

EASTERN SHORE

If you want to escape into the fog, away from summer crowds, this pristine region is the place to explore. Running from the outskirts of Dartmouth, across the harbor from Halifax, to Cape Canso at the extreme eastern tip of the mainland, the Eastern Shore has no large towns and the main road is almost as convoluted as the rugged shoreline it follows. For those seeking wildlife and barely touched wilderness, and opportunities to enjoy hiking, kayaking or fishing, this is your heaven.

Historically, villages in the region were linked only by boat, then by rail, which was later taken away. Spirited and resilient, these close-knit communities have upheld and maintained their family histories and traditions for decade upon decade.

Sights

★**Memory Lane Heritage Village** MUSEUM
(☎877-287-0697; https://heritagevillage.ca; 5435 Clam Harbour Rd, Lake Charlotte; adult/child $8/3; ⌚9:30am-4pm Jun-Sep) A 20-minute drive from Tangier, this place is an outstanding

example of how a community can work together to preserve its history. It recreates a 1940s Eastern Shore village in a series of lovingly relocated and restored buildings, chock-full of hands-on antiques, as if frozen in time. You'll find vintage cars, a farmstead with animals (great for kids), a schoolhouse, a church, a miner's hut, a blacksmithery, shipbuilding shops and so much more. A must for history buffs of any kind.

From 11:30am to 3pm, 1940s-style chow is served in the cookhouse.

★Sherbrooke Village MUSEUM
(☎902-522-2400; http://sherbrookevillage.novascotia.ca; 42 Main St, Sherbrooke; adult/child $15.95/4.95; ⏲9:30am-5:30pm Jun-Oct) This living-history village offers a chance to really step back in time: you can chat with people in period costume as you wander the streets of a typical Nova Scotian village as it might have looked before WWI. Among the 80 buildings, 25 of which you can step inside, are a blacksmith's shop, a printery, a woodworkers' workshop, a weaving house and a traditional tearoom.

Fisherman's Life Museum MUSEUM
(☎902-889-2053; http://fishermanslife.novascotia.ca; 58 Navy Pool Loop, Jeddore Oyster Pond; adult/child $4/3; ⏲9am-4pm Wed-Sun Jun, Tue-Sun Jul-Sep) The tiny Fisherman's Life Museum, 35km west of Tangier, paints a convincing picture of the tough lives of the people – particularly the women – who lived along the Eastern Shore at the turn of the 20th century. The museum is dotted with family memorabilia, and costumed guides offer tea, tales and hospitality.

Musquodoboit Harbour Railway Museum MUSEUM
(☎902-889-2689; www.mhrailwaymuseum.com; 7895 Hwy 7, Musquodoboit Harbour; by donation; ⏲9am-5pm Jun-Sep) This wonderful little railway museum, loved by train buffs and kids alike, looks a little incongruous in its surroundings: it's hard to believe there was once a passenger service through here. Housed in the 1918 station, the museum has train memorabilia inside and rolling stock outside. There are also some picnic tables on the grounds.

Activities

There are beautiful, long, white-sand beaches all along the Eastern Shore and, although the water never gets very warm, brave souls venture in for a swim or a surf, particularly if the fog stays offshore.

The busiest of the Eastern Shore beaches, 1km-long **Rainbow Haven** has washrooms, showers, a canteen and a boardwalk with wheelchair access to the beach.

The most popular destination for surfers, cobblestone **Lawrencetown Beach** faces directly south and often gets big waves, compliments of hurricanes or tropical storms hundreds of kilometers away. It boasts a supervised swimming area, washrooms and a canteen.

The longest swimming beach in Nova Scotia and the prettiest in the area, with more than 3km of grass-backed white sand, is **Martinique Beach**. Even if you find the water too cold for a swim, it's a beautiful place to walk, watch birds or play Frisbee.

About 10km southwest of Taylor Head Provincial Park, Tangier is one of the best settings for kayaking in the Maritimes.

★Coastal Adventures Sea Kayaking KAYAKING
(☎902-772-2774; www.coastaladventures.com; half/full-day tour $85/125; ⏲Jun-Sep) Based at Mason's Cove, off Hwy 7, this hugely experienced sea-kayaking company (in business since 1980) offers some of the best day trips in Nova Scotia, exploring the isolated '100 Wild Islands' along the east coast. It also

WORTH A TRIP

TAYLOR HEAD PROVINCIAL PARK

A little-known scenic highlight of Nova Scotia, this spectacular **park** (☎902-772-2218; http://parks.novascotia.ca/content/taylor-head; 20140 Hwy 7, Spry Bay) encompasses a peninsula jutting 6.5km into the Atlantic. On one side is a long, very fine, sandy beach fronting a protected bay. Some 17km of hiking trails cut through the spruce and fir forests. The **Headland Trail** is the longest at 8km round-trip and follows the rugged coastline to scenic views at Taylor Head. The shorter **Bob Bluff Trail** is a 3km round-trip hike to a bluff with good views.

In spring you'll see colorful wildflowers, and this is a great bird-watching area. Pack a picnic and plan to spend a full day hiking, lounging and – if you can brave the cool water – swimming.

has a simple lodge, the **Paddlers' Retreat** (rooms $65 to $100).

East Coast Surf School SURFING
(☎902-449-9488; www.ecsurfschool.com; 4348 Lawrencetown Rd, East Lawrencetown; lessons from $75) Daily surfing lessons are conducted on Lawrencetown Beach by Nova Scotia's first and only professional surfer, Nico Manos, and his team. Board and wetsuit rentals are also available.

Festivals

Stan Rogers Folk Festival MUSIC
(www.stanfest.com; ⌚Jul) Most people who come to Canso come for the Stan Rogers Folk Festival, the biggest event in Nova Scotia. It quadruples the town's population, with six stages showcasing folk, blues and traditional musicians from around the world.

Sleeping & Eating

Murphy's Camping on the Ocean CAMPGROUND $
(☎902-772-2700; www.murphyscamping.ca; 291 Murphy's Rd; tent/RV sites $30/40; ⌚May-Oct; P) This is oceanside camping at its finest, with plenty of secluded sites (serviced and unserviced) spread out under the trees with views over the 100 Wild Islands. Tuck into a bowl of freshly steamed mussels by the communal campfire. The owners also run boat trips.

Liscombe Lodge Resort RESORT $$
(☎902-779-2307; www.liscombelodge.ca; 2884 Hwy 7, Liscomb; r/chalets from $155/189; ⌚May-Oct; P) A nature-lover's dream, this rambling country lodge comprises 30 spacious, nicely decorated riverside rooms in the main lodge, five rustic four-room cottages, and 17 sweeter-than-sweet chalets with fireplaces as well as decks overlooking the woodsy grounds and river. There's loads to keep kids occupied, including an indoor pool, a tennis court, free bikes and kayaking.

Dobbit Bakehouse BAKERY $
(☎902-889-2919; 7896 Hwy 7, Musquodoboit Harbour; baked goods $2-6; ⌚7am-5pm Mon-Fri, 8am-5pm Sat;) Come chat with the friendly baker, a font of local knowledge, at this wonderful country bakery, which boasts rustic fresh breads and baked goods free from preservatives and using only seasonal local ingredients wherever possible. The selection changes daily. Make sure you try the fair-trade coffee and grab a pie to take with you on your journey.

Rare Bird MICROBREWERY
(☎902-533-2128; www.rarebirdbeer.com; 80 Main St; ⌚10am-5pm mid-Jun–Oct) The first man to set up a brewery in Guysborough was Nicolas Denys, way back in 1659, and the beer-heads at Rare Bird are proud to continue that legacy with their brews. Check out the seasonal beers, made with spruce, maple and pumpkin.

Getting There & Away

The Eastern Shore runs from Eastern Passage, south of Dartmouth, to Canso at the eastern tip of the mainland. It is serviced by a veiny network of ancient roads (you'll need your own wheels) that vary in condition depending on the time of year – some communities are cut off during winter storms. Hwy 7 forms the spine of the Eastern Shore but heads inland, due north, at Liscomb.

New Brunswick

Includes ➡

Best Places to Eat

- ➡ Fresco (p152)
- ➡ La Terrasse à Steve (p149)
- ➡ 11th Mile (p119)
- ➡ Tipsy Tails Restaurant (p141)
- ➡ The Chandler Room (p126)

Best Places to Stay

- ➡ Cielo (p149)
- ➡ Compass Rose (p133)
- ➡ Earle of Leinster Inn (p136)
- ➡ Château Albert (p150)
- ➡ Evandale Resort (p119)

Why Go?

Once the favored stomping grounds of millionaires and celebrities who journeyed here for silver, salmon-filled rivers and rustic lodges deep in primeval forests, New Brunswick's beauty and abundance has slipped off most bucket lists in recent decades. Living in the shadows of its more fashionable neighbors, Prince Edward Island (PEI) and Nova Scotia, New Brunswick is regularly referred to as the 'forgotten' or 'drive-through' province. Those who do explore its majestic, brown-sugar beaches, culturally rich Acadian villages, quaint coastal islands and vast tracks of forests brimming with wildlife are richly rewarded. Whether you're kayaking through the world's highest tides, wandering through world-class museums, or bibbing up for a lobster feast, it'll often just be you and the locals. Visit before the secret gets out.

When to Go

Fredericton

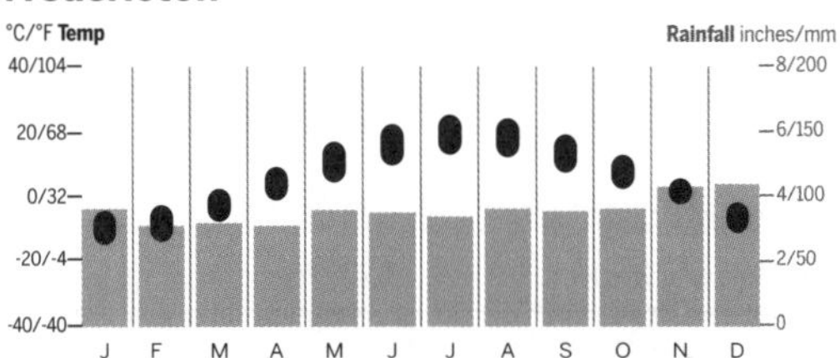

Jul–Sep St Andrews By-The-Sea bustles with crowds of whale-watchers.

Aug Acadians unleash their Franco-Canadian spirit for the Festival Acadien in Caraquet.

Nov–Mar Cross-country skiers hit the groomed trails of Fundy National Park.

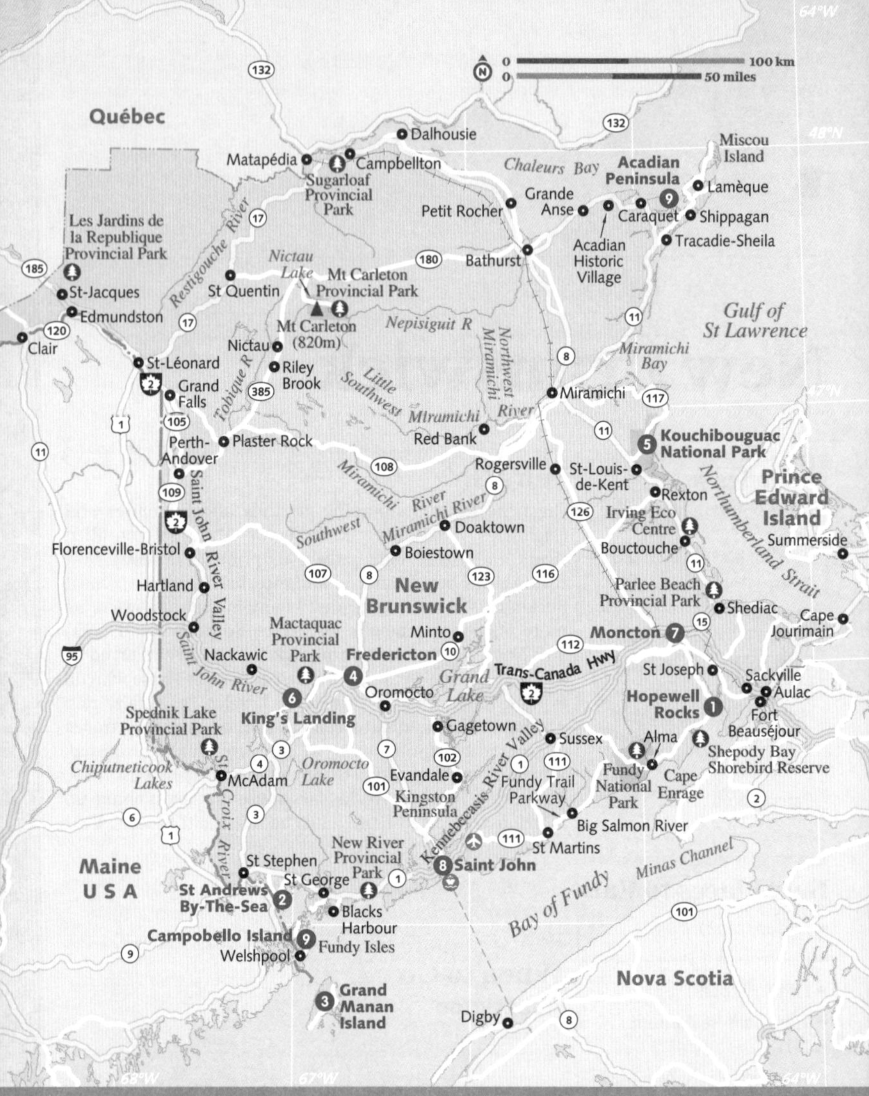

New Brunswick Highlights

1 Hopewell Rocks (p140) Feeling the power of the highest tides in the world.

2 St Andrews By-The-Sea (p124) Exploring the history and bustling streets of this picturesque seaside town.

3 Grand Manan Island (p132) Breathing in the fresh sea air on this peaceful island.

4 Fredericton (p115) Soaking up culture in a world-class art gallery.

5 Kouchibouguac National Park (p148) Setting up camp in this award-winning, beach- and lagoon-laden park.

6 Kings Landing (p116) Living Acadian history at this reconstructed scene.

7 Moncton (p141) Enjoying the hopping music scene in the province's biggest small city.

8 Saint John (p134) Buying food and artisans' wares at the spirited morning market.

9 Acadian Peninsula (p149) Soaking up Acadian culture and sunshine on this string of stunning islands.

History

What is now New Brunswick was originally the land of the Mi'kmaq and, in the western and southern areas, the Maliseet First Nations. Many places still bear their indigenous names, although the First Nation people (who today number around 17,000) are now mainly concentrated in small communities.

Following in the wake of explorer Samuel de Champlain, French colonists arrived in the 1600s. The Acadians, as they came to be known, farmed the area around the Bay of Fundy. In 1755 they were expelled by the English, many returning to settle along the Bay of Chaleur. In the years following, the outbreak of the American Revolution brought an influx of British Loyalists from Boston and New York seeking refuge in the wilds of New Brunswick. These refugees settled the valleys of the Saint John and St Croix Rivers, established the city of Saint John and bolstered the garrison town at Fredericton.

Through the 1800s, lumbering and shipbuilding boomed, and by the start of the 20th century, other industries, including fishing, had developed. That era of prosperity ended with the Great Depression. Today pulp and paper, oil refining and potato farming are the major industries.

Language

New Brunswick is Canada's only officially bilingual province; one-third speak French as their first language. Many of these are concentrated around Edmundston, the Acadian Peninsula, along the East Coast, and Moncton. You will rarely have a problem being understood in English or French.

Information

There are tourist information centers at most border crossings and in many towns. Opening times vary, but these are open from June to October only. **Tourism New Brunswick** (☎800-561-0123; www.tourismnewbrunswick.ca) publishes useful information on its excellent website.

Getting There & Away

AIR

Air Canada has several daily flights from cities across Canada into Moncton, Saint John, Fredericton and Bathurst. WestJet serves Moncton and Fredericton.

BOAT

The **Bay Ferries** (☎877-762-7245; www.bayferries.com; adult/child/senior $49/34/39, car/bicycle $118/10) sails between Saint John and Digby, Nova Scotia, year-round. The three-hour crossing is pricey but can save a lot of driving.

Free government ferries service Deer Island and White Head Island; East Coast Ferries (p128) runs between Campobello Island and Deer Island. Another private ferry company also serves Grand Manan Island. Reserve ahead.

BUS

Maritime Bus (☎800-575-1807; www.maritimebus.com) services the major transportation routes in New Brunswick, with service to Nova Scotia, PEI and into Québec as far as Rivière-du-Loup, where buses connect with **Orléans Express** (☎833-449-6444; www.orleansexpress.com) services to points west.

CAR & MOTORCYCLE

For drivers, the main access points into New Brunswick are the cities of Edmundston from Québec and Houlton or Calais from Maine. Many enter the province from Nova Scotia or over the bridge from PEI. If you're going to PEI, there's no charge to use the Confederation Bridge eastbound from Cape Jourmain – you pay on the way back. Traffic is generally light, although crossing the Maine borders sometimes means a delay at customs.

TRAIN

VIA Rail (☎888-842-7245; www.viarail.ca) operates passenger services between Montréal and Halifax, with stops in Campbellton, Bathurst, Miramichi and Moncton.

> **NEW BRUNSWICK FAST FACTS**
>
> ➡ Population: 747,100
>
> ➡ Area: 73,400 sq km
>
> ➡ Capital: Fredericton
>
> ➡ Quirky fact: Home to the world's biggest fake lobster (Shediac), axe (Nackawic) and fiddlehead (Plaster Rock).

FREDERICTON

POP 58,200

The Saint John River curves lazily alongside the provincial capital, watched over by stately historic buildings, tree-lined banks and walking paths. On warm weekends, 'The Green,' as it's known, looks like something out of a watercolor – families strolling, kids kicking soccer balls and couples picnicking.

The small downtown commercial district is a neat grid of redbrick storefronts set on a flat, broad curve in the riverbank. Surrounding it are residential streets lined with tall, graceful elms shading beautifully maintained Georgian and Victorian houses and abundant flower beds.

Sights

The two-block strip along Queen St between York and Regent Sts is known as the Historic Garrison District. It comprises **Barracks Square** (497 Queen St; Guard House 9:30am-5pm Fri-Wed, to 8pm Thu May-Oct) FREE and **Officers' Square** (www.historicgarrisondistrict.ca; btwn Carleton & Regent Sts; ceremonies 11am & 4pm daily, plus 7pm Tue & Thu Jul & Aug). In 1875 Fredericton became the capital of the newly formed province of New Brunswick, and the garrison housed British soldiers for much of the late 18th and early 19th centuries. It's now a lively multiuse area with impressive stone architecture.

★ Kings Landing HISTORIC SITE
(506-363-4999; www.kingslanding.nb.ca; 5804 Rte 102, Prince William; adult/youth/family $31/22/72; 10am-5pm mid-Jun–Oct) A visit to Kings Landing, 36km west of Fredericton, is a somewhat surreal step back in time. The majority of the early-19th-century buildings are original, moved here and beautifully restored to create a Loyalist village with homes, churches, a schoolhouse, general store, sawmill and print shop. Staff role-play actual people who lived and worked here and are busy with everyday 19th-century life, chatting about the village's goings on. Don't be shy – ask lots of questions to learn and experience the most.

★ Beaverbrook Art Gallery MUSEUM
(www.beaverbrookartgallery.org; 703 Queen St; adult/student/child $10/5/free; 10am-5pm Mon-Wed, Fri & Sat, to 9pm Thu, noon-5pm Sun) This excellent gallery was a gift to the town from Lord Beaverbrook. The exceptional collection includes works by international heavyweights and is well worth an hour or so. Among others you will see Dalí, Freud, Gainsborough and Turner, Canadian artists Tom Thompson, Emily Carr and Cornelius Krieghoff, as well as changing contemporary exhibits of Atlantic art.

New Brunswick Sports Hall of Fame MUSEUM
(www.nbsportshalloffame.com; 503 Queen St; adult/student/family $3/2/8; noon-5pm Tue-Fri, 10am-5pm Sat mid-Jun–Aug) Housed in the 19th-century customs office, this museum and gallery celebrates the province's star teams and athletic achievements. Learn about local athletes including hockey player Gordie Drillon, tennis player Ethel Babbitt and baseballer Jason Dickson. Test out the sports simulator, peek inside the virtual locker room and explore momentum and center of gravity in the hands-on biomechanics exhibit.

Fredericton Region Museum MUSEUM
(506-455-6041; www.frederictonregionmuseum.com; Officers' Sq; adult/student $6/4; 10am-4pm Apr-Jun & Sep-Nov, to 5pm Jul & Aug, by appointment Dec-Mar) What this museum lacks in gloss, it makes up for in care and some serious creativity. Housed in the 19th-century officers' quarters on the western side of Officers' Sq, the artifact-filled displays take you through the city's past with stories of merchants, military, Acadians and Loyalists. Don't miss the Coleman Frog, a 42lb creature of Fredericton legend. Real or plaster? Decide for yourself.

Government House HISTORIC BUILDING
(www.gnb.ca/lg/ogh; 51 Woodstock Rd; 10am-4pm Mon-Sat, noon-4pm Sun) FREE This magnificent sandstone palace was erected for the British governor in 1826. The representative of the queen moved out in 1893 after the province refused to continue paying his expenses, and during most of the 20th century the complex was a Royal Canadian Mounted Police (RCMP) headquarters. It now evocatively captures a moment in time with tours led by staff in period costume.

New Brunswick Legislative Building HISTORIC BUILDING
(506-453-2506; www.gnb.ca/legis; 706 Queen St; 10am-5pm, last tour 4:30pm Jul & Aug, 9am-4pm Sep-Jun by appointment) Following a fire that destroyed the original Provincial Hall, the impressive stone Legislative Building opened its doors to New Brunswick's Provincial Government in 1882. Join a half-hour tour to check out the 41m central domed tower and the dramatic spiral staircase in the entrance hall. Next door is the Education Building, built in 1816 and Fredericton's oldest surviving public building; it now houses the Opposition Offices.

Activities

Fredericton is blessed with parkland. Lovely **Wilmot Park** is popular with families, of-

Fredericton

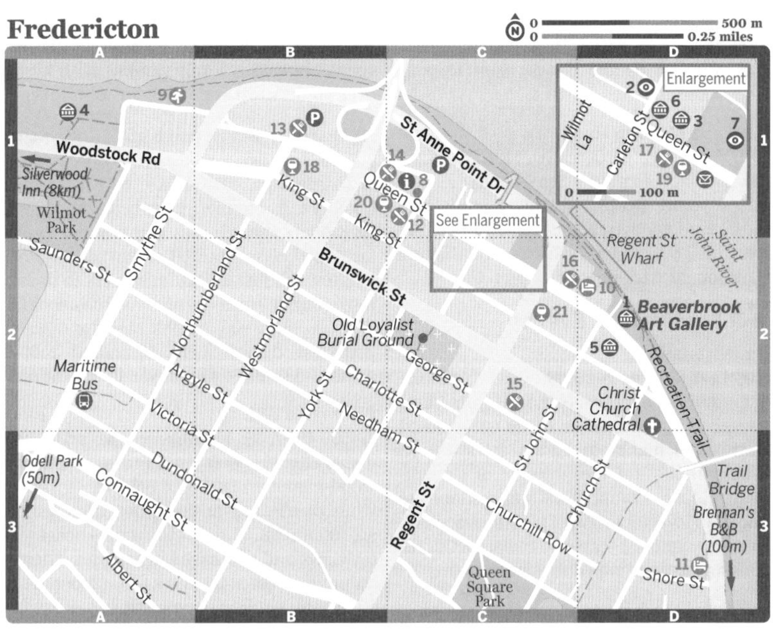

Fredericton

Top Sights
1 Beaverbrook Art Gallery D2

Sights
2 Barracks Square D1
3 Fredericton Region Museum D1
4 Government House A1
5 New Brunswick Legislative Building D2
6 New Brunswick Sports Hall of Fame D1
7 Officers' Square D1

Activities, Courses & Tours
8 Heritage Walking Tours C1
9 Second Nature Outdoors A1

Sleeping
10 Crowne Plaza Fredericton-Lord Beaverbrook D2
11 Quartermain House B&B D3

Eating
12 11th Mile C1
540 Kitchen & Bar .... (see 17)
13 Byblos B1
14 Chess Piece Patisserie & Cafe C1
15 Fredericton Boyce Farmers Market C2
16 Isaac's Way C2
17 The Abbey D1

Drinking & Nightlife
18 Graystone Brewing B1
19 Red Rover Craft Cider D1
20 The Capital Complex B1
21 The Muse C2

fering shade, lots of lawn for picnics, playgrounds and a water park. In the southwest of town, massive **Odell Park** has botanical gardens, an arboretum and and a huge wooded expanse of trails to explore. Parking is off Prospect Rd or Cameron Court.

For trail maps visit the information center or www.frederictontrailscoalition.com.

Second Nature Outdoors BOATING
(www.secondnatureoutdoors.com; off Woodstock Rd; kayak/paddle board/canoe per hr $17/17/22, half-day bike rental $15; ⌚May-Sep) Operating out of the Small Craft Aquatic Centre, on the Saint John River beside Government House, Second Nature Outdoors rents out canoes, double and single kayaks, paddleboards and

bikes, along with children's attachments. They will drop you at Heart Island Resort and you can paddle downstream to your heart's and muscle's content.

Heritage Walking Tours WALKING
(☎506-457-1975; 796 Queen St; ⊙10am & 2:30pm daily Jul & Aug, 4pm Jun & Sep–mid-Oct) Enthusiastic young people wearing historic costumes lead good, free hour-long tours of the river, the government district or the Historic Garrison District, departing from City Hall.

Festivals & Events

New Brunswick Highland Games Festival CULTURAL
(http://highlandgames.ca; ⊙late Jul) Kilts, clans and all things positively Celtic are exposed at this fun highlands games extravaganza held annually on the grounds of Government House. Competitors and visitors are drawn to its celebration of all things Scottish culture: dancing, caber-toss competitions, whiskey tastings, piped music and more.

Harvest Jazz & Blues Festival MUSIC
(www.harvestjazzandblues.com; ⊙Sep) This weeklong event transforms the downtown area into the 'New Orleans of the North.' Jazz, blues and Dixieland performers arrive from across North America to fill three stages with more than 100 performances.

Silver Wave Film Festival FILM
(www.swfilmfest.com; ⊙early Nov) Three days of New Brunswick, Canadian and international films and lectures organized by the NB Filmmakers' Cooperative.

Sleeping

Silverwood Inn MOTEL $
(☎506-458-8676; www.silverwoodinn.ca; 3136 Woodstock Rd; r from $90;) A 10-minute drive towards Kings Landing, this friendly motel is a bit of a steal with clean, spacious rooms, some with kitchenettes, and a small, well-kept outdoor pool. Don't worry – the trippy night lighting can be turned off.

University of New Brunswick UNIVERSITY ACCOMMODATIONS $
(☎506-447-3227; http://stay.unb.ca; 20 Bailey Dr; s/d with bath $41/65, ste $85-115; ⊙7am-11pm May–mid-Aug; P) Fredericton's only budget accommodations is located at the university. It's a great deal, but rooms are available in summer only. Traditional rooms have shared bathrooms and include a light continental breakfast and pass to the university pool and fitness rooms. Suites have private bathrooms and kitchenettes. Rooms may be a bit sparse, but it's a lovely campus with views over Fredericton and the Saint John River.

★**Quartermain House B&B** B&B $$
(☎506-206-5255; www.quartermainhouse.com; 92 Waterloo Row; r $110-145; P) The former home of a premier, this beautiful 1840s B&B offers three rooms that epitomize old-fashioned class. Located on enviable Waterloo Row, it's just a 10-minute walk to downtown. Subtle touches, such as fresh cookies and tea, push way up the uber-great scale. Breakfast dishes such as braised maple pears and soufflés will set you up for the day.

Brennan's B&B B&B $$
(☎506-455-7346; 146 Waterloo Row; s $115-195, d $125-210; P@) Built for a wealthy wood-merchant family in 1885, this turreted white riverfront mansion is now a handsome six-room B&B. Three of the rooms boast water views and two have kitchenettes. There's stunning original fretwork throughout. It's a 10-minute stroll to downtown.

Crowne Plaza Fredericton-Lord Beaverbrook HOTEL $$$
(☎506-455-3371; www.cpfredericton.com; 659 Queen St; r $180-220; P) Looking rather lacklustre from its beaver-mosaiced exterior, this 1948 vintage hotel is all vintage glamour once you step inside. Wrought-iron railings and a sweeping staircase are leftovers from when Lord Beaverbrook owned the place. Spacious rooms are renovated and modern if a little lacking in character. Ever-popular, it pays to book ahead.

Eating

Fredericton Boyce Farmers Market MARKET $
(www.frederictonfarmersmarket.ca; 665 George St; ⊙6am-1pm Sat) This Fredericton institution is great for picking up fresh fruit, vegetables, meat, cheese and dessert. Many of the 150 or so stalls recall the city's European heritage, with everything from German-style sausages to French duck pâtés to British marmalade. There is also an eatery where Frederictonians queue to chat and people-watch. Pick up souvenirs from the many artisan stalls.

The Abbey VEGETARIAN $
(www.facebook.com/abbeycafegallery; 546 Queen St; $9-11; ⊙9am-9pm Mon-Fri, 11am-9pm Sat, noon-6pm Sun;) If you're vegan, this place will get your stomach giddy. Burritos with cashew

cheese, pulled pork that's actually jackfruit, and hot and cold bowls of veggie goodness will fill you up. You'll find it in the back of the Red Rover ciderhouse. Regular events such as comedy nights and music are held in the basement. Check the website for listings.

Chess Piece Patisserie & Cafe CAFE $
(☎506-459-1969; www.chesspiece.ca; 361 Queen St; snacks $3-8; ⏰7am-9pm Mon-Fri, 8am-9pm Sat, 10am-4pm Sun) This tiny cafe has an in-house patisserie bakery creating to-die-for macaroons, mini cheesecakes and pastries. There's also soup, quiche and sausage rolls but they're hard to notice amid all of that caramel and chocolate. The coffee here is top-notch, too.

★**11th Mile** CANADIAN $$
(☎506-443-1187; www.11thmile.ca; 79 York St; small plates $12-18) All class, the muted colors of this new-to-the-scene, chef-owned restaurant belie the bright flavors of its food. An ever-changing menu of small plates goes the distance with dishes such as roasted broccoli with walnut crema, seared coulotte steak and salmon with salsa verde. Bespoke cocktails are exceptional. The secret is well and truly out; book ahead.

540 Kitchen & Bar CANADIAN $$
(☎506-449-5400; http://540kitchenandbar.com; 540 Queen St; mains $16-25; ⏰11:30am-9pm Mon & Tue, to 10pm Wed & Thu, to 11pm Fri & Sat; ✎) Fashionable and just classy enough to not feel like a pub, this place has a stellar, seasonal menu with locally sourced produce and nearly everything made from scratch. Wash down the likes of pork-belly gnocchi, wild-mushroom risotto or panko and lemon haddock with one of 10 local beers on tap. Get here early or reserve ahead; it's popular.

Isaac's Way CANADIAN $$
(☎506-474-7222; www.isaacsway.ca; 649 Queen St; mains $15-22; ⏰11am-10pm Mon-Fri, 10am-10pm Sat & Sun; 👪) Using local products, Isaac's has quickly become a favorite of locals, especially in summer for its patio with river views. Big portions of burgers, seafood and pasta keep families happy, and while the menu isn't unique, dishes are created with care and a real knack for flavor. There are plenty of options for vegetarians and weekend breakfasts are a hit.

Byblos LEBANESE $$
(☎506-454-5552; 215 Queen St; meals $15-19; ⏰11:30am-8pm Mon-Fri, 5-9pm Sat) Crazy popular, this elegant Lebanese restaurant has a bustling atmosphere. Linger over garlic-laced dishes, marinated meats and homemade pita bread.

WORTH A TRIP

EVANDALE

A century ago, tiny **Evandale** was bustling, where a dance band would entertain passengers stopping off here for the night. These days, you can stop for an outdoor swim, patio drink – and maybe a night – at **Evandale Resort** (☎506-468-2222; www.evandaleresort.com; 3500 Rte 124, Evandale; r $100-170; ⏰May-Oct; ❄📶🏊), restored to its grandeur as an 1889 riverboat hotel. Even if you're not a guest, you can swim ($5) and enjoy pub meals on the patio overlooking the dock.

The cable ferry at Evandale Ferry Landing takes you across the short, rapid St John river to Rte 124 and the Belleisle Ferry to rural Kingston Peninsula.

Drinking & Nightlife

In the evening the bars, pubs and rooftop patios of King and Queen Sts come alive. There's a prerequisite brewery and a great ciderhouse here. Younger things hit the multi-venue Capital Complex.

★**The Muse** COCKTAIL BAR
(www.facebook.com/musecafefredericton; 86 Regent St; ⏰8:30am-6pm Mon & Tue, to 10pm Wed-Sun) If you're feeling drinky in the afternoon, come here for cool cocktails or coffee alongside bagels and gourmet cream cheese with muddled raspberry or vermouth and oregano. Beer, cider, prosecco and kombucha are all on tap. Most evenings there's live music by touring or local musicians. See the website for listings.

Graystone Brewing BREWERY
(www.graystonebrewing.com; 221 King St; ⏰11am-11pm Mon-Thu, to midnight Fri & Sat, noon-9pm Sun) Somewhat industrial with a hopping street patio, the cool cats hang out here to sip on Graystone and other local brews. Although still in its infancy, the brewery is already expanding. A food truck outside serves fancy hearty naanwiches, rice bowls, lettuce wraps and poutine.

Red Rover Craft Cider BAR
(www.redrovercider.com; 546 Queen St; ⏰5-9pm Mon, noon-9pm Tue-Thu, noon-10pm Fri & Sat) This convivial ciderhouse serves craft brews made by New Brunswick's original (and very

FLORENCEVILLE-BRISTOL

The tidy, green riverside village of **Florenceville-Bristol** is ground zero of the global french-fry industry. It's home to the McCain Foods frozen-foods empire, which is sustained by the thousands of hectares of potato farms that surround it in every direction. Started by the McCain brothers in 1957, the company produces one-third of the world's french-fry supply at its Florenceville factory. That adds up to 453,600kg of chips churned out every hour and $5.8 billion in annual net sales. To get your head around the spud industry, head to **Potato World** (www.potatoworld.ca; Rte 110; tours adult/family $5/16, experiential tours $10/32; ⌚9am-6pm Mon-Fri, to 5pm Sat & Sun Jun-Aug, 9am-5pm Mon-Fri Sep–mid-Oct), an interactive exposition of the history of the humble potato in these parts.

Twenty kilometers further south, the tiny country hamlet of **Hartland** is home to the granddaddy of New Brunswick's many wooden covered bridges. The photogenic and functioning 390m-long **Hartland Bridge** over the Saint John River was erected in 1897 and is the world's longest.

passionate) cider producers. Try all four on tap with a short flight ($10), sit back with a glass or a pint, or buy a few tall tins to take with you.

The Capital Complex CLUB
(www.thecapitalcomplex.com; 362 Queen St; ⌚4pm-midnight Mon, to 2am Tue-Fri, 6pm-2am Sat) A series of balconies, floors, clubs, bars and venues, this complex is where it's at on summer nights. Whether you're into beer, cocktails, live comedy or owning the dance floor, the Capital Complex doesn't disappoint. Enter down Piper's Lane off Queen St, or through the Tannery shopping complex on King St.

Information

The entire CBD is wired for free internet access.

Main post office (☎506-444-8602; 570 Queen St; ⌚8am-5pm Mon-Fri)

Visitor Information Centre (☎506-460-2129; www.tourismfredericton.ca; City Hall, 397 Queen St; ⌚10am-8pm Jul & Aug, to 5pm Jun & Sep, to 4:30pm May & Oct) Fredericton's main tourist office provides free three-day city parking passes to visitors. A secondary office opens in summer at **Kings Landing** (42 Prince William Rd, Prince William; ⌚10:30am-5:30pm Jun-Oct).

Getting There & Away

AIR

Fredericton International Airport (YFC; ☎506-460-0920; www.frederictonairport.ca) is located on Hwy 102, 14km southeast of town. Air Canada has flights between Fredericton and the US, including New York City and Orlando (via other Canadian cities), as well flights to London, UK. Fredericton is also part of a good network of domestic flights.

BUS

The **Maritime Bus** (☎506-455-2049; www.maritimebus.com; 105 Dundonald St; ⌚8am-8pm Mon-Fri, 10am-8pm Sat & Sun) terminal is a few kilometers southwest of downtown. Some useful destinations include Moncton ($42, 2¼ hours, three daily), Charlottetown, PEI ($69, 5½ hours, two daily) and Saint John ($26, 1½ hours, three daily).

CAR & MOTORCYCLE

Cars with out-of-province license plates are eligible for a free three-day parking pass for downtown Fredericton from May to October; pick one up from the visitor center at City Hall. In-province visitors can get a one-day pass.

Major car-rental agencies all have desks at the airport.

Getting Around

A taxi to the airport costs $18 to $22.

The city has a decent bus system; tickets cost $3 and include free transfers. Service runs Monday through Saturday from 6:15am to 11pm. Most city bus routes begin at King's Place Mall, on King St between York and Carleton.

Bicycle rentals are available at **Radical Edge** (☎506-459-3478; www.radicaledge.ca; 386 Queen St; rental per day $25).

UPPER ST JOHN RIVER VALLEY

The St John River winds along the western border of the province past forests and lush farmland. It drifts through Fredericton between tree-lined banks and around flat islands between rolling hills before emptying into the Bay of Fundy 700km later. The river is the province's dominant feature and for centuries has been its major thoroughfare.

The valley's eye-pleasing landscape along the Trans Canada Trail (TCT) follows the river for most of its length.

Two automobile routes carve through the valley: the quicker Trans-Canada Hwy (Hwy 2), mostly on the western side of the river, and the more scenic old Hwy 105 on the eastern side, which meanders through many villages. Branching off from the valley are Hwy 17 (at St-Léonard) and Rte 385 (at Perth-Andover), which cut northeast through the Appalachian highlands and lead to rugged Mt Carleton Provincial Park.

Mt Carleton Provincial Park & the Tobique Valley

The 17,427-hectare provincial park is one of the region's best-kept secrets. It offers visitors a wilderness of mountains, valleys, rivers and wildlife including moose, deer and bear. The park's main feature is a series of rounded glaciated peaks and ridges, including Mt Carleton (820m), the Maritimes' highest. This range is an extension of the Appalachian Mountains, which begin in Georgia, USA, and end in Québec.

The park is open from mid-May to October. All roads are gravel-surfaced. The nearest towns are Riley Brook, 40km to the south, and St Quentin, 42km to the west, so bring all food and a full tank of gas.

Activities

Canoeing

The Mt Carleton area boasts superb wilderness canoeing. In the park itself, the Nictau and Nepisiguit chains of lakes offer easy day-tripping through a landscape of tree-clad mountains. For experienced canoeists, the shallow and swift Little Tobique River rises at Big Nictau Lake, winding in tight curls through dense woods until it joins the Tobique itself at Nictau. The more remote Nepisiguit River flows out of the Nepisiguit Lakes through the wilderness until it empties into the Bay of Chaleur at Bathurst, more than 100km away.

The lower reaches of the Tobique, from Nictau, through minute Riley Brook and down to Plaster Rock is a straight, easy paddle through forest and meadow that gives way to farmland as the valley broadens, with a couple of waterfront campgrounds along the way. The easy 10km between Nictau and the Bear's Lair landing in Riley Brook make for a relaxing afternoon paddle.

Guildo Martel WATER SPORTS
(☎506-235-0286; 8162 Rte 385; kayak & canoe rental per day $40, plus transport $15, tubing adult/child $20/15; ⏲Jun-Sep) Guildo Martel rents canoes and kayaks for the day and will deliver them where required. He's located 4km from the park toward St Quentin. He will guide for a total of $100 on top of rental prices (for up to six people).

Bill Miller CANOEING
(☎506-356-2409; www.millercanoes.com; 4160 Rte 385, Nictau) Bill Miller welcomes visitors to his cluttered canoe-making workshop in Nictau (population roughly eight), on the forested banks of the Tobique River, where he and his father and grandfather before him have handcrafted wooden canoes since 1922.

Bear's Lair KAYAKING
(☎506-356-8351; www.bearslairhunting.com; 3349 Rte 385, Riley Brook; kayak/canoe rental per day $35/45) Owners will drop you off upriver so you can paddle and float your way downstream and back to home base, Bear's Lair (p122), the cozy lodge.

Hiking

The best way to explore Mt Carleton is on foot. The park has a network of nearly 70km of trails: most of them are loops winding to the handful of rocky knobs that are the peaks. The International Appalachian Trail (IAT) passes through here.

The easiest peak to climb is **Mt Bailey**; a 7.5km loop trail to the 564m hillock begins near the day-use area. Most hikers can walk this route in three hours. The highest peak is reached via the **Mt Carleton Trail**, a 10km route that scales rocks to reach the 820m knob, where there's a fire tower. Plan on five hours for the trek, wear good footwear and pack your parka; the wind above the tree line can be brutal.

TOBIQUE SALMON BARRIER

Each spring, the government-funded **Tobique Salmon Barrier** (4320 Rte 385; ⏲May-Sep) FREE holds back salmon from swimming upstream, protecting them from low water levels and poachers. From the viewing platform, you can see the barrier as well as flashes of 30lb Atlantic salmon that return every two years to spawn. At the end of September, the barrier is removed and the salmon swim free.

WORTH A TRIP

NEW BRUNSWICK BOTANICAL GARDEN

Working-class Edmundston has a large paper mill, a utilitarian town center and a mainly bilingual French citizenry. Much of the downtown seems to be for sale or closed down but there are some nearby sights that are worthy of your time – especially the **New Brunswick Botanical Garden** (506-737-4444; www.jardinnbgarden.com; off Rte 2, St-Jacques; adult/student/child/family $18/15/8/40; 9am-5pm May, Jun & Sep, to 8pm Jul & Aug). Located in the small community of St-Jacques, this 7-hectare garden has peaceful paths, an unusual Celestial Garden, more than 80,000 plants and a team of artists-in-residence at work in small pavilions. The cafe here is a popular lunch spot for locals.

The most challenging hike (and the most rewarding for the views) is the **Sagamook Trail**, a 6km loop to a 777m peak with superlative vistas of Nictau Lake and the highlands area to the north of it; allow four hours for this trek. The **Mountain Head Trail** connects the Mt Carleton and Sagamook Trails (the latter being part of the Appalachian Trail), making a long transit of the range possible.

All hikers intending to follow any long trails must register at the visitor center before hitting the trail. Outside the camping season (mid-May to mid-September), you should call ahead to make sure the main gate will be open, as the Mt Carleton trailhead is 13.5km from the park entrance.

Festivals & Events

World Pond Hockey Tournament SPORTS
(http://worldpondhockey.ca; Rte 109, Plaster Rock; admission free; Feb) Every February, the forest town of Plaster Rock (population 1200), 84km from Mt Carleton, hosts the World Pond Hockey Tournament. More than 20 rinks are plowed on Roulston Lake, which is ringed by tall evergreens, hot-chocolate stands and straw-bale seating for the thousands of spectators drawn to the four-day event. More than 120 amateur four-person teams come from around the world.

Fiddles on the Tobique MUSIC
(506-356-2409; late Jun/early Jul) Fiddles on the Tobique is a weekend festival held annually in Nictau and Riley Brook. It is a magical idea: a round of community-hall suppers, jam sessions and concerts culminating in a Sunday-afternoon floating concert down the Tobique River from Nictau to Riley Brook. Upward of 800 canoes and kayaks join the flotilla each year – some stocked with musicians, some just with paddlers – and 8000 spectators line the riverbanks to watch.

Sleeping

Heritage Cottages COTTAGE $
(506-235-0793; https://parcsnbparks.ca; Mt Carleton Provincial Park; d $60-90) These damn cute log cabins dating from the late 1800s sit on Bathurst Lakes and at Little Nictau right within the park. You must bring everything, including bedding, pots and pans. Some share facilities; others have their own kitchens and bathrooms.

Armstrong Brook Campground CAMPGROUND $
(506-235-0793; https://parcsnbparks.ca; campsites $28; May-Oct) The park's largest campground has 88 sites nestled among the spruce on the northern side of Nictau Lake, 3km from the entrance. It has toilets, showers and a kitchen shelter, but no sites with hookups. RV drivers often have their noisy generators running, so tenters should check out the eight tent-only sites on the northern side of the campground.

Bear's Lair INN $
(506-356-8351; www.bearslairhunting.com; 3349 Rte 385, Riley Brook; r from $80, 4-/8-person cabin $150/175; May-Sep; P) Even if you aren't planning to hunt, you need to be fine with taxidermy to feel comfortable here. Moose and his friends festoon the walls of this log hunting lodge on the banks of the Tobique River. Rooms are very basic but spick-and-span and right on the river.

The lodge's friendly owners offer meals and canoe and kayak rentals. Be aware that since this is predominantly a hunting lodge, you might be sharing with those who partake in this activity.

Information

A **visitor center** (506-235-0793; www.nbparks.ca; off Rte 385; per vehicle $10; 8am-8pm May-Sep, to 6pm Oct) at the park entrance has maps and information. Park entry is paid here; cash only. At the time of research, an interpretive center was also being built inside the park.

WESTERN FUNDY SHORE

Almost the entire southern edge of New Brunswick is presided over by the constantly rising and falling waters of the Bay of Fundy.

The resort town of St Andrews By-The-Sea, the serene Fundy Isles, fine seaside scenery and rich history make this easily one of the most appealing regions of the province. Whale-watching is a thrilling activity here with fin, humpback and minke commonly seen along with the occasional but increasingly rare right whale. Porpoises and dolphins are plentiful. And let's not overlook the seafood – it's bountiful and delicious.

St Stephen

POP 4420

Right on the US border across the river from Calais, ME, St Stephen is a busy entry point with small-town charm. Elegant historic homes line the residential streets and the tidy downtown has a handful of shops, cafes and an honest-to-goodness chocolate factory that you can tour.

The Ganong family has been making chocolate since 1873, sending its products across Canada and the world. Long-standing treats include the once 5¢ Pal-o-Mine (a fudge and peanut bar) and 'chicken bones' (cinnamon-flavored candy filled with chocolate). They are also credited with the heart-shaped box of chocolates seen everywhere on Valentine's Day. Today their factory is on the edge of town with the original location now a **museum** (☎506-466-7848; www.chocolatemuseum.ca; 73 Milltown Blvd; adult/student/family $10/8.50/30; ⊙10am-6pm Jul & Aug, 10am-4pm Mon-Sat Apr-Jun & Sep-Nov, shop 9am-7pm Mon-Fri, to 6pm Sat, 11am-5pm Sun) with taste-testing-filled tours and the chance to see chocolate hand-dippers at work.

The town celebrates its love of chocolate during the **Chocolate Fest** (www.chocolate-fest.ca; ⊙early Aug), which features a parade, tours of the local Ganong factory and unlimited sampling of the goods (yes, really!).

Sleeping & Eating

Winsome Inn MOTEL **$$**

(☎506-466-2130; www.winsomeinn.com; 198 King St; d/q $112/125; ❄ 📶) Located on the edge of town, this motel is super-clean, friendly and – some might even say – winsome. Standard rooms are smartened up with some modern furnishings. It's a drive into town but a short walk to Carmen's Diner. This is the best (read: only) deal in town. Watch for the colorful, giant lawn chairs.

Blair House INN **$$**

(☎506-466-2233; www.blairhouseheritageinn.com; 38 Prince William St; r incl breakfast $105-140; ⊙mid-Apr–Dec; P ⊖ ❄ 📶) Three rather beautiful and extremely comfortable rooms are complemented by a quiet garden at this fabulous Victorian home. A generous cooked breakfast is served at the large dining table and tea, lemonade and cookies are available in the evening in the living room. It's an easy walk from here to downtown.

Carman's Diner DINER **$**

(☎506-466-3528; 164 King St; mains $5-15; ⊙7am-9pm) Home cooking is served up at this 1960s throwback with counter stools and your own mini (and working) jukeboxes at the tables. There's everything from burgers to sandwiches, but the homemade pies are the things to go for. It's only really convenient if you have a car, as it's not in the center of town.

Getting There & Away

Across the border in Calais, **West's Coastal Connection** (☎800-596-2823; www.westbusservice.com; 189 Main St, Calais, Maine) buses

WORTH A TRIP

GRAND FALLS

Grand Falls lives up to its name. Dropping 25m into a narrow gorge with walls towering 80m, the falls are the focal point of the town. The Grand Falls are best when the dam gates are open, often after rain. During spring freshet, 6 million litres of water cascade over the falls every second – nine-tenths the volume of Niagara Falls. In summer much of the water is diverted for generating hydroelectricity – yet the gorge is pretty at any time.

To see the falls, follow the boardwalk trails from the tourist center (www.grandfallsnb.com/malabeam) on the western side of the bridge, Lovers' Lane is a garden trail with fabulous views.

Maritime Bus services (www.maritimebus.com) stop at the Esso station, just west of downtown, with departures to Fredericton ($42, two hours 40 minutes, one or two daily), Moncton ($73, 5½ hours, daily) and Quebec City ($86, four hours, twice daily) via Riviere Du Loup.

head to Bangor (one-way ticket $27, four hours, one daily), connecting with Bangor airport.

There are no transport options from here to other provincial destinations. You'll need your own wheels.

St Andrews By-The-Sea

POP 1790

St Andrews is a genteel summer resort town. Blessed with a fine climate and picturesque beauty, it also has a colorful history and feels much like a living museum. Founded by Loyalists in 1783, it's one of the oldest towns in the province, with plaques of the original owners next to many of the stately Georgian homes. It's extremely busy with holidaymakers and summer residents in July and August, but the rest of the year there are more seagulls than people.

The town sits on a peninsula pointing southward into the Bay of Fundy. Its main drag, Water St, is lined with quaint buildings, restaurants and boutiques.

Sights

Ministers Island ISLAND

(☎506-529-5081; www.ministersisland.ca; adult/student/child under 8yr $15/13/free; ⊙May-Oct) This picturesque tidal island was once used as a retreat by William Cornelius Van Horne, builder of the Canadian Pacific Railway and one of Canada's wealthiest men. As well as touring the island on foot along 20km of marked trails, you can visit Covenhoven, his splendid 50-room Edwardian cottage, plus the towerlike stone bathhouse, tidal swimming pool and stunning, château-like barn (the largest freestanding wooden structure in Canada).

Important: the island can only be visited at low tide, when you can drive (or walk, or bike) on the hard-packed sea floor. At high tide, it's 3m under water but staff will kick you off in plenty of time. To get to Ministers Island from downtown St Andrews, follow Rte 127 northeast for about 1km and then turn right on Bar Rd. If you walk over, take Cedar Lane just past the toll booth, which was planted in the 1800s as a dust-free path to Covenhaven.

Ross Memorial Museum HISTORIC BUILDING

(☎506-529-5124; www.rossmemorialmuseum.ca; 188 Montague St; ⊙10am-4:30pm Tue-Sat Jun-Sep, plus Mon Jul & Aug) Hark back to a time when beds were so high, you needed an ornate step stool to climb in. This 1820s home was bought by the wealthy Ross couple who traveled the world and filled their eclectic home with souvenirs. Fine furnishings and artifacts successfully turn back the clock to the early 1900s. Knowledgeable staff will give you a tour or you can wander independently.

St Andrews By-The-Sea

Sights

1 Kingsbrae Garden D2
2 Ross Memorial Museum C3
3 St Andrews Blockhouse A3

Activities, Courses & Tours

4 Eastern Outdoors C4
5 Jolly Breeze C4
Quoddy Link Marine .... (see 5)

Sleeping

6 Algonquin Resort B2
7 Picket Fence Motel A1
8 Treadwell Inn B4

Eating

9 Niger Reef Tea House A3
The Chandler Room .... (see 8)

Drinking & Nightlife

10 Something's Brewing C4

Fundy Discovery Aquarium AQUARIUM

(www.huntsmanmarine.ca; 1 Lower Campus Rd; adult/child $14.25/10; ⊙10am-7pm Jun-Sep) Linked to a nonprofit research center, this impressive aquatic center has a 20,000-sq-ft aquarium containing most specimens found in Bay of Fundy waters. In addition to the exhibits, try to see the seal, seahorse and salmon feedings; arrive at 10am or 3pm to get a chance to take it all in. Brave the touch pool reserved just for slippery skates and join a behind-the-scenes tour ($10, ages eight and up).

St Andrews Blockhouse HISTORIC BUILDING

(Joe's Point Rd; by donation; ⊙10am-6pm Jun-Aug) Built in 1812 by town folk anticipating an attack by the USA, this wooden blockhouse was run by local militia. Restored and set up to look like 1812 inside, it is one of the few surviving blockhouses in Canada. At low tide, there's a path extending from the blockhouse across a great stretch of beach and the tidal flats.

Kingsbrae Garden GARDENS

(☎506-529-3335; www.kingsbraegarden.com; 220 King St; adult/student/family $16/12/38, tours per person $3; ⊙9am-7pm May-Oct) Extensive, multihued Kingsbrae Garden is considered one of the most beautiful horticultural displays in Canada. Check out the wollemi pine, one

St Andrews By-The-Sea

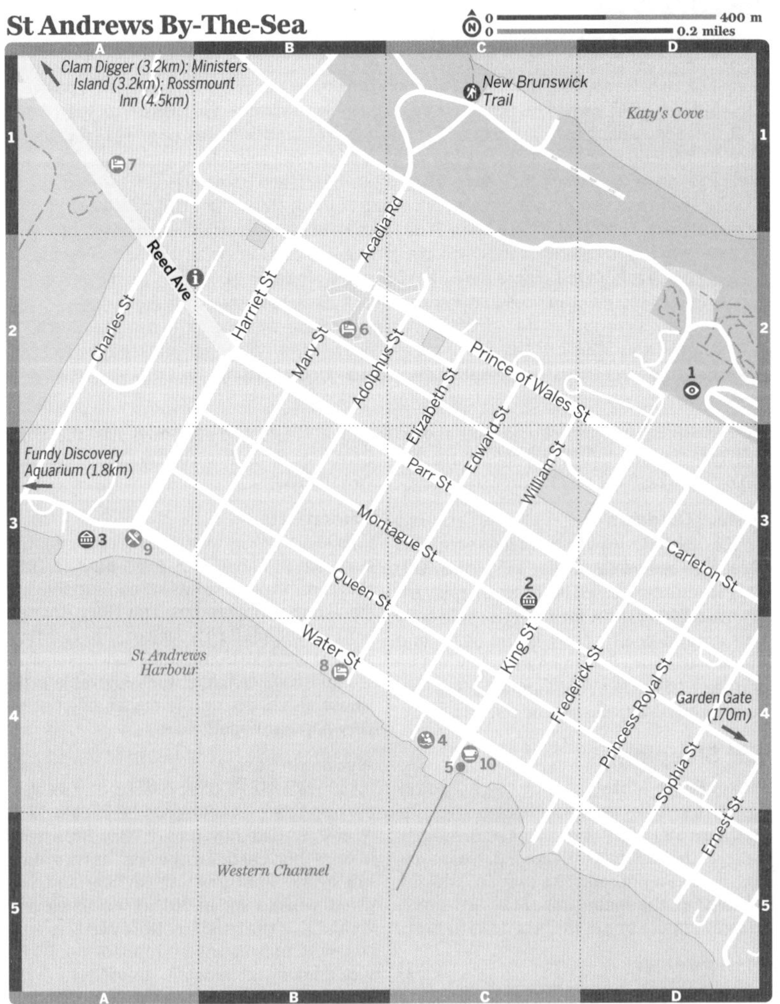

of the world's oldest and rarest trees, and the functioning Dutch windmill. In summer, try to time your visit for the daily 12:30pm alpaca walk on the lawn or the 2pm ladybug release in the rose garden.

Activities

Numerous companies offering boat trips and whale-watching cruises have offices by the wharf at the foot of King St. They're open from mid-June to early September. The cruises (around $60) take in the lovely coast with its seabirds and whales. The ideal waters for whale-watching are further out in the bay, so if you're heading for the Fundy Isles, do your trip there.

Jolly Breeze BOATING
(☎506-529-8116; www.jollybreeze.com; Quoddy Link Marine; adult/child $67/45; ⊙tours 9am, 12:45pm & 4:30pm Jun-Oct) This antique-style tall ship sails around Passamaquoddy Bay looking for seals and whales as well as porpoises and eagles. Trips are 3½ hours long, with a 95% success rate of whale encounters.

Quoddy Link Marine BOATING
(☎506-529-2600; http://quoddylinkmarine.com; adult/youth/child $69/49/39; ⊙mid-Jun–Oct)

WORTH A TRIP

NEW RIVER PROVINCIAL PARK

Just off Hwy 1, about 35km west of Saint John on the way to St Stephen, this large **park** (☎506-755-4046; www.tourismnewbrunswick.ca; Jun-Sep per vehicle $10) has one of the best beaches along the Fundy shore, a wide stretch of sand bordered on one side by the rugged coastline of Barnaby Head. During camping season the park charges a fee per vehicle for day use, which includes parking at the beach and Barnaby Head trailhead.

You can spend an enjoyable few hours hiking Barnaby Head along a 5km network of nature trails. The **Chittick's Beach Trail** leads through coastal forest and past four coves, where you can check the catch in a herring weir or examine tidal pools for marine life. Extending from this loop is the 2.5km **Barnaby Head Trail**, which hugs the shoreline most of the way and rises to the edge of a cliff 15m above the Bay of Fundy.

The park's **campground** (☎506-755-4046; https://parcsnbparks.ca; 78 New River Beach Rd; tent/RV sites $28/31; ⏲May-Sep) is across the road from the beach and features 100 secluded sites, both rustic and with hookups, in a wooded setting.

Serious whale-watchers should hop aboard this catamaran, staffed by trained marine biologists. There are one to three tours daily.

Eastern Outdoors KAYAKING
(☎506-529-4662; www.easternoutdoors.com; 165 Water St; kayak rental per day $65; ⏲May-Oct) This St Andrews–based outfitter offers a variety of kayaking trips, including a three-hour tour around nearby Navy Island ($79), and full-day trips to Passamaquody Bay ($155) and Deer Island ($159). Mountain bikes (per hour/day $20/30) can also be rented here.

Sleeping

Picket Fence Motel MOTEL $
(☎506-529-8985; www.picketfencenb.com; 102 Reed Ave; r $90-110; P ❄ 📶) This retro-looking motel is the real deal. Although dated, rooms are neat-as-a-pin and it's within walking distance of the main drag. Staff are super-friendly and it's one of the best deals in town.

Rossmount Inn INN $$
(☎506-529-3351; www.rossmountinn.com; 4599 Rte 127; r $140-150; ⏲Apr-Dec; P ❄ 📶 🏊) Flags flap in the breeze in front of this stately yellow summer cottage, perched atop a manicured slope overlooking Passamaquoddy Bay. Inside the 17 elegant rooms have hand-carved wooden furniture and white linens. The feather overlays on the beds make for a cloud-like sleep. Dinner is available in the classy dining room by reservation only, as is breakfast.

Treadwell Inn B&B $$
(☎888-529-1011, 506-529-1011; www.treadwellinn.com; 129 Water St; r $140-210; ⏲mid-Jun–Oct; 🚭 ❄ 📶) You will feel very at home in these big, handsome rooms in an 1820 ship chandler's house. The pricier rooms have private decks and ocean views. With wooden beams and a sleigh bed, Room 6 has the edge. Breakfast is buffet continental. Minimum two nights.

Garden Gate B&B $$
(☎506-529-4453; www.bbgardengate.com; 364 Montague St; r from $150; P 📶) Built in 1910, this beautiful house has six comfortable but small and simple rooms. The Tilley Room is worth nabbing for its Jacuzzi tub. Excellent cooked breakfasts and small touches such as tea and cookies make it an enjoyable experience. Prices are on the higher side but it's very popular nonetheless.

Algonquin Resort HOTEL $$$
(☎506-529-8823, 855-529-8693; www.algonquinresort.com; 184 Adolphus St; r from $230; P ❄ 📶 🏊) The doyenne of New Brunswick hotels, this 'Castle-by-the-Sea' has sat on a hill overlooking town since 1889 and was given a makeover in 2015. With its elegant verandah, gardens, rooftop terrace, golf course, tennis courts and indoor pool with waterslides, it's a world unto itself. Prices vary according to seasons and demand; check the website for deals.

Eating & Drinking

Clam Digger SEAFOOD $
(4468 Hwy 127, Chamcook; mains $6-15; ⏲11:30am-3pm & 5-9pm Apr-Sep) Cars park three-deep outside this teeny red-and-white seafood shack, a summertime tradition in these parts. Order your clams, burger, scallops, poutine and milkshakes at the window and claim one of the red-painted picnic tables. It's 3.5km north of the visitor center.

★**The Chandler Room** CANADIAN $$
(www.treadwellinn.com/the-chandler-room; 129 Water St; share plates $10-18; ⏲4-10pm Wed-Sun)

Polished yet comfortable, this tapas-style restaurant is yards above the competition. Simple-sounding dishes such as beef carpaccio, spicy cauliflower and local seafood are elegantly presented and bursting with flavor. Expect a carefully chosen wine and whiskey list and bespoke cocktails. Inside it's candlelit and intimate; outside the deck views are substantial.

Rossmount Inn Restaurant CANADIAN **$$**
(☎506-529-3351; www.rossmountinn.com; 4599 Rte 127; mains $18-30; ⏲5-9:30pm) The Swiss chef-owner makes wonderful use of local bounty in this warm, art-filled dining room. The ever-changing menu might include local ingredients such as wild mushrooms, periwinkles or New Brunswick lobster turned into exquisite dishes such as lobster with nasturtium-flower dumplings and vanilla bisque. By reservation only. The restaurant is 3km north of town.

Niger Reef Tea House CANADIAN **$$**
(☎506-529-8005; https://niger-reef-tea-house.business.site; 1 Joes Point Rd; mains lunch $14-21, dinner $22-30; ⏲11am-3pm & 5-8pm May-Oct) Built in 1926 and used as a teahouse to raise money for charity until WWII, this tiny, atmospheric place is a popular spot for well-prepared meals such as loaded seafood sandwiches and homemade soup. Next to the St Andrews Blockhouse, it has an enviable location overlooking the water. The impressive and unmissable murals on the walls were discovered during restoration in the 1990s. The teahouse is named after the reef on the outer approaches of St Andrews.

Something's Brewing CAFE
(☎506-529-4702; www.facebook.com/somethingsbrewingcafestandrews; 209 Water St; bistro $10-15; ⏲7:30am-5pm Mon-Wed, to 8pm Thu-Sun, bistro Thu-Sun only) Down by the water, this tiny cafe-bar is dynamite. Grab a spot on the big deck for morning coffee or afternoon cocktails, wine and New Brunswick beer. The bistro menu will wow you with shareable and main dishes. Everything is local or homemade, from the cheeses to the smoked salmon and the blueberry-ale ice-cream sandwich.

Information

Tourist Office (www.townofstandrews.ca; 46 Reed Ave; ⏲9am-7pm Jul & Aug, to 5pm May, Jun, Sep & Oct; 📶)

FUNDY ISLES

The thinly populated, unspoiled Fundy Isles are ideal for a tranquil, nature-based escape. With grand scenery, colorful fishing wharves tucked into coves, supreme whale-watching, uncluttered walking trails and steaming dishes of seafood, the islands will make your everyday stresses fade away. The three main islands each have a distinct personality. Outside the summer season, all are nearly devoid of visitors and most services are shut.

Deer Island

Deer Island, the closest of the three main Fundy Isles to the mainland, is an unassuming fishing settlement with a lived-in look. Just 16km-by-5km, the island has been inhabited since 1770. Around 1000 people live here year-round, kept company by the many deer that reside in the island's dense forests. Lobster is the main catch with wharves and lobster pounds dotted around the island.

Deer Island can be easily explored on a day trip. Narrow, winding roads run south down each side toward Campobello Island and the ferry.

Sights & Activities

Whales usually arrive in mid-June and stay until October. You can be lucky enough to spot these offshore; for a closer look, head out on a kayak tour with Seascape Kayak Tours.

Old Sow Whirlpool WATERFRONT
(Deer Island Point Park) From the shores of the pretty, community-run 16-hectare Deer Island Point Park, Old Sow, the world's second-largest natural tidal whirlpool, is seen offshore a few hours before high tide. Check at the tourist information center (p128) for tide times. Whales pass occasionally, too.

Seascape Kayak Tours KAYAKING
(☎506-747-1884; www.seascapekayaktours.com; 40 NW Harbour Branch Rd, Richardson; half-/full-day trips $85/150, sunset trips $65; ⏲mid-May–mid-Sep) Fabulous guided paddling excursions around Deer Island and Passamaquoddy Bay with experienced guides. Multiday island-jumping camping trips also available.

Sleeping & Eating

Deer Island Inn GUESTHOUSE **$**
(☎506-747-1998; www.deerislandinn.com; 272 Rte 772, Lords Cove; r incl breakfast $95-105;

Fundy Isles

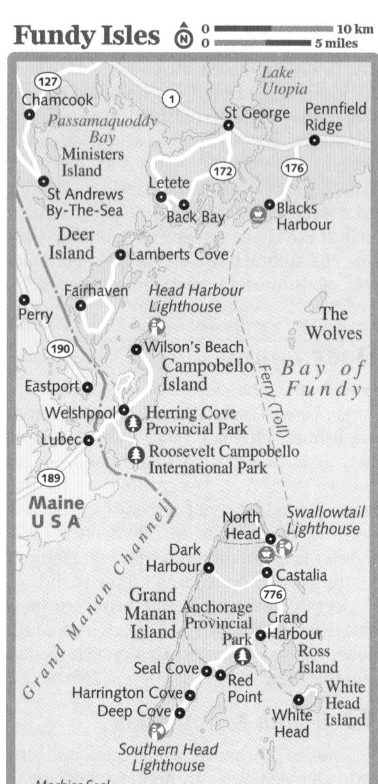

May–mid-Oct) If island stays are your thing, this excellent-value home brings a touch of Deer Island heritage with its five pleasantly appointed rooms. Excellent full breakfasts set you up for taking on the local sights. The inn is conveniently located along the main road in Lords Cove, close to a shop and the information center.

Deer Island Point Park CAMPGROUND $
(506-747-2423; www.deerislandpointpark.com; 195 Deer Island Point Rd; tent sites $25-30; Jun-Sep) Set up your tent on the high bluff and spend an evening watching the Old Sow whirlpool. The campground is directly above the Campobello ferry landing with a rocky beach and a few wilderness sites. There is no swimming here due to the dangerous pull of Old Sow.

45th Parallel Restaurant & Motel DINER $
(www.45thparallel.ca; 941 Rte 772; mains; restaurant 11am-7:30pm, shorter hours Oct-May, motel Jul & Aug;) Slide into a wooden booth or park yourself at a gingham-checked table and fill up on good home cooking. Family-run for more than 50 years, this diner-style restaurant serves up local seafood and burgers. Big pancake breakfasts are for motel guests only, who also enjoy clean, basic rooms (single/double/twin $50/60/70), an outdoor pool, firepit and tremendous hospitality.

Information

Tourist information (506-747-0119; www.deerisland.nb.ca; 193 Rte 772, Lords Cove; 10am-5pm Jul-Sep) Based in Lord's Bay community with helpful staff.

Getting There & Away

A free government-run ferry (25 minutes) carries vehicles and passengers to the northern end of Deer Island from Letete, which is 14.5km south of St George on Hwy 172 via Back Bay. The ferry runs year-round every half-hour from 6am to 7pm, and hourly from 7pm to 10pm. Get in line early on a busy day.

In summer **East Coast Ferries** (506-747-2159; www.eastcoastferries.nb.ca; car & driver $22, additional passenger $5; 9am-7pm) services Campobello Island.

Campobello Island

POP 800

The wealthy have long been enjoying Campobello as a summer retreat, with private estates that aren't much in tune with the rustic feel of the rest of the island. Like many moneyed families, the Roosevelts bought property here at the end of the 1800s and the house and its surrounding park is now the island's main attraction. With a bridge to Maine, it feels as much a part of the USA as of Canada, and most of the tourists here are day-tripping Americans.

Once billed as unspoiled and ideal, Campobello's residents are dealing with a lack of garbage disposal, few medical services and limited groceries. With the ferry running only during summer months, residents must travel through US customs to reach mainland Canada, and many are feeling exiled.

Sights & Activities

★ **Roosevelt Campobello International Park** PARK
(www.fdr.net; Hwy 774; Roosevelt Cottage 10am-6pm mid-May–mid-Oct) FREE Southernmost Campobello Island is home to this 1133-hectare park. Its star attraction is **Roo-**

sevelt Cottage, the 34-room lodge where Franklin D Roosevelt came with his family between 1905 and 1921 and visited periodically throughout his US presidency (1933–45). The surprisingly rustic structure is furnished with original Roosevelt furniture and artifacts; well-versed tour guides give insight into the Roosevelts' personal lives. Adjacent Hubbard House, built in 1891 and home to an insurance broker and concert pianist, is far more glamorous.

Head Harbour Lighthouse LIGHTHOUSE
(210 Lighthouse Rd; $5) The oldest surviving lighthouse in New Brunswick, and one of the most photographed, this 51ft structure was built in 1829 and decorated with a distinctive St George red cross. Also called East Quoddy Lighthouse, you can visit and climb it at low tide only; tide water comes in here at 5ft per hour and can leave you stranded. Whales are regular visitors offshore and many people sit along the rocky coast with binoculars enjoying the sea breezes.

Mulholland Park Lighthouse LIGHTHOUSE
(81 Narrows Rd; 10am-6pm) A favorite spot for seal-watching, the diminutive Mulholland Lighthouse was built in 1884 to guide ships through Lubec Narrows. Next door the Marine Interpretive Centre displays info on local marine life and the work of the Whale Emergency Network that operates off the island.

Herring Cove Provincial Park PARK
FREE On the southeastern side of the island, Herring Cove Provincial Park has 10km of walking trails and a rocky-sandy beach arching for 1.5km. A century ago, this was the stomping ground of the wealthy who would follow the 1.9km Gibraltar Trail to Glensevern Lake, which separates the forest from the sea and was once the site of a teahouse. There is also a golf-course restaurant, campground and picnic tables here.

Island Cruises Whale Watch CRUISE
(506-752-1107; www.bayoffundywhales.com; 62 Harbour Head Rd, Wilson's Beach; adult/child $58/48; mid-Jun–Oct) Offers daily 2½-hour whale-watching cruises with guaranteed sightings.

Sleeping & Eating

Herring Cove Provincial Park CAMPGROUND $
(506-752-7010; www.campobello.com/cmpgrdfe.html; 136 Herring Cove Rd; tent/RV sites $28/31, rustic shelter $43; Jun-Sep) This 76-site park on the eastern side of the island, 3km from the Deer Island ferry, has some nice secluded sites in a forest setting, plus there's a sandy beach and ample hiking.

Owen House B&B B&B $$
(506-752-2977; www.owenhouse.ca; 11 Welshpool St, Welshpool; d private/shared bath from $115/105; P) This large, wooden manor on the water hales from yesteryear, complete with antique spool beds made up with quilts, cozy reading nooks and lots of windows looking out to the ocean.

The Pier CANADIAN $
(506-752-2200; www.facebook.com/thepierwaterfront; 6 Pollac Cove Rd; mains $9-18; 11:30am-9pm) It's a difficult choice whether to eat inside the nautically themed dining room with big windows and regular live music, or outside on the killer patio alongside the ocean. Filling burgers and smoked or baked seafood dinners are strong contenders on the menu and local craft beers are on tap. There's a kids' menu, too.

The Prince Cafe CAFE $
(459 Rte 774, Roosevelt Campobello National Park; meals $10-14; 10am-4pm mid-May–mid-Oct) Next to Roosevelt's Cottage, get your lunch canteen-style. On a nice day, sit on the verandah for a sea view. Soups, salads, sandwiches and baking is all freshly prepared and scrumptious. We can't help but think that even Franklin would approve.

Family Fisheries Restaurant SEAFOOD $$
(1977 Rte 774, Wilson's Beach; mains $6-18; 11:30am-9pm Apr-Sep) Part of a fresh-fish market, this ultra-casual seafood shack specializes in fish-and-chips (all the seafood is caught by family members), plus lip-smacking chowders and lobster grilled cheese.

Information

Visitor Center (506-752-2922; www.fdr.net; Hwy 774; 10am-5pm) Co-billed as an Adventure Centre, this is principally an information center for the Roosevelt Campobello International Park with maps and information on local flora and wildlife. Nevertheless, they also carry information on activities and accommodation elsewhere on the island.

Getting There & Away

East Coast Ferries (p128) connects Deer Island to Welshpool (25 minutes, half-hourly) on Campobello Island. In reality, it's a tugboat pulling and pushing a barge across the open sea. The island has no gas station; arrive prepared.

(Continued on page 132)

1. Old City Market (p137)
One of New Brunswick's top markets is located in Saint John and is home to produce, artisan and sourvenir stalls.

2. Hopewell Rocks (p140)
Sandstone erosion formations rising from the ocean floor, the Rocks resemble giant arches, stone mushrooms and animals.

3. St Andrews By-The-Sea (p124)
A genteel summer resort town on the Bay of Fundy, it has a colorful history and feels much like a living museum.

4. Kings Landing (p116)
A surreal step back in time, this recreated village has staff role-playing people who lived and worked here.

KHANH NGO PHOTOGRAPHY/GETTY IMAGES ©

TERRY CARPENTER/ALAMY STOCK PHOTO ©

3

JHVEPHOTO/SHUTTERSTOCK ©

(Continued from page 129)

Grand Manan Island

Grand Manan is a peaceful, unspoiled place. There are no fast-food restaurants, no nightclubs, no traffic lights and no traffic. Just a ruggedly beautiful coastline of high cliffs and sandy coves, spruce forests and fields of long grass. Wonderful lighthouses, including the famous Swallowtail Lighthouse, stand guard above cliffs, looking out over the fishing weirs. Along the eastern shore and joined by a meandering coastal road sit a string of pretty and prosperous fishing villages. There is plenty of fresh sea air, amazing beaches and that rare and precious commodity in the modern world: silence, broken only by the rhythmic ocean surf. Some people make it a day trip, but lingering is recommended.

Sights

★Swallowtail Lighthouse LIGHTHOUSE
(www.swallowtaillighthouse.com; 50 Lighthouse Rd; adult/under 12yr $5/free; ⏲10am-6pm Jul & Aug) Clinging to the clifftop about 1km north of the ferry wharf, atmospheric Swallowtail Lighthouse (1860) is the island's signature vista. Climb down 53 stairs and across a wooden footbridge to enter. Inside you'll find tales of shipwrecks and survivors, artifacts left by lighthouse keepers' families, and fascinating equipment from yesteryear. Climb four flights of curved stairs plus a ladder to the light at the tippy top. If you want to visit a lighthouse, here's the one.

Fishing Weirs LANDMARK
Those round contraptions of wooden posts that you see dotting the waters around Grand Manan are based on the design of ancient fishing traps; some of those you see date back to the 19th century. They were formerly labeled with names such as 'Ruin,' 'Winner,' 'Outside Chance' and 'Spite,' evoking the heartbreak of relying on an indifferent sea for a living.

Grand Manan Art Gallery GALLERY
(☎506-662-3662; www.grandmananartgallery.com; 21 Cedar St, Castalia; adult/child $2/free; ⏲noon-6pm Mon-Sat, 1pm-5pm Sun mid-Jun–late Sep) Housed in what looks like a 1970s church, this lovely, nonprofit local gallery showcases local and regional artists, as well as well-known historic and emerging figures. Exhibits change regularly. Watch for a sign off the main highway, just south of North Head.

Grand Manan Historical Museum MUSEUM
(☎506-662-3524; www.grandmananmuseum.ca; 1141 Rte 776, Grand Harbour; adult/student & senior $5/3; ⏲9am-5pm Mon-Fri Jun-Sep, plus 9am-5pm Sat, 1-5pm Sun Jul & Aug) This museum makes a good destination on a foggy day. Its diverse collection of local artifacts provides a quick primer on island history. You can see a display on shipwreck lore and the original kerosene lamp from nearby Gannet Rock lighthouse (1904). There is also a room stuffed with 200-plus taxidermied birds (including the now-extinct passenger pigeon).

Seal Cove HISTORIC SITE
For a century, smoked herring was king on Grand Manan. A thousand men and women worked splitting, stringing and drying fish in 300 smokehouses up and down the island. The last smokehouse shut down in 1996 but you can still see many clustered around the tidal creek mouth at tiny Seal Cove village.

Tours

Sea Watch Tours BIRD-WATCHING
(☎877-662-8552, 506-662-8552; www.seawatchtours.com; Seal Cove Fisherman's Wharf; Machias Seal Island per person $150, whale-watching adult/child $75/55; ⏲Mon-Sat late Jun-late Sep) From late June until the end of July, make the pilgrimage out to isolated **Machias Seal Island** to see the Atlantic puffins waddle and play on their home turf. Access is limited to 15 visitors a day, so reserve well in advance. Getting onto the island can be tricky, as the waves are high and the rocks slippery. Wear sturdy shoes. Tours to see humpback, finback and Altantic right whales run from July until the end of September.

Adventure High KAYAKING
(☎506-662-3563; www.adventurehigh.com; 83 Rte 776, North Head; half-/full-day tours $65/110, evening tours $45, bicycles per half-day/day/week $18/25/125; ⏲May-Oct) This outfitter offers tours of the Grand Manan coastline ranging from lovely two-hour sunset paddles to multiday Bay of Fundy adventures. In addition to high-quality mountain bikes, they also rent double bikes and bike trailers.

Sleeping

Anchorage Camping CAMPGROUND $
(☎506-662-7022; https://parcsnbparks.ca; 136 Anchorage Rd, Anchorage; tent/RV sites $24/26; ⏲May-Sep) Family-friendly camping in a large field surrounded by the tall evergreens of Anchorage Provincial Park. Located be-

tween Grand Harbour and Seal Cove, the campground has a kitchen shelter, playground, laundry and a long pebbly beach. The area adjoins marshes, which comprise a migratory bird sanctuary, and there are several short hiking trails and bird hides.

★Compass Rose B&B $$
(☎506-662-3563; www.compassroseinn.com; 65 Rte 776, North Head; r $100-165; P ❄ ☎) It's hard to go wrong at this quaint little spot, which has seven airy rooms with wrought-iron beds, sea views and access to the beach. It's within walking distance of the ferry dock, and has one of the island's most tasteful restaurants (mains $20 to $25) with big windows, daily fresh menus and sumptuous desserts.

Island Home B&B B&B $$
(☎506-662-8777; http://islandhomebnb.ca; 22 Rte 776, North Head; r $125; ⏱year-round; ❄ ☎) Directly across from the ferry and set in a tranquil yard, this six-bedroom guesthouse is like stepping into the pages of a gorgeous magazine layout. Beautiful linens, furnishings and bathrooms will make you want to stay in all day. There's also a lovely patio, sitting room and dining room where equally beautiful breakfasts are served. It shouldn't be surprising that a professional decorator lives here.

Inn at Whale Cove INN $$
(☎506-662-3181; www.whalecovecottages.ca; Whistle Rd, North Head; s/d incl breakfast $145/155; ⏱May-Oct; ❄ ☎) 'Serving rusticators since 1910,' including writer Willa Cather, who wrote several of her novels here in the 1920s and '30s. The main lodge (built in 1816) and six shingled cottages (two with fully equipped kitchens) retain the charm of that earlier era. They are fitted with polished pine floors and stone fireplaces, antiques, chintz curtains and well-stocked bookshelves.

Eating

The island's dining options are decent if not plentiful in summer but nearly nonexistent in the off-season. The majority are found around North Head or south in Grand Harbour. Be sure to try dulse, a dark-purple seaweed harvested locally and eaten like crisps (chips) by locals. Chefs use it as a seasoning. You might even see a 'DLT sandwich' on the menu (yep, that's dulse instead of bacon).

Old Well House Cafe CAFE $
(☎506-662-3232; www.facebook.com/theoldwellhousecafe; 56 Rte 776, North Head; meals $9-15; ⏱8am-4pm) This shingled cottage from 1832 is a local meeting place. Get comfy on a couch, perch at a wooden table or relax outside at a picnic table. Order excellent coffees, homemade soups, grilled wraps and some of the best baking you'll find in New Brunswick (try the flourless peanut butter cookies). The bagels are shipped from Montréal.

Sunrise Seafoods SEAFOOD $
(☎506-660-0156; Woodwards Cove Breakwater Rd; $8-18; ⏱11am-9pm) Right down by the fisheries, with a smokehouse pluming into the air, this place is the real deal. Get your chowders, chips, scallops and clams, lobster roll and fish, all as fresh as fresh can be. There are a few picnic tables or take it to go. Cash only.

Trapped SEAFOOD $$
(☎506-662-3696; 7 Norman Rd, Grand Harbour; meals $18-24; ⏱noon-7pm Mon-Sat Jul & Aug) A family-owned fishery since 1969, these guys know their lobster. Chill out on the deck with a beer or a smoothie and hot lobster or spinach dip to share. The 'Trapped' clothing in the attached store makes for great souvenirs.

Inn at Whale Cove CANADIAN $$$
(☎506-662-3181; www.whalecovecottages.ca; Whistle Rd; mains $22-28; ⏱5-7pm) Wonderful food in a relaxed country setting on Whale Cove. The menu changes daily, but includes mouthwatering upscale meals such as pulled pork and tagliatelle, seafood bouillabaisse and a to-die-for hazelnut crème caramel for dessert. Come early and have a cocktail by the fire in the cozy, old-fashioned parlor.

Roland's Sea Vegetables MARKET
(☎506-662-3468; 174 Hill Rd; per pound $11.50; ⏱9am-5pm year-round) Grand Manan is one of the few remaining producers of dulse, a type of seaweed that is used as a snack food or seasoning. Dulse gatherers wade among the rocks at low tide to pick the seaweed, then lay it out on beds of rocks to dry, just as they've been doing for hundreds of years. For three generations, Roland's has been producing dulse and shipping it as far as Japan and Hawaii. Buy it here by the bag full.

Information

Visitor Information Centre (☎506-662-3442; www.grandmanannb.com; 130 Rte 776, North Head; ⏱mid-Jun–late Aug) Locally run tourist organization that has maps, brochures and ferry schedules.

Getting There & Away

The only way to get from Blacks Harbour on the mainland to North Head on Grand Manan is by a private ferry company, **Coastal Transport** (☎506-662-3724; http://grandmanan.coastaltransport.ca; adult/child/car/bicycle $12/6/36/4.10). The crossing takes 1½ hours, and there are around three to four daily departures from each port in summer. Reserve and pay in advance as it gets busy. It's best to pay for a return trip, rather than one way, so you don't get stuck on the island. Watch for harbor porpoises and whales en route.

The ferry dock is within walking distance of several hotels, restaurants, shops and tour operators. To explore the whole of the island, bring your own car, as there is no rental company on Grand Manan.

Getting Around

The ferry disembarks at the village of North Head at the northern end of the island. The main road, Rte 776, runs 28.5km down the length of the island along the eastern shore. You can drive from end to end in about 45 minutes. The western side of Grand Manan is uninhabited and more or less impenetrable: a sheer rock wall rising out of the sea, backed by dense forest and bog, broken only at Dark Harbour where a steep road drops down to the water's edge. Hiking trails provides access to this wilderness.

Adventure High (p132) rents out bicycles. The roads are winding and keen cyclists will enjoy the undulating routes.

SAINT JOHN

POP 67,600

Saint John has long been a force to be reckoned with. Once a gritty port city, and the original economic engine of the province, it has since cleaned up its act. Its lively historic core is home to one of New Brunswick's top markets and there's a dynamic restaurant and pub scene worth exploring. Wander past beautifully preserved redbrick and sandstone 19th-century architecture, down narrow side streets that offer glimpses of the sea, or along the harbor where the mighty Saint John and Kennebecasis Rivers empty into the Bay of Fundy. Check out the city's unique museums and zip-line over the Reversing Falls. Sure, some of the surrounding natural beauty is diminished by pulp mill smokestacks and an oil refinery but Saint John will welcome you with open arms and knows how to show you a good time.

Sights

★New Brunswick Museum MUSEUM
(www.nbm-mnb.ca; 1 Market Sq; adult/student/family $10/6/22; ⏰9am-5pm Mon-Wed & Fri, to 9pm Thu, 10am-5pm Sat, noon-5pm Sun) The New Brunswick Museum has a varied and interesting collection. There's a surprisingly captivating section on industrial history with 1908 figurines by Acadian Alfred Morneault and an outstanding section on marine life, including a life-size specimen of a whale. There are also hands-on exhibits, models of old sailing ships and a stunning collection of Canadian and international artwork on the top floor. This is the province's top museum and worth a visit.

Reversing Rapids NATURAL FEATURE
The Bay of Fundy's phenomenal tides are a defining characteristic along this coast. Here, where the Saint John River nears this tidal bay, one of the province's best-known sights occurs. Known as the Reversing Rapids, the real action is happening underwater, where a 61m waterfall drops into a plunge pool. What you see from above is the high tides of the Bay of Fundy colliding with the strong river current, causing rapids, standing waves and the water to flow upstream.

Irving Nature Park PARK
(www.facebook.com/IrvingNaturePark; Sand Cove Rd; ⏰8am-dusk May-Oct) For those with a vehicle and who like nature, Irving Nature Park, 9km southwest of Saint John, has rugged, unspoiled coastal topography. It's also a remarkable place for bird-watching, with hundreds of species regularly spotted, while seals sometimes gather on the rocks offshore. Seven trails lead around beaches, cliffs, woods, mudflats, marsh and rocks. Wear sturdy footwear.

Loyalist House HISTORIC BUILDING
(☎506-652-3590; www.loyalisthouse.com; 120 Union St; adult/child/family $5/2/7; ⏰10am-5pm late May-Oct) Dating from 1810, this Georgian-style Loyalist House was maintained with minimal changes for five generations until the family moved out in 1959. As one of the city's oldest unchanged buildings and a survivor of the 1877 fire, it's now a museum, depicting the Loyalist period. Tours led by guides in period dress take 30 to 45 minutes.

Saint John

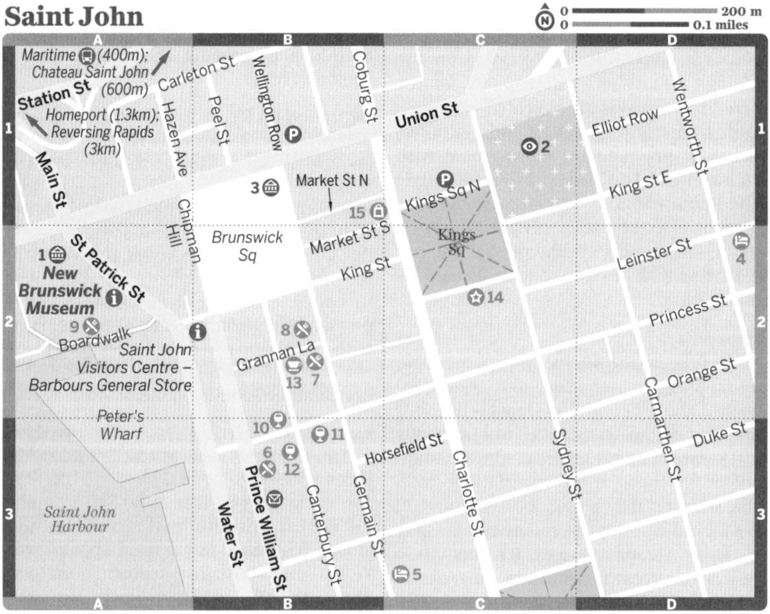

Saint John

Top Sights
1 New Brunswick Museum A2

Sights
2 Loyalist Burial Ground C1
3 Loyalist House B1

Sleeping
4 Earle of Leinster Inn D2
5 Mahogany Manor C3

Eating
Billy's Seafood Company .... (see 15)
6 East Coast Bistro B3
7 Italian By Night B2
8 Port City Royal B2
9 Saint John Ale House A2

Drinking & Nightlife
10 Big Tide Brewing Company B3
11 Happinez Wine Bar B3
12 O'Leary's B3
Picaroons ....(see 13)
13 Rouge B2

Entertainment
14 Imperial Theatre C2

Shopping
15 Old City Market B1

Activities & Tours

Saint John Adventures ADVENTURE SPORTS
(☎506-634-9477; www.saintjohnadventures.ca; Fallsview Park; per person $65) Five lines are strung between six towers allowing you to zip over the Reversing Rapids on Saint John River. The zip-line course takes one to two hours.

Walks 'n' Talks with David Goss WALKING
(☎506-672-8601; walks free-$5; ⏱7pm Tue & Fri Jun-Sep) Local storyteller David Goss leads themed walks throughout the city and natural environments. The walks have so much flair that locals as well as visitors frequent the fun. Departure locations and hours vary; check with the visitor center. Friday-night ghost walks leave from New River Beach.

Sleeping

Saint John motels sit primarily along Manawagonish Rd, 7km west of uptown. There are also a couple of upscale chain hotels uptown and some great B&Bs.

★ **Earle of Leinster Inn** B&B $$
(☎506-652-3275; www.earleofleinster.com; 96 Leinster St; r from $110;) Come for the original, atmospheric rooms; stay for the incredible breakfasts. Located a quick stroll from the city center, this fabulous B&B has nine unique rooms, some with kitchenettes. The Rocky Mountain–style Pine Room with the bear rug may be your thing or else the rather ornate Fitzgerald Room. The owners are the perfect balance of discreet and welcoming with a wealth of information.

Homeport B&B $$
(☎506-672-7255,888-678-7678;www.homeportinn.ca; 60 Douglas Ave; r $135-180; P) Perched above once-grand Douglas Ave, this imposing Italianate-style B&B was originally two separate mansions belonging to shipbuilder brothers. It has a boutique-hotel vibe, with a stately parlor, a full bar and 10 elegant old-world guest rooms (try to snag the lovely Veranda Queen). It's about 1km west of the uptown peninsula, en route to the Reversing Rapids.

Mahogany Manor B&B $$
(☎506-636-8000; http://mahoganymanor.ca; 220 Germain St; d from $125; P) Tucked into the heart of Uptown, this beautiful Victorian B&B is a wonderful place to call home. Rooms are fairly standard but comfortable, and there are antique sitting rooms and sun porches to relax in. The upbeat owners know more about the city than you'll be able to absorb.

Chateau Saint John BUSINESS HOTEL $$
(☎506-644-4444; www.chateausaintjohn.ca; 369 Rockland Rd; r from $185; P) Situated on a main road on the edge of the CBD, behemoth Chateau Saint John has large, spacious rooms and city views. Professional service and the price-to-quality ratio make it a good choice. It's a 15-minute walk into town and there's ample parking on-site. It's popular with groups and business people.

Eating

★ **Port City Royal** INTERNATIONAL $$
(☎506-631-3714; www.portcityroyal.com; 45 Grannan St; small plates $12-18, mains $23-29; ⊙4-11pm Tue-Thu, to late Fri & Sat) With exposed brick and peeling plaster, the interior of this vintage historic building defies its well-cared-for and elegant menu. Small shareable plates are perfect for the intimate atmosphere and the ever-changing mains are a fresh take on traditional ingredients. The cocktail menu is equally original.

★ **Italian By Night** ITALIAN $$
(☎506-214-8259; www.italianbynight.com; 97 Germain St; mains $15-30; ⊙5-9pm Mon-Thu, to 10pm Fri & Sat) Big and open, and with a slightly rustic feel, this is a little bit of Italy in the center of Saint John. Big windows look out to the street but you'll be too absorbed with what's on your plate to notice. Think fresh pasta, stone-baked pizzas and second plates such as lamb with butter-poached potatoes or pistachio-crusted salmon. The wine list is honed and cocktails divine.

East Coast Bistro FRENCH $$
(☎506-696-3278; www.eastcoastbistro.com; 60 Prince William St; mains $24-30; ⊙11am-9pm Tue-Thu, to 10pm Fri, 10am-10pm Sat) Combining French flair with local ingredients, this chic, brick-walled bistro is all about flavor. Watch elegant dishes featuring seafood, duck or steak being created in the open kitchen.

Billy's Seafood Company SEAFOOD $$$
(www.billysseafood.com; 49 Charlotte St; mains lunch $15-30, dinner $24-36; ⊙11am-10pm Mon-Thu, to 11pm Fri & Sat, 4-10pm Sun, closed Sun Jan-Mar, raw bar 6-9pm Mon-Sat) Next to the City Market, locals and visitors alike come here to dine on satisfying seafood dishes. Try bayou seafood stew, white-wine garlic mussels or lobster with warm butter. Oysters at the raw bar are $2.50 a pop. In summer, the polished restaurant opens up onto a sidewalk patio.

Saint John Ale House MODERN AMERICAN $$$
(www.sjah.ca; 1 Market Sq; mains $18-40; ⊙11am-late Mon-Fri, 10:30am-late Sat & Sun) On summer evenings this place is popular for its big, wharfside patio and long list of beers on tap. Head upstairs for a menu of locally sourced dishes such as bacon maple scallops, market chowder or giant lobster roll. It's also a favorite spot for weekend brunch.

Drinking & Nightlife

★ **Rouge** COFFEE
(☎506-639-6011; 36 Grannan Lane; ⊙7am-6pm Mon-Fri, 8am-5pm Sat & Sun) Hands down the best coffee in town, if not the province. If

your curiosity peaks, you can also try elderflower mimosa, pink lemonade or a variety of cold brews. The funky interior is entirely welcoming or the flower-bedecked patio has outdoor seating. You'll find it tucked off Grannan Lane.

Picaroons BREWERY
(☎506-648-9834; http://picaroons.ca; 32 Canterbury St; ⏲10am-10pm Mon & Tue, to 11pm Wed-Sat, noon-8pm Sun) With a mothership in Fredericton, this cool brewery creates six beers on-site. With a long wooden table wound around the room and additional barrel tables next to big, often open windows, it a great place to chill out. If you like it a lot, grab a growler to go.

Happinez Wine Bar BAR
(www.happinezwinebar.com; 42 Princess St; ⏲4pm-midnight Wed & Thu, to 1am Fri, 5pm-1am Sat) If you want a break from beer, duck into this intimate little wine bar. The list is mainly international, and while cellar wines by the bottle come with a hefty price tag, there's a good selection available by the glass.

Big Tide Brewing Company BREWERY
(www.bigtidebrew.com; 47 Princess St; ⏲11am-midnight Mon-Sat, 3-9pm Sun) This subterranean brewpub is a local hangout and a cozy spot for a pint (try the Confederation Cream Ale or the Whistlepig Stout). They have five beers on tap that are brewed right here.

Imperial Theatre THEATER
(☎506-674-4100; www.imperialtheatre.nb.ca; 24 Kings Sq S) Now restored to its original 1913 splendor, this is the city's premier venue for performances ranging from classical music to live theater.

Shopping

★Old City Market MARKET
(☎658 2820; 47 Charlotte St; ⏲7:30am-6pm Mon-Fri, to 5pm Sat) Wedged between North and South Market Sts, this sense-stunning food hall has been home to wheeling and dealing since 1876. The impressive brick interior is packed with produce stalls, bakeries, fishmongers and butcher shops, as well as numerous counters selling the full meal deal. There are also plenty of skilled artisans with stalls, making this a top place to pick up unique souvenirs.

Information

MEDICAL SERVICES

Saint John Regional Hospital (☎506-648-6000; 400 University Ave; ⏲24hr) Located northwest of the town center.

POST

Main Post Office (126 Prince William St)

TOURIST INFORMATION

Saint John Visitors Centre – Barbours General Store (St Andrew's Bicentennial Green; ⏲10am-6pm mid-May–Sep) Conveniently located in the old-fashioned Barbours General Store, at the central St Andrew's Bicentennial Green.

Saint John Visitors Centre – Reversing Rapids (450 Bridge Rd; ⏲9am-6pm mid-May–Sep, to 7pm Jul & Aug)

Visitor & Convention Bureau (☎506-658-2990; www.discoversaintjohn.com; City Hall, 15 Market Sq; ⏲9am-6pm mid-May–mid-Oct, to 7pm Jul & Aug) Knowledgeable, friendly staff. Ask for the self-guided walking-tour pamphlets.

Getting There & Away

AIR

The airport is 5km east of town on Loch Lomond Rd toward St Martins. Air Canada runs daily flights to Toronto, Montréal and Halifax.

BOAT

The Bay Ferries (p115) sails daily between Saint John and Digby, Nova Scotia, year-round. The three-hour crossing can save a lot of driving.

Arrive early or call ahead for vehicle reservations, as the ferry is very busy in July and August. Even with a reservation, arrive an hour before departure. Walk-ons and cyclists should be OK at any time. There's a restaurant and a bar on board.

BUS

Long-haul bus services are operated by **Maritime Bus** (☎506-672-2055; www.maritimebus.com; 125 Station St; ⏲8am-8pm Mon-Fri, 9am-8pm Sat & Sun). Routes include Fredericton ($25.50, 1½ hours) and Moncton ($34, two to four hours).

Getting Around

Downtown (known as Uptown) Saint John sits on a square, hilly peninsula between the mouth of the Saint John River and Courtenay Bay. Kings Sq marks the nucleus of town, and its pathways duplicate the pattern of the Union Jack.

West over the Harbour Bridge is Saint John West. Many of the street names in this section of the city are identical to those of Saint John proper, and to avoid confusion, they end in a west designation, such as Charlotte St W. Saint John West has the ferries to Digby, Nova Scotia.

EASTERN FUNDY SHORE

Much of the rugged, unspoiled Eastern Fundy Shore from Saint John to Hopewell Cape has been incorporated into the Fundy Trail Parkway, a 30km-long road with sweeping coastal views and countless trails to explore by foot or bike. Nature-lovers will be enchanted by this marvelous coast, edged by dramatic cliffs and tides.

The plan to link the parkway to Fundy National Park had been delayed due to the discovery of traditional Mi'kmaq hunting grounds; the new link was expected to open in 2021.

St Martins

POP 276

A 40km drive east of Saint John, St Martins is a winsome seaside hamlet surrounded by steep cliffs and flower-studded pastureland. Once a major wooden shipbuilding center, this relaxed community springs to life in summer. Hikers, bikers and scenic-drivers flock to the 30km Fundy Trail Parkway, which starts just 10km east of the village and winds along a jaw-dropping stretch of coastline. In town, check out the impressive red sandstone sea caves at Mac's Beach, accessible by foot when the tide is low. The village's twin covered bridges are also a popular photo op.

Activities

Red Rock Adventure OUTDOORS
(☎506-833-2231; www.bayoffundyadventures.com; 415 Main St; walking tours per person $25-130, kayaking/boat trips $65; ⏲9am-5pm) Located opposite the St Martins Wharf, Red Rock Adventures offers walking tours, including multiday treks in the parkway, kayaking adventures and scenic boat trips.

River Bay Adventures KAYAKING
(☎506-663-9530; www.riverbayadventures.com; tours from $80) Runs two- to three-hour guided sea-kayaking trips from St Martins Harbour to the sea caves at nearby Mac's Beach, under the bridges, along the coast and to nearby islands.

Sleeping & Eating

Fundy Woods Campground & Cottages CAMPGROUND $
(www.fundywoods.com; 2644 Rte 111; tent sites $30, RV sites $40-50, cottages $120; ⏲mid-May–Sep; 📶🐾) Just a few minutes from Main Street, this wooded campground offers friendly services and fully kitted-out cottages that sleep four.

Salmon River B&B B&B $$
(☎506-833-1110; www.salmonriverbandb.com; 4 Snows Lane; r $115-125; ⏲mid-May–mid-Oct; ❄📶) Eight plain but pleasant rooms named after local personalities. It's in a handy location bang in the middle of town, above Fiori's restaurant.

Octopus Ice Cream ICE CREAM $
(www.octopusicecream.com; 404 Main St; $3-8; ⏲10am-7pm May-Oct) Come to this place right on the harbor to be spoiled by choice. Black cherry, pistachio, chocolate peanut butter and countless other flavors come as cones, milkshakes, banana splits and sundaes. And then there's the toppings. Be sure to try the homemade fish-shaped waffle cones.

The Caves SEAFOOD $
(www.cavesrestaurant.com; 82 Big Salmon River Rd; mains $10-27; ⏲11am-7pm May, Jun, Sep & Oct, to 8:30pm Jul & Aug) One of two seaside spots known for their creamy chowder sitting side by side on Mac's Beach. Get your fill of seafood with toasted lobster tail or seafood casserole, or grab a salad or burger, all served next to the gorgeous sand with views of the caves.

Seaside Restaurant & Take Out SEAFOOD $$
(80 Big Salmon River Rd; mains $10-20; ⏲11am-8pm Mar-Nov) Right on Mac's Beach, the simple but spacious Seaside Restaurant serves fish-and-chips, scallops, chowder and more next to the sand and with views of the caves. Now you know you are on holiday.

Fundy National Park

Fundy National Park (www.pc.gc.ca/eng/pn-np/nb/fundy; daily permit adult/under 17yr/family $7.80/free/15.70; ⏲May-Oct) is understandably the region's most popular sight. Highlights include the world's highest tides, the irregularly eroded sandstone cliffs and the wide beach at low tide that makes exploring the shore for small marine life and debris such a treat. The park is delightfully wooded

DON'T MISS

FUNDY TRAIL PARKWAY

Stretching east from St Martins for 30 glorious kilometers, this magnificent **parkway** (www.fundytrailparkway.com; adult/youth $9.50/5.50; ⏲9am-5pm mid-May–Jun & Sep, 8am-8pm Jul–mid-Aug, 9am-7pm late Aug) provides big ocean views and access to a large network of trails and footpaths along the Bay of Fundy coast. The parkway offers numerous viewpoints, picnic areas and beach access points while trails lead to waterfalls, suspension bridges and more sandy beaches. The parkway was expected to extend to Fundy National Park in 2021.

At Big Salmon River visit the **Big Salmon River Interpretive Center** (Fundy Trail Pkwy; ⏲9am-5pm mid-May–Jun & Sep, 8am-8pm Jul–mid-Aug, 9am-7pm late Aug), which has exhibits from when a logging community lived here, plus lots of information on hikes. Nearby, a suspension bridge crosses over the crystal-clear river, leading to the 61km Fundy Footpath, a solid five-day trek from Big Salmon River to Goose River in Fundy National Park for which you must register at either end.

If you're looking for something a little less giant, try the 4.4km **Long Beach Footpath** or the beautiful and non-strenuous 2.3km trail to **Walton Glen Gorge** beginning at the end of the parkway. Running parallel to the parkway is an accessible 10km-long multiuse trail for walkers and cyclists. In the off-season, the main gate is closed, but you can park at the entrance and hike or pedal in. On weekends, a shuttle runs within the parkway to various trail heads.

and lush, and features an extensive network of impressive hiking trails and lakes. Unusual for a national park, you'll also find a motel, a golf course and an outdoor saltwater swimming pool.

Activities

Hiking

Fundy features 120km of walking trails, where it's possible to enjoy anything from a short stroll to a three-day trek. Several trails require hikers to ford rivers, so be prepared.

The most popular backpacking route is the **Fundy Circuit**, a three-day trek of 45km through the heart of the park. Hikers generally spend their first night at Tracy Lake and their second at Bruin Lake, returning via the Upper Salmon River. You must reserve your wilderness campsites online (https://reservation.pc.gc.ca; $20 per night).

Enjoyable day hikes in Fundy National Park include the **Matthews Head Loop**, a 4.5km stretch with the nicest coastal views of the park (ranked moderate to difficult); and the **Third Vault Falls Trail**, a challenging one-way hike of 3.7km to the park's tallest falls. Alternatively, a short and pleasant stroll along a boardwalk takes you to **Dickson Falls**.

For serious, experienced hikers, the most popular one-night backcountry trek is the **Goose River Trail**. It joins the **Fundy Footpath** (not to be confused with Fundy Circuit). The Fundy Footpath is an undeveloped five-day wilderness trek and one of the most difficult in the province. While you can cycle to Goose River, the trail beyond can only be done on foot.

Pick up maps and trail condition information at Headquarters Visitors Centre (p140). In summer rangers lead a variety of family-friendly educational programs, including night hikes.

Mountain Biking

Mountain biking is permitted on 10 trails, including both easy routes suitable for beginners and moderate trails for those after a challenge. Park maps detail where bikes are permitted; on all trails, you share the path with hikers. Adult and child mountain bikes can be rented at Chignecto South (half/full day $30/50).

Swimming

The ocean is pretty bracing here. A solar-heated saltwater **swimming pool** (off Wolfe Point Rd; ⏲11am-6:30pm Jul & Aug), located near the park's southern entrance, was recently renovated and is the perfect place to cool off.

Sleeping

Chignecto North CAMPGROUND **$**
(☎877-737-3783; http://reservation.pc.gc.ca; tent/RV sites $26/36) This beautifully wooded campground (with 251 sites in total) is popular with families as it has playgrounds and

DON'T MISS

HOPEWELL ROCKS

The **Hopewell Rocks** (www.thehopewellrocks.ca; off Hwy 114; adult/child/family $10/8/25.50, shuttle per person $2; 9am-5pm May-Oct, longer hours in summer;) are bizarre sandstone erosion formations known as 'flowerpots,' rising from the ocean floor. They resemble giant arches, stone mushrooms and animals. Many come to marvel at their Dr Seussian look, making the rocks New Brunswick's top attraction and certainly one of its most crowded. You can only walk amid the rocks at low tide; at high tide, the rock towers are still visible from the well-trafficked trails that wind through the woods above, or you can join a kayaking tour to bob around them.

Check the tide tables at any tourist office or area hotel. From the interpretive center at the entrance to the rocks, you can walk 20 minutes or take a shuttle that stops steps away from the main viewing deck. It is free for those with a disability and anyone accompanying them. Hopewell Rocks is located 38km southwest of Moncton.

good facilities. Sites are secluded and private, despite its generous size, and it's just a 4km drive from the beach. There are also yurts and Otentiks (both $100).

Point Wolfe Campground CAMPGROUND **$**
(877-737-3783; http://reservation.pc.gc.ca; tent sites $26, RV sites $33-35, Otentiks $100) This lovely campground (with 146 sites and 10 Otentiks), 8km southwest of the Headquarters Visitor Center, is a little more secluded than the park's other main campgrounds and it's the closest of all the campgrounds to the water. Twelve sites have water and electricity for RVs.

Headquarters Campground CAMPGROUND **$**
(877-737-3783; http://reservation.pc.gc.ca; tent/RV sites $26/35, Otentiks/yurts $100/115) Of all the campsites in Fundy National Park, this is the most mainstream, and the only one close to both the beach and Alma village. It has 101 sites and offers yurts and Otentiks for those who don't have their own camping gear. It's not entirely wooded but the tent sites are grassy and a couple have excellent bay views.

Fundy Highlands Motel & Chalets CABIN, MOTEL **$$**
(506-887-2930, 888-883-8639; www.fundyhighlands.com; 8714 Hwy 114; d $110, cabins $125-135; May-Oct) The only private accommodations in Fundy National Park, this spot has charming little cabins, all with decks, kitchenettes and superlative views. On the same premises is a small, well-kept motel that offers big rooms with kitchenettes that open onto a lovely lawn. While it's not luxurious, it's spotless and has friendly owners and an appealing touch of retro 1950s.

Eating

Be prepared to bring your own supplies. The village of Alma does a good job at servicing the park; while there aren't supermarkets, it has many restaurants, a couple of decent takeouts and a good bakery.

Information

Headquarters Visitors Centre (506-887-6000; Rte 114 & Wolfe Point Rd; 10am-6pm May & Aug-Oct, to 8pm Jun & Jul) Just inside the park's southern entrance, the park rangers at this center have information on trail conditions, dole out maps and info and can take reservations for campsites.

Getting There & Away

If heading east, it's not yet possible to drive directly along the coastline from St Martins to Fundy National Park; instead, a detour inland by Sussex is necessary. There's no public transport in the area.

Alma

POP 213

The tiny, cheerful fishing village of Alma is bustling in the summertime. A worthwhile stop in its own right, it also serves as a supply center for Fundy National Park, with accommodation, restaurants, a grocery store and laundry. Most facilities close in winter when the only one left standing is Molly Kool (OK, statue of), the first female sea captain on the continent. The beach on the edge of town offers a sandy stretch at low tide and views of the colorful fishing fleet.

Fresh Air Adventure (506-887-2249, 800-545-0020; www.freshairadventure.com; 16 Fundy View Dr; 2-/3hr tours from $50/62; Jun-Sep) offers myriad kayaking tours, from two-hour trips to multiday excursions, in and around Fundy. For experienced paddlers

WORTH A TRIP

CAPE ENRAGE

Perched at the top of a suitably windblown and rocky precipice since 1840, **Cape Enrage Lighthouse** (www.capeenrage.ca; 650 Cape Enrage Rd; adult/child $6/5; 10am-6pm mid-May–Oct, to 8pm Jul & Aug) is one of the oldest in the province. The 150-year-old clifftop lightstation, with its lighthouse, former lighthouse-keeper's house (now a restaurant) and a small gallery, provides dramatic views. The more adventurous can do on-site rappelling ($90 per person for two hours) and zip-lining ($45 per person for three runs). Or you can simply wander the beach looking for fossils (low tide only).

At Mary's Point, 22km east of Cape Enrage, is the **Shepody Bay Shorebird Reserve** (Mary's Point Rd, off Hwy 915) FREE, where hundreds of thousands of shorebirds, primarily sandpipers, gather from mid-July to mid-August to fuel up before their southern migration. The interpretive center is open from late June to early September, but you can use the 6.5km of trails any time. The only way to reach the cape is with your own wheels or on a tour; there is no public transport to the cape.

and serious adventurers, they offer surf-ski wave-riding tours.

Sleeping & Eating

Alpine Motor Inn MOTEL $$
(866-87-2052; www.alpinemotorinn.ca; 8591 Main St; r $105-160; May–mid-Oct;) This busy, renovated motel has clean, standard rooms, the majority of which have bay views. Colorful lawn chairs next to the sea are a relaxing place to be, and the staff is both helpful and welcoming.

Parkland Village Inn INN $$
(506-887-2313; www.parklandvillageinn.com; 8601 Main St; r $125-165; May–mid-Oct;) Originally a garrison moved from Sussex in 1949, Parkland Village Inn has standard, renovated rooms, some with balconies and killer Bay of Fundy views. Breakfast is only included out of high season.

★**Tipsy Tails Restaurant** CANADIAN $$
(506-887-2190; www.facebook.com/tipsytails; 8607 Main St; mains $13-30; 11am-9:30pm May–mid-Oct) With a patio looking out over the marina and a chef who winters as a fisherman, this new-on-the-scene restaurant serves top-quality grub. Local seafood, PEI beef ribs and pulled pork with house-made kimchi all grace the menu. There's nothing standard about this place. Be sure to try the loaded corn on the cob.

Alma Lobster Shop SEAFOOD $$
(506-887-1987; www.thankfultoo.com; 36 Shore Lane; mains $16-25; 11am-9pm) Get your seafood straight from the source – this is where local fishing boats unload. Dine on the beach or buy it to take away, but either way check out the touch tank with its 14lb lobsters and ask to peek in the back room to see the hundreds of incoming lobsters being sorted into size.

Holy Whale Brewery BREWERY
(506-887-1999; 8576 Main St; noon-10pm Mon-Fri, 10am-10pm Sat & Sun) Housed in a converted church, this lively brewery is making a name for itself across the Maritimes. The punchy Devil's Half Acre IPA and creamy Medusa Milk Stout are often accompanied by sessionals such as the Creamsicle Pale. You'll also find Buddha Bear Coffee Roaster here, a summertime menu and regular live music.

SOUTHEASTERN NEW BRUNSWICK

The southeastern corner of New Brunswick province is a flat coastal plain sliced by tidal rivers and salt marshes. Moncton, known as 'Hub City,' is a major crossroads with two well-known attractions where nature appears to defy gravity. Southeast, toward Nova Scotia, are significant historical and birdlife attractions.

Moncton

POP 71,900

Once a major wooden shipbuilding port and then in a slump, Moncton is now the fastest-growing city in the Maritime provinces with the motto: 'I will rise again.' And thanks to a new economy built on transportation and call centers drawn here by the bilingual workforce, it is rising quickly. Its small, red-brick downtown along the glistening banks

OFF THE BEATEN TRACK

FORT BEAUSÉJOUR

Sitting atop a hill overlooking green fields rolling down to the Bay of Fundy and across to Nova Scotia, this **historical site** (☎506-364-5080; www.pc.gc.ca/fortbeausejour; 111 Fort Beauséjour Rd, Aulac; adult/child $3.90/free; ⊙interpretive center 9am-5pm late Jun-early Sep) is well worth a visit. Built in 1751 to hold back the British and later reinforced by the British invaders, it was used as a stronghold during the American Revolution and War of 1812. The fort's unique star-shaped design, with angles and corners, made it trickier to hit. Exploring underground barracks and casement rooms makes for an atmospheric adventure.

of the Petitcodiac River has a lively pub and restaurant scene. There is also a bustling Acadian farmers market, a couple of worthwhile museums and popular nearby sights including Hopewell Rocks and Magnetic Hill. To top it off, Moncton's event calendar is full in summer.

Sights

Resurgo Place & Moncton Museum MUSEUM
(☎506-856-4383; www.resurgo.ca; 20 Mountain Rd; adult/youth/child/family $10/7/5/24; ⊙10am-5pm Mon-Sat, noon-5pm Sun, closed Mon Sep-May) This modern, engaging museum inside Resurgo Place follows the story of Moncton. Steer a car-cart over a giant floor map to see video footage and learn the history of landmarks and check out impressive artifacts such as a French Bible from 1747. The transportation exhibit is kid-tastic; drive a train, build a truck and a boat, pilot a sub and launch a rocket. Stop by the traveling exhibitions as well.

Magnetic Hill AMUSEMENT PARK
(☎506-877-7720; Mountain Rd; per car $6; ⊙8am-8pm May-Sep) There is a hint of nostalgia about Magnet Hill, one of Canada's earliest tourist attractions. It continues to draw crowds and is worth visiting purely for the novelty. Since the 1930s, motorists noticed they had to accelerate to go downhill and coasted uphill – that gravity appeared to work in reverse. During the summer, expect a half-hour wait for your turn. There is also a colorful boardwalk nearby with restaurants and shops, a covered bridge, water park and zoo.

Magnetic Hill is about 10km northwest of downtown off Mountain Rd.

Thomas Williams House HISTORIC BUILDING
(☎506-857-0590; 103 Park St; entrance by donation, high tea $15; ⊙house 10am-5pm, tea 11am-5pm Wed-Sun Jun-Sep) Williams arrived in Canada from England in 1864 when he was just 18. He went on to become the treasurer of the Canadian Railway. Built in 1883, the house has been restored to its former glory of the late 1800s when he lived here with his wife and 11 children. Enjoy tea or lemonade and some homemade sweets in the dining room or patio.

Acadian Museum MUSEUM
(☎506-858-4088; Pavillon Clément-Cormier, 405 University Ave, University of Moncton; adult/student/child/family $5/3/2/10; ⊙9am-5pm Mon-Fri, 1-5pm Sat & Sun Jun-Sep, 1-4:30pm Tue-Fri, 1-4pm Sat & Sun Oct-May) Follow the engaging, bilingual exhibits along the story of the Acadians from when the first French pioneers arrived in 1524, through their expulsion by the British to present day. A generous number of artifacts, interesting side tales and examples of the cultural Acadian renaissance keep it interesting.

Tidal Bore NATURAL FEATURE
(Main St; ⊙high tide, times vary) Witnessing the tidal bore is something of a right of passage for tourists. As the giant tide rises in the Bay of Fundy, it pushes upstream against the flow of the chocolate-colored Petitcodiac River. The result is a solid wave unfurling like a carpet down the riverbed in one dramatic gesture. The height of this oncoming rush can vary from just a few centimeters to over 1m; it's usually somewhere in between.

Tide times are posted everywhere, including on the digital billboard outside Tidal Bore Park – the place to see the action. You may see locals surfing the wave; in 2013 they broke a world record by riding it for 29km. Unless you're an experienced surfer with knowledge of the river, don't try it.

Blue Roof Distillers DISTILLERY
(☎506-538-7767; www.blueroofdistillers.com; 4144 Rte 16, Malden; tours $5; ⊙9am-5pm Mon, 10am-5pm Tue-Sat, noon-4pm Sun) This isn't your average potato farm. Just 10km west of Cape Jourimain, en route to Moncton, this sixth-generation farmstead has decided to

Moncton

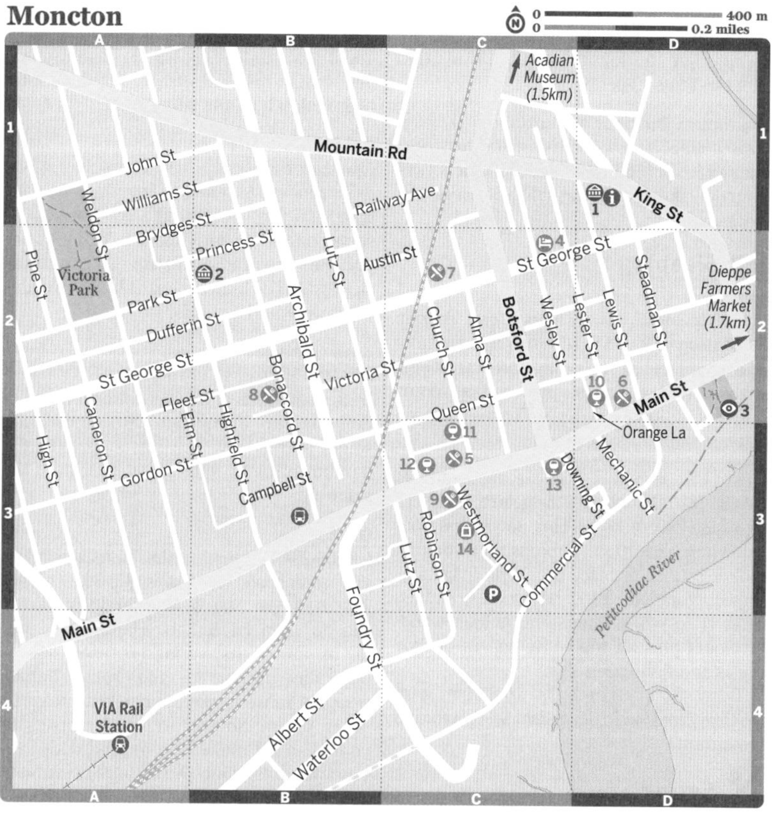

Moncton

Sights
1 Resurgo Place & Moncton Museum D1
2 Thomas Williams House B2
3 Tidal Bore D2

Sleeping
4 Glory Inn C2
L'Hotel St James .... (see 11)

Eating
5 Cafe C'est la Vie C3
6 Café Cognito D2
7 Calactus C2
8 Co Pain Bread Company B2
9 Gusto C3

Drinking & Nightlife
10 Pump House D2
11 Saint James' Gate C3
12 The Furnace Room C3
13 Tide & Boar C3

Shopping
14 Moncton Market C3

try something new. Taking the province's prized possession, skin and all, it works its magic on them using a unique process of cooking, mashing, fermenting and distilling with custom fabricated machinery to create premium vodka. See the process and have a taste test on a tour of the micro-distillery.

Tours

Roads to Sea BUS

(☎506-850-7623; www.roadstosea.com; per person $174; ⊙May-Oct) Roads to Sea offers nine-hour bus tours to Hopewell Rocks and the Bay of Fundy (including the Fundy National Park and Cape Enrage, plus lighthouses and covered bridges). The company's unique marketing pitch is that you get to see extreme high and low tides in the same day. The bus seats 12 people.

Baymount Outdoor Adventures KAYAKING
(☎877-601-2660; www.baymountadventures.com; tours adult/child $69/59; ⌚Jun-Sep) Offers two-hour kayaking tours around the Hopewell Rocks.

Sleeping

Glory Inn INN $
(☎506-858-9888; www.bbcanada.com/gloryinn; 89 St George St; r $75-115; P❄📶) Friendly and well-located, this tidy inn has rooms with a few antiques, private bathrooms and lots of home comforts. There's a shared kitchen too.

L'Hotel St James BOUTIQUE HOTEL $$$
(☎888-782-1414; www.st-jamesgate.ca; 14 Church St; r $180-290; P❄📶) This downtown boutique hotel has 10 sleek rooms that wouldn't look a bit out of place in a style magazine. Expect gorgeous tiled bathrooms, sunken tubs, crisp white linens and golden wooden floors plus all the conveniences of iPod docks and flat-screen TVs.

Downstairs there's a popular **pub** (⌚11am-2am Mon-Fri, 10am-2am Sat & Sun) and restaurant.

Eating

Two excellent markets, the **Dieppe Farmers Market** (www.marchedieppemarket.com; cnr Acadie Ave & Gauvin Rd, Dieppe; ⌚7am-1:30pm Sat, express market 11:30am-6:30pm Wed & Fri) and **Moncton Market** (www.marchemoncton market.ca; 120 Westmoreland St; ⌚7am-2pm Sat), are the places to buy fresh produce, baked goods and all kinds of food from many of Moncton's diverse cultures.

Co Pain Bread Company BAKERY $
(http://copainbread.ca; 98 Bonaccord St; snacks $3-6; ⌚7am-7pm Tue-Sat) Follow your nose to this amazing bakery for fresh bread, scones, raisin rolls and almond croissants. Cheese and sliced meat is also available for a full picnic.

Calactus VEGETARIAN $
(☎506-388-4833; www.calactus.ca; 125 Church St; mains $12-18; ⌚11am-10pm; 🌱) Busy, bright and welcoming with a bit of a hippy vibe, this vegetarian restaurant excels with unexpected dishes such as lasagna and burgers. You'll also find filling salads, falafel plates and Indian-inspired dishes. Fabulous local beer makes it all the better.

Cafe C'est la Vie CAFE $
(www.cafecestlavie.ca; 75 Main St; $8-14; ⌚7:30am-6pm Mon-Wed, to 8pm Thu & Fri, 9am-6pm Sat & Sun) This bright, well-loved spot serves panini, risottos and salads along with organic soups and *bibimbap* (Korean mixed rice dish). The bulletin board here is weighted down with local info.

Café Cognito CAFE $
(581 Main St; snacks $3-8; ⌚7:30am-5:30pm Mon-Fri, 8:30am-3pm Sat) Get your morning joe at Café Cognito, a tiny cafe with sandwiches, soups and all-day breakfasts served at a handful of bistro tables that spill onto the sidewalk.

Gusto ITALIAN $$
(☎506-204-7177; http://gustoitaliangrill.ca; 130 Westmorland St; mains $18-30; ⌚11am-2pm & 4-9pm Sun & Mon, to 10pm Wed & Thu, to 11pm Fri & Sat) Handmade pasta in all of its variations, rich sauces and the option to add some butter-poached lobster, roasted chicken breast or other scrumptiously prepared morsels to your dish all make this multi-leveled restaurant a busy spot. Downstairs is intimate and classy; upstairs is open and brighter. But the eight types of cheesecake taste divine wherever you sit.

Drinking & Nightlife

Main St, between Lester and Robinson, and the blocks spilling north along here offer a good choice of pubs and bars including some great microbreweries.

The Furnace Room PUB
(☎506-229-5559; www.facebook.com/thefurnace roommoncton; 191 Robinson St; ⌚2pm-2am Jun-Sep, 4pm-2am Oct-May) In an alley behind the Capitol Theatre, this leafy patio with big wooden barrel tables and strings of lights is a lovely place to while away an evening. Inside the pub has a comfortable rustic look with a glossy wooden bar and a long list of provincial beers. This intimate place is where locals escape the crowds. Shhhh...

Tide & Boar PUB
(☎506-857-9118; www.tideandboar.com; 700 Main St; mains $15-30; ⊙11am-midnight Mon-Wed, to 2am Thu-Sat, noon-midnight Sun) A classy gastropub that serves it's own and other local beer, plus wines and fancy cocktails. When its smoker is going, order brisket, ribs, pulled pork or smoked wings with corn on the cob. Other mains include fried-chicken sandwiches, beer-battered cod or boar poutine.

This place is hopping and there's often live music on weekends. It's shaded patio is an oasis in summer.

Pump House BREWERY
(www.pumphousebrewery.ca; 5 Orange Lane; mains $12-15; ⊙11am-late Mon-Sat, noon-midnight Sun) At the laid-back Pump House, duck into a booth and devour a good burger, fish-and-chips or wood-fired pizza. Beers brewed here are understandably popular; try the Blueberry Ale or Muddy River Stout. This is where locals gather; above the bar hangs 400-plus steins with names on the bottoms, many of them used daily.

Information

Visitors Information Centre (20 Mountain Rd, Resurgo Palace; ⊙10am-5pm Mon-Sat, noon-5pm Sun) A well-stocked and helpful center in the lobby of the Moncton Museum. There is a second visitor center in Tidal Bore Park.

Getting There & Away

AIR

Greater Moncton International Airport (YQM; ☎506-856-5444; www.gmia.ca) is about 6km east of Champlain Place Shopping Centre via Champlain St. Air Canada runs daily flights to Toronto and Montréal.

BUS

Maritime Bus (☎506-854-2023; www.maritimebus.com; 1240 Main St) has multiple daily services to Fredericton ($41.75, 2½ hours), Saint John ($33.75, two hours), Charlottetown, PEI ($41.75, three hours) and Halifax ($53.25, four hours).

CAR & MOTORCYCLE

There are six municipal parking lots around town, plus several private lots. Public parking meters cost $1 to $2.50 per hour. The municipal parking lot at Moncton Market on Westmorland St is free on Saturday, Sunday and evenings after 6pm. The city uses HotSpot Parking, a mobile payment service where you can pay for parking (and top up your metered space parking time) with your cell phone. Rates and maps can be found at www.moncton.ca.

TRAIN

Services depart **VIA Rail Station** (☎506-857-9830; www.viarail.ca; 1240 Main St) on the Ocean line (Montreal–Halifax), passing through northern New Brunswick, including Miramichi ($37, two hours) and Campbellton ($77, 5½ hours), and into Québec, on its way to Montréal ($167, 17½ hours). The train to Halifax (from $61, four hours) departs three days a week.

Getting Around

The airport is served by bus 20 from Champlain Pl nine times a day on weekdays. A taxi to the town center costs about $20.

While downtown is very walkable, if you want to go further afield, Codiac Transit (www.codiactranspo.ca) is the local bus system, with 40 wi-fi-equipped buses going all over town.

If you need wheels, there are car-rental desks at the airport, or try **Discount Car Rentals** (☎506-857-2309; www.discountcar.com; 470 Mountain Rd, cnr High St; ⊙7:30am-5:30pm Mon-Fri, 8am-noon Sat) in town.

> **OFF THE BEATEN TRACK**
>
> **CAPE JOURIMAIN**
>
> Set on the Northumberland Strait, this 675-hectare **nature center** (☎506-538-2220; www.capejourimain.ca; Rte 16; $5; ⊙8am-7pm May-Oct) has 13km of walking trails. A four-storey tower affords great views of the Confederation Bridge that crosses to Prince Edward Island, and the Cape Jourimain Lighthouse that was built in 1869. It's a twitcher's favorite for the migratory birds, with tours available upon request. The red, sandy beach is long and beautiful.

Sackville

POP 5300

Sackville is a small university town with big green spaces and flanked by grand old homes. The **Sackville Waterfowl Park** (⊙24hr) FREE is on a major bird migration route with more than 180 species sighted and 35 breeding within the grounds. From May to August is the best time to visit.

The **Black Duck Cafe** (www.theblackduck.ca; 19 Bridge St; meals $5-12; ⏲7am-9pm, brunch 9am-3pm) is the most popular hangout in town, serving up yummy lunches such as kimchi grilled cheese or strawberry and Brie panini, plus brunches of eggs Benny, buttermilk biscuits and the drool-worthy Quack Madam – an egg-battered sandwich with bacon, old cheddar, maple and spinach.

Information

Sackville Visitor Centre (https://sackville.com/explore-sackville/visitor-information; 34 Mallard Dr; ⏲9am-5pm May-Oct, to 8pm Jul & Aug)

Getting There & Away

Buses run between Sackville and Moncton ($14.25, 45 minutes, three daily).

NORTHUMBERLAND SHORE

New Brunswick's Northumberland Shore stretches from the Confederation Bridge in the south to Kouchibouguac National Park and is dotted with fishing villages and summer cottages. Shediac, on all lobster-lovers' itineraries, is a popular resort town in a strip of summer seaside and beach playgrounds. A good part of the population along this coast is French-speaking, and Bouctouche is an Acadian stronghold. Further north, Kouchibouguac National Park protects a large swath of scenic coastal ecosystems.

Shediac

POP 6700

Shediac, a self-proclaimed lobster capital, is a busy summer beach town and home of the annual Lobster Festival in July. Nearby are plenty of sandy beaches, including Canada's golden child, **Parlee Beach** (per vehicle $9), which has the country's warmest sea water.

After dinner at one of the town's relaxed seafood restaurants, catch a flick at the wonderfully retro **Neptune Drive-In** (www.neptunedrivein.ca; 691 Main St; adult/child/couple/carload $10/5/18/25; ⏲box office 8pm, movie starts 9pm Jun-Sep).

Sights & Activities

Homarus Eco-Centre AQUARIUM
(☎506-878-9315; www.ecocentrehomarus.org; Pointe-du-Chêne Wharf; adult/child $7/4; ⏲10am-6pm Mon-Sat Jun-Aug, plus noon-5pm Sun Jul & Aug) Focusing on the local bay's marine life with particular attention to it's star, the lobster, 20-minute tours of the eco-centre begin in the hatchery and include the chance to get up close with the rare blue and albino lobsters. The impetus behind nonprofit Homarus was to increase the local lobster population. You can adopt a baby lobster and, with the certificate number, follow its release. Since 2002, more than five million baby lobsters have been delivered to the sea.

Shediac Paddle Shack ADVENTURE SPORTS
(☎506-532-8914; www.shediacpaddleshack.com; 229 Main St; paddleboard or kayak 1-/3hr $25/47, party board/tandem kayak 1hr $55/35; ⏲Jun-Sep) Next to the information center, this shack will meet all of your paddling needs. Party boards fit up to six people. They also run regular lesson including SUP yoga and paddle-with-your-dog.

Shediac Bay Cruises CRUISE
(☎506-532-2175, 888-894-2002; www.lobstertales.ca; 60 Pointe-du-Chêne Wharf; lobster tales adult/child/family $79/56/245, bay tour adult/child/family $24/19/75) The popular Lobster Tales cruise takes passengers out on the water, pulls up lobster traps, then prepares a feast complete with Acadian music. The Bay Cruise is a 75-minute scenic boat ride around the bay.

Sleeping & Eating

Maison Tait INN **$$**
(☎506-532-4233; www.maisontaithouse.com; 293 Main St; r incl breakfast from $100; 📶) Lodgings at Maison Tait, a luxurious 1911 mansion, consist of nine classy, sun-drenched rooms, some with four-poster beds and zen bathtubs. There's a steakhouse and bar on-site. Excellent hot breakfast served.

Shediac Lobster Shop SEAFOOD **$**
(☎506-533-1437; www.shediaclobster.ca; 261 Main St; whole cooked lobster $10; ⏲10am-7pm) Just before the bridge at the northern end of town, get your lobster wholesale, ready to eat, with crackers and all. There are also scallops and clams along with canned goods to take home. If you're feeling flush, you can have a lobster shipped anywhere in Canada.

Paturel's Shore House SEAFOOD **$$**
(☎506-532-4774; www.paturelrestaurant.ca; 2 Blvd Cap Bimet, Grand-Barachois; mains $17-33; ⏲4-10pm Tue-Sun Jun–mid-Sep) Locals have

WORTH A TRIP

MIRAMICHI RIVER VALLEY

The 217km-long Southwest Miramichi River flows from near Hartland through forest to Miramichi where it meets the Northwest Miramichi. This area holds potent cultural significance for the Mi'kmaq Nation who have lived on the river's banks for 3000 years. Forty kilometers northwest of Miramichi, on the Esk River, the **Metepenagiag Heritage Park** (☎506-836-6118; www.metpark.ca; 2156 Micmac Rd, Red Bank; adult/child $8/6; tipis 2/4 people $85/150; ⏰10am-5pm May-Oct, to 3pm Nov-Apr) has interpretive tours of Mi'kmaq culture and history on a 3000-year-old archaeological site.

Throughout the region is a web of rivers and tributaries draining much of central New Brunswick. These waterways have inspired reverent awe for their tranquil beauty and incredible Atlantic salmon fly-fishing. Famous business tycoons, international politicians, sports and entertainment stars along with Prince Charles have all wet lines here. Even Marilyn Monroe is said to have dipped her toes in the water.

You can learn about the valley's storied fishing history at the **Atlantic Salmon Museum** (www.atlanticsalmonmuseum.com; 263 Main St, Doaktown; adult/child $8/5; ⏰9am-5pm Mon-Sat, noon-5pm Sun Jun-Oct) in Doaktown, 90km southwest of Miramichi, then swing by **WW Doak & Sons** (www.doak.com; 331 Main St, Doaktown; ⏰8am-5pm Mon-Sat), one of Canada's finest fly-fishing shops.

There are no tours to the Miramichi River Valley Area. Having your own vehicle is useful, especially to explore some off-piste roads and river areas.

been hauling themselves out to this seafood restaurant located on the seashore, 7km east of Shediac, for years. It's hard to know if it's the lobster chowder or bacon-wrapped scallops that keep drawing them back, but to join them, turn off Main St and head north on Blvd Cap Bimet.

Information

Visitors Information Centre (☎506-533-7925; www.shediac.ca; 229 Main St; ⏰9am-5pm May-Sep, to 9pm Jul & Aug) On the northern edge of town, this center provides excellent information on New Brunswick and maps of Shediac and surrounds. It's next to the world's largest lobster. (No, really...)

Getting There & Away

Maritime Bus (www.maritimebus.com; 167 Main St) runs from Shediac to Moncton ($12.25, 30 minutes, one daily) and Fredericton ($46, three hours, one daily); you must reserve three hours in advance. Buses also run from Shediac to Halifax, Nova Scotia.

Bouctouche

POP 2360

This small, surprisingly busy waterside town is an Acadian cultural focal point. The visitor center at the town's southern entrance features an impressive boardwalk that extends over the salt marsh, across the bridge and along the waterfront.

Sights

★Irving Eco Centre PARK

(www.irvingecocentre.com; 1932 Rte 475, St-Édouard-de-Kent; ⏰interpretive center 10am-6pm late May-late Sep) Just 9km northeast of Bouctouche, Irving Eco Centre makes accessible 'La Dune de Bouctouche,' a gorgeous, powder-soft sandspit jutting into the strait. The interpretive center has worthwhile displays, but the highlight is the 800m boardwalk that weaves above the sea grass along the dunes. The peninsula itself is 12km long, taking more than four hours to hike over the loose sand and back. If you're short on time, walk the boardwalk and return along the beautiful beach, taking a dip along the way.

There's a 12km hiking and cycling trail through mixed forest to Bouctouche town, which begins at the Eco Centre parking lot.

Le Pays de la Sagouine PARK

(☎506-743-1400; www.sagouine.com; 57 Acadie St; adult/student/family $22/17/55; ⏰10am-5:30pm Jul & Aug) Sitting on a small island in the Bouctouche River, this Acadian village is constructed to bring to life the setting from La Sagouine, a play by writer Antonine Maillet. Monologues from the play are acted out throughout the village, sometimes over the soup pot or local handicrafts and often accompanied by music. Several cafes serve old-fashioned Acadian cuisine, and in July and August there are regular supper theater performances (tickets from $63; French only).

Olivier Soapery MUSEUM
(www.oliviersoaps.com; 831 Rte 505, Ste-Anne-de-Kent; ⏲10am-6pm Jun-Aug, 8:30am-4:30pm Mon-Fri Sep-May) If you're a market-goer, you've likely already seen Olivier Soap around New Brunswick. In their old-fashioned soap factory, you can sit on a wooden bench and see a batch of soap being made while learning about its history. The attached shop sells beautiful and often delicious-smelling wares. Check out the lobster-shaped butter soap, sage and clay or carrot soap.

Sleeping & Eating

Gite de la Sagouine B&B $
(www.sagouinerestaurant.com; 43 Irving Blvd; d $85-100, q $125; P ❄ ☎) Conveniently located on the edge of the town center, this six-room inn has clean, comfortable accommodation. Check the website for deals that include a night's stay and dinner in the attached restaurant.

Chez les Maury CAMPGROUND $
(☎506-743-5347; 2021 Rte 475, St-Édouard-de-Kent; campsites with/without hookups $25-30; ⏲May-early Oct) On the grounds of a family-run vineyard, 200m from the Irving Eco Centre, this sweet campground is set in the field next to the farmhouse. The welcoming owner rings a bell at 6:30pm for the 7pm free sampling of wares such as elderberry and strawberry wine. Facilities are clean and there's a private beach across the way.

SCKS Société culturelle Kent-Sud CAFE $
(www.sckentsud.com; 5 Irving Blvd; snacks $9-11; ⏲8am-4pm Tue-Sat Sep-May, to 5pm daily Jun-Aug) Full of local art, baked goods, salads and soups, this little nonprofit cafe is a pleasant place to stop for coffee and simple French-style snack lunches using, where possible, local produce.

Restaurant La Sagouine ACADIAN $
(www.sagouine.nb.ca; 43 Irving Blvd; mains $8-18; ⏲6am-10pm) With seafood in its various presentations alongside fried chicken and crepes for good measure, this old-fashioned spot has a summer patio for great sidewalk gazing.

Information

The **Visitors Information Center** (☎506-743-8811; www.tourismnewbrunswick.ca; 14 Acadie St; ⏲10am-3pm late May-late Sep, longer hours in summer) has lots of info on the surrounding area.

Getting There & Away

No public transport services Bouctouche; you'll need your own wheels.

Kouchibouguac National Park

Beaches, lagoons and offshore sand dunes stretch for a gorgeous 25km, inviting strolling, bird-watching and clam-digging. The **park** (www.pc.gc.ca; Rte 117; adult/youth $7.80/free; ⏲8am-dusk year-round) encompasses hectares of forest and salt marshes, crisscrossed or skirted by bike paths, hiking trails and groomed cross-country ski tracks. Kouchibouguac (*koosh*-e-boo-gwack), a Mi'kmaq word meaning 'River of Long Tides,' is home to moose, deer and sometimes black bear.

Activities

Hiking

The calm, shallow water between the shore and the dunes, which run for 25km north and south, makes for a serene morning paddle. For a real adventure, head out to the sandy barrier islands in a **Voyageur Canoe** (☎506-876-2443; per person $30) to see hundreds of seals and birds and learn about the Mi'kmaq way of life along the way.

Kayaking

The park has 10 trails, mostly short and flat. The excellent **Bog Trail** (1.9km) is a boardwalk beyond the observation tower, and only the first few hundred meters are crushed gravel. The **Cedars Trail** (1.3km) is a lovely boardwalk trail with interpretation boards. The **Osprey Trail** (5.1km) is a loop trail through the forest. **Kelly's Beach Boardwalk** (600m one way) floats above the grass-covered dunes. When you reach the beach, turn right and hike around 6km to the end of the dune (the limits vary according to the location of the piping plover's nesting grounds). Take drinking water.

Sleeping

Kouchibouguac has two drive-in campgrounds and three primitive camping areas totalling 360 sites. The camping season is from mid-May to mid-October, and the park is very busy throughout July and August, especially on weekends. Camping reservations are necessary for the majority of sites. Park entry costs extra.

THE ACADIAN PENINSULA

The northeastern tip of the province is breathtaking. A chain of low-lying islands pointing across the Gulf of St Lawrence to Labrador, it offers a surprising slew of fantastic sights, plenty of opportunities to unwind by the sea and cheerful Acadian culture. Rte 113 cuts across salt marsh, arriving first in **Shippagan**, home of the province's largest fishing fleet. Get up close to life under the Atlantic, touch blue lobsters and feed the seals at the worthwhile **New Brunswick Aquarium** (506-336-3013; www.aquariumnb.ca; 100 Aquarium Rd, Shippagan; adult/child $9.50/6; 9am-6pm Jun-Sep).

Hop the bridge to **Lamèque**, with its modern windmills and tidy fishing village that has hosted the **Lamèque International Baroque Festival** (506-344-5846; www.festivalbaroque.com; late Jul) for more than 30 years. Nearby, the **Ecological Park** (506-344-3223; 65 Ruisseau St, Lamèque; 9:30am-5:30pm Jun-Sep) FREE offers a boardwalk to a bird-filled 2.6km forested loop trail. Watch for the endangered piping plover, kingfishers and great blue herons. Definitely stop at the unbelievable **Sainte Cécile Church** (8166 Rte 313, Petite-Rivière-de-l'Ile; 8am-5pm, shorter hours in winter) FREE. Built in 1913 and unremarkable from the outside, the inside was repainted in the 1960s by one psychedelic reverend who opted for a kaleidoscope of color. Grab a light lunch at the **Aloha Café-Boutique** (41 Principale St, Lamèque; mains $7-9; 7am-4pm Mon-Thu, to 9pm Fri, 8:30am-4pm Sat & Sun;) then continue north over the arched bridge to **Miscou Island**.

Stretch your legs over at the peaceful **Cheniere Lake Boardwalk** and learn about the local peat industry. The road dead-ends at a **Miscou Lighthouse** (506-344-7203; Rte 113, Miscou Island; adult/child $6/4; 9am-5pm Jun-Sep), built in 1856 and one of New Brunswick's most impressive. Climb 100ft to the top for killer views and then relax in the cafe next door. On your way south down the island, stop at **Miscou Beach** for sugar-like sand and great swimming. Just before you cross the bridge, gorge yourself on stuffed, steamed or oven-baked lobster and seafood at **La Terrasse à Steve** (9650 Rte 113, Quai de Miscou, Miscou Island; mains from $20; noon-8pm May-Sep). Near here, at very low tide, you can see the ruins of New Brunswick's first church, built in 1634 by Catholic missionaries.

Back on Lamèque, you can spend the night at the homey **Aux Peupliers B&B** (506-344-5145; https://aux-peupliers.business.site; 66 North Pêcheur Rd, Lamèque; d $95;). Otherwise, continue on to Shippagan where the ultra-cool **Cielo** (501-601-8005; www.glampingcielo.com; 232 Haut-Shippagan Dr; 2/4 people $180/240, min 2 nights; bar 10am-8pm Sun-Wed, to 11pm Thu-Sat;) has otherworldly domes to stay in, complete with stargazing lofts, hand-built hot tubs and green-egg barbecues. Even if you can't stay, hit their bar for a local brew and a look-see. Dinner can be had at **Pinokkio** (506-336-0051; 121 16e St, Shippagan; mains $13-25; 4:30-8pm daily, from 11:30am Wed-Fri Jun-Sep) with its fresh pasta and seafood. All three of the islands also have campgrounds and information centers with local maps.

The three primitive campgrounds cost $16 per person per night; they have only vault (pump) toilets and you must take your own water.

Cote-a-Fabien CAMPGROUND $
(877-737-3783; www.pccamping.ca; Kouchibouguac National Park; campsites Otentiks/walk-in $120/16) On the northern side of Kouchibouguac River, Cote-a-Fabien is the best choice for those seeking a bit of peace and privacy. There is water and vault toilets, but no showers. Some sites are on the shore, others nestled among the trees, with a dozen walk-in sites (100m; wheelbarrows are provided for luggage) for those who want a car-free environment.

South Kouchibouguac CAMPGROUND $
(877-737-3783; www.pccamping.ca; Kouchibouguac National Park; campsites with/without hookup $27/38, equipped camping/Otentiks $70/100) South Kouchibouguac is the largest campground. It's 13km inside the park near the beaches in a large open field ringed by trees, with oTENTiks (a type of yurt) and equipped tents sites, plus showers and a kitchen shelter. You can also rent bikes and all kinds of water toys here, including kayaks, paddleboards and pedal boats.

Information

Visitor Center (506-876-2443; www.pc.gc.ca/kouchibouguac; 186 Rte 117; 8am-4:30pm

Oct-May, to 8pm Jul-Sep) Has maps and helpful staff with good information. If the center is closed, visit the administration office opposite, which is open year-round.

NORTHEASTERN NEW BRUNSWICK

The North Shore, as it is known to New Brunswickers, is the heartland of Acadian culture in the province. The region was settled 250 years ago by French farmers and fishers, starting from scratch again after the upheaval of the Expulsion, frequently marrying the original Mi'kmaq inhabitants. The coastal road north from Miramichi, around the Acadian Peninsula and along Chaleurs Bay to Campbellton, passes through small fishing settlements with peaceful ocean vistas and soft, sandy beaches. At Sugarloaf Provincial Park, the Appalachian Mountain Range comes down to the edge of the sea. Behind it, stretching hundreds of kilometers into the interior of the province, is a vast, trackless wilderness of rivers and dense forest, rarely explored.

Caraquet

POP 4250

The oldest of the Acadian villages, Caraquet was founded in 1757 by refugees from forcibly abandoned homesteads further south. It's now the commercial center of the peninsula's French community. Caraquet's colorful, bustling wharf on Ave du Carrefour has shops, bars, restaurants and sea breezes. Downtown is spread along Rte 145, divided into East and West Blvd St-Pierre.

Caraquet is the self-proclaimed 'cultural capital of Acadia.' Each August the town is the proud host of the massive Festival Acadien, a historic occasion that celebrates their survival. It's also the closest town to the popular Acadian Historic Village.

Sights

★ Acadian Historic Village PARK

(www.villagehistoriqueacadien.com; 14311 Rte 11; adult/student/family mid-Jun–Sep $20/16/45, early Jun & Oct $9.50/8/21.50; ⏲10am-6pm mid-Jun–Sep, to 5pm early Jun & Oct) Just 15km west of Caraquet, this village of old is 33 original buildings relocated to this historical site. Staff in period costumes reflect life from 1780 to 1880. Several hours are required to have a good look, then head for a traditional meal at La Table des Ancêtres. Join Madame Savoie in her 1860s kitchen for a lesson in Acadian cooking ($75, twice daily) or get your kids kitted with costumes and a day full of historical activities ($35).

Founding Cultures Museum MUSEUM

(☎506-732-3003; 184 Rte 11, Grande-Anse; by donation; ⏲9am-5pm Jun-Sep) If you're traveling down Rte 11 and feel the need to be wowed, stop in at the Founding Cultures Museum in Grande-Anse. Sure, there are detailed displays on Scottish, English, Irish, First Nation and Acadian cultures, but the real wowzer is an unlikely and very intricate scale model of the St Peter's Basilica in Rome. Crafted by European artisans in the 1890s, it's precise down to the final statue on the colonnades. If you need a place to unwind afterwards, there is a popular beach around the corner with a popular canteen.

Festivals & Events

Festival Acadien CULTURAL

(www.festivalacadien.ca; ⏲Aug) The largest annual Acadian cultural festival, Festival Acadien, is held here the first two weeks of August. It draws 100,000 visitors, and more than 200 performers including singers, musicians, actors, dancers from Acadia and other French regions (some from overseas).

Sleeping

Motel Bel Air MOTEL $

(☎506-727-3488; www.motelbelair.ca; 655 W St-Pierre Blvd; r from $90; ❄📶) With new owners, this motel has been given a serious makeover. The stylish and extremely comfortable rooms are a true bargain. But word is out – book ahead.

Maison Touristique Dugas INN $

(☎506-727-3195; www.maisontouristiquedugas.ca; 683 Blvd St-Pierre W; campsites serviced/unserviced $23/30, r/cabins from $70/100) Five generations of the ultra-friendly Dugas family have run this rambling, something-for-everyone property, 8km west of Caraquet. The homey, antique-filled 1926 house has 11 rooms, four with shared bathrooms. There are also five clean, cozy cabins with private bathrooms and cooking facilities, a guesthouse with private and family rooms, and a quiet, tree-shaded campground.

★ Château Albert INN $$

(☎506-726-2600; https://villagehistoriqueacadien.com/en/hotel; Acadian Historic Village; d incl dinner & site visit $100-150; P) For complete immersion in Acadian culture, spend the night in a Historical Village – no TV and no phone, just 15 quiet rooms restored to their original 1909 splendor, complete with claw-foot tubs. The hotel bar pours local brews and Acadian cocktails. The original Albert stood on the main street in Caraquet until it was destroyed by fire in 1955.

Hotel Paulin HOTEL $$$

(866-727-9981, 506-727-9981; www.hotelpaulin.com; 143 Blvd St-Pierre W; r incl breakfast $195-315; P) The somewhat shabby outside of Hotel Paulin is not a reflection of what's inside. This vintage seaside hotel overlooking the bay was built in 1891 and has been run by the Paulin family since 1905. Good old-fashioned service remains and the rooms are sunny and polished, done up in crisp white linens, lace and quality antiques. But there's no denying that it's pricey.

The hotel has earned a reputation for fine cuisine, so make a reservation to sample the fiddlehead fern soup followed by Acadian chicken fricot with herb dumplings (three-course meal $48).

Eating

Pro-Mer SEAFOOD $$

(506-727-7931; 9 Quai St; meals $15-23; 11am-9pm Sun-Thu, to 10pm Fri & Sat) The is *the* place to eat seafood in town. Next to the bobbing boats in the marina, get your fill of breaded clam poutine, seafood lasagna or whole lobster in a relaxed restaurant setting or on the patio. In the attached shop, you can buy oysters on ice or jars of your favorite crustaceans to take home.

Origines ACADIAN $$$

(506-727-2717; www.originescuisinemaritime.com; 49a W St-Pierre Blvd; 5-course meal $68; 5-9pm Thu-Sat) While the seaside restaurant may be new on the scene, the chef isn't. This culinary artist has returned to his hometown to create five-course meals from local, seasonal producte. In summer, it's largely seafood based. Flavor-filled and polished, it's as much an experience as a meal.

Information

Visitor Centre (202-726-2676; www.caraquet.ca/en/tourism/discover-caraquet; 39 W Blvd St-Pierre; 9am-5pm Jun-Sep) Information on all things local, and the Acadian Historic Village.

Bathurst

POP 11,900

Set on a pretty harbor and sheltered by Carron and Alston Point, tiny Bathurst is a former mining town that's morphed into a relaxed seaside destination. The town itself is joined by a bridge that spans the harbor, with most things of interest for the tourist on the southern side.

Join locals in stretching your legs on the boardwalk at the revamped harborfront, home to the tourist office and a couple of restaurants. There are no less than three local microbreweries to sample and plenty of fresh seafood. Not far from town is the gorgeous Youghall Beach and Pabineau Falls.

Bathurst's original name was Nepisiguit, a Mi'qmaq word meaning 'Rough Waters.'

Sights

Pabineau Falls WATERFALL

(Pabineau Falls Rd, Pabineau First Nation) On the territory of the Mi'kmaq Pabineau Nation, this pretty waterfall tumbles down the Nepisiguit River, about 14km south of Bathurst. The drive here is scenic and many people picnic on the banks. Check with locals about conditions before swimming.

Note: ask the tourist office (p152) for directions, as there is limited signage. It's on property owned by a former paper mill (you enter at own risk etc).

Point Daly Reserve NATURE RESERVE

(Carron Dr) Stop in at the interpretive center before heading out on one of this nature reserves' nine marked trails, all courtesy of a former mining company. Just 5km from Bathurst, come here to see Canada geese on their migratory voyage, along with eagles, osprey and the rare maritime ringlet butterfly that appears at the end of July.

Sleeping & Eating

Auberge & Bistro l'Anjou B&B $$

(http://aubergedanjou.com; 587 Principale St, Petit-Rocher; r $90-110; P) About 20 minutes northwest of Bathurst in the village of Petit-Rocher, this lovely B&B with very comfortable rooms is a home away from home – and you're just minutes away from the local beach. The on-site bistro is a favorite with locals and visitors; don't miss the Acadian sugar pie.

LOCAL KNOWLEDGE

BON AMI ICE CREAM

From Campbellton, take the coastal Rte 134 27km east to Dalhousie, where Bon Ami Ice Cream serves 24 flavors of ice cream and 20 flavors of frozen yoghurt. Locals have been coming here for more than 20 years – and with lactose-free, sugar-free and tofu options, there's a cone for everyone.

L'Étoile du Havre B&B B&B $$

(506-545-6238; www.etoileduhavre.com; 405 Youghall Dr; r $125; P ❄) Situated in a tranquil location opposite a golf course, and en route to Youghall Beach, this designer-sleek, open-plan, ultra-contemporary B&B with six rooms looks like it's out of the pages of an LA showroom magazine. Cooked breakfasts are served in the massive open-plan kitchen-lounge room.

★ **Fresco** CANADIAN $$$

(506-546-1061; 224 King St; $25-40; 5-9pm Tue, to 10pm Wed-Sat) Following on from a successful food truck and an appearance on Canada's *Top Chef*, Joel Aubie is working his culinary magic in his own open-kitchen restaurant. The well-honed menu uses local ingredients and everything is made from scratch, from hand-rolled pasta to pâté and stocks. These gourmet dishes are so good, you'll want to lick your plate. Make reservations if you can.

Information

Tourist office (506-548-0412; www.bathurst.ca; 86 Douglas Ave, Bathurst Harbor; 9am-4pm Mon-Fri Sep-Apr, to 5pm May, to 8pm Jun-Aug) This helpful office will direct you to nature-based activities around Bathurst and rents bikes (half/full day $25/40).

Getting There & Away

Maritime Bus (506-544-9892; www.maritimebus.com; 896 Main St) services Bathurst. Handy links include Fredericton ($68.50, six hours, one daily), Campbellton ($25.50, 1½ hours, one daily), Saint John ($63.50, 6¼ hours, one daily) and Moncton ($46, 3¼ hours, one daily). Note: for Shediac ($41.75, 2¾ hours, one daily) you must book 24 hours ahead. See the website for services to Sydney, Nova Scotia.

Campbellton

POP 6900

Campbellton is a pleasant humdrum mill town on the Québec border. The lengthy Restigouche River, which winds through northern New Brunswick and then forms the border with Québec, empties to the sea here. The Bay of Chaleur is on one side and dramatic rolling hills surround the town on the remaining sides. Across the bridge to Québec lies Pointe-à-la-Croix and Hwy 132 leading west to Mont Joli and east to Gaspé.

The last naval engagement of the Seven Years' War was fought in the waters off this coast in 1760. The Battle of Restigouche marked the conclusion of the long struggle for Canada by Britain and France.

The town is dominated by Sugarloaf Mountain, which rises nearly 400m above sea level and looks vaguely like one of its other namesakes in Rio. **Sugarloaf Provincial Park** (www.parcsugarloafpark.ca; 596 Val d'Amours Rd, Atholville; Downhill Bike Park full/half-day/single ride $30/25/5; 8am-dusk late May-late Sep) is located off Hwy 11 at exit 415. From the base, it's just a half-hour walk to the top – well worth it for the extensive views of the town and part of the Restigouche River. The park also has 76 lovely **campsites** (506-789-2366; www.parcsugarloafpark.ca; 596 Val d'Amours Rd; tent sites $28, RV sites with hookup $36, yurts $43; late May-late Sep;).

Getting There & Away

Maritime Bus (506-753-6714; www.maritimebus.com; 157 Roseberry St; 6am-9pm) services stop at the Pik-Quik convenience store, near Prince William St. Buses departs daily for Fredericton ($82, 7½ hours) and Moncton ($59, five hours).

The **VIA Rail station** (www.viarail.ca; 99c Roseberry St) is conveniently central. Trains depart three times weekly to Montréal ($243, 12 hours).

Prince Edward Island

Includes ➡

Best Places to Eat

- FireWorks (p167)
- Blue Mussel Cafe (p172)
- Dunes Studio Gallery & Cafe (p169)

Best Places to Stay

- Fairholm National Historic Inn (p160)
- Great George (p160)
- Barachois Inn (p172)
- Johnson Shore Inn (p166)

Why Go?

Fringed by grassy bluffs, flat pastures and miles of rust-red sand, Prince Edward Island (PEI) presents a postcard-worthy picture of pastoral Canada. Every summer, thousands of tourists descend on the island to visit its beaches and seaside villages, many of which lie within the boundaries of Prince Edward Island National Park. Famed for its shellfish, lobsters and oysters, the island excels in farm-to-table dining, and it's a great place to experience modern Canadian cuisine at its finest.

But for many visitors, it's the adventures of a red-headed, straw-hatted little girl that will forever define PEI in their imaginations. Published in the early 1900s, Lucy Maud Montgomery's *Anne of Green Gables* tales are as popular as ever. The astonishing thing is how little the island's landscape has changed since then: farmhouses, fields, creeks and dunes straight out of a children's storybook. Cycling the 435km-long Confederation Trail makes a fine way to explore.

When to Go

Charlottetown

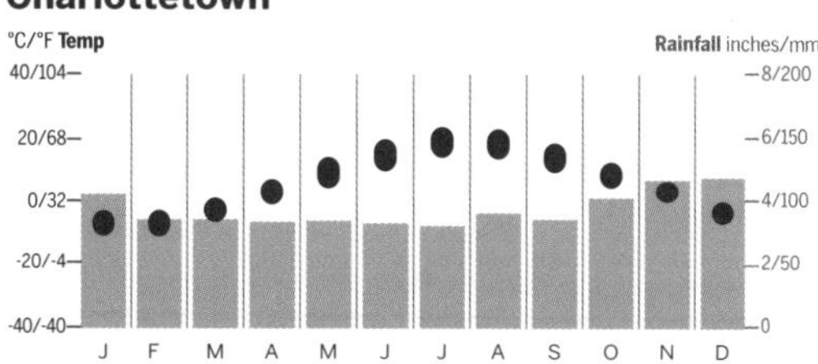

Jun Enjoy the spring calm and blooming wildflowers before the crowds hit.

Jul & Aug The entire island is in festival mode with live music and lobster suppers nightly.

Sep Traditional music and a bevy of food events mark PEI's Fall Flavours Festival.

Prince Edward Island Highlights

1. **Charlottetown** (p157) Wandering the elegant streets of PEI's compact capital.
2. **Cavendish** (p176) Following in Anne of Green Gables' fictional footsteps around the home of author LM Montgomery.
3. **Basin Head Provincial Park** (p167) Stepping on the strange squeaking sands of this far-easterly beach.
4. **Lennox Island** (p180) Learning Mi'kmaq lore on a guided walk of this forested isle.
5. **FireWorks** (p167) Devouring the barbecue-of-a-lifetime at celeb chef Michael

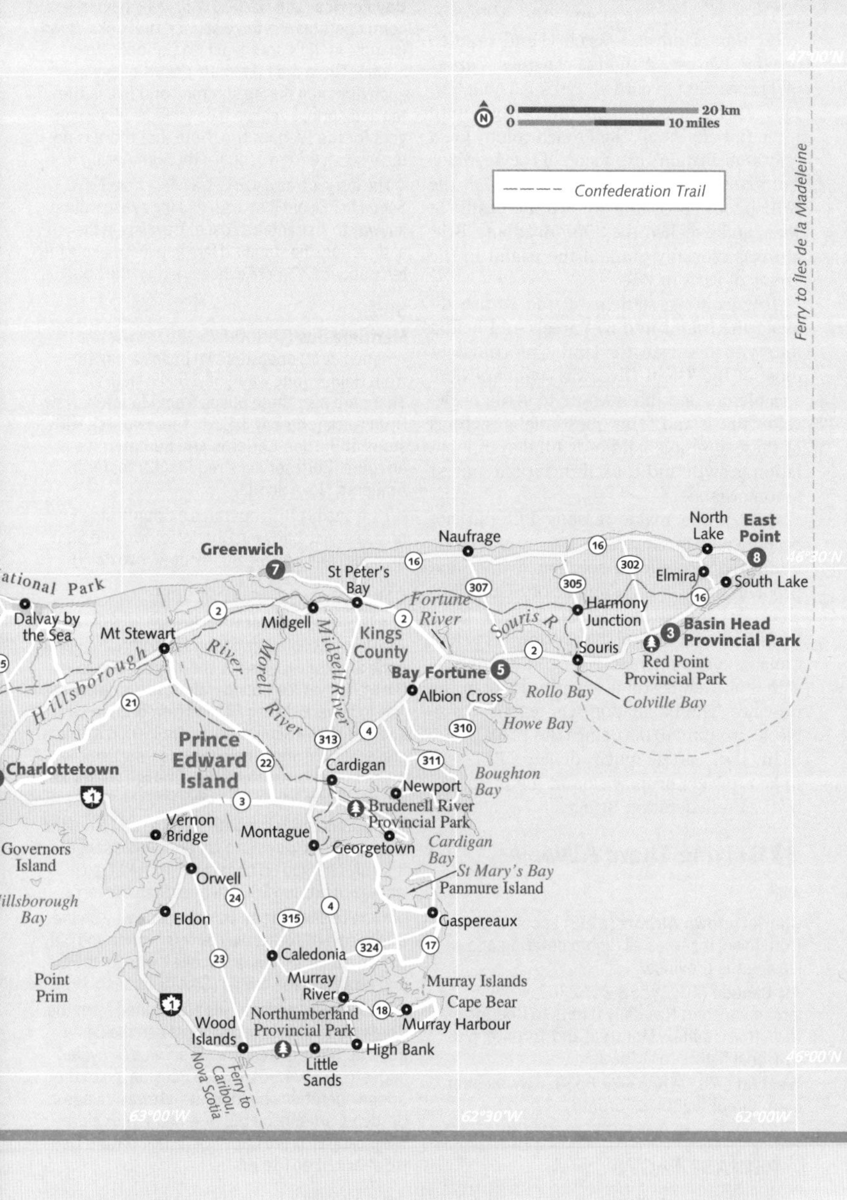

Smith's culinary HQ in Bay Fortune.

6 **New Glasgow Lobster Supper** (p173) Cracking your way through the island's original lobster extravaganza.

7 **Greenwich Dunes** (p168) Walking the floating boardwalk into a world of dunes.

8 **East Point Lighthouse** (p165) Climbing up the tower of this historic lighthouse.

9 **Confederation Trail** (p161) Spinning along a section of this fabulous railway-turned-bike-trail.

History

Its Indigenous inhabitants, the Mi'kmaq, knew the island as Abegeit (Land Cradled on the Waves). Although Jacques Cartier of France first recorded PEI's existence in 1534, European settlement didn't begin until 1603. Initially small, the French colony grew only after Britain's expulsion of the Acadians from Nova Scotia in the 1750s. In 1758 the British took the island, known then as Île St Jean, and expelled the 3000 Acadians. Britain was officially granted the island in the Treaty of Paris of 1763.

To encourage settlement, the British divided the island into 67 parcels and held a lottery to give away the land. Unfortunately, most of the 'Great Giveaway' winners were speculators and did nothing to settle or develop the island. The questionable actions of these absentee landlords hindered population growth and caused incredible unrest among islanders.

One of the major reasons PEI did not become part of Canada in 1867 was because union did not offer a solution to the land problem. In 1873 the Compulsory Land Purchase Act forced the sale of absentee landlords' land and cleared the way for PEI to join Canada later that year. Foreign land ownership, however, is still a sensitive issue in the province. The population has remained stable, at around 140,000, since the 1930s.

In 1997, after much debate, PEI was linked to New Brunswick and the mainland by the Confederation Bridge.

Getting There & Away

AIR

Charlottetown Airport (p163) Located 8km from town, it serves all flights entering and leaving the province.

Air Canada (AC; ☎888-247-2262; www.aircanada.com) Has daily flights to Charlottetown from Halifax, Montréal and Toronto, plus seasonal flights to Ottawa.

WestJet (WS; ☎888-937-8538; www.westjet.com) Direct flights to Toronto.

PEI FAST FACTS

- Population: 142,907
- Area: 5700 sq km
- Capital: Charlottetown
- Quirky fact: 1.3 billion kilograms of potatoes produced per year

BOAT

Bay Ferries (☎877-762-7245; www.bayferries.com) operates the ferry service that links Wood Islands, in PEI's southeast, to Caribou, Nova Scotia. There are up to nine daily sailings in each direction during summer, and five in the fall and spring. Vehicle fees include all passengers for the 1¼-hour trip. Note that there is no ferry service from January through April.

The ferry is free if you're traveling from Nova Scotia to PEI, but it's worth making a reservation anyway to guarantee a space. Traveling in the other direction, the standard fare applies, making the ferry about $30 more expensive than the bridge.

BUS

Maritime Bus (☎800-575-1807; www.maritimebus.com) operates two buses a day to/from Halifax (one way $58.25, 4½ hours). There are also three buses from Moncton, New Brunswick (one way $41.75, three hours), with stops at Borden-Carleton and Summerside en route. Both services require a transfer in Amherst, Nova Scotia.

T3 Transit (p163) operates a County Line Express service between Charlottetown and Summerside (one way $9, 80 minutes, two daily).

CAR, BICYCLE & MOTORCYCLE

The 12.9km **Confederation Bridge** (☎902-437-7300; www.confederationbridge.com; car/motorcycle $47.75/19; ⌚24hr), the longest bridge in the world over ice-bound waters, is the quickest way to travel between PEI and New Brunswick, and on to Nova Scotia. Opened in 1997, it's an impressive sight and a major engineering achievement, but unfortunately the 1.1m-high guardrails rob you of any hoped-for view.

The standard toll covers travel to and from the island, and includes one car and all passengers. It's only charged on departure from PEI, so it works out around $30 cheaper than the ferry.

If you're planning on traveling one way on the bridge and the other way by ferry, since you only pay on exit, it's cheaper to take the ferry to PEI and return via the bridge ($47.75 versus $79).

Cyclists and pedestrians are banned from the Confederation Bridge and must use the 24-hour, demand-driven shuttle service (bicycle/pedestrian $9/4.50). On the PEI side, go to the bridge operations building at Gateway Village in Borden-Carleton; on the New Brunswick side, the pickup is at the Cape Jourimain Nature Centre at exit 51 on Rte 16.

Getting Around

Bus services are fairly limited on the island; what services there are are provided by Maritime Bus and T3 Transit (p163).

While your easiest option to get around the island is by car, bicycle is also a fine choice. The flat and well-maintained Confederation Trail runs the length of the island through some beautiful countryside and small towns. For details, check out www.tourismpei.com/pei-confederation-trail.

CHARLOTTETOWN

902 / POP 44,739

If there's a prettier provincial capital in Canada than Charlottetown, we're yet to find it (even its name sounds quaint). Eschewing the headlong rush for concrete and glass that characterizes many big Canadian cities, Charlottetown has stayed true to its small-town roots, with a low-rise downtown that retains many of the redbrick facades and Victorian buildings of its late-19th-century heyday. Covering just a few blocks inland from the harbor, the old part of town was designed to be walkable, and it pays to wander and soak up the sights – including its impressive mock-Gothic cathedral and a surfeit of heritage homes, browsable shops and colorful clapboard buildings. The town's fast-growing food and craft-beer scene is boosted by the presence of the Culinary Institute of Canada downtown.

History

Charlottetown is named after the consort of King George III. Her African roots, dating back to Margarita de Castro Y Sousa and the Portuguese royal house, are as legendary as they are controversial.

While many believe the city's splendid harbor was the reason Charlottetown became the capital, the reality was less glamorous. In 1765 the surveyor-general decided on Charlottetown because he thought it prudent to bestow the poor side of the island with some privileges.

As every Canadian schoolkid knows, Charlottetown's main historical event of note was its role as host of the 1864 Confederation Conference – the event that led to the founding of modern Canada.

Sights

In terms of 'attractions,' Charlottetown isn't top-heavy on sights. That said, think of the whole of the downtown area (known as Old Charlottetown), with its beautifully preserved, quaint and colorful colonial buildings, and the wealth of boutiques, bistros and bars they contain, as the main event. The significant sights are all in this downtown area.

★ Victoria Park PARK

(www.discovercharlottetown.com/listings/victoria-park) Dedicated in 1873, Charlottetown's most popular and beautiful waterfront green space has 16 hectares of lush loveliness for you to enjoy on a fine day. A boardwalk runs along the park's southern edge.

St Dunstan's Basilica NOTABLE BUILDING

(902-894-3486; www.stdunstanspei.com; 45 Great George St; 9am-5pm) FREE Rising from the ashes of a 1913 fire, the three towering stone spires of this Catholic, neo-Gothic basilica are now a Charlottetown landmark. The marble floors, Italianate carvings and decoratively embossed ribbed ceiling are surprisingly ornate.

Beaconsfield Historic House NOTABLE BUILDING

(902-368-6603; www.peimuseum.ca; 2 Kent St; adult/student/family $5/4/14; 10am-4pm daily Jul & Aug, Mon-Fri May, Jun, Sep & Oct, from noon Mon-Fri Nov-Apr) Charlottetown has its fair share of impressive period buildings, but this handsome mansion is the finest. Designed and built by the prominent PEI architect WC Harris in 1877 for James Peake, a wealthy shipowner, and his wife Edith, it sports all the fashionable features of the day: elegant 19th-century furnishings, gingerbread trim, a grand verandah and a crowning belvedere.

COWS Creamery FACTORY

(902-566-5558; www.cowscreamery.ca/tours; 397 Capital Dr; 10am-6pm) FREE Apart from the potato, the ice cream produced here is arguably PEI's best-known export (there's even a COWS in Beijing these days). So it would be a crime not to sample some – you can take a self-guided tour of the factory, step into a cheese cave, try some Avonlea Clothbound Cheddar and, of course, eat enough ice cream to make yourself ill.

Tours

★ Confederation Players Walking Tours WALKING

(800-565-0278; www.confederationcentre.com/heritage/confederation-players; 6 Prince St; adult/child $17/12; Jul & Aug) There is no better way to tour Charlottetown. Playing the fathers and ladies of Confederation, actors garbed in 19th-century dress educate and

Charlottetown

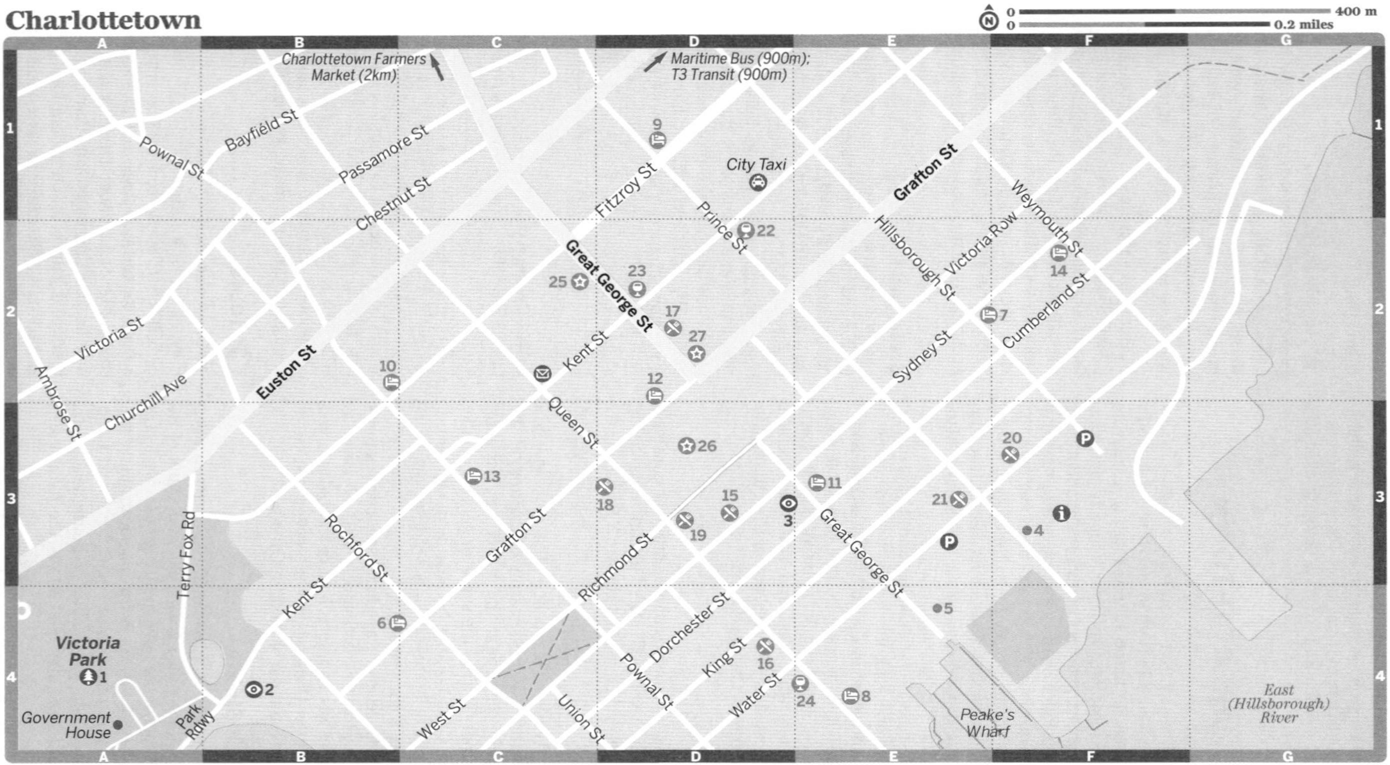

0 — 400 m
0 — 0.2 miles

Charlottetown Farmers Market (2km)
Maritime Bus (900m); T3 Transit (900m)
Pownal St
Bayfield St
Passamore St
Chestnut St
Fitzroy St
City Taxi
Grafton St
Weymouth St
Victoria Row
Hillsborough St
Prince St
Great George St
Cumberland St
Victoria St
Euston St
Kent St
Sydney St
Ambrose St
Churchill Ave
Queen St
Terry Fox Rd
Rochford St
Grafton St
Richmond St
Great George St
Kent St
Dorchester St
King St
Pownal St
Water St
Union St
West St
Park Rdwy
Victoria Park
Government House
Peake's Wharf
East (Hillsborough) River

Charlottetown

Top Sights

1 Victoria Park A4

Sights

2 Beaconsfield Historic House B4
3 St Dunstan's Basilica D3

Activities, Courses & Tours

4 Confederation Players Walking Tours F3
5 Peake's Wharf Boat Cruises E4

Sleeping

6 Charlotte's Rose Inn B4
7 Charlottetown Backpackers Inn E2
8 Delta Prince Edward E4
9 Fairholm National Historic Inn D1
10 Fitzroy Hall B&B B2
11 Great George E3
12 Holman Grand Hotel D2
13 Hotel on Pownal C3
14 Sydney Boutique Inn & Suites F2

Eating

15 Brickhouse Kitchen & Bar D3
16 Kettle Black D4
17 Leonhard's D2
18 Pilot House D3
19 Receiver Coffee D3
20 Sugar Skull Cantina F3
21 Water Prince Corner Shop & Lobster Pound E3

Drinking & Nightlife

22 Charlottetown Beer Garden D2
23 Craft Beer Corner D2
Hopyard .... (see 23)
24 Merchantman E4

Entertainment

25 Baba's Lounge C2
26 Confederation Centre of the Arts D3
27 Mack D2

entertain visitors as they walk through the town's historic streets. Tours leave from the Visitor Information Centre (p163) at Founders' Hall, with a variety of themes and itineraries to choose from.

Peake's Wharf Boat Cruises CRUISE
(☎902-566-4458; www.charlottetownboattours.com; 1 Great George St; tours from $40; ⊙Jun-Sep) Observe sea life, hear interesting stories and witness a wonderfully different perspective of Charlottetown from the waters of its harbor aboard the 45ft good ship *Fairview*. Assorted itineraries of varying durations are available.

Festivals & Events

Fall Flavours FOOD & DRINK
(☎866-960-9912; www.fallflavours.ca; ⊙Sep) Now one of the island's largest festivals, this massive, month-long kitchen party merges traditional music with incredible cuisine. Don't miss the oyster-shucking championships or the chowder challenge.

Farm Day in the City FOOD & DRINK
(www.discovercharlottetown.com/events/farm-day-in-the-city; ⊙Oct) PEI farmers get their big day out in early October, when 150 producers and food stalls, a beer garden and tasting events take over the center of Charlottetown.

PEI International Shellfish Festival FOOD & DRINK
(www.peishellfish.com; ⊙mid-Sep) Crustaceans and shellfish take center stage at this high-profile seafood fest.

PEI Burger Love FOOD & DRINK
(www.peiburgerlove.ca; ⊙Mar) Although a province-wide event, this month-long celebration of the humble burger has gained cult-like status in the restaurants of Charlottetown, which try to outdo each other for the title of PEI's most-loved burger.

Festival of Small Halls MUSIC
(www.smallhalls.com; ⊙mid-Jun) Island musicians, dancers and storytellers who have 'made it' out of the province return to their homeland to perform in rural community halls around PEI during this popular festival.

Charlottetown Festival PERFORMING ARTS
(☎800-565-0278; www.confederationcentre.com; ⊙Jun-Sep) This long-running festival organized by the Confederation Centre of the Arts (p162) features free outdoor performances, a children's theater and dance programs.

Sleeping

Charlottetown Backpackers Inn HOSTEL $
(☎902-367-5749; www.charlottetownbackpackers.com; 60 Hillsborough St; dm/r incl breakfast $34/95; 📶) Impossible to miss with its bright red-and-white paint job and happy

hostellers milling about on the lawn, this superbly happening backpackers has single-sex or mixed dorms, a good kitchen and a quirky common room with a turntable and a rather epic vinyl collection. Be prepared for spontaneous barbecues and pub outings.

★Great George BOUTIQUE HOTEL **$$**
(☎902-892-0606; www.thegreatgeorge.com; 58 Great George St; d/ste from $199/259; ❄📶) This colorful collage of celebrated buildings along Charlottetown's most famous street has rooms ranging from plush and historic to bold and contemporary. Its room designs cover all bases – from multiroom layouts (ideal for families) to self-contained suites.

Hotel on Pownal HOTEL **$$**
(☎902-892-1217; www.thehotelonpownal.com; 146 Pownal St; d from $189; P📶) Charlottetown can be pricey, which makes this motel-conversion hotel a handy find. Rooms are boxy but well appointed, and rates include parking and a complimentary breakfast – and they stay reasonable even in the height of summer. Ask for an upper-floor room, as the ground-floor ones can feel a bit dingy. Soundproofing isn't the best; bring earplugs.

Holman Grand Hotel HOTEL **$$**
(☎877-455-4726; www.theholmangrand.com; 123 Grafton St; d/ste from $209/299) Rising rather incongruously above Charlottetown's red-brick facades, this central and practical hotel is an excellent base. Rooms are modern and rather functional, but some have added bonuses like outside terraces and floor-to-ceiling windows.

Charlotte's Rose Inn INN **$$**
(☎902-892-3699; www.charlottesrose.com; 11 Grafton St; apt/d from $150/165; ❄📶) Frilly as a pair of lace curtains, this feminine B&B has attractive, antique-filled rooms, mostly named after PEI notables (LM Montgomery, Jacques Cartier and John A Macdonald), as well as a spacious loft suite with its own private deck. Creaky hallways and vintage decor add to the charm – as do the complimentary tea and cakes.

Fitzroy Hall B&B B&B **$$**
(☎866-627-9766; www.fitzroyhall.com; 45 Fitzroy St; d/ste from $199/249; 📶) Built for a banker in 1872, this Victorian house brims with antiques: original fireplaces, mahogany beds, wing-back chairs, secretary desks and period styling to match. It's definitely not one for minimalists, though.

★Fairholm National Historic Inn INN **$$$**
(☎902-892-5022; www.fairholminn.com; 230 Prince St; d $179-309; 📶) Always hankered to stay in a museum? Well, the Fairholm can oblige, with a gorgeous selection of rooms inside a stunning, bay-windowed period inn dating from 1838, plus self-catering rooms and apartments in several other period properties just along the street. It feels seriously luxurious – it's well worth bumping up to the king rooms for architectural bragging rights.

Sydney Boutique Inn & Suites BOUTIQUE HOTEL **$$$**
(☎902-367-5888; www.sydneyinn.com; 55 Weymouth St; d/ste from $199/349; P❄📶) You won't find a more imposing facade in Charlottetown than the Sydney's – converted from the town's old Notre Dame Convent (built 1857), it's a redbrick eye-catcher. Rooms are smart, in shades of cream and pale yellow, ranging from 'micro' doubles to roomy self-catering suites. It's worth bumping up the price bracket for more space and views.

Delta Prince Edward HOTEL **$$$**
(☎902-566-2222; www.marriott.com; 18 Queen St; d/ste from $211/321; P⊜❄📶🏊) The town's traditional choice for delegates and overnighting business travelers (it's linked to the Convention Centre), the Marriott-owned Delta might belong to a big chain, but you can't beat its waterfront location. Rooms are mostly fresh and modern, and there are the usual upscale amenities like a fitness room and spa.

Eating

Sugar Skull Cantina MEXICAN **$**
(☎902-367-5141; www.sugarskullcantina.ca; 83 Water St; mains $9-13; ⊙noon-8pm) *Arriba!* This on-trend Mexican joint is one of the funnest places to eat in town, with its zingy Mexicano decor, outside deck and pitchers of pink lemonade, sangria and blueberry mojitos. There's a choice of dining styles – go classic with fish tacos, spit-roasted chicken or a burrito bowl, or pick a 'share-and-compare' platter of taquito fingers or street corn.

DON'T MISS

THE CONFEDERATION TRAIL

Following the course of the railway that once cut right across PEI but was finally abandoned for good in 1989, the Confederation Trail (www.tourismpei.com/pei-confederation-trail) is one of the best cycling routes in Canada. Winding through a varied landscape of fields, forests, rivers, valleys and coastline, it's a pleasure to cycle – not least because it's almost entirely flat. Some sections of the trail are completely canopied; in late June and the early weeks of July the trail is lined with bright, flowering lupines, and in fall the changing colors of the foliage are a wonder.

The tip-to-tip distance from Tignish in the northwest to Elmira in the northeast is 273km, but branch trails bring the total possible distance to 435km. You don't necessarily have to do the trail in one go: it's easily done in sections, since the main trail passes through major towns including Summerside, Kensington and Mt Stewart, with branches to other towns including Charlottetown, Souris and Montague.

Distance is measured from west to east (Tignish is at 0km, Elmira at 273km); since prevailing winds on PEI blow from the west and southwest, cycling in this direction is easier.

You can download a trail map and route guide from the Tourism PEI website, and information centers can help with route guidance, accommodations and bike rental.

Receiver Coffee DINER **$**
(www.receivercoffee.com; 128 Richmond St; coffee $2-5; ⏲7am-7pm Sun-Thu, to 8pm Fri & Sat) Receiver is the coffee connoisseurs' choice in Charlottetown. Come here for the perfect flat white made with ethically sourced Ethiopian single-origin beans. And don't miss the muffins. It's on the attractive pedestrianized part of Richmond St known as Victoria Row (look out for the wrought-iron sign).

Charlottetown Farmers Market MARKET
(☎902-626-3373; www.charlottetownfarmersmarket.com; 100 Belvedere Ave; ⏲9am-2pm Sat) Enjoy some prepared island foods or peruse the cornucopia of fresh organic fruit and vegetables. The market is north of the town center, off University Ave.

Kettle Black CAFE **$**
(☎902-370-0776; www.kettleblackpei.com; 45 Queen St; light lunches $9; ⏲7am-7pm) Every town needs its coffee corner, and this place is Charlottetown's, with hand-written menus and sofas to lounge around on while indulging in your flat white and home-baked muffin. The brunch menu and lunchtime falafels are good too.

Leonhard's CAFE **$**
(☎902-367-3621; www.leonhards.ca; 142 Great George St; mains from $10; ⏲9am-5pm) A little slice of PEI countryside comes to downtown Charlottetown with this friendly, frilly spot serving generous sandwiches, German pastries, all-day breakfasts and country-style dishes. Get in early around lunchtime.

★ **Water Prince Corner Shop & Lobster Pound** SEAFOOD **$$**
(☎902-368-3212; http://waterprincelobster.ca; 141 Water St; mains $12-36; ⏲9:30am-8pm) When locals want seafood they head to this inconspicuous, sea-blue eatery near the wharf. It is deservedly famous for its scallop burgers, but it's also the best place in town for fresh lobster. You'll probably have to line up for a seat; otherwise order take-out lobster, which gets you a significant discount.

Brickhouse Kitchen & Bar CANADIAN **$$**
(☎902-566-4620; http://brickhousepei.com; 125 Sydney St; mains $16-30; ⏲11am-10pm) An upscale-grub pub that's crammed with rough-bricked, industrial chic, from the trendy booth seats and open-view kitchen to the pop-art prints on the walls. Dishes take their cue from PEI ingredients – chef Seth's seafood chowder is a favorite, as is the tandoori-spiced roasted hen.

Pilot House CANADIAN **$$$**
(☎902-894-4800; www.thepilothouse.ca; 70 Grafton St; mains $25-33; ⏲11am-10pm Mon-Sat) The old Roger's Hardware building has now become this smart gastropub, but the old wood beams, brick columns and etched windows have been left in situ for character. There's a choice of pub classics or upscale dining, washed down with a generous supply of beers, wines and whiskies.

WORTH A TRIP

THE ROAD TO POINT PRIM

If you're looking for a sweet, kid-friendly, half-day trip from Charlottetown and have had your fill of *Anne of Green Gables* action, head east on Rte 1. After about 30km, you'll come to **Orwell Corner Historic Village** (☎902-651-8510; www.orwellcornervillage.ca; Resource Rd 2, Vernon Bridge; adult/child $10.30/5.18; ⏲8:30am-4:30pm daily Jul & Aug, Mon-Fri Jun), a recreation of a rustic 19th-century farming community with animals, antiques and costumed locals. Further down the road, the **Sir Andrew MacPhail Homestead** (☎902-651-2789; www.macphailhomestead.ca; 271 MacPhail Park Rd, Vernon Bridge; ⏲9:30am-4:30pm Tue-Fri Jun-Sep) is open for tea on summer afternoons. Its beautiful grounds, with a nursery, vegetable garden and woods, are a delight to wander.

The real delight of the excursion is found continuing south on Rte 1 for a further 11km, where you'll come to signs for Point Prim. This skinny spit of land is covered in wild rose, Queen Anne's lace and wheat fields through summer and has views of red-sand shores on either side. At the tip is the **Point Prim Lighthouse** (☎902-659-2768; www.pointprimlighthouse.com; 2147 Point Prim Rd, Belfast; adult/child $5/3.50; ⏲10am-6pm mid-Jun–mid-Sep): the province's oldest and, we think, prettiest. If you're lucky, you'll be able to climb to the top to pump the foghorn.

Round out your day with a cup of chowder by the ocean at **Point Prim Chowder House** (☎902-659-2187; www.chowderhousepei.com; 2150 Point Prim Rd, Belfast; mains $9-46; ⏲11am-3pm & 4:30-8pm mid-Jun–Sep) – there is no place on PEI with a finer sundown-er view – then head back to Charlottetown, or continue south to Wood Islands (30km) for your ferry to Nova Scotia.

Drinking & Nightlife

★Hopyard BAR

(☎902-367-2599; 131 Kent St; ⏲11am-midnight) It's almost too-cool-for-school, this place – with craft beer on tap, racks of vinyl to browse and a regularly changing menu of small plates to snack on. It's a big hit locally, and has since spawned a sister establishment over in Halifax.

Craft Beer Corner BREWERY

(Upstreet Craft Brewing; ☎902-894-0543; www.upstreetcraftbrewing.com; 156 Great George St; ⏲noon-midnight) Charlottetown's premier craft brewer now has a downtown location for its trendy taproom, where you can sip brews like the Commons Pilsner, White Noize IPA and unusual strawberry-rhubarb Rhuby Social. The brewery serves sharing plates too.

Charlottetown Beer Garden BEER GARDEN

(☎902-367-6070; www.beergardenpei.com; 190-192 Kent St; ⏲4pm-1am or 1:30am Mon-Fri, from 2pm Sat & Sun) This building on Hunter's Corner has been many things – house, tearoom, bike shop, tattoo parlor – but its current incarnation as a beer garden seems to be the most popular. Pan-Canadian brews on tap, with a special focus on beers from Nova Scotia, New Brunswick and PEI.

Merchantman BAR

(☎902-892-9150; www.merchantman.ca; 23 Queen St; ⏲11am-9pm) Merchantman wears many hats; it's a bar, it's a restaurant, it's a takeout. In summer months, the patio tables are a great place to soak up the sun and enjoy a drink while you work up your appetite for fresh PEI oysters, seafood or all manner of upscale pub grub.

☆ Entertainment

★Confederation Centre of the Arts THEATER

(☎902-566-1267; www.confederationcentre.com; 145 Richmond St) This modern complex's large theater and outdoor amphitheater host concerts, comedic performances and elaborate musicals. *Anne of Green Gables – The Musical* has been entertaining audiences here as part of the Charlottetown Festival since 1964, making it Canada's longest-running musical.

You'll enjoy it, and your friends will never have to know.

Mack THEATER
(☎902-566-1267; www.confederationcentre.com/venues/the-mack; 128 Great George St) An intimate venue where guests sit at round tables for (mainly) comedy gigs. Bookings are handled through the Confederation Centre Box Office.

Baba's Lounge LIVE MUSIC
(☎902-892-7377; 181 Great George St; ⏲11am-midnight) Known to locals just as Baba's, this small upstairs venue is the place to go for local bands.

Benevolent Irish Society LIVE MUSIC
(☎902-963-3156; 582 North River Rd; $10; ⏲8pm Fri) On the north side of town, this is a great place to catch a ceilidh. Come early, as seating is limited.

Information

MEDICAL SERVICES

Polyclinic Professional Centre (☎902-629-8810; www.polycliniconline.com; 199 Grafton St; ⏲5:30-8pm Mon-Fri, 9:30am-noon Sat) Charlottetown's after-hours, walk-in medical clinic.

Queen Elizabeth Hospital (☎902-894-2111; 60 Riverside Dr; ⏲24hr) Emergency room.

POST

Main Post Office (☎902-628-4400; 101 Kent St; ⏲9am-5pm Mon-Fri) Central post office.

TOURIST INFORMATION

Charlottetown Visitor Information Centre (☎902-368-4444; viccharlottetown@gov.pe.ca; 6 Prince St; ⏲9am-5pm) The island's main tourist office at Founder's Hall has all the lowdown you need on Charlottetown and the wider island, plus a plethora of brochures and maps, and free wi-fi.

Getting There & Away

AIR

Charlottetown Airport (YYG; ☎902-566-7997; www.flypei.com; 250 Maple Hills Ave) is 8km north of the city center. A taxi to/from town costs $16, plus $5 for each additional person.

BUS

T3 Transit County Line Express (T3 Transit; ☎902-566-9962; www.t3transit.ca; 7 Mt Edward Rd) runs between Charlottetown and Summerside ($9, 1½ hours, Monday to Friday only).

Maritime Bus (p338) also runs a bus service to/from Halifax ($58.25 one way, 4½ hours, two daily).

CAR & MOTORCYCLE

Rental cars, available from a variety of providers with city and airport depots, are the preferred method of transportation to/from Charlottetown. Cars are in short supply during summer, so be sure to book ahead.

Getting Around

BICYCLE

MacQueen's Bicycles (☎902-368-2453; www.macqueens.com; 430 Queen St; rental per day/week $40/210) Rental bikes for getting around town and the Confederation Trail.

BUS

Limited public transportation is provided by T3 Transit, but walking or renting a bike are both great ways to get around this compact city.

TAXI

City Taxi (☎902-892-6567; www.citytaxipei.com; 195 Kent St)

Yellow Cab PEI (☎902-566-6666; www.yellowcabpei.com; 1-14 MacAleer Dr)

EASTERN PRINCE EDWARD ISLAND

Outside the summer beach season, few folk make the trek out to explore the eastern part of PEI, and that's a real shame – it's every bit as pretty as the middle of the island, and arguably offers a truer picture of the island's rural character. From stretches of neatly tended homesteads to the sinuous eastern shore with its sheltered harbors, country inns, historic lighthouses and white, sandy beaches, it's well worth the road trip – and easily doable in a day from Charlottetown.

The 338km Points East Coastal Drive (www.pointseastcoastaldrive.com) makes a full circuit around the eastern headland of PEI. Planning tools and maps are available on the website.

Wood Islands

☎902 / POP 470

The strung-out coastal settlement of Wood Islands is principally of interest if you're planning on catching a ferry to Nova Scotia – boats chug across the channel at least once a day. If you have time to spare, it's worth detouring via the artsy little fishing community of Murray River, and the historic lighthouses at Cape Bear and Wood Islands, which can be reached along the coastal Rte 18.

Sights

Cape Bear Lighthouse & Marconi Station LIGHTHOUSE

(www.capebearlighthouse.com) This three-story lighthouse looks like many others in PEI, but it has its own unique place in history. Built in 1881, it was chosen in 1905 as the site of a Marconi Wireless Telegraph Station. Seven years later, on the night of April 14, 1912, operator Thomas Bartlett was the first person to receive a distress call from a passenger vessel that was sinking somewhere off the coast of Newfoundland. That vessel's name? The *Titanic*.

Wood Islands Lighthouse LIGHTHOUSE

(www.woodislands.ca; 9:30am-5:30pm Jun-Sep) If you'll be waiting a while at the ferry terminal, it's worth visiting this 1876 lighthouse, which has a good gift shop, a small shipbuilding gallery and fabulous views from its tower. Tours run from June to September.

Newman Estate Winery WINERY

(902-962-4223; www.newmanestatewinery.com; 9404 Gladstone Rd, Gladstone; by appointment) Head toward the coast from Murray River along Rte 348 (Gladstone Rd) to find Newman Estate Winery. This lovely place specializes in blueberry wines, but has recently begun making white wine from its grapes, too.

Rossignol Estate Winery WINERY

(902-962-4193; www.rossignolwinery.com; 11147 Shore Rd, Murray River; 10am-5pm Mon-Sat, from noon Sun May-Oct) For wine tasting on a grand scale, cruise over to Little Sands, 9km from the Wood Islands Ferry, where Rossignol Estate Winery has free tastings and specializes in fruit wines. The blackberry mead has won a string of gold medals and the wild rose liqueur made from rose hips is also well worth a try; call ahead for winter hours.

Information

Wood Islands Visitor Information Centre (902-962-7411; 13054 Shore Rd; 10:30am-5pm mid-May–mid-Oct) Right on the Confederation Trail, this is the main visitor center for those arriving on PEI by ferry.

Getting There & Away

Wood Islands is 51km southeast of Charlottetown and the boarding point for Bay Ferries (p335) services to Caribou, Nova Scotia (adult/child $20/free, 1¼ hours). A standard vehicle costs $79, bicycles $20.

Montague & Georgetown

The fact that Montague isn't flat gives it a unique, inland feel. Perched on either side of the Montague River, the busy little town is the service center for Kings County; its streets lead from the breezy, heritage marina area to modern shopping malls, supermarkets and fast-food outlets.

Around the peninsula, the many historic buildings in Georgetown are testament to the town's importance as a shipbuilding center in the Victorian era. Today it's a mix of sleepy village and tourist spot thanks to its great places to eat and its waterfront setting.

The **Panmure island Powwow** (902-892-5314; mid-Aug) is held in mid-August with drumming, crafts and a sweat tent – it attracts around 5000 visitors, so don't expect to find any secluded beaches around here during that time.

Sights & Activities

Panmure Head Lighthouse LIGHTHOUSE

(www.panmureislandlighthouse.ca; 62 Lighthouse Rd, Panmure Island; tours $5; 10am-6pm mid-Jun–mid-Sep) Completely restored by community volunteers in 2015, this 1853 lighthouse was constructed to guide shipping vessels into Georgetown Harbour. It has an unusual octagonal design, shingled in wood and laid out over four stories, measuring 17.5m from base to vane. Tours of the lighthouse are available in the summer season.

Garden of the Gulf Museum MUSEUM

(902-838-2467; www.montaguemuseumpei.com; 564 Main St, Montague; adult/child under 12yr $5/free; 9am-5pm Tue-Sat Jul & Aug, Mon-Fri Sep) On the southern side of the river, the statuesque former post office and customs house (1888) overlooks the marina, and since 1958 has been home to this small community museum (the oldest on PEI, apparently). The displays are strictly local-interest: historic photos of the town, Mi'kmaq artifacts and a recreation of an old general store.

Tranquility Cove Adventures FISHING

(902-969-7184; www.tcapei.com; Fisherman's Wharf, 1 Kent St, Georgetown; half-day tours from $45) Starfish hunting, deep-sea fishing and a giant bar clam dig are just a few of the activities offered by this adventure company based at the Georgetown wharf. In winter, it arranges snowmobile tours.

Sleeping

Brudenell River Provincial Park CAMPGROUND $

(902-652-8966; www.tourismpei.com/provincial-park/brudenell-river; off Rte 3, Cardigan; tent sites $28-30, RV sites $32-37; May-Oct; P) Development meets nature at Brudenell River Provincial Park, a park and resort complex just north of town. Tent and RV sites are available, as well as cottages and motel-style accommodations. Activities range from kayaking to nature walks and golf on two championship courses.

Georgetown Inn & Dining Room INN $$

(902-652-2511; www.peigeorgetownhistoricinn.com; 62 Richmond St, Georgetown; d from $120;) Eight island-themed rooms are on offer at this fine old Georgetown house, including a spacious captain's room with jet tub and a shared outside deck, a bay-windowed harbor room and (of course) a Green Gables suite. The restaurant is good too (mains from $15).

Eating & Drinking

Clam Diggers SEAFOOD $$

(902-583-3111; www.clamdiggerspei.com; 6864 Water St, Georgetown; mains $12-35; 11:30am-9pm) This popular creekside seafood diner is a brilliant place for brunch, lunch or dinner, with local specialties such as breaded clams, old-fashioned shanty bake (basically fish pie) and hot scallop caesar.

Wheelhouse Inn DINER $$

(902-652-2474; www.wheelhouseingeorgetown.com; 7 West St, Georgetown; mains $15-36; 11:30am-9pm) This waterside pub has the best dinner views in Georgetown, looking clear across the harbor. The menu is divided into 'lower deck' (casual dishes like fish-and-chips and lobster melt), 'upper deck' (mains of fish, meat and steaks) or big 'shareables' platters of mussels, seafood and snow crab. There's a fun cocktail menu – try the Terry's berries blueberry lemonade.

★ **Cardigan Lobster Suppers** SEAFOOD $$$

(902-583-2020; www.peicardiganlobstersuppers.com; 4557 Wharf Rd, Cardigan; seafood mains $25-35; 5-9pm Jun-Oct) In tiny Cardigan, enjoy a five-course lobster supper in a heritage building on the harbor. There's also good-quality pub grub – fish cakes, Irish stew, steak sandwiches – on offer in 1888, housed in a separate building next door.

★ **Copper Bottom Brewing** BREWERY

(902-361-2337; www.copperbottombrewing.com; 567 Main St, Montague; 11am-10pm Mon-Wed, to 11pm Thu-Sat, noon-8pm Sun) The first craft brewery and taproom to open in King's County, this lively establishment serves up a range of ales to its Montague clientele, including an intriguing Blueberry Sour and an extra-hoppy double IPA, Parkman Ave. Founder Ken Spears learned his craft at Propeller (p69) in Halifax, so he really knows his beers, as does his equally ale-crazy wife, Ashley Condon.

Getting There & Away

Georgetown is 52km east of Charlottetown. Montague is 16km west of Georgetown.

Souris & Around

902 / POP 1173

Wrapped around the waters of Colville Bay is the bustling fishing community of Souris (*sur*-rey). It owes its name to the French Acadians and the gluttonous mice (*souris* in French) who repeatedly ravaged their crops. It's now known more for its joyous annual music festival than for the hungry field rodents of old.

This is a working town that's a friendly jumping-off point for cycling the coastal road (Rte 16) and the Confederation Trail, which comes into town. Souris is also the launching point for ferries to the Îles de la Madeleine in Québec.

The wooded coast and lilting accents along this stretch of coastline offer some welcome variety from the patchwork of farms found inland. Giant white windmills march across the landscape. North Lake and Naufrage harbors are intriguing places to stop and, if you feel so inclined, join a charter boat in search of a monster 450kg tuna.

Sights

★ **East Point Lighthouse** LIGHTHOUSE

(902-357-2106; www.eastpointlighthouse.ca; adult/child $6/3.50; 10am-6pm Jun-Aug) Built in 1867 (the same year as Confederation), the East Point Lighthouse still guards PEI's northeastern shore. As you climb the 67 steps to the top, you'll see a collection of old lenses, a gallery of former lighthouse keepers and the original lantern machinery, before topping out on the 5th floor for wraparound views of East Point.

The lighthouse has been moved twice. After its original location inland was blamed for the 1882 wreck of the British *Phoenix*, the lighthouse was moved a half-mile closer to shore in 1885 using a system of weighs, capstan and horses. The lighthouse was moved again in 1908 due to coastal erosion, and to accommodate the expansion of the foghorn building, which now houses a pleasant craft shop (open 9am to 7pm in summer).

Elmira Railway Museum MUSEUM
(902-357-7234; Rte 16A; adult/student/family $5/4/10; 9:30am-4pm daily Jul & Aug, Mon-Fri Jun & Sep) Once upon a time, the station at Elmira represented the end of the line for PEI's railway; it now marks the eastern end of the Confederation Trail. This little museum explores the railway's history, and is home to the largest model railway collection in Canada. There's also a miniature train (adult/student/family $6/4/15) that winds through the surrounding forest.

Festivals & Events

PEI Bluegrass & Old Time Music Festival MUSIC
(902-569-3153; http://peibluegrass.tripod.com; early Jul) The PEI Bluegrass & Old Time Music Festival draws acts from as far away as Nashville. Come for just a day, or camp out for all three.

Sleeping & Eating

Johnson Shore Inn INN $$
(902-687-1340; www.jsipei.com; 9984 Northside Rd, Hermanville; r from $120; May-Jan;) Coastal luxury and stunning views of St Lawrence Bay are the calling cards at this lovely seaside inn, clad in white clapboard and full of Atlantic Canadian character. Rooms are priced according to the quality of the sea view, but they're all extremely elegant.

★ **Inn at Bay Fortune** INN $$$
(902-687-3745; https://innatbayfortune.com; 758 Rte 310, Bay Fortune; r from $225; P) Without doubt the plushest place to stay (and dine) on the whole of PEI, this swanky inn is the domain of celebrity chef Michael Smith. Built in 1913 as a 20-hectare summer residence for Broadway playwright Elmer Harris and family, it's been renovated with serious style. There's a choice of palatial rooms in the main inn or the attached towers.

21 Breakwater CANADIAN $$
(902-687-2556; 21 Breakwater St; mains $12-28; 11:30am-8pm or 9pm Mon-Sat) Owners Pedro and Betty have made their little restaurant in Souris a destination for casual fine dining. Yes, you'll find mussels and fish chowder on the menu, but also poached haddock, Portuguese fish-and-chips and brined pork steak. It's in a handsome mansion overlooking the waterfront.

WORTH A TRIP

PEI DISTILLERIES

Two distinctly different distilleries operate on PEI, echoing the province's fame for bootlegging during Prohibition. Even today many families distill their own moonshine (which is technically illegal) and this is what is often mixed in punch and cocktails at country weddings and parties.

Prince Edward Distillery (902-687-2586; www.princeedwarddistillery.com; Rte 16, Hermanville; 11am-6pm) has two varieties on its list: the original potato vodka (this is PEI, after all!), and a more recent one that's made from wild blueberries. You can take a tour of the distillery and try your hand at mixology with a cocktail-making masterclass.

Myriad View Distillery (902-687-1281; www.straitshine.com; 1336 Rte 2, Rollo Bay; 10am-6pm Mon-Sat, 11am-5pm Sun) produces Canada's first and only legal moonshine. The hard-core, double-distilled Straight Lightning Shine is 75% alcohol and so potent it feels like liquid heat before it evaporates on your tongue. Take our advice and start with a micro-sip. A gulp could knock the wind out of you. The 50% alcohol Straight Shine lets you enjoy the flavor a bit more. Myriad View also brews a brandy, pastis, gin, whiskey, rum, vodka and even a unique dandelion 'shine. Tours and tastings are free.

It's about 17km along Rte 307 between the two distilleries.

★ **FireWorks** CANADIAN $$$

(☎902-687-3745; https://innatbayfortune.com/fireworks; 758 Rte 310, Bay Fortune; per person $155; ⏰from 5pm) Since taking over the Inn at Bay Fortune in 2015, Food Network star Michael Smith has created one of PEI's most unique dining experiences: the 'Fire-Works feast,' based around a monstrous 7.5m brick-lined, wood-burning oven. It features a smorgasbord of oysters, hot-smoked fish, flame-grilled steaks, seafood chowder and fire-oven bread, served at long butcher-block tables: a truly epic barbecue banquet.

Guests staying at the Inn automatically receive a reservation at the feast. The event also includes a tour of the kitchen garden and farm.

Getting There & Away

Souris is 72km east of Charlottetown and located in the northeast corner of the island. Souris is also the boarding point for the **CTMA Ferry** (☎902-687-2181; www.traversierctma.ca/en) to Québec's Îles de la Madeleine (one way from $54.30 in high season, $101.25 with car, five hours).

St Peter's Bay to Mt Stewart

The area between the villages of St Peter's Bay and Mt Stewart is a hotbed for cycling. The section of the Confederation Trail closest to St Peter's Bay flirts with the shoreline and rewards riders with an eyeful of coastal views. In Mt Stewart, three riverside sections of the Confederation Trail converge, giving riders and hikers plenty of attractive options within a relatively compact area.

★ **Trailside Cafe & Inn** CAFE $$

(☎902-628-7833; www.trailside.ca; 109 Main St, Mt Stewart; mains $12-17) This stomping venue is one of the best places in eastern PEI to catch some live music – owners Pat and Meghann are passionate music lovers, and they attract top artists to their nighttime performances. The shingled building, dating from 1897, makes an intimate space, and you can dine on pizzas, cheese and charcuterie platters while you enjoy the show.

There are also four rooms upstairs. If you can't make a dinner show, try and catch the Hillsborough River Gospel Brunch ($22), held on summer Sundays in July and August.

DON'T MISS

BASIN HEAD PROVINCIAL PARK

The star attraction of **Basin Head Provincial Park** (www.tourismpei.com/provincial-park/basin-head; Basin Head) is the sweeping sand of golden **Basin Head Beach**. Many islanders rank this as their favorite beach and we have to agree. The sand is also famous for its singing – well, squeaking – when you walk on it. Unfortunately, the sand only performs when dry, so if it's been raining, it's no show. Five minutes of joyous 'musical' footsteps south from the park's fisheries museum and you have secluded bliss – enjoy!

CENTRAL PRINCE EDWARD ISLAND

Central PEI contains a bit of all that's best about the island: verdant fields, quaint villages and forests undulating north to the dramatic sand-dune-backed beaches of Prince Edward Island National Park.

The main attraction for many people is Cavendish, the fictional home of Anne of Green Gables, the engaging heroine of Lucy Maud Montgomery's 1908 novel – but in truth, the town has changed a bit since Lucy's day (unless we missed the passages filled with parking lots, gift shops and chain hotels). It's still worth visiting for die-hard fans, but everyone else will be much better rewarded by taking a leaf out of PEI-ers' books and heading straight to the beach.

Information

For those entering central PEI via the Confederation Bridge, it's worth stopping at the **Borden-Carleton Visitor Information Centre** (☎902-437-8570; Hwy 1; ⏰8:30am-8pm), just off the bridge on the PEI side, for its free maps, brochures and restrooms.

Victoria

☎902 / POP 100

A place to wander and experience more than 'see,' this lovely little fishing village has

DON'T MISS

GREENWICH DUNES

Massive, dramatic and ever-shifting sand dunes epitomize the amazing area west of Greenwich. These rare parabolic giants are fronted by an awesome, often empty beach. Preserved by Parks Canada in 1998, this 6km section of shore is now part of Prince Edward Island National Park. Learn about it all in the **Greenwich Interpretation Centre** (902-961-2514; Rte 13; 9:30am-7pm Jul & Aug, to 4:30pm May, Jun, Sep & Oct).

shaded, tree-laden lanes that scream character and charm. The entire village still fits neatly in the four blocks laid out when the town was formed in 1819. Colorful clapboard and shingled houses are home to more than one visitor who was so enthralled by the place they decided to stay. There's a profusion of art, cafes and eateries, as well as an excellent summer theater festival.

By the Sea Kayaking (902-658-2572; www.bytheseakayaking.ca; 1 Water St; kayak rentals per hour/day from $25/50) rents kayaks or stand-up paddleboards by the hour, or you could sign up for a guided expedition to the local sea colony at Granville Island or to the Confederation Bridge. They also offer kayak-and-clamming expeditions ($90), where you get to learn to dig like a true PEI-er on the Tryon Shoal.

Sleeping & Eating

Treetop Haven TREEHOUSE $$
(902-439-0267; www.treetophaven.ca; 1210 Mount Tryon Rd; pods from $200) And now for something a little different: five geodesic 'tree-pods,' hidden away in woodland about 19km from Victoria. The pods range in size, but all have proper beds, kitchen, wooden deck and private hot tub, and you can listen to the sounds of nature as you nod to sleep. Glamping's not for everyone, but it's a change from boring B&Bs.

★ **Landmark Oyster House** CAFE $$
(902-658-2286; www.landmarkcafe.ca; 12 Main St; mains lunch $13-22, dinner $19-34; 11am-9pm or 10pm daily May-Oct, 9am-2pm Sat-Sun only Nov & Dec) Despite the name, there's a lot more on offer at this super-friendly cafe-diner than oysters (although you can certainly sample the holy bivalves if you want, choosing 'em raw, deep-fried or baked). The menu is a catch-all treat of island flavors: pot pies, fish cakes, surf and turf, as well as a selection of sumptuous platters.

Lobster Barn Pub and Eatery PUB
(902-658-2722; 19 Main St; noon-10pm) This gorgeous little pub in an old barn is a great place for a beer, but the food's good too – and yes, there's lobsterr.

Getting There & Away

Victoria is midway between Summerside (37km) and Charlottetown (36km) on the Trans-Canada Hwy.

Prince Edward Island National Park

For most Canadians, if you mention PEI, the image that comes immediately to mind is the sprawling, dune-backed beaches of the north shore – nearly all of which are encompassed within the borders of Prince Edward Island National Park. Established in 1937, the park runs in a narrow strip for 42km along the island's north coast, ranging in width from a few kilometers to just a few hundred meters.

Beaches lined with marram grasses and wild rose span almost the entire length of the park's 42km coastline: from west to east, the main ones are Cavendish (the largest and busiest), MacNeills Brook, North Rustico, Brackley, Stanhope and Dalvay. Greenwich Beach, on the west side of Tracadie Bay, is also inside the national park. The beaches further east tend to be quieter.

In summer, it's sunbathing central – finding a free patch of sand (or a parking space) can be a challenge. But outside July and August, the beaches are much quieter – and in winter, the park's pretty much deserted.

A beautiful bike lane runs all the way along the coast.

PEI National Park Campgrounds CAMPGROUND $
(800-414-6765; www.pc.gc.ca/eng/pn-np/pe/pei-ipe/visit.aspx; campsites $27.40-35.30; Jun-Aug) Parks Canada operates three campgrounds: at Cavendish, Robinsons Island and Stanhope, spread along the park's length. You can request a campground, but not a specific campsite. Booking online is the most sensible option: 80% of sites can be booked in advance; the remaining sites are first-come, first-served, so it's wise to arrive early.

Getting There & Away

The park's western entrance is in Cavendish, 37km from Charlottetown. Its eastern gate in North Rustico is 25km from Charlottetown.

Brackley Beach

At the eastern end of Prince Edward Island National Park, Brackley Beach isn't so much a town as a rural area, with a few hotels, restaurants and cafes dotted on or around the coastline. The main attraction here is, of course, the eponymous beach.

A few miles east along the coast, Stanhope is a tranquil corner of the national park, popular with beachgoers and golfers, as well as *Green Gables* tourists wanting afternoon tea at the historic hotel Dalvay by the Sea, a frequent location used in the 1980s miniseries. It's also of interest to historians: Stanhope was the site of one of the first communities of British settlers in PEI, who arrived in the late 18th century.

Sleeping & Eating

Brackley Beach Hostel HOSTEL $

(902-672-1900; www.brackleybeachhostel.com; 37 Britain Shore Rd; dm/d/tr/f from $39.10/79.35/108.10/143.75; P) For near-the-beach budget digs you won't find better than this clean and super-friendly hostel housed in a big barn about 2km from the shoreline. There are several eight-bed dorm rooms, plus a few private doubles and family-size rooms, as well as plenty of showers, a game room and an equipped kitchen.

Shaw's Hotel & Cottages COTTAGE $$

(902-672-2022; www.shawshotel.ca; 99 Apple Tree Rd; d/cottages from $135/175;) With its red roof, geranium-filled window boxes and stripy awnings, Shaw's offers a cheery welcome – as befits Canada's oldest family-operated inn (founded 1860!). Unsurprisingly, rooms feel old-fashioned – flock wallpaper, dated furnishings – but have a certain homey charm. Self-catering chalets offer more comfort (although older cottages don't have kitchens), and the beach is just a 600m walk away.

The dining room is open to outside guests (mains $18 to $30); reservations are recommended for the popular Sunday-evening buffet (held in July and August).

★ **Dalvay by the Sea** HISTORIC HOTEL $$$

(902-672-2048; www.dalvaybythesea.com; 16 Cottage Cres, Dalvay; d/cottages from $189/389; May-Oct;) Built in 1895 by businessman Alexander MacDonald, this gabled mansion will be immediately familiar to *Anne of Green Gables* fans – it featured in the TV series as the White Sands Hotel. It's a sprawling, old-fashioned affair: Adirondack armchairs, huge fireplaces, an enormous dining room and a choice of fusty rooms or self-contained two-room cabins on the hotel's lavishly lawned grounds.

Richard's Seafood SEAFOOD $

(902-672-3030; www.richardsfreshseafood.com; 9 Wharf Rd, Covehead; mains $8-15; noon-8:30pm Jun-Sep) Lobster rolls, fish sandwiches, sea-scallop burgers – when it comes to seafood on the north shore, Richard's longstanding shack is the place to go to try it. But it's the crispy haddock and Burbank fries that keep the customers flocking back.

★ **Dunes Studio Gallery & Cafe** FUSION $$

(902-672-2586; www.dunesgallery.com; 3622 Brackley Point Rd; dinner mains $11-30; cafe 11:30am-9pm Jun-Aug, gallery 9am-6pm or later May-Sep) Wow – this place is worth the trip. Buddha statues, gleaming glass, island artworks and Canadian crafts aplenty in the gallery; a lovely garden filled with exotic plants and blooms; and a great cafe serving sophisticated dishes like Thai mussels, pan-seared scallops and a PEI ploughman's board. Chef Norman Day scooped up the coveted 'Taste Our Island' award in 2018.

Rustico & North Rustico

902 / POP 583

Acadian culture lives on in these two seafront settlements, separated by around 5km

DON'T MISS

BRACKLEY DRIVE-IN THEATRE

Generations of PEI-ers have grown up catching the features at this drive-in **movie theater** (902-672-3333; www.drivein.ca; 3164 Brackley Point Rd; adult/child from $12/7.50; May-Sep). Screening since the 1950s, the drive-in was restored in 1992 – making this a real island experience that's not to be missed. Check the website for forthcoming attractions. Adult prices include a soft drink.

Around PEI National Park

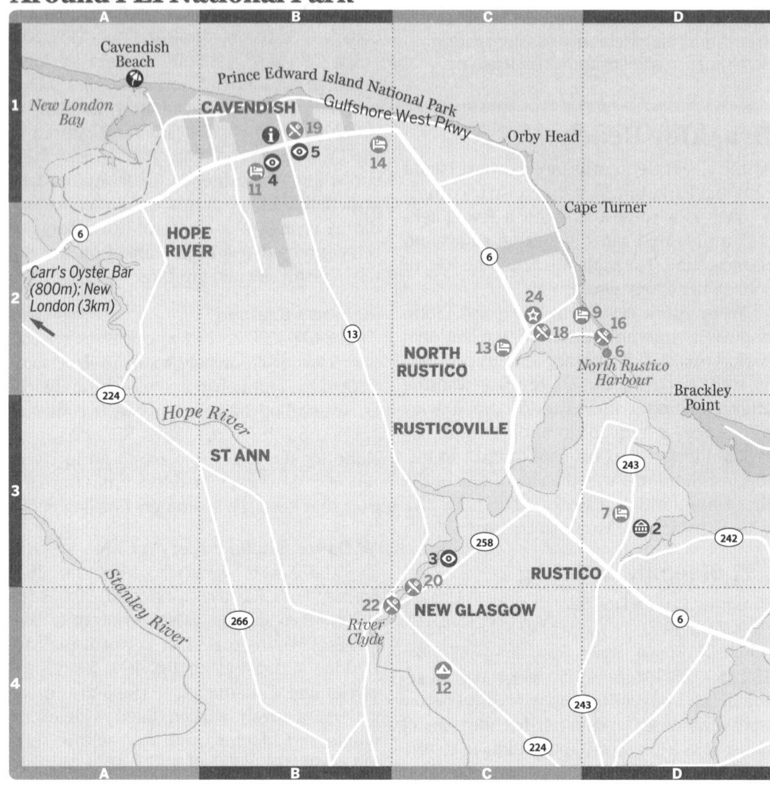

Around PEI National Park

Top Sights
1 Prince Edward Island National Park E3

Sights
2 Farmer's Bank of Rustico & Doucet House D3
3 Glasgow Glen Farm C3
4 Green Gables Heritage Place B1
5 Lucy Maud Montgomery's Cavendish Homestead B1

Activities, Courses & Tours
6 Outside Expeditions D2

Sleeping
7 Barachois Inn D3
8 Brackley Beach Hostel F4
9 Canada's Rotating House – Around the Sea C2
10 Dalvay by the Sea H3
11 Kindred Spirits Inn & Cottages B1
12 New Glasgow Highlands Camping & Cabins C4
13 North Rustico Motel & Cottages C2
14 Parkview Farms Tourist Home & Cottages B1
15 Shaw's Hotel & Cottages F3

Eating
16 Blue Mussel Cafe D2
17 Dunes Studio Gallery & Cafe F3
18 Fisherman's Wharf Lobster Suppers C2
19 Lost Anchor Pub B1
20 New Glasgow Lobster Supper C4
Prince Edward Island Preserve Company .... (see 22)
21 Richard's Seafood F3
22 The Mill in New Glasgow C4

Entertainment
23 Brackley Drive-In Theatre F4
24 Watermark Theatre C2

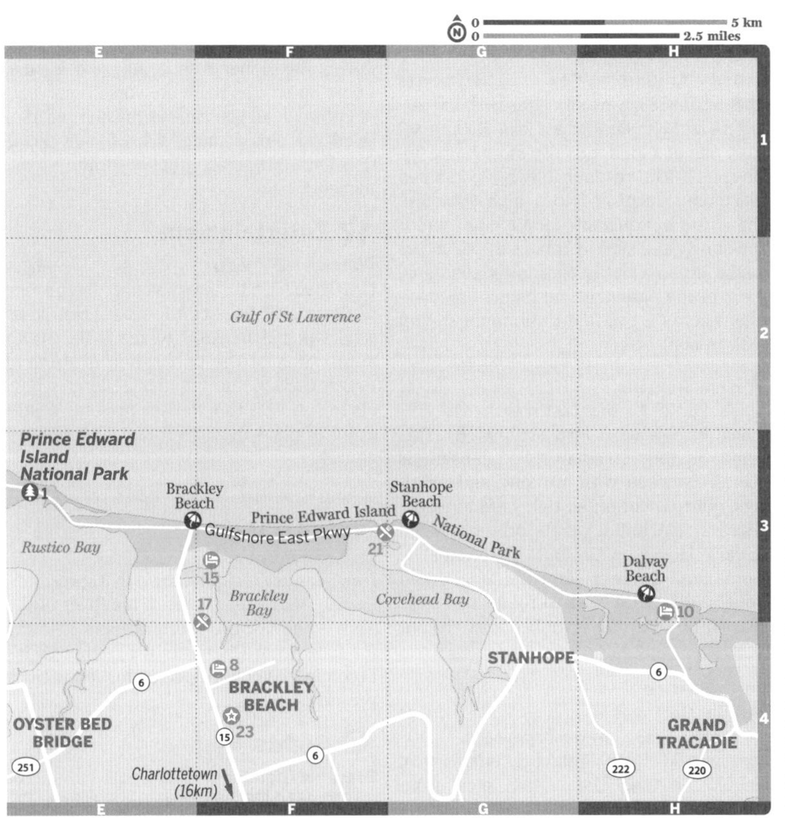

along Rte 6. The first Acadians put down roots here in the 1700s: you can still see several fine historic buildings, and visit the old farmer's bank, now an intriguing museum.

Of the two, North Rustico is the more attractive, with rickety, boxy fisher's houses painted in navies, brick reds and beiges. Taking a walk east from the pier along the boardwalk is a great way to take in the sights, sounds and smells of this atmospheric little village and its busy harbor packed with fishing boats.

Sights & Activities

Farmer's Bank of Rustico & Doucet House MUSEUM

(902-963-2194; www.farmersbank.ca; Church Rd, Rustico; adult/student $6/3.50; 9:30am-5:30pm Mon-Sat, 1-5pm Sun Jun-Sep) The solid red-stone Farmer's Bank of Rustico operated here between 1864 and 1894, and served an important role in providing funds for local Acadian communities. It's now a museum describing the settlement and the importance of the bank's role in local history.

Beside the bank is Doucet House, a wooden-clad Acadian dwelling that's believed to be one of the oldest such structures in the province. It's been carefully restored and contains some interesting Acadian items and 19th-century artifacts.

Outside Expeditions OUTDOORS

(902-963-3366; www.getoutside.com; 374 Harbourview Dr, North Rustico; tours from $45; May-Oct) Situated at the far end of the harbor in a bright-yellow fishing shed, this outdoors company runs regular guided kayak tours, and rents canoes (from $30 per hour), stand-up paddleboards (from $25 per hour) and bikes. Beginners can go for the 1½-hour introductory 'Beginner Bay' tour, but the three-hour 'Harbour Passage' ($65) and two-hour evening 'Cavendish Coves' ($55) tours offer more coastal scenery.

Sleeping

★Canada's Rotating House – Around the Sea APARTMENT $$

(☎866-557-8383; www.aroundthesea.ca; 130 Lantern Hill Dr, North Rustico; apt from $169; P 📶) Truly one of a kind, this two-story home 'in-the-round' features four fully self-contained apartments furnished to a high standard. The entire building sits atop a giant motor that slowly and silently rotates the structure so the ocean view is constantly changing. Tours of the basement mechanics are available. There's a two-night minimum stay in peak season.

★Barachois Inn B&B $$

(☎902-963-2906; www.barachoisinn.com; 2193 Church Rd, Rustico; r from $140; ❄📶) This grand, historic Acadian-style mansion is liberally stocked with antiques and paintings, not to mention an 1890s grand piano. There are two buildings: the original gabled Gallant House, with four Victorian-style rooms; and a newer copy, the MacDonald House, with more modern rooms and a fitness suite. Both are a refined and elegant treat.

North Rustico Motel & Cottages MOTEL $$

(☎902-963-2253; www.cottages-pei.ca; 7103 Cavendish Rd, North Rustico; r/cottages from $99/135; P📶🏊) Take your pick from motel-style suites, wood-paneled cottages and B&B rooms in the original house: all are simple and pleasant, and the grounds are lovely.

Eating

★Blue Mussel Cafe SEAFOOD $$

(☎902-963-2152; www.bluemusselcafe.com; 312 Harbourview Dr, North Rustico; mains $15-30; ⊙11:30am-8pm or 9pm mid-May–Oct) Simple seafood fresh off the boats is the order of the day at this stylish harborside cafe: Daisy Bay oysters, seared halibut, seafood bubbly bake and a banquet-worthy lobster dinner. The space is light and modern, with glass doors and a wooden-decked interior that seems to bring the outside in. Nothing pretentious here: just great grub. No reservations.

Fisherman's Wharf Lobster Suppers SEAFOOD $$$

(☎902-963-2669; www.fishermanswharf.ca; 7230 Rustico Rd, North Rustico; lobster dinners from $35; ⊙noon-8:30pm late Jun-Aug, 4-8pm Sep–mid-Oct) This huge place has lines out the door during the dinner rush in July and August. Come hungry, as there are copious servings of chowder, all-you-can-eat mussels, an 18m salad bar plus a main dish of your choice (lobster, snow crab, jumbo shrimp – you name it).

Entertainment

Watermark Theatre THEATER

(☎902-963-3963; www.watermarktheatre.com; 57 Church Hill Ave, North Rustico; ticket prices vary) Opened in 2008 to mark the 100th anniversary of the publication of *Anne of Green Gables,* the popular children's novels set on PEI, this theater presents a program of plays in a renovated 19th-century church.

New Glasgow

☎902 / POP 1240

New Glasgow is a quiet town that spreads elegantly across the shores of the River Clyde. This is the favorite lobster-supper getaway for folks from Charlottetown, although it's becoming equally respected for its luscious preserves.

Sights

Glasgow Glen Farm FARM

(☎902-963-2496; http://glasgowglenfarm.ca; 190 Lower New Glasgow Rd; ⊙10am-5pm Mon-Sat May-Oct) Blessed are the cheesemakers, or so they say. This one produces numerous variants of Gouda, which makes the perfect addition to any picnic hamper. Otherwise, the cheesy goodness is liberally applied to the island's most delicious pizzas.

Sleeping & Eating

★New Glasgow Highlands Camping & Cabins CAMPGROUND $

(☎902-964-3232; www.newglasgowhighlands.com; 2499 New Glasgow Rd, Hunter River; tent/RV sites from $38/48, cabins from $65; ⊙Apr-Nov; 📶🏊) This lovely wooded campground with well-spaced sites, each with a fire pit, is located in Hunter River, 7km south of New Glasgow. For rainy days there are simple cooking facilities in the lodge. There are also bright cabins, each with two bunks, a double bed, a sofa and a picnic table, but no linens or pillows; bathrooms are shared.

Be sure to book ahead and don't even think about making late-night noise. It's all about the peace and quiet here. There's a laundry, a small store and a mystifying absence of bugs.

★**The Mill in New Glasgow** CANADIAN **$$**
(☎902-964-3313; www.themillinnewglasgow.com; 5592 Rte 13; mains $18-35; ⊙noon-3pm & 5-9pm Wed-Sun) Chef Emily Wells has turned this lakeside restaurant into a destination address since winning the 'Taste Our Island' competition in 2015. The ethos is comfort food with an upscale twist, often with an Asian-inspired or Provençal flair (fish cakes with sriracha lime mayo, or chicken stuffed with arborio rice, feta, parmesan, almonds and dried cranberries).

Prince Edward Island Preserve Company CAFE **$$**
(☎902-964-4300; www.preservecompany.com; 2841 New Glasgow Rd; mains $12-26; ⊙9am-8pm; 🖉) This place carries on the old island tradition of making preserves, chutneys, marmalades, jellies and curds, many from local fruit. There's a cafe too, serving island dishes like hodgepodge haddock, seafood bubbly pie and maritime fish cakes – not to mention a bakeshop and a gift store.

★**New Glasgow Lobster Supper** SEAFOOD **$$$**
(☎902-964-2870; www.peilobstersuppers.com; 604 Rte 258; lobster dinners from $37.95; ⊙4-8pm Jun–mid-Oct) There are plenty of places to get a lobster supper these days, but this spot claims to be the original – in any event, it's been serving these shellfish feasts since 1958. Getting messy while you crack your crustacean is part of the fun – but leave room for chowder, mussels, salads, breads and a mile-high lemon pie.

New London

The patchwork of fields and dune-fringed coastline around New London is quintessential *Anne of Green Gables* country: author Lucy Maud Montgomery was born nearby, and drew much of the inspiration for her novels from the island scenery. Gift shops and antique boutiques give it a quaint heritage feel, but the tiny village gets pretty overrun in summer.

Sights

Anne of Green Gables Museum MUSEUM
(☎902-886-2884; www.annemuseum.com; 4542 Rte 20; adult/child $6/2; ⊙9am-5pm Jul & Aug, 10am-4pm Jun & Sep, 11am-4pm May & Oct) This homestead is an important part of the *Anne of Green Gables* mythos. Set in 110 hectares of fields and woodland, the house was built by author Lucy Maud Montgomery's uncle and aunt; she called the house the 'wonder castle of my childhood' and used it as the inspiration for Silver Bush. It's full of memorabilia, including Lucy Maud's writing desk, the original 'enchanted bookcase,' a patchwork quilt made by her, autographed 1st editions and a gallery of hand-tinted photos.

The house was so dear to Lucy Maud, she chose it as the venue for her own wedding: in 1911 she was married to Presbyterian minister Ewan Macdonald in the parlor. Visitors here can also take a horse carriage down to Campbell's Pond, the real-life 'Lake of Shining Waters.'

Lucy Maud Montgomery Birthplace MUSEUM
(☎902-886-2099; www.lmmontgomerybirthplace.ca; cnr Rtes 6 & 20; $5; ⊙9am-5pm mid-May–Thanksgiving) Author Lucy Maud Montgomery was born in this humble little white-and-green clapboard house on November 30, 1874. Fans of *Anne of Green Gables* will thrill at the prospect of visiting the writer's childhood bedroom, and seeing her wedding books and scrapbooks; everyone else might feel a little underwhelmed.

Eating & Drinking

★**The Table Culinary Studio** COOKING
(☎902-314-9666; www.thetablepei.com; 4295 Graham's Rd; dinner $75-80, courses from $70; ⊙dinner around 7pm mid-May–Sep) Under the stained glass and wooden beams of the old New London United Church, this place is part cooking school, part fine-dining restaurant. Chef Derrick Hoare provides custom culinary courses exploring everything from bread-making to PEI potatoes, and every evening there's a slap-up island-themed supper served on platters at the central harvest table.

Blue Winds Tea Room BRITISH **$**
(☎902-886-2860; http://bluewindstearoom.blogspot.com; 10746 Rte 6; meals $10-14; ⊙2-5pm Mon-Thu, from 11:30am Fri-Sun) A most charming place to stop for a bite and a cup of tea,

(Continued on page 176)

1

BRYTTA/GETTY IMAGES ©

V J MATTHEW/SHUTTERSTOCK ©

1. Charlottetown (p157)
Provincial capital of Prince Edward Island, Charlottetown is named after the consort of King George III.

2. East Point Lighthouse (p165)
Built in 1867, the East Point Lighthouse has been moved twice and still guards PEI's northeastern shore.

3. Confederation Trail (p161)
See beautiful coastline, forests and farmland along the course of PEI's decommissioned railway.

4. Greenwich Dunes (p168)
These dramatic and ever-shifting sand dunes are part of the Prince Edward Island National Park.

4

EMILIE NGUYEN/SHUTTERSTOCK ©

(Continued from page 173)

surrounded by English gardens. Of course, like everything else in this region, the fare can be very *Anne of Green Gables*–centric and perhaps too twee for some. Order a raspberry cordial or 'new moon pudding' – both recipes have been taken from author Lucy Maud Montgomery's journals.

Sou'West BAR
(902-886-3000; www.souwest.ca; 6457 Rte 20; noon-11pm May-Oct) Dining on the water-view deck or quaffing some sundowner beers: that's what you come to Sou'West for. There's an oyster bar plus a standard range of seafood-y mains and a good selection of beers on tap. There might be some live music too.

Shopping

★ **Village Pottery** CERAMICS
(902-886-2473; www.villagepottery.ca; 10567 Rte 6; 10am-5pm) PEI's longest-running pottery studio is a family affair and a labor of love – it's been operated by the same clan since opening in 1973. The colorful pots, cups and ceramics make great souvenirs, and if you're lucky you might meet current owner Suzanne Scott. There's also a lovely little ice-cream parlor and cafe next door.

Kensington

902 / POP 1619

Kensington is a busy market town about halfway between Cavendish and Summerside. It's a good place to replenish supplies and the closest service center for those attending the popular **Indian River Festival** (www.indianriverfestival.com; Jul-Sep).

Malpeque Bay Kayak Tour Ltd (902-836-3784, 902-266-5706; www.peikayak.ca; Princetown Point; 2½hr kayak tour $55) offers guided kayak tours out to Ram Island, an important migratory stop-off for birds including eagles, cliff swallows, osprey, geese and blue herons. It can also arrange one-on-one stand-up paddleboard and kayak lessons, plus private rentals. It's a 15km drive from Kensington.

Home Place Inn INN $$
(902-836-5686; www.thehomeplace.ca; 21 Victoria St E; d from $99; May-Oct; P) Constructed in 1915 by a local merchant (the brilliantly named Parmenius Orr), this fine, verandah-encircled house exudes period elegance. It's still decorated with vintage furnishings, photographs and paintings, and each of the five rooms is named after a different family member. Breakfast is a home-cooked treat.

★ **Malpeque Oyster Barn** SEAFOOD $$
(902-836-3999; www.facebook.com/malpequeoysterbarn; 10 Malpeque Wharf Rd; 6 oysters from $14; 11am-9pm Jun-Sep) If you want to sample Malpeque's legendary bivalves, this harborside fisherman's barn in Kensington is the place to do it. Experienced eaters take them straight-up raw, fresh-shucked with maybe a twist of lemon; first-timers might perhaps prefer pan-fried with a sauce. If oysters aren't your thing, there are other dishes like fish tacos, lobster rolls and fried haddock, too.

Cavendish

902 / POP 266

Cavendish is famous across Canada as the hometown of Lucy Maud Montgomery (1874–1942), author of the beloved *Anne of Green Gables* stories (around here she's known simply as Lucy Maud or LM). While it provided the model for the fictional town of Avonlea, fans of the stories might be in for a bit of a shock on arrival in Cavendish. Far from a quaint country village filled with clapboard houses and clip-clopping horses, these days the town has become a full-on tourist mecca, crisscrossed by busy roads, swallowed up by parking lots and populated with a mishmash of attractions of questionable value.

Sights

Lucy Maud Montgomery's Cavendish Homestead HISTORIC SITE
(902-963-2231; www.lmmontgomerycavendishhome.com; 8523 Cavendish Rd; adult/child $6/free; 9:30am-5:30pm Jul & Aug, 10am-5pm May, Jun & Oct) This restored homestead arguably offers a more authentic picture of author Lucy Maud Montgomery's life and times than the more heavily marketed Green Gables Heritage Place. Lucy Maud lived here from 1876 to 1911 with her maternal grandparents Alexander and Lucy Macneill, after her mother Clara died of tuberculosis. It's here that she wrote books including *Anne of Green Gables* and *Anne of Avonlea*. There's a small museum and an Anne-themed bookstore.

Green Gables Heritage Place HISTORIC SITE
(902-672-7874; www.pc.gc.ca/en/lhn-nhs/pe/greengables; 8619 Hwy 6; adult/child $7.80/free; 10am-5pm May-Oct) Owned by author LM Montgomery's grandfather's cousins, the now-famous House of Green Gables and

its Victorian surrounds inspired the setting for *Anne of Green Gables* and other stories. Now a National Historic Site, the house has been carefully restored to reflect how it would have appeared in Anne's day, including the furniture, furnishings and decor. Tour guides and audiovisual displays are on hand to provide context – you might even spy Anne herself wandering about.

Outside, you can explore the grounds and woodlands, including the original Lover's Lane. A 1.1km trail leads through the 'Haunted Wood' to Lucy Maud Montgomery's Cavendish Homestead.

Sleeping & Eating

Parkview Farms Tourist Home & Cottages GUESTHOUSE $
(902-963-2027; www.parkviewfarms.com; 8214 Cavendish Rd; r/cottages from $70/180;) Simple tourist-home rooms and self-contained cottages are both on offer at this working dairy farm, 2km east of Cavendish: expect plenty of frills and floral wallpaper.

Kindred Spirits Inn & Cottages INN $$
(902-963-2434; www.kindredspirits.ca; 46 Memory Lane; r from $165; P) This prim, spread-out complex goes big on the storybook style. Rooms are every *Anne of Green Gables* fan's dream, with dotty floral prints, glossy wood floors and fluffy, comfy beds: they're split between the main inn and a separate gatehouse.

Lost Anchor Pub PUB $$
(902-388-0118; www.lostanchorpei.com; 8572 Cavendish Rd; mains $14-29; noon-9pm) If all the talk of Cavendish's favorite fictional orphan Anne of Green Gables is driving you to drink, here's where to come. Simple but hearty pub meals are available: lobster mac 'n' cheese, fish-and-chips and pork-belly tacos.

Carr's Oyster Bar SEAFOOD $$
(902-886-3355; www.carrspei.ca; 32 Campbellton Rd, Stanley Bridge; mains $16-40; 11am-8pm) Dine on oysters straight from Malpeque Bay, or lobster, mussels and seafood you've never even heard of, like quahogs from Carr's own saltwater tanks (the menu helpfully divides dishes up into raw, steamed, fried or baked). There is also plenty of fish on offer.

Information

Cavendish Visitor Information Centre
(902-963-7830; cnr Rte 6 & Hwy 13; 9am-5pm) *Anne of Green Gables* fans will want to chat with the happy, friendly staff here; they really know their stuff about all things Lucy Maud Montgomery, the series' author.

Getting There & Away

Cavendish is 37km northwest of Charlottetown via Rtes 224 and 13. The junction of Rtes 6 and 13 is the tourist center and the area's commercial hub.

WESTERN PRINCE EDWARD ISLAND

Separated from the central part of PEI by a narrow stretch of land, bordered to north and south by Malpeque and Bedeque Bays, the western third of the island is a picture of pastoral peace and quiet. Inland, you'll find arable and potato farms, sleepy villages, and tractors chugging down country roads; along the coast, quiet beaches, fishing towns and pockets of rugged shore. Apart from the area's main town, Summerside, and the lonely headland at North Cape, there are no major sights to speak of, but that doesn't mean it's an area not worth exploring: this is quintessential rural PEI, ideal for a day's road-tripping.

There's culture too: Lennox Island has a lively Mi'kmaq community, while Egmont and Bedeque Bays have clung on to their French Acadian roots.

The 350km-long North Cape Drive (www.northcapedrive.com) is an organized route that hits all the area's major sights.

Summerside

902 / POP 13,814

PEI's second-largest city, Summerside lacks the cosmopolitan cachet of Charlottetown, but it makes a more practical base for exploring the western side of the island. Recessed deep within Bedeque Bay, this tiny seaside town possesses a modern waterfront and quiet streets lined with leafy trees and grand old homes, although sadly many of the old farmsteads have been swallowed up by a tangle of roads and sprawling development. The town's most attractive parts are along, or near to, Water St, which runs parallel to the waterfront.

Sights

★ **Maisons de Bouteilles** ARCHITECTURE
(Bottle Houses; 902-854-2987; www.bottlehouses.com; Rte 11, Cape Egmont; adult/child $8/3;

Summerside

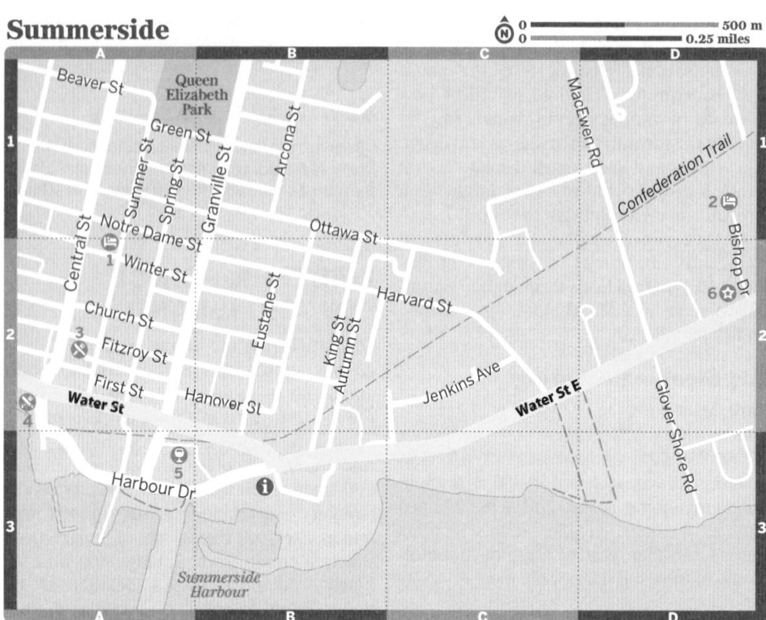

Summerside

Sleeping

1 Summerside Bed & Breakfast ... A2
2 Willowgreen Farm ... D1

Eating

3 Holman's Ice Cream Parlour ... A2
4 Samuel's Coffee House ... A2

Drinking & Nightlife

5 Evermore Brewing Company ... A3

Entertainment

6 College of Piping & Celtic Performing Arts ... D2

9am-8pm July & Aug, to 6pm May, Jun, Sep & Oct) This amazing place brings a new meaning to recycling. The three buildings here are constructed entirely from reclaimed bottles, collected from the local community by fisherman, carpenter and lighthouse keeper Edouard Arsenault. The first, six-gabled house was built in 1980 from 12,000 bottles; a second, hexagonal 'tavern' was added in 1982 from 8000 bottles, followed by a chapel (10,000 bottles) in 1983, complete with altar. The light refracted through the bottles creates a unique effect: come at sunset for maximum impact.

★ West Point Lighthouse LIGHTHOUSE
(902-859-3605; www.westpointlighthouse.ca; West Point; 9am-8:30pm mid-May–mid-Oct) Built in 1875, this striking lighthouse is immediately recognizable thanks to its black-and-white paint job. At 21m high, it's the tallest lighthouse in PEI, and is now home to a small museum exploring the structure's history (it was manned until 1963), as well as a craft shop and inn.

Near the lighthouse, the **Cedar Dunes Provincial Park** (902-859-8785; www.tourismpei.com/provincial-park/cedar-dunes; tent sites $28-30, RV sites $32-37) offers some lovely stretches of sand, although it can be a little windy out this way.

Acadian Museum MUSEUM
(902-432-2880; http://museeacadien.org/an; 23 Maine Dr E, Miscouche; $4.50; 9:30am-5pm Jul & Aug, 9:30am-5pm Mon-Fri & 1-4pm Sun Sep-Jun) The very worthwhile Acadian Museum, in Miscouche, uses 18th-century Acadian artifacts, texts, visuals and music to enlighten visitors about the tragic and compelling history of the Acadians on PEI since 1720. An introspective video introduces a fascinating theory that the brutal treatment of the Acadians by the British may have backhandedly helped preserve a vestige of Acadian culture on PEI.

Sleeping

West Point Lighthouse B&B $$
(902-859-3605; www.westpointlighthouse.ca; d from $169; P) This lighthouse toward West Point ranks as one of PEI's quirkiest places to stay. Located on the lighthouse's 2nd floor, the tower room commands breathtaking views over the Northumberland Strait. Less impressive (but probably more practical) is the adjacent 11-room inn, which has simple modern rooms, all with private balconies. You can also sleep in the former lighthouse-keeper's quarters.

Summerside Bed & Breakfast B&B $$
(902-620-4993; www.summersideinnbandb.com; 98 Summer St; r from $125;) The pick of Sumerside's B&Bs, in a handsome Queen Anne Revival house on the corner of Summer and Winter Sts. The winter room is the prettiest, with a four-poster bed and clawfoot tub; the spring room is even more spacious, with a twinset of original window seats, while the blue room offers arguably the best value.

Willowgreen Farm B&B $$
(902-436-4420; www.willowgreenfarm.com; 117 Bishop Dr; r from $100;) A slice of homespun Summerside here, on one of the town's oldest farmsteads. Rambling rooms filled with antiques, homemade textiles, creaky floorboards and wooden furniture make for a really cozy stay, and a generous breakfast is served communally in the downstairs dining room. It feels surprisingly rural, even though you're just moments from downtown Summerside.

Eating & Drinking

Holman's Ice Cream Parlour ICE CREAM $
(1-800-350-1367; www.facebook.com/Holmansicecream; ice creams from $3.50; noon-10pm Mon-Sat) This ice-cream emporium is where everyone in Summerside comes for their fix: 100% homemade, served in a cake cone or waffle cone, and with delicious flavors like peanut butter fudge swirl, sticky bun and maple walnut. Holman's also has an 80-year-old soda fountain for that extra retro cred.

Samuel's Coffee House CAFE $
(902-724-2300; https://samuelscoffeehouse.ca; 4 Queen St; mains $8-14; 7:30am-6pm Mon-Thu, to 9pm Fri, 8am-5pm Sat & Sun) A perennially popular hangout for morning coffee, lunchtime wraps and afternoon muffins, this stylish cafe is enclosed in a redbrick building in downtown Summerside. With its arched windows and wooden floors, it feels a bit Brooklyn-esque: try the grilled-cheese sandwich with your choice of PEI cheeses.

★ **Evermore Brewing Company** CRAFT BEER
(www.facebook.com/evermoorebrewing; 192 Water St; noon-8:30pm Mon-Wed, to 11pm Thu-Sat, 11am-5pm Sun) This on-trend brewery serves up a choice of ales, sours, seasonal brews and punchy stouts (you can see the stainless-steel vats from the bar). Located in Summerside's former railway station since 2018, the building's original architecture is still in evidence: look out for the original station telephone. Bar snacks and regular bands complete the craft-beer package.

Entertainment

College of Piping & Celtic Performing Arts LIVE MUSIC
(902-436-5377; www.collegeofpiping.com; 619 Water St E) Schooling students in the traditional instruments of Celtic music since the 1980s – from bagpipes to fiddles – this highly regarded music college also stages an impressive Celtic concert called 'Highland Storm' (adult tickets $46) in summer. Expect plenty of step dancing, stirring drums and haunting pipes.

In July and August, there are also hourly mini-concerts ($7) between 11am and 3pm Monday to Friday.

Information

Visitor Information Centre (902-888-8364; www.exploresummerside.com; 124 Heather Moyse Dr; 9am-7pm Jul & Aug, reduced hours May, Jun, Sep & Oct;) Summerside's information center has plenty of local listings, information on the Confederation Trail and self-guided tours. There's also free wi-fi.

Getting There & Away

Summerside is 61km west of Charlottetown on Rte 2.

T3 Transit (p163) operates a twice-daily service between Summerside and Charlottetown ($9, 1½ hours, Monday to Friday only).

Maritime Bus (p56) services from Halifax to Charlottetown stop in Summerside en route.

Tyne Valley

This area, famous for its Malpeque oysters, is one of the most scenic in the province. The village, with its cluster of ornate hous-

WORTH A TRIP

TIGNISH & NORTH CAPE

Tignish is a quiet town tucked up near the North Cape; it sees only a fraction of PEI's visitors. The main reason to make the journey is simply to say you've been to PEI's northern point; it's an impressively remote (and windblown) spot, home to the Wind Energy Institute of Canada and the longest natural rock reef on the continent. At low tide, it's possible to walk out 800m, exploring tide pools and searching for seals.

The **North Cape Interpretive Centre** (902-882-2991; www.northcape.ca; Rte 12, North Cape; $6; 9am-8pm Jul & Aug, 10am-6pm May, Jun, Sep & Oct) provides displays dedicated to wind energy, local history and wildlife, as well as a small aquarium. The Black Marsh Nature Trail (2.7km) leaves the interpretive center and takes you to the west side of the cape – at sunset these crimson cliffs glow against the deep-blue waters. There's also a restaurant.

es, gentle river and art studios, is definitely worth a visit.

Set in the mouth of Malpeque Bay, sheltered behind Hog Island, is Lennox Island and its 250 Mi'kmaq people. The island is connected by a causeway, making it accessible from the town of East Bideford off Rte 12.

Sights

★Lennox Island Cultural Centre CULTURAL CENTRE
(866-831-2702; www.lennoxisland.com; 2 Eagle Feather Trail, Lennox Island; by donation; 10am-6pm Jun-Aug, to 5pm Sep) Mi'kmaq culture remains strong on the little 535-hectare wooded islet known as Lennox Island, and this cultural center provides a decent primer on understanding the history, beliefs and traditions of this ancient First Nations people. It's also the starting point for the Path of Our Forefathers, a **nature trail** that winds through the island's forests and along the coastline.

There's a choice of two trails, one 3km and the other 10km; in July and August, you can follow them in the company of a Mi'kmaq guide, who can tell you all about the local plants, wildlife and traditional medicines.

Canadian Potato Museum MUSEUM
(902-859-2039; www.canadianpotatomuseum.info; 1 Dewar Lane, O'Leary; $10; 9:30am-5pm mid-May–mid-Oct) It had to happen: a museum dedicated to the humble spud, and where better than in potato-capital-of-Canada PEI? Admittedly it's a niche affair, with displays exploring the history of potato farming alongside antique farm machinery and period photos, but it's worth visiting for the **Potato Country Kitchen** (mains $5-12; 11am-5pm mid-May–mid-Oct), where you can try numerous spud-based dishes.

Green Park Shipbuilding Museum & Yeo House MUSEUM
(902-831-7947; www.peimuseum.ca; 360 Green Park Rd; adult $5.75; 9am-4:30pm daily Jul & Aug, Mon-Fri Jun) This museum tells the story of the booming shipbuilding industry in the 19th century. It's located in a painstakingly restored Victorian-era home known as the Yeo House, once home to a prominent local shipbuilder, James Yeo.

Festivals & Events

Tyne Valley Oyster Festival FOOD & DRINK
(www.tvoysterfest.ca; Aug) Four days of shucking and slurping slimy oysters.

Sleeping & Eating

Green Park Campsites CAMPGROUND $
(902-831-7912; www.greenparkcampground.com; 364 Green Park Rd; tent sites $25, with hookups $30, cabins without bath $50; Jun-Sep) The park has 58 campsites spread within a mixed forest. The dozen cabins are a steal.

★Tyne Valley Teas Cafe CAFE $
(902-831-3069; www.teastynevalley.com; 6980a Rte 12; mains $7.50-11; 9am-3:30pm Mon-Fri, 10am-3pm Sat & Sun) This cute village cafe is the top place for lunch in Tyne Valley. There's a great selection of food, from teahouse crepes to Montréal bagels, but it's the cakes and puddings that will have you drooling – served on tradition English bone-china plates, and accompanied by a bewildering choice of teas.

Newfoundland & Labrador

Includes ➡

Best Places to Eat

- ➡ Boreal Diner (p206)
- ➡ Merchant Tavern (p193)
- ➡ Bonavista Social Club (p206)
- ➡ Norseman Restaurant (p221)
- ➡ Piatto (p192)

Best Places to Stay

- ➡ Fogo Island Inn (p214)
- ➡ Artisan Inn (p204)
- ➡ Skerwink Hostel (p204)
- ➡ Green Point Campground (p218)
- ➡ Blue on Water (p189)

Why Go?

They call Newfoundland 'the Rock', a fitting name, as this is an island of thoroughly elemental attractions and aesthetics. The muskeg and cliffs are barren and salt-drenched. The trees give off the smell of spruce like the air is spiced. The ocean roils, flecked with icebergs and spouting whales. The wind roars, and at any time, a storm may scream across the bights and coves.

If you enjoy the rugged and the rough, there are few more beautiful places. Yet ever contrasting the harsh geography is a culture that is, simply, magic. Bright houses painted like rainbows spill over the cliffs; menus advertise cod tongue and crowberries; at night, fiddles compete with the howling wind; and the ever-present chill is countered by the warmest locals you'll ever meet. This, then, is Canada's easternmost, most idiosyncratic province, a marriage of land and salt and storm all its own.

When to Go

St John's

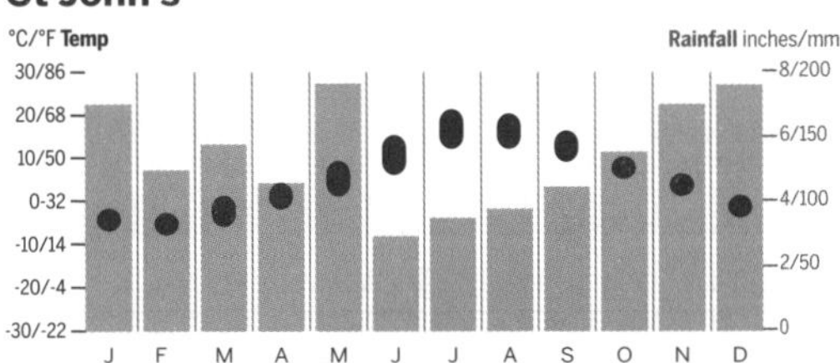

Jun Icebergs glisten offshore, though the weather can be wet and foggy.

Jul & Aug Whales cavort, festivals rock the weekends, and the province is at its sunniest.

Dec & Jan Skiers hit the slopes as Marble Mountain receives most of its 5m of snow.

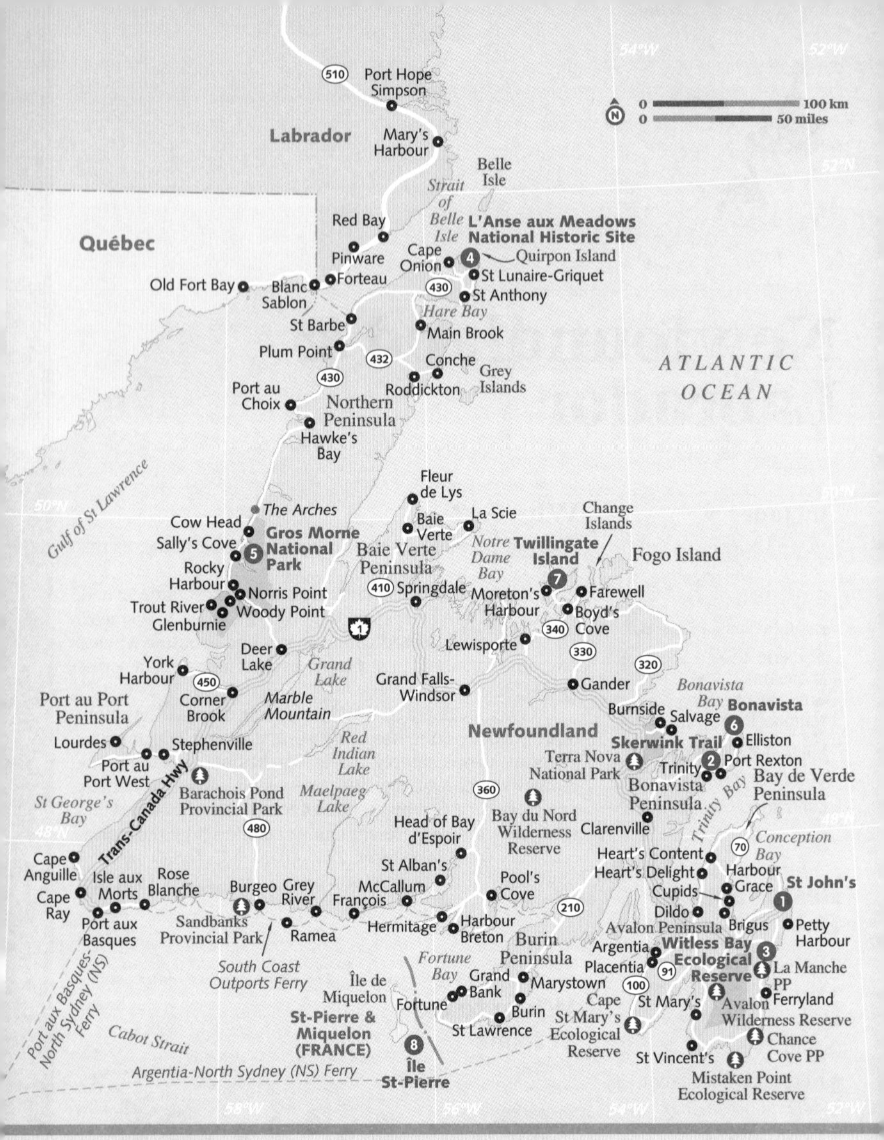

Port Hope Simpson
Labrador
Mary's Harbour
Belle Isle
Strait of Belle Isle
Québec
Red Bay
Pinware
L'Anse aux Meadows National Historic Site
Cape Onion
Quirpon Island
Old Fort Bay
Blanc Sablon
Forteau
St Lunaire-Griquet
St Anthony
Hare Bay
St Barbe
Main Brook
Plum Point
Conche
Grey Islands
Port au Choix
Roddickton
Northern Peninsula
Hawke's Bay
ATLANTIC OCEAN
Gulf of St Lawrence
Fleur de Lys
The Arches
Cow Head
Gros Morne National Park
Sally's Cove
Baie Verte
La Scie
Change Islands
Baie Verte Peninsula
Notre Dame Bay
Twillingate Island
Fogo Island
Rocky Harbour
Norris Point
Springdale
Moreton's Harbour
Farewell
Trout River
Woody Point
Glenburnie
Boyd's Cove
Lewisporte
Deer Lake
Grand Lake
York Harbour
Corner Brook
Grand Falls-Windsor
Gander
Port au Port Peninsula
Marble Mountain
Bonavista Bay
Burnside
Salvage
Bonavista
Newfoundland
Lourdes
Stephenville
Red Indian Lake
Skerwink Trail
Elliston
Port au Port West
Terra Nova National Park
Trinity
Port Rexton
Barachois Pond Provincial Park
Maelpaeg Lake
Bonavista Peninsula
Bay de Verde Peninsula
Trinity Bay
St George's Bay
Trans-Canada Hwy
Head of Bay d'Espoir
Bay du Nord Wilderness Reserve
Clarenville
Conception Bay
Cape Anguille
Heart's Content
Heart's Delight
Harbour Grace
St John's
Isle aux Morts
Rose Blanche
Burgeo
Grey River
St Alban's
McCallum
François
Pool's Cove
Cupids
Cape Ray
Port aux Basques
Sandbanks Provincial Park
Ramea
Hermitage
Harbour Breton
Dildo
Avalon Peninsula
Brigus
Petty Harbour
Burin Peninsula
Argentia
Witless Bay Ecological Reserve
Placentia
South Coast Outports Ferry
Fortune Bay
Grand Bank
Marystown
La Manche PP
Île de Miquelon
Fortune
Cape St Mary's Ecological Reserve
St Mary's
Avalon Wilderness Reserve
Ferryland
Port aux Basques-North Sydney (NS) Ferry
St-Pierre & Miquelon (FRANCE)
Burin
St Lawrence
Cabot Strait
Chance Cove PP
Île St-Pierre
St Vincent's
Argentia-North Sydney (NS) Ferry
Mistaken Point Ecological Reserve
0 — 100 km
0 — 50 miles

Newfoundland & Labrador Highlights

1. **St John's** (p184) Hoisting a drink, taking a ghost tour and soaking up the history of North America's oldest city.
2. **Skerwink Trail** (p204) Trekking through magnificent coastal scenery.
3. **Witless Bay Ecological Reserve** (p198) Sharing the waves with whales and puffins.
4. **L'Anse aux Meadows National Historic Site** (p220) Visiting Leif Eriksson's sublime 1000-year-old Viking pad.
5. **Gros Morne National Park** (p216) Hiking the ridges and kayaking the fjord-like lakes.
6. **Bonavista** (p205) Exploring a synthesis of modern Canada and old outport.
7. **Twillingate Island** (p210) Ogling icebergs, hiking and seeing whales every morning.
8. **St-Pierre** (p208) Getting your French fix – wine, chocolate éclairs and baguettes.

History

The Paleo-Indians walked into Labrador 9000 years ago. They hunted seals, fished for salmon and tried to stay warm. The Vikings, led by Leif Eriksson, washed ashore further south at L'Anse aux Meadows in Newfoundland in CE 1000 and established North America's first European settlement.

John Cabot (Italian-born Giovanni Caboto) sailed around the shores of Newfoundland next. It was 1497, and he was employed by England's Henry VII. Cabot's stories of cod stocks so prolific that one could nearly walk on water spread quickly throughout Europe. Soon the French, Portuguese, Spanish and Basques were also fishing off Newfoundland's coast.

The 1713 Treaty of Utrecht ceded all of Newfoundland to England. The land remained a British colony for most of the next two centuries, with life revolving around the booming fishing industry. Newfoundland's Indigenous people, the Beothuk, did not fare well after settlement began. Diseases and land conflicts contributed to their demise by 1829.

Ever true to its independent spirit, Newfoundland was the last province to join Canada, doing so in 1949. While Labrador was always part of the package, it wasn't until 2001 that it became part of the provincial name.

Language & People

Two hundred years ago, coastal fishing families from Ireland and England made up almost the entire population. Since then, as a result of living in isolated outposts, their language has evolved into almost 60 different dialects. Strong, lilting inflections, unique slang and colorful idioms pepper the language, sometimes confounding even residents.

The authoritative source is the *Dictionary of Newfoundland English* (www.heritage.nf.ca/dictionary).

Inuit and Innu have occupied Labrador for thousands of years. Until the 1960s they were the sole inhabitants, alongside a few longtime European descendants known as 'liveyers,' who eked out an existence by fishing and hunting from tiny villages that freckled the coast. The interior was virgin wilderness.

While populations of both groups can be found in Labrador, remember that 'Inuit' and 'Innu' are not interchangeable terms, but rather two distinct peoples. The Inuit are an Arctic people who inhabit a broad swath of the globe stretching from Greenland through Canada (mainly Nunavut) to the USA (Alaska). The Innu can be found throughout Labrador and eastern Québec; they refer to this homeland as Nitassinan.

NEWFOUNDLAND FAST FACTS

- Population: 525,355
- Area: 405,212 sq km
- Capital: St John's
- Quirky fact: Newfoundland has 82 places called Long Pond, 42 called White Point and one called Jerry's Nose

Land & Climate

They don't call it the Rock for nothing. Glaciers tore through here, leaving behind a rugged landscape of boulders, lakes and bogs. Newfoundland's interior remains barren, while the island's cities and towns congregate at its edges near the sea.

Labrador is sparser than Newfoundland, puddled and tundra-like, with mountains thrown in for good measure.

Temperatures peak in July and August, when daytime highs average 20°C (68ºF). These are also the driest months; it rains or snows about 15 out of every 30 days. Wintertime temperatures hover at 0°C (32°F). Fog and wind plague the coast much of the year (which makes for a lot of canceled flights).

Parks & Wildlife

Whales, moose and puffins are Newfoundland's wildlife stars, and most visitors see them all. Whale-watching tours depart from all around the province and will take you close to the sea mammals (usually humpback and minke). Puffins – the funny-looking love child of the penguin and parrot – flap around Witless Bay and Elliston. Moose nibble shrubs near roadsides throughout the province, so keep an eye out while driving. Some visitors also glimpse caribou near the Avalon Wilderness Reserve, which is special because usually these beasts can only be seen in the High Arctic. Caribou herds also roam in Labrador, though their numbers have been declining sharply in recent years.

Getting There & Away

AIR

St John's International Airport (p196) is the main hub for the region, though **Deer Lake Airport** (YDF; 709-635-3601; www.deerlakeairport.com; 1 Airport Rd;) is an excellent option for

NEWFOUNDLAND ITINERARIES

Five Days

Start in St John's by visiting Signal Hill (p185) and Cape Spear (p196). Both are historical sites, but they also offer walking trails and views where you just may see an iceberg, a whale or both. At night sample St John's eateries, funky shops and music-filled pubs.

After a couple of days of 'big city' life, move onward through the Avalon Peninsula. Cruise to see whales and puffins at Witless Bay Ecological Reserve (p198), plan a picnic in Ferryland (p199) or visit the birds at Cape St Mary's Ecological Reserve (p202).

Spend the last day or two soaking up the historical eastern communities of Trinity (p203) and Bonavista (p205), and the cliffside hikes in between.

Ten Days

Do the five-day itinerary and then go west, possibly via a quick flight to Deer Lake (p183), and reap the reward of viewing the mighty fjords of Gros Morne National Park (p216) and the monumental Viking history at L'Anse aux Meadows National Historic Site (p220). With a few extra days you could sail across the Strait of Belle Isle and slow waaay down among the wee towns and bold granite cliffs of the Labrador Straits (p228).

visitors focusing on the Northern Peninsula. Airlines flying in include **Air Canada** (☎888-247-2262; www.aircanada.com), PAL Airlines (p196), Porter (p196) and United (p196).

BOAT

Marine Atlantic (☎800-341-7981; www.marineatlantic.ca) operates two massive car/passenger ferries between North Sydney (NS) and Newfoundland. There's a daily six-hour crossing to Port aux Basques (western Newfoundland) year-round, and a thrice-weekly 14-hour crossing to Argentia (on the Avalon Peninsula) in summer. Reservations are recommended, especially to Argentia.

Provincial Ferry Service (www.gov.nl.ca/ferryservices) runs the smaller boats that travel within the province to various islands and coastal towns. Each service has its own phone number with up-to-the-minute information; it's wise to call before embarking.

BUS

DRL (p196) sends one bus daily each way between St John's and Port aux Basques (13½ hours), making dozens of stops en route. Other than DRL, public transportation consists of small, regional shuttle vans that connect with one or more major towns. Although not extensive, the system works pretty well and will get most people where they want to go.

CAR & MOTORCYCLE

The Trans-Canada Hwy (Hwy 1) is the main cross-island roadway. Driving distances are deceptive, as travel is often slow going on heavily contorted, single-lane roads. Watch out for moose, especially at dusk.

Be warned: rental-car fleets are small (thanks to the island's remoteness and short tourist season), which means loads of visitors vie for limited vehicles in midsummer. Costs can rack up to $100 per day (including taxes and mileage fees). Reserve well in advance – April or May is recommended if you're traveling during the mid-July-to-early-August peak – and confirm the booking before you arrive.

St John's to Port aux Basques 905km
St John's to Gros Morne 708km
Gros Morne to St Anthony 372km

ST JOHN'S

POP 114,000

Newfoundland is an island of austere, washed-out beauty and vast unpopulated wilderness. Yet here, in its capital and largest city, one finds scads of homes colored like tropical fruit, plus bustling street life and a dim urban (yet small-town friendly) buzz. For all that, North America's oldest city doesn't just contrast the province it dominates. St John's exudes wry wit, stoicism and lust for life, and to this end embodies some of Newfoundland's best values.

The town paints the steep slopes of a harbor that shelters hectares of green space, winding paths, rainbow row houses, artists, technocrats and engineers – St John's is by far the most economically dynamic corner of Newfoundland; not coincidentally, it's also where you'll find the province's only university and ethnic enclaves. Signal Hill dominates the topography, while new restaurants, an active outdoors scene, and nights on the town dominate the social life.

Sights

Most sights are downtown or within a few kilometers, though be prepared for some serious uphill walking.

★Signal Hill National Historic Site HISTORIC SITE
(709-772-5367; www.pc.gc.ca/signalhill; 230 Signal Hill Rd; grounds 24hr, visitor center 10am-6pm; P) The city's most famous landmark is worth it for the glorious view alone, though there's much more to see. The tiny castle atop the hill is **Cabot Tower** (8:30am-5pm Apr-Nov) FREE, built in 1898 to honor both John Cabot's arrival in 1497 and Queen Victoria's Diamond Jubilee. In midsummer, soldiers dressed as the 19th-century Royal Newfoundland Company perform a tattoo (p195) and fire cannons.

The **Signal Hill Visitor Centre** (adult/child $3.90/1.90; 10am-6pm May-Oct) features interactive displays on the site's history. The last North American battle of the Seven Years' War took place here in 1762, and Britain's victory ended France's renewed aspirations for control of eastern North America. The tattoo takes place next to the center at O'Flaherty Field.

You can see cannons and the remains of the late-18th-century British battery at **Queen's Battery & Barracks** further up the hill. Inside Cabot Tower, educational displays relay how Italian inventor Guglielmo Marconi received the first wireless transatlantic message from Cornwall, England, at the site in 1901. An amateur radio society operates a station in the tower in July and August.

Various activities and events kick off throughout the year, including guided walks, ghost tours ($15) and beer tastings ($39.50). Call ahead or check the website for details.

An awesome way to return to downtown is along the 1.7km North Head Trail (p188). The trailhead isn't marked; look for it right before you enter the lot. It's the path leading furthest to the right. Because much of the trail runs along the bluff's sheer edge, this walk is not something to attempt in icy, foggy or dark conditions. Free maps are available at Cabot Tower. If you're looking for an easier walk, take the 710m hike to the Ladies Lookout (p188). The site sits 1.5km from downtown, up Signal Hill Rd.

★The Rooms MUSEUM
(709-757-8000; www.therooms.ca; 9 Bonaventure Ave; adult/child $10/5, 6-9pm Wed free; 10am-5pm Mon, Tue, Thu & Sat, to 9pm Wed, to 10pm Fri, noon-5pm Sun, closed Mon Oct-Apr;) Not many museums offer the chance to see a giant squid, hear avant-garde sound sculptures and peruse ancient weaponry all under one roof. But that's The Rooms, the province's all-in-one historical museum, art gallery and archives. The building itself, a massive stone-and-glass complex, is impressive to look at, with views that lord it over the city. Has an on-site cafe and excellent restaurant.

Quidi Vidi VILLAGE
Over Signal Hill, away from town, is the tiny picturesque village of Quidi Vidi. Check out the 18th-century battery and the lakeside regatta museum, but make your first stop Quidi Vidi Brewery (p195), which whips up Newfoundland's most popular microbrews. Located in an old fish-processing plant on the small wharf, it's a scenic place to slake your thirst.

Nearby there's one of the oldest cottages in North America, the 1750s-era Mallard Cottage (p193), a restaurant that serves Newfoundland comfort food. Nearby is the Inn of Olde Pub (p193), a dive bar located in what is not the oldest cottage in North America, but sure feels like it. Also in this vicinity is the **Quidi Vidi Village Plantation** (709-570-2038; http://qvvplantation.com; 10 Maple View Pl; 10am-4pm Wed-Sat, 11am-4pm Sun), an arts center that hosts a rotating collection of local creatives.

The 1762 **Quidi Vidi Battery**, atop the hill end of Cuckold's Cove Rd, was built by the French after they took St John's. The British quickly claimed it, and it remained in military service into the 1800s.

Inland from the village, **Quidi Vidi Lake** is the site of the St John's Regatta (p188). The **Royal St John's Regatta Museum** (709-576-8921; cnr Lakeview Ave & Clancy Dr, off Forest Rd; by appointment May-Aug 15) FREE is on the 2nd floor of the boathouse. A popular walking trail leads around the lake.

Quidi Vidi is about 2km from the northeast edge of downtown. Take Plymouth Rd, go left on Quidi Vidi Rd, then right on Forest Rd (which becomes Quidi Vidi Village Rd). For the brewery, bear right onto Barrows Rd. For the battery, veer off on Cuckold's Cove Rd. For the regatta museum, take a left off Forest Rd onto Lakeview Ave. You can also

St John's

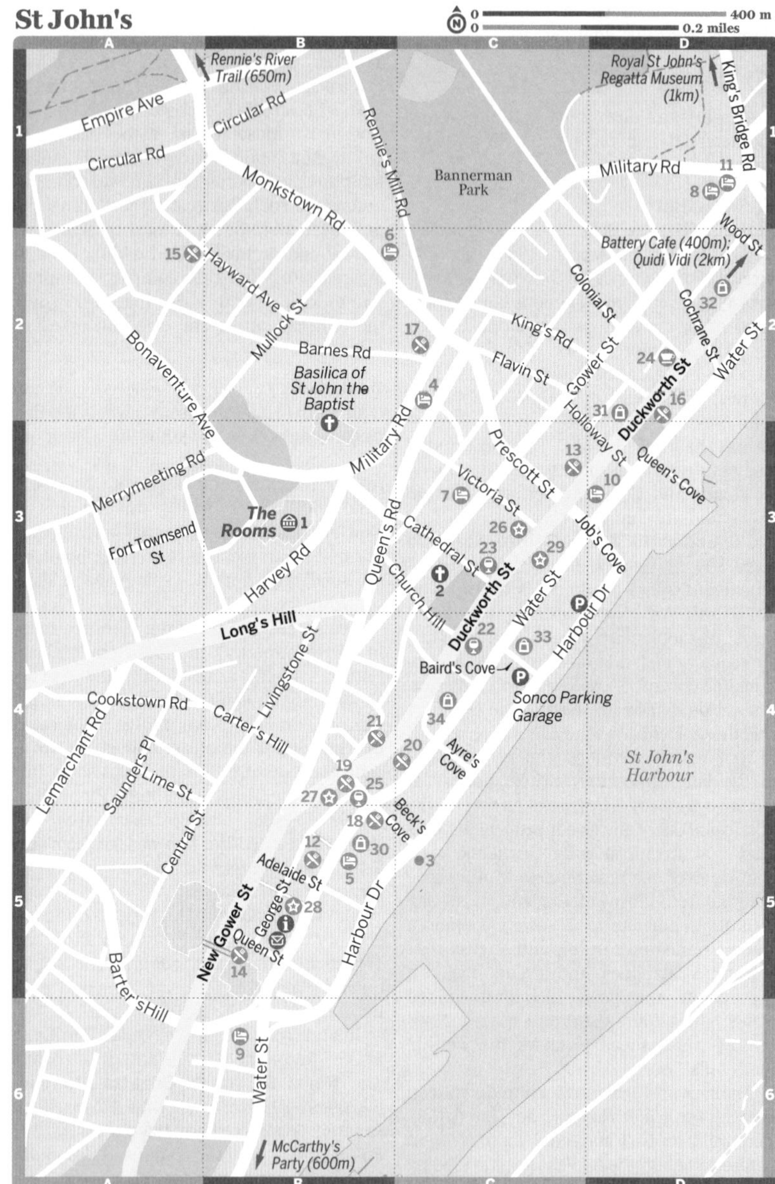

walk from Signal Hill via the Cuckold's Cove Trail, which takes about 30 minutes.

CA Pippy Park PARK

(www.pippypark.com;) The feature-filled 13-sq-km CA Pippy Park coats downtown's northwestern edge. Recreational facilities include walking trails, picnic areas, playgrounds, a golf course and a campground. **Memorial University**, the province's only university, is here too. The university's botanical garden is at Oxen Pond, at the park's western edge off Mt Scio Rd.

St John's

Cultivated areas and a nature reserve fill the botanical landscape. Together, these and the park's **Long Pond** marsh give visitors an excellent introduction to Newfoundland's flora, habitats (including boreal forest and bogs) and animals (look for birds at Long Pond and the occasional moose). Take the 3km **Long Pond Walk** for the full effect.

The **Fluvarium** (709-754-3474; www.fluvarium.ca; 5 Nagle's Pl; adult/child/family $8/6/25; 9am-5pm Mon-Fri, from 10am Sat & Sun Jul & Aug, reduced hours Sep-Jun; P), a glass-sided cross-section of a 'living' river, is located across the street from the campground.

To get here from downtown, take Bonaventure Ave north to Allandale Rd and follow the signs; it's about 2km.

Memorial University Botanical Garden GARDENS
(709-737-8590; www.mun.ca/botgarden; 306 Mt Scio Rd, CA Pippy Park; adult/child $9/6; 10am-5pm May-Aug, reduced hours Sep-Apr) The premier botanical garden of the province, with nature trails, a large cultivated garden and a greenhouse within a 100-acre nature reserve.

Johnson Geo Centre MUSEUM
(709-737-7880; www.geocentre.ca; 175 Signal Hill Rd; adult/child $12/6; 9:30am-5pm) Nowhere in the world can geo-history, going back to the birth of the earth, be accessed so easily as in Newfoundland. The Geo Centre does a grand job of making snore-worthy geological information perk up with appeal via its underground, interactive displays.

Anglican Cathedral of St John the Baptist CHURCH
(709-726-5677; www.stjohnsanglicancathedral.org; 16 Church Hill; 10am-4pm Mon-Sat) Serving Canada's oldest parish (1699), this Anglican cathedral is one of the finest examples of ecclesiastical Gothic architecture in North America. Although originally built in the 1830s, all but its exterior walls were reduced to ashes by the Great Fire of 1892. Rebuilt in 1905, its Gothic ribbed ceiling, graceful stone arches and long stained-glass windows are timeless marvels. High tea (adult/child $10/6) is offered in the crypt on weekday afternoons in July and August.

Activities

★ Rennie's River Trail WALKING

(access at Carpasian Rd) FREE It takes a city as understated as St John's to not make a big deal about this trail, which must be one of the most pleasant urban walks anywhere. Right in the middle of the city is a 2.9-mile (5km) trail, much of which runs alongside the rushing Rennie's River, which forms natural waterfalls and is flanked by grassy banks.

★ North Head Trail WALKING

(Signal Hill) You only have to go to Signal Hill (p185) to get a taste of Newfoundland's majestic, rugged beauty. The North Head Trail (1.7km) connects Cabot Tower (p185) with the harborfront Battery neighborhood, and is a beloved local gem. The walk departs from the tower's parking lot and traces the cliffs, imparting tremendous sea views and sometimes whale spouts.

Ladies Lookout HIKING

(Signal Hill) The North Head Trail is justifiably the most famous walk in St John's, but it's demanding. The nearby Ladies Lookout (710m) is much easier, and still yields superlative views. The walk was so named because sailors' wives would supposedly head here watching for their husbands (the trail also gives a view of Cuckold's Cove; make of that what you will).

Grand Concourse WALKING

(☎709-737-1077; www.grandconcourse.ca) The Grand Concourse is an ambitious 160km-long network of trails all over town and linking St John's with nearby Mt Pearl and Paradise via downtown sidewalks, trails, river corridors and old railway beds.

Tours

★ St John's Haunted Hike WALKING

(www.hauntedhike.com; adult/child $10/5; ⏲9:30pm Sun-Thu Jun-Sep) As you may expect, the oldest city on the continent has generated its share of ghost stories, and you can explore this phantasmal heritage on these popular adventures. Departure is from the Anglican Cathedral's west entrance. On midsummer Fridays and Saturdays, the action moves to Signal Hill (p185) for a seated, indoor show of ghost stories (8pm, tickets $15).

Outfitters KAYAKING

(☎800-966-9658, 709-579-4453; www.theoutfitters.nf.ca; 220 Water St; half-/full-day tour $89/189; ⏲10am-6pm Mon-Wed & Sat, to 9pm Thu & Fri, noon-5pm Sun) Popular kayak tours at Bay Bulls, with shuttle service (round-trip $60 for up to two people) from the Outfitters (p195) store downtown.

Fairy Door Tours WALKING

(☎709-682-9724; http://fairydoortours.com; $9; ⏲Sat 11am & 1pm; 👪) If there are faeries in North America, there must be a few in Newfoundland, one of the most magical islands anywhere. On these tours you'll be on the lookout for hand-painted miniature doors set in trees and the like, leading to other worlds and lots of excitement if you've got kids (or kids at heart).

The tour kicks off near the Fluvarium (p187); the hosts will give you an exact location. You won't be walking more than a kilometer, and the tour lasts around 75 minutes.

McCarthy's Party BUS

(☎888-660-6060, 709-579-4444; www.mccarthysparty.com; 566 Water St; 3hr tour adult/child from $60/35) A seasoned tour company with wonderful guides that will give you a true sense of local culture. Offerings range from half-day tours of St John's and Cape Spear to 12-day trips around the island ($3470).

Iceberg Quest BOATING

(☎709-722-1888; www.icebergquest.com; Pier 6; 2hr tour adult/child $70/30) Departs from St John's Harbour and makes a run down to Cape Spear in search of icebergs in June and whales in July and August. There are multiple departures daily.

Festivals & Events

Royal St John's Regatta SPORTS

(http://stjohnsregatta.ca; ⏲1st Wed Aug) The streets are empty, the stores are closed and everyone migrates to the shores of Quidi Vidi Lake. This rowing regatta officially began in 1825 and is now the oldest continuously held sporting event in North America. Postponed if the rowing conditions are poor.

Shakespeare by the Sea Festival THEATER

(☎709-722-7287; www.shakespearebytheseafestival.com; tickets $20-25; ⏲early Jul–mid-Aug) Live outdoor productions are presented at Signal Hill, local parks and other venues. Buy all tickets on-site; cash only. Some performances are free.

Downtown Busker Festival CARNIVAL

(www.downtownstjohns.com; ⏲early Aug) Jugglers, magicians, acrobats, comedians and more take their performances to the streets for a long weekend. Performances are centered on Water St.

Newfoundland & Labrador Folk Festival MUSIC
(www.nlfolk.com; Bannerman Park; early Aug) This three-day event celebrates traditional Newfoundland music, dancing and storytelling. It's held the weekend after the regatta.

George Street Festival MUSIC
(www.georgestreetlive.ca; daily/weekly tickets from $30/199; late Jul/early Aug) The mighty George St becomes one big nightclub for a fabulous week of daytime and nighttime musical performances.

Sleeping

Scores of B&Bs offer a place to rest your head in the heart of St John's; they're usually better value than the hotels and motels. They fill fast, so book ahead. Many have a two-night minimum-stay requirement. The ones listed here all serve a hot breakfast. The city's 17% tax is not included in prices listed here. Parking is available at or near all accommodations.

Memorial University Rooms ACCOMMODATION SERVICES $
(877-730-7657; www.mun.ca/stay; r with shared bath $69; late Jun-Aug; P) One of the best deals in town, the local university offers summer accommodations in its dormitory housing with shared washroom facilities. There's the option of twin or double beds in modern, pleasant rooms. Guests have access to kitchen facilities, a pool and fitness center. There are no TVs.

HI St John's HOSTEL $
(709-754-4789; www.hihostels.ca; 8 Gower St; dm/r $38/79; @) It's everything a good hostel should be: well located near the action, with spick-and-span facilities, not too big (16 beds in all), and helpful. A whiteboard lists everything of interest happening in town each day. The hostel also books reasonably priced tours.

★ **Blue on Water** BOUTIQUE HOTEL $$
(709-754-2583; www.blueonwater.com; 319 Water St; r $199-249; @) One of the more stylish hotels in the St John's lineup, Blue on Water has all the fresh, modern dressings the hip hotel-hopper desires: crisp white sheets, exposed brick, distressed accents, and a downstairs bar that attracts the attractive. The central location on Water St (imagine that) is a serious draw.

PLANNING YOUR TRIP

- Book ahead for rental cars and accommodations. If you're arriving during the mid-July to early August peak, secure a car by April or May and don't wait much longer to book a room. **Newfoundland & Labrador Tourism** (800-563-6353; www.newfoundlandlabrador.com) has listings.
- Driving distances are lengthy, so have realistic expectations of what you can cover. For instance, it's 708km between St John's and Gros Morne National Park, and a lot of those kilometers are curving and twisty. The Road Distance Database (www.stats.gov.nl.ca/DataTools/RoadDB/Distance) is a good reference.
- Know your seasons for puffins (May to August), icebergs (June to early July) and whales (July to August). Icebergs, in particular, can be tricky to predict. Check Iceberg Finder (www.icebergfinder.com) to get the drift.

JAG BOUTIQUE HOTEL $$
(844-564-1524; www.steelehotels.com; 115 George St W; r $216-286, ste $366;) What's not to like about a hotel that blasts the Stones or Dylan in the lobby? This rock-and-roll-themed boutique hotel occupies a tall multistory building with harbor views. Spacious rooms have a sleek look of muted colors with pleated leather headboards and oversize windows (double-paned with blackout curtains specially made for rock stars).

Cabot House B&B $$
(709-754-0058; www.abbainn.com; 26 Monkstown Rd; r/ste $209/259; P) A stunning 1904 Queen Anne-revival mansion, this sprawling house full of antiques and stained-glass windows makes for a subdued stay. Gorgeous, spacious rooms are mostly restored to their original layout, with the addition of bathrooms and a Jacuzzi suite. With no on-site host, the experience is more hotel-like.

Leaside Manor B&B $$
(709-722-0387; www.leasidemanor.com; 39 Topsail Rd; r $229; @) The rooms in this old merchant's home have been updated with boutique-hotel contemporary flourishes,

(Continued on page 192)

1

4

3

K.L DENMAN/SHUTTERSTOCK ©

1. Twillingate Island (p210)
A good place for spotting whales and icebergs, Twillingate is located at the top of the Central Coast.

2. Witless Bay Ecological Reserve (p198)
Four islands off Witless Bay, and southward, represent one of the top seabird breeding areas in eastern North America.

3. St John's (p184)
North America's oldest city, and Newfoundland's capital, has a bustling streetlife and a friendly buzz.

4. Skerwink Trail (p204)
This 5km-long trail near Trinity offers dramatic coastal vistas of sea stacks, early-summer icebergs and a lighthouse.

(Continued from page 189)

including big tubs, plush beds (some with canopies), fireplaces, sitting areas and Jacuzzis, which explains why the *Globe and Mail* designated Leaside one of Canada's 'most romantic destinations.' Each room has its own individual vibe, but they're all plush and comfortable.

The Roses B&B **$$**
(☎877-767-3722; www.therosesnl.com; 9 Military Rd; r $99-169;) The Roses boasts a dozen nicely appointed guest rooms spread out over two Victorian properties located near the heart of the St John's action. Breakfasts vary by day, and can include Newfoundland berry pancakes, a breakfast sandwich and hash browns. Rooms have en suite bathrooms, and duvets filled with Canadian goose down.

Abba Inn B&B **$$**
(☎709-754-0058; www.abbainn.com; 36 Queen's Rd; r $135;) The Abba shares a building with **Balmoral House** (☎709-754-5721; www.balmoralhouse.com; 38 Queen's Rd; r $129-159;), and both B&Bs have similar amenities and ambience. Rooms are surprisingly large and absolutely comfortable, and the townhouse setting is attractive. If Abba is full, the owner also has nearby **Gower House** (☎709-754-0058; www.abbainn.com; 180 Gower St; r $129;) and Cabot House (p189), which are comparable. There's often no on-site host; guests let themselves in with a lock code.

★ **Luxus** BOUTIQUE HOTEL **$$$**
(☎844-722-8899; www.theluxus.ca; 128 Water St; r $439-599;) Opened by a businessman originally from the area, the Luxus' amenities read like a wish list of those who travel for a living. Bose speakers, check. Dual-jet shower and freestanding tub, check. Electronic Japanese toilet, check. All the luxurious rooms boast harbor views, minibar and a whopping 70-inch (178cm) flat-screen TV. Don't miss happy hour at the ambient cocktail bar.

Eating

★ **Adelaide Oyster House** INTERNATIONAL **$**
(☎709-722-7222; www.facebook.com/theadelaideoysterhouse; 334 Water St; small plates $8-17; ⏲5-11pm Mon-Wed, to midnight Thu, to 1am Fri, 11am-3pm & 5pm-1am Sat, 11am-3pm & 5pm-midnight Sun) The Adelaide is a stylish sliver of a bar and restaurant where the specialty is small plates such as fish tacos, Kobe beef lettuce wraps topped with spicy kimchi, and, of course, fresh oysters from both coasts, plus some brick-strong cocktails to get the party started.

★ **Georgestown Cafe and Bookshelf** CAFE **$**
(☎709-579-7134; https://georgestowncafe.wordpress.com; 73 Hayward Ave; mains $5-10; ⏲8am-5pm Mon-Sat, from 10am Sun;) If you've got younger kids and you need to kill time before heading to The Rooms (p185), Georgestown Cafe is here to answer your every prayer. It's a cafe, sure, serving fair-trade coffee and yummy treats such as granola, bagels, scones and muffins, but there's also a bookstore on-site, and a play area stacked with kids' books and toys.

Rocket Bakery BAKERY **$**
(☎709-738-2011; www.rocketfood.ca; 272 Water St; mains $3-10; ⏲7:30am-9pm Mon-Sat, to 6pm Sun;) Cheery Rocket is the perfect spot for a cup o' joe, a groovy sandwich or a sweet treat. Try the hummus on crusty homemade multigrain bread, or maybe a croissant with lemon curd. The fish cakes also win raves. Order at the counter, then take your goodies to the tables in the adjoining room.

Hungry Heart CAFE **$**
(☎709-738-6164; www.hungryheartcafe.ca; 142 Military Rd; mains $13-16; ⏲8am-3pm Tue-Sat) Eat in this warm-toned cafe and you're helping abused women and others in need to train in food service. Try the curry mango chicken or pulled-pork sandwiches. Saturday brunch brings out the cheese scones with crisp, house-cured bacon and cherry bread pudding. Lots of baked goodies too.

Sprout VEGETARIAN **$**
(☎709-579-5485; www.thesproutrestaurant.com; 364 Duckworth St; mains $10-15; ⏲11:30am-8:30pm Mon-Wed, to 9:30pm Thu-Sat;) Full-on vegetarian food is almost unheard of in rural Newfoundland, but Sprout almost makes up for the difference in St John's. Take a seat and savor your marinated tofu burger, walnut-pesto-melt sandwich and brown rice poutine (fries served under miso gravy) before leaving town. Sandwiches feature thick slices of homemade bread. Cash and debit only.

★ **Piatto** PIZZA **$$**
(☎709-726-0709; www.piattopizzeria.com; 377 Duckworth St; mains $12-19; ⏲11:30am-10pm Mon-Thu, to 11pm Fri & Sat, to 9pm Sun;) Offering a

great night out without breaking the bank, cozy brick Piatto wood-fires pizza like nobody's business. Go trad or try a thin-crust pie topped with prosciutto, figs and balsamic. It's all good. There are nice fresh salads, wine and Italian cocktails. Children's books plus pizza and ice-cream specials for kids make this a good option for families.

Bagel Cafe CANADIAN **$$**
(709-739-4470; http://thebagelcafe.ca; 246 Duckworth St; mains $10-28; 7am-9pm) For a moment, disregard the name of this spot and note the crowds, which absolutely pack this downtown eatery, especially on weekend mornings. Now back to the name: of course the Bagel Cafe has many variations of its eponymous circle of doughy delight, but you'll also find poutine hash browns, burgers, toutons (pancakes) with baked beans and bologna, and strong coffee.

Get Stuffed CANADIAN **$$**
(709-757-2480; www.facebook.com/getstuffedsj; 190 Duckworth St; mains $15-26; noon-3pm & 5:30-10pm Tue-Sat, to 9pm Sun) Contemporary Canadian and home-cooking kicked up a notch, served in a comfortably laid-back atmosphere, is the name of the game at Get Stuffed, where the food will get you – well – stuffed. Fancy cheese 'n' doo (mac 'n' cheese) is cooked with Gruyère and sharp cheddar, while a lovely meatloaf comes with a nice scoop of mushroom demi-cream.

★**Merchant Tavern** CANADIAN **$$$**
(709-722-5050; http://themerchanttavern.ca; 291 Water St; mains $21-40; 11:30am-10pm Tue-Fri, from 10:30am Sat, 10:30am-2:30pm Sun) An elegant tavern housed in a former bank building, this restaurant is a fine choice for a splurge. Gorgeous seafood stews, duck and lentils, and cod with parsnip make for near culinary perfection – just bear in mind this is a seasonal, changing menu (but always solid). Some seating faces the open-view kitchen – good for chatting with the cooks.

Dinner is served until 10:30pm, then it's just bar food. Reservations recommended.

Chinched CANADIAN **$$$**
(709-722-3100; www.chinchedbistro.com; 7 Queen St; mains $14-35; 5:30-9:30pm Mon-Sat) Quality dishes without the white-tablecloth pretense – think octopus tacos or Newfoundland wild mushroom risotto served in a warm, dark-wood room. On an ever-changing menu, meat figures prominently – don't skip the charcuterie boards or homemade pickles. The young chefs' creativity extends to the singular desserts (say, wild-nettle ice cream) and spirits (partridgeberry vodka) made in-house. If you don't want to commit to a full meal, the bar menu lets you sample dishes for $6 to $10.

Mallard Cottage CANADIAN **$$$**
(709-237-7314; www.mallardcottage.ca; 2 Barrows Rd; mains $19-35; 10am-9pm Wed-Sat, to 6:30pm Sun, to 5pm Mon & Tue) A lot of restaurants give lip service to 'local and sustainable,' but this one is spot-on and devilishly good. The blackboard menu changes daily. Think turnips with yogurt and crispy shallots or brined duck with spaetzle and fried rosemary. The adorable Mallard Cottage, which dates from the 1750s, is a historical site in and of itself.

Drinking & Nightlife

★**Inn of Olde Pub** BAR
(709-576-2223; 67 Quidi Vidi Village Rd; noon-2am) Step inside the Inn of Olde and you'll feel like you've walked into the collective attic of the city, with a jumble of laminate tables, dusty hockey gear, black-and-white photos, framed newspaper clippings and faded NHL jerseys. Presiding over everything is Linda, who has been tending bar and bending ears for as long as anyone can remember.

Fair warning: the hours can be pretty flexible.

★**Geeks Public House** BAR
(709-746-8469; www.facebook.com/geekspublichouse; 288 Duckworth St; 6pm-midnight Wed, Thu, Sun & Mon, to 1am Fri & Sat;) This bar serves its own butterbeer and scores a +5 bonus for getting customers happily buzzed while they peruse all five editions of the *Dungeons & Dragons Player's Handbook*. If that last sentence got you excited, you'll love this place. If it made you scratch your head, you'll likely still love this spot, dedicated to nerdy pursuits and affectations.

Video gaming consoles are scattered around, as is tabletop and role-playing paraphernalia, plus art inspired by all things geek.

★**Battery Cafe** CAFE
(709-722-9167; www.batterycafe.ca; 1 Duckworth St; 7:30am-5:30pm Mon, Tue & Thu, to 9pm Wed, 7am-5:30pm Fri, 8am-9pm Sat, 8am-5:30pm Sun) This bright, cozy espresso bar and cafe brews some of the finest caffeine jolts in

LOCAL KNOWLEDGE

GEORGE STREET: PUB CRAWL LIKE A PRO

Tell a Canadian you've been to St John's, and almost inevitably someone will say, 'So you went to George Street' with a knowing smile. Though only two blocks long, this thoroughfare is known nationally as one of Canada's prime party promenades.

You'd never pick up on this vibe during the day. Under the harsh, sober glare of the sun, George St emanates the stale smell of dried booze and sick, set adjacent to shuttered bars and clubs. Throughout the day a lonely truck will drop off kegs and bar supplies, but there's little movement otherwise. By early evening, confused tourists wander by businesses that have opened their doors but are still largely empty.

But show up at midnight and you'll find a weird cross between a fraternity rager, a Newfoundland house party and a karaoke concert. For all of the diversity of those nightlife genres, the bars here are more or less interchangeable. Folks come here to get smashed and sing, and the local landlords have catered their businesses to provide this opportunity. The crowd is largely students, tourists, and folks from the province hitting the town for a big night. If you're after a quiet spot for some craft cocktails or a hard-to-find Riesling, you may want to drink elsewhere.

A few rules of thumb:

➡ George St does not get going until 11pm. Show up beforehand and you'll be wondering what all the fuss is about.

➡ Bring some identification with you, especially if you're under 30. The doormen at George St bars all seem to err on the side of checking ID.

➡ St John's does not have ride-sharing services, but if you need a taxi, they tend to queue all around George St.

➡ You can find food – greasy mystery meat on a bun – at almost any hour of the night. We assume these sausage vendors are vampires, because they seem to vanish into the foggy air as the sun cracks the horizon.

town; there are also good sandwiches and baked goods. Has outdoor picnic-table seating in good weather.

★Duke of Duckworth PUB

(☎709-739-6344; www.dukeofduckworth.com; McMurdo's Lane, 325 Duckworth St; ⌚noon-2am; 📶) 'The Duke,' as it's known, is an unpretentious English-style pub that represents all that's great about Newfoundland and Newfoundlanders. Stop in on a Friday night and you'll see a mix of blue-collar and white-collar workers, young and old, and perhaps even band members from Great Big Sea plunked down on the well-worn red-velour bar stools.

The kitchen cooks the ultimate in chicken pot pie, fish-and-chips and other comfort foods, and 14 beers (including the local Quidi Vidi) flow through the taps. The popular *Republic of Doyle* CBC TV series filmed here, which explains all the people taking photos of the sign by the door.

Newfoundland Chocolate Company CAFE

(☎709-579-0099; www.newfoundlandchocolatecompany.com; 166 Duckworth St; ⌚10am-6pm Mon-Wed & Sat, to 8pm Thu & Fri, noon-5pm Sun) This small local chain dishes out bonkers-good artisan chocolates, including cups of hot chocolate ($5 to $7) with flavors including sea salt, caramel, and local berries that will make your head spin. Look for a big Newfoundland-as-chocolate-paradise mural near this flagship location. There's another branch in the Signal Hill Visitor Centre (p185) that's open from 9am to 8pm daily.

Yellow Belly Brewery PUB

(☎709-757-3780; www.yellowbellybrewery.com; 288 Water St; ⌚11am-1am Sun & Mon, 11:30am-2am Tue-Thu, to 3am Fri, 11am-3am Sat) Refreshing brews crafted on-site are front and center at this casual meeting spot, a brick behemoth dating back to 1725. Everyone's having a good time and there's decent pub grub to soak up the brews. For extra ambience descend to the underbelly – a dark basement bar with a speakeasy feel.

Quidi Vidi Brewery BREWERY

(☎709-738-4040; www.quidividibrewery.ca; 35 Barrows Rd; tasting or tour $10; ⌚tastings 11am, taproom noon-10pm Sun-Wed, to midnight Thu-

Sat) This microbrewery is located in an old fish-processing plant on the tiny wharf. It's a swell place to enjoy a drink. Call ahead to book a tasting, which lasts around 45 minutes. Locals prefer you to park on the outskirts of town and walk in.

The fee includes ample tastings and a bottle to sip while touring. Be sure to try the Iceberg brand, made with water from the big hunks.

On Friday nights, the brewery hosts a kitchen party with Irish music kicking off at 6pm. A seafood boil occurs on Saturdays starting at noon.

Entertainment

Check out www.musicnl.ca for updated listings. Perhaps because this is such an intimate city, word of mouth and flyers slapped on light poles are also major vehicles for entertainment information. Venues are close together – have a wander and enjoy.

Ship Pub LIVE MUSIC
(709-753-3870; www.facebook.com/TheShipPubKitchen; 265 Duckworth St; noon-late) Attitudes and ages are checked at the door of this little pub, tucked down Solomon's Lane. You'll hear everything from jazz to indie, and even the odd poetry reading. The pub closes when things slow down, but tends to stay open until 3am on weekends.

Resource Centre for the Arts PERFORMING ARTS
(709-753-4531; www.rca.nf.ca; 3 Victoria St) Sponsors indie theater, dance and film by Newfoundland artists, all of which play downtown in the former longshoremen's union hall (aka LSPU Hall).

Shamrock City LIVE MUSIC
(709-758-5483; www.shamrockcity.ca; 340 Water St; noon-2am) Bands playing everything from Newfoundland folk to '80s hair ballads take the stage nightly at this all-ages pub.

Signal Hill Tattoo LIVE MUSIC
(709-772-5367; www.signalhilltattoo.org; Signal Hill National Historic Site; $10; 11am & 3pm Wed & Thu, Sat & Sun Jul & Aug) This award-winning historical reenactment program recreates 19th-century British military drills with cannon fire, mortars and muskets, all backed by a fife and drum band.

Shopping

Outfitters SPORTS & OUTDOORS
(709-579-4453; www.theoutfitters.nf.ca; 220 Water St; 10am-6pm Mon-Wed & Sat, to 9pm Thu & Fri, noon-5pm Sun) At this camping and gear shop you can get the local outdoorsy lowdown (check the bulletin board) and good rentals. Hikers should note this spot sells East Coast Trail (p198) maps and butane canisters.

Fred's MUSIC
(709-753-9191; www.fredsrecords.com; 198 Duckworth St; 9:30am-9pm Mon-Fri, to 6pm Sat, noon-5pm Sun) This is the premier music shop in St John's. It features local music from blue-chip provincial artists such as Hey Rosetta, Buddy Wasisname, Ron Hynes, Amelia Curran, The Navigators and Great Big Sea.

Invasion ART
(709-746-8469; www.facebook.com/invasionnl; 114 Duckworth St; 11am-6pm Mon & Wed-Fri, from 10am Sat, noon-5pm Sun) Pop art, comic books, science fiction and geek culture gets mashed up with St John's cityscapes and Newfoundland photography at this oddball art gallery. Think pictures of Godzilla rampaging through Quidi Vidi, or sketches of Marvel Comics villains kissing the cod.

Living Planet GIFTS & SOUVENIRS
(709-739-6811; www.livingplanetstudio.com; 181 Water St; 9am-3pm Mon-Thu, 8am-4pm Fri) Head here for quirky tourist T-shirts and buttons with Newfoundland slang even locals are proud to wear.

Information

MEDICAL SERVICES

Health Sciences Complex (709-777-6300; 300 Prince Phillip Dr; 24hr) A 24-hour emergency room.

MONEY

Banks stack up near the Water St and Ayre's Cove intersection.

CIBC (709-576-8800; 215 Water St; 9:30am-5pm Mon-Fri)

Scotia Bank (709-576-6000; 245 Water St; 10am-5pm Mon-Fri)

POST

Central Post Office (709-758-1003; 354 Water St; 8am-4pm Mon-Fri)

WORTH A TRIP

CAPE SPEAR

A 15km drive southeast of St John's leads you to the most easterly point in North America, with spectacular coastal scenery and whale-watching during much of the summer.

In a stunning windswept setting, **Cape Spear National Historic Site** (709-772-2191; www.pc.gc.ca/en/lhn-nhs/nl/spear; Blackhead Rd; adult/child $3.90/free; 10am-6pm) includes an interpretive center, a refurbished 1835 lighthouse, and the heavy gun batteries and magazines built in 1941 to protect the harbor during WWII. The remains of the concrete bunkers are particularly atmospheric, and under the right light, pretty darn spooky. Hikers can join up with the East Coast Trail here.

Heed all signs warning visitors off the coastal rocks, as rogue waves have knocked people into the water.

TOURIST INFORMATION

Visitors Center (709-576-8106; www.stjohns.ca; 348 Water St; 9am-4:30pm Mon-Fri May-early Oct) Excellent resource with free provincial and city road maps, and staff to answer questions and help with bookings. There's another outlet at the Quidi Vidi Village Plantation (p185) open from 10am to 4pm Tuesday to Saturday, and noon to 4pm Sunday. The **Airport Visitors Center** (709-758-8515; St John's International Airport; 10am-5pm) is the only St John's visitor center that's open year-round.

Some useful websites:

City of St John's (www.stjohns.ca) The 'Visiting Our City' category has descriptions of and links to attractions, accommodations, eateries and events.

Downhome (www.downhomelife.com) A folksy, *Reader's Digest*–style monthly for the region.

St John's Telegram (www.thetelegram.com) The city's daily newspaper.

Getting There & Away

AIR

St John's International Airport (YYT; 709-758-8500; www.stjohnsairport.com; 100 World Pkwy;)

Air Canada offers a daily direct flight to and from London; WestJet goes direct to Dublin and Gatwick. **United Airlines** (800-864-8331; www.united.com) flies to the USA.

The main carriers:

Air Canada (p184)

PAL Airlines (800-563-2800; www.palairlines.ca)

Porter Airlines (888-619-8622; www.flyporter.com)

WestJet (888-937-8538; www.westjet.com)

BUS

DRL (709-263-2171; www.drl-lr.com) sends one bus daily each way between St John's and Port aux Basques ($126, cash only, 13½ hours) via the 905km-long Hwy 1, making 25 stops en route. It leaves at 7:30am from Memorial University's Student Centre, in CA Pippy Park (p186).

CAR & MOTORCYCLE

Avis, Budget, Enterprise, Hertz, National and Thrifty have offices at the airport or adjacent to it (in the latter case, they'll pick you up in a free shuttle).

SHARE TAXIS

These large vans typically seat 15 and allow you to jump on or off at any point along their routes. You must call in advance to reserve. They pick up and drop off at your hotel. Cash only.

Newhook's Transportation (709-682-4877; griffinevlynn@hotmail.com) Travels down the southwestern Avalon Peninsula to Placentia ($35, two hours), in sync with the Argentia ferry schedule.

Shirran's Taxi (709-468-7741) Plies the Bonavista Peninsula daily, making stops at Trinity ($50, 3½ hours) and Bonavista ($40, four hours), among others.

Getting Around

BUS

The **Metrobus** (709-570-2020; www.metrobus.com) system covers most of the city (fare $2.50). Maps and schedules are online and in the Visitors Center. Bus 3 is useful; it circles town via Military Rd and Water St before heading to the university. **The Link** loops around the main tourist sights, including Signal Hill, between 10am and 5:30pm Wednesday to Sunday from late June to September. Hop-on/hop-off fare is $10.

CAR & MOTORCYCLE

The city's one-way streets and unique intersections can be confounding. Thankfully, citizens are incredibly patient. The parking meters that line Water and Duckworth Sts cost $1.50 per hour. **Sonco Parking Garage** (709-754-1489; cnr Baird's Cove & Harbour Dr; 6:30am-11pm) is central, but there are several others; most charge around $2 per hour.

TAXI

Except for the trip from the airport, all taxis operate on meters. A trip within town should cost around $8 to $10. **Jiffy Cabs** (709-722-2222; www.facebook.com/jiffycabs) provides dependable service. As of this writing, there were no ride-sharing services (ie Uber or Lyft) in St John's.

AVALON PENINSULA

The landscape along the coastline's twisting roads is vintage fishing-village Newfoundland. Many visitors make day trips to the peninsula's sights from St John's, which is easily doable, but there's something to be said for burrowing under the quilt at night, with the sea sparkling outside your window, in Cupids or Branch. Four of the province's six seabird ecological reserves are in the region, as are 28 of its 41 national historical sites.

Much of the East Coast Trail (p198) runs through the area; keep an eye out for free guided hikes. The ferry to Nova Scotia leaves from Argentia.

Southeastern Avalon Peninsula

This area, sometimes called the South Shore, is known for its wildlife, archaeology, boat and kayak tours, and unrelenting fog. Scenic Rtes 10 and 90, aka the **Irish Loop** (www.irishloop.nf.ca), lasso the region. For a quick taste, visit the **Cape Spear Lighthouse** (709-772-2191; www.pc.gc.ca/en/lhn-nhs/nl/spear; Blackhead Rd, Cape Spear; entry incl with Cape Spear National Historic Site; 10am-6pm Jun-Aug, reduced hours May, Sep & Oct) and the fishing village of Petty Harbour, though sites further south are well worth exploring. Highlights include watching the puffins and whales in Witless Bay, exploring La Manche Provincial Park (p199) and hiking the East Coast Trail (p198).

Goulds & Petty Harbour

Backed against steep slopes, beautiful, pocket-sized Petty Harbour sits like an opal embedded into the coast. While you'll spot many tourists experiencing what may be their first settlement outside of St John's, it's worth noting the weathered boats in the active port are the real deal – this is a true fishing village. Check out the harbor, learn to fish, and pet some aquatic creatures at the aquarium. Nearby Goulds is a useful stop for groceries.

> **DON'T MISS**
>
> **RUNNING THE GOAT**
>
> The active printing press **Running the Goat** (709-334-3239; http://runningthegoat.com; Cove Rd, Tors Cove; 10:30am-5:30pm Thu-Tue mid-May–Oct), south of St John's, is a bibliophile's dream. Owner Marnie Parsons gives tours of her presses, one from 1830s London. In addition to handmade poetry chapbooks and manifestos, there's a wonderful selection of local artists' prints, and good adult and children's books authored by Newfoundlanders.

Sights & Activities

★Fishing for Success FISHING
(709-740-3474; www.islandrooms.org; 10d Main Rd, Petty Harbour; adult/child $99/50) Run by Kimberly and Leo, a local fishing family, this nonprofit organization seeks to rescue the local fishing traditions by teaching them to local kids and visitors. Dory trips include rowing lessons in a traditional wood dory (boat) and cod jigging. There's also a full-day option that includes net-knitting, rope work and a historical wharf tour.

For $50 extra they can cook up your catch and serve it to you Newfoundland-style right on the pier.

Harbour Lookout VIEWPOINT
(Main Rd, Petty Harbour) Drive or hike up to this outcrop, popular with local road-trippers, find a spot to sit (or stand), then enjoy the stellar views of icebergs and fishing ships returning home (or setting out).

North Atlantic Zip Lines ADVENTURE
(709-368-8681; www.zipthenorthatlantic.com; 32 Main Rd, Petty Harbour; adult/child $130/95) Canada's longest zip-line course has 10 zip lines ranging from 300ft to 2200ft in length. Tours run at 11am, 3pm and 6pm.

Eating & Drinking

Tinkers Ice Cream Shop ICE CREAM $
(709-747-1629; www.facebook.com/tinkersicecream; 20 Main Rd, Petty Harbour; ice cream $3-6;

⏲11am-9pm Jun-Sep) Every summer holiday escape deserves a great ice-cream place, and Tinker's is the spot in Petty Harbour. The house specialty is an iceberg – *of course* – a scoop of vanilla placed on a flavored slushie. You can also get floats, milkshakes and ice-cream tacos (the shell is a waffle cone).

Chafe's Landing SEAFOOD **$$**
(☎709-747-0802; www.chafeslanding.com; 11 Main Rd, Petty Harbour; mains $9-19; ⏲11am-9pm) A lot of folks here day-trip from St John's specifically for the fish-and-chips, which are quite good (if not particularly mind-blowing). Lines get long and parking might be impossible, but it's worth it. Chafe's also serves locally made moose sausage, beer-steamed mussels, and salads.

WaterShed CAFE
(☎709-747-0500; 24a Main Rd, Petty Harbour; ⏲10am-5pm Jun-Sep; 📶) Joy is here: real espresso drinks at a refurbished waterfront shed. Owner Karen loves talking local lore; she also makes a mean hiker cookie, packed with seeds. There's also great baked treats and sandwiches. If you have an extra few hours to chill out, spend them on the deck.

Witless Bay Ecological Reserve & Around

This is a prime area for whale-, iceberg- and puffin-watching. Several boat tours will take you to see them from the towns of Bay Bulls (35km south of St John's) and Mobile (10km south of Bay Bulls). Midway between the towns, there's lodging in Witless Bay.

Four islands off Witless Bay and southward are preserved as the **Witless Bay Ecological Reserve** (www.flr.gov.nl.ca/natural_areas/wer/r_wbe) and represent one of the top seabird breeding areas in eastern North America.

The best months for trips are late June and July, when the humpback and minke whales arrive to join the birds' capelin (a type of fish) feeding frenzy. If you really hit the jackpot, in early summer an iceberg might be thrown in too.

Tours

Tours from Bay Bulls visit Gull Island, which has the highest concentration of birds in the Witless Bay Ecological Reserve. Tours that depart to the south around Bauline East head to nearby Great Island, home to the largest puffin colony. Bauline East is closer to the reserve, so less time is spent en route, but you see the same types of wildlife on all of the tours.

Also popular, kayaking provides a special perspective on wildlife. After all, you don't just see a whale while paddling, you feel its presence.

You can't miss the boat operators – just look for signs off Rte 10. Sometimes the smaller companies cancel tours if there aren't enough passengers; it's best to call ahead to reserve and avoid such surprises. They operate from mid-May through mid-September. Most depart several times daily between 9:30am and 5pm.

Captain Wayne's BOATING
(☎709-763-8687; www.captwaynes.com; Northside Rd, Bay Bulls; tour $80) Descended from

THE EAST COAST TRAIL

Skirting gaping cliffs, fairy-tale forests and fields of edible berries, the world-class **East Coast Trail** (☎709-738-4453; www.eastcoasttrail.ca) is a through-hiker's delight. It stretches 265km from Cape St Francis (north of St John's) south to Cappahayden, with an additional 275km still under way.

Its 26 sections range in difficulty from easy to challenging, but most make good day hikes. For a sample, try the scenic 9.3km path between Cape Spear and Maddox Cove (near Petty Harbour); it should take between four and six hours.

For seasoned hikers, the ECT can also be walked as a through-hike, combining camping with lodging in villages along the way. Campsites generally feature pit toilets and a good water source nearby. Fires are prohibited. A local taxi service operates at the trailheads and can bring you to nearby lodging or your vehicle.

Topographical maps are available in St John's at Outfitters (p188) or **Downhome** (☎709-722-2970; http://shopdownhome.com; 303 Water St; ⏲10am-5:30pm Mon-Wed & Sat, to 8:30pm Thu & Fri, noon-5pm Sun). Check out the ECT trail website for detailed 'how to' information and the lowdown on guided hikes.

generations of Newfoundland fishermen, Captain Wayne really knows his coast and his enthusiasm proves contagious. Best of all, he only does small, 12-person tours in his custom boat. The three-hour tour includes puffin- and whale-watching. There are several departures daily, but photographers should go at 5pm for best light.

Molly Bawn Tours BOATING
(☎709-334-2621; www.mollybawn.com; Rte 10, Mobile; adult/child/child under 5yr $50/45/free; 👪) These popular tours cruise over the waves on a small, 10m boat. Mobile is halfway between Bay Bulls and Bauline East.

Outfitters KAYAKING
(☎800-966-9658, 709-579-4453; www.theoutfitters.nf.ca; 18 Southside Rd, Bay Bulls; half-/full-day tour $89/189) Popular half-day kayak tours leave at 9am and 2pm; full-day tours depart at 9:30am and travel beyond the inner bay of Bay Bulls to the top of the eco-reserve. There is a shuttle service from St John's that leaves from Outfitters (p195) at 220 Water St; rates are $30 per person.

Gatherall's BOATING
(☎800-419-4253; www.gatheralls.com; Northside Rd, Bay Bulls; tour adult/child $62/29, family (2 adults & 2 children) $155; 👪) This large, fast catamaran is a good choice for people prone to seasickness.

Sleeping & Eating

Armstrong's Suites MOTEL $
(☎709-334-2201; 236 Main Hwy, Witless Bay; r $80; 📶) Though this is just your run-of-the-mill roadside motel, it's unlikely that even your own grandmother could better receive your visit. The kind owner thinks nothing of going the extra mile, providing extra cots and towels and breakfast fixings to East Coast Trail through-hikers.

Bears Cove Inn B&B $$
(☎866-634-1171; https://thebearscoveinn.ca; 15 Bears Cove Rd, Witless Bay; r $135-165; 📶) A pleasant place to stay, this seven-room B&B has all the amenities you could want, including water views and a lovely garden and barbecue area. Rooms feature country decor and flat-screen TVs. The helpful owners also run a local pub and speak French.

Bread & Cheese B&B $$
(☎709-334-3994; www.breadandcheeseinn.com; 22a Bread & Cheese Rd, Bay Bulls; r $155-175; 📶) This gorgeous country house with a wrap-around porch and sprawling lawn is a sight for sore feet, located a short stroll from the East Coast Trail. Rooms are smart and modern, with one wheelchair-accessible option. Our only wish is for a cheerier welcome.

OFF THE BEATEN TRACK

AVALON WILDERNESS RESERVE

Dominating the interior of the region is the 1070-sq-km **Avalon Wilderness Reserve** (☎709-637-2081; www.flr.gov.nl.ca/natural_areas/wer/r_aw; free permit required). Illegal hunting dropped the region's caribou population to around 100 in the 1980s; 30 years later, a couple of thousand roam the area. Permits for hiking, canoeing and bird-watching in the reserve are available at La Manche Provincial Park.

Even if you don't trek into the wilds, you still might see caribou along Rte 10 between Chance Cove Provincial Park and St Stevens.

La Manche Provincial Park

Diverse birdlife, along with beaver, moose and snowshoe hare, can be seen in this lush **park** (www.tcii.gov.nl.ca/parks/p_lm; NL 10, Tors Cove) FREE only 53km south of St John's. A highlight is the 1.25km trail to the remains of La Manche, a fishing village that was destroyed in 1966 by a fierce winter storm. Upon arrival, you'll see a beautiful suspension bridge dangling over the narrows – it's part of the East Coast Trail. Find the trailhead at the park's fire-exit road, past the main entrance.

There is excellent camping, with many sites overlooking large La Manche Pond, which is good for swimming. There is also a drive-through entry kiosk with information and fee collection for camping.

Ferryland

POP 414

Ferryland, one of North America's earliest settlements, dates to 1621, when Sir George Calvert established the Colony of Avalon and figured the winters here weren't too bad. A few Newfoundland seasons of ice and snow later and he was scurrying for Maryland, where he eventually became the first Lord Baltimore. Other English families arrived

WORTH A TRIP

MISTAKEN POINT ECOLOGICAL RESERVE

Designated a World Heritage site in 2016, the **Mistaken Point Ecological Reserve** (☎709-438-1011; www.flr.gov.nl.ca/natural_areas/wer/r_mpe; Portugal Cove South) FREE protects 575-million-year-old multicelled marine fossils – the oldest in the world. The only way to reach it is via a free ranger-guided hike from the **Edge of Avalon Interpretive Centre** (☎709-438-1100; www.edgeofavalon.ca; Rte 10, Portugal Cove; adult/child $8/5; ⏲10am-6pm mid-May–Oct) in Portugal Cove South.

You can also drive the bumpy gravel road between here and Cape Race. At the end, a lighthouse rises up beside an artifact-filled replica 1904 Marconi wireless station. It was the folks here who received the fateful last message from the *Titanic*.

The 'Mistaken Point' name, by the way, comes from the blinding fog that blankets the area and has caused many ships to lose their way over the years.

later and maintained the colony despite it being razed by the Dutch in 1673 and the French in 1696. These days, Ferryland and surrounding communities make the most of showcasing both the history and arts of the region.

For gorgeous windswept panoramas, don't miss the 2km walk out to the lighthouse.

Sights

Colony of Avalon ARCHAEOLOGICAL SITE
(☎709-432-3200; www.colonyofavalon.ca; Rte 10; adult/child $15/11.50; ⏲10am-6pm Jun-Sep; P 🚸 🐾) The seaside surrounds of the Colony of Avalon archaeological site only add to the rich historical atmosphere that permeates Ferryland. Join a tour and you'll see archaeologists unearthing everything from axes to bowls. The worthwhile interpretation center is very kid friendly and houses beautiful displays of the artifacts that have been recovered. Guided 45-minute tours are offered upon request. Leashed dogs are allowed on the site (but probably shouldn't do their own digging).

Historic Ferryland Museum MUSEUM
(☎709-432-2711; www.manl.nf.ca/ferrylandmuseum; Baltimore Dr; adult/child $3/2; ⏲10am-4pm Mon-Sat, 1-4pm Sun Jun-Aug) The village's former courthouse is now the small Historic Ferryland Museum. The towering hill behind the museum was where settlers climbed to watch for approaching warships, or to escape the Dutch and French incursions. After seeing the view, you'll understand why the settlers named the hill 'the Gaze.'

Eating

★**Lighthouse Picnics** SANDWICHES $$
(☎709-363-7456; www.lighthousepicnics.ca; Lighthouse Rd; per person $26; ⏲11:30am-4:30pm Wed-Sun Jun-Sep; 🐾) Lighthouse Picnics has hit upon a winning concept: it provides a blanket and organic picnic meal (say, a curried chicken sandwich, mixed-green salad and lemonade from a Mason jar) that visitors wolf down while sitting in a field overlooking explosive ocean views. Reserve in advance.

It's at Ferryland's old lighthouse, off Rte 10; you have to park and hike 2km to reach it, but oh it's worth it.

Southern Shore Folk Arts Council Dinner Theatre THEATRE
(☎709-432-2052; www.ssfac.com; The Pool; adult/child $54/38; ⏲7pm Tue, Thu & Fri Jul & Aug) Get a taste of local cuisine and Irish–Newfoundland sketch humor and folk songs at this well-regarded dinner-theater production. Expect the entire show to wrap up around 10pm. A lunch production also runs on select days while the theater operates; the cold-plate meal kicks off at noon and runs $40. Note 'The Pool' is the name for an actual road.

Along Route 90

The western arm of the Irish Loop (p197) doesn't receive as much attention as the east-coast stretch, partly because tourism infrastructure is simply not as developed. That said, this is still an area rife with dramatic scenery, and when it comes to the road between St Vincent's to St Mary's, potential wildlife spotting. This stretch of the loop is great for seeing whales, particularly humpbacks, which feed close to shore. Otherwise, even as rural Newfoundland goes, this a quiet area of little villages clinging to rocks and a sense of time gone by.

The stony beach at **St Vincent's** (Rt 90, St Vincent's; P) FREE is raw even by Newfoundland standards. It's also a brilliant spot to engage in a bit of whale-watching (your best bet is throughout summer), and all without having to board a boat. The paved path means that whale-watching here is wheelchair accessible. Even if there aren't whales around, this is a beautiful cove that's photogenic on its own merits.

Baccalieu Trail

The Bay de Verde Peninsula sticks out like a hitchhiker's thumb just west of St John's, marking what is for many visitors their first Newfoundland peninsular road trip. The scenic route here is known as the Baccalieu Trail. Fishing villages and pirate haunts stretch endlessly along Conception Bay's scenic western shore, and make for a wonderful day trip a mere 80km from the provincial capital. Highlights include Brigus, in all its Englishy, rock-walled glory combined with North Pole history, and Cupids, a 1610 settlement complete with an archaeological dig to explore. To the west, thick forest and serenity define Trinity Bay.

Brigus

POP 720

If you took an English countryside village, scooped it out of the green hills of that rainy island, and then dumped it on the rocky shores of *this* rainy island, you'd get Brigus. Walk around postcard-perfect stone-walled streams and watch them meander slowly past old buildings and colorful gardens before emptying into the serene Harbour Pond. Seriously, if this place was any more idyllic it would vanish into the mists every 100 years.

Back in its heyday as a busy port, Captain Abram Bartlett needed a new deepwater berth. Brigus was ideal, but the surrounding cliffs made docking tricky. His solution? Blast a hole through the rock with the help of Cornish miner John Hoskins. Four months, some drill bits and a lot of gunpowder later, their efforts yielded the **Brigus Tunnel** (The Walk): about 24m long, and tall enough for a horse and carriage to traverse. It's now a cool, damp landmark.

The town's most famous son, Captain Robert Bartlett, made more than 20 Arctic expeditions, and in 1909 cleared a trail in the ice that enabled US commander Robert Peary to make his celebrated dash to the North Pole. Bartlett's old home, **Hawthorne Cottage** (709-528-4004; www.pc.gc.ca/en/lhn-nhs/nl/hawthorne; 1 South St, cnr Irishtown Rd & South St; adult/child $3.90/free; 10am-6pm Jun-Aug), is an ornate example of a wealthy Newfoundland mariner's mansion, and is today managed as a national historical site and museum.

The best place to stay is **Seasalt & Thyme** (709-528-9100; www.seasaltandthyme.ca; 1 Convent Lane; r/ste $150/195;), a combination gastropub and B&B whose rooms balance understated wood accents with historical details, and end up feeling classy without a whiff of vintage chintz – a nice accomplishment in Brigus.

Cupids

POP 740

This atmospheric village is imbued with rich history and surrounded by towering sea cliffs. Those rock formations didn't ward off merchant John Guy, who sailed here in 1610 and staked out England's first colony in Canada.

The first English colony, **Cupids Cove Plantation Provincial Historic Site** (709-528-3500; www.seethesites.ca/the-sites/cupids-cove-plantation.aspx; Seaforest Dr; adult/child $6/free; 9:30am-5pm May-Oct; P) features an ongoing archaeological dig that's worth touring. A stone's throw down the road is the **Cupids Legacy Centre** (709-528-1610; www.cupidslegacycentre.ca; Seaforest Dr; adult/child $8/4; 9:30am-5pm Jun-Oct; P), with fascinating exhibits.

There are a couple of local trails to tackle: the 2.5km **Burnt Head Trail**, with good views, forests, picnic areas and a sea arch; and the **Spectacle Head Trail**, a bumpy 100m climb that ends at the 'American Man,' a cairn that has overlooked Conception Bay for generations.

Afterwards, you can warm up at the **Cupid's Haven Tea Room** (709-528-1555; www.cupidshaven.ca; Burnt Head Loop; r $119-169;) or treat yourself to a tipple at the **Newfoundland Distillery Company** (709-786-0234; www.thenewfoundlanddistillery.com; 97 Conception Bay Hwy; noon-9pm Mon-Wed, to 10:30pm Thu-Sat, 1-6pm Sun).

Harbour Grace & Around

Notable historic figures have paraded through Harbour Grace over the past 500

DON'T MISS

CAPE ST MARY'S ECOLOGICAL RESERVE & AROUND

Tucked away amidst the sea and cliffs and incessant winds that braid around the southwestern tip of the peninsula, you'll find the **Cape St Mary's Ecological Reserve** (709-277-1666; www.flr.gov.nl.ca/natural_areas/wer/r_csme) FREE, one of the most accessible large-bird colonies in North America. You will smell before you see some 70,000 birds, including gannets, kittiwakes, murres and razorbills, but when you do spy all of those winged beasts, your heart won't soon forget the sight. The nearest town is little St Bride's, but services here are limited.

The best-known viewpoint is **Bird Rock**, reached via an easy footpath through fields of sheep and blue irises; suddenly you're at the cliff's edge facing a massive, near-vertical rock swarmed by squawking birds.

A small **Interpretive Centre** (709-277-1666; 9am-5pm May-Oct; P) offers info on nesting seabirds and the local ecology.

Placentia is 45km to the north, while St John's is 180km to the northeast.

years, including the pirate Peter Easton and aviator Amelia Earhart. Their stories are told at **Conception Bay Museum** (709-596-5465; www.conceptionbaymuseum.com; 1 Water St; adult/child $3/2; 10am-4pm Jun, to 5pm Jul & Aug). Nearby **Harbour Grace Airfield** (www.hrgrace.ca/site/tourism-heritage/attractions/airstrip; Earhart Rd; sunrise-sunset) is the site where Earhart launched her historic solo Atlantic flight.

It's hard to miss the large ship beached at the mouth of the harbor. This is the **SS Kyle** (1913), wrecked during a 1967 storm. Locals liked the look of it so much they paid to have it restored instead of removed.

Clinging to cliffs at the northern end of the peninsula are the remote and striking villages of Bay de Verde and Grates Cove. Hundreds of 500-year-old **rock walls** line the hills around Grates Cove and have been declared a national historical site.

Further offshore, in the distance, is the inaccessible **Baccalieu Island Ecological Reserve**, which is host to three million pairs of Leach's storm petrel, making it the largest such colony in the world.

Dildo

POP 1200

Oh, go on – take the obligatory sign photo. For the record, no one knows definitively how the name came about; some say it's from the phallic shape of the bay, others think it's named for an oar pin. Nevertheless, proud and stalwart locals have denied several campaigns to change the town name, which makes sense: tourists flock here to say they've had a romantic evening on Dildo Harbour. All jokes aside, Dildo is a lovely village and its shore is a good spot for whale-watching.

The **Dildo Interpretation Centre** (709-582-3339; Front Rd; adult/child $2/1; 10am-4:30pm Jun-Sep) has a whale skeleton and exhibits on the ongoing Dorset Eskimo archaeological dig on Dildo Island. It's not terribly exciting, but outside you can snap a picture with a fisherman in a yellow rain slicker dubbed Captain Dildo, and a giant squid, and really, how many times do you get to say that happened?

Cape Shore

The ferry to Nova Scotia, French history and lots of birds fly forth from the Avalon Peninsula's southwesterly leg.

Information

A provincial **Visitors Center** (709-227-5272; Rte 100; hours vary) is 3km from the ferry on Rte 100. Its opening hours vary to coincide with ferry sailings.

Getting There & Away

Newhook's Transportation (p196) runs a taxi service that connects the towns of Argentia and Placentia to St John's. The 14-hour Argentia **ferry** (800-341-7981; www.marineatlantic.ca; Charter Ave; adult/child $121/59, per car/motorcycle $244/122; mid-Jun–late Sep) links Newfoundland to Nova Scotia.

Placentia

POP 3500

In the 17th century, Placentia – then Plaisance – was the French capital of Newfoundland, a place where French fishermen laid out their cod catches and French militia plotted raids against the English, including the 1696 Avalon Peninsula Campaign, when Pierre Le Moyne d'Iberville effectively annihilated English Newfoundland – for a year.

Today Placentia is more of a working town than a tourism hub, although tourists do come here. That said, they're almost always passing through on their way to or from Nova Scotia via the ferry, which sails out of nearby Argentia. Still, there are a few historical sites around that are worth some exploration.

Sights & Activities

Castle Hill National Historic Site HISTORIC SITE
(709-227-2401; www.pc.gc.ca/en/lhn-nhs/nl/castlehill; Old Castle Hill Rd; adult/child $3.90/free; 10am-6pm Jun-Aug) French and British forces spent almost a decade fighting over this land, all in the name of expanding their fisheries and seizing control of the North American continent. This historical site commemorates that conflict; the rubble of an old stone fort can be seen here.

Great Beach Boardwalk WALKING
(Beach Rd) You'll find nice views of Placentia Bay on this 1.4km-long boardwalk. It's a simple, easy walkway, and it's worth noting it's one of the few wheelchair-accessible means of enjoying the province's natural beauty. There are multiple access points along Beach Rd.

Sleeping & Eating

Rosedale Manor B&B B&B $$
(877-999-3613; www.rosedalemanor.ca; 40 Orcan Dr; r $120-150;) This beautiful heritage B&B has flower gardens, romantic rooms with claw-foot tubs, and waterfront views that will make you sigh with happiness.

Philip's Cafe CAFE $
(709-227-6596; 170 Jerseyside Hill; mains $5-12; 7:30am-3:30pm Wed-Mon;) A must pre- or post-ferry stop for yummy baked goods and creative sandwiches such as apple and sharp cheddar on molasses-raisin bread. The breakfasts are the stuff of legend around here; come early to skip the wait. Note that this spot may be closed or have reduced hours outside of summer.

Three Sisters PUB FOOD $$
(709-227-0124; www.facebook.com/thethreesisterspub; 2 Orcan Dr; mains $8-30; 11am-9pm daily, bar closes 11pm Sun-Tue, midnight Wed, Thu & Sat, 1am Fri) Lovely pub grub and chilly pints of beer are served in this atmospheric Placentia house. It's often busy, and come evening, it's the best nightlife going in town.

Getting There & Away

It's a 10-minute drive from the Argentia ferry, and about 14km from here to St John's.

EASTERN NEWFOUNDLAND

Two peninsulas, webbing like a pair of amoeba arms into the Atlantic, comprise eastern Newfoundland. The beloved, well-touristed Bonavista Peninsula projects northward. Historic fishing villages freckle its shores, and windblown walking trails swipe its coast. Clarenville (www.clarenville.net) is the Bonavista Peninsula's access point and service center, though there's not much for sightseers.

To the south juts the massive but less-traveled Burin Peninsula, with fishing villages struggling to find their way in the post-cod world. You will need your passport to hop the ferry from Fortune to the nearby French islands of St-Pierre and Miquelon, a regional highlight complete with wine, éclairs and Brie.

Getting There & Away

The region is a half-day drive from St John's, and you really need your own wheels to properly explore. From Fortune you can take a fast ferry to St-Pierre and Miquelon, from where you can fly to St John's.

Trinity

POP 170

Before we wax on about how ridiculously picturesque and scenic Trinity is, let's set the record straight: Trinity is the Bonavista Peninsula's most popular stop, a historic town of crooked seaside lanes, storybook heritage houses, and gardens with white picket fences. Trinity Bight, on the other hand, is the name given to the 12 communities in the vicinity, including Trinity, Port Rexton and New Bonaventure.

If it all looks familiar, it may be because *The Shipping News* was partly filmed here. While the excitement has faded, there are still historic buildings, stunning hiking and theater along with whale-watching.

First visited by Portuguese explorer Miguel Corte-Real in 1500 and established as a town in 1580, Trinity is one of the oldest settlements on the continent.

Sights & Activities

One admission ticket (adult/child $20/free) lets you gorge on seven buildings scattered throughout the village of Trinity. They are run by both the **Trinity Historical Society** (709-464-3599; www.trinityhistoricalsociety.com; 41 West St) and the provincial government (www.seethesites.ca), and are open from 9:30am to 5pm, May to mid-October.

Trinity Museum MUSEUM
(709-464-3599; www.trinityhistoricalsociety.com; Church Rd; 7-site admission adult/child $20/free; 9:30am-5pm mid-May–mid-Oct) This creaking collection of bric-a-brac displays more than 2000 pieces of historical relics, including North America's second-oldest fire wagon. It's got that whole 'attic of fascinating stuff' vibe.

Random Passage Site FILM LOCATION
(709-464-2233; www.randompassagesite.com; Main Rd, New Bonaventure; adult/child $10/3.50; 9:30am-5:30pm) Back in 2002, the CBC and Ireland's RTÉ made a miniseries out of Bernice Morgan's 1992 novel *Random Passage*. The show was partially filmed at a pretty cove a little south of Trinity, and the set, a painstakingly recreated 19th-century Newfoundland outport (small fishing village), is open to the public for guided tours. You'll learn a lot about the miniseries and a bit about historical Newfoundland – we'd appreciate more of the latter than the former, but this is still a good detour.

★ **Skerwink Trail** HIKING
(www.theskerwinktrail.com) This 5km loop is well worth the effort, with dramatic coastal vistas of sea stacks, early summer icebergs and a lighthouse. Be on guard for moose. The trailhead is near the church in Trinity East, off Rte 230.

Trinity Eco-Tours BOATING
(709-464-3712; www.trinityecotours.com; Zodiac/kayaking tours $90/109) Head out on the water, either in an inflatable Zodiac or a sea kayak, and spot whales, icebergs and the rest while enjoying the crazy beautiful coast of this corner of Newfoundland.

Rugged Beauty Tours WILDLIFE
(709-464-3856; www.ruggedbeautyboattours.net; 3hr tour adult/child $90/60; 10am & 2pm May-Oct) Unique trips with Captain Bruce, who takes you to abandoned outports and makes their history come alive. You might even see an eagle along the way.

Sleeping

★ **Skerwink Hostel** HOSTEL $
(709-436-3033; www.skerwinkhostel.com; Rocky Hill Rd; campsite $5-15, dm $34, r $85-120; May-Oct; P) Travelers of all ages stay at homey, community-oriented Skerwink. With two six-bed dorms (with squishy, plastic-coated mattresses) and two private rooms, it's part of Hostelling International. Many locals drop by to chat and play guitar with the staff. Fresh bread and weak coffee are included for breakfast, and the fabulous Skerwink Trail is across the street. Located off Rte 230.

★ **Artisan Inn & Campbell House** INN $$
(709-464-3377; www.trinityvacations.com; 57 High St; r incl breakfast $159-235; mid-May–Oct;) A fantasy coastal getaway, these gorgeous properties are adjacent to each other and managed by the same group. Both have ocean vistas. The three-room inn hovers over the sea on stilts; set further back, Campbell House has lush gardens.

Fishers' Loft INN $$
(709-464-3240; http://fishersloft.com; Rocky Hill Rd, Port Rexton; r incl breakfast $160-309;) Featuring traditional 19th-century local architecture, this colonial is a favorite of return travelers. Rooms and suites are bright and spacious with fluffy duvets and down pillows; the treetop rooms offer stunning views of the bay. It's kitted out perfectly, with iPod docks, hiking poles and binoculars.

Eriksen Premises B&B $$
(709-464-3698; www.mytrinityexperience.com/eriksen-premises; 8 West St; r $119-190; mid-May–mid-Oct;) This 19th-century merchant home offers elegance in accommodations and dining (mains $20 to $30, open lunch and dinner). It also manages four other properties, ranging from small B&Bs to furnished apartment rentals, in the village.

Eating & Drinking

Skipper Bob's CANADIAN $
(50 Church Rd; mains $8-16; 7am-8pm) This simple spot has friendly service and a juicy

moose burger that's as good as much fancier versions plied at much more expensive restaurants. Also serves a basic, tasty menu of soups and sandwiches.

★ **Twine Loft** CANADIAN $$$

(☎709-464-3377; www.trinityvacations.com/our-restaurant; 57 High St; prix fixe $55) The upscale restaurant of the Artisan Inn serves a three-course, prix-fixe meal of local specialties, with wonderful seafood and wine selections guided by an in-house sommelier. Reservations are necessary, but you can also stop by for a sunset drink on the deck. Check the daily menu posted out front.

Two Whales Cafe COFFEE

(☎709-464-3928; http://twowhales.com; 99 Main Rd, Port Rexton; ⏲10am-6pm) An adorable coffee shop serving the full-octane variety and lemon blueberry cake that's off the charts. It also does good vegetarian fare and organic salads.

☆ Entertainment

Trinity Pageant THEATER

(adult/child $20/15; ⏲2pm Wed & Sat) One of the mainstays of the Rising Tide theater company is this outdoor dramedy, a heartfelt (and at times hilarious) theatrical exploration of Trinity's identity and history, held at the **Rising Tide Theatre** (☎888-464-3377; www.risingtidetheatre.com; 40 West St; ⏲Jun-Sep).

ℹ Information

The town website (www.townoftrinity.com) has lots of tourism information. Make sure to pop into the **Trinity Visitor Centre** (☎709-464-2042; www.seethesites.ca; West St; ⏲9:30am-5pm mid-May–mid-Oct).

ℹ Getting There & Away

Trinity is 259km from St John's and is reached via Rte 230 off Hwy 1. **Shirran's Taxi** (☎709-468-7741) offers a daily taxi service to St John's.

Bonavista

POP 3450

The town of Bonavista is one of the highlights of the peninsula that bears the same name. It has a lashing of historic sites, plus creative restaurants, businesses and accommodations that have worked in concert to effect a small, innovative downtown revival. Visitors should understand Bonavista is a working town. This is no assemblage of painstakingly elegant historical homes à la Trinity, and the village does not spill down a raw rock face like settlements on the Irish Loop. Rather, Bonavista remains something of a fishing village, all cottages starting to peel and sag, plus modern convenience stores. But peel back a layer and you'll find a living, functioning community, where the warmth and friendliness is vital and sincere, even compared to other Newfoundland towns, and raw natural beauty is a quick hike away.

Sights & Activities

Dungeon Park PARK

(Cape Shore Rd, off Rte 230; P) FREE The sheer power of the ocean is more than evident at the Dungeon, a deep chasm 90m in circumference that was created by the collapse of two sea caves. The thunderous waves that shattered the caves now slam the coast, and are often shrouded in pea-soup fogs.

Cape Bonavista Lighthouse LIGHTHOUSE

(☎709-468-7444; www.seethesites.ca; Rte 230; adult/child $6/free; ⏲9:30am-5pm late May–mid-Oct) This brilliant red-and-white-striped lighthouse dates from 1843. The interior has been restored to the 1870s, and includes the original lead-weight pulley device that kept the lighthouse lights turning automatically, as well as period costumes curious tourists can try on. A puffin colony lives just offshore; the birds put on quite a show around sunset.

Ye Matthew Legacy HISTORIC SITE

(☎709-468-1493; www.matthewlegacy.com; Roper St; adult/child $7.25/3; ⏲9:30am-5pm Jun-Sep) Enter this structure and discover a wonderful replica of John Cabot's 15th-century ship *Matthew*, which Cabot sailed into Bonavista. Travelers who love history, especially those of a nautical bent, will love the attention to detail that's been put into this reconstruction. While the *Matthew* is smaller than many contemporary sailing yachts, it sailed halfway around the world.

Ryan Premises National Historic Site HISTORIC SITE

(☎709-468-1600; www.pc.gc.ca/en/lhn-nhs/nl/ryan; Ryans Hill Rd; adult/child $3.90/free; ⏲10am-6pm Jun-Sep) Explore a restored 19th-century saltfish mercantile complex at this National Historic Site, which consists of a slew of white clapboard buildings. The exhibits honor five centuries of fishing in Newfoundland via multimedia displays and interpretive programs.

WORTH A TRIP

ELLISTON

The Root Cellar Capital of the World, aka Elliston, lies 6km south of Bonavista on Rte 238. The teeny town was struggling until it hit upon the idea to market its 135 subterranean veggie storage vaults, and then presto – visitors came a knockin'. Actually, what's most impressive is the **puffin colony** just offshore and swarming with thousands of chub-by-cheeked, orange-billed birds from mid-May to mid-August. A quick and easy path over the cliffside brings you quite close to them and also provides whale and iceberg views.

Stop at the Elliston Visitors Center as you enter town, and the kindly folks will give you directions to the site along with a map of the cellars (which you're welcome to peek inside). If you're interested in the local practice of sealing, make sure to stop by the **Sealers Interpretation Centre** (John C. Crosbie Sealers Interpretation Centre; 709-476-3003; www.homefromthesea.ca; Elliston; $7; 9am-5:30pm May-Oct; P), which provides a careful examination of this hunting tradition.

Work up an appetite while you're here, because **Nanny's Root Cellar Kitchen** (709-468-5050; 177 Main St, Elliston; mains $8-16; 8am-8pm; P) in historic Orange Hall cooks a mighty fine lobster, Jiggs dinner (roast meat with boiled potatoes, carrots, cabbage, salted beef and pea-and-bread pudding) and other traditional foods, plus it's licensed.

In September, the **Roots, Rants & Roars Festival** (www.rootsrantsandroars.ca; Elliston; mid-Sep) celebrates the province's top chefs, who prepare outdoor feasts in a dramatic setting.

From the adjoining hamlet of **Maberly**, a gorgeous 17km **coastal hiking trail** winds over the landscape to Little Catalina.

Seas the Day Boat Tours BOATING

(709-468-8810; www.seasthedayboattours.com; Station Rd; adult/child $60/35; tours depart 10am, 1pm, 4pm & 7pm May-Sep) Come for the punny name, stay for the boat tours all along the nearby coast. Spot whales, puffins and icebergs – plus, if you're lucky, the staff might show you how to gut a codfish. Memories!

Sleeping

HI Bonavista HOSTEL $

(709-468-7741; www.hihostels.ca; 40 Cabot Dr; dm $35, r $79; @) This tidy white-clapboard hostel offers four private rooms, two shared dorm rooms, free bike use, and kitchen and laundry facilities. It's a short walk from the center of town.

Russelltown Inn & Vacation Homes INN $$

(www.russelltowninn.com; 134 Coster St; r $140-193, pods $80, cottages $275-350) This property manages several accommodations throughout town: a main inn with clean, understated but attractive rooms; several guest cottages (minimum two-night stay); and 'glamping' in eco pods – effectively, nicely renovated studio shacks – with solar lighting. All of the options are well executed and comfortable.

Harbourview B&B B&B $$

(709-468-2572; www.harbourviewgetaway.com; 21 Ryans Hill Rd; r $139; Jun-Sep;) The name doesn't lie: you get a sweet view and pretty historical accents at this simple, four-room B&B, plus an evening snack (crab legs) with owners Florence and Albert. Breakfast has a gluten-free option.

Eating & Drinking

★ **Boreal Diner** CANADIAN $$

(709-476-2330; www.theborealdiner.com; 61 Church St; mains $13-19; noon-9pm Mon-Thu, to 10pm Fri & Sat, 5-9pm Sun;) In a bright-red colonial house, this innovative restaurant manages what many others aspire to: creative, international takes on local Newfoundland ingredients. Thus crab pot stickers, cod in tarragon sauce, and polenta with wild mushroom stew are all potential options on the ever-shifting menu. It also does vegan and gluten free. Real espresso drinks keep you wired.

Bonavista Social Club CANADIAN $$

(709-445-5556; www.bonavistasocialclub.com; Upper Amherst Cove; mains $12-26; 11am-8pm Tue-Sun) Social Club's innovative meals are sourced on-site and served with a view to die for. From incredible wood-fired breads and pizzas to rhubarb lemonade and moose burgers with partridgeberry ketchup, the kitchen is on fire (literally; there's a wood-burning oven for those pizzas). The goats roaming the grounds provide milk for cheese, while the chickens lay the eggs. Reserve ahead.

The rustic restaurant is about 15 minutes from Bonavista via Rte 235 (turn left when you see the sign for Upper Amherst Cove). The chef's dad carved all the beautiful wood decor in his workshop next door.

Quintal Cafe CAFE
(☎709-476-2191; www.facebook.com/TheQuintalCafe; 63 Church St; ⌚8am-6pm Mon-Thu, to 8pm Fri-Sun) The folks at the Boreal Diner also operate this friendly little coffee shop, which has strong caffeinated goodness and a bunch of board games if you just feel like passing the time.

☆ Entertainment

Garrick Theatre THEATER
(☎709-468-5777; www.garricktheatre.ca; 18 Church St) The artfully restored Garrick is an anchor for downtown Bonavista. The theater screens mainstream and indie films, and hosts live-music performances that often showcase a rich tableau of local talent.

Shopping

Newfoundland Salt Company FOOD
(☎709-770-7412; https://newfoundlandsaltcompany.com; 45 Church St; ⌚11am-5pm Tue-Fri, from 10am Sat, from noon Sun) As creative gifts go, it doesn't get much more unique than the locally sourced sea salt sold at this little storefront. We're particularly enamored of its flavored salts, including a green alder sea salt that makes your food taste as though it's been seasoned with a forest (in a good way).

ℹ Information

The town website (www.townofbonavista.com) has tourism information.

ℹ Getting There & Away

Bonavista is a scenic 50km drive north of Trinity along Rte 230. **Shirran's** (☎709-468-7741; www.facebook.com/ShirransTransportation) offers a daily shuttle service from St John's ($40 one way).

Burin Peninsula

This is a foggy, isolated peninsula, a place where the towns have been depressed by the loss of fishing and the spruce-furred cliffs are wet and massive. But as with anywhere in Newfoundland, locals are over-the-top welcoming, and you can easily lose a day or two wandering down coastal walks before embarking toward the baguettes of France (aka St-Pierre).

Marystown is the peninsula's largest town; it's jammed with big-box retailers but not much else. **Burin** is the area's most attractive town, with a gorgeous elevated boardwalk over the waters of its rocky shoreline. **St Lawrence** is known for fluorite mining and scenic coastal hikes. In **Grand Bank**, there's an interesting self-guided walk past historic buildings and along the waterfront. Just south is fossil-rich **Fortune**, the jumping-off point for ferries to St-Pierre.

◉ Sights

Fortune Head Geology Centre MUSEUM
(☎709-832-3569; www.fortunehead.com; Bunker Hill Rd, Fortune; adult/child $7.50/5; ⌚9am-5pm Thu-Tue, 8am-7pm Wed Jun-Aug) Exhibits examine the geology of the Burin Peninsula, minerals and rocks, the 1929 Grand Banks tsunami and prehistoric animals. Kids will appreciate this interactive center with fossils to touch from Fortune Head Ecological Reserve; it's in town by the St-Pierre ferry dock. It also offers a children's day camp with a daily rate. Daily tours go to the reserve (adult/child $20/10).

Fortune Head Ecological Reserve PARK
(☎709-637-2081; www.flr.gov.nl.ca/natural_areas/wer/r_fhe; off Rte 220; ⌚24hr) The reserve protects fossils dating from the planet's most important period of evolution, when life on earth progressed from simple organisms to complex animals some 550 million years ago. The reserve is about 3km west of Rte 220, by the Fortune Head Lighthouse.

Sleeping & Eating

Thorndyke B&B B&B **$$**
(☎709-832-0820; www.thethorndyke.ca; 33 Water St, Grand Bank; r $165; ⌚May-Oct; 🚭) This handsome old captain's home overlooks the harbor. Antique wood furnishings fill the four light and airy rooms (each with private bathroom). The hosts will provide dinner with advance notice.

Sharon's Nook & the Tea Room CAFE **$**
(☎709-832-0618; 12 Water St, Grand Bank; mains $7-12; ⌚8:30am-6pm Mon, Tue & Sat, to 9pm Wed-Fri, 11am-7pm Sun) This kitschy and countrified eatery serves up lasagna, chili, sandwiches and over a dozen varieties of heavenly cheesecake.

Getting There & Away

The Burin Peninsula is accessed via Rte 210 off Hwy 1. The drive from St John's to Grand Bank is 359km and takes just over four hours; this is a narrow road, and in heavy rains you'll want to pace yourself. **Matthew's Taxi** (☎709-832-0491) runs from St John's down the peninsula as far as Fortune.

ST-PIERRE & MIQUELON

POP 6100

Twenty-five kilometers offshore from the Burin Peninsula floats a little piece of France. The islands of St-Pierre and Miquelon aren't just French-like with their berets, baguettes and Bordeaux – they *are* France, governed and financed by the *tricolore*. Locals kiss their hellos and pay in euros, sweet smells waft from myriad pastry shops, and French cars crowd the tiny one-way streets. It's a world away from Newfoundland.

St-Pierre is the more populated and developed island, with most of its 5500 residents living in the town of St-Pierre. Miquelon is larger geographically but has only 600 residents overall.

Jacques Cartier claimed the islands for France in 1536, after they were discovered by the Portuguese in 1520. At the end of the Seven Years' War in 1763, the islands were turned over to Britain, only to be given back to France in 1816. And French they've remained ever since.

Sights & Activities

When Prohibition dried out the USA's kegs in the 1920s, Al Capone decided to slake his thirst – and that of the nation – by setting up shop in St-Pierre.

He and his mates transformed the sleepy fishing harbor into a booming port crowded with warehouses filled with imported booze. Bottles were removed from their crates, placed in smaller carrying sacks and taken secretly to the US coast by rum runners. The piles of Cutty Sark whiskey crates were so high on the docks that clever locals used the wood both to build and heat houses. At least one house remains today and is known as the 'Cutty Sark cottage'; most bus tours drive by.

The tourist information center offers a special two-hour Prohibition tour (adult/child €20/10) that covers sites related to the theme. If nothing else, drop by the Hotel Robert near the tourist information center and check out Al Capone's hat; it hangs in the gift shop.

Miquelon & Langlade ISLAND

(☎508-416-187; mne@ct975.fr; adult/child 3hr tour €45/35; ⊙Jun-Sep) The island of Miquelon is less visited and far less developed than St-Pierre. The village of Miquelon, centered on the church, is at the northern tip of the island. From nearby l'Étang de Mirande a walking trail leads to a lookout and waterfall. From the bridge in town, a scenic 25km road leads across the isthmus to the wild and uninhabited island of Langlade. There are some wild horses, and around the rocky coast you'll see seals and birds.

Tours are operated by the Comite Regional de Tourisme.

Île aux Marins VILLAGE

(☎508-410-435; 3hr tour adult/child €30/25; ⊙9am & 1:30pm May-Sep) The magical Île aux Marins ('Sailor Island'; often translated as 'Pioneer Island') is a beautiful abandoned village on an island out in the St-Pierre harbor. A bilingual guide will walk you through colorful homes, a small schoolhouse museum, lonely cemeteries and a grand church, built in 1874. Book tours at **L'Arche Museum** (☎508-410-435; www.arche-musee-et-archives.net; Rue du 11 Novembre; adult/child €7/5; ⊙9am-5pm Jul & Aug, 9:30am-noon & 1:30-4:30pm May, Jun & Sep). You can also go over on a ferry (€6; 10 to 15 minutes) sans guide during July and August; boats run roughly every two hours.

Zodiac Tours BOATING

(☎508-414-736; adult/child €41/35; ⊙Jun-Sep) Full-day bilingual tours by Zodiac cover both Miquelon and Langlade. Book at the visitor center. Rates include snacks.

Festivals & Events

Bastille Day CULTURAL

(⊙Jul 14) The largest holiday of the year, both in this part of France and that other bit of France across the Atlantic.

Basque Festival CULTURAL

(⊙mid-Aug) A weeklong festival with music, marching and invigorating street fun.

Sleeping

★ **Auberge St Pierre** B&B $$

(☎508-414-086; www.aubergesaintpierre.fr; 16 Rue Georges Daguerre; d €88-179; 📶) Guests rave about the warm service and lovely atmosphere of this family-run island B&B.

Arrive to chilled wine and cheese. Remodeled rooms feature flat-screen TVs and hydromassage showers; they're also stocked with robes and extra towels. Transportation to and from the ferry and island tours included.

Nuits St-Pierre B&B $$
(☎508-412-027; www.nuitssaintpierre.com; 10 Rue du Général Leclerc; r €140-200;) An upscale lodging aimed at the honeymoon crowd. The five rooms, each with private bath and blissful, downy beds, are named after famous French authors. There's free pickup from the airport or ferry. The attached tea salon is open every afternoon from 2pm to 6pm; it's a must for a restorative beverage and slice of cake.

Hotel Robert HOTEL $$
(☎508-412-419; www.hotelrobert.com; 2 Rue du 11 Novembre; r €80-133, ste $105-165;) Most visitors end up in this decent-value hotel, the largest on the island. Rooms are pleasant, with crisp white sheets and powerful showers. Some are dated. A downstairs restaurant serves breakfast (not included). It's within close walking distance of the ferry.

Eating

★Guillard Gourmandises BAKERY $
(☎508-413-140; 31 Rue Boursaint; pastries €2-5; 7am-noon & 2-5:30pm Tue-Sat, 7:30am-12:30pm Sun) It's worth memorizing the complicated schedule to make good on this slice of *la belle* France. After all, these cream-plumped chocolate éclairs, macarons, piping-hot pastries and gateaux are the reason you came, right?

Tiffin ASIAN $$
(☎508-552-531; www.facebook.com/pg/tiffin.spm; 9 Rue Saveaur Ladret; mains €12-18, multicourse set meals from €40; noon-1pm & 6-8pm Wed, Fri & Sat) At this creative pan-Asian restaurant, there isn't a restaurant. Rather, you order set meals served in Indian-style tiffins – stackable metal lunchboxes – that you eat on the go. The meals span the Asian continent, ranging from garlic cauliflower and Indonesian *gado gado* (vegetable salad) to Vietnamese *banh mi* (baguette) laced with mint and coriander to coconut chicken and basmati rice.

Le Feu de Braise FRENCH $$
(☎508-419-160; www.feudebraise.com; 14 Rue Albert Briand; mains €12-23; noon-1:30pm & 7-9:30pm) As French restaurants go, this one is wonderfully old-school, serving a master class in stick-to-your-ribs rural classic cuisine: steak in Roquefort sauce, duck breast, and grilled sausage in mustard sauce. Everything is delicious, and you'll have to roll yourself through the narrow streets after polishing off *crème brûlée* for dessert.

Crêperie Restaurant du Vieux Port FRENCH $$
(☎508-412-700; www.facebook.com/creperiesrestaurantduvieuxport; 10 Rue du 11 Novembre; €8-25; 7am-10pm Jul & Aug, noon-1:30pm & 7-9:30pm Sep-Jun) This *crêperie* boasts a fantastic location overlooking St-Pierre's old port, and a kitchen to match the view: dine out on crepes stuffed with cod and chorizo, beef in a shallot and wine sauce, or just enjoy some excellent scallops. Should you have some good wine to wash everything down? You really should.

Information

Americans, EU citizens and all visitors except Canadians need a passport for entry. Those staying longer than 30 days also need a visa. Other nationalities should confirm with their French embassy if a visa is needed prior to arrival. Canadians can enter with a driver's license.

To merit the duty-free waiver on alcohol, you must stay on the islands at least 48 hours.

MONEY

Most vendors accept credit cards. Some accept the loonie, though they return change in euros. If you're staying more than an afternoon, it's probably easiest to get euros from the local ATMs.

OPENING HOURS

Most shops and businesses close between noon and 1:30pm. Some stores also close on Saturday afternoons, and most are closed on Sunday.

TELEPHONE

Calling the islands is an international call, meaning you must dial 011 in front of the local number. Phone service links to the French system, so beware of roaming charges on your mobile.

TIME

The islands are half an hour ahead of Newfoundland Time.

TOURIST INFORMATION

Office de Tourisme (Tourist Information; ☎508-410-200; www.spm-tourisme.fr; Place du Général de Gaulle; 8:30am-8pm;) The visitors center, near the ferry dock, provides a map showing all the banks, restaurants etc. Staff also provide information on the islands' hotels and tours, and make bookings for free. The same organization operates conventional tours, boat tours and guided hikes.

Getting There & Away

AIR

Air St-Pierre (508-410-000, 877-277-7765; www.airsaintpierre.com; round-trip from St John's $360) flies to St John's, Montréal and Halifax. There are two to three flights weekly to each city. Taxis to/from the airport cost around €5.

BOAT

From Fortune on Newfoundland, the **St-Pierre Ferry** (508-410-875; www.spm-ferries.fr; 14 Bayview St, Fortune; adult/child return from Fortune €74/50) makes the hour-long trip to and from the island once daily (twice on Wednesdays) in July and August. It runs less often the rest of the year. Departure times vary, so check the website. Boats carry foot passengers only, though plans are in the works for two car ferries. Ferry staff coordinate Fortune parking in lots near the dock (per day $10). Buy tickets in advance and arrive 30 minutes early (or one hour before departure if you need to leave a car).

Getting Around

Much can be seen on foot. Roads are steep, so prepare to huff and puff. Car-rental agencies are resistant to renting to tourists, who admittedly have difficulty navigating the unsignposted, narrow one-way streets.

The visitor center (p209) rents bicycles (per day €13) as well as motorized bicycles. Local ferries head to Miquelon (adult/child return €24/13) and Langlade (adult/child return €17/8); check the tourist office for departure times.

CENTRAL NEWFOUNDLAND

Central Newfoundland elicits fewer wows per square kilometer than the rest of the province, but that's because huge chunks of the region are virtually inaccessible hinterlands of bogland and trees. Still, this area is in every way as beautiful as the rest of Newfoundland, as evidenced by the misty islands of Notre Dame Bay – particularly Twillingate, which is whale-and-iceberg central – and the long, forested vistas of Terra Nova National Park.

Gander

POP 11,700

Gander sprawls across the juncture of Hwy 1 and Rte 330, which leads to Notre Dame Bay. It's a convenient stopping point and offers a couple of sights for aviation buffs; it's also the site of a major Canadian Forces air base. This is the region's main town – it may not feel quintessentially 'Newfoundland' with its glut of big-box retailers and lack of anything resembling scenery, but this is one of the few places in the province that isn't experiencing population loss. If you need to stock up on anything, do it here.

The **Gander Airport** (YQX; 709-256-6677; www.ganderairport.com) gets a fair bit of traffic. **DRL** (709-263-2171; www.drl-lr.com) buses stop at the airport en route to St John's (four hours) and Port aux Basques (nine hours).

Twillingate Island & New World Island

Pastel houses, the rock-ribbed coast, the steel-gray ocean, a breaching whale, a turquoise iceberg: all in a day's sightseeing here at the top of the central coast. Twillingate (comprised of two barely separated islands, North and South Twillingate) is one of Newfoundland's most popular tourism towns, and with good reason. The area is connected to 'mainland' Newfoundland by narrow causeways, and between local trails, endless views and friendly locals, it's a tough place to tear yourself away from.

Sights

★**Prime Berth Fishing Museum** MUSEUM
(709-884-2485; www.primeberth.com; Main Tickle Causeway; $5, tour $8; 10am-5pm Jul & Aug) Run by an engaging fisherman, this private museum, with its imaginative and deceptively simple concepts (a cod-splitting show!), is brilliant, and fun for mature scholars and schoolkids alike. It's one of the first places you see as you cross to Twillingate.

Long Point Lighthouse LIGHTHOUSE
(709-884-2247; 10am-6pm) FREE Long Point provides dramatic views of the coastal cliffs. Travel up the winding steps, worn from lighthouse-keepers' footsteps since 1876, and gawk at the 360-degree view. Located at the tip of the north island, it's an ideal vantage point for spotting icebergs in May and June.

Isles Wooden Boat Museum MUSEUM
(709-884-5841; www.isleswoodenboatbuilders.com; 4 St Peters Church Lane; $10; 9am-5pm mid-May–Sep; P) Wooden boats were once as common as cod in Newfoundland, but

WORTH A TRIP

TERRA NOVA NATIONAL PARK

In the popular imagination, Newfoundland's beauty, to say nothing of her population, is constantly associated with the coast. But there is a magic to the island's interior, a strange, alluring blanket of bogs, boreal forest and cloud-cloaked hills. **Terra Nova National Park** (☎709-533-2801; www.pc.gc.ca/terranova; adult/child/family per day $5.80/free/11.75) is the province's best showcase of this sort of inner-island scenery. You can lose days here hiking amidst moss-floored and spruce forest, mere physical meters and an entire wilderness world away from the nearby Trans-Canada Hwy.

All that said, this area does include oceanside real estate – the park is fronted by the salty waters of Clode and Newman Sounds.

Terra Nova's 14 hiking trails total almost 100km; pick up maps at the **Visitors Center** (☎709-533-2942; Hwy 1; ⏲10am-6pm Jul & Aug, to 4pm May, Jun & Sep). The epic **Outport Trail** (48km) provides access to backcountry campgrounds and abandoned settlements along Newman Sound. The loop in its entirety is rewarding, but be warned: parts are unmarked, not to mention mucky. A compass, a topographical map and ranger advice are prerequisites for this serious route.

Camping is the only option within the park itself. Those with aspirations of a bed should head to Eastport; it's near the park's north end on Rte 310, about 16km from Hwy 1. For camping reservations (recommended on summer weekends), call **Parks Canada** (☎877-737-3783; www.pccamping.ca; reservation fee $10.80) or go online.

The park is 259km northwest of St John's. While buses on the Trans-Canada Hwy can drop you near the east and west entrances of the park, the interior is best accessed by private vehicle.

these classic craft have since been largely replaced by fiberglass vessels. This museum, staffed by both passionate youngsters and old timers committed to the craft of their forefathers, keeps the wooden boatbuilding tradition alive. In many ways it's as much boatbuilding studio as learning institution; every few months, the museum creates a new wooden boat, and you can see the process unfold in real time.

Auk Island Winery WINERY
(☎709-884-2707; www.aukislandwinery.com; 29 Durrell St; tastings $3, with tour $5; ⏲10am-6:30pm Jul & Aug, reduced hours Sep-Jun) Visit the grounds that produce Moose Joose (blueberry-partridgeberry), Funky Puffin (blueberry-rhubarb) and other fruity flavors using iceberg water and local berries. There's also ice cream made from iceberg water.

Twillingate Museum MUSEUM
(☎709-884-2825; www.tmacs.ca; 1 St Peters Church Rd; admission by donation; ⏲9am-5pm May-Sep) Housed in a former Anglican rectory off Main St, this museum tells the island's history since the first British settlers arrived in the mid-1700s. The exhibits feel a bit dated, but the docents are kind and you'll likely learn a little something. There's a historical **church** next door.

Activities

Fun two-hour tours to view icebergs and whales depart daily from mid-May to early September.

★**Lower Little Harbour Trail** HIKING
(Lower Little Harbour Rd) This 4.8km loop, rated moderate-difficult, takes in just about everything that makes Newfoundland special: big root cellars, a 9m natural sea arch, cliffs, coast, forests and the remains of a community, since resettled. The abandoned houses you'll wander by give parts of this trail the whole icy-fingers-on-the-neck vibe.

Rock Adventures KAYAKING
(☎709-884-9801; www.rockadventures.ca; 185 Main St; 2hr tour $75) The frigid waters off Twillingate may seem foreboding when all that's between them and you is a little bit of kayak hull. But paddling around this area with Rock Adventures is an exercise in repeatedly having your mind blown by nature's sheer beauty and Newfoundland's deep reserve of this quality.

Iceberg Man Tours BOATING
(☎800-611-2374; www.icebergtours.ca; 50 Main St; adult/child $50/25) Captain Cecil's popular two-hour tours depart at 9:30am, 1pm and 4pm. Guests rave about the service.

Twillingate Adventure Tours BOATING
(☎888-447-8687; http://twillingateadventuretours.com; Wharf; adult/child $60/40) Whale-watching and iceberg-spotting tours depart from Twillingate's wharf off Main St at 10am, 1pm and 4pm (and sometimes 7pm).

Sleeping

Despite a glut of lodging options, Twillingate gets very busy in the summer. Book early.

HI Tides Hostel HOSTEL $
(☎709-884-8477; www.twillingateandbeyond.com; 94 Main St; dm/d/q $35/75-80/99;) This hostel occupies a saltbox home built way back in 1885. It must have been built pretty well, because this is a warm, welcoming spot, although that probably partly comes down to the budget-traveler vibe. Berry pancakes, coffee and tea are on the house.

Anchor Inn Hotel HOTEL $$
(☎709-884-2777; www.anchorinntwillingate.com; 3 Path End; r $150-190; Mar-Dec; P) The waterfront Anchor has attractive rooms with deliciously soft beds and heart-melting scenic vistas. Amenities include the hotel's view-worthy deck and the barbecue grill for do-it-yourself types.

Captain's Legacy B&B B&B $$
(☎709-884-5648; www.captainslegacy.com; Hart's Cove; r $115-160; May-Oct; P) A real captain named Peter Troake once owned this historical 'outport mansion,' now a gracious four-room B&B overlooking the harbor.

Eating

★ **Doyle Sansome & Sons** SEAFOOD $$
(☎709-628-7421; www.sansomeslobsterpool.com; 25 Sansome's Place, Hillgrade; mains $8-24; 11am-9pm; P) Head out of your way for this classic cash-only seafood spot, serving crisp cod, fish cakes with rhubarb relish, and fresh lobster. If it's a nice day, the dock seating provides a fine view. Don't be fooled by the name – a slew of friendly women cook here. The village of Hillgrade is about 17km from Twillingate.

Annie's Harbour Restaurant SEAFOOD $$
(☎709-884-5999; www.anniesrestaurant.ca; 128 Main St; mains $11-22; 8:30am-9pm) Annie's is a solid choice if you want to eat all of the denizens of the ocean you've been admiring from Twillingate's shores (speaking of which, this spot has some nice waterfront views). Fish-and-chips are firm and flavorful, and the cod melt burger is a standout.

Georgie's Restaurant CANADIAN $$
(☎709-884-2777; www.georgiesrestaurant.com; 3 Path End; mains $17-29; 8am-10am & 5-8pm) Upscale your Twillingate dining experience at this pretty waterfront spot, a romantic setting for dining on sesame-crusted scallops, shrimp penne and root-cellar bisque.

Drinking & Nightlife

★ **Crow's Nest Café** CAFE
(☎709-893-2029; www.facebook.com/CrowsNestCafe; Main St, Crow Head; 10am-5pm Tue-Sat & 8-10pm Wed, Fri & Sat, 11am-4pm Sun) True to its name, the Crow's Nest occupies a high hill overlooking Twillingate. Even better than the views are the coffee, scones, cakes and other baked goods ($3 to $6) – all superlatively delicious and made with care. There's a bohemian vibe and plenty of local art on the walls.

The main cafe is in Crow Head, about 5km north of Twillingate, but there's a takeout stand at 127 Main St near 'downtown.'

Stage Head Pub BREWERY
(☎709-893-2228; www.splitrockbrewing.ca; 119 Main St; noon-midnight) This pub, which exudes contemporary stylized charm, is attached to the local brewmasters at Split Rock Brewing. The minimalist drinking hall is a good spot to meet someone from around, enjoy the occasional live-music performance or just sink a local beer. Note that the bar closes when it wants to.

Information

For tourist information, travelers should visit the websites for the town (www.townoftwillingate.ca) and the island (www.visittwillingate.com).

Getting There & Away

From the mainland, Rte 340's causeways almost imperceptibly connect Chapel Island, tiny Strong's Island, New World Island and Twillingate Island.

Fogo Island & Change Islands

POP 2400

All across Newfoundland, you'll find fishing villages that have struggled to sustain themselves off the tourism trade. This rugged island chain seems to have figured out the formula, which is partly down to creating an ambitious, arts-oriented tourism infrastructure, and partly down to anchoring said infrastructure with an internationally renowned hotel.

Founded in the 1680s, Fogo is both an outport and a (by and large) well-heeled artists' colony. It's a unique and beautiful place, cut through by lovely trails and art studios, a slice of 21st-century cosmopolitan chic in the middle of a salt-battered province at the edge of the world.

Sights

On Fogo, the village of **Joe Batt's Arm**, backed by rocky hills, is a flashback to centuries past – though it now has a mod twist thanks to the luxe Fogo Island Inn (p214). A **farmers market** takes place at the ice rink on Saturday mornings.

Nearby **Tilting** is perhaps the most engaging village on the island. Irish roots run deep here and so do the accents. The inland harbor is surrounded by picturesque fishing stages and flakes, held above the incoming tides by weary stilts.

The **Newfoundland Pony Sanctuary** (☎709-884-6953, 709-621-6381; www.nlponysanctuary.com; 12 Bowns Rd, Change Islands; admission by donation; ⏲by appointment) maintains the world's largest herd of endangered Newfoundland ponies. The small creatures are renowned as hardy workers (especially in winter) with gentle temperaments. Pony rides may be available. Call first to make sure someone is on-site before visiting.

Activities

Turpin's Trail HIKING

(NL 334, Tilting) Set aside the better part of a day for this roughly 8km trail, which crosses a tableau of sea barrens, coastal views and windy heath that is simply jaw dropping. While this is a longer hike than most on the island, the elevation changes aren't too terrible. The trail begins at **Lane House**, a historical saltbox home.

Brimstone Head HIKING

(off Sargents Rd, Fogo) Near the village of Fogo, the indomitable Brimstone Head rises from the sea like a rocky knob. This is a short (2km there and back) but steep hike; the rewards are an almost mystical view of the ocean. To begin the hike, look for signs for Brimstone Head Park.

Lion's Den Trail HIKING

The Lion's Den Trail (4.2km) forms a loop that begins at a Marconi radio site (an early long-distance radio transmitter), where there is a small interpretation center. The route passes tons of gorgeous scenery; hikers should keep an eye out for the caribou and fox that roam the area.

Sleeping

★**Tilting Harbour B&B** B&B $

(☎709-658-7244; www.tiltingharbourbnb.ca; 10a Kelley's Island Rd, Tilting; r $98-110;) Outstanding in hospitality, this traditional 100-year-old home has four spotless rooms with renovated bathrooms. While angles are sharp, it's comfortable and cozy. Best of all, the owner Tom is an accomplished chef who offers wonderful, social dinners ($35)

THE ART STUDIOS OF FOGO ISLAND

Newfoundland is an ancient place, geologically but even spiritually – this is an island with an old soul. Yet on Fogo Island you may notice buildings that appear to have been plucked from a science fiction film. Iconic art studios dot local walking trails, serving as a work space for painters, filmmakers, authors and photographers from around the world.

The studios were designed by Newfoundland native Todd Saunders, who also designed the Fogo Island Inn. They're sleek assemblages of clean, sharp angles, almost jarring in their modernity. But they are also encased in spruce shells and stand on stilts, a nod to Newfoundland. The intended effect is of a minimalist, futuristic take on the local fishing shed.

The studios serve as residencies for visiting artists, so you can't just peek your head in, but you're free to walk by and take a picture that will inevitably provoke a reaction on your preferred social media platform. Check out http://saunders.no/work for more information on these structures.

featuring fresh local seafood. Breakfast scones are also a big hit.

If you're lucky, Phil Foley's shed will be open next door. It's a very improvised speakeasy with local musicians and merriment.

★**Old Salt Box Co** ACCOMMODATION SERVICES $$
(☎709-658-7392; www.theoldsaltboxco.com; home rental $180;) The Old Salt Box Co operates heritage-home rentals across the province, and three of their best properties are here. These may be historical homes, but their interiors are exercises in contemporary minimalist design, with sleek staircases, fresh furnishings, lots of natural light and gorgeous views. Warning: these book up fast. Your booking will be for a whole home rental.

★**Fogo Island Inn** INN $$$
(☎709-658-3444; www.fogoislandinn.ca; Joe Batt's Arm; 2-night stay incl meals $1975-2875; P) The Fogo Island Inn is a groundbreaking exploration of the concept of local sourcing. *Everything* in this place comes from at least as close as Newfoundland, including the community guides every visiting party is paired with. Architecturally, the Inn is a jaw-dropper, starkly minimalist yet growing organically from the rugged island landscape.

Eating

Growler's ICE CREAM $
(☎709-658-7015; www.facebook.com/GrowlersIceCream; 125 Main Rd, Joe Batt's Arm; cones $5; ⏱noon-8pm) It would be a pity to miss this seaside stop, serving homemade partridgeberry-pie ice cream flecked with cinnamon and salty crumbs of crust.

Scoff Restaurant CANADIAN $$
(☎709-658-3663; www.scoffrestaurant.com; 159 Main Rd, Joe Batt's Arm; mains $12-26; ⏱11am-3pm & 5-10pm) Scoff – Newfoundland slang for a good meal – serves fancy takes on local cuisine in a cozy yet upscale setting. Salt beef comes with split pea 'fries,' smoked herring is served with marmalade, fresh toast and onion-and-fennel salad, and salt cod pierogies pair with fried onions and scruncheons (fried pork fat). A beautiful setting for original eats.

Fogo Island Inn Restaurant CANADIAN $$$
(☎709-658-3444; www.fogoislandinn.ca; Joe Batt's Arm; lunch mains $20-48, prix-fixe dinner $115; ⏱7-10am, noon-3pm & 6-9pm, by reservation only) With sparkling sea views, this tiny gourmet eatery dishes up innovative three-course dinners sourced as locally as possible. The menu changes daily. Think delicate preparations of snow crab with sea salt, Prince Edward Island grass-fed beef, and rye ice cream with nettles. Nonguests should reserve at least three days ahead and park roadside, a five-minute walk from the inn.

Information

Valuable sources of local information are www.changeislands.ca and www.townoffogoisland.ca.

Getting There & Away

Rte 335 takes you to the town of Farewell, where the ferry sails to the Change Islands (20 minutes) and then onward to Fogo (45 minutes). Demand is heavy in summer – it is worth arriving two hours before your departure to ensure a spot for your vehicle. Note that bad weather can cause ferries to be cancelled, so you want to leave a day's grace period when traveling here to account for unforeseen climatic conditions.

Five boats leave between 7:45am and 8:30pm. Schedules vary, so check with **Provincial Ferry Services** (☎709-627-3492; www.gov.nl.ca/ferryservices; round-trip Fogo vehicle/passenger $25.50/8.50). Note it is about 25km from Fogo's ferry terminal to Joe Batt's Arm.

Central South Coast

If you're looking to get far away from just about everything, hop on Rte 360. This windy road runs 130km through the center of the province to the south coast, another land of long vistas, little towns and isolated coves. It's a long way down to the first settlements at the end of **Bay d'Espoir**, a gentle fjord. **St Alban's** is on the west side of the fjord. You'll find a few motels with dining rooms and lounges around the end of the bay.

Further south is a concentration of small fishing villages. The scenery along Rte 364 to **Hermitage** is particularly impressive, as are the landscapes around **Harbour Breton**. The largest town (population 1700) in the region, it huddles around the ridge of a gentle inland bay.

To access this remote area it's best to go by private vehicle. **Provincial Ferry Services** (☎709-729-3835; www.tw.gov.nl.ca/ferryservices) serve Hermitage, making the western south-coast outports accessible from here.

Assuming you do drive, gas up often, as service stations are spaced pretty far apart.

New-Wes-Valley

Tell someone in St John's you've been to New-Wes-Valley and they might ask, 'Where?' This is a little-known detour off the main Newfoundland tourism trail, but no less beautiful than the rest of the island. It's a land of foggy coves and rocky shorelines and great friendliness. Here you'll also find a living history museum and one of the province's more appealing offshore islands.

New-Wes-Valley is the name of a small town; it takes its name as a portmanteau of several other nearby towns – Newtown, Wesleyville and Valleyfield.

Sights

★Greenspond ISLAND
(Greenspond Rd) This windy island, which seems to dangle somewhere between the Atlantic and the end of the world, is one of Newfoundland's oldest continuously inhabited outports. While connected to the mainland by bridge, Greenspond (and its population of roughly 270 souls) still has the feel of existing somewhere out of time. Walking trails thread over this 2.85-sq-km island, some winding through cemeteries, others dipping past rocky coves and bays. It's a 30km drive from New-Wes-Valley.

Barbour Living Heritage Village HISTORIC SITE
(709-536-3220; www.barbour-site.com; Newtown; adult/child $10/5; 10am-4pm mid-Jun–early Sep; P) Get a taste of the life of the Barbours, a prosperous merchant family, at this village consisting of 19 homes (two of which are historically registered). The exhibits and staff provide insight on multiple generations of family history, spanning 1873 to 1960. Visit is by guided tour. Frequent live-music performances kick off around the village on many summer evenings. From Tuesday to Thursday you can buy an 'inside-out' ticket ($25), which adds a guided kayaking excursion to your visit.

Pool's Island ISLAND
(Quay Rd) Drive alllll the way to the end of the road and you'll get to Pool's Island, an outcrop of smoothed boulders and pebbly beach often cloaked in a thick pea-soup fog. There's not a ton to do but soak up the lonely ambience and walk along several informal trails, all of which lead to somewhere haunted and beautiful.

Sleeping & Eating

★Aunt Christi's B&B $$
(709-658-7392; www.theoldsaltboxco.com/aunt-christis-greenspond; Main St, Greenspond; whole home (sleeps four) $180; P) This lovely B&B is located by the ocean in Greenspond, within walking distance of some convenience stores and stark, wind-lashed stretches of moorland and coast. Despite the old-school exterior of the building, the interior drips with hanging lanterns and other contemporary design features.

Audrey's Tickle Bliss B&B $$
(709-536-3220; www.barbour-site.com/accommodations; Barbour Living Heritage Village, Newtown; r $110; P) This place sounds like one of those naughty tricks they recommend in men's and women's magazines, but in fact it's a really cute B&B with quilted bedspreads and, yes, blissful views of a nearby tickle (Newfoundland English for a narrow strait). Audrey's is located at the Barbour Living Heritage Village, and was formerly the Director's residence.

Norton's Cove Cafe CANADIAN $$
(709-536-2633; www.nortonscove.com/pages/cafe; 114 Main St, Brookfield; mains $8-22; 10am-8pm Thu-Tue; P) This gorgeous cafe boasts a light, airy interior, brilliant waterfront views, and a menu that takes enjoyable license with local cuisine; try cod with basmati rice and vegetables, or local squid stir-fried Korean style. On-site coffee and baked goods are excellent.

Getting There & Away

NL 320 is the main road through this area, and connects to Gander on one side via NL 330, and the Trans-Canada Hwy near Gambo. You need your own car to explore the area.

NORTHERN PENINSULA

The Northern Peninsula points upward from the body of Newfoundland like an extended index finger, and you almost get the feeling it's wagging at you saying, 'Don't you dare leave this province without coming up here.'

Heed the advice. Two of the province's World Heritage–listed sites are here: Gros Morne National Park (p216), with its fjord-like lakes and geological oddities, rests at the peninsula's base, while the sublime, 1000-year-old Viking settlement (p220) at

OFF THE BEATEN TRACK

ROW, ROW, ROW YER BOAT

There are oodles of boat tour companies in Newfoundland; what sets **Hare Bay Adventures** (☎709-537-2028; www.harebayadventures.com; Rogers Lane, Hare Bay; rowboat tour $95) apart is their use of wooden boats to explore the region. Three-hour rowboat trips allow visitors an uncommon, quiet and gentle communion with the rugged landscape. Hiking treks, birding trips and fishing trips can also be arranged.

Hare Bay is about 67km east of Gander, and 55km south of New-Wes-Valley.

L'Anse aux Meadows stares out from the peninsula's tip. Connecting these two famous sites is the **Viking Trail** (www.vikingtrail.org), aka Rte 430, an attraction in its own right that holds close to the sea as it heads resolutely north past the ancient burial grounds (p219) of Port au Choix and the ferry jump-off point to big, brooding Labrador.

The region continues to gain in tourism, yet the crowds are nowhere near what you'd get at Yellowstone or Banff, for example.

Getting There & Away

Visitors to Gros Morne National Park usually fly into the Deer Lake Airport (p183). Long-distance **DRL** (☎709-263-2171; www.drl-lr.com) buses transit the Trans-Canada Hwy.

It's a five- to six-hour drive from Deer Lake at the peninsula's southern edge to L'Anse aux Meadows at its northern apex. Towns and amenities are few and far between, so don't wait to fuel up.

Gros Morne National Park

The stunning flat-top mountains and deeply incised waterways of this **national park** (☎709-458-2417; www.pc.gc.ca/grosmorne; per day adult/child/family $9.80/free/19.60) are simply supernatural playgrounds. Designated a World Heritage site in 1987, the park offers special significance to geologists as a blueprint for the planet. The bronze-colored Tablelands feature rock from deep within the earth's crust, supplying evidence for theories such as plate tectonics. Nowhere else in the world is such material as easily accessed as it is in Gros Morne.

Several small fishing villages dot the shoreline and provide amenities. Bonne Bay swings in and divides the area: to the south is Rte 431 and the towns of **Glenburnie**, **Woody Point** and **Trout River**; to the north is Rte 430 and **Norris Point**, **Rocky Harbour**, **Sally's Cove** and **Cow Head**. Centrally located Rocky Harbour is the largest village and most popular place to stay. Nearby Norris Point and further-flung Woody Point also make good bases.

Sights

The park is quite widespread – it's 133km from Trout River at the south end to Cow Head in the north – so it takes a while to get from sight to sight; you could easily spend an hour on the road driving between two of the visitor centers (which have interpretive programs and guided walks).

Tablelands NATURAL FEATURE
(Rte 431) Dominating the southwest corner of the park, near Trout River, are the unconquerable and eerie Tablelands. This huge flat-topped massif was part of the earth's mantle before tectonics raised it from the depths and planted it squarely on the continent. Its rock is so unusual that plants can't even grow on it. You can view the barren golden phenomenon up close on Rte 431, or catch it from a distance at the stunning **photography lookout** above Norris Point.

Bonne Bay Marine Station AQUARIUM
(☎709-458-2550; www.bonnebay.ca; Rte 430, Norris Point; adult/child/family $6.25/5/15; ⏲9am-5pm Jun-Aug; 👪) At the wharf in Norris Point is this small research facility, which is part of Memorial University. Every half-hour there are interactive tours, and the aquariums display the marine ecological habitats in Bonne Bay. For children, there are touch tanks, whale bones and an activity room.

Gros Morne Wildlife Museum MUSEUM
(☎709-458-3396; https://grosmornewildlifemuseum.ca; 76 Main St N, Rocky Harbour; adult/child $8/5; ⏲10am-6pm Jun, 9am-9pm Jul & Aug) While this spot falls into the kitschy-but-fun attraction-cum-gift-shop category, we want to stress: it *is* fun. Several rooms, each themed around a Gros Morne ecosystem, are filled with the taxidermied bodies of some of the park's most iconic animals. Kids love this spot, especially seeing as the owners give guests a scavenger hunt activity to complete.

Lobster Cove Head Lighthouse LIGHTHOUSE
(709-453-2127; Rocky Harbour; included in park admission; 10am-5:30pm mid-May–mid-Oct;) Overlooking the Gulf of St Lawrence, this lighthouse is picturesque enough to grace the cover of a nautically inclined calendar. Inside you'll find parks staff and exhibits dedicated to the cultural history of this part of Newfoundland; outside are trails winding through the tuckamore to a rocky coast studded with tide pools. Kids can play dress-ups with period clothes, and locals come here to whale-watch and fly kites. Sunsets over the St Lawrence defy hyperbolic description.

During summers the lighthouse hosts a slew of events, including guided walks, drum and fire circles, and evening music and storytelling ($14.70; call to reserve a spot).

Shallow Bay BEACH
The gentle, safe, sand-duned beach at Shallow Bay seems out of place, as if transported from the Caribbean by some bizarre current. The water, though, provides a chilling dose of reality, as it rarely gets above 15°C (59°F).

Arches Provincial Park PARK
(off Rt 430, Portland Creek; 8am-11pm;) FREE The relentless force of the ocean has carved out these scenic arched rocks on Rte 430, north of Parsons Pond. The area is nice for a picnic assuming the wind isn't howling (which it usually is).

SS Ethie SHIPWRECK
(Rte 430, past Sally's Cove) Follow the sign off the highway to a parking lot, and from here take a short path to where the waves batter the rusty and tangled remains of the SS *Ethie*. The story of this 1919 wreck, and the subsequent rescue, was the inspiration for the folk song 'Wreck of the Steamship *Ethie*'.

Broom Point Fishing Camp HISTORIC SITE
(Rte 430, Broom Point; 10am-5:30pm May-Oct) FREE This restored fishing camp sits a short distance north of Western Brook Pond. The three Mudge brothers and their families fished here from 1941 until 1975, when they sold the entire camp, including boats, lobster traps and nets, to the national park. Everything has been restored; it's staffed by guides.

Activities

Hiking

Twenty maintained trails of varying difficulty snake through 100km of the park's most scenic landscapes. The gem is the 16km **Gros Morne Mountain Trail** (www.pc.gc.ca/en/pn-np/nl/grosmorne) to the peak of Gros Morne, the highest point at 806m. The 16km **Green Gardens Trail** is almost as scenic and challenging, and has the added advantage of stunning views over water.

Shorter scenic hikes are **Tablelands Trail** (4km), which extends to Winterhouse Brook Canyon; **Lookout Trail** (5km), which starts behind the Discovery Centre (p219) and loops to the site of an old fire tower above the tree line; **Lobster Cove Head Trail** (2km), which loops through tidal pools; and **Western Brook Pond Trail** (Rte 430), the most popular path.

The granddaddies of the trails are the **Long Range Traverse** (35km) and **North Rim Traverse** (27km), serious multiday treks over the mountains. Permits and advice from park rangers are required.

If you plan to do several trails, invest in a copy of the *Gros Morne National Park Trail Guide,* a waterproof map with trail descriptions on the back, which is usually available at the visitor centers.

Kayaking/Boating

Kayaking in the shadow of the Tablelands and through the spray of whales is truly something to be experienced. Companies such as **Gros Morne Adventures** (709-458-2722; www.grosmorneadventures.com; Norris Point Wharf; 2hr kayak tour adult/child $59/49) can help get you on the water.

Bon Tours (709-458-2016; www.bontours.ca; Norris Point Wharf) will get you cod jigging ($40) or, during July and August, take you on a sunset cruise ($47). If you haven't purchased a park pass, you must do so before embarking. Reserve tickets well in advance. Bon also runs the phenomenal **Western Brook Pond boat tour** (105 Pond Rd, Rocky Harbour; 2hr trip per adult $58-65, child $26-30) every hour between 10am and 5pm.

Festivals & Events

Trails Tales Tunes Festival MUSIC
(www.facebook.com/trailstalestunes; Norris Point; late May) This 10-day festival blends all of the things that make Newfoundland great: walks into the rugged landscape, folk music

on small stages, and kitchen parties with screech. Lots of screech.

Writers at Woody Point Festival LITERATURE
(☎709-453-2900; www.writersatwoodypoint.com; Woody Point; tickets from $20; ⊙mid-Aug) Authors from across Newfoundland, Canada and the world converge at the Woody Point Heritage Theatre to do readings. There are also live-music events.

Sleeping

Sometimes it feels like every house in the region turns into a B&B or short-term rental come summer. However, places fill fast in July and August. Rocky Harbour has the most options; Woody Point and Norris Point are also good bets.

For backcountry campsites reachable by hiking, inquire at the Main Visitor Centre. Five developed campgrounds (☎877-737-3783; www.pccamping.ca; campsites $25.50-32.50, oTENTik & cabins per night $120; ⊙Jun-Sep; P) lie within the park: Berry Hill, Lomond, Trout River, Green Point and Shallow Bay.

Aunt Jane's Place B&B $
(☎709-453-2485; www.grosmorneescapes.com; Water St, Woody Point; d $75-95; ⊙May-Oct; ⊖) This welcoming B&B is an excellent spot to post up in Woody Point, Your lodging is a classic historical home with authentic accents (including bureaus and shelving made by the original owner). Rooms are smallish, but clean, comfy and good value. The owners manage local whole-home rentals as well.

Bonne Bay Inn BOUTIQUE HOTEL $$
(☎709-453-2223, 709-400-6583; www.woodypointmagic.com; 145 Main Rd, Bonne Bay; r $199-219, ste 249-299; ❄) There's a nice spread of options at this spot, from a main hillside hotel with nicely sized rooms that afford great views out to the fjords, to more plush suites on the Bonne Bay main drag with small outdoor seating areas.

Gros Morne Cabins CABIN $$
(☎709-458-2020; www.grosmornecabins.ca; 72 Main St S, Rocky Harbour; cabins $149-209;) While backed by tarmac, most of these beautiful log cabins are fronted by nothing but ocean (ask when booking to ensure a view). Each has a full kitchen, TV and pullout sofa for children. Bookings can be made next door at Endicott's variety store.

Wildflower Country Inn INN $$
(☎709-458-3000; www.wildflowerscountryinn.ca; 108 Main Street N, Rocky Harbour; r $109-119, cabin $129; P) This 90-year-old home boasts four warm, wood-accented rooms with en suite bathrooms, plus two more spacious cabins (only available during the summer) if you need a little more room to stretch out after your hike. Located near the heart of Rocky Harbour's main drag. Rates drop by about $10 between October and May.

Eating & Drinking

Earle's CANADIAN $
(☎709-458-2577; 111 Main St S, Rocky Harbour; mains $8-14; ⊙11am-9pm;) Earle is an institution in Rocky Harbour. This spot gets packed with tourists and locals, from pensioners to families, and has great ice cream, decent moose burgers, plenty of pizzas and traditional Newfoundland fare that you can chomp on the patio.

Java Jack's CAFE $$
(☎May-Sep 709-458-2710; https://javajacks.ca; 88 Main St, Rocky Harbour; mains $12-28; ⊙7:30am-8:30pm Wed-Mon May-Sep, closed Oct-Apr; P) Escape the tyranny of fried food and head to Jack's, the outpost for an artsy crowd into locally sourced fare. There's a vintage-but-hip vibe, and Gros Morne's best coffees, wraps and soups by day. At night, the upstairs dining room fills hungry post-hike bellies with fine seafood, caribou and vegetarian dishes. Greens come fresh from the property's organic garden.

Black Spruce CANADIAN $$$
(☎709-458-3089; www.theblackspruce.ca; 7 Beach Rd, Norris Point; mains $26-40; ⊙5-9pm) Named for the province's most iconic tree, the Black Spruce has brought fine dining to Norris Point. It's got a luxury-lodge ambience and an atmosphere underlined by dishes such as cider-brined chicken and parsnip puree, or lobster and squid ink fettuccine. Scrub the trail dirt off your boots and treat yourself.

★**Galliott Studios** CAFE
(☎709-453-2328; www.galliottstudios.blogspot.com; 10 Water St, Bonne Bay; ⊙8am-7pm Jun-Sep) Part espresso house, part cheesemonger, part beer bar, part artists' gallery, all awesome: Galliott is a highlight of any visit to the Woody Point side of Gros Morne. Make sure to enjoy the phenomenal view from the back porch. It's a favorite hangout for those attending the Writers at Woody Point Festival.

Shopping

★The Hunky Dory ARTS & CRAFTS
(709-453-2304; 60 Main Rd, Woody Point; hours vary) Besides the great punny name, this is a brilliant spot to pick up local folk arts and crafts, including stuff you genuinely can't find in other shops. The owners live next door, so knock on their door at a reasonable hour and they'll be happy to show you around.

Information

Park admission includes the trails, the Discovery Centre and all day-use areas.

Discovery Centre (709-453-2490; Rte 431, Woody Point; 9am-6pm May-Oct) Has interactive exhibits and a multimedia theater explaining the area's ecology and geology. There's also an information desk with maps, daily interpretive activities and a small cafe.

Main Visitor Centre (709-458-2066; Rte 430; 8am-8pm May-Oct) As well as issuing day and backcountry permits, it has maps, books, Viking Trail (p216) materials and an impressive interpretive area.

Park Entrance Kiosk (Rte 430, Wiltondale; 9am-5pm May-Oct) Near Wiltondale.

Rocky Harbour (www.rockyharbour.ca) Online information about lodging, restaurants and attractions in Rocky Harbour.

Western Newfoundland Tourism (www.gowesternnewfoundland.com)

Getting There & Away

Deer Lake Airport (p183) is 71km south of Rocky Harbour. There are shuttle-bus services (p224) from the airport to Rocky Harbour, Woody Point and Trout River.

Port au Choix

POP 790

Dangling on a stark peninsula 13km off the Viking Trail (p216), Port au Choix houses a large fishing fleet, a quirky art gallery , and a worthy archaeological site that delves into ancient burial grounds.

Sights

Port au Choix National Historic Site HISTORIC SITE
(709-861-3522; www.pc.gc.ca/portauchoix; Point Riche Rd; adult/child $3.90/1.90; 9am-6pm Jun-Sep; P) This site is dedicated to the ancient burial grounds of three different Indigenous groups that date back 5500 years. The modern **visitors center** tells of creative survival in this rough area and of one group's unexplained disappearance 3200 years ago. Several good trails around the park let you explore further. Reached by walking, **Phillip's Garden**, a site with vestiges of Paleo-Eskimo houses, is a highlight.

Ben's Studio GALLERY
(709-861-3280; 24 Fisher St; hours vary) FREE At the edge of town is Ben Ploughman's capricious studio of folk art. Pieces such as *Crucifixion of the Cod* are classic and the artist himself is happy to bend your ear for a while. Ben lives next door, so just knock if it's a decent hour and he'll open the studio for you if he's not already working there.

Sleeping & Eating

Jeannie's Sunrise B&B B&B $
(709-861-2254; www.jeanniessunrisebb.com; Fisher St; r $99-119; P) Jeannie radiates hospitality through her spacious rooms, bright reading nook and demeanor as sweet as her muffins. Guests rave about the big breakfasts with homemade jam. Rooms at the lower end of the price spectrum share a bathroom.

★Anchor Cafe SEAFOOD $$
(709-861-3665; Fisher St; mains $12-18; 11am-8pm; P) You can't miss this place – the front half is the bow of a boat – and don't, because it has great service and some of the best seafood on the Northern Peninsula. Perfect fries and cod, rich moose stew and original salads are served in cozy leather booths with *lots* of nautical-themed decorations. There's a kids' menu for the little ones.

Getting There & Away

Port au Choix sits in the middle of the Viking Trail (p216) on Rte 430. Most travelers come on a day trip by car.

L'Anse aux Meadows & Around

As the Viking Trail (p216) winds ever north, the land gets more, well, Viking-esque. Muskeg and hills framed by snow-capped mountains edge onto the bays, themselves peppered with sailing icebergs. At St Barbe, the waters of the gulf quickly narrow, so ferries can ply the desolate shores of Labrador. Further on, at Eddies Cove, the road leaves the coast and heads inland.

WORTH A TRIP

THE FRENCH SHORE

From 1783 until 1904, the eastern coast of the Northern Peninsula was visited by seasonal fishermen from Brittany, France. These men arrived thanks to 18th-century treaties, all part of the colonial chess game that characterized so much of early North American history.

The French Shore of the Northern Peninsula has thus always been a land apart, even from Newfoundland, itself a bit of a place apart from the rest of Canada. While the area is hardly Francophone, its unique history is captured in the stunning *French Shore Tapestry*, a 66m-long work of art that tells the story of this strand of woods, cliffs and sea from prehistoric days to the modern era. The tapestry draws clear influence from the 11th-century *Bayeux Tapestry*, and was created by women from the tiny outport of Conche.

The tapestry really has to be seen to be appreciated. One panel might show a Newfoundland dog shaking hands with a Canadian beaver, representing the Confederation debate. Another may show battles between Native Americans and Vikings, while another depicts diplomatic missives between the kings and queens of England and France.

To take in this stunning work of folk art, head to Conche itself, where the tapestry is displayed at the **French Shore Interpretation Centre** (☎709-622-3500; www.frenchshoretapestry.com; Rt 434, Conche; adult/child $8/free; ⏲9am-5pm Mon-Fri, from 1pm Sat & Sun May-Sep; P). Conche is a good 150km (two hours) south of St Anthony, and part of the road is unpaved (hard-packed gravel) – strap in for a bumpy ride.

So what else awaits on the French Shore? Keep an eye out for the turnoff to the **Tuckamore Lodge** (☎709-865-6361; www.tuckamorelodge.com; Main Brook; r incl breakfast $155-180; P@ 📶), an assemblage of chalet-style lodgings in the middle of the woods that comes with excellent home-cooked meals and, if you're into it, fishing, hunting or birding classes.

As you approach the northern tip of the peninsula, Rte 430 veers off toward St Anthony, and two new roads wind through foggy passes and scraggly woods to L'Anse aux Meadows National Historic Site. Rte 436 hugs the eastern shore and passes through a series of tiny fishing villages, including (from south to north) St Lunaire-Griquet, Gunners Cove, Straitsview and L'Anse aux Meadows village, which has a stunning end-of-the-road ambience.

Sights

★L'Anse aux Meadows National Historic Site HISTORIC SITE

(☎709-623-2608; www.pc.gc.ca/lanseauxmeadows; Rte 436; adult/child $11.70/free; ⏲9am-6pm Jun-Sep; P) Leif Eriksson and his Viking friends lived here circa CE 1000. Visitors can see the remains of their waterside settlement: eight wood-and-sod buildings, now just vague outlines left in the spongy ground, plus three replica buildings inhabited by costumed docents. The latter have names such as 'Thora' and 'Bjorn' and simulate Viking chores such as spinning fleece and forging nails. Allow two or three hours to walk around and absorb the ambience.

The premise may seem dull – visiting a bog in the middle of nowhere and staring at the spot where a couple of old sod houses once stood – but somehow this site, lying in a forlorn sweep of land, turns out to be one of Newfoundland's most stirring attractions.

Be sure to browse the interpretive center and watch the introductory film, which tells the captivating story of Norwegian explorer Helge Ingstad and his wife, archaeologist Anne Stine, who rediscovered the site in 1960. Also worthwhile is the 3km trail that winds through the barren terrain and along the coast surrounding the interpretive center.

Whale Point HILL

(Ship Cove) Phew, that view. This windswept hill overlooks the cold ocean, drifting icebergs and breaching whales. It's located at the end of the road in the 'town' of Ship Cove, adjacent to a series of fantastically atmospheric geographic nomenclature, including Cape Onion, Diable Cove and Savage Cove. The lonely, end-of-the-world atmosphere is underlined by a nearby cemetery.

Norstead HISTORIC SITE
(☎709-623-2828; www.norstead.com; Rte 436; adult/child/family $10/6.50/30; ⏲9:30am-5:30pm Jun-Sep) Can't get enough of the long-bearded Viking lifestyle? Stop by Norstead, just beyond the turnoff to the national historic site. This recreated Viking village features costumed interpreters smelting, weaving, baking and telling stories around real fires throughout four buildings. Sounds cheesy, but they pull it off with class. There's also a large-scale replica of a Viking ship on hand.

Activities

★ **Quirpon Lighthouse Inn** ADVENTURE SPORTS
(☎709-634-2285; www.linkumtours.com; Main Rd, Quirpon; 2-person package incl boat transfer $425-450, Zodiac tour only $55; ⏲May-Sep) Whales and icebergs skim by this island located 9km west of L'Anse aux Meadows. As remote getaways go, it would be hard to beat the on-site 10-room inn, close by a working lighthouse. Package stays include hiking, Zodiac tours and guided kayaking; if you don't want to shell out big bucks, you can just book a Zodiac iceberg/whale-watching tour.

Cape Raven HIKING
(Off Hwy 436) This wonderful, moderately difficult trail takes you up a fairly steep incline to the spot where James Cook supposedly surveyed Noddy Bay. On the way up you'll pass through spruce woods, over fast streams, before reaching a terminus that overlooks a spectacular vista of cliffs, gray ocean, fishing villages and speckled icebergs.

Dark Tickle Expeditions WILDLIFE
(☎844-999-2374; www.darktickle.com; 75 Main St, St Lunaire-Griquet; tours adult/child $65/40) The Dark Tickle complex offers its own Zodiac tours to connect visitors to marine life and icebergs. It's a wild tour that guests rave about.

Festivals & Events

Iceberg Festival CULTURAL
(☎877-778-4546; www.theicebergfestival.ca; ⏲early Jun) Well, that settles it: there's a festival for everything. We joke: it makes sense that Northern Peninsula folks celebrate the iceberg, given how crucial these frozen chunks are to tourism, and how iconic they are to the seascape. This party, lasting a week at least, includes music, lectures, food demonstrations and more at locations near L'Anse aux Meadows.

Sleeping & Eating

Valhalla Lodge B&B B&B $$
(☎709-754-3105; www.valhalla-lodge.com; Rte 436, St Lunaire-Griquet; r $120-175, cottage $175-270; ⏲May-Sep; P 📶) Sea views from this hilltop location inspired Pulitzer Prize–winning author Annie Proulx, who penned *The Shipping News* here. Sleep in a cottage (the more expensive ones can sleep up to four people) or in the more modern main lodge with a cozy living-room fireplace and a deck to watch icebergs in comfort. It's only 8km from the Viking site.

Burnt Cape Cabins CABIN $$
(☎709-452-3521; www.burntcape.com; 4 Main St, Raleigh; cabins $129-189; P 📶) The lonely town of Raleigh sits west of L'Anse aux Meadows, and makes for a less touristed base for exploring the region. These rustic wood cabins are located near the Raleigh harbor and include satellite TVs and comfortable beds. The owners run **Burnt Cape Tours** (☎709-452-3521; www.burntcape.com; $75; ⏲9am late-Jun-early Sep). There's a convenience store and gas station next door.

★ **Daily Catch** SEAFOOD $$
(☎709-623-2295; 112 Main St, St Lunaire-Griquet; mains $10-26; ⏲11am-9pm) A stylish little restaurant serving finely prepared seafood and wine. The basil-buttered salmon gets kudos. Fish cakes, crab au gratin and cod burgers also please the palate. There's live music on Wednesday nights during the summer.

★ **Norseman Restaurant & Art Gallery** SEAFOOD $$$
(☎709-754-3105; www.valhalla-lodge.com; Rte 436, L'Anse aux Meadows village; mains $20-38; ⏲noon-9pm May-Sep; P) This lovely waterfront outpost ranks among Newfoundland's best. Emphasizing local products and creative preparations, the menu will have you wavering between options such as perfectly grilled lamb chops, kale Caesar salad with Arctic char, seared scallops or tender Labrador caribou tenderloin. Espresso drinks are served and cocktails come chilled with iceberg ice.

Shopping

Dark Tickle FOOD
(www.darktickle.com; 75 Main St, St Lunaire-Griquet; ⏲9am-9pm) Dark Tickle is a shop in the grand tradition of the Québécois *économusée:* a place that showcases a particular

THE VIKINGS

Christopher Columbus gets the credit for 'discovering' North America, but the Vikings were actually the first Europeans to walk upon the continent. Led by Leif Eriksson, they sailed over from Scandinavia and Greenland some 500 years before Columbus and landed at L'Anse aux Meadows. They settled, constructed houses, fed themselves and even smelted iron out of the bog to forge nails, attesting to their ingenuity and fortitude. That it was all accomplished by a group of young-pup twenty-somethings is even more impressive.

Norse folklore had mentioned a site called 'Vinland' for centuries. But no one could ever prove its existence – until 1968, when archaeologists found a small cloak pin on the ground at L'Anse aux Meadows. Archaeologists now believe the site was a base camp, and that the Vikings ranged much further along the coast.

kind of heritage craft. In this case, it's the jam-making of Newfoundland and Labrador. You'll learn how the people of this province take northern fruit – bakeapple, crowberries, partridgeberries and more – and create preserves that would make an angel sigh.

On-site, you'll also find loads of gifts, souvenirs and artwork. The owners speak French, and the excellent **Cafe Nymphe** (709-623-2354; www.darktickle.com/content/18-cafe-nymphe; 75 Main St, St Lunaire-Griquet; mains $7-15; 9am-9pm) is located upstairs.

Getting There & Away

The road to the Northern Peninsula is narrow and often potholed. Travel extra slow in the rain. You'll need your own wheels to explore the area.

A ferry travels between St Barbe and Blanc Sablon, Québec (near the Labrador border), daily. The 1¾-hour trip across the Strait of Belle Isle is run by **Labrador Marine** (866-535-2567; www.tw.gov.nl.ca/ferryservices/schedules/j_pollo.html; adult/child/vehicle $11.75/9.50/35.25); see the website for schedules. You'll want to show up at least an hour ahead of time to reserve your spot in the car line, even if you've already purchased tickets (which is a good idea).

St Anthony

Congratulations. You've made it to the end of the road, your windshield has culled the insect population and you have seen two World Heritage sites. After such grandeur, St Anthony may be a little anticlimactic. Though not pretty, it possesses a rough-hewn charm, and inspiring hiking and whale- and iceberg-watching.

Grenfell is a big name around here. Sir Wilfred Grenfell was a local legend and, by all accounts, quite a man. This English-born and educated doctor first came to Newfoundland in 1892 and, for the next 40 years, traveling by dogsled and boat, built hospitals and nursing stations and organized much-needed fishing cooperatives along the coast of Labrador and around St Anthony. A number of local sites pertaining to the pioneering doctor can be visited round town, including the doctor's own house, now an intriguing **museum** (709-454-4010; www.grenfell-properties.com; multisite admission adult/child/family $10/3/22; 8am-5pm Jun-Sep).

The main road through town ends at **Fishing Point Park**, where a lighthouse and towering headland cliffs overlook the sea. The **Iceberg Alley Trail** and Whale Watchers Trail both lead to cliff-top observation platforms – the names say it all.

If you want to get closer, **Northland Discovery Tours** (709-454-3092, 877-632-3747; www.discovernorthland.com; 2½hr tour adult/child $63/27; 9am, 1pm & 4pm Jun-Sep) offers highly recommended cruises for whale- or iceberg-viewing that leave from the dock behind the Grenfell Interpretation Centre on West St. This far north, the chances of spotting either icebergs or whales are excellent, so this tour is great value for money.

The St Anthony Airport is 35km (22 miles) northwest of town. **PAL Airlines** (800-563-2800; www.provincialairlines.ca; St Anthony Airport) makes the trip from St John's daily.

If you're leaving St Anthony by car, you have two options: backtrack entirely along Rte 430, or take the long way via Rte 432 along the east coast and Hare Bay. This will meet up with Rte 430 near Plum Point, between St Barbe and Port au Choix.

WESTERN NEWFOUNDLAND

Western Newfoundland presents many visitors with their first view of the Rock, thanks to the ferry landing at Port aux Basques. It's big, cliffy, even a bit forbidding with all those wood houses clinging to the jagged shoreline against the roaring wind. From Port aux Basques, poky fishing villages cast lines to the east, while Newfoundland's second-largest town, Corner Brook, raises its wintry head (via its ski mountain) to the northeast.

Corner Brook

POP 19,800

Where St John's is a Newfoundland city on the cusp of globalization, Corner Brook, the province's number-two town, is local to the core. This is a city for mill workers and fisher folk, as well as tour outfitters who work in Gros Morne. While Newfoundland attracts visitors from all over, Corner Brook attracts many from Newfoundland itself, specifically skiers who love the handsome Humber Valley, about 10km east. The valley offers adventure-sport junkies places to play, while the city itself sprawls with big-box retailers and a smoke-belching pulp-and-paper mill.

Sights

Captain James Cook Monument MONUMENT

(Crow Hill Rd) While this cliff-top monument is admirable – a tribute to James Cook for his work in surveying the region in the mid-1760s – it's the panoramic view over the Bay of Islands that is the real payoff. Cook's names for many of the islands, ports and waterways you'll see, such as the Humber Arm and Hawke's Bay, remain today.

Railway Society of Newfoundland MUSEUM

(709-634-2720; Station Rd, off Humber Rd; admission $3; 9am-8pm Jun-Aug) Within historical Humbermouth Station, the Railway Society of Newfoundland has a good-looking steam locomotive and some narrow-gauge rolling stock that chugged across the province from 1921 to 1939.

Activities

Cycle Solutions CYCLING

(709-634-7100; www.cyclesolutions.ca; 35 West St; 9am-6pm Mon-Wed & Sat, to 8:30pm Thu & Fri) This sweet bike shop runs local cycling and caving tours; it's attached to the Brewed Awakening (p224) coffee shop.

Marble Zip Tours ADVENTURE SPORTS

(709-632-5463; www.marbleziptours.com; Thistle Dr; 2hr tour adult/child $99/89) The highest zip line in eastern Canada. Strap in near the mountaintop, and zigzag platform to platform down a gorge traversing Steady Brook Falls. It'll take your breath away. Tours depart four to five times daily. The office is past Marble Mountain's lodge, behind the Tim Hortons.

Marble Mountain SKIING

(709-637-7616; www.skimarble.com; Hwy 1; day pass adult/child $60/35; 10am-4:30pm Sat-Thu, 9am-9:30pm Fri Dec-Apr) Marble Mountain is the lofty reason most visitors come to Corner Brook. With 35 trails, four lifts, a 488m vertical drop and annual snowfall of 5m, it offers Atlantic Canada's best skiing. There are snowboarding and tubing parks, as well as night skiing on Friday, plus Oh My Jesus (you'll say it when you see the slope).

Sleeping & Eating

Brookfield Inn B&B $

(709-639-3111; brookfieldinn@gmail.com; 2 Brookfield Ave; r $70-90;) A cool couple runs this B&B. The white-frame house has homey rooms with hardwood floors and plump beds. In the morning make your own breakfast from the eggs, bacon, cheeses and breads in the well-stocked kitchen. In the evening watch the sunset from the deck. The house dogs will amble up for a scratch if you want.

Glynmill Inn HOTEL $$

(709-634-5181; www.steelehotels.com; 1 Cobb Lane; r incl breakfast $125-165;) Lawns and gardens surround the gracious Tudor-style Glynmill. It was built originally for the engineers supervising the pulp mill's construction in the 1920s, at that time the largest project in the history of papermaking. The property retains an elegant if somewhat faded ambience.

★ **Harbour Grounds** CAFE $

(709-639-1677; 9 Humber Rd; mains $7-12; 7:30am-6pm Mon-Fri, from 9am Sat, 9am-5pm Sun) This excellent breakfast and lunch spot boasts great views and one of the most consistently good menus in Corner Brook. Garden-pesto paninis, Irish stew, omeletes and steak-and-Guinness pie are all complemented by friendly service and some very fine coffee.

Corner Brook

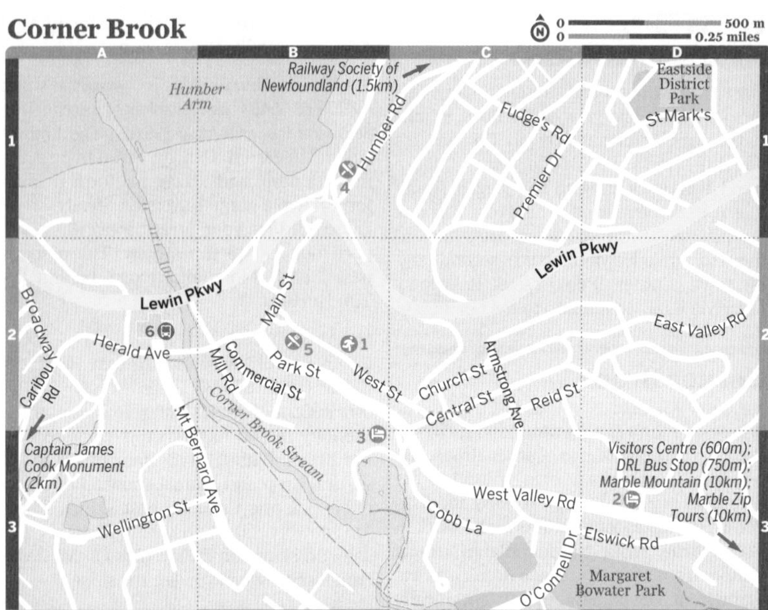

Brewed Awakening COFFEE
(☎709-634-7100; www.brewedawakening.ca; 35 West St; ⊙7am-6pm Mon-Fri, from 8am Sat, from 9am Sun; 📶) This small, funky, art-on-the-wall coffee shop pours fair-trade organic java done right. It's attached to the groovy bike shop Cycle Solutions (p223). Baked goods $3 to $7.

Information

Visitors Center (☎709-639-9792; www.cornerbrook.com; 15 Confederation Dr; ⊙9am-5pm) Just off Hwy 1 at exit 5. Has a craft shop.

Getting There & Away

Corner Brook is a major hub for bus services in Newfoundland. **DRL** (☎709-263-2171; www.drl-lr.com; Confederation Dr) stops on the outskirts of town at the Irving Gas Station, just off Hwy 1 at exit 5 across from the Visitors Center.

All other operators use the bus station in the Millbrook Mall building. Prices listed for the following shuttle vans are one way; you must make your own reservations.

Burgeo Bus (☎709-886-7777; bus station, Millbrook Mall) Runs to Burgeo ($40 cash only, two hours) departing at 3pm Monday through Friday. Leaves Burgeo between 8am and 9am.

Deer Lake Airport Shuttle (☎709-634-4343) Picks up from various hotels en route to Deer Lake Airport ($22, 45 minutes) three to five times daily.

Gateway (☎709-695-9700; bus station, Millbrook Mall) Runs to Port aux Basques ($40, three hours) on weekdays at 3:45pm. Departs Port aux Basques at 7:45am.

Martin's (☎709-634-7777; martins.transportation@nf.sympatico.ca; bus station, Millbrook Mall) Operates weekdays, departing for Woody Point ($18, 1½ hours) and Trout River ($20, two hours) at 4:30pm. Returns from Trout River at 9am.

Pittman's (☎709-458-2486; bus station, Millbrook Mall) Runs to Rocky Harbour ($35, two hours) via Deer Lake on weekdays at 4:30pm. Departs Rocky Harbour at noon.

Blomidon Mountains

The Blomidon Mountains (aka Blow Me Down Mountains) – heaved skyward from a collision with Europe around 500 million years ago – run along the south side of the Humber Arm, west of Corner Brook. They're tantalizing for hikers, providing many sea vistas and glimpses of the resident caribou population. Some of the trails, especially those up on the barrens, are not well marked; topographical maps and a compass are essential for all hikers.

Corner Brook

Activities, Courses & Tours
1 Cycle Solutions B2

Sleeping
2 Brookfield Inn D3
3 Glynmill Inn B3

Eating
4 Harbour Grounds B1
5 Shez West B2

Drinking & Nightlife
Brewed Awakening .... (see 1)

Transport
6 Burgeo Bus A2
Gateway .... (see 6)
Martin's .... (see 6)
Pittman's .... (see 6)

Further on, Blow Me Down Provincial Park has beaches and scenery.

The only accommodations option is a provincial-park **campground** (709-681-2430; www.nlcamping.ca; Rte 450; campsites $18, per vehicle $5; Jun-Aug).

Activities

Copper Mine Trail HIKING
(York Harbour) This moderately difficult 7km trail by York Harbour provides awesome views of the Bay of Islands and also links to the International Appalachian Trail (IAT).

Blow Me Down Brook Trail HIKING
(Frenchman's Cove) One of the easiest and most popular trails in the Blomidon range, this 5km trail begins west of Frenchman's Cove at a parking lot. The trail can be followed for an hour or so; for more avid hikers it continues well into the mountains, where it becomes part of the International Appalachian Trail (IAT).

Port au Port Peninsula

Jutting into the Gulf of St Lawrence like a nose bitten raw by the chilly ocean winds is the Port au Port Peninsula, the only officially bilingual corner of Newfoundland. While everyone here speaks English, Francophones may find many residents engaging them in a distinctive French dialect that is neither of Québec or France itself.

The peninsula is simply stunning, all jaw-dropping sea cliffs and wild views, and there is a lot to be said for taking a long, lazy day to drive NL 460 and 463, which tie a loop around the entire landmass.

Sights

Boutte du Cap VIEWPOINT
(Cape St George; P) The southwestern tip of the peninsula is one of those Newfoundland places where the wind blows and the ocean rumbles and you generally feel as if you're about to fall off the face of the Earth. The loneliness is underlined by a memorial to the Acadians – French Canadians who were expelled from the region after the British conquest of Canada – and their exile.

The Gravels LANDMARK
The spit of land that connects Port au Port to the mainland looks as if it could be snipped away with a pair of dull scissors. In fact, this isthmus is great for bird-watching, and a parking lot allows access to about 3.5km of lovely walking trails.

Sleeping & Eating

Inn at the Cape INN $$
(888-484-4740; www.innatthecape.com; 1250 Oceanview Dr, Cape St George; s/d incl breakfast $99/129; P) At this nicely run inn, you'll find nine comfortable rooms, decks with excellent views, and a buffet supper along with a full breakfast.

Oliver's Restaurant CANADIAN $
(709-642-5178; 42 NL 463; mains $8-16; 11am-8pm) Head to this friendly roadside restaurant for great-quality fish-and-chips and some of the meanest poutine you'll ever devour outside of Québec.

Secret Cove Brewing BREWERY
(709-648-2683; www.secretcovebrewing.com; 92-96 Main St, Port au Port; 1-9pm Mon-Thu, noon-midnight Fri & Sat, 1-6pm Sun) It's not enough that this isolated peninsula has great natural beauty and one of the world's rarest dialects of French; thanks to Secret Cove, there's a very fine brewery, complete with beer garden, here as well. Pop in for a craft beer, some live music, good camaraderie and other reminders of the joys of life.

Getting There & Away

Access the peninsula via private vehicle. Stephenville is the closest large town. It's about 91km to Corner Brook. Fair warning: the roads here are twisty, even by Newfoundland standards, and a distance of a few kilometers will take longer to drive than you may initially think.

Port aux Basques

POP 4070

Traditional wood houses painted aqua, scarlet and sea-green clasp the stony hills, but it's all about the ferry in Port aux Basques. Most visitors come here to jump onto the Rock from Nova Scotia, or jump off for the return trip. That doesn't mean the town isn't a perfectly decent place to spend a day or night. Laundry blows on the clotheslines, boats moor in backyard inlets and locals never fail to wave hello to newcomers.

Port aux Basques (occasionally called Channel-Port aux Basques) was named in the early 16th century by Basque fishers and whalers who came to work the waters of the Strait of Belle Isle.

The town is a convenient place to stock up on food, fuel and money before journeying onward.

Hotel Port aux Basques HOTEL **$$**
(☎709-695-2171; www.hotelpab.com; 1 Grand Bay Rd; r $109-189; ❄📶) This is an older hotel, but it's clean, comfortable and has a lot of character. An executive suite features a Jacuzzi tub. Kids stay for free, and the hotel has an autism-friendly sensory room.

St Christopher's Hotel HOTEL **$$**
(☎800-563-4779, 709-695-3500; www.stchrishotel.com; Caribou Rd; r $140; ❄📶) This is the most professional hotel in town, with a small fitness room and a seafood restaurant called the **Captain's Room** (☎709-695-3500; 146 Caribou Rd; mains $10-19; ⏱7am-1:30pm & 5-10pm). Odd-numbered rooms have harbor views.

Alma's CANADIAN **$**
(☎709-695-3813; www.facebook.com/almasfamilyrestaurant; Grand Bay Mall, Grand Bay Rd; mains $7-15; ⏱7:30am-8pm Mon-Wed, to 9pm Thu & Fri, to 7pm Sat, 9:30am-7pm Sun) Follow the locals

Port aux Basques

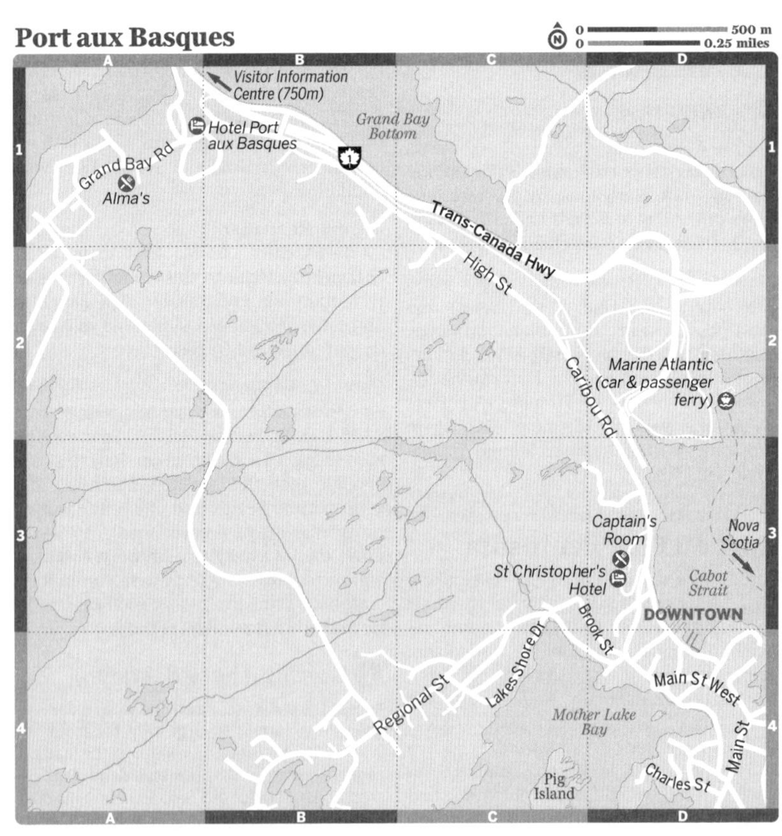

into this no-frills family diner for heaping portions of cod, scallops, fish cakes and berry pies. Your best bet for a good meal in town, it serves breakfasts, burgers and sandwiches too.

Information

Visitors Center (709-695-2262; www.portauxbasques.ca; Hwy 1; 9am-5pm Mon-Fri May-Oct) Information on all parts of the province; sometimes open later to accommodate ferry traffic.

Getting There & Away

The car and passenger **ferry** (800-341-7981; www.marineatlantic.ca; adult/child/car $45/21/119) goes to Nova Scotia. Buses (p196) go on to St John's and Corner Brook. If you exhaust stuff to do around here, Corner Brook is the nearest large town, 'only' 220km to the north.

OFF THE BEATEN TRACK

CAPE ANGUILLE

The westernmost point of Newfoundland is Cape Anguille, located 58km north of Port aux Basques. Drive out to explore the windswept lighthouse, where you can watch blue whales and stay in an adjoining lightkeeper's **cottage** (709-634-2285; www.linkumtours.com; 1 Lighthouse Rd; r incl breakfast $130-160; May-Sep). Don't expect phones or TVs – the idea is to get away here. Spring $10 extra for an ocean view. Dinner with locally sourced fish and berries is available ($30).

It's 45 minutes north of Port aux Basques in moose country; pay particular attention if driving at dusk or at night.

Cape Ray

Adjacent to **John T Cheeseman Provincial Park** (709-637-2040; www.tcii.gov.nl.ca/parks/p_jtc; Rte 408; sunrise-sunset) FREE and 19km north of Port aux Basques is Cape Ray. The coastal scenery is engaging, and the road leads up to the windblown **Cape Ray Lighthouse** (Cape Ray; P) FREE. This area is the southernmost-known Dorset Paleo-Eskimo site, dating from 400 BCE to CE 400. Thousands of artifacts have been found here and some dwelling sites can be seen.

There's camping at **John T Cheeseman Provincial Park** (877-214-2267; www.nlcamping.ca; Rte 408; campsites $18-28, per vehicle $5; Jun-Sep).

South Coast

Visitors often ignore Rte 470, and that's a shame because it's a beauty. Heading east out of Port aux Basques for 45km and edging along the shore, the road rises and falls over the eroded, windswept terrain, looking as though it's following a glacier that plowed through yesterday.

Isle aux Morts (Island of the Dead) got its name from the many shipwrecks that occurred just offshore over some 400 years. Named after a family famous for daring shipwreck rescues, the **Harvey Trail** (7km) twists along the rugged shore and makes a stirring walk. Look for the signs in town.

Another highlight is the last settlement along the road, **Rose Blanche**, an absolutely splendid, traditional-looking village nestled in a cove with a fine natural harbor – a perfect example of the classic Newfoundland fishing community. From here follow the signs to the restored **Rose Blanche Lighthouse** (709-956-2052; www.roseblanchelighthouse.ca; Rose Blanche; admission $6; 9am-9pm May-Oct).

KILLICK COAST

The peninsula just north and west of St John's is known as the Killick Coast, a 55km one-way journey that makes a good day trip. The main things to see out here are some quiet beaches (that can get not quite so quiet during summer weekends), a kid-friendly aquarium, and a mine where it gets so dark, you can't actually see anything at all.

To reach Bell Island (p228), go 14km northwest from St John's to Portugal Cove and the ferry.

Ocean Sciences Centre AQUARIUM
(709-864-2459; www.mun.ca/osc; Marine Lab Rd; 10am-5pm Jun-Aug;) FREE Right out of *20,000 Leagues Under the Sea,* this university center examines the salmon life cycle, seal navigation, ocean currents and life in cold oceanic regions. The outdoor visitors area consists of local sea life in touch tanks. It's about 8km north of St John's, just before Logy Bay.

From the city, take Logy Bay Rd (Rte 30), then follow Marine Dr to Marine Lab Rd and take it to the end.

Bell Island Community Museum MUSEUM

(☎709-488-2880; www.bellislandminetour.com; Compressor Hill; museum & mine tour adult/child $12/5; ⏲11am-6pm Jun-Sep) Miners here used to work in shafts under the sea at the world's largest submarine iron mine. Conditions were grim: the museum tells tales of adolescents working 10-hour days by candlelight. Visitors can also go underground; dress warmly.

Bell Island ISLAND

(www.tourismbellisland.com) The largest of Conception Bay's little landmasses makes an interesting day trip from St John's. It was the only place on the continent hit by German forces in WWII. U-boats torpedoed the pier and 80,000 tonnes of iron ore in 1942. At low tide, you can still see the aftermath. The island sports a pleasant mélange of beaches, coastal vistas, lighthouses and trails.

Getting There & Away

Visitors will need a car to explore the Killick Coast. The **Bell Island Ferry** (☎709-895-6931; www.tw.gov.nl.ca; per passenger/car $4/10; ⏲hourly 6am-10:30pm) provides quick transit between Portugal Cove and the island.

LABRADOR

POP 27,000

Welcome to the 'Big Land': an undulating expanse of spruce woods, muskeg, bog and tundra that stretches from St Lawrence to the Arctic Circle and back again. The vast landscape contains military bases, little towns, Inuit and Innu villages, and some of the world's oldest geologic formations, the latter a most fitting addition to this most primeval of landscapes.

The simplest means of access is the Labrador Straits region, which connects to Newfoundland via a daily ferry. From there, a solitary road – the stark, rough Trans-Labrador Hwy – connects the interior's main towns. The Indigenous-influenced northern coast is accessible only by plane or supply ferry. Here, Torngat Mountains National Park offers a privileged glimpse into ultra-remote wilderness.

Labrador is cold, wet and windy, and its bugs are murderous. Facilities are few and far between throughout the behemoth region, so planning ahead is essential.

Getting There & Away

Wabush and Goose Bay have flight connections to Newfoundland, Nova Scotia and Québec. **Air Borealis** (☎800-563-2800; www.palairlines.ca) flies to small communities in far north Labrador.

Overland visitors enter Labrador via Québec at Labrador West or the Labrador Straits village of L'Anse au Clair.

Those taking the ferry from Newfoundland to Labrador arrive in Blanc Sablon, 6km from L'Anse au Clair.

Labrador Straits

And you thought the Northern Peninsula was commanding? Sail the 28km across the Strait of Belle Isle and behold a landscape even more windswept and black-rocked. Clouds rip across aqua-and-gray skies, and the water that slaps the shore is so cold it's purplish. Unlike the rest of remote Labrador, the Straits region is easy to reach and exalted with sights such as Red Bay and a slew of great walking trails that meander past shipwreck fragments and old whale bones.

'Labrador Straits' is the colloquial name for the communities that make up the southern coastal region of Labrador.

Information

The Straits' excellent **Gateway to Labrador Visitors Center** (☎709-931-2013; www.labradorcoastaldrive.com; Rte 510, L'Anse au Clair; ⏲9am-5pm Jun-Oct) is in an old church that doubles as a small museum. Be sure to pick up hiking trail information for the region.

Getting There & Away

Labrador Marine (☎709-535-0811, 866-535-2567; www.labradormarine.com; adult/child/vehicle $11.75/9.50/35.25; ⏲May-early Jan) sails the two hours between St Barbe in Newfoundland and Blanc Sablon from May to early January. The boat runs one to three times daily between 8am and 6pm. Schedules vary from day to day. In July and August, it's not a bad idea to reserve in advance. Note that the ferry terminal in Blanc Sablon operates on Newfoundland Time and not Eastern Time (as in the rest of Québec).

PAL Airlines (☎800-563-2800; www.palairlines.ca) has flights to Blanc Sablon from St John's and St Anthony. Just to confuse you,

OFF THE BEATEN TRACK

SOUTH COAST OUTPORTS

If you have the time and patience, a trip across the south coast with its wee fishing villages – called outports – is the best way to witness Newfoundland's unique culture. They're some of the most remote settlements in North America, reachable only by boat as they cling to the convoluted shore. **Burgeo** (population 1460) is accessible by an easy road trip, while **Ramea** (population 525) is an island just offshore from Burgeo.

In Burgeo, you could climb the stairs to **Maiden Tea Hill**, or head for the 7km of white-sand beaches at **Sandbanks Provincial Park**, possibly the best in the entire province. Author Farley Mowat lived in Burgeo for several years, until he penned *A Whale for the Killing*, which tells the story of how Burgeo's townsfolk treated an 80-tonne fin whale trapped in a nearby lagoon. Let's just say the outcome was not a happy one for the whale. Locals can point out the lagoon and Mowat's old house, though expect to get an earful about it.

The other outports are great areas for remote camping, hiking and fishing; ask locals or at the visitor center in Port aux Basques about arranging a guide. Tiny **François**, surrounded by towering walls of rock, is particularly gorgeous.

A good base is **Ramea Retreat** (Island View Lodge; ☎709-625-2522; www.easternoutdoors.com; 2 Main St, Ramea; dm/r/house $39/89/195; ⏲May-Nov; 📶), an adventure lodge with 10 hostel beds and options for kayaking, bird-watching, hiking and fishing tours. The lodge owners also rent rooms in various vintage clapboard houses scattered around Ramea.

departure times from the airport are on Eastern Time versus Labrador Straits (ie Newfoundland) Time.

Rental cars are available at the airport from **Eagle River Rent-a-Car** (☎709-931-2292, 709-931-3300; Forteau).

Blanc Sablon to Pinware

After arriving by ferry or plane in Blanc Sablon, Québec, and driving 6km northeast on Rte 510 you come to Labrador and the gateway town of L'Anse au Clair.

The town makes a good pre-ferry base, with sleeping and basic dining options and a useful visitor center.

Heading northeast on Rte 510 you'll pass a glut of blink-and-miss-it towns: Forteau, L'Anse Amour, L'Anse au Loup, West St Modeste and Pinware. Scattered among these settlements are fascinating historical sites, pretty walks and a few other interesting detours as you make your way to Red Bay.

Sights & Activities

Point Amour Lighthouse LIGHTHOUSE
(☎709-927-5825; www.pointamourlighthouse.ca; L'Anse Amour Rd; adult/child $6/4; ⏲9:30am-5pm May-Oct) At 109ft, this is the tallest lighthouse in Atlantic Canada, with 127 steps to climb. When you reach the top, you will be rewarded with a spectacular 360-degree view of the coastline. The HMS *Raleigh* went aground here in 1922 and was destroyed in 1926.

L'Anse Amour Burial Mound HISTORIC SITE
(L'Anse Amour Rd) A pile of stones, placed here by the Maritime Archaic Indigenous people, is the oldest burial monument in North America. A small roadside plaque marks the 7500-year-old site.

Labrador Adventures TOURS
(☎709-931-2840; www.tourlabrador.ca) Provides knowledgeable guides for Straits-oriented day tours by SUV ($450). It also arranges all-inclusive overnight packages. This is a good way to see the area if you're without a car.

Sleeping & Eating

Grenfell Louie A Hall B&B B&B $$
(☎709-931-2916; www.grenfellbandb.ca; Willow Ave, Forteau; r $110-125, cottages $165; ⏲May-Oct; P 📶) This charming B&B is in the old nursing station where generations of Labrador Straits folk were born – there's also rumor of a few ghosts floating around. With quilts and country decor, the five simple rooms share two bathrooms. Some have sea views.

Max's House HISTORIC HOTEL $$$
(Point Amour Lighthouse; ☎709-931-2840; www.tourlabrador.ca; Point Amour Lighthouse; cottage $325; ⏲Jun-early Oct; 📶) On the grounds of the Point Amour Lighthouse, this historic building was the residence of lighthouse keeper Max Sheppard. The house features

Labrador

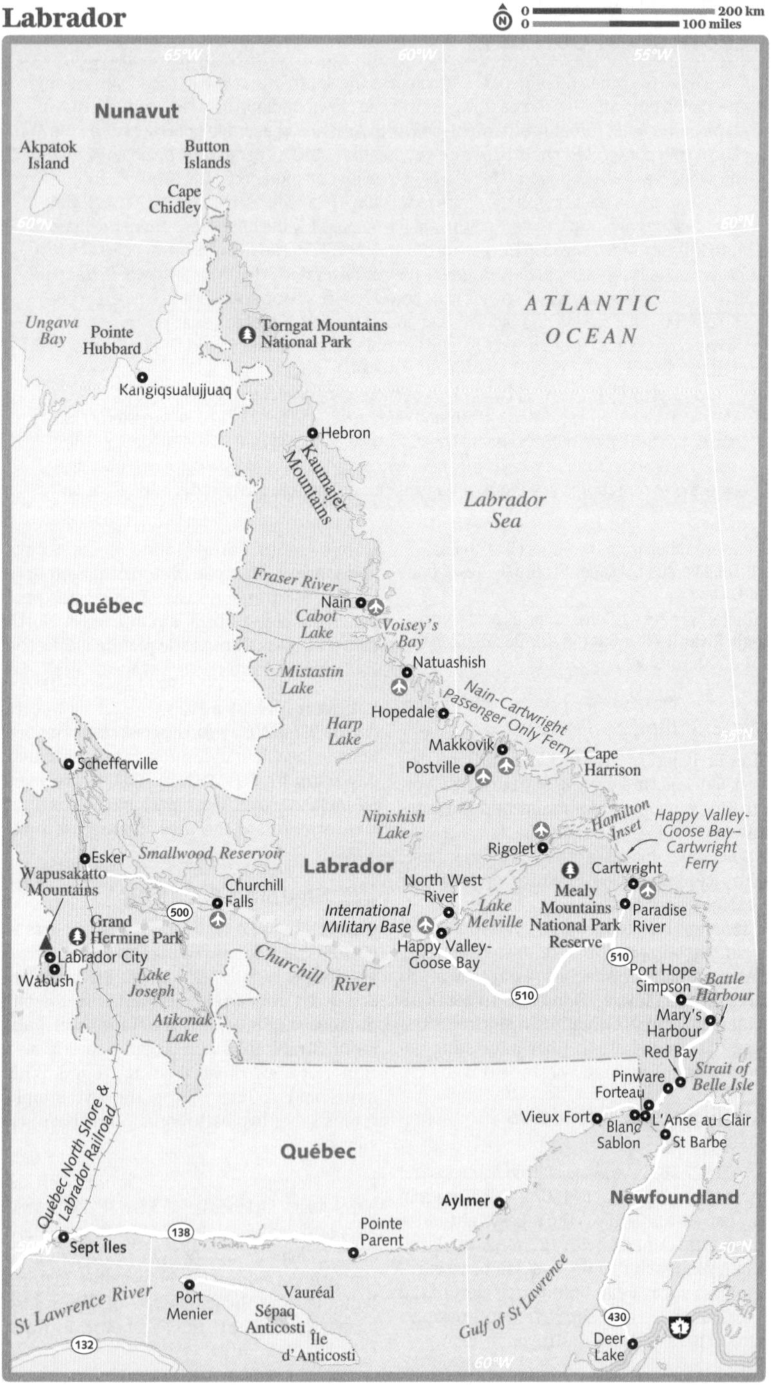

0 200 km
0 100 miles

65°W
60°W
55°W
60°N
55°N
50°N
Nunavut
Akpatok Island
Button Islands
Cape Chidley
ATLANTIC OCEAN
Ungava Bay
Pointe Hubbard
Torngat Mountains National Park
Kangiqsualujjuaq
Hebron
Kaumajet Mountains
Labrador Sea
Fraser River
Québec
Nain
Cabot Lake
Voisey's Bay
Natuashish
Mistastin Lake
Nain-Cartwright Passenger Only Ferry
Hopedale
Harp Lake
Makkovik
Cape Harrison
Postville
Schefferville
Nipishish Lake
Hamilton Inset
Happy Valley-Goose Bay–Cartwright Ferry
Rigolet
Esker
Smallwood Reservoir
Labrador
Wapusakatto Mountains
Churchill Falls
North West River
Cartwright
Mealy Mountains National Park Reserve
Paradise River
500
International Military Base
Lake Melville
Grand Hermine Park
Labrador City
Happy Valley-Goose Bay
510
Wabush
Churchill River
Port Hope Simpson
Battle Harbour
Lake Joseph
Mary's Harbour
Atikonak Lake
Red Bay
Strait of Belle Isle
Pinware
Forteau
Vieux Fort
Blanc Sablon
L'Anse au Clair
St Barbe
Québec North Shore & Labrador Railroad
Québec
Aylmer
Newfoundland
Sept Îles
138
Pointe Parent
St Lawrence River
Port Menier
Vauréal
Sépaq Anticosti
Île d'Anticosti
Gulf of St Lawrence
430
Deer Lake
1
132

five guest rooms with quilted bedcovers, a well-stocked kitchen and two bathrooms, accommodating 10. Dinner is served in the lighthouse; there's also whale- and iceberg-viewing. No phones on-site.

Seaview Restaurant CANADIAN $$
(Rte 510, Forteau; mains $10-25; ⏲11am-9pm) Enjoy some fresh seafood or chow down on the famous fried chicken and tender caribou. A grocery store and jam factory are also on-site.

Red Bay

Spread between two venues, **Red Bay National Historic Site** (☎709-920-2051, 709-458-2417; www.pc.gc.ca/en/lhn-nhs/nl/redbay; W Harbour Dr; adult/child $7.80/free; ⏲9am-5pm Jun-Sep) – declared a Unesco World Heritage site in 2013 – uses different media to chronicle the discovery of three 16th-century Basque whaling galleons on the seabed here. Well-preserved in the ice-cold waters, the vestiges of the ships tell a remarkable story of what life was like here some four centuries ago. For many visitors, this is as far as they travel in Labrador, and if you're going to terminate your trip to the Big Land, this harbour – lined with icebergs and creaking salt box shacks – is a scenic place to do so.

Rarely does a walking trail live up to its atmospheric name like Red Bay's **Boney Shore Trail** (Tracey Rd). This is where Basque whalers tossed bits of skeleton from the whales they killed, and even today, discarded vertebrae still litter the shore. This 1km out-and-back route also skirts windswept fields of lichen and muskeg, and affords some great views of Red Bay.

Whaler's Station INN $$
(☎709-920-2156; www.redbaywhalers.ca; 72-76 West Harbour Dr; r $125-150) Divided between several buildings, these rustic but comfortable lodgings provide a central base for visits to the historic site. Some rooms offer water views. They all have private bathrooms, TV, a microwave and refrigerator. There's also an on-site restaurant.

Whaler's SEAFOOD $$
(☎709-920-2156; www.redbaywhalers.ca; W Harbour Dr; mains $9-20; ⏲8am-8pm) For fish-and-chips with partridgeberry pie, look no further than this friendly restaurant, a focal point for visitors to the bay. It also serves substantial breakfasts, and picnickers can order boxed lunches.

Getting There & Away

Red Bay is about 80km northeast of the ferry landing at Blanc Sablon. Past here, the road is paved, but it is...lonely, to say the least. It's another 90km northeast to Mary's Harbour.

Battle Harbour

Sitting on an island in the Labrador Sea is the elaborately restored village and saltfish premises of Battle Harbour. Now a national historic district, it used to be the unofficial 'capital' of Labrador during the early 19th century, when fishing schooners lined its docks. Another claim to fame: Robert E Peary gave his first news conference here after reaching the North Pole in 1909.

★ **Battle Harbour Heritage Properties** INN $$
(☎709-921-6325; http://battleharbour.com; dm $50, r $195-335, cottages $245-800; ⏲Jun-Sep; 🛜) In addition to a classic inn, there are adorable heritage homes and cottages throughout the settlement. Think decks with sea views and little distraction: there are no cars, cell signal or TVs on the island. Instead you will find hiking trails with good berry-picking prospects and boat rides.

Battle Harbour Dining Room CANADIAN $$
(Battle Harbour Inn; meals incl with lodgings; ⏲8am-6pm) If you're staying on the island, you get a package deal that includes gourmet dining at this fine restaurant.

Getting There & Away

Battle Harbour is accessed by boat from Mary's Harbour (departure at 11am, one hour). The passenger ferry is included with accommodations. The return ferry leaves Battle Harbour daily at 9am.

Central Labrador

Making up the territorial bulk of Labrador, the central portion is an immense, sparsely populated and ancient wilderness. Paradoxically, it also has the largest town in Labrador, Happy Valley-Goose Bay, home to a military base. The town (population 7600) has all the usual services, but unless you're an angler or hunter, there isn't much to see or do.

Goose Bay was established during WWII as a staging point for planes on their way to Europe, and has remained an aviation center. The airport is also an official NASA alternate landing site for the space shuttle.

OFF THE BEATEN TRACK

TORNGAT MOUNTAINS NATIONAL PARK

Named from the Inuktitut word *torngait* (place of spirits), the **Torngat Mountains National Park** (☎709-922-1290; www.pc.gc.ca/torngat) is the ancestral home of Inuit and their predecessors. Its spectacular wilderness features herds of caribou, polar bears and even seals in a freshwater habitat. The park comprises 9700 sq km, extending from Saglek Fjord in the south, including all islands and islets, to the very northern tip of Labrador.

Visitation is difficult since there is only plane and boat access. The **Torngat Mountains Base Camp and Research Station** (☎709-635-4336; www.thetorngats.com; Torngat Mountains National Park; 4-night all-inclusive packages from $6212; ⏲Jul & Aug) offers package tours with four-night and seven-night options, including air transportation from Happy Valley-Goose Bay. You sleep in comfortable yurts or more luxuriant dome tents with heat and electricity, and spend your days hiking, boating and heli-touring (if you wish, you can spend just a few nights at base camp and the rest of the time in the wilderness with Inuit guides). Meals are provided, and an electrified fence keeps out polar bears.

No superlatives can do the beauty of this place justice.

Sights & Activities

Labrador Interpretation Centre MUSEUM
(☎709-497-8566; www.therooms.ca/labrador-interpretation-centre; 2 Portage Rd, North West River; ⏲9am-4:30pm Mon-Sat, 1-4:30pm Sun) FREE Officially opened by Queen Elizabeth II in 1997, the Labrador Interpretation Centre is the provincial museum, which holds some of Labrador's finest works of art and a fine slew of historical exhibits. It's in North West River, via Rte 520.

Northern Lights Building DEPARTMENT STORE
(☎709-896-5939; 170 Hamilton River Rd, Happy Valley-Goose Bay; ⏲10am-5:30pm Tue-Sat) The Northern Lights Building is a one-stop shop for a good range of winter, fishing and hunting gear, and a ton of souvenirs and random gifts – because you didn't come all the way to Labrador to not get the refrigerator magnet. The sheer massive everything-and-the-kitchen-sink nature of the place makes it worth a visit.

Sleeping & Eating

Emma's Suites B&B $$
(☎709-896-8694; www.emmassuites.ca; 214 Kelland Dr, Happy Valley-Goose Bay; r from $149; 📶🐾) This pet-friendly spot has clean rooms, decent wi-fi, a gym and satellite TVs – in other words, it has all the comforts of home way up in Labrador. As creature comforts go, this is one of the better options in town.

Royal Inn & Suites HOTEL $$
(☎709-896-2456; www.royalinnandsuites.ca; 5 Royal St, Happy Valley-Goose Bay; s/d/ste from $120/130/150; ❄📶) The good-looking Royal has a variety of well-lit, blue-and-white rooms to choose from; many of them have kitchens. The inn also loans out satellite phones to drivers through the region-wide safety program.

Mariner's Galley SEAFOOD $$
(☎709-896-9301; 25 Loring Dr, Happy Valley-Goose Bay; mains $7-24; ⏲6am-9pm) Come here for fried cod tongues with scruncheons (pork rind) or crab cocktail. Visitors rave about the friendly service and buffet options.

Information

Visitor Information Centre (☎709-896-8787; www.tourismlabrador.com; 6 Hillcrest Rd, Happy Valley-Goose Bay; ⏲8:30am-8pm Mon-Fri, 9am-5pm Sat & Sun; 📶) Provides information on Central Labrador, plus brochures and maps. Events are announced on its Facebook page.

There's also a useful town website (www.happyvalley-goosebay.com).

Getting There & Away

AIR

Daily flights are available to Happy Valley-Goose Bay from St John's via Deer Lake and Halifax. Montréal has daily flights to Wabush. The following also offer services:

Air Canada (☎888-247-2262; www.aircanada.com)

Air Inuit (☎800-361-2965; www.airinuit.com)

PAL Airlines (Provincial Airlines; ☎800-563-2800; www.palairlines.ca)

BOAT

You can reach Happy Valley-Goose Bay by a seasonal, passenger-only ferry via **Nunatsiavut Marine** (☎855-896-2262; www.labradorferry.

ca; Main Dock, Happy Valley-Goose Bay; adult/child to Nain $99/70; ⌚Jul-Aug).

CAR & MOTORCYCLE

From Happy Valley-Goose Bay you can take the mostly gravel Rte 500 west to Churchill Falls and then on to Labrador City. The drive to Labrador City takes about seven hours. There are no services until Churchill Falls, so stock up. The Royal Inn & Suites has free satellite phones you can take on the road (part of a region-wide safety program).

The partially paved Rte 510 heads southeast toward Cartwright (383km) and L'Anse au Clair (623km).

Before leaving, contact the Department of Transportation & Works (www.roads.gov.nl.ca) for the latest conditions. Many rental-car agreements prohibit driving on the Trans-Labrador Hwy or will not provide insurance; some have vehicles specifically designated for the route. You can hire cars from **National** (☎709-896-5575; www.nationalcar.com), among others.

Labrador West

Just 5km apart and 15km from Québec, the twin mining towns of Labrador City (population 8600) and Wabush (population 1900) are referred to collectively as Labrador West. This is where the province's western population is concentrated. The largest open-pit iron ore mine in the world is in Labrador City, a place that is mining town and wilderness outpost all at once. Out here the landscape is massive, and the celestial polychromatic artwork can expand throughout the entire night sky.

From Wabush, 39km east on Rte 500 is **Grande Hermine Park** (☎709-282-5369; ⌚Jun-Sep), which has a beach and some fine scenery. The Menihek hiking trail (15km) goes through wooded areas with waterfalls and open tundra.

Sleeping & Eating

Wabush Hotel HOTEL $$
(☎709-282-3221; www.wabushhotel.com; 9 Grenville Dr, Wabush; r $165-175; ❄📶) Centrally located in Wabush, this chalet-style, 68-room hotel has spacious and comfortable rooms and an old-world ski lodge vibe. The dining room has a popular dinner buffet.

Sushi Lab SUSHI $
(☎709-944-4179; www.facebook.com/sushilabrador; 118 Humphrey Rd, Labrador City; mains $6-16; ⌚noon-2pm & 5-10pm Mon-Fri, 5-10pm Sat & Sun) The dining experience here is nouveau-Labrador all the way. Order from a selection of dozens of sushi rolls, then expect a bit of a long wait, although the food does tend to be worth it once it arrives. For less adventurous diners, there's also Chinese food or pizza.

Baba Q's CANADIAN $$
(☎709-944-2355; www.facebook.com/BabaQs; 211 Drake Ave, Labrador City; mains $8-23; ⌚6:30am-11pm Sun-Thu, to midnight Fri) After a day in the woods, a nice slab of grilled or smoked pure meaty goodness goes down a treat. At this smokehouse you can wolf down rib eyes, burgers and similar carnivore friendly fare; the on-site bar can get pretty busy too.

Information

Destination Labrador (www.destinationlabrador.com) is a comprehensive tourism website with special events, services and tips, and there's a **visitors center** (☎709-944-5399; www.labradorwest.com; 1365 Rte 500) just west of Labrador City, in the Gateway Labrador building.

Getting There & Away

AIR

Air Canada (☎888-247-2262; www.aircanada.com), **PAL Airlines** (Provincial Airlines; ☎800-563-2800; www.palairlines.ca), and Air Inuit fly into Happy Valley-Goose Bay and Wabush, with some other destinations.

CAR & MOTORCYCLE

Fifteen kilometers west from Labrador City along Rte 500 is Fermont, Québec. From there, Rte 389 is mainly paved (with some fine gravel sections) and continues south 581km to Baie Comeau.

Happy Valley-Goose Bay is a seven-hour drive east on Rte 500, considered a good gravel road. **Budget** (☎709-282-1234; www.budget.ca; 1 Airport Rd) has an office at the airport; rental cars may not be driven on Rte 500.

Understand Nova Scotia, New Brunswick & Prince Edward Island

History

The history of this long-inhabited region, which has had its fair share of hardship, colonization, enforced exodus, genocide and disaster, is a complicated one, with a number of disparate cultures at different times laying claim to land that was inhabited for millennia by indigenous groups. Add to that an environment whose beauty can be outweighed by its brutality and you begin to get a sense of the resilient people who have chosen to call Eastern Canada home.

The First Fishers

Atlantic Canada's first inhabitants, the Paleoindians, walked into Labrador 9000 years ago. Next came the Maritime Archaic Indians, hunter-gatherers who ranged throughout Atlantic Canada, Maine and parts of Labrador between 7500 and 3500 years ago. Known for their ceremonial burials and other religious and magical practices, evidenced at sites such as Newfoundland's Port au Choix, they mysteriously disappeared around 1000 BCE.

Next to tend the land were the Mi'kmaq and Maliseet peoples in the Maritimes and the Beothuk people in Newfoundland – all members of the Algonquin-speaking eastern woodlands tribes. The Mi'kmaq and Maliseet practiced agriculture and lived in fairly permanent settlements. The Beothuk were semi-nomadic and paddled the area in birch-bark canoes. It was the Beothuk and their ceremonially ocher-coated faces who were dubbed 'red men' by Europeans, a name soon applied to all of North America's indigenous groups.

None of these people fared well once Europeans arrived, bringing with them disease and conflict. While the Mi'kmaq and Maliseet still occupy parts of Atlantic Canada, the last person of Beothuk ethnicity died in 1829, and a unique language and culture was lost forever.

The Age of European Discovery

Viking celebrity Leif Erikson and his tribe of adventurous seafarers from Iceland and Greenland were the first Europeans in North America. Around the year 1000, they poked around the eastern shores of Canada, establishing winter settlements and way stations for repairing ships and

TIMELINE

1000 BCE

After hanging around for a few thousand years eating fish and seals and developing complex ceremonial practices, the Maritime Archaic Indians inexplicably disappear.

CE 1000

Viking Leif Erikson and crew wash up at L'Anse aux Meadows, create the New World's first European settlements, repair their ships and smelt iron.

1492

Christopher Columbus, under the crown of Spain, stumbles upon the Bahamas and gets credit for 'discovering' America; John Cabot sails five years later and lands on Cape Breton and Newfoundland.

restocking supplies, such as at L'Anse aux Meadows in Newfoundland. The local Canadian indigenous groups did not exactly roll out the welcome mat for these intruders, who eventually tired of the hostilities and withdrew.

The action didn't heat up again until after 1492, when Christopher Columbus stumbled upon some small islands in the Bahamas. Other European monarchs, excited by his 'discovery,' quickly sponsored expeditions of their own. In 1497 Giovanni Caboto, better known as John Cabot, sailed under a British flag as far west as Newfoundland and Cape Breton. Although there's no evidence of where he first made landfall, the village of Bonavista in eastern Newfoundland usually gets the nod.

Cabot didn't find a passage to China but he did find cod, then a much-coveted commodity in Europe. Soon, hundreds of boats were shuttling between Europe and the fertile new fishing grounds. Several were based at Red Bay in Labrador, which became the world's biggest whaling port during the 16th century.

About this time, French explorer Jacques Cartier was also sniffing around Labrador. He was looking for gold and precious metals, but found only 'stones and horrible rugged rocks,' as he wrote in his journal in 1534. So he moved on to Québec – but not before bestowing Canada with its name. Scholars say it comes from *kanata,* a Huron-Iroquois word for village or settlement, which was written in Cartier's journal and later transformed by mapmakers to Canada.

First Nations Culture

Lennox Island First Nation, Price Edward Island

Goat Island, Cape Breton, Nova Scotia

Port au Choix National Historic Site, Newfoundland

Bear River First Nation Heritage & Cultural Centre, Nova Scotia

Settlers Move In

Fish, furs and nice juicy chunks of land – is it any wonder Europe started salivating?

St John's in Newfoundland lays claim to being the oldest town in North America, first settled around 1528. It belonged to no nation; rather it served fishing fleets from all over Europe. By 1583 the British claimed it, and St John's had the distinction of being the first colony of the empire.

The French weren't just sitting on their butts during this time. In 1604 explorer Samuel de Champlain and his party spent the winter on St Croix Island, a tiny islet in the river on the present international border with Maine. The next year Champlain and his fur-trader patron Sieur de Monts moved their small settlement to Port Royal in the Annapolis Valley, which would soon become an English–French flashpoint.

Nova Scotia – 'New Scotland' – was so-named by the 1st Earl of Stirling, Sir William Alexander of Menstrier in 1621. Stirling was convinced that Scotland was being left behind in the rush to the New World, and appealed to King James I (also James VI of Scotland) for permission to establish a new colony in Scotland's name. James granted Stirling a royal charter that established him as mayor of a huge swathe of territory encompassing modern Nova Scotia, New Brunswick and parts of the

1528

The fishing village of St John's bobs up as North America's first European settlement but belongs to no nation; instead it serves fishing fleets from around the world.

1621

The 1st Earl of Stirling successfully lobbies the Scottish crown for the creation of a new colony – Nova Scotia ('New Scotland').

1755

English round up and deport thousands of French Acadians from the Bay of Fundy region for not pledging allegiance to the Crown. Many move to Louisiana to become known as Cajuns.

1763

The Treaty of Paris boots France out of Canada after France loses the Seven Years' War. France retains St Pierre and Miquelon, however, which remain an overseas French territory to this day.

The earliest Scottish settlers to arrive in Nova Scotia landed at Pictou on 15th September 1773 aboard the ship *Hector*; a replica of the ship can still be visited along the harborside.

northeastern US. Stirling founded a small colony at Port Royal (governed by his son), but expended such a vast fortune on it that it effectively bankrupted him – an effort that ultimately came to naught when the region returned to French control in 1632 (although Stirling's coat-of-arms still appears on the Nova Scotian flag).

The French also revved up their colonization by bringing in a load of immigrants to LaHave on Nova Scotia's south shore. More settlers arrived in 1635, and soon the French had spread throughout the Annapolis Valley and the shores of the Bay of Fundy – a rich farming region they called Acadia.

French & English at War

The French were galling the English, and the English were infuriating the French. Both had claims to the land – hadn't Cabot sailed here first for England? Or was it Cartier for France? – but each wanted regional dominance. They skirmished back and forth in hostilities that mirrored those in Europe, where wars raged throughout the first half of the 18th century.

Things came to head in 1713 with the Treaty of Utrecht, which ended Queen Anne's war (1701–13) overseas. Under its provisions the majority

AVAST! PIRATES ON THE HORIZON

Pirates began to ply and plunder Atlantic Canada's waters soon after Europeans arrived to colonize the area. Peter Easton was one of the region's most famous pirates. He started out as an English naval officer in 1602. But when King James downsized the Royal Navy the next year, stranding Easton and his men in Newfoundland without any money, they understandably weren't pleased and decided to use the resources at hand (ie boats and a bad attitude) to become pirates. By 1610 Easton was living large in Harbour Grace, commanding a fleet of 40 ships and a crew of 5000 men. The money piled in for several more years, until he eventually retired to France, married a noblewoman and became the Marquis of Savoy.

Black Bart, aka Bartholomew Roberts, was another boatsman who made quite a splash in the local plundering business. He became a pirate after being captured by another, and he took to the lifestyle. Sort of. He liked the booty and the clothing it enabled (crimson waistcoat, scarlet plumed hat, gold necklaces), but he disliked booze and gambling. He also encouraged prayer among his employees. No one mutinied though, because his pirating prowess was legendary. For example, in 1720 he sailed into Newfoundland's Trepassey Bay aboard a 10-gun sloop with a crew of 60 men, where they were able to capture 21 merchant ships manned by 1200 sailors.

Halifax put a unique spin on its pirate history when the local government began sponsoring the plunder. The pirates were called privateers, and during the War of 1812 the government sanctioned them to get the goods and then provided them with waterfront warehouses to store it all. You can see where the action took place at the Privateer's Warehouse. The South Shore town of Liverpool commemorates the era by hosting a rollicking Privateer Days festival.

1769

The colony of Prince Edward Island is created from the larger Nova Scotia and will one day become Canada's smallest province; English is the official language.

1784

New Brunswick is created as a separate province from Nova Scotia in order to appease the tension between the huge influx of Loyalists from the US with the original settlers.

1840

The Cunard Line shipping company is founded in Halifax, providing the fastest link to England and boosting the region's economy; immigrants from around Europe and the UK arrive in droves.

1864

Fathers of the Confederation meet in Charlottetown and create the framework for a new country called Canada. The deal is sealed by the *British North America Act* in London three years later.

LOYALIST COLONIES IN THE MARITIMES

Some Acadians returned to Canada, but *merde alors,* they hadn't seen the end of English-speaking colonization. Many American colonists who remained loyal to the King of England during the American Revolutionary War fled or were driven out of the US once the British were defeated; these families resettled throughout the British Empire, including the Maritime provinces, while others went to the British West Indies.

Loyalists were offered free land by the British and their arrival meant a sudden influx of English-speakers. This new division of language and culture divided the country into predominantly British 'Upper Canada' and French 'Lower Canada.' It also led to the division of Nova Scotia into two provinces, modern-day Nova Scotia and New Brunswick.

Meanwhile, many Loyalists from the American south brought their slaves as they were assured by law that their slaves would remain their property. However, there were also freed black Loyalists who had been granted their freedom by fighting for the British during the Revolution. The government helped these ex-slaves resettle in Canada but they were met far less kindly than their white compatriots.

Ultimately, the influx of Loyalists to Canada helped strengthen ties with Britain and increased antipathy to the US, which contributed to keeping Canada an independent country in North America.

of Nova Scotia and Newfoundland went to the British (no longer just the English, following the landmark Act of Union in 1707, which united England, Scotland, Wales under the same flag for the first time), while Cape Breton Island, Prince Edward Island and what is today New Brunswick went to the French. That Acadia was now British was a particularly bitter spoonful for the French; the Brits had even overtaken Port Royal and renamed it Annapolis Royal, after Queen Anne.

The French reorganized and decided to give regional dominance another shot. In 1719 they began construction of a fortress at Louisbourg on Cape Breton Island to protect their interests. Bit by bit the fortified town grew. The British took note and in 1745 sent out a colonial army from Massachusetts to capture Louisbourg. It fell after a 46-day siege. A treaty a few years later returned it to France.

And so it went, with control of the region ping-ponging, until 1754 when the French and Indian Wars (sometimes called the Seven Years' War) began and ramped up the fighting to a new level.

Early European Settler Sites

- *Highland Village Museum, Cape Breton, Nova Scotia*
- *Colony of Avalon, Newfoundland*
- *Cupids, Newfoundland*
- *Kings Landing, New Brunswick*
- *Port Royal National Historic Site, Nova Scotia*

Memo to Acadians: Get Out

Charles Lawrence, the security-conscious British governor of Nova Scotia, had had enough. A war was going on and when the French Acadian citizens refused to swear allegiance to Britain, his suspicions mounted to fever pitch. In 1755 he ordered the Acadians to be rounded up and deported.

1912

Titanic sinks off the southern coast of Newfoundland and rescue ships are sent from Halifax – most of the recovered bodies are buried in Halifax.

1917

A munitions ship collides with another ship in Halifax Harbour creating the 'Halifax explosion,' the largest man-made explosion before the A-bomb, killing some 1900 people.

1921

The fabled fishing schooner and racing yacht *Bluenose* is launched out of Lunenburg, winning her first International Fishermen's Trophy in October of the same year.

1925

Cape Breton coal miners stage a 155-day strike and end up with a 7% pay cut. The industry continues to decline from here on.

The Nova Scotia government maintains a website of all things *Titanic* (www.novascotia.ca/titanic), including a list of passengers buried in local graveyards and artifacts housed in the local museums.

In a tragic chapter of history known as the Great Expulsion, the British burned villages and forced some 14,000 men, women and children onto ships. (The exact number is unknown.) Grand Pré was the heart of the area from which the Acadians were removed. Many headed for Louisiana and New Orleans; others went to various Maritime points, the Caribbean or back to Europe.

The government gave their lands in the Annapolis Valley to 12,000 New England colonists called 'planters.' After peace was restored some Acadians chose to return from exile, but they were forced to settle on the less favorable 'French Shore' between Yarmouth and Digby.

In 1758 the key French stronghold of Louisbourg was besieged for a second time, with the British sending more than 13,000 troops and 150 ships to ensure victory. The fortress fell after seven weeks, and in order to neutralise it for good the British troops demolished the walls and put much of the fort to the torch.

Ultimately the British won the French and Indian Wars, and the French colonial era in the region ended. At the Treaty of Paris in 1763, France handed Canada over to Britain – except for two small islands off the coast of Newfoundland, named St Pierre and Miquelon, which remain staunchly French to this day.

Following the peace settlements, large numbers of settlers arrived in eastern Canada from all over Great Britain, particularly from Scotland. Many established themselves around Antigonish and Pictou, with anoth-

THE TITANIC'S CORONER, UNDERTAKER & MOURNER

By Jon Tattrie, Halifax-based author and journalist

When RMS *Titanic* sank in April 1912 the rescue and recovery effort started in Halifax, the nearest port city with rail connections. John Snow, owner of JA Snow Funeral Homes, sailed to the disaster site to pull bodies from the ocean, bringing with him 125 coffins, ice, iron and all the embalming fluid in the city.

Some bodies were buried at sea (the iron ensured the coffins sank) and others were brought back to Snow's funeral home. (The building now houses the Five Fishermen restaurant (p68); the bodies were stored in today's wine cellar.) Snow helped devise a system to match bodies with possessions so they could be identified and returned to their families, or buried with a marked tombstone. Eventually 150 bodies were interred in Halifax, earning the town the grim title of '*Titanic*'s coroner, undertaker and mourner.'

Five years later the city was struck by another tragedy, known as the Halifax Explosion, when two ships collided in Halifax Harbour. Snow came out of retirement to help Halifax deal with hundreds of bodies, and ensure as many as possible got a proper burial. Snow's Funeral Home still operates out of Halifax (nowadays in the far northwest of town at 339 Lacewood Dr). It unveiled a *Titanic* memorial placard in its front garden in 2012.

1942

Bell Island, Newfoundland, is torpedoed by German forces and 69 people are killed; this is the only location on the American continent to receive a German hit during WWII.

1962

The Trans-Canada Hwy officially opens, spanning 7821km from St John's to Victoria, British Columbia, and linking Canada's 13 provinces – it is completed in 1971.

1969

New Brunswick extends its Equal Opportunity Plan when it passes the *Official Languages Act*, making it the only constitutionally bilingual province in Canada.

1992

A cod fishing moratorium is imposed and thousands of fisherfolk lose their livelihood. While hoped to be only a temporary measure, the cod stocks do not make a comeback.

er wave putting down roots on Cape Breton. These areas retain a strong Celtic connection.

A Perfect Union in Prince Edward Island

Throughout the first half of the 19th century, shipbuilding made New Brunswick and Nova Scotia wealthy, and Nova Scotia soon boasted the world's fourth-largest merchant marine. The Cunard Line was founded at Halifax in 1840, and immigration from Scotland and Ireland flourished.

In 1864 Charlottetown on Prince Edward Island served as the birthing room for modern Canada. At the town's Province House, a group of representatives from Nova Scotia, New Brunswick, Prince Edward Island, Ontario and Québec got together and hammered out the framework for a new nation. It took two more meetings – one in Québec City, the other in London – before parliament passed the *British North America Act* in 1867. And so began the modern, self-governing state of Canada. The date the act became official, July 1, is celebrated as Canada's national holiday.

Newfoundland, ever true to its independent spirit, did not join the confederation until 1949.

Military Sites

Fortress of Louisbourg (French), Nova Scotia

Citadel Hill (British), Nova Scotia

Fort Anne National Historic Site (French), Nova Scotia

Grassy Island Fort (British), Nova Scotia

Quidi Vidi (French & British), Newfoundland

World Wars

During both world wars Atlantic Canada played a key role as a staging area for the convoys that supplied Britain. The wars also boosted local economies and helped transition the region from an agricultural to an industrial base.

Halifax was the only city in North America to suffer damage during WWI. In December 1917 the *Mont Blanc,* a French munitions ship carrying TNT and highly flammable benzol, collided with the *Imo* in Halifax Harbour. The 'Halifax Explosion' ripped through the city, leveling most of Halifax's northern end, injuring 9000 and killing 1900 people.

Newfoundland had the dubious honor of being the only place in North America directly attacked by German forces during WWII. In 1942, just offshore from Bell Island near St John's, German U-boats fired on four allied ore carriers, sinking them; 69 died. The Germans fired a torpedo at yet another carrier, but the projectile missed and instead struck inland at Bell Island's loading pier – thus making it the sole spot on the continent to take a straight-on German hit. That same year the Germans also torpedoed a Newfoundland ferry sailing in the Cabot Strait near Port aux Basques; 137 people died.

Antigonish hosts the longest-running Highland Games outside Scotland: they've been held every year since 1861, a testament to the town's strong Scottish roots.

Modern Times

It wasn't until 1960 that Canada's Indigenous people were finally granted Canadian citizenship. Even into the late 1960s, Indigenous children were being removed from their families and sent away to residential schools to

1997

The 12.9km Confederation Bridge linking PEI and New Brunswick opens at a cost of $1 billion.

1998

On September 2 Swissair Flight 111 crashes into the Atlantic Ocean in St Margaret's Bay, killing all 229 passengers.

2001

Cape Breton's last coal mine shuts down, paving the way for outward migration and the clean-up of Sydney Tar Ponds, Nova Scotia, North America's largest toxic-waste site.

2003

Hurricane Juan hits Halifax, passing through central Nova Scotia and Prince Edward Island leaving extensive destruction, eight fatalities and $30 million worth of damage.

Top History Museums

Canadian Museum of Immigration at Pier 21 (Halifax, Nova Scotia)

Maritime Museum of the Atlantic (Halifax, Nova Scotia

Fisheries Museum of the Atlantic (Lunenburg, Nova Scotia)

Alexander Graham Bell Museum (Baddeck, Cape Breton Island, Nova Scotia)

Black Loyalist Heritage Centre (Shelburne, Nova Scotia)

Kings Landing (Fredericton, New Brunswick)

'civilize' them; many were abused. Land-rights claims and settlements regarding the schools are still winding their way through Canadian courts, while the damage such policies inflicted continues to haunt the Indigenous communities.

Meanwhile, in Newfoundland in the 1950s, the provincial government also was enforcing a resettlement program. People living in isolated fishing communities (aka outports) were being strongly 'encouraged' to move inland where the government could deliver schools, health care and other services more economically. One method for encouraging villagers was to cut ferry services. Many communities had no road access so this effectively made them inaccessible.

The later 20th century was particularly harsh to the region's biggest industries: coal mining and fishing. Cape Breton's coal mines started to tank in the 1960s as its product fell out of favor in the marketplace; the mines shut for good in the 1990s. In 1992 a cod fishing moratorium was put in place, and many fisherfolk and fish-plant workers – a huge percentage of the population, especially in Newfoundland – lost their livelihoods. The offshore oil and tourism industries have been trying to pick up the slack, but many people are leaving the region to find work elsewhere in Canada.

Ironically, immigration to some parts of the Maritimes from overseas has picked up markedly – particularly Prince Edward Island, where a controversial law was introduced that granted immediate permanent residency to overseas residents who were looking to establish a business in the province, and could provide a refundable escrow deposit of $200,000. The initiative helped attract large numbers of applicants – in 2017, PEI was officially Canada's fastest-growing province – but was widely accused of being open to fraud, leading to formal investigations by Canada Border Services.

As in the rest of Canada, the COVID-19 pandemic in 2020 and 2021 caused havoc across all four of the Atlantic provinces, although case numbers and deaths were both statistically low (at the time of writing, Newfoundland and Labrador had the second-lowest death rate in the country).

Tragically, the pandemic was not the only event to rock the region in 2020. In April, a series of horrific shootings occurred in the seaside community of Portapique, 130km north of Halifax. Dressed as a police officer, the shooter went on a 13-hour killing spree that left 22 people dead and three injured, including an RCMP constable, before being shot dead by police. The attacks – the worst in Canadian history – prompted a public inquiry, which led to 1500 models of "military-grade assault-style" weapons being banned nationwide.

2005

Canada legalizes gay marriage. Most provinces and territories permitted it anyway, but now hold-out Prince Edward Island has joined the ranks.

2010

Civil rights activist Viola Desmond is granted a posthumous free pardon (the first in Canada), overturning a 64-year-old conviction for refusing to leave a whites-only area of a cinema in New Glasgow in 1946.

2018

In line with the rest of Canada, the four Maritime provinces legalize cannabis on October 17.

2020

Twenty-two people are killed in a tragic shooting spree in Nova Scotia, the deadliest such attack in Canadian history.

Maritimes Music

If Atlantic Canada were a bowl of chowder, music would be the stock in which everything floats. As a visitor you'll run into live performances everywhere, be they called ceilidhs (*kay*-lees), shindigs or kitchen parties. Even if you never gave fiddle music a second thought, the festive ambience will make you want to join in, sing along or tap your feet surreptitiously in time.

Indigenous

Indigenous cultures who populated the Atlantic coast for thousands of years are known to have sung, played music and danced, but details are few. Today, native music has been strongly influenced by the power of the fiddle. The most recent famous Mi'kmaw musician was Lee Cremo (1939–99), whose fiddle-playing talents mixing Mi'kmaw, Scottish and Irish music took him as far as Nashville and Hollywood. It's said that no one played quite like Lee, and he was ranked by many as one of the top 10 fiddle players of his time in North America.

The Mi'kmaw word that most roughly translates into the English word for music is *welta'q* which literally means 'it sounds good.' This is a broad definition that has come to encompass the poetry of Rita Joe (1932–2007), who is often referred to as the poet laureate of the Mi'kmaq people. Joe's poems are frequently set to music for school performances, but even as spoken word are considered to 'sound good' and thus be as agreeable and entertaining as a song. Over her lifetime, Joe published seven books of poetry which can be found online and in bookstores around Nova Scotia.

Your best chance of hearing traditional music is at one of several pow-wows held around the region; for modern indigenous sounds, head to music festivals that highlight the region's culture, such as Celtic Colours in Nova Scotia. One of the best acts is the Newfoundland band Tipatshimun, whose lyrics are in the Innu language.

What's On?

Nova Scotia: www.thecoast.ca

Newfoundland: www.thetelegram.com

New Brunswick: www.musicrunsthroughit.com

Prince Edward Island: www.buzzon.com

Scottish & Irish

Bagpipes wail mysteriously from a blustery hilltop and a lone fiddler serenades you at lunch. Yes, Scottish music is the dominant influence in the region, particularly in Nova Scotia and Prince Edward Island (PEI). Highland Scots who settled here didn't leave their fiddles at home, and the lively, fun piano-and-fiddle combos were quick to catch on. To this day, these folksy sounds define the Atlantic Canadian music scene. Most modern music produced from the music-heavy regions of Cape Breton Island and Halifax still sound quite a bit like the folk music of old, blending the fiddle with some electric guitar but still little percussion.

Popular Cape Breton musicians include fiddlers Ashley MacIsaac, Buddy MacMaster and Natalie MacMaster, and multi-instrumentalist JP Cormier. Banjo-strumming Old Man Luedecke, hailing from Chester, is often touring around the region in summer. And then there's the multi-generational Rankin family, hailing from Mabou, Cape Breton – they've been going since the 1970s, passing on their Celtic-tinged tunes down the generations.

They haven't released any new music in a while, but you can often hear one (or more) of the sisters play at their fantastic Red Shoe Pub in Mabou. Halifax has also produced a number of acts who've gained wider acclaim, including indie crooners Wintersleep, the electronica-tinged Jimmy Swift Band, hip-hop artist Buck 65 and alt-rockers Nap Eyes.

Bagpipes might not often be found in popular music but you will hear them in the area – a lot. Between the College of Piping & Celtic Arts in PEI and the Gaelic College of Celtic Arts & Crafts on Cape Breton, bagpipers are pumped out by the dozen to play at historical sites, busk along the streets of cities and create a mysterious air in some of the most out-of-the-way places, taking you away to the Scottish Highlands.

Up Newfoundland and Labrador way, expect to hear more Irish-tinged tunes that move at a faster pace and generally tell a story, with the dialogue dominating the accompaniment – if you've ever listened to the Pogues, you know what we're talking about. This music generally emanates from Irish pubs where accents start to lilt as more beer is consumed. Singer-songwriter Ron Hynes was a longstanding local favourite. He passed away in 2015, but his tunes remain pub staples. Also listen out for the gritty sound of the Navigators, known for their driving Celtic tunes. Bands who can still be seen touring the region include folk trio The Once and indie-popsters Repartee, both based in St John's, and rock-and-rollers the Novaks, with shades of Tom Petty. But the band that most successfully translates this music to a larger stage is Great Big Sea. They tour throughout the US and Canada, filling mighty venues with their Celtified rave-ups and kitchen-party enthusiasm. If they happen to be touring, they're a definite must-see.

Acadian

Men of the Deeps, a choral group of retired coal miners in Nova Scotia, can be found playing around the province and invariably pull a crowd.

The Acadians are scattered in small groups throughout Atlantic Canada and were often very remote and isolated before the modern advent of roads; Acadian music has therefore evolved in many different directions. Scottish influences are very apparent in areas such as Cape Breton, and as you move up the Cabot Trail from Mabou's Scottish fiddling to Chéticamp's Acadian kitchen parties, you'll be struck by how similar the sounds are. Generally, Acadian music is a little more soulful than Scottish music, with more percussion from tricky hand-clapping, foot-tapping and the spoons. The lyrics, of course, are in French.

CEILIDHS & KITCHEN PARTIES

What exactly is a ceilidh, you might ask. Well, in the broadest sense, a ceilidh is a gathering where traditional Gaelic music is played and people can dance – kind of like a rural, family-style disco with an accordion instead of heavy bass. Sometimes it's just a solo fiddle player playing during lunch hours at a restaurant; other times it can be families dressed in their full clan tartan performing for folks in town halls, or larger, more professional groups playing in front of big audiences. Whatever the size, ceilidhs are always laid-back affairs where the musicians mingle with the audience and hold no airs of being anything more than another local who just happens to play an instrument rather well. There are usually many more locals in the audience than visitors, and everyone goes crazy when, say, Cyril and Betty's seven-year-old son Timmy gets up and step dances – and you'll be into it, too, because chances are little Timmy is really, really good.

The terms ceilidh and kitchen party are often used interchangeably, but the latter is a term more likely to be used by Acadians (along with the Acadian French term: '*party de cuisine*'), non-Celtic folks or by anyone on Cape Breton Island in Nova Scotia. A kitchen party is also more likely to actually be at someone's house and to have food and drink, although this is not always the case.

FOLK & TRADITIONAL PLAYLIST

This playlist will get you in the mood for highland hills, long stretches of Atlantic coastline and perhaps a stop for some step dancing on the way. These old and new favorites are a little bit folk and a little bit country.

- *Guysborough Train*, Stan Rogers
- *The Silver Spear*, Natalie MacMaster
- *These Roads*, David Gunning
- *Rant and Roar*, Great Big Sea
- *Home I'll Be*, Rita MacNeil
- *Walk With Me*, Pogey
- *My Nova Scotia Home*, Hank Snow
- *Wrong Side of the Country*, Old Man Luedecke
- *Maritime Express*, Eddie LeGere
- *Maple Sugar*, Don Messer
- *Snow Bird*, Anne Murray
- *Sail Away to the Sea*, The Once

In southwestern Nova Scotia the local music is far more influenced by rock, bluegrass and country, as well as Cajun styles introduced by descendants of those caught up in the Great Expulsion. The most popular Acadian band today, Blou, is from this region, and they call their sound 'Acadico' – a mix of Acadian, Cajun and zydeco (American Creole folk music). The group's accordion-based rock tunes regularly win the East Coast Music Award title for Best Francophone recording of the year. Meanwhile, from the same region, Jacobus et Maleco, which eventually became Radio Radio, was the first Acadian rap group, and internationally renowned Grand Dérangement sings movingly of Acadian reality through its traditional tunes.

Many Acadian groups head to Montréal where there's a much stronger Francophone music scene and it's easier to get recognized. New Brunswick Acadian groups are often influenced by the traditional Québecois poetic style. Acts from Atlantic Canada that have made names for themselves include Marie-Jo Thério (soothing and lyrical from New Brunswick), Suroît (Cajun and fiddle from the Magdalen Islands), Borlico and Barachois (lively kitchen-party-style duo from PEI), and Felix and Formanger (an accordion-and-guitar group from Newfoundland).

African Influences

Many Black Canadians arrived as freed slaves and Loyalists to the British Crown during the American War of Independence. Social inequalities and marginalization (Nova Scotia's racism earned it the moniker 'Mississippi of the North') stopped the black community from making a huge mark in the Maritime music scene in the past, but nowadays it's adding a lot of spice to the region's music scene. The influence had been largely gospel music, but today hip-hop, jazz, blues, R&B, pop and classical music are all holding some cultural sway.

Portia White from Truro, Nova Scotia, was one of the first African-Canadians to make it big in the region when she won a silver cup at the Nova Scotia Music Festival in 1928 at the age of 17. She went on to become a powerful and well-known contralto classical vocalist and stage presence through the early '40s. Nova Scotian R&B musician Gary Beals placed second in the first season of *Canadian Idol,* and Faith Nolan, a

PARTYING AT THE PUB

Pubs are by far the best way to experience local music and, fortunately, finding a good one isn't difficult. With Halifax and St John's vying for the title of most pubs per capita, you'll actually have a harder time finding a nightspot that's not hosting a live gig. The following is a list of our favorites:

Red Shoe Pub (p100) Mabou, Cape Breton, Nova Scotia; folk and fiddle

Seahorse Tavern (p69) Halifax, Nova Scotia; indie, punk and metal

Benevolent Irish Society (p163) Charlottetown, PEI; Irish

Ship Pub (p195) St John's, Newfoundland; anything and everything

mixed-heritage African, Mik'maq and Irish jazz singer, songwriter and guitarist, has made music with powerful political statements.

Recent breakthrough artists include Reeny Smith and Keonté Beals, whose R&B-influenced sounds have scored them big audiences and major awards.

Top Music Festivals

Beyond pubs and concerts, Canada's Atlantic provinces swell with music festivals, especially during the summer. The following are the most renowned:

Stan Rogers Folk Festival (p112) Camp out in remote Canso for three days of live music from fine bluegrass and folk songwriters and performers.

Celtic Colours International Festival (p99) Watch the trees turn color in several Cape Breton locations while enjoying nine days of Celtic music from around the world.

Cavendish Beach Music Festival (www.cavendishbeachmusic.com; Cavendish Beach Events Centre, 8779 Rte 6; ⏲early Jul) Big names such as Taylor Swift make it to this five-day camp-out, which features a big stage and an audience that pours in from all around Canada and the US.

Halifax Pop Explosion (p63) Catch breaking acts at venues all over Halifax for this lively introduction to Atlantic Canada's contemporary music scene.

Deep Roots Festival (p91) Folk and roots music are highlighted at this weekend festival, which also includes music workshops.

Indian River Festival (p176) Classical, folk, jazz and world music resonate through the acoustically blessed St Mary's Church in Kensington.

Sound Symposium (☎709-754-1242; www.soundsymposium.com; tickets from $10; ⏲early Jul) Amazing diversity from jazz, world music and classical musicians; nine days and nights of artistic jamming in St John's.

Atlantic Canadian Art

Canada's Atlantic provinces attract artists like kids to cupcakes. That ever-present sea, the blend of blues and greens on the horizon, bucolic quiet and low cost of living make the region a prime place to swipe oil paints on canvas or whittle an old log into something astonishing. Indigenous Canadians have been taking nature's bounties, from porcupine quills to ash wood, and crafting them into beautiful daily objects for thousands of years.

Where to Find What

The Art Gallery of Nova Scotia has the largest collections with state-of-the-art galleries in both Halifax and Yarmouth. Here you'll find the stars: Alex Colville, Maud Lewis, Arthur Lismer and many more, as well as temporary shows of up and comers and renowned artists 'from away.' But there's an incredible richness to be discovered outside the museum as well. Drive around Cape Breton and it seems that every town has a shop selling arts and crafts, be that outrageous hats, forged iron sculptures, pottery or paintings hanging randomly from trees in a forest.

Other regions may not be so thickly dotted with artisans, but wherever you go, you'll find a plentiful array of creative folk turning out beautiful works. Drive slowly, ask about local artisans at visitor centers and browse small town galleries and craft shops. If you're looking to buy something special you'll be spoiled for choice.

Indigenous

Many of Canada's most ancient artistic artifacts hail from the eastern subarctic areas of the country including the Atlantic provinces. The tribes that lived here were nomadic and crafted elaborate headdresses with feathers, sewed patterns of beads and porcupine quills onto clothing, and wove patterns into their basketware. Art was something that embellished practical objects or was used for religious purposes. You'll find displays full of these works of refined design at museums large and small throughout the region.

It's been argued that art for art's sake wasn't a concept in indigenous culture until the 20th century. But even then, stereotypes of what indigenous art should look like (prehistoric) made it difficult for modern-day artists to have their works seen, appreciated or sold. Norval Morrisseau (1931–2017), an Ojibwa from Ontario, has been called the 'Grandfather of Canadian Native Art' for his paintings that capture Ojibwa cultural and spiritual images in a striking, colorful and modern style – his work is simply stunning. Morrisseau and several other artists began to make an impression on the art world through the late 1960s and the 1970s, paving the way for the future.

Today indigenous Canadian art is an incredibly rich terrain, and in the Eastern provinces inspiration is drawn mostly from Mi'kmaw and Maliseet cultures. Some standouts in this region include Ned Bear, who carves Pawakan (spirit guide) wooden masks and 'living trees' throughout New Brunswick. Alan Syliboy is one of the better-known artists in the

Artisan & Gallery Hot Spots

St Ann's Bay, Nova Scotia

Lunenburg, Nova Scotia

St Andrews By-The-Sea, New Brunswick

Fogo Island, Newfoundland

Twillingate Island, Newfoundland

Charlottetown, PEI

MAUD LEWIS

By far the most well-known and beloved folk artist in Nova Scotia is Maud Lewis. Born in 1903, she was uncommonly small, had almost no chin and suffered from juvenile rheumatoid arthritis. She spent much of her childhood alone and she never traveled beyond Yarmouth and Digby counties. After being left with no money once her parents died in the 1930s, she married Everett Lewis and the couple spent the rest of their lives in a roughly 12ft by 12ft house. But what a house it was! Lewis painted every surface with colorful, happy scenes of the life and community around her, making what many would have considered a place of poverty into a beautiful piece of beguiling art. She died in Digby in 1970, but continued to paint right up until the end.

In 1984, 14 years after Lewis passed away, the house was bought by the province of Nova Scotia as a landmark; it was restored in 1996. Since 2008 the entire house can be seen in the heart-wrenching Maud Lewis Room at the Art Gallery of Nova Scotia. Bring a hanky.

But Maud's artistic endeavors didn't end with her house. She began her career making Christmas cards as a child, and as an adult she was an incredibly prolific painter. The small, often 8in-by-10in paintings she sold out of her house back in the 1950s for $2 are now sold at auction for up to $22,000. Lewis, who never sold a painting for more than $10, would have hardly believed it.

In 2016 a moving biopic, *Maudie*, was released, starring Sally Hawkins in the title role, and Ethan Hawke as her fishmonger love interest.

region and paints scenes from Mi'kmaw mythology with a striking modern style; prints and note cards of David Brook's stylized animal paintings are found in many indigenous shops; Dozay Christmas specializes in dreamlike paintings of ghostly animals or people in monocolored natural settings; Ursula Johnson takes traditional basketry to new realms, including nonfunctional colorful pieces and incorporating techniques into performance art pieces; high-realism of the natural world is painted by Nova Scotian Leonard Paul; and in Newfoundland, Jerry Evans specializes in detailed lithographs.

Big Art Museums

Art Gallery of Nova Scotia, Halifax, Nova Scotia

Art Gallery of Nova Scotia, Yarmouth, Nova Scotia

The Rooms Provincial Art Gallery, St John's, Newfoundland

Beaverbrook Art Gallery, Fredericton, New Brunswick

Confederation Centre of the Arts, PEI

Folk Art

Back when roads were few and budgets were lean, many Canadians in these provinces had limited to no opportunities to visit art museums or learn about art beyond their local sphere. Folk art is the embodiment of what happens when artistic people create works without any influence from the outside world. Today the movement continues with its charming mix of simplicity and sophistication with avant-garde and tradition.

Painters include Joe Norris who depicted classic Maritime scenes from nesting ducks to sailboats in a simple colorful way; and Joseph Sleep who creates massive, childlike tableaux of animals and plants, using everything from cardboard to felt tip markers. The most famous painter, of course, was Maud Lewis (p250).

Folk art goes far beyond paint on paper, though. Well-known wood artists include Ralph Boutilier, known for his lifelike human-sized wood carvings and mechanical wooden birds; Sidney Howard, who made more rustic polychrome wood sculptures of people, fish, birds and animals; Bradford Naugler, who has carved life-size wood sculptures of the Ten Fathers of the Confederation, the Obama family and British royals William and Kate among others; and Collins Eisenhauer who is considered the master of appealing, stylized poultry sculptures.

Marine-Inspired Art

Nearly any artist who has spent time in these provinces could be slotted into this category for at least some of their work. And really, how can you paint, sculpt or get creative here without getting inspiration from

The Rooms, St John's (p185)

the surrounding sea that provides jobs, food, briny smells and a never-ending calming swish that rocks you to sleep?

Halifax native John O'Brien (1831–91) was one of the best-known artists of the region in his generation; he painted detailed, realistic seascapes that have greatly helped historians studying maritime history. Next came Edith Smith, who held the position of Arts Mistress at Halifax Ladies College for nearly 40 years; she was influential in many artists' education, the shaping of the first collections for the Art Gallery of Nova Scotia (AGNS), and most importantly for her masterful realist seascape, landscape and portrait paintings. One of the artists Edith Smith chose for the AGNS collections was Arthur Lismer, another Haligonian who first made his name painting WWI camouflaged naval ships in the harbor; he also sketched the Halifax Explosion of 1917. A few years later Lismer became a part of the 'Group of Seven,' a collaboration of the seven most revered nature artists at that time in Canada who were (contentiously) promoted as Canada's national school of painters.

ARTS FESTIVALS

Nova Scotia Folk Art Festival (Lunenburg; www.nsfolkartfestival.com; late Jul/early Aug) This fun, four-hour festival would be more aptly named the 'Folk Art Auction.' Entry ($5) to the auction includes the chance to win a lucky door prize.

Studio Rally (Nova Scotia; www.studiorally.ca; end Jul) For more than 20 years artists all over Nova Scotia have opened their doors to visitors on this special weekend.

Victoria Park Lantern Festival (St John's, Newfoundland; http://lanternfest.ca; last weekend of July) Public lantern-making workshops are held during this popular event that concludes with a lantern-lighting ceremony featuring music, dance and theatrical performances.

Other marine artists include HM Rosenberg, who was the principal at the Victoria School of Art and Design (now known as NSCAD University) in Halifax from 1898 to 1910. Rosenberg took a mix of European styles from Gauguin to Sargent to create his own realistic yet stylized approach that's universally appealing. Many of his works can be seen today in the permanent collection at the AGNS.

The Maritime Museum of the Atlantic's art collection focuses on ship-related marine works, but the AGNS has a substantial collection as well.

Art Trails & Resources

Halifax Art Map (www.halifax-artmap.com) An online guide to the city's art hot spots.

Cape Breton Centre for Craft & Design (www.capebretoncraft.com) Find out about makers and craftspeople to visit on the trail.

Arts & Heritage Trail (www.artsandheritagepei.com) Download the app for pointers to PEI's best artists and creatives.

Realism

The 20th century was dominated by the realists. Alex Colville, whose family moved to Amherst, Nova Scotia, from Toronto when he was nine years old, is Atlantic Canada's most famous artist. While Colville is known as a realist, many of his works are reminiscent of the American Precisionist movement of the 1930s and he was greatly influenced by the American realist Edward Hopper. There's a dreamy aspect to Colville's work that make the seemingly innocuous Canadian scenes he painted a shade darker, then they become more enigmatic the longer you examine them. Colville died peacefully at the age of 92 in 2013 in Wolfville, Nova Scotia.

Power artist couple Christopher and Mary Pratt met at Mount Allison University in Sackville, where they both studied under and were influenced by Alex Colville. While Christopher's stark, streamlined landscape pieces are nearly photographic in quality, Mary employed color and design more boldly in her still life, portrait and domestic scenes. Mary Pratt passed away in 2018, but Christopher's works still figure prominently in the Bay Roberts Heritage Society's art gallery (www.bayrobertsheritage.com).

Another student of Colville's, Tom Forrestall, has been called a magic realist, a moniker given to many East Coast Canadian artists after WWII. Forrestall's works are very Maritime in theme (think crab traps on wood docks and ice fields).

Newfoundland painter David Blackwood takes the magic a little further with starlit dark images of ghostly people or stormy sea vistas from the shore. In 2003 he was named Honorary Chairman of the Art Gallery of Ontario, although he still maintains a studio in Wesleyville, Newfoundland.

Landscapes & Wildlife

From unexplored wilderness to dramatic coastlines and phenomenal wildlife, the provinces of Atlantic Canada are a nature-lover's dream. It's a place where you are as likely to see thousands of seabirds resting on a passing iceberg as a moose crossing the road, and if you're lucky, you may spot feeding blue whales or a wandering polar bear in Newfoundland or Labrador.

A Geologist's Dream

For geologists this region hides great wealth, not just in rich ore deposits but in the record of earth history preserved by the rocks. Two significant geologic provinces converge here: Labrador forms the eastern rim of the vast Canadian Shield, the greatest exposure of ancient rocks on the earth's surface; while the other Atlantic provinces perch themselves at the northern tip of the Appalachian Mountains.

Above Moose, Cape Breton Island

Sitting at this great convergence, Atlantic Canada offers a snapshot of more than one billion years of earth history, from the red sandstone cliffs of Northumberland Strait to the granite headlands at Peggy's Cove, Nova Scotia. Even more fascinating are the many signs of the massive Pleistocene ice sheet that smothered the region with ice a mile deep as recently as 20,000 years ago: the fjords of the north, the rounded mounds of Nova Scotia (known as drumlins) and the tens of thousands of small shallow lakes.

At the Fundy Geological Museum, you can visit a lab where excavated dinosaur bones are being cleaned, catalogued and reassembled.

In its simplest form, the geological story is that Atlantic Canada formed from the fragments and pieces left over after North America and Africa collided and crushed an ocean between them 400 million years ago. In the collision, the two continents compressed and folded seafloor sediments into a giant mountain chain that has eroded over millions of years into what we now call the Appalachian Mountains. When North America and Africa went their separate ways 180 million years ago, they each left part of their coastline behind. This may be best observed in Newfoundland: its western third is a remnant of the ancestral North American coastline, its middle third is a slice of ancient seafloor, and its eastern third once belonged to northern Africa. Fossils buried in the coastline around the Bay of Fundy mostly date from the Carboniferous Era (sometimes called the Coal Age), around 300 million years ago.

Critters of the Great North

Whether you come for a glimpse of caribou, whales or moose, Atlantic Canada's wildlife is plentiful, if elusive. Many people travel to the region to see the incredible numbers of seabirds and whales that can be spotted from coastal bluffs or on whale-watching trips, and these sightings are certainly spectacular, though never guaranteed. Polar bears, however quintessentially Canadian they may be, are only present in the far north of this region.

The plants and animals of Atlantic Canada are even more amazing when you realize that the entire region was completely buried in ice only 20,000 years ago and was not suitable for life until about 10,000 years ago.

Animals

If you needed one single reason to visit Atlantic Canada, it's surely to see the whales that gather in these food-rich waters. Around 22 species of whale and porpoise can be seen on whale-watching tours, which are offered from countless coastal harbors. Leaping and diving humpback whales are most common throughout the region, but you might also catch a glimpse of the highly endangered North Atlantic right whale or even the largest leviathan of all, the blue whale.

Closer to shore or out on the ice, it's common to see seals, including the snowy white young of the harp seal in winter. Harbor and gray seals are easily observed, though in winter they seek out the edges of the pack ice.

FABULOUS FOSSILS

Kids will be especially intrigued by the region's fossils, many of which are on display in various parks and museums. They include fossil footprints, dinosaur bones and fossilized creatures that look like they're from outer space. Nova Scotia holds the most accessible fossil viewing at the Unesco-listed Joggins Fossil Cliffs (p94). More fossils are on show at the Fundy Geological Museum (p93) in nearby Parrsboro, and you can even search for fossils and semiprecious stones in the low-tide flats (but note that if you find any, you can't actually keep the fossils).

ATLANTIC CANADA'S TOP NATURAL AREAS

PARK	FEATURES	ACTIVITIES	BEST TIME TO VISIT
Nova Scotia			
Cape Chignecto Provincial Park	Largest and newest park in the province, rugged wilderness; old-growth forest, deer, moose, eagles	Hiking, backcountry camping	Jun-Oct
Kejimkujik National Park	Pristine wilderness, network of glacial lakes; otter, loon, bald eagles	Canoeing, camping, hiking	late Sep–early Oct
Cape Breton Highlands National Park	Dramatic oceanside cliffs, world-famous scenic drive; whales, bald eagles, seabirds, bear, moose, wild orchids	Hiking, camping, sightseeing, whale-watching	May-Oct
New Brunswick			
Fundy National Park	Sandstone cliffs, extensive beach, dramatic tides; bear, moose, beaver, peregrine falcons	Mountain biking, bird-watching, hiking	year-round
Kouchibouguac National Park	Lagoons, white-sand beaches; moose, deer, bear	Strolling, clam digging, cycling, skiing, kayaking, bird-watching	year-round
Prince Edward Island			
Prince Edward Island National Park	Red sandstone bluffs, dunes, beaches; red foxes, piping plover, sandpipers	Bird-watching, beach walking, swimming, picnicking	May-Sep
Newfoundland			
Cape St Mary's Ecological Reserve	Rugged ocean cliffs; one of the most accessible seabird colonies in North America, nesting gannets, whales	Bird-watching	Mar-Aug
Terra Nova National Park	Craggy cliffs, many sheltered inlets, lakes, bogs; moose, beaver, bald eagles, whales	Kayaking, fishing, camping	mid-May–mid-Oct
Witless Bay Ecological Reserve	Offshore islands, icebergs; more than one million breeding seabirds, feeding whales	Bird-watching, whale-watching	Jun-Aug

Land animals are also a powerful draw. Fox, bear and otter are widespread throughout the region. Rabbits are everywhere. On Newfoundland there are more than 100,000 moose and there are many more on Cape Breton Island. They do stick to the woods, however, so unless you're a hiker, the highest likelihood of seeing them is on the road – a very good reminder to drive slow (hitting a moose often does more damage to the car and driver than it does the moose).

As you travel north the animals become even more exotic. From Newfoundland north you will find polar bear, arctic fox, wolf, lynx and musk ox. Labrador has the largest herd of caribou in the world, as well as wolves that follow the long lines of migrating caribou.

The white hairs on a polar bear are hollow and trap sunlight to help keep the animal warm in frigid temperatures.

Birds

Seabirds are the primary wildlife attraction in Atlantic Canada. There are few places in North America where it's easier to see outstanding numbers of seabirds such as razorbill, Atlantic puffin, common murre

Northern gannets

and northern gannet. Huge nesting colonies on rocky islands and promontories may contain more than a million birds, but these merely hint at the numbers that once nested here before hunters slaughtered uncounted millions of birds.

Birds of Eastern Canada (2013) is a handy field guide to have in your pocket, with clear photos and descriptions that will help you identify sightings.

Mudflats and shorelines, especially along the Bay of Fundy, are famous for the tremendous quantities of shorebirds they attract during the May and August migration. Upwards of two million birds stop here annually. On nearby beaches, the endangered piping plover tries to hold its own against the trespass of invading sunbathers and beach walkers – please respect signs that warn you of this bird's home.

On Cape Breton Island and in Newfoundland and Labrador you're very likely to see bald eagles, Canada's largest bird of prey and the only eagle exclusive to North America. The birds can weigh up to 6.8kg (females are larger than males) and the wing span is around 2m. Besides their sheer size, you'll know them when you see them thanks to their distinctive white heads and brown bodies. Keep an eye out for their massive nests, often high in the trees along the coast, that weigh around 2 tons. In some coastal areas you may also see fish eagles (ospreys).

Fish

More than any other animal, fish have placed Atlantic Canada on the map, in particular the northern cod. With the collapse of the great cod fishery, other species such as halibut, mackerel, haddock and herring have grown in economic importance. In the region's many lakes and rivers, fishers seek out trout, bass, salmon and river herring (with the quaint name 'alewives'). And then, of course, there are lobsters galore – the Maritime provinces land more lobster than anywhere else in Canada, and export their crustaceans far and wide.

Insects & Other Creatures

Although it is easy to focus on the region's showiest animals, we cannot ignore the one that is smallest but not least in Atlantic Canada. It has been said that the diminutive black fly has single-handedly maintained the wild splendor of Labrador. This may sound like an exaggeration until you set foot onto the shore in midsummer and are blanketed in insects against which you are defenseless. Second only to the black fly are prolific mosquitoes. If it's any consolation, every animal from ant to moose is tormented equally by these creatures, so they're not picking on you.

But what can be most troubling to those unaccustomed to them are North American leeches (also called freshwater leeches or medicinal leeches) found in many fresh-water lakes, slow-moving streams and marshes. These 5cm long parasites usually spend their days chilling out under rocks or leaves in the cool, mucky bottoms, but water disturbances (such as a splash of diving in or stepping out into the water for a swim) are a bit akin to a dinner bell and out they swim looking for grub. While being a meal for a leech can be very disturbing, the bites are painless and the critters carry no diseases. If you do get bitten, you can opt either to let the leech eat its fill and drop off, or try to release its suction with a fingernail or sharp flat object before gently pulling it off. Salt or insect repellent can work to suffocate the leech.

Plants

Although Atlantic Canada presents some tree diversity in its southern reaches with a mix of birch, maple and ash, vast areas of forest are completely dominated by spruce as you head north. And at some point even those homogenous forests give way to soggy tundra that stretches to the Arctic. Surprisingly, the area can be rich with abundant wildflowers during the short growing season.

The yellow dandelion-like flowers of the coltsfoot may be the first ones to come out each spring, but far more attention is given to the region's delightful midsummer orchid displays, including showy lady's slipper, which may carpet entire boggy areas. Blue lupines seem to bloom everywhere, and many other varieties and colors can be found.

The most common shrubs, especially in Newfoundland and Labrador, are those in the heath family, including blueberries, cranberries and other delicious berries that grow in profusion in August. Wild roses bloom along the coasts from late June through August.

Perhaps the most curious plant is the odd lichen called caribou moss. Growing in such a dense spongy carpet that other plants cannot get a toehold, this pale greenish moss may be the most dominant plant in the northern forests. It is an important food source for caribou, hence its name, and is often mixed with seal meat to vary the diets of sled dogs.

THE GRAND BANKS

Banks are a funny name for a shallow area, but in the case of the Grand Banks off Newfoundland's southeast coast it's no laughing matter. Until recently this was considered the greatest site in the world for ocean fish and the animals that came to feed on them. Even today, with the fish nearly hunted out, millions of seabirds and uncounted whales come to feed in the rich waters. This area is incredibly productive because the continental shelf off the coast of Newfoundland sticks out like a thumb to intercept the south-flowing waters of the frigid Labrador Current right at the point where they mingle with the warm north-flowing waters of the Gulf Stream. The mix of warmth and nutrient-rich Arctic waters creates an explosion of plankton that feeds everything from the smallest fish to the biggest whale. And because the shallow waters allow sunlight to penetrate to the ocean floor, the food chain is active at all depths.

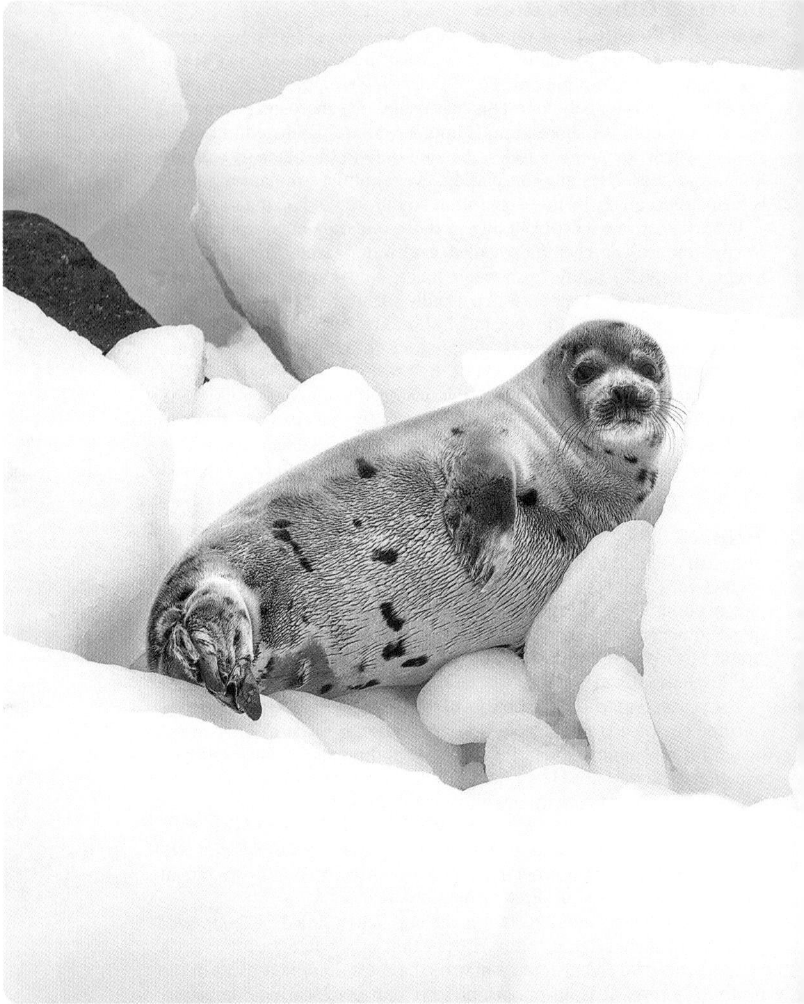

THREEROCKSIMAGES/SHUTTERSTOCK ©

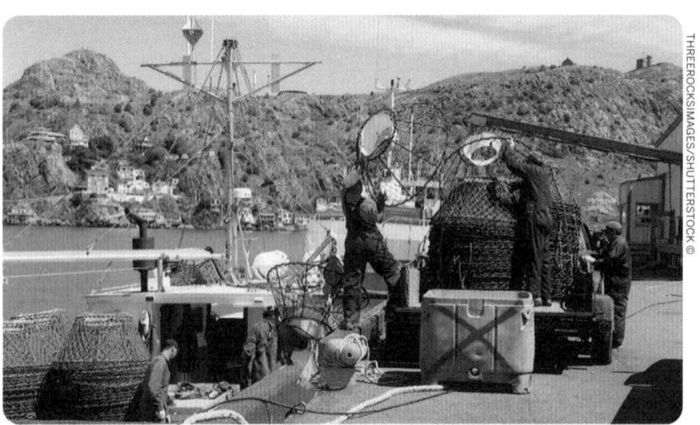

Top Harp seal

Bottom Crab pots, St John's Harbour

Environmental Issues

Early European explorers were dumbfounded by the apparently inexhaustible numbers of animals they encountered in Atlantic Canada. It was a scene of such incredible abundance that they thought it would never end, so they bent their will toward exploiting and profiting from the natural wealth in every way possible. The result is only too predictable and sad: animals lost forever include the mythical great auk, the Labrador duck and the sea mink. Today Atlantic Canada is facing the horrifying prospect that the greatest fishery in the world, the uncounted millions of cod that sustained their provincial livelihood for 400 years, may have come to an end when cod were listed as endangered in 2003.

Even with fishing limitations the recovery of stocks is hindered by the proliferation of species that cod and other predator fish once fed on, such as herring and snow crab, which eat fish eggs, making it even more difficult for the fish to make a comeback. In the end, not only has the environment suffered great damage, but so have the villages and traditions that needed the fish for their survival.

Recent studies have showed conflicting pictures of the current state of Atlantic cod stocks; populations seem to have recovered in some areas thanks to management and fishing moratoriums, but have declined markedly in others. At the time of writing, there is only one commercial cod fishery operating in Newfoundland, which is being closely monitored by the Marine Stewardship Council (www.msc.org); recent estimates tentatively suggest stocks may be showing signs of recovery, but

THE SEAL HUNT DEBATE

Canada's annual seal hunt, which occurs in March and April off Newfoundland's northeast coast and in the Gulf of St Lawrence around the Îles de la Madeleine and Prince Edward Island, is a topic of fierce debate around the world.

The debate pits animal-rights activists against sealers (typically local fishers who hunt in the off-season). The main issues revolve around the following questions:

Are baby seals being killed? Yes and no. Whitecoats are newborn harp seals, and these are the creatures that have been seen in horrifying images. But it has been illegal to hunt them for decades. After seals lose their white coats at 12 to 14 days old, they're considered fair game.

Are the animals killed humanely? Sealers say yes, that their guns and/or clubs kill the seals humanely. Animal activists dispute this, saying seals are injured and left on the ice to suffer until the sealers come back later and finish the job.

Is the seal population sustainable? The Canadian government says yes, and sets the yearly quota based on the total seal population in the area (estimated at 7.3 million). For 2018, some 60,000 harp seals were taken, despite market decline.

Is the seal hunt really an important part of the local economy? Activists say no, that it represents a fraction of Newfoundland's income. The province disagrees, saying for some sealers it represents up to one-third of their annual income. And in a province with unemployment near 16%, that's significant.

In 2009 the EU banned the sale of seal products, which hurt the industry considerably. For more on the two perspectives, see the Canadian Sealers Association (www.sealharvest.ca) or visit the Sealers Interpretation Centre (p206) in Elliston. For the other side's perspective, visit the website of the Humane Society of the United States (www.protectseals.org). With all that said, the topic of the seal hunt is a fairly settled matter in Newfoundland and Labrador itself. Locals, including many who would identify as progressive environmentalists, tend to consider the seal hunt an important element of a seasonal hunting and fishing cycle that has defined the cultural life of generations of Newfoundlanders.

Razorbills, Witless Bay Ecological Reserve (p198)

World Heritage Sites

Gros Morne National Park, Newfoundland

L'Anse aux Meadows National Historic Site, Newfoundland

Old Town Lunenburg, Nova Scotia

Joggins Fossil Cliffs, Nova Scotia

The Landscape of Grand Pré, Nova Scotia

it will be many years before cod fishing off Atlantic Canada returns to anything like its former scale.

Unfortunately, resource exploitation continues unabated on several other fronts. Some $3 billion a year is generated from logging, with half of the production coming from New Brunswick. Vast ore deposits are being explored and developed all the time, with huge areas stripped of their forest and soil cover to access coal, iron, nickel and other mineral resources.

The newest threat to the environment, yet a perk for jobs and suffering local economies, is hydraulic fracturing for natural gas exploration (often called fracking). The technique involves drilling into shale or coal-bed deposits and injecting a water and chemical fracking fluid filled with ceramic beads into the holes. The beads hold open the cracks allowing natural gas to rise to the surface and be collected. The environmental risks here are many, including a huge use of valuable fresh water and the risk of fracking chemicals leaking into the water table and ocean. Fracking rigs also emit large amounts of greenhouse gases into the atmosphere. What is particularly troubling is how much exploitation occurs in seldom-visited parts of Labrador, where there is little public scrutiny or attention.

MARC BRUXELLE/SHUTTERSTOCK ©

Survival Guide

Directory A–Z

Accessible Travel

Many public buildings, including museums, tourist offices, train stations, shopping malls and cinemas, have access ramps and/or lifts. Most public restrooms feature extra-wide stalls equipped with hand rails. Many pedestrian crossings have sloping curbs.

➡ Newer and recently remodeled hotels, especially chain hotels, have rooms with extra-wide doors and spacious bathrooms.

➡ Interpretive centers at national and provincial parks are usually accessible, and many parks have trails that can be navigated in wheelchairs.

➡ Car rental agencies offer hand-controlled vehicles and vans with wheelchair lifts at no additional charge, but you must reserve them well in advance.

➡ For accessible air, bus, rail and ferry transportation check Access to Travel (www.accesstotravel.gc.ca), the federal government's website. In general, most transportation agencies can accommodate people with disabilities if you make your needs known when booking. For more information, download Lonely Planet's free *Accessible Travel* guide from https://shop.lonelyplanet.com/categories/accessible-travel.com.

Accommodations

Book in advance during Atlantic Canada's short-lived tourist season, which runs from around June to September. Be mindful of the many summer festivals and events that always pull a crowd.

Amenities

➡ Most properties offer wi-fi. It's typically free in budget and midrange lodgings, while top-end hotels can sometimes still charge a fee, although this trend is diminishing.

➡ The majority of hotels and B&Bs properties are now smoke-free.

➡ Air-conditioning is not standard at most budget and midrange places. If you want it, be sure to ask about it when you book.

Discounts

➡ In winter prices can plummet by as much as 50%.

➡ Online booking websites are convenient, but it can often be as cheap (or cheaper) to book direct..

➡ Membership of the American Automobile Association (AAA), American Association of Retired Persons (AARP) or other organizations also yield modest savings (usually 10%).

B&Bs

➡ B&Bs are common in Atlantic Canada.

➡ BBCanada.com (www.bbcanada.com) is the main booking agency.

➡ In Canada, B&Bs (known as *gîtes* in French) are essentially converted private homes whose owners live on-site.

➡ Standards vary widely. The cheapest rooms tend to be small with few amenities and a shared bathroom. Nicer ones have added features such as a balcony, a fireplace and an en suite bathroom. Breakfast is nearly always included in the rates (though it might be continental instead of a full cooked affair).

➡ Not all B&Bs accept children.

➡ Minimum stays (usually two nights) are common, and many B&Bs are only open seasonally.

Camping

Canada's Maritime and Atlantic provinces are filled with campgrounds – some federal or provincial, others privately owned. Private campgrounds sometimes cater only to trailers (caravans) and recreational vehicles (RVs), and may feature convenience stores, playgrounds and swimming pools. It is a good idea to phone ahead to make sure the size of sites and the services provided at a particular campground are suitable for your vehicle.

Season Most campsites are open from May to September. Some remain open for maintenance year-round and may let you camp at a reduced rate in the off-season. Winter camping, though, is only for the hardy.

Facilities Vary widely. Backcountry sites offer little more than pit toilets and fire rings, and have no potable water. Unserviced (tent) campgrounds come with access to drinking water and a washroom with toilets and sometimes showers. The best-equipped sites feature flush toilets and hot showers and water, and electrical and sewer hookups for RVs. The most popular national parks usually have some permanent tents (called oTENTiks), cabins and even yurts: these swanky digs (by camping standards) are popular and sell out fast.

Fees In national and provincial parks fees range from about $25 to $35 for tents and up to $45 for full hookup sites per night; fire permits often cost a few dollars extra. Backcountry camping costs about $16 to $18 per night. Private campgrounds tend to be a bit pricier.

Availability A first-come, first-served basis is used at most government-run sites, which fill up quickly, especially in July and August. Many national parks now require online bookings at www.pccamping.ca.

SLEEPING PRICE RANGES

Prices listed here are for peak-season travel and, unless stated otherwise, do not include taxes (which can be up to 17%). If breakfast is included and/or a bathroom is shared, that information is included in the listing.

$ less than $100

$$ $100–250

$$$ more than $250

Homestays & Holiday Rentals

If you're content to stay in one place, renting a holiday home can be a good way of keeping costs down, especially for families. Most campgrounds offer self-catering cabins or lodges where you can get the camping-out vibe in relative comfort, or if you fancy something a little more luxurious, online listings can be found on all the usual homestay and short-term rental websites. Tourist offices usually also keep a list of self-catering places.

Hostels

Canada has independent hostels as well as those affiliated with Hostelling International (HI). All have dorms ($25 to $35 per person on average), which can sleep from two to 10 people, and many have private rooms (from $60) for couples and families. Rooms in HI hostels are generally gender segregated and the consumption of alcohol and smoking is prohibited; nonmembers pay a surcharge of about $4 per night.

Bathrooms are usually shared and facilities include a kitchen, lockers, internet access, laundry room and common TV room. Most hostels, especially those in big cities, are open 24 hours. If not, ask if you can make special arrangements if you're arriving late.

For additional information and online reservations, try Backpackers Hostels Canada (www.backpackers.ca) for independent hostels, or Hostelling International Canada (www.hihostels.ca).

Hotels & Motels

Most hotels are part of international chains, and the newer ones are designed for either the luxury market or business people. Rooms generally have cable TV and wi-fi, and other facilities may include swimming pools and fitness and business centers. Rooms with two double- or queen-sized beds sleep up to four people, although there is usually a small surcharge for the third and fourth person. Many places advertise that 'kids stay free,' but sometimes you have to pay extra for a crib or a rollaway (portable bed).

In Canada, like the US (both lands of the automobile), motels are ubiquitous. They dot the highways and cluster in groups on the outskirts of towns and cities. Although most motel rooms won't win any style awards, they're usually clean and comfortable and offer good value for travelers. Many regional motels remain your typical mom-and-pop operations, but plenty of North American chains have also opened up around the region.

University Accommodations

In the lecture-free summer months, some universities and colleges rent beds in their student dormitories to travelers of all ages. Most rooms are quite basic, but with rates ranging from $40 to $80 a night, often including breakfast, you know you're not getting the Ritz. Students usually qualify for small discounts.

Customs Regulations

The Canada Border Services Agency (www.cbsa.gc.ca) has the customs lowdown. A few regulations to note:

Alcohol You can bring in 1.5L of wine, 1.14L of liquor or 24 355mL beers duty-free.

Gifts You can bring in gifts totaling up to $60.

Money You can bring in/take out up to $10,000 cash; larger amounts must be reported to customs.

Personal effects Camping gear, sports equipment, cameras and laptop computers can be brought in without much trouble.

BOOK YOUR STAY ONLINE

For more accommodations reviews by Lonely Planet authors, check out www.lonelyplanet.com. You'll find independent reviews, as well as recommendations on the best places to stay. .

Declaring these to customs as you cross the border might save some hassle when you leave, especially if you'll be crossing the US-Canadian border multiple times.

Pets You must carry a signed and dated certificate from a veterinarian to prove your dog or cat has had a rabies shot in the past 36 months.

Prescription drugs You can bring in/take out a 90-day supply for personal use (though if you're bringing it to the USA, know it's technically illegal, but usually overlooked for individuals).

Tobacco You can bring in 200 cigarettes, 50 cigars, 200g of tobacco and 200 tobacco sticks duty-free.

Discount Cards

Discounts are commonly offered for seniors, children, families and people with disabilities, though no special cards are issued (you get the savings on-site when you pay). AAA and other automobile association members also receive various travel-related discounts. Many cities have discount cards for local attractions.

- **International Student Identity Card** (www.isic.org) Provides students with discounts on travel insurance and admission to museums and other sights. There are also cards for nonstudents under 26 and for full-time teachers.
- **Parks Canada Discovery Pass** (www.pc.gc.ca/en/voyage-travel/admission; adult/child/family $67.70/free/136.40) Provides access to nearly 100 national parks and historic sites around Canada for a year. Can pay for itself over daily entry fees in as few as seven visits; also provides quicker entry into sites, as you're allowed to bypass the ticket kiosks.

Embassies & Consulates

All countries have their embassies in Ottawa, although a few maintain consulates in Nova Scotia, New Brunswick and/or Newfoundland.

Food

The following price ranges refer to a main course.

$ less than $15

$$ $15–25

$$$ more than $25

Health

Before You Go

HEALTH INSURANCE

Canada offers some of the finest health care in the world. The problem is that, unless you are a Canadian citizen, it can be prohibitively expensive. It's essential to purchasetravel health insurance if your regular policy doesn't cover you when you're abroad. Check www.lonelyplanet.com/bookings for supplemental insurance information.

Bring medications you may need clearly labeled in their original containers.

A signed, dated letter from your physician that describes your medical conditions and medications, including generic names, is also a good idea.

Electricity

Type A
120V/60Hz

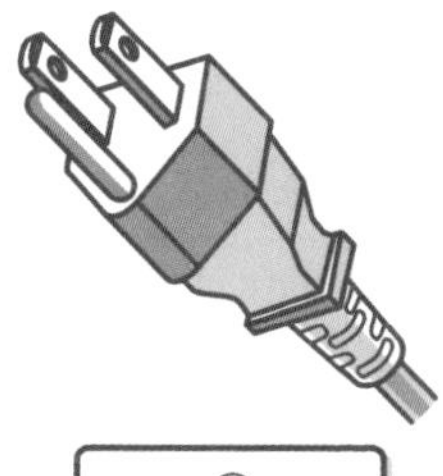

Type B
120V/60Hz

VACCINATIONS

No special vaccines are required or recommended for travel to Canada. All travelers should be up to date on routine immunizations.

MEDICAL CHECKLIST

- acetaminophen (eg Tylenol) or aspirin
- anti-inflammatory drugs (eg ibuprofen)

- antihistamines (for hay fever and allergic reactions)
- antibacterial ointment (eg Neosporin) for cuts and abrasions
- steroid cream or cortisone (for poison ivy and other allergic rashes)
- bandages, gauze, gauze rolls
- adhesive or paper tape
- safety pins, tweezers
- thermometer
- DEET-containing insect repellent for the skin
- permethrin-containing insect spray for clothing, tents and bed nets
- sunblock
- motion-sickness medication

COVID-19

At the time of writing, all travelers to Canada must have been double vaccinated, and provide proof of a negative result taken within 72 hours of your arrival date (or a previous positive test taken no less than 10 days and no more than 180 days prior).

All travelers are required to upload proof of vaccination via the ArriveCAN portal (available either as an iOS/ Android app, or online at https://arrivecan.cbsa-asfc.cloud-nuage.canada.ca/welcome). Once approved, you will receive a notification that you should present to border officials; be aware that you could also be selected for a test on arrival. All travelers should monitor themselves for symptoms for 14 days after arrival.

For the latest rules, see https://travel.gc.ca/travel-covid. For provincial advice, including on border restrictions and mask wearing, consult each province's COVID-19 response pages:

- https://novascotia.ca/coronavirus/travel/
- https://www.princeedwardisland.ca/en/topic/travel
- https://www2.gnb.ca/content/gnb/en/corporate/promo/covid-19/travel.html
- https://www.gov.nl.ca/covid-19/travel/arriving-in-newfoundland-and-labrador/travelling

In Canada

AVAILABILITY & COST OF HEALTH CARE

Medical services are widely available. For emergencies the best bet is to find the nearest hospital and go to its emergency room. If the problem isn't urgent, call a nearby hospital and ask for a referral to a local physician, which is usually cheaper than a trip to the emergency room (where costs can be $500 or so before any treatment).

Pharmacies are abundant, but prescriptions can be expensive without insurance. However, Americans may find Canadian prescription drugs to be cheaper than drugs at home. You're allowed to take out a 90-day supply for personal use (note that it's technically illegal to bring them into the USA, but usually overlooked for individuals).

ENVIRONMENTAL HAZARDS

Cold exposure This can be a significant problem, especially in the northern regions. Keep all body surfaces covered, including the head and neck. Watch out for the 'Umbles' – stumbles, mumbles, fumbles and grumbles – which are signs of impending hypothermia.

Heat exhaustion Dehydration is the main contributor. Symptoms include feeling weak, headache, nausea and sweaty skin. Lay the victim flat with their legs raised, apply cool, wet cloths to the skin, and rehydrate.

INFECTIOUS DISEASES

Most are acquired by mosquito or tick bites, or environmental exposure. The **Public Health Agency of Canada** (www.phac-aspc.gc.ca) has details on all listed here.

Giardiasis Intestinal infection. Avoid drinking directly from lakes, ponds, streams and rivers.

Lyme disease Occurs mostly in southern Canada. Transmitted by deer ticks in late spring and summer. Perform a tick check after you've been outdoors.

PRACTICALITIES

Newspapers The most widely available newspaper is the Toronto-based *Globe and Mail* (www.globeandmail.com). *Maclean's* (www.macleans.ca) is Canada's weekly news magazine. The Maritimes' regional principal dailies are the *Chronicle Herald* (www.chronicleherald.ca) in Halifax, the *Guardian* (www.theguardian.pe.ca) in Charlottetown, the *New Brunswick Telegraph-Journal* (www.telegraphjournal.com) in Saint John and the *Telegram* (www.thetelegram.com) in St John's.

Smoking Banned in all restaurants, bars and other public venues nationwide. The majority of hotels and B&Bs are also smoke-free.

Television The Canadian Broadcasting Corporation (CBC) is the dominant nationwide network for both radio and TV. CTV Atlantic is the major competition.

Weights & measures Officially Canada uses the metric system, but imperial measurements are common for many day-to-day purposes.

West Nile virus Mosquito-transmitted in late summer and early fall. Prevent by keeping covered (wear long sleeves, long pants, hats, and shoes rather than sandals) and apply a good insect repellent, preferably one containing DEET, to exposed skin and clothing.

TAP WATER

Tap water in Canada is safe to drink.

Insurance

Make sure you have adequate travel insurance, whatever the length of your trip. At a minimum, you need coverage for medical emergencies and treatment, including hospital stays and an emergency flight home. Some policies specifically exclude 'dangerous activities' such as skiing or even hiking. Make sure to check the fine print if you plan on doing any outdoor activities. Medical treatment for non-Canadians is very expensive.

Also consider insurance for luggage theft or loss. If you already have a homeowners' or renters' policy, check what it will cover and only get supplemental insurance to protect against the rest. If you have prepaid a large portion of your vacation, trip cancellation insurance is worthwhile.

Internet Access

Wi-fi is widely available throughout Atlantic Canada and free public wi-fi hot spots are becoming increasingly prevalent. Hotels, restaurants, cafes, bars and libraries, as well as tourist information centers, all generally offer free wi-fi.

Legal Matters

Drugs & Alcohol

The blood-alcohol limit is 0.08% and driving cars, motorcycles, boats and snowmobiles while drunk is a criminal offense. If you are caught, you may face stiff fines, license suspension and other nasty consequences.

Consuming alcohol anywhere other than at a residence or licensed premises is also a no-no, which puts parks, beaches and the rest of the great outdoors off limits, at least officially.

In October 2018, recreational marijuana was legalized in Canada, but the way the legislation is implemented is different for every province and territory. There are a few common rules to take note of, however: you need to be 19 to buy it; it's generally illegal to consume cannabis in public places; it's illegal to drive under the influence; and there's a 30g limit on how much you can carry on your person at any time.

All other drugs remain illegal: penalties if you get caught may entail heavy fines, possible jail time, deportation and a criminal record.

Police

If you're arrested or charged with an offense, you have the right to keep your mouth shut and to hire any lawyer you wish (contact your embassy for a referral, if necessary). If you cannot afford one, be sure to ask to be represented by public counsel. There is a presumption of innocence.

LGBTIQ+ Travelers

Canada is one of the most LGBTIQ+-friendly countries on the planet, although you might still come across uncommon pockets of prejudice in rural areas. In 2005 Canada became the fourth country in the world to legalize same-sex marriage.

Halifax is by far this region's gayest city, with a humming nightlife scene, publications and lots of associations and support groups. It has a sizable Pride celebration, too, which attracts big crowds. While very low-key, Prince Edward Island also has a decent-sized gay population and has a small pride event in July.

Resources

The following are good resources for LGBTIQ+ travelers; they include Canadian information, though not all are exclusive to the region.

Canadian Government (https://travel.gc.ca/travelling/health-safety/lgbt-travel)

Gay Canada (www.gaycanada.com) Search by province or city for queer-friendly businesses and resources.

Purple Roofs (www.purpleroofs.com) Website listing queer accommodations, travel agencies and tours worldwide.

Xtra (www.xtra.ca) Source for gay and lesbian news nationwide.

CANNABIS BY PROVINCE

New Brunswick The legal retailer is Cannabis NB (www.cannabis-nb.com), which has outlets in cities and sizable towns.

Newfoundland & Labrador Twenty licensed retailers across the province, from St John's to Labrador City.

Nova Scotia Sold through authorized NSLC (www.mynslc.com) stores, including Halifax's cannabis-only NSLC Clyde St (p69).

Prince Edward Island Four PEI Cannabis (www.peicannabiscorp.com) retail stores are located in Charlottetown, Summerside, O'Leary and Montague.

Maps

Most tourist offices distribute free provincial road maps.

For extended hikes or multiday backcountry treks, it's a good idea to carry a topographic map. The best are the series of 1:50,000 scale maps published by the government's Centre for Topographic Information. These are sold by map dealers across the country. For details, see www.nrcan.gc.ca/earth-sciences/geography/topographic-information.

Money

Canadian coins come in 5¢ (nickel), 10¢ (dime), 25¢ (quarter), $1 (loonie) and $2 (toonie) denominations. The gold-colored loonie features the loon, a common Canadian waterfowl, while the two-toned toonie is decorated with a polar bear.

Canada has a full series of plastic/polymer notes in circulation. The currency comes in $5 (blue), $10 (purple), $20 (green) $50 (red) and $100 (gold) denominations.

In larger cities, currency exchange offices may offer better rates than banks.

ATMs

Many grocery and convenience stores, airports, and bus, train and ferry stations have ATMs. Most are linked to international networks, the most common being Cirrus, Plus, Star and Maestro. The exchange rate tends not to be very favorable, and you may be charged transaction fees on top. Most ATMs also spit out cash with a major credit card, but service fees are very high.

Visitors heading to more remote regions (such as Newfoundland) won't find an abundance of ATMs, so it is wise to cash up beforehand.

Scotiabank, common throughout Canada, is part of the Global ATM Alliance. If your home bank is a member, fees may be less if you withdraw from Scotiabank ATMs.

TIPPING

Tipping is standard practice in Canada, as it is across North America. Generally accepted rates are as follows:

Bar staff $1 per drink

Hotel bellhop $1 to $2 per bag

Hotel room cleaners $2 per day

Restaurant waitstaff 15% to 20%

Taxis 10% to 15%

Cash

Most Canadians don't carry large amounts of cash for everyday use, relying instead on credit and debit cards. Still, carrying some cash, say $100 or less, comes in handy when making small purchases. In some cases, cash is necessary to pay for rural B&Bs and shuttle vans; inquire in advance to avoid surprises. Note that shops and businesses rarely accept personal checks.

Credit Cards

Major credit cards such as MasterCard, Visa and American Express are widely accepted in Canada, except in remote, rural communities where cash is king. You'll find it hard or impossible to rent a car, book a room or order tickets over the phone without having a piece of plastic. Note that some credit-card companies charge a transaction fee (which is around 3% of whatever you purchased); ensure you check with your provider to avoid surprises.

Taxes & Refunds

Canada's federal goods and services tax (GST), variously known as the 'gouge and screw' or 'grab and steal' tax, adds 5% to just about every transaction. Most provinces also charge a provincial sales tax (PST) on top of it. Taken together, they are known as the Harmonized Sales Tax (HST), which currently stands at 15%.

You might be eligible for a rebate on some of the taxes. If you've booked your accommodation in conjunction with a rental car, plane ticket or other service (ie if it all appears on the same bill from a 'tour operator'), you should be eligible to get 50% of the tax refunded from your accommodation. Fill out the GST/HST Refund Application for Tour Packages form available from the Canada Revenue Agency at www.cra-arc.gc.ca/E/pbg/gf/gst115.

Opening Hours

The following list provides standard opening hours for high-season operating times.

Banks 10am to 5pm Monday to Friday; some open 9am to noon Saturday.

Bars 5pm to 2am.

Clubs 9pm to 2am Wednesday to Saturday.

Museums 10am to 5pm; may close on Monday.

Restaurants 8am to 11am and 11:30am to 2:30pm Monday to Friday, 5pm to 9:30pm daily; some open 8am to 1pm weekends.

Shops 10am to 6pm Monday to Saturday, noon to 5pm Sunday.

Supermarkets 9am to 8pm; some open 24 hours.

Post

Canada's national postal service, Canada Post/Postes Canada (www.canadapost.ca), is neither quick nor cheap, but it is reliable. Stamps are available at post offices, drugstores, convenience stores and hotels. Many Shopper's Drug Mart branded pharmacies have Canada Post agencies in the rear of the store, though the counters do not always have the same opening hours as the pharmacies themselves.

Postcards or standard letters cost $1.05 within Canada, $1.27 to the USA and $2.65 to all other countries. Travelers often find they have to pay high duties on items sent to them while in Canada, so beware.

Public Holidays

Canada observes 10 national public holidays and more at the provincial level. Banks, schools and government offices close on these days.

National Holidays

New Year's Day January 1

Good Friday March or April

Easter Monday March or April

Victoria Day Monday before May 25

Canada Day July 1; called Memorial Day in Newfoundland

Labour Day First Monday of September

Thanksgiving Second Monday of October

Remembrance Day November 11

Christmas Day December 25

Boxing Day December 26

Provincial Holidays

Some provinces also observe local holidays, with Newfoundland leading the pack.

St Patrick's Day Monday nearest March 17

St George's Day Monday nearest April 23

National Day Monday nearest June 24 in Newfoundland

Orangemen's Day Monday nearest July 12 in Newfoundland

Civic Holiday First Monday of August everywhere *except* Newfoundland and PEI

School Holidays

Children have summer holidays from late June to early September. University students get even more time off, usually May to early/mid-September. Most people take their big annual vacation during these months.

Safe Travel

Atlantic Canada is generally an extremely safe place to visit. There is a general sense of mutual respect where members of communities look out for each other.

➡ There are small pockets of illicit drug use and the crime it attracts, but hard drugs don't have a place here and the majority of violent crimes are fuelled by alcohol.

➡ There are no venomous snakes or spiders, but you might come across the odd bear or moose. If you do, it pays to know what to do: get up to speed at https://www.pc.gc.ca/en/docs/v-g/oursnoir-blackbear.

➡ Blackflies and mosquitoes can be a major annoyance in the summer. Bring insect repellent and clothing to cover up, especially in northern, woodsy regions.

➡ In winter, exercise caution when driving and always be sure to have enough warm clothes, food and fuel.

Telephone

Canada's phone system is almost identical to the US system.

UNIQUELY CANADIAN CELEBRATIONS

National Flag Day (February 15) Commemorates the first time the maple-leaf flag was raised above Parliament Hill in Ottawa, at the stroke of noon on February 15, 1965.

Victoria Day (late May) This day was established in 1845 to observe the birthday of Queen Victoria and now celebrates the birthday of the British sovereign who's still Canada's titular head of state. Victoria Day marks the official beginning of the summer season (which ends with Labour Day on the first Monday of September). Some communities hold fireworks.

National Aboriginal Day (June 21) Created in 1996, it celebrates the contributions of Indigenous peoples to Canada. Coinciding with the summer solstice, festivities are organized locally and may include traditional dancing, singing and drumming, storytelling, arts and crafts shows, canoe races and lots more.

Canada Day (July 1) Known as Dominion Day until 1982, Canada Day was created in 1869 to commemorate the creation of Canada two years earlier. All over the country, people celebrate with barbecues, parades, concerts and fireworks.

Thanksgiving Day (mid-October) First celebrated in 1578 in what is now Newfoundland by explorer Martin Frobisher to give thanks for surviving his Atlantic crossing, Thanksgiving became an official Canadian holiday in 1872 to celebrate the recovery of the Prince of Wales from a long illness. These days, it's essentially a harvest festival involving a special family dinner of roast turkey and pumpkin, very much as it is practiced in the US.

Cell Phones

Local SIM cards can be used in unlocked GSM 850/1900 compatible phones.

If you have an unlocked GSM phone, you should be able to buy a SIM card from local providers such as Telus, Rogers or Bell. Bell has the best data coverage, though reception can be poor in rural areas, regardless of your carrier.

US residents can often upgrade their domestic cell phone plan to extend to Canada. Verizon provides good results.

Domestic & International Dialing

Canadian phone numbers consist of a three-digit area code followed by a seven-digit local number. In many parts of Canada you must dial all 10 digits preceded by 1, even if you're calling across the street. In other parts of the country, when you're calling within the same area code, you can dial the seven-digit number only, but this is slowly changing. The pay phone or phone book where you are should make it clear which system is used.

For direct international calls, dial 011 + country code + area code + local phone number. The country code for Canada is 1 (which is the same as for the USA, although international rates still apply for all calls made between the two countries).

Toll-free numbers begin with 800, 877 or 866 and must be preceded by 1. Some of these numbers are good throughout Canada and the USA, others only work within Canada, and some work in just one province.

Phone Cards

Prepaid phonecards usually offer the best per-minute rates for long-distance and international calling. They come in denominations of $5, $10 and $20 and are widely sold in drugstores, supermarkets and convenience stores. Beware of cards with hidden charges such as 'activation fees' or a per-call connection fee. A surcharge ranging from 30¢ to 85¢ for calls made from public pay phones is common.

Time

Canada spans six of the world's 24 time zones. The Eastern zone in Newfoundland is unusual in that it's only 30 minutes different from the adjacent zone. The time difference from coast to coast is 4½ hours.

Canada observes daylight saving time, which comes into effect on the second Sunday in March, when clocks are put forward one hour, and ends on the first Sunday in November.

In Francophone areas, times are usually indicated by the 24-hour clock.

Time difference between cities

Halifax, Fredericton & Charlottetown	7pm
London	11pm
New York City, Toronto & Montréal	6pm
Newfoundland	7:30pm
Vancouver	3pm

Tourist Information

The Canadian Tourism Commission (www.canada.travel) is loaded with general information, packages and links.

All provincial tourist offices maintain comprehensive websites with information helpful in planning your trip. Staff also field telephone inquiries and, upon request, will mail out free maps and directories about accommodations, attractions and events. Some offices can also help with making hotel, tour or other reservations.

For detailed information about a specific area, contact the local tourist office, aka visitor center. Just about every city and town has at least a seasonal branch with helpful staff, racks of free pamphlets and books and maps for sale.

Provincial tourist offices:

Borden-Carleton Visitor Information Centre (902-437-8570; Hwy 1; 8:30am-8pm)

Newfoundland & Labrador Tourism (800-563-6353; www.newfoundlandlabrador.com)

Tourism New Brunswick (800-561-0123; www.tourismnewbrunswick.ca)

Tourism Nova Scotia (800-565-0000; www.novascotia.com)

Visas

With the exception of US nationals, all visitors to Canada require either an electronic travel authorization (eTA; visa-waiver) or a formal visa.

Visa Requirements

Currently, visas are not required for citizens of 46 countries – including most EU members, Australia and New Zealand – for visits of up to six months.

To find out if are required to apply for a formal visa, go to www.cic.gc.ca/english/visit/visas.asp.

Visitor visas – aka Temporary Resident Visas (TRVs) – can be applied for online at www.cic.gc.ca/english/information/applications/visa.asp. Single-entry TRVs ($100) are usually valid for a maximum stay of six months from the date of your arrival in Canada.

A separate visa is required for all nationalities if you plan to study or work in Canada.

Visiting the USA

Admission requirements are subject to frequent change. The US State Department (http://travel.state.gov) has the latest information, or check with a US consulate in your home country.

Under the US visa-waiver program, visas are not required for citizens of 38 countries – including most EU members, Australia and New Zealand – for visits of up to 90 days (no extensions allowed), as long as you can present a machine-readable passport (e-Passport) and are approved under the Electronic System for Travel Authorization (www.cbp.gov/esta). Note you must register at least 72 hours before arrival and there's a US$14 fee for processing and authorization.

All visitors, regardless of their country of origin, are subject to a US$6 entry fee at land border crossings. Note that you don't need a Canadian multiple-entry TRV for repeated entries into Canada from the USA, unless you have visited a third country.

Volunteering

Volunteering provides the opportunity to interact with local folks and the land in ways you never would just passing through. Many organizations charge a fee, which varies depending on the program's length and the type of food and lodging it provides. The fees usually do not cover travel to Canada. Groups that take volunteers include:

Churchill Northern Studies Centre (www.churchillscience.ca) Volunteer for six hours per day (anything from stringing wires to cleaning) and get free room and board at this center for polar bear and other wildlife research.

New Brunswick Association for Community Living (www.nbacl.nb.ca) Nonprofit facilitating volunteer placements in various areas of NB.

Volunteer Nova Scotia (www.volunteerns.ca) Volunteering opportunities across NS.

Volunteer PEI (www.princeedwardisland.ca/en/topic/volunteer-opportunities) Official volunteer advice from the PEI government.

Women Travelers

Canada is generally a safe place for women to travel, even alone and in the cities. Simply use the same common sense as you would at home.

In bars and nightclubs, solo women are likely to attract a lot of attention, but if you don't want company, most men will respect a firm 'no thank you.' If you feel threatened, protesting loudly will often make the offender slink away – or will at least spur other people to come to your defense. Note that carrying mace or pepper spray is illegal in Canada.

Physical attack is unlikely, but if you are assaulted, call the police immediately or contact a rape crisis center. A complete list is available from the **Canadian Association of Sexual Assault Centres** (☎604-876-2622; www.casac.ca).

Her Own Way (www.travel.gc.ca/travelling/publications/her-own-way) is published by the Canadian government for Canadian travelers, but contains a great deal of general advice.

Work

Finding Work

Students aged 18 to 30 from over a dozen countries, including the US, UK, Australia, New Zealand, Ireland and South Africa, are eligible to apply for a spot in the Student Work Abroad Program (www.swap.ca). If successful, you get a six-month to one-year, non-extendable visa that allows you to work anywhere in Canada in any job you can get.

Even if you're not a student, you may be able to spend up to a year in Canada on a working-holiday program with International Experience Canada (www.canada.ca/en/immigration-refugees-citizenship/services/work-canada/iec.html). The Canadian government has an arrangement with several countries for people aged 18 to 30 to come over and get a job; check the website for participants. The Canadian embassy in each country runs the program, but basically there are quotas and spaces are filled on a first-come, first-served basis.

Permits

In almost all cases, you need a valid work permit to work in Canada. Obtaining one may be difficult, as employment opportunities go to Canadians first. Before you can even apply, you need a specific job offer from an employer who in turn must have been granted permission from the government to give the position to a foreign national. Applications must be filed at a visa office of a Canadian embassy or consulate in your home country. Some jobs are exempt from the permit requirement. For full details, check with Citizenship & Immigration Canada (www.cic.gc.ca).

RESPONSIBLE TRAVEL

Overtourism is a problem in many of the region's most popular areas, such as Peggy's Cove, Lunenburg and along the Cabot Trail: you can help ease pressures by visiting outside the busy summer months, and exploring less frequented areas. Public transport is limited, which means nearly everyone explores by car. Electric vehicles and charging points are a rarity; if you do drive, select the most fuel efficient vehicle you can, and travel with as many people as possible to reduce your carbon footprint.

Equally important, especially in national and provincial parks, is the idea of Leave No Trace (www.leavenotrace.ca): stick to established trails, respect wildlife, camp responsibly, and take nothing home except your own waste.

Transportation

GETTING THERE & AWAY

Entering the Region

Visitors to Canada must hold a valid passport with at least six months remaining before its expiration. Visitors from visa-exempt countries (with the exception of the US) are required to purchase an electronic travel authorization (eTA; $7; see the 'Electronic Travel Authorization (eTA)' section at www.canada.ca), similar to the USA's ESTA visa-waiver, before departing their home country. It's all done online, so the process is fairly streamlined.

Visitors from non-visa waiver countries must apply for the appropriate visa, prior to arriving in Canada.

Many of Canada's larger airports are transitioning to automated passport gates; you'll need your passport and eTA documents to hand when you use one. If you can't use the automated gates, you'll be directed to a border officer, who will ask you a few questions about the purpose and length of your visit. Questioning may be more intense at land border crossings and your car may be searched. Once the immigration officer has verified your passport, eTA/ visa and travel plans, you'll go through customs.

For updates (particularly regarding land border crossing rules), check the websites for the US State Department (http://travel.state.gov) and Citizenship & Immigration Canada (www.cic.gc.ca).

Having a criminal record of any kind, including any drunk-driving related charges, may keep you out of Canada. If this affects you, be sure to contact the Canadian embassy or consulate in your home country.

Passports

All international visitors, with the exception of travelers from the US, require a passport to enter Canada.

Visitors from the US require a valid US passport, passport card, enhanced drivers license or NEXUS card to enter Canada at a land or sea border crossing. However, when traveling by air to/from Canada, US citizens are required to present a US passport or NEXUS card only.

Air

Airports

While Halifax has the region's largest airport, with direct flights to major US, Canadian and European cities, Moncton is also busy and may offer lower fares than Halifax. Often cheaper fares connect through another Canadian or US hub airport: watch out for long layovers.

PEI's airport in Charlottetown also has direct connections to Canadian cities including Halifax, Montréal, Ottawa and Toronto (mostly with Air Canada).

For visitors heading to Newfoundland, Deer Lake is a great option if you are centering your travels on the west coast.

Main airports:

Charlottetown, Prince Edward Island (YYG; ☎902-566-7997; www.flypei.com; 250 Maple Hills Ave)

Deer Lake, Newfoundland (YDF; ☎709-635-3601; www.deerlakeairport.com; 1 Airport Rd; Wi-Fi)

Fredericton, New Brunswick (YFC; ☎506-460-0920; www.frederictonairport.ca)

Halifax, Nova Scotia (YHZ; ☎902-873-4422; www.hiaa.ca; 1 Bell Blvd)

Moncton, New Brunswick (YQM; ☎506-856-5444; www.gmia.ca)

St John's, Newfoundland (YYT; ☎709-758-8500; www.stjohnsairport.com; 100 World Pkwy; Wi-Fi)

Sydney, Nova Scotia (www.sydneyairport.ca)

Airlines

The majority of flights are via the national flagship carrier Air Canada or the discount airline WestJet. Major US airlines also serve Atlantic Canada.

CLIMATE CHANGE & TRAVEL

Every form of transport that relies on carbon-based fuel generates CO_2, the main cause of human-induced climate change. Modern travel is dependent on airplanes, which might use less fuel per kilometer per person than most cars but travel much greater distances. The altitude at which aircraft emit gases (including CO_2) and particles also contributes to their climate change impact. Many websites offer 'carbon calculators' that allow people to estimate the carbon emissions generated by their journey and, for those who wish to do so, to offset the impact of the greenhouse gases emitted with contributions to portfolios of climate-friendly initiatives throughout the world. Lonely Planet offsets the carbon footprint of all staff and author travel.

Airlines operating to/from the region include:

Air Canada (AC;888-247-2262; www.aircanada.com)

Air St-Pierre (PJ;877-277-7765; www.airsaintpierre.com)

Air Transat (TS;877-872-6728; www.airtransat.com)

American Airlines (AA;800-433-7300; www.aa.com)

Delta (DL;800-241-4141; www.delta.com)

Porter Airlines (PD;888-619-8622; www.flyporter.com)

Provincial Airlines (SPR; 800-563-2800; www.palairlines.ca)

United Airlines (UA;800-241-6522; www.united.com)

WestJet (WS;888-937-8538; www.westjet.com)

Land

There are three major border crossings between New Brunswick, Canada, and Maine, USA: Calais–St Stephen, Madawaska–Edmundston, and Houlton–Woodstock. The Canadian Border Services Agency (www.cbsa-asfc.gc.ca) website has details on estimated wait times. In general, waits rarely exceed 30 minutes, except during the peak summer season and holidays.

When returning to the US, check the website for the US Department for Homeland Security (http://apps.cbp.gov/bwt) for border wait times.

Bus

Maritime Bus (800-575-1807; www.maritimebus.com) plies the roads from Saint John (New Brunswick), as far as Rivière-du-Loup (Québec), up through Charlottetown (PEI) and to Nova Scotia as far as Halifax and up to Cape Breton Island to North Sydney (for ferry connections to Newfoundland). From Rivière-du-Loup, you can connect onto the **Orléans Express** (833-449-6444; www.orleansexpress.com) to head further afield into Québec. The changeover is pretty seamless.

Car & Motorcycle

The US's extensive highway network connects directly with the Canadian system at numerous key points along the border. These Canadian highways then go on to meet up with the east–west Trans-Canada Hwy, an excellent way to traverse the country.

If you're driving into Canada, you'll need the vehicle's registration papers, proof of liability insurance and your home driver's license. Cars rented in the US usually can be driven into Canada and back, but make sure your rental agreement says so. If you're driving a car registered in someone else's name, bring a letter from the owner authorizing use of the vehicle in Canada.

Train

VIA Rail (888-842-7733; www.viarail.ca), Canada's national rail line, offers one service to the Atlantic region: a Montréal to Halifax overnight train (advance purchase $223, 22 hours, one daily except Tuesday) that includes several stops in New Brunswick and Nova Scotia. It leaves Montréal at 7pm, and arrives in Halifax at 5:51pm the next day.

Visitors coming from the USA can hop aboard America's national rail line, Amtrak (www.amtrak.com), which has daily service connecting New York City and Montréal.

Sea

Various (although dwindling) ferry routes connect Atlantic Canada to the US and the French territory of St Pierre and Miquelon:

New Brunswick East Coast Ferries (www.eastcoastferriesltd.com) links Deer Island to Campobello Island, which lies just east of the US-Canada border at Lubec.

Newfoundland (www.spm-ferries.fr) Links the Burin Peninsula to the French territory of St Pierre and Miquelon.

Nova Scotia (www.ferries.ca) Links Yarmouth and Portland, Maine.

GETTING AROUND

Air

Most regional flights within the Maritimes are operated by Air Canada. Small provincial airlines fly out to the more remote portions of the region. Fares in such noncompetitive markets can be high.

Other carriers flying within Atlantic Canada include **Air St-Pierre**, **Porter Airlines** and **Provincial Airlines**.

Bicycle

The Maritime provinces, particularly Prince Edward Island, are ideal for bicycle touring.

Cycling Rules & Resources

➡ Cyclists must follow the same rules of the road as vehicles, but don't expect drivers to always respect your right of way.

➡ Since 2015, it has been mandatory for cyclists in all Maritime provinces to wear an approved helmet.

➡ The Better World Club (www.betterworldclub.com) offers emergency roadside assistance for cyclists. Membership costs $39.95 per year.

Transportation

➡ By air: most airlines will carry bikes as checked luggage without charge on international flights, as long as they're in a box. Always check details before you buy the ticket.

➡ By bus: **Maritime Bus** (☎800-575-1807; www.maritimebus.com) charges $20 plus tax per bike and also sells bike bags ($10) to pack them in. Bikes only travel on the same bus as the passenger if there's enough space. To ensure that yours arrives at the same time as (or before) you do, ship it a day early.

➡ By train: **VIA Rail** (☎888-842-7733; www.viarail.ca) will transport your bicycle for $25. There are no trains with bike racks that run through this part of Canada so you'll have to dismantle and pack your bike to put on as baggage.

Rental

Outfitters renting bicycles exist in most tourist towns. Rentals cost around $15 per day for touring bikes and $25 per day for mountain bikes. The price usually includes a helmet and lock. Most companies require a security deposit of $20 to $200.

Boat

The watery region hosts an extensive ferry system. Walk-ons and cyclists should be OK anytime, but call ahead for vehicle reservations or if you require a cabin berth. This is especially important during peak season (July and August) on popular services such as the Pictou-Wood Islands ferry between Nova Scotia and PEI.

Bus

Maritime Bus (☎800-575-1807; www.maritimebus.com) is the main operator of services within the Maritimes and has routes around and between all four provinces. **DRL** (☎888-263-1854; www.drl-lr.com) operates services on the island of Newfoundland.

Bus travel is cheaper than other means of transport, and advance ticket purchase (four, seven or 14 days) saves quite a bit, too.

Tickets can be bought online or at bus terminals for Maritime and on the bus (cash). Tickets for DRL services can only be purchased on the bus, with cash: there are no phone or online sales. Show up at least 30 to 45 minutes prior to departure.

Sample fares and journey times:

➡ Halifax to Moncton Airport ($49, 3½ to four hours)

➡ Halifax to Charlottetown ($58.25, 5½ hours)

➡ Charlottetown to Moncton ($41.75, three hours)

➡ Charlottetown to Halifax ($58.25, 4½ hours).

➡ St John's to Port aux Basques ($126, 13½ hours).

Car & Motorcycle

Automobile Associations

Auto-club membership is a handy thing to have in Canada. Try the following:

Better World Club (www.betterworldclub.com) Donates 1% of its annual revenue to environmental cleanup efforts. It offers service throughout the USA and Canada, and also has a roadside-assistance program for bicycles.

Canadian Automobile Association (www.caa.ca) Offers services, including 24-hour emergency roadside assistance, to members of international affiliates such as AAA in the USA, AA in the UK and ADAC in Germany. The club also offers trip-planning advice, free maps, travel-agency services and a range of discounts on hotels, car rentals etc.

Bring Your Own Vehicle

There's minimal hassle driving into Canada from the USA as long as you have your vehicle's registration papers, proof of liability insurance and your home driver's license.

Driver's Licenses

Visitors can legally drive for up to three months with their home driver's license.

If you're spending considerable time in Canada, think about getting an international driving permit (IDP), which is valid for one year. Your automobile association at home can issue one for a small fee. Always carry your home license together with the IDP.

Fuel & Spare Parts

➡ Gas is sold in liters.

➡ Prices are higher in remote areas.

➡ Fuel prices in Canada are usually higher than in the

USA, so fill up south of the border.

- Most gas stations are self-service.
- Finding a gas station is generally easy except in sparsely populated areas such as Labrador and Newfoundland's South Coast.
- When traveling in remote regions always bring some tools and a spare tire. Finding spare parts can be difficult far from big cities.

Insurance

Canadian law requires liability insurance for all vehicles, to cover you for damage caused to property and people. The minimum requirement is $200,000 in all Maritime provinces.

Americans traveling to Canada in their own car should ask their insurance company for a nonresident interprovince motor vehicle liability insurance card (commonly known as a 'yellow card'), which is accepted as evidence of financial responsibility anywhere in Canada. Although not mandatory, it may come in handy in an accident.

Car-rental agencies offer liability insurance. Collision damage waivers (CDW) reduce or eliminate the excess (the amount you'll have to reimburse the rental company if there's damage to the car itself). Some credit cards cover CDW for a certain rental period, if you use the card to pay for the rental, and decline the policy offered by the rental company. Always check with your card issuer to see what coverage they offer in Canada.

Personal accident insurance (PAI) covers you and any passengers for medical costs incurred as a result of an accident. If your travel insurance or your health insurance policy at home does this as well (and most do, but check), then this is one expense you can do without.

Rentals

CAR

To rent a car in Canada you generally need to:

- be at least 25 years old
- hold a valid driver's license (an international one may be required if you're not from an English- or French-speaking country)
- have a major credit card

Some companies will rent to drivers between the ages of 21 and 24 for an additional charge.

You should be able to get an economy-sized vehicle for about $30 to $65 per day. Child safety seats are compulsory (reserve them when you book) and cost about $13 per day.

Car-rental prices can double in July and August, and it's essential to book ahead in prime tourist spots such as Charlottetown or St John's, as there often just aren't enough cars to go around.

International car-rental companies usually have branches at airports and in city centers; note that ferry terminals often do not have branches.

On-the-spot rentals often are more expensive than prebooked packages (ie rental cars booked online or with your flight).

MOTORCYCLE

The Motorcycle Tour Guide (www.motorcycletourguidens.com) is a great reference for motorcyclists visiting Nova Scotia.

Northeastern Motorcycle Tours (☎802-463-9853; www.motorcycletours.com) runs tours along the Cabot Trail from Maine, USA.

RECREATIONAL VEHICLE

Rentals cost roughly $160 to $275 per day in high season for midsize vehicles, although insurance, fees and taxes add a hefty chunk. Diesel-fueled RVs have considerably lower running costs.

Road Conditions & Hazards

Road conditions are generally good, but keep the following in mind:

- Fierce winters can leave potholes the size of landmine craters. Winter travel in general can be hazardous due to heavy snow and ice, which may cause roads and bridges to close periodically. Transport Canada (www.tc.gc.ca) provides links to road conditions and construction zones for each province.
- If you're driving in winter or in remote areas, make sure your vehicle is equipped with four-seasonal radial or snow tires, and emergency supplies in case you're stranded.
- Distances between services can be long in sparsely populated areas so keep your gas filled up whenever possible.
- Moose, deer and elk are common on rural roadways, especially at night. There's no contest between a 534kg bull moose and a Subaru, so keep your eyes peeled.

Road Rules

- Canadians drive on the right-hand side of the road.
- Seat-belt use is compulsory. Children under 18kg must be strapped in child-booster seats, except infants who must be in rear-facing safety seats.
- Motorcyclists must wear helmets and drive with their headlights on.
- Distances and speed limits are posted in kilometers. The speed limit is generally 40km/h to 50km/h in cities and 90km/h to 110km/h outside town.
- Slow down to 60km/h when passing emergency vehicles (such as police cars and ambulances) stopped on the roadside with their lights flashing.

- Turning right at red lights after coming to a full stop is permitted in all provinces.
- Driving while using a hand-held cell phone is illegal in Newfoundland, Nova Scotia and Prince Edward Island.
- Radar detectors are not allowed. If you're caught driving with a radar detector, even one that isn't being operated, you could receive a fine of $1000 and your device may be confiscated.
- The blood-alcohol limit for drivers is 0.08%. Driving while drunk is a criminal offense.
- You are not allowed to smoke cannabis in a vehicle, or drive under the influence. If you are carrying cannabis, it must be kept inside a sealed container at all times.

Hitchhiking

Hitchhiking is never entirely safe in any country and we don't recommend it. That said, in remote and rural areas in Canada it is not uncommon to see people thumbing for a ride. If you do decide to hitch, understand that you are taking a small but potentially serious risk. Remember that it's safer to travel in pairs and let someone know where you are planning to go.

Hitchhiking is illegal on some highways and in the provinces of Nova Scotia and New Brunswick, although you'll see people hitching there anyway.

Local Transportation

Bicycle

Cycling is more of a recreational activity than a means of local transportation in Atlantic Canada. City bike paths are not common. Still, most public transportation allows bicycles to be brought on at certain times of day.

Bus

The only cities in the region with municipal bus services are Fredericton, Saint John, Moncton, Halifax, Sydney, Charlottetown and St John's. The Annapolis Valley has a regional bus service between Wolfville and Bridgetown. Elsewhere the car is king.

Taxi & Ride Sharing

Taxis are usually metered, with a flag-fall fee of $3 and a per-kilometer charge around $1.75. Drivers expect a tip of between 10% and 15%. Taxis can be flagged down or ordered by phone.

At the time of writing, rideshare apps such as Uber and Lyft are not operating in the Maritime provinces, but there has been much talk that they're on the way soon.

Many hostels have rideshare boards that can be a boon if you're traveling without a car.

Train

Train travel is limited within the region. Prince Edward Island and Newfoundland have no train services. Nova Scotia and New Brunswick are served along the **VIA Rail** (☎888-842-7733; www.viarail.ca) Montréal–Halifax route. For a train schedule, check the website. Most stations have left-luggage offices.

Classes

There are four main classes:

Economy class Buys you a fairly basic, if indeed quite comfortable, reclining seat with a headrest. Blankets and pillows are provided for overnight travel.

Sleeper class Available on shorter overnight routes. You can choose from compartments with upper or lower pullout berths, and private single, double or triple roomettes, all with a bathroom.

Touring class Available on long-distance routes and includes Sleeper Class accommodations plus meals, access to the sightseeing car and sometimes a tour guide.

Business class Provides access to a business lounge with spacious seats, free nonalcoholic beverages, high-speed wi-fi and more.

Costs

Taking the train is more expensive than the bus, but most people find it a more comfortable way to travel. June to mid-October is peak season, when prices are about 40% higher. Buying tickets in advance (even just five days before) can yield significant savings.

Passes

VIA Rail offers the **Canada Pass** (www.viarail.ca/en/fares-and-packages/rail-passes/canada-pass; from $649), which offers a choice of six, 12 or unlimited one-way trips over 15, 30, or 60 days.

All seats are in economy class, but the pass qualifies you for a 40% discount on upgrades to Business and Touring class. On sleeper trains, you get a 25% discount on upgrading to a cabin, or 40% for berths.

Reservations

Tickets and train passes are available for purchase online, by phone, at VIA Rail stations and from many travel agents. Seat reservations are highly recommended, especially in summer and for sleeper cars.

Language

English and French are the official languages of Canada. You'll see both on highway signs, maps, tourist brochures, packaging etc.

New Brunswick is Canada's only officially bilingual province, although only about one third of the population speaks both French and English. French is widely spoken, particularly in the north and east of the province. Nova Scotia also has a significant French-speaking population. The strongest French Acadian ancestry on Prince Edward Island is found in Région Évangéline, where some 6000 residents still speak French as their first language.

You'll find that the French spoken in Canada is essentially the same as in France, and locals will have no problem understanding more formal French.

French pronunciation is pretty straightforward for English speakers, as the sounds can almost all be found in English. The exceptions are nasal vowels (represented in our coloured pronunciation guides by o or u followed by an almost inaudible nasal consonant sound m, n or ng), the 'funny' *u* (ew in our guides) and the deep-in-the-throat *r*. Bearing this in mind and reading the pronunciation guides in this chapter as if they were English, you shouldn't have problems being understood. Syllables in French words are, for the most part, equally stressed. English speakers tend to stress the first syllable, which is unusual in French, so try adding a light stress on the final syllable to compensate.

WANT MORE?

For in-depth language information and handy phrases, check out Lonely Planet's *French Phrasebook*. You'll find it at **shop.lonelyplanet.com**, or you can buy Lonely Planet's iPhone phrasebooks at the Apple App Store.

BASICS

Hello.	*Bonjour.*	bon·zhoor
Goodbye.	*Au revoir.*	o·rer·vwa
Excuse me.	*Excusez-moi.*	ek·skew·zay·mwa
Sorry.	*Pardon.*	par·don
Yes./No.	*Oui./Non.*	wee/non
Please.	*S'il vous plaît.*	seel voo play
Thank you.	*Merci.*	mair·see
You're welcome.	*De rien.*	der ree·en

How are you?
Comment allez-vous? — ko·mon ta·lay·voo

Fine, and you?
Bien, merci. Et vous? — byun mair·see ay voo

My name is ...
Je m'appelle ... — zher ma·pel ...

What's your name?
Comment vous appelez-vous? — ko·mon voo·za·play voo

Do you speak English?
Parlez-vous anglais? — par·lay·voo ong·glay

I don't understand.
Je ne comprends pas. — zher ner kom·pron pa

ACCOMMODATIONS

Do you have any rooms available?
Est-ce que vous avez des chambres libres? — es·ker voo za·vay day shom·brer lee·brer

How much is it per night/person?
Quel est le prix par nuit/personne? — kel ay ler pree par nwee/per·son

Is breakfast included?
Est-ce que le petit déjeuner est inclus? — es·ker ler per·tee day·zher·nay ayt en·klew

a ... room	*une chambre ...*	ewn shom·brer ...
single	*à un lit*	a un lee
double	*avec un grand lit*	a·vek un gron lee

air-con	*climatiseur*	klee·ma·tee·zer
bathroom	*salle de bains*	sal der bun
campsite	*camping*	kom·peeng
dorm	*dortoir*	dor·twar
guesthouse	*pension*	pon·syon
hotel	*hôtel*	o·tel
window	*fenêtre*	fer·nay·trer
youth hostel	*auberge de jeunesse*	o·berzh der zher·nes

DIRECTIONS

Where's ...?
Où est ...? oo ay ...

What's the address?
Quelle est l'adresse? kel ay la·dres

Could you write the address, please?
Est-ce que vous pourriez écrire l'adresse, s'il vous plaît? es·ker voo poo·ryay ay·kreer la·dres seel voo play

Can you show me (on the map)?
Pouvez-vous m'indiquer (sur la carte)? poo·vay·voo mun·dee·kay (sewr la kart)

at the corner	*au coin*	o kwun
at the traffic lights	*aux feux*	o fer
behind	*derrière*	dair·ryair
in front of ...	*devant ...*	der·von ...
far (from ...)	*loin (de ...)*	lwun (der ...)
left	*gauche*	gosh
near (to ...)	*près (de ...)*	pray (der ...)
next to ...	*à côté de ...*	a ko·tay der...
opposite ...	*en face de ...*	on fas der ...
right	*droite*	drwat
straight ahead	*tout droit*	too drwa

EATING & DRINKING

A table for (two), please.
Une table pour (deux), s'il vous plaît. ewn ta·bler poor (der) seel voo play

What would you recommend?
Qu'est-ce que vous conseillez? kes·ker voo kon·say·yay

What's in that dish?
Quels sont les ingrédients? kel son lay zun·gray·dyon

I'm a vegetarian.
Je suis végétarien/ végétarienne. zher swee vay·zhay·ta·ryun/ vay·zhay·ta·ryen (m/f)

I don't eat ...
Je ne mange pas ... zher ner monzh pa ...

KEY PATTERNS

To get by in French, mix and match these simple patterns with words of your choice:

Where's (the entry)?
Où est (l'entrée)? oo ay (lon·tray)

Where can I (buy a ticket)?
Où est-ce que je peux (acheter un billet)? oo es·ker zher per (ash·tay un bee·yay)

When's (the next train)?
Quand est (le prochain train)? kon ay (ler pro·shun trun)

How much is (a room)?
C'est combien pour (une chambre)? say kom·buyn poor (ewn shom·brer)

Do you have (a map)?
Avez-vous (une carte)? a·vay voo (ewn kart)

Is there (a toilet)?
Y a-t-il (des toilettes)? ee a teel (day twa·let)

I'd like (to book a room).
Je voudrais (réserver une chambre). zher voo·dray (ray·ser·vay ewn shom·brer)

Can I (enter)?
Puis-je (entrer)? pweezh (on·tray)

Could you please (help)?
Pouvez-vous (m'aider), s'il vous plaît? poo·vay voo (may·day) seel voo play

Do I have to (book a seat)?
Faut-il (réserver une place)? fo·teel (ray·ser·vay ewn plas)

Cheers!
Santé! son·tay

That was delicious.
C'était délicieux! say·tay day·lee·syer

Please bring the bill.
Apportez-moi l'addition, s'il vous plaît. a·por·tay·mwa la·dee·syon seel voo play

Key Words

appetiser	*entrée*	on·tray
bottle	*bouteille*	boo·tay
breakfast	*déjeuner*	day·zher·nay
children's menu	*menu pour enfants*	mer·new poor on·fon
cold	*froid*	frwa
delicatessen	*traiteur*	tray·ter
dinner	*souper*	soo·pay
dish	*plat*	pla

food	*nourriture*	noo·ree·tewr
fork	*fourchette*	foor·shet
glass	*verre*	vair
grocery store	*épicerie*	ay·pees·ree
highchair	*chaise haute*	shay zot
hot	*chaud*	sho
knife	*couteau*	koo·to
local speciality	*spécialité locale*	spay·sya·lee·tay lo·kal
lunch	*dîner*	dee·nay
main course	*plat principal*	pla prun·see·pal
market	*marché*	mar·shay
menu (in English)	*carte (en anglais)*	kart (on ong·glay)
plate	*assiette*	a·syet
spoon	*cuillère*	kwee·yair
wine list	*carte des vins*	kart day vun
with	*avec*	a·vek
without	*sans*	son

Meat & Fish

beef	*bœuf*	berf
chicken	*poulet*	poo·lay
fish	*poisson*	pwa·son
lamb	*agneau*	a·nyo
pork	*porc*	por
turkey	*dinde*	dund
veal	*veau*	vo

Fruit & Vegetables

apple	*pomme*	pom
apricot	*abricot*	ab·ree·ko
asparagus	*asperge*	a·spairzh
beans	*haricots*	a·ree·ko
beetroot	*betterave*	be·trav
cabbage	*chou*	shoo
celery	*céleri*	sel·ree
cherry	*cerise*	ser·reez
corn	*maïs*	ma·ees
cucumber	*concombre*	kong·kom·brer
gherkin (pickle)	*cornichon*	kor·nee·shon
grape	*raisin*	ray·zun
leek	*poireau*	pwa·ro
lemon	*citron*	see·tron
lettuce	*laitue*	lay·tew
mushroom	*champignon*	shom·pee·nyon
peach	*pêche*	pesh
peas	*petit pois*	per·tee pwa
(red/green) pepper	*poivron (rouge/vert)*	pwa·vron (roozh/vair)
pineapple	*ananas*	a·na·nas
plum	*prune*	prewn
potato	*pomme de terre*	pom der tair
prune	*pruneau*	prew·no
pumpkin	*citrouille*	see·troo·yer
shallot	*échalote*	eh·sha·lot
spinach	*épinards*	eh·pee·nar
strawberry	*fraise*	frez
tomato	*tomate*	to·mat
turnip	*navet*	na·vay
vegetable	*légume*	lay·gewm

Other

bread	*pain*	pun
butter	*beurre*	ber
cheese	*fromage*	fro·mazh
egg	*œuf*	erf
honey	*miel*	myel
jam	*confiture*	kon·fee·tewr
lentils	*lentilles*	lon·tee·yer
oil	*huile*	weel
pasta/noodles	*pâtes*	pat
pepper	*poivre*	pwa·vrer
rice	*riz*	ree
salt	*sel*	sel
sugar	*sucre*	sew·krer
vinegar	*vinaigre*	vee·nay·grer

Drinks

beer	*bière*	bee·yair
coffee	*café*	ka·fay
(orange) juice	*jus (d'orange)*	zhew (do·ronzh)
milk	*lait*	lay
red wine	*vin rouge*	vun roozh

Signs

Entrée	Entrance
Femmes	Women
Fermé	Closed
Hommes	Men
Interdit	Prohibited
Ouvert	Open
Renseignements	Information
Sortie	Exit
Toilettes/WC	Toilets

tea	*thé*	tay
(mineral) water	*eau (minérale)*	o (mee·nay·ral)
white wine	*vin blanc*	vun blong

EMERGENCIES

Help!
Au secours! o skoor

I'm lost.
Je suis perdu/perdue. zhe swee pair·dew (m/f)

Leave me alone!
Fichez-moi la paix! fee·shay·mwa la pay

There's been an accident.
Il y a eu un accident. eel ya ew un ak·see·don

Call a doctor.
Appelez un médecin. a·play un mayd·sun

Call the police.
Appelez la police. a·play la po·lees

I'm ill.
Je suis malade. zher swee ma·lad

It hurts here.
J'ai une douleur ici. zhay ewn doo·ler ee·see

I'm allergic to ...
Je suis allergique ... zher swee za·lair·zheek ...

Where are the toilets?
Où sont les toilettes? oo son lay twa·let

SHOPPING & SERVICES

I'd like to buy ...
Je voudrais acheter ... zher voo·dray ash·tay ...

May I look at it?
Est-ce que je peux le voir? es·ker zher per ler vwar

I'm just looking.
Je regarde. zher rer·gard

I don't like it.
Cela ne me plaît pas. ser·la ner mer play pa

How much is it?
C'est combien? say kom·byun

It's too expensive.
C'est trop cher. say tro shair

Can you lower the price?
Vous pouvez baisser le prix? voo poo·vay bay·say ler pree

Question Words

How?	*Comment?*	ko·mon
What?	*Quoi?*	kwa
When?	*Quand?*	kon
Where?	*Où?*	oo
Who?	*Qui?*	kee
Why?	*Pourquoi?*	poor·kwa

There's a mistake in the bill.
Il y a une erreur dans la note. eel ya ewn ay·rer don la not

ATM	*guichet automatique de banque*	gee·shay o·to·ma·teek der bonk
credit card	*carte de crédit*	kart der kray·dee
internet cafe	*cybercafé*	see·bair·ka·fay
post office	*bureau de poste*	bew·ro der post
tourist office	*office de tourisme*	o·fees der too·rees·mer

TIME & DATES

What time is it?
Quelle heure est-il? kel er ay til

It's (eight) o'clock.
Il est (huit) heures. il ay (weet) er

It's half past (10).
Il est (dix) heures et demie. il ay (deez) er ay day·mee

morning	*matin*	ma·tun
afternoon	*après-midi*	a·pray·mee·dee
evening	*soir*	swar

yesterday	*hier*	yair
today	*aujourd'hui*	o·zhoor·dwee
tomorrow	*demain*	der·mun

Monday	*lundi*	lun·dee
Tuesday	*mardi*	mar·dee
Wednesday	*mercredi*	mair·krer·dee
Thursday	*jeudi*	zher·dee
Friday	*vendredi*	von·drer·dee
Saturday	*samedi*	sam·dee
Sunday	*dimanche*	dee·monsh

January	*janvier*	zhon·vyay
February	*février*	fayv·ryay
March	*mars*	mars
April	*avril*	a·vreel
May	*mai*	may
June	*juin*	zhwun
July	*juillet*	zhwee·yay
August	*août*	oot
September	*septembre*	sep·tom·brer
October	*octobre*	ok·to·brer
November	*novembre*	no·vom·brer
December	*décembre*	day·som·brer

TRANSPORTATION

Public Transportation

boat	*bateau*	ba·to
bus	*bus*	bews
plane	*avion*	a·vyon
train	*train*	trun

I want to go to ...
Je voudrais aller à ... zher voo·dray a·lay a ...

Does it stop at ...?
Est-ce qu'il s'arrête à ...? es·kil sa·ret a ...

At what time does it leave/arrive?
À quelle heure est-ce qu'il part/arrive? a kel er es kil par/a·reev

Can you tell me when we get to ...?
Pouvez-vous me dire quand nous arrivons à ...? poo·vay·voo mer deer kon noo za·ree·von a ...

I want to get off here.
Je veux descendre ici. zher ver day·son·drer ee·see

first	*premier*	prer·myay
last	*dernier*	dair·nyay
next	*prochain*	pro·shun

a ... ticket	*un billet ...*	un bee·yay ...
1st-class	*de première classe*	der prem·yair klas
2nd-class	*de deuxième classe*	der der·zyem las
one-way	*simple*	sum·pler
return	*aller et retour*	a·lay ay rer·toor

aisle seat	*côté couloir*	ko·tay kool·war
cancelled	*annulé*	a·new·lay
delayed	*en retard*	on rer·tar
platform	*quai*	kay
ticket office	*guichet*	gee·shay
timetable	*horaire*	o·rair
train station	*gare*	gar
window seat	*côté fenêtre*	ko·tay fe·ne·trer

Driving & Cycling

I'd like to hire a ...	*Je voudrais louer ...*	zher voo·dray loo·way ...
car	*une voiture*	ewn vwa·tewr
bicycle	*un vélo*	un vay·lo
motorcycle	*une moto*	ewn mo·to

Numbers

1	*un*	un
2	*deux*	der
3	*trois*	trwa
4	*quatre*	ka·trer
5	*cinq*	sungk
6	*six*	sees
7	*sept*	set
8	*huit*	weet
9	*neuf*	nerf
10	*dix*	dees
20	*vingt*	vung
30	*trente*	tront
40	*quarante*	ka·ront
50	*cinquante*	sung·kont
60	*soixante*	swa·sont
70	*soixante-dix*	swa·son·dees
80	*quatre-vingts*	ka·trer·vung
90	*quatre-vingt-dix*	ka·trer·vung·dees
100	*cent*	son
1000	*mille*	meel

child seat	*siège-enfant*	syezh·on·fon
diesel	*diesel*	dyay·zel
helmet	*casque*	kask
mechanic	*mécanicien*	may·ka·nee·syun
petrol/gas	*essence*	ay·sons
service station	*station-service*	sta·syon·ser·vees

Is this the road to ...?
C'est la route pour ...? say la root poor ...

(How long) Can I park here?
(Combien de temps) Est-ce que je peux stationner ici? (kom·byun der tom) es·ker zher per sta·syo·nay ee·see

The car/motorbike has broken down (at ...).
La voiture/moto est tombée en panne (à ...). la vwa·tewr/mo·to ay tom·bay on pan (a ...)

I have a flat tyre.
Mon pneu est à plat. mom pner ay ta pla

I've run out of petrol.
Je suis en panne d'essence. zher swee zon pan day·sons

I've lost my car keys.
J'ai perdu les clés de ma voiture. zhay per·dew lay klay der ma vwa·tewr

Where can I have my bicycle repaired?
Où est-ce que je peux faire réparer mon vélo? oo es ker zher per fair ray·pa·ray mon vay·lo

Behind the Scenes

SEND US YOUR FEEDBACK

We love to hear from travelers – your comments keep us on our toes and help make our books better. Our well-traveled team reads every word on what you loved or loathed about this book. Although we cannot reply individually to your submissions, we always guarantee that your feedback goes straight to the appropriate authors, in time for the next edition. Each person who sends us information is thanked in the next edition.

Visit **lonelyplanet.com/contact** to submit your updates and suggestions or to ask for help. Our award-winning website also features inspirational travel stories and news.

Note: We may edit, reproduce and incorporate your comments in Lonely Planet products such as guidebooks, websites and digital products, so let us know if you are happy to have your name acknowledged. For a copy of our privacy policy visit lonelyplanet.com/legal.

WRITER THANKS

Oliver Berry

Big thanks to Ben Buckner for the chance to return to write about Canada, to the Lonely Planet editors for whipping my work into shape, and to my fellow writers for making this book what it is. Heartfelt thanks to Rosie Hillier for putting up with my wanderlust, and to Susie Berry for long-distance correspondence. Thanks also to Sam White, Justin Foulkes, Deborah Gill, Anna Louis and many others for useful Canadian tips and much-needed hospitality.

Adam Karlin

Big thanks to Ben Buckner, for getting me on this project, Anna Kaminski, my commiserator in chief, my fellow co-authors, Carolyn and Adam in St John's, Gordon in Bonavista, the construction crews of the New Wes Valley, mom and dad, my wild little Isaac, and my favorite traveling companions: Rachel, who can layer for anything, and Sanda, who endures the road better than her daddy.

Korina Miller

Thank you to Ben Buckner for inviting me to join this project, to my fellow authors for their enthusiasm and to Imogen Bannister for her support. Huge thanks to my parents who kept things ticking while I was away, to Kirk for being my rock and to my daughters, Simone and Monique, who make coming home the best part of traveling. To the people of New Brunswick, *merci* for sharing your truly beautiful province with me.

ACKNOWLEDGMENTS

Climate map data adapted from Peel MC, Finlayson BL & McMahon TA (2007) 'Updated World Map of the Köppen-Geiger Climate Classification', *Hydrology and Earth System Sciences*, 11, 1633–44.

Cover photograph: Puffins, Nova Scotia, Greg and Jan Ritchie/Shutterstock ©

THIS BOOK

This 6th edition of Lonely Planet's *Nova Scotia, New Brunswick & Prince Edward Island* guidebook was curated by Oliver Berry and researched and written by Oliver, Adam Karlin and Korina Miller, who also wrote the previous edition. This guidebook was produced by the following:

Destination Editor Ben Buckner

Senior Product Editors Kate Chapman, Grace Dobell, Martine Power, Saralinda Turner

Cartographer Corey Hutchison

Product Editors Andrea Dobbin, Bruce Evans, Kate Kiely

Book Designers Virginia Moreno, Ania Bartoszek, Gwen Cotter

Assisting Editors Sarah Bailey, Melanie Dankel, Victoria Harrison, Jennifer Hattam, Gabrielle Innes, Charlotte Orr, Claire Rourke, Tamara Sheward, James Smart

Cover Researcher Gwen Cotter

Thanks to Bailey Freeman, Clare Healy, Sonia Kapoor

Index

Map Pages **000**
Photo Pages **000**

N

O

P

Map Pages **000**
Photo Pages **000**

Y

Z

Map Legend

Sights
- Beach
- Bird Sanctuary
- Buddhist
- Castle/Palace
- Christian
- Confucian
- Hindu
- Islamic
- Jain
- Jewish
- Monument
- Museum/Gallery/Historic Building
- Ruin
- Shinto
- Sikh
- Taoist
- Winery/Vineyard
- Zoo/Wildlife Sanctuary
- Other Sight

Activities, Courses & Tours
- Bodysurfing
- Diving
- Canoeing/Kayaking
- Course/Tour
- Sento Hot Baths/Onsen
- Skiing
- Snorkeling
- Surfing
- Swimming/Pool
- Walking
- Windsurfing
- Other Activity

Sleeping
- Sleeping
- Camping
- Hut/Shelter

Eating
- Eating

Drinking & Nightlife
- Drinking & Nightlife
- Cafe

Entertainment
- Entertainment

Shopping
- Shopping

Information
- Bank
- Embassy/Consulate
- Hospital/Medical
- Internet
- Police
- Post Office
- Telephone
- Toilet
- Tourist Information
- Other Information

Geographic
- Beach
- Gate
- Hut/Shelter
- Lighthouse
- Lookout
- Mountain/Volcano
- Oasis
- Park
- Pass
- Picnic Area
- Waterfall

Population
- Capital (National)
- Capital (State/Province)
- City/Large Town
- Town/Village

Transport
- Airport
- BART station
- Border crossing
- Boston T station
- Bus
- Cable car/Funicular
- Cycling
- Ferry
- Metro/Muni station
- Monorail
- Parking
- Petrol station
- Subway/SkyTrain station
- Taxi
- Train station/Railway
- Tram
- Underground station
- Other Transport

Routes
- Tollway
- Freeway
- Primary
- Secondary
- Tertiary
- Lane
- Unsealed road
- Road under construction
- Plaza/Mall
- Steps
- Tunnel
- Pedestrian overpass
- Walking Tour
- Walking Tour detour
- Path/Walking Trail

Boundaries
- International
- State/Province
- Disputed
- Regional/Suburb
- Marine Park
- Cliff
- Wall

Hydrography
- River, Creek
- Intermittent River
- Canal
- Water
- Dry/Salt/Intermittent Lake
- Reef

Areas
- Airport/Runway
- Beach/Desert
- Cemetery (Christian)
- Cemetery (Other)
- Glacier
- Mudflat
- Park/Forest
- Sight (Building)
- Sportsground
- Swamp/Mangrove

Note: Not all symbols displayed above appear on the maps in this book

OUR STORY

A beat-up old car, a few dollars in the pocket and a sense of adventure. In 1972 that's all Tony and Maureen Wheeler needed for the trip of a lifetime – across Europe and Asia overland to Australia. It took several months, and at the end – broke but inspired – they sat at their kitchen table writing and stapling together their first travel guide, *Across Asia on the Cheap*. Within a week they'd sold 1500 copies. Lonely Planet was born.

Today, Lonely Planet has offices in the US, Ireland and China, with a network of over 2000 contributors in every corner of the globe. We share Tony's belief that 'a great guidebook should do three things: inform, educate and amuse'.

OUR WRITERS

Oliver Berry

Nova Scotia, Prince Edward Island Oliver Berry is a writer and photographer from Cornwall. He has worked for Lonely Planet for more than a decade, covering destinations from Cornwall to the Cook Islands, and has worked on more than 30 guidebooks. He is also a regular contributor to many newspapers and magazines, including Lonely Planet *Traveller*. His writing has won several awards, including The Guardian Young Travel Writer of the Year and the TNT Magazine People's Choice Awards. His latest work is published at www.oliverberry.com. Oliver also wrote the Plan, Understand and Survive sections.

Adam Karlin

Newfoundland & Labrador Adam has contributed to dozens of Lonely Planet guidebooks, covering an alphabetical spread that ranges from the Andaman Islands to the Zimbabwe Border. As a journalist he has written on travel, crime, politics, archeology, and the Sri Lankan Civil War, among other topics. He has sent dispatches from every continent barring Antarctica (one day!) and his essays and articles have featured in the BBC, NPR, and multiple non-fiction anthologies. Learn more at http://walkonfine.com/, or follow on Instagram @adamwalkonfine.

Korina Miller

New Brunswick Korina grew up on Vancouver Island and has been exploring the globe independently since she was 16, visiting or living in 36 countries and picking up a degree in Communications and Canadian Studies, an MA in Migration Studies and a diploma in Visual Arts en route. As a writer and editor, Korina has worked on nearly 60 titles for Lonely Planet and has also worked with LP.com, BBC, the *Independent*, the *Guardian*, BBC5 and CBC, as well as many independent magazines. She has currently set up camp back in Victoria, soaking up the mountain views and the pounding surf.

Published by Lonely Planet Global Limited
CRN 554153
6th edition – Aug 2022
ISBN 978 1 78868 459 0

10 9 8 7 6 5 4 3 2 1
Printed in China